THE TRIAL OF THE FOUR

THE TRIAL OF THE FOUR

A collection of materials on the case of

GALANSKOV, GINZBURG

DOBROVOLSKY & LASHKOVA

1967–68

Compiled, with commentary, by
PAVEL LITVINOV

English text edited and annotated by
PETER REDDAWAY

With a Foreword by
LEONARD SCHAPIRO

Translated by
Janis Sapiets, Hilary Sternberg & Daniel Weissbort

The Viking Press   New York

The Russian original, under the title *Protsess chetyryokh*,
was published in Amsterdam in 1971
© 1971 Alexander Herzen Foundation, Amstel 268, Amsterdam
English translation and edition Copyright © 1972
Longman Group Limited

Published in 1972 by The Viking Press, Inc.
625 Madison Avenue, New York, N.Y. 10022

SBN 670-73017-3

Library of Congress catalog card number: 70-186735
Printed in U.S.A.

ACKNOWLEDGMENT

Harvard University Press: From *Soviet Criminal Law and
Procedure—RSFSR Codes* by Burman and Spindler

CONTENTS

FOREWORD

This book contains an account of one of the most important political trials to have taken place in the Soviet Union in recent years; and many documents and materials relating to it. Mr Reddaway's Introduction contains the information necessary to explain the significance of this trial in Soviet political life. But, it may be asked, what general interest does it hold for the serious student of Soviet affairs? I think its main value lies in the light which it throws on the chequered fate of legal order in the Soviet Union since the death of Stalin in 1953.

One of the most hopeful features of the Khrushchev era for those for whom the freedom of the individual is still the pre-eminent value was the attempt after 1953 to create some kind of respect for law as a standard determining relations between the citizen and the state. The extraordinary and unlimited powers of the security forces over life and liberty were repealed at the end of the year. The powers of the Procurators were strengthened and, what was more important, these officials were allowed and indeed encouraged to exercise the duty laid upon them to protect the individual which they have long enjoyed, but equally long neglected. On Christmas Day 1958 new Fundamental Principles of Criminal Law and Procedure were enacted. These removed some of the most arbitrary features of Soviet criminal law; and for the first time in Soviet history enacted some of the safeguards which are traditionally associated with any civilized legal system. Even more encouraging was the beginning of legal debate among the academic lawyers and in the press. For a time matters such as the right to challenge an arrest in the courts, the right to seek legal redress against officials for abuse of power or greater facilities for the conduct of defence at trials were debated with relative freedom. The new climate was for a time reflected in the practice of the courts and in their relative independence from party influence. It looked as if the Soviet rulers were at last making a genuine effort to put the horrifying past behind them.

Unhappily all this was short-lived. The notorious anti-parasite laws opened up a whole new area of arbitrary repression (in flagrant contravention of the Fundamental Principles of 1958) and gave the authorities a new weapon for harassing dissenters and hounding critics. The death penalty was extended to a new wide range of 'economic' crimes: what was worse, the new laws were often applied with complete disregard for the safeguards contained in the Fundamental Principles and, on one occasion at least, retrospectively. Severe penalties were enacted for the spreading in verbal or written form of 'deliberate lying inventions vilifying the Soviet political and social system'—a provision which the courts were soon interpreting to cover any criticism, however justified, which the authorities resented; and were to turn into an instrument of control over all intellectual life.

The turning-point was marked by the trial of the writers Sinyavsky and Daniel in February 1966: the appointment a short time afterwards of two high-ranking security service officers as judges of the Soviet Supreme Court took on a new significance in the light of this trial and of those which followed it, including the Trial of the Four. The new role which the courts were called on to play was a grimly ironical answer to the persistent efforts which the members of the dissent movement had been making to ensure the observance of legality in Soviet life.

The significance of this trial does not lie in the severity of the laws which the courts are called on to apply: severity of laws is not incompatible with legal order, if the laws are fairly applied. What appear most notable about the Trial of the Four, and about all the similar trials of which reports are now available, are the abuse and disregard of the law which they record, and which the pages which follow document beyond any doubt or question. The very heart of the offence according to the article under which the defendants were charged is the 'slanderous' nature of the statements which they made: yet all evidence designed to show that the criticism they made was fair and true was rigorously excluded by the judge as irrelevant. This alone, apart from the innumerable violations of procedural rules, is enough to show that the trial was a rigged and predetermined political farce.

However, the picture is not all black: even though the Soviet authorities may have recoiled in fear from the relative liberalism of the early Khrushchev era, the seeds sown in that short spring of reform have not all fallen on barren soil. For a small band of courageous and determined men and women the struggle to see that Soviet law, even if imperfect, is at all events strictly observed in practice has become the main aim of their lives. Their influence and example have already spread beyond their own number: witness, for example, in this trial the brave and honest effort of counsel for the defence to do their utmost in very adverse conditions for their clients. This is something that has not been known in the Soviet Union for generations—or indeed, with few exceptions, at all. Note again the success with which the friends and supporters of the defendants in these political trials have hitherto been able at the cost of great risk to their own liberty to make public the proceedings at the trials which the authorities have done their best to distort or to suppress altogether. No one can confidently prophesy how long they will be able to continue in this valiant effort. But at least it is right that the record of their endeavours and their courage should be made available to the rest of the world.

LEONARD SCHAPIRO

London School of Economics and Political Science
March 1972

viii

INTRODUCTION

Thanks to Pavel Litvinov's skill as a compiler, the task of editing the English translation of such a large and complex book as *The Trial of the Four* has been comparatively light. Virtually no rearrangement of the material has proved necessary, only a slight pruning of it, plus the addition of some extra notes for the English reader. Scholars who wish to study the full, original text may refer to the Russian edition.[1]

Mr Litvinov's editorial competence did not emerge in 1968 from nowhere: it had been maturing in the atmosphere of an already established tradition. In 1964 the novelist Frida Vigdorova performed her last brave act before her early death by compiling a verbatim account of the trial in Leningrad of the young poet Iosif Brodsky.[2] Two years later, in the increasingly cold post-Khrushchev climate, Alexander Ginzburg did the same for the trial of the writers Sinyavsky and Daniel, adding to his *White Book* a wide selection of comments and protests relating to the whole case. And then in 1967 Mr Litvinov entered the field by compiling a record of two further political trials, which arose out of a demonstration organized by the now well-known dissenter, Vladimir Bukovsky.[3]

So this book, put together in 1968, has notable predecessors. Also successors. For after Litvinov and seven of his friends had demonstrated on Red Square against the invasion of Czechoslovakia on 25 August 1968, his own trial became the subject of such a book. This is the fascinating *Red Square at Noon*, by the poet Natalya Gorbanevskaya. In addition, many other trial records, shorter but similar in nature, have since appeared in the dissenters' chief *samizdat* (i.e. typescript) journal, the *Chronicle of Current Events*,[4] among them that of Gorbanevskaya's trial in 1970 for compiling *Red Square at Noon*.[5] These records concern trials not only against dissenters of the 'mainstream' of the human rights movement but also against Ukrainians and Jews, Crimean Tatars and Orthodox Christians. Also available, outside the pages of the *Chronicle*, are lengthy records of trials of Baptists.[6]

But apart from occupying an outstanding position—as the largest compilation—in this new genre of Soviet literature, *The Trial of the Four* is also a key work for understanding the emergence in the USSR of the Human Rights (or Democratic) Movement. For it was the Galanskov-Ginzburg trial of January 1968, and the unprecedented protests it provoked, which in fact gave birth to the movement, all this finding its reflection, first in the *Chronicle*[7] and then in this book. But the pale, if clear outlines visible in the first two *Chronicles* (April and June 1968) hardly prepared *samizdat* readers for the full magnificence, detail and three-dimensional images of *The Trial of the Four*. Here were the full texts of letters not just from Muscovites but also from individuals and groups in Leningrad, Kiev, Odessa, Latvia, Novosibirsk, Gorky and Pskov. Here were not merely the hundred-odd protest signatures of the Sinyavsky-Daniel trial but those of more than a thousand Soviet citizens, from a variety of professions and backgrounds. Here was the evidence that intellectuals and students, writers and scientists, Crimean Tatars and Ukrainians, neo-Leninists and liberals, Christian socialists and Marxists, were all concerned about the same thing: the prevention of injustices which indicated neo-Stalinist tendencies in the regime. Here was proof that the different groups had become aware of each other and established contacts, that a loose but nonetheless real movement had been born.

Here one could read, too, of the breaking of long-established Soviet taboos. An important appeal was handed openly and directly to foreign reporters by Litvinov and Larissa Daniel; all four defence counsel pleaded for their clients with a deep sense of commitment, thereby revealing all the more nakedly the injustice of the court and the illegalities of its KGB 'bouncer', Colonel Tsirkunenko; and foreigners began to demonstrate in Moscow, almost in the KGB's back-yard, in defence of the victims.[8]

Not surprisingly, the authorities took fright at the appearance of this independent public opinion and resolved to nip it in the bud. A systematic series of threats, interrogations, sackings and expulsions began, directed at all the 'signers', and especially at the organizers of the protests and petitions. Details of these appear in document V: 46 and in the index.

But the campaign had only partial success. Many 'signers' were intimidated, but others were not and, seeing the wave of intimidation as confirmation of their fears, determined to continue the struggle with even greater resolve.

Over the next big political trial, however, the KGB made things more difficult for them. Whereas 'the four' had languished in pre-trial detention for twelve long months, Litvinov and his colleagues spent there a mere one and a half. In consequence the dissenters had much less time to organize, and partly for this reason the number of protesters did not exceed a hundred. Another factor which kept the numbers down was the less savage sentencing at the trial: Litvinov, for example, received five years, to be served not in a camp but in the—in his case at least—less uncomfortable conditions of exile on the Manchurian border.[9]

While Litvinov, however, experienced the consolation of being joined in exile by his family, what, we may ask, was the fate of the central figures of his magnum opus? Vera Lashkova had been released immediately after the trial and rejoined the ranks of the dissenters.[10] Aleksei Dobrovolsky served no more than a year in the camps, before returning to a suspiciously good job near Moscow.[11] But their co-defendants were struggling—in the Mordovian labour-camps, three hundred miles southeast of Moscow—for their very survival. Yury Galanskov and Alexander Ginzburg were, in fact, continuing there—in conditions unimaginable to most of us in the comfortable west—to live out the humane and self-sacrificial values by which they had lived previously.[12] Time and again they joined in hunger-strikes in defence of one or another victim of injustice among their fellow-prisoners, even though this brought the chronically sick Galanskov to the very brink of death. Ginzburg's finest hour was his success in marrying his fianceé Irina in the camp. This happened in August 1969, after two and a half years of trying, and a hunger-strike of twenty-five days which was strongly supported by his camp comrades, among them Galanskov and Yuly Daniel. A remarkable *samizdat* booklet tells the story of this strike.[13]

Galanskov and Ginzburg also found the courage—and the means—to make known to the outside world the fearful conditions in which the 20,000 camp inmates of Mordovia (like the million-odd such prisoners throughout the whole Soviet Union) live and sometimes die. Ginzburg used a home-made tape-recorder to transmit a message on this theme,[14] and Galanskov wrote a long reflective essay on Soviet penal policy.[15] And both of them sent letters, on two occasions, to political and cultural figures in Moscow, arguing at length for radical improvements in the barbaric treatment of prisoners.[16]

In August 1970 the authorities hit especially hard at Ginzburg. For his strikes and his 'negative influence on other prisoners' he was sentenced at a camp-trial to be transferred to the infamous prison at Vladimir, a little east of Moscow. Here, in even tougher conditions, he sat out his last seventeen months, before returning in January 1972 to his wife and mother in Moscow. At this point Galanskov faced two more years of permanent damp and continual hunger.

Of him, therefore, one could not say what Ivy Litvinov, once Ivy Lowe of Hampstead, said in September 1971 about her much loved grandson Pavel and his Siberian exile, which was due to end in 1972. Questioned by a BBC reporter, she replied, with the sort of stoic resilience typical of the Democratic Movement: 'Well, so what? He's all right. He'll be coming back. His mother has been to see him. We write to him, he writes to us. He's very well. He has a new baby.'[17]

PETER REDDAWAY

London, March 1972

A Note on the Translation

The transliteration system used is eclectic in principle, but consistent in application. Its main aim is to give the lay reader some idea of correct pronunciation.

As for translation, these points should be noted: (1) the Communist League of Youth appears normally as 'Komsomol', the Russian acronym for its title; (2) the words Procurator and Procuracy have been used: Soviet Procurators have a dual function, not only prosecuting in criminal cases but also being responsible for the observation of legality throughout the Soviet legal system; (3) the RSFSR—the Russian Soviet Federated Socialist Republic, by far the largest of the USSR's fifteen constituent republics—appears normally just as Russia; (4) although the terms *kandidat nauk* and *doktor nauk* appear as Master of Science and Doctor of Science, it should be noted that the former is more or less on the level of an average Western Ph.D. and the latter, not normally attained before the age of forty, is well above it.

A few cases of discrepancies between pieces of dialogue as recorded by Mr Litvinov and as printed in Soviet press reports are to be explained by the absence of any official stenographic record of the trial. Mr Litvinov's discussion of this point (pp. 41-2) leads one to suppose that the Soviet journalists concerned either took notes inaccurately, or, perhaps, deliberately distorted certain sentences, and also that his own text is always the reliable one.

Finally, (1) passages in square brackets and in Roman script are commentary by Mr Litvinov; (2) passages in square brackets and in italics are commentary by the editor; and (3) notes at the bottom of the page are all by Mr Litvinov, except where the editor is indicated. Further notes by the editor appear at the end of the book.

THE TRIAL OF THE FOUR

PREFACE

The compiler of the present collection has set himself two main tasks. In the first place, to inform Soviet and world opinion of all the circumstances surrounding 'the case of the four' that are known to him, publicity having always and everywhere served as the indispensable and chief condition for the observation of legality. In the second place, to bring the 'case of the four' once more to the attention of those responsible for conducting this and similar trials in our country: the supreme legislative, executive and judicial organs of the USSR. In carrying out these tasks, he has compiled the present collection and is now, firstly, going to do his utmost to secure its publication in the USSR as well as abroad, and, secondly, to send it to the Chairman of the Presidium of the USSR Supreme Soviet.

The compiler has striven for the highest degree of objectivity; whether he has achieved this aim, he leaves to the judgment of his readers. He recognizes the defects of the collection but would like to point out that, in the first place, work on it took place under very difficult conditions, and, in the second, that the methodology of constructing such collections has not yet been adequately developed. For obvious reasons the compiler has not been able everywhere to indicate the source of his information sufficiently clearly or to evaluate the authenticity of certain facts; however, he has carefully checked everything and is prepared to vouch personally for all the information presented in the collection where the source has not been given. This relates particularly to the verbatim reports of the court sessions. The compiler wishes to emphasize that, though in many instances the record is not a word-for-word rendering, the general sense is absolutely accurate.

The collection is divided into the following sections:

  (I)   The Background: Personality of the Accused
  (II) Before the Trial
 (III) The Trial
 (IV) Letters and Appeals by Soviet Citizens
  (V) Press Coverage of the Case
 (VI) The Appeal Hearing

The compiler has felt it advisable to limit himself exclusively to letters and statements of Soviet citizens about the trial, and to material published by the Soviet press as this interested him in the first place and constituted the one task he might hope to execute on a sufficiently extensive scale. Within the sections the materials are set out in chronological order and where their authors have not indicated the dates, the compiler has added them in brackets. All the documents within the sections are numbered, references being made to the number of the section and the number of the document (for example, II: 1, i.e. Section II, Document 1).

The compiler, in anticipation, wants to thank all those who will help to publish and circulate the present collection.

Moscow, 24 August 1968   PAVEL LITVINOV

I

THE BACKGROUND:
PERSONALITY OF
THE ACCUSED

In the view of the compiler of the present collection, the trial of
Galanskov, Ginzburg, Dobrovolsky and Lashkova was an extension
of the case of Sinyavsky and Daniel, who in 1966 were sentenced
to seven and five years' strict-regime camp respectively on account
of their literary works. The trial of the four was an extension of this
case as much in substance, in that the activities that placed the
principal defendants in the dock sprang from their reactions to the
1966 case, as in form, in that a considerable part of the materials
that officially incriminated Galanskov and Ginzburg were connected
with the earlier case.

In the compiler's view, the Sinyavsky and Daniel case combined
two contradictory features. On the one hand, it was an expression
of the growing tendency that has begun to assert itself in recent years,
towards the 'formalization' of legal life in the Soviet Union, a
tendency to be guided by existing laws and decrees and not only by
the circumstances in any particular instance. Sinyavsky and Daniel
were tried for what they had actually done under that all-embracing
article of the Russian Criminal Code that covered their activities.
They were not declared 'mentally ill' or 'parasites', 'hooligans',
'agents of imperialist espionage', as might have been done to facilitate
penalizing them. Similarly, although they were persistently censured
from a moral standpoint, they were not formally accused of publishing their works under pseudonyms and abroad, since publication
under a pseudonym or abroad is not in itself criminally punishable.
All they were accused of was that *in publishing abroad* they were
disseminating their *anti-Soviet works*, and that their willingness to be
published was proof of their anti-Soviet intent. Intent is a necessary

3

condition for the application of article 70 of the Russian Criminal Code—anti-Soviet agitation and propaganda. (The compiler is speaking here not of the observation of the essence of the law, but of a purely superficial tendency to be guided by the letter of the law. In his view, the possibility of a violation of the law is already implied in the fact that there is no commentary attached to article 70 of the Criminal Code formally interpreting the concept of 'anti-Soviet agitation and propaganda', this being wholly left to the discretion of the investigation and the court.)

On the other hand, in the Sinyavsky and Daniel trial circumstances played a crucial part. In organizing the trial and according it a great deal of publicity, the authorities tried to check the uncontrolled flow of foreign publications of Soviet authors. It was as though they were addressing all Soviet writers, those of standing as well as beginners; this is what you can expect if works by you that are not published and not approved of here appear abroad!

If this was, indeed, the object of the Sinyavsky and Daniel trial, then, as is now clear, it was not achieved. On the contrary, the organizers of the trial unexpectedly discovered that, besides the writers who in their works transgressed the official limits, there also existed in our country a body of public opinion ready to support these writers. Many representatives of Soviet society—writers, scientists, artists, students—openly expressed their disagreement with the court's decision, demanded a review of the case and the release of the prisoners, or at least the mitigation of their harsh sentences. Public opinion had been latently forming during the ten years since the dismantling of the Stalin cult; now it showed itself openly and took its first steps. This was the most astonishing and significant result of the trial.

Our country's friends abroad reacted even more sharply than the Soviet public to the trial and conviction of Sinyavsky and Daniel. The majority of them being ill-informed about the true state of affairs in our country, they were shocked that such a trial could take place, a trial not of saboteurs, spies or members of terrorist groups, but of writers whose only fault was that they had written and published works which in content and style departed from the officially approved canons of Soviet literature.

The great interest the trial aroused in Soviet and world public opinion of course called for information as complete and objective as possible. Although Soviet and foreign papers and magazines published a considerable amount about the trial, their articles were often tendentious or included inaccurate information, while verbatim reports published abroad contained errors. Being issued at different times in various languages and publications, this material moreover was widely dispersed, while a great amount simply remained unpublished and existed only in an extremely limited number of manuscript copies. Thus there was the unquestionable need for a single collection bringing together all or the most significant materials on the trial, regardless of the point of view expressed in them, which would simultaneously satisfy the public demand for information and, perhaps, act as a stimulus for a review of the case.

It is not surprising that this notion arose independently in the Soviet Union and abroad and was independently expressed. In the Soviet Union, Alexander Ginzburg assembled such a collection, animated, in his own words, by the desire to provide not so much the public as the responsible Soviet leaders with as full information as possible, and thereby to bring about a repeal of the court's, in his view, unjust decision.*

Alexander Ilich GINZBURG was born on 21 November 1936 in Moscow. His father died when he was two years old and the boy was brought up by his mother Lyudmila Ginzburg, an economist by training, but who had taken an interest in art all her life and had passed on this interest to her son. At school he was attracted by poetry and acted in the school's theatre. His idol at that time was Mayakovsky and he often won prizes for reciting the latter's verse. Subsequently he became interested in rowing and in 1954 came first in the All-Union youth competition (in the pairs, kayak and canoe events). After completing secondary school he worked as a lathe-operator in a factory and at the same time as a reporter for the newspaper *Moskovsky Komsomolets*. In 1956 he took evening courses at the faculty of journalism of Moscow University. In 1957 he participated in the work of the Soviet Preparatory Committee of the Sixth International Youth and Student Festival in Moscow and worked as an assistant producer on the films about the festival. In 1958, continuing his university course by correspondence, he got a job as an actor in the Kimry Dramatic Theatre,† where he worked for about two years. In 1959 he fell from the window of his third-floor flat, broke his arm, and consequently had to give up his acting career.

In the late 'fifties new cultural tendencies manifested themselves

* Abroad a similar collection was compiled by Leopold Labedz and Max Hayward, *On Trial: the Case of Sinyavsky (Tertz) and Daniel (Arzhak)*, London and New York, 1967.
† Kimry is a town in the Kalinin Region, 120 km to the north of Moscow, with a population of about 100,000.

in our country. Several writers and artists who had already won official recognition began dealing with hitherto forbidden topics and seeking new forms of expression. Young artists and poets also emerged, the nature of whose work had hitherto virtually excluded the possibility of getting published or having an exhibition in the immediate future in the Soviet Union, not so much because of anything political, as because of their artistic orientation, which puzzled and annoyed the philistines. It may be said that an avant-garde of sorts sprang up in our country. However, the artists and poets were very isolated, knew little about each other and were almost totally unknown to the public. The need for mutual contact, for a certain popularization of the new art was, so to speak, 'in the air', and Ginzburg felt that here he could make a contribution. In 1959-60 he helped to organize several unofficial exhibitions of young artists, and also began publishing the typewritten magazine *Syntax*. His flat became a regular meeting place for young artists, writers and poets.

The magazine *Syntax*, of which three numbers in all appeared,[1] contained only poems. Most of its contributors—notably B. Akhmadulina, A. Glazkov, V. Nekrasov, B. Okudzava, B. Slutsky —either were being published already in official publications or were to be in the next few years. However, the KGB regarded the attempt to publish uncensored, typewritten collections as dangerous. In 1960 a satirical article by A. Ivashchenko, 'The idlers storm Parnassus', appeared in *Izvestia*. Ginzburg was expelled from university, arrested, thrown into the Lubyanka prison and an investigation under article 70 of the Russian Criminal Code was initiated by the organs of the KGB. Over a hundred witnesses were called, but the KGB was evidently unable to bring a convincing indictment against Ginzburg. The only evidence that could be used related to the rather strongly worded comments Ginzburg had made on certain Soviet works of literature at the time of his interrogation, but this was really too insignificant for a criminal case. Besides, the slogan 'there are no political prisoners in the USSR' was still current and the case had already gained too much publicity for Ginzburg to be tried in secret. It was then decided to use another incident to incriminate Ginzburg. Shortly before his arrest he had taken a school-leaving certificate examination on behalf of a friend he wanted to help, switching photographs in his identity card for this purpose. The investigation under article 70 was now dropped, but under article 196, paragraph 1 (forgery of documents), Ginzburg received the maximum two-year sentence, the balance of which, after the trial, he spent in an ordinary-regime camp. (Without in any way condoning Ginzburg's action, it should be pointed out that taking exams for someone else occurs fairly frequently. If it is found out, the examination results are annulled and measures of social pressure are brought to bear on the guilty party, so the institution of criminal proceedings in Ginzburg's case was unique.)

On his return to Moscow in 1962, Ginzburg met with great difficulties. He barely managed to get permission to live in Moscow with his mother, was unable to get a place anywhere to study and found it very hard to get a job. He worked at first in a sewage-disposal trust, then as a lighting engineer in television, a lathe-operator in a home-construction factory, a librarian and an employee in the Museum of Literature. It was only in 1966 that he succeeded in getting on to an evening course in the Historical Archives Institute. In spite of all these difficulties, Ginzburg persevered in his attempts to promote a rapprochement and mutual understanding among various artists and writers, to reduce the spiritual isolation of our young people from world culture. As before, this provoked the open displeasure of the KGB. In 1963 Ginzburg organized a number of showings of French films about artists (Picasso, Utrillo and others) in his own and in friends' homes; although many of these films were subsequently shown in Soviet cinemas, they were confiscated from Ginzburg, and *Izvestia* published a satirical article about him by M. Sturua and V. Kassis, 'The Windbags Ask for Europe'. In 1964 he obtained books on American and European culture from the guides at the Exhibition of American Graphics in Moscow; these books were confiscated from him by the KGB and he was again accused of 'circulating anti-Soviet literature'. (Perhaps the grounds for this accusation lay in the fact that Ginzburg also received several books of a political character—which included M. Djilas's *The New Class*, a book that profoundly irritated the KGB officials.)

He spent several days in the Lubyanka prison again, but, as in 1960, the investigation was broken off because of the obvious groundlessness of the charge. Nevertheless, the KGB did not relax its pressure on Ginzburg. He was informed that he might be arrested or banished from Moscow at a moment's notice if he did not publicly renounce his 'former activities'. This pressure continued for a year and finally Ginzburg wrote the letter demanded of him. It was published in *Evening Moscow*, with a number of additions made by the editorial staff. (The letter, headed 'Answer to Mr Hughes', appeared in the issue of 3 June 1965. The paper informed its readers that it was publishing this 'in the hope that A. Ginzburg has frankly confessed his errors and is setting out firmly on the right path'.

Ginzburg himself writes that, with his interest in literature and art, he had not displayed the necessary political maturity and, therefore, that Western 'propaganda' and 'Western intelligence'—a typical representative of which was Loran Hughes, a journalist—tried to use his naïvety and impulsiveness for their own ends in the following manner: 'An underground writer and public figure is unearthed. I obviously looked like an entirely suitable subject to Western propagandists. Having invested me with an aura of sanctity on my return from prison, they decided, probably for want of anyone better, to use me as one of the cogs in their machine.' Ginzburg declined this role and he ends his letter: 'The glory of the fighter for Western rottenness is the glory of the leper.') This letter greatly surprised Ginzburg's friends and was apparently a source of considerable anguish to Ginzburg himself. It was very important for him to be able to demonstrate to everyone, above all to himself, that he had not, in fact, altered and had remained true to his former convictions regarding the need for creative freedom.

In September[2] 1965 Sinyavsky and Daniel were arrested, and their trial took place in February 1966. Regarding the court's sentence as unjust and the information about the trial as inadequate, Ginzburg decided to produce a collection of all the materials on the trial available to him, with the object of acquainting the representatives of Soviet society and the organs of government with the facts, and thereby securing a review of the case.

Ginzburg started work on the collection shortly after the trial, and the collection was complete towards the end of November 1966. While working on it Ginzburg made no attempt to keep the matter a secret and a considerable number of people were aware of what he was doing and of its exact purpose. Five typewritten copies of the collection were made and Ginzburg immediately handed one of them over to the KGB, intending the other copies for a number of Supreme Soviet deputies. (It is known that he succeeded in informing I. Ehrenburg about it. Whether any other deputies or politicians saw the collection is not known. After Ginzburg had been arrested, the collection, a copy of which had somehow or other got abroad, was published in France under the title *The White Book*.[3]) He notified the KGB about this approach to the deputies, to avoid making the circulation of the book appear clandestine.

In December 1966 Ginzburg was summoned to the City of Moscow and Moscow Region KGB office. He was urged to repudiate his collection, to stop circulating it altogether, and to bring all copies to the KGB and state who had helped him compile it. Ginzburg refused to comply with these demands and was informed that consequently he would soon be arrested and tried under article 190-1 (the circulation of deliberately false fabrications defaming the Soviet political and social order).

The Sinyavsky and Daniel trial made a similarly deep impression on another individual convicted in the trial of the four: Yury Galanskov.

Yury Timofeyevich GALANSKOV was born on 19 June 1939 in Moscow into a worker's family. His father, Timofei Galanskov, worked as a lathe-operator in a factory; his mother, Ekaterina Galanskova, was an office-cleaner. Galanskov grew up under hard conditions, and from early youth had to earn his own living. He worked as an electrician in various theatres, at the same time attending school. Subsequently he worked in the administration of the Machine-tool Technical School, then as an employee in the Museum of Literature. Interested in history and sociology, he studied for two years at the historical faculty of Moscow University, but was expelled. Later, in 1965, he enrolled as an evening student at the Historical Archives Institute, where he studied until the time of his arrest.

Galanskov wrote poetry and in 1959-60 frequently read his verse in Mayakovsky Square, which at the time was a meeting place for young poets. None of his poems was published in the Soviet Union, but later many of them were published several times abroad. However, he did not have a real vocation for poetry; as he said, what always interested him was not the artistic but the social aspect of art. Social problems came to preoccupy him increasingly year by year.

To his mind, there was a discrepancy between the just order envisaged by the founders of socialism and the one actually prevailing in our country. He felt that the 1917 Revolution, like every revolution, was bound to cost something and be subject to certain temporary deviations, but that it was the duty of every honest individual to do his utmost to bring about the gradual revival of the true aims of the revolution. The fact that the lofty ideas of the revolution were later used as a cover for terror and cruel exploitation did not, in his opinion, invalidate them, but he felt that they should be revived not by coercive but by peaceful means: by the widest possible dissemination of the views held by himself. Furthermore, it was necessary to protest against injustice not only in his own country but throughout the world. In his opinion socialist and pacifist

9

propaganda might gradually alter the appearance of the whole world, end wars, hunger and social inequality. If all means of propaganda were monopolized by the state, then one should act on one's own initiative. With this object in mind, he issued the type-written miscellany *Phoenix*[4] in 1961.

From then on Galanskov began to be periodically subjected to enforced periods in psychiatric hospitals. Although he was, in all probability, perfectly healthy to start with, this gradually began to affect his mental state. Nevertheless, he felt it necessary to persevere in his work. In 1965 he staged a one-man demonstration in front of the United States Embassy in Moscow, protesting against American intervention in the Dominican Republic. It was then that he conceived the idea of publishing a pacifist magazine or miscellany bearing, again, the title *Phoenix*, and started collecting material for it.

However, the Sinyavsky and Daniel trial brought about a change in his plans. Shocked by the injustice and severity of the sentence, Galanskov decided to give his material a somewhat different slant. Sinyavsky and Daniel had been accused of circulating their uncensored works; he decided to produce a miscellany of literary, religious and political works that the official publishing houses had refused to publish or that the censorship had not passed. Possibly he thought of publishing similar collections periodically. Acting completely openly and putting his own signature to *Phoenix-'66*,[5] he compiled it on his own from material circulated among the Moscow intelligentsia, including in it his letter to M. Sholokhov in which he harshly condemned the writer for his position on the Sinyavsky and Daniel case. The miscellany was ready at the end of December 1966.

As neither Ginzburg nor Galanskov made a secret of their work, and Ginzburg had even taken a copy of his collection to the KGB, the KGB was able to keep well informed of their activity. (That the KGB was aware of the preparations for *Phoenix* is borne out, in particular, by the following: in November 1966 several pages typed by Lashkova were stolen by two visiting detectives, when she went out into the corridor to answer the door. The detectives called on the pretext of questioning her about the recently deceased religious writer, Mark Dobrokhotov.) Those wishing to prevent the appearance of more collections on the political trials and the circulation of uncensored literature possibly saw the arrest and trial of Ginzburg and Galanskov as the only solution. This, they might hope, would not only deprive Galanskov and Ginzburg of the opportunity to circulate their material, but would also frighten others. However, the hostile reaction of Soviet and world public opinion to the trial of persons convicted on account of their works was still fresh in the memory. For this reason those favouring a trial decided to invent a plot to secure a conviction on quite different grounds. Once again, as in the 1966 trial, they were trying to intimidate the Soviet intelligentsia—you see, this is what you can expect!—and at the same time to shrug off world public opinion with the claim that 'we are not trying writers but conspirators!'

To put the trial in this light it was necessary, in the first place, somehow to link the work being done by Ginzburg and Galanskov, to prove that they were jointly compiling the *Collection of Materials on the Sinyavsky and Daniel Trial* and *Phoenix-'66*. In this respect, they could use the fact that the two had known each other for about seven years, had recently been working in the same museum and studying at the same institute. Furthermore, the same typist had done some of the typing for both of them. However, even if this 'evidence' was to be taken seriously, their joint efforts in the compilation of both collections hardly amounted to an 'anti-Soviet plot'.

The missing link turned out to be Aleksei Dobrovolsky. During and after the trial the view was frequently expressed that Dobrovolsky had for some years been a KGB stool-pigeon, deliberately placed, right at the beginning, in the psychiatric hospital where Bukovsky was confined and afterwards, for a few months before their arrest, fixed up with a job in the Museum of Literature where Ginzburg and Galanskov worked. (In 1965 Vladimir Bukovsky was in a prison psychiatric hospital on a charge of anti-Soviet activity. He was accused of making photocopies of Milovan Djilas's book *The New Class*. There he became acquainted with Dobrovolsky and reported favourably on him when released. In January 1967 Bukovsky was one of the organizers of the demonstration demanding the release of Galanskov, Dobrovolsky, Lashkova and Radziyevsky, who had been arrested shortly before. The same year he was sentenced on account of this to three years of ordinary-regime camp.[6]) Supposedly Dobrovolsky had become more intimate with them to describe their allegedly anti-Soviet and conspiratorial activity and links with foreign organizations during the investigation and trial. However, there are no very strong grounds for such a view and probably the matter was more complicated.

Aleksei Alexandrovich DOBROVOLSKY was born on 13 October 1938 in Moscow. His father died when Dobrovolsky was two years old and he was raised by his mother, Natalya Dobrovolskaya, an aeronautical engineer by profession. He was brought up to revere the existing social order, the government and, in particular,

Stalin. Khrushchev's anti-Stalinist speech at the 20th Party Congress and the subsequent de-Stalinization campaign deeply shocked him, provoking his first conflict with society: he was expelled from the Komsomol for pro-Stalinist speeches. A mentally unbalanced person by nature, with the desire frequent among schizophrenics to play a more significant part than his capabilities allowed him to, Dobrovolsky grew more and more embittered, leaping more and more rapidly from one extreme to the other the more ruthlessly he was treated by the society in which he lived. His attitude swiftly altered from extreme pro-Stalinism to extreme anti-Stalinism and in 1957 he was arrested for distributing pamphlets of an anti-Soviet nature and sentenced to six years.[7] (Both here and below the compiler is discussing Dobrovolsky's anti-Soviet sentiments not on the basis of the verbal content of the various sentences passed on him, but on the grounds of his own personal statements as reported by his friends after his appearance in court in January 1968. Dobrovolsky himself denied in court that he now held anti-Soviet views. It should also be pointed out that, in view of the total absence of a legal definition of the word 'anti-Soviet', the compiler is taking as anti-Soviet those actions or statements regarded as such by their perpetrators.) According to other prisoners, he kept to himself in the camp, not collaborating with the camp administration, frequently undergoing various kinds of disciplinary action; nevertheless he was released after half his term had been served.[8] The symptoms of a profound mental disturbance that subsequently deepened had already been observable in the camp. The circumstances of Dobrovolsky's life were conducive to this: the KGB arrested him twice more and investigated him on the charge of anti-Soviet agitation; the first time the investigation was called off, the second time he was confined to the prison psychiatric hospital in Leningrad by court order. He several times underwent medical examinations and compulsory treatment on the basis of the usual diagnosis, 'psychopathy', the last occasion being in 1966. He had no means of continuing his studies and took up all kinds of casual occupations which gave him little satisfaction; only in 1966 was he able to get on to an evening course at the Moscow Institute of Culture. Even in his youth religious questions had interested him and, under the pressure of life's shocks this religiosity became, on the surface at least, increasingly fanatical. At the same time, according to those who knew him, petty calculation, greed, stinginess and a purely physical cunning became more and more salient features of his character.

The Sinyavsky and Daniel trial made a deep impression on him too. He saw in it additional proof of the correctness of his anti-Soviet sentiments. He got to know Galanskov at this time and nearly tried to take part in several public protests, but their legal and democratic character was profoundly alien to him; he aspired to extremist actions of a conspiratorial kind. Apparently he proposed something like this to Galanskov, and Galanskov's refusal deeply offended him, calling forth feelings of vindictiveness and petulance. The question as to whether Dobrovolsky was connected with any foreign anti-Soviet organization, in particular the NTS,* deserves consideration. There are two indirect pieces of evidence: in the first place, when his flat was searched, various materials that might have come from the NTS (NTS literature, pamphlets, a hectograph and money) were confiscated; in the second place, he told his friend Vera Lashkova that he could enroll her in the NTS†. Several of Dobrovolsky's friends subsequently stated that they often saw dollars at his flat and heard him express the intention of printing pamphlets in Moscow, supposedly in the name of the NTS, but there are no means now of verifying these statements. Thus, although there are no grounds for asserting categorically that Dobrovolsky had a link with the NTS, such a link is not improbable, particularly as it is not inconsistent with Dobrovolsky's views. If so, it is not unlikely that the KGB was to a greater or lesser extent aware of these links and able to take

* NTS—*Narodno-trudovoi soyuz (rossiiskikh solidaristov)* or The People's Labour Alliance (of Russian Solidarists)—is an organization of political émigrés from the USSR, with headquarters in Frankfurt-on-Main, West Germany. The Alliance was set up in the 'thirties[9] in Belgrade largely by the second generation of émigrés, when it was called The National Labour Alliance (of the Younger Generation), or *Natsionalno-trudovoi soyuz (molodogo pokoleniya)*. Unlike the majority of émigré organizations, the NTS actively strove to penetrate Soviet society, in which it occupied anti-Soviet and anti-bolshevist positions. It appears that the NTS, at least as regards many of its members, collaborated with the Germans during the war,[10] and after the war with the Americans. After the war the NTS filled up with new members from among the so-called displaced persons, but it retained its anti-Soviet orientation. Its programme envisages the overthrow of the Soviet system by force and the establishment of a system based on the solidarist philosophy. As before, the NTS tries actively to influence Soviet society by publishing and circulating various kinds of books, magazines and pamphlets, and also by making personal contact with Soviet citizens abroad and in the USSR. Tourist trips to the USSR of other nationals who are sympathetic to the NTS are turned to account. The NTS frequently distributes its materials to people with whom it has no contact, acquiring their addresses from various reference books. Thus receiving or harbouring NTS literature is in no way proof of any connection with the organization. Also many NTS emissaries may get to know various Soviet citizens while not revealing to them that they belong to the NTS, but simply stressing their interest in Soviet social life or literature.

† In court Dobrovolsky himself explained this by alleging that Galanskov had entrusted all these materials to him, and that he had simply been joking with Lashkova. There is another version that explains the presence of NTS material in Dobrovolsky's flat by his prior agreement with the KGB (see p. 111).

them into account, trying Dobrovolsky on the same charge as Galanskov and Ginzburg.

In the autumn of 1966 Dobrovolsky became a bookbinder in the Museum of Literature where Galanskov and Ginzburg were already working. He had no contact with Ginzburg at all, never discussed anything with him and never visited his home. With Galanskov, on the other hand, he maintained contact and agreed to the publication in *Phoenix* of his article 'The Interrelation of Knowledge and Faith'[11] and the anonymous work 'A Description of Events in the Pochayev Monastery'[12] that had originated in religious circles and was being circulated by him. Although, according to what he said at the trial, he was indifferent as to whether these things appeared in *Phoenix* or not, he could now, all the same, be regarded as an indirect participant in Galanskov's activity. (As was revealed during the investigation, there may also have been some sort of monetary arrangement between Dobrovolsky and Galanskov. Galanskov testified that he received $560 from Dobrovolsky, initially for the purchase of a typewriter and subsequently to convert them into Soviet roubles. Dobrovolsky denied this and in turn maintained about the 2000 Soviet roubles found at his place that he had received them from Galanskov. Although it is impossible at present to confirm either testimony, it seems to the compiler that Galanskov's is more trustworthy, when the falseness of much of Dobrovolsky's evidence and his line of defence are taken into account.)

The typist Vera Lashkova typed part of the material for *Phoenix* and the *Collection on the Sinyavsky and Daniel case*. She was the fourth person put on trial with Galanskov, Ginzburg and Dobrovolsky. Other typists also typed some of the material for *Phoenix*, some of whom were called as witnesses, others not being called at all. Most likely Lashkova was brought to trial because she typed for Ginzburg as well as for Galanskov and for that reason might serve as a connecting link between them, and also because she was already known to the KBG on account of her friendship with several young poets. She was later accused also of circulating anti-Soviet literature, but the fact that she had shown books published by the NTS to two people apparently came to light only during the course of the investigation.

Vera Iosifovna LASHKOVA was born on 18 June 1944 in Moscow. Her father, Iosif Belogorov, a railway employee, and her mother, Anna Lashkova, a cook, separated when she was only a little girl. She lived at first with her mother, but when she was sixteen she was on her own; the mother went to join her husband in Smolensk. No one helped Lashkova and she had to rely on her own

resources. After she left school, she worked as a messenger, a laboratory assistant, a cleaner and a typist in various establishments. In
1965 she entered the extra-mural department of stage management
at the Moscow Institute of Culture.

The trial of Sinyavsky and Daniel and the public protests it provoked made a great impression on her. In late 1965 she met
Dobrovolsky and in summer 1966 Galanskov, who later introduced
her to Ginzburg. She saw in them people who were apparently
guided not by hopes of material gain and the desire to improve their
position in life somehow or other, but primarily by idealistic considerations, even if this got them into trouble. It was for this reason,
evidently, and also out of interest in the materials themselves, that
she undertook to type a number of pieces at Dobrovolsky's request
and afterwards for Galanskov and Ginzburg. Both Galanskov and
Ginzburg, in their turn, wanted to help Lashkova. Galanskov gave
her his typewriter, thanks to which she was able to earn money as a
home-typist, and Ginzburg brought her money and provisions during
the time she was typing for him. Thus it can be said that Ginzburg
paid for her work as a typist, although they had made no formal
arrangement about a definite sum. None of the materials she typed,
according to Galanskov and Ginzburg as well as Lashkova, were
anti-Soviet in character, nor could they constitute grounds for the
three being involved in the same case. Both the men warned
Lashkova not to conceal the work she was doing and, if any government agencies enquired as to whom she was typing for, to tell them
the truth.

So by January 1967 the *Collection of Materials on the Sinyavsky and
Daniel Trial* was ready and Ginzburg, having sent one copy to the
KGB, started circulating the remainder among deputies of the
Supreme Soviet. The miscellany *Phoenix* too was ready and Galanskov
was preparing to acquaint the Moscow literary public with it. Those
anxious to curtail their activity were faced with the choice of either
permitting these collections to be circulated or stopping this activity
at once.

II

BEFORE THE TRIAL

On 17 January 1967 Vera Lashkova was accosted in the institute where she worked by persons with Ministry for the Maintenance of Public Order [MMPO] identification cards. They informed her that her flat had been burgled and that she must accompany them there. However, they took her to the Moscow and Moscow Region KGB reception centre where she was soon shown a search warrant, whereupon they proceeded to her home for the search. On 18 January she was interrogated for the first time and taken to the Lefortovo prison, but it was only on 21 January that the KGB managed to obtain the Procurator's approval of her arrest.

That same day, 17 January, searches were carried out in Galanskov's home (Document II: 1),* Ginzburg's (Document II: 2) and Dobrovolsky's. Galanskov and Dobrovolsky were arrested on 19 January and Ginzburg on the 23rd. Approval of the arrests of all three was obtained only after their detention, when they were all already in the Lefortovo prison. Radziyevsky, with whose aid Dobrovolsky tried to duplicate a series of manuscripts, was arrested a little before, but was released after a few days, once he had given the KGB the evidence they required. The entire operation, it appears, was conducted by General A. A. Skvortsov, and the investigation of the case was carried out by Major V. I. Eliseyev.

It is impossible now to give any detailed account of the circumstances surrounding the preliminary investigation. It is known that initially the investigation centred on the matter of the leaflets of 4 December 1966[13] and the collections compiled by Ginzburg and Galanskov; this merged with an investigation of the demonstration of 22 January 1967. But it was February–March, when definite collaboration between the KGB and Dobrovolsky became noticeable, that the allegation of links between the defendants and the NTS was first heard and increasingly emphasized. A second search was

* References to the documents in this section are in brackets. All the documents available to the compiler relating to the investigation and to the public reaction to it and the impending trial are there, given in chronological order.

16

carried out at Dobrovolsky's home and NTS materials were discovered. The fact that nothing of the sort had been found during the first search led some people to assume that all these articles had been purposely placed there by the KGB with Dobrovolsky's consent, but it is impossible to be absolutely certain about this.

A forensic medical diagnosis of Galanskov and Dobrovolsky, who were registered in psycho-neurological health centres, was carried out, and they were both judged to be of sound mind. It must be noted that the conclusions of the diagnoses, especially with regard to Dobrovolsky, are not sufficiently convincing.

However, it was precisely Dobrovolsky's evidence that became the main basis for the charges. Dobrovolsky showed great, at times even excessive, willingness to collaborate with the investigation. Thus he requested in writing that he be allowed to speak on radio and television and tell the whole story of his own criminal activity and that of the others under investigation, and thereby warn young people against acts of disloyalty; he also gave information as to the existence of caches where undiscovered copies of *The White Book* and *Phoenix* could allegedly be found. As a result, the public garden near Ginzburg's home, for example, was dug up by KGB men. Dobrovolsky gave evidence of the existence of an allegedly broad 'anti-Soviet front', starting with academics and ending with young poets, and he wrote notes to Galanskov from the psychiatric institute where the diagnosis was made, urging the latter to give the KGB the evidence it needed, etc. Galanskov began to comply in the hope, possibly, of making things easier for Dobrovolsky by taking the blame on himself; however, when he got to know of Dobrovolsky's testimony, he repudiated his own. Nevertheless, the interrogator succeeded in blackmailing Galanskov with the prospect of a long drawn-out investigation and a harsh sentence into reaffirming his false testimony and it was only to the court itself that he finally repudiated it. In the summer, during the course of the investigation of a group of currency operators, it was revealed, furthermore, that Galanskov had sold one of them dollars through Entin and Borisova, and a new charge was added to the accusation against him. A second search was carried out at Galanskov's home and an inventory of his property was drawn up (Documents II: 10 and 11). Lashkova too confirmed that she had seen dollars at Galanskov's home and recounted several episodes involving Galanskov along the lines required by the investigation, for example, how she took a cipher letter at his dictation. Ginzburg alone refused to give the KGB the evidence it wanted; furthermore, the KGB had no evidence against him, although he was intended to be the central figure in the trial. A further search was carried out in his home in September which produced no results (Document II: 12).

About fifty witnesses were examined during the course of the investigation. Searches were carried out in the homes of many of the witnesses; typewriters and typewritten and printed material were confiscated.

The investigation was closed on 21 September and by 12 October the accused had familiarized themselves with all the materials relating to the case. (In all, there were nineteen volumes of it.) They were all charged under article 70, paragraph 1 of the Russian Criminal Code, Galanskov being, in addition, charged under article 88, paragraph 1. All the accused took defence counsels; Galanskov took D. I. Kaminskaya; Ginzburg, B. A. Zolotukhin; Dobrovolsky, V. Ya. Shveisky; Lashkova, S. L. Ariya. The case was handed over to the Moscow City Court and the hearing was set for 11 December. By this time the period during which the prisoners had been held in custody had exceeded the legally permitted maximum by over one and a half months. However, the trial did not even start on 11 December. It can be assumed that this was for reasons of expediency: the investigation was not sure of the cogency of its arguments and, as its last trump, was waiting for the arrival from abroad of some NTS emissary, which the organs of the KGB might have known about beforehand. The trial was finally set for 8 January 1968. It may be that in order to justify such a lengthy pre-trial detention period a special decree of the Presidium of the Russian Supreme Soviet was issued—but this is only supposition.

Since public opinion linked this case with Sinyavsky's and Daniel's trial, it received considerable publicity right from the start. The first public reaction to the arrests was a demonstration on 22 January 1967 in Pushkin Square in Moscow, demanding the release of Galanskov, Dobrovolsky, Lashkova and Radziyevsky, in which about forty people took part; five were detained and four appeared in court and received one- to three-year sentences. (V. Khaustov and V. Bukovsky received three years; E. Kushev and V. Delone, one year's suspended sentence each, all of them under article 190-3 of the Russian Criminal Code. I. Gabai spent several months in the Lefortovo prison and the investigation of his case was dropped. With regard to this, see *The Case of the Demonstration of 22 January 1967*, edited by P. Litvinov, London, 1968.[14])

As soon as it became known that a collection on the Sinyavsky and Daniel case had been compiled, several foreign correspondents in Moscow wanted to meet its authors. Rumours of arrests and the demonstration stimulated this interest still further. Alexander Ginzburg and Olga Timofeyeva, the wife of Galanskov, were supposed to meet correspondents on 24 January. However, Ginzburg was arrested on the evening before and Olga Timofeyeva saw the correspondents alone and told them of Galanskov's and Ginzburg's arrest and of the reasons for this. Thus the Soviet public and the world learnt about the beginning of the case.

From the very beginning then, it was clear that the Soviet public was not going to remain indifferent. On 11 February Academician A. D. Sakharov appealed to the Central Committee of the Soviet communist party asking for the Ginzburg and Galanskov trial to be called off; he received no reply. (This is A. D. Sakharov's account in his pamphlet 'Reflections on progress, peaceful co-existence and intellectual freedom', dated June 1968: 'Is it not a disgrace that Ginzburg, Galanskov and others were arrested, imprisoned for twelve months without trial and sentenced to five and seven years for activities which basically consisted in defending civil liberties and, as regards people, to give one example, Daniel and Sinyavsky? On 11 February 1967 the author of these lines appealed to the Central Committee of the Soviet communist party requesting that the case against Ginzburg and Galanskov be dismissed. However, he received no reply whatsoever to his appeal, nor any clarification of the matter. Only much later did he learn that an attempt, evidently on the initiative of the former KGB chairman Semichastny, had been made to slander him and a number of other persons with the help of false testimony elicited from one of the accused in the Galanskov and Ginzburg case. Subsequently the testimony of this very same defendant—Dobrovolsky—was used by the prosecution at the trial of Ginzburg and Galanskov as evidence of a link between these defendants and a foreign anti-Soviet organization, all of which inevitably gives rise to doubts.') On 16 March the *Figaro Littéraire* (Paris) published an interview with the writer Yu. Kazakov, who described Ginzburg in extremely unfavourable terms. Granted, Kazakov later explained that he had confused Ginzburg with another person (Document II: 9). At the end of February Ginzburg's mother sent a letter to the leaders of party and state in which she wrote of the illegality of her son's arrest and the hard conditions of his pre-trial imprisonment. She received no effective reply in respect of these questions. In November she sent another letter in which she pointed out a series of violations of the law that had taken place during the course of the investigation.

Again she received no effectual reply (Documents II: 3, 4, 5, 6, 7, 8, 13, 14 and 15).

As the trial approached, the fear grew that it would, in effect, be a closed one like the Sinyavsky and Daniel trial or that of the demonstrators. There had already been violations of the law (the long duration of the pre-trial detention periods, the infringement of the established time limits within which cases should be brought before the court and heard) and they gave an additional cause for anxiety. For this reason on 30 November a group of 116 citizens addressed a letter to the Procurator-General of the Soviet Union and the Chairman of the Moscow City Court, asking for assurances that the legal proceedings would be public and that friends of the accused would be allowed into court (Document II: 16). There was no reply to the letter. A few days before 11 December when the trial was expected to begin a group of forty-two citizens, mainly from among the signatories of the previous letter, again wrote to the same authorities requesting that infringements of the law be eliminated and that the trial be guaranteed publicity. Finally, at the beginning of January 1968, a group of thirty-one citizens wrote to the Moscow City Court, pointing out the unlawfulness, in their opinion, of Ginzburg's arrest and demanding that his trial be conducted in public (Documents II: 17 and 18).

There was no reply, but perhaps it was these very protests, and also the information about the impending trial put out by foreign stations, that persuaded the persons concerned not to conduct it unobtrusively, as for example in the case of the demonstrators, but to focus public attention on it, stressing the alleged link between the accused and the NTS. On 3 January a brief item appeared in *Izvestia* on the arrest of the NTS emissary Brox-Sokolov; on the 9th, the second day of the trial, there was a long article on the NTS and Brox-Sokolov; on the 10th he appeared in the trial as a witness; and on the 16th *Izvestia*, counting on a primed readership, wrote categorically of the links between the accused and the NTS. (The Brox-Sokolov case is only indirectly related to the case of Ginzburg, Galanskov, Dobrovolsky and Lashkova and is interesting merely from the point of view of the propagandist methods of the KGB, all the materials on him have been consigned to a special appendix.*)

Under these conditions the trial began and was conducted.

* Appendix I in Litvinov's collection. It is omitted in this edition, the material on Brox-Sokolov being for the most part either irrelevant to the Ginzburg–Galanskov case or included already in other parts of the collection. The four documents reproduced by Litvinov are: 'In the KGB' (article in *Izvestia*, 3 January 1968); 'The Depths' (*Izvestia*,

[margin annotations: Cnjctrs ++ prts | lttrs & atten to case in forgn press convcd auths to cover it extnsly & emph the supp cnnctn b/w NTS & dfndnts]

Document II: 1

RECORD OF SEARCH

Moscow, 17 January 1967

Captain Sedov, investigator in the Investigation Section of the Directorate of the KGB under the Council of Ministers of the USSR for the City and Region of Moscow, and Captain Kustov, Senior Lieutenants Vasyukin, Balakirev and Karamas, members of the same Directorate, together with search witnesses Alexander Semyonovich Tishchenko, resident of Moscow, ul. Profsoyuznaya, d. 43, korp. B, kv. 39; Victor Vasilevich Lozenko, resident of Moscow, ul. Profsoyuznaya, d. 43, korp. B, kv. 39; Victor Ivanovich Surnev, ul. Profsoyuznaya, d. 43, korp. B, kv. 39; Sergei Petrovich Chamarya, resident of ul. Kedrova, d. 3, korp. 6, kv. 24 [presumably the search witnesses too were members of the KGB, as they took an active part in the search and furthermore were living in KGB houses]; and in the presence of Yury Timofeyevich Galanskov, his wife Olga Valentinovna Timofeyeva, and his mother Ekaterina Alekseyevna Galanskova; in accordance with the requirements of articles 169-171 and 176-177 of the Russian Criminal Code and on the basis of the decision of 17 January 1967 of the Investigations Section of the Directorate of the KGB under the Council of Ministers of the USSR for the City and Region of Moscow, on the instruction of Chief Investigator comrade Major Eliseyev, conducted a search of Yu. T. Galanskov's flat at the following address: Moscow, 3-i Golutvinsky per., dom. 7/9, kv. 4.

It was explained to the above-named persons that they were entitled to be present during the entire course of the investigator's activities and to make statements regarding any of these activities. In addition, it was explained to the witnesses that it was their duty, under article 135 of the Russian Criminal Code, to attest to the act, procedures and results of the search.

The search was begun at 13.40 hours and was completed at 18.30 hours.

Before the search was started it was suggested to Yu. T. Galanskov that he voluntarily surrender the handwritten, typewritten and other documents of an anti-Soviet content mentioned in the warrant authorizing the search. Yury Timofeyevich Galanskov declared that no such documents were in his possession.

Subsequently a search was carried out in the flat of Yu. T. Galanskov and in the Galanskov family's wood-shed.

During the search the following items were discovered and confiscated:

1. A book entitled *Your Firm Constitution*, in Russian, printed in West Germany in May 1963, 153 pages, in dark blue covers [a book about the constitution of the United States].

---

9 January 1968); 'A Familiar Name' (*Izvestia*, 10 July 1968); and 'A Sabotage Enterprise and its Finale' (*Isvestia*, 11 July 1968). Ed.

2. Two copies of a typewritten text starting with the words: 'Open Letter' and ending with the words: 'Letter signed by', each copy on ten sheets.

3. Typewritten text, ten pages, entitled 'The Interrelation of Knowledge and Faith: an Exercise in Apologetics by Aleksei Dobrovolsky'.[15]

4. Typewritten text, six pages, starting with the words: 'G. Pomerants: Paper delivered at the Institute of Philosophy'.[16] On the last page is the date: '3 December 1965'.

5. Typewritten text, nine pages of white paper, starting with the words: 'Open Letter to the Presidium of the Central Committee of the Communist Party'. On the last page is the signature: 'A. Levltin (Krasnov). 28 July 1965'.

6. Assembled pages of a typescript in a yellow cover, forty-six pages in all, the text beginning with the words: 'Culture, Truth, Russia. *Russian Word*.'[17] Typewritten on the last page is: 'Editor Khokhlov'. [Typewritten magazine *Russian Word* issued by V. Khokhlov.]

7. Typescript of nine pages on white paper, the text beginning with the words: 'To the Commission of the USSR Supreme Soviet' and ending with the words: 'Collection of signatures to the petition continues'.

8. Typescript of seventy-one pages on white paper, beginning with the words: 'Preamble. Article 1' and ending with the words: 'Constitutes a most serious crime'. [Items 7 and 8 refer to a draft for a new constitution of the USSR, drawn up by a group of Soviet citizens, and their appeal to the USSR Supreme Soviet.]

9. Typewritten miscellany entitled *Phoenix*, 379 pages. Typewritten on the first page: 'Edited by Yu. Galanskov, Moscow, 1966'. On the last page is typed the list of contents of *Phoenix*, with page numbers 1 to 376.

10. Visiting-card of the Japanese Embassy on which the following address is written: 'Gruzinsky Per., dom 3, kv. 236'. [Visiting-card of a Japanese Embassy official Minoru Tamba.]

11. Sheet of white paper with a note written in pencil starting with the words: 'Short waves' and ending with the words: 'Free Europe—40'.[18]

12. Four sheets of white paper bearing the seal of the Machine-tool Technical Evening School of Moscow.

13. Blank forms of the Machine-tool Technical Evening School of Moscow, eleven pages, three of which forms bear the seal of the above-mentioned technical school.

14. Application forms of the Machine-tool Technical Evening School bearing the round seal of the said school, one of which is filled out in the name of Yury Timofeyevich Galanskov and dated 1 December 1965. [Items 12-14: Galanskov worked in this technical school as a secretary until he joined the Museum of Literature.]

15. Two forms from the philosophical faculty of Moscow University with stamps in the corner. [Galanskov became a student in this faculty of Moscow University.]

16. Small-calibre cartridges in four clips, 154 in all. [The cartridges belonged to Galanskov's father, a hunter.]

17. Handwritten texts consisting of eighteen pages.

18. Three sheets of blank white paper, from a packet of typing paper made by the Kommunar Factory, artel 76, paper size 203 × 208 mm.

19. One sheet of black and one sheet of red carbon-paper.

20. Various kinds of blank white paper, fifty-six sheets in all.

21. Typewritten text on sheets of white paper, 411 pages in all.

22. Photocopies of typewritten text on photographic paper, size 17 × 12 cm.

23. Note-book with dark-blue leatherette covers.

24. Dark green cloth-bound note-book containing sheets of music paper.

25. Photocopies of typewritten text on 112 sheets of photographic paper, size 12 × 18 cm. Objects and texts listed in this record, items 17-25 inclusive, have been stamped with sealing wax stamp No. 8.

26. Rectangular metal box, size 30 × 22 × 10 cm, without a lid.

27. Half-litre bottle containing congealed black dye.

28. Piece of congealed white substance, wrapped in vinyl plastic film.

29. Piece of dark-red paint.

30. (Glass) pipette, stained with dye.

31. Roller, made from a large nail and two rubber tubes, with traces of dye, 26 cm long.

32. Piece of black rubber tubing, 12 cm long.

33. Piece of bent hollow copper tubing.

34. Piece of black substance.

35. Metal plate, 17 cm long.

36. Fifteen heavy white metal plates of various shapes, with printer's type along the edge. [Items 26-36: The articles belong to Yu. Galanskov's father, who had previously worked in a printing house and brought them home for personal domestic use. For example, the metal plates he used as plummets for fishing.]

37. Small grey metal box, with a metal fastening, containing a liquid (found in desk).

Items 26 to 36 inclusive were found in a wooden trunk in the wood-shed outside.

The confiscated items 26 to 36 were parcelled up and sealed with the sealing wax stamp of No. 3 investigator. Three photographs were taken of the confiscated objects during the search.

Statements or comments with regard to the search made by persons taking part in the search or present during it: Yu. T. Galanskov stated that the nature of the texts confiscated from him did not correspond to the substance of the search warrant.

The record was read out by the investigator: it had been correctly made.

Signature of persons whose premises have been searched: Galanskov, Timofeyeva, Mrs Galanskov. Signature of persons taking part in the search—Witnesses: Tishchenko, Lozenko, Surnev, Chamarya; Investigators: Sedov, Kustov, Vasyukin, Balakirev, Karamas. Copy of search record received by Galanskov.*

Document II: 2

RECORD OF SEARCH

Moscow, 17 January 1967

Captain Smelov, senior investigator in the Investigation Section of the Directorate of the KGB under the Council of Ministers of the USSR for the City and Region of Moscow, Senior Lieutenant Zabaluyev, Lieutenants Baryshev, Guganov, Semashkin and expert Khorinov, together with search witnesses Anna Fyodorovna Kiryagina and Kuzma Sergeyevich Denisov, residents of g. Moskva, ul. B. Polyanka, d. 11/14, kv. 25, and in the presence of Lyudmila Ilinichna Ginzburg, in accordance with the requirements of articles 169-171, 176 and 177 of the Russian Criminal Code conducted a search of Alexander Ilich Ginzburg's flat, kv. 25, d. 11/14, ul. Bolshaya Polyanka, with the object of finding and confiscating anti-Soviet manuscripts and literature and also other articles bearing on the case.

It was explained to the above-named persons that they were entitled to be present during the entire course of the investigator's activities and to make statements regarding any of these activities. In addition, it was explained to the witnesses that it was their duty, under article 135 of the Russian Criminal Code, to attest to the act, procedures and results of the search.

The search was begun at 13.40 hours and completed at 20.15 hours.

Before the search began a warrant of 17 January 1967 was produced by the investigator, after which it was suggested to L. I. Ginzburg (A. I. Ginzburg's mother) that she surrender the manuscripts and literature mentioned in the warrant, to which L. I. Ginzburg declared that she knew nothing about any such documents. At 14.00 hours Alexander Ilich Ginzburg returned to the flat and he also was shown the search warrant, after which he declared that there were no manuscripts or literature of an anti-Soviet nature at his home.

During the search the following items were discovered and confiscated, to be handed over to the Moscow City and Regional Directorate of the KGB.

1. Standard sheet of white paper on which was noted: 'Moskva M-461, Kherson, d. 4, kv. 38, bus 101 to Khersonskaya St. 1, AV 9-31-30 34, 481, Kovenadsky, AD 1-14-54'.

2. Poetic text on a sheet of white unruled paper dedicated to A. Agin, beginning with the words: 'O, soul, do not fly from the body . . .' and ending: 'Lifts us straight up to the stars'.

* Six-page record, each page signed.

3. The same poetry text as in item two, entitled 'Plebeian Song'.

4. Typescript on six sheets stitched together. At the top of the first sheet, written in red ink: 'Remaining in Moscow for the summer, I imitate the Chinese writers (poem in thirty quatrains)'. The typescript ends with the words: 'The old grey-headed curator sleeps, napping on the books'.

5. 'Anthology of Soviet Pathology', typewritten poetry collection marked 'Leningrad SkhS 1962', thirty pages. On the last page is written: 'United Publishers "Kapa" and "Beta".'

6. Typescript on a sheet of white unruled paper, beginning with the words: 'To the Politbureau of the Central Committee of the Soviet Communist Party, to the Presidium of the Supreme Soviet of the USSR, to the Session of the Supreme Soviet of the RSFSR, to the Session of the Supreme Soviet of the USSR. Dear Comrades! We, a group of Soviet citizens, regard it as our duty . . .' and ends: ' . . . may become an obstacle to the implementation of liberties guaranteed under the Constitution of the USSR.'

[Protest of a group of Soviet citizens against the introduction of articles 190-1 and 190-3 into the Russian Criminal Code.][19]

7. Typewritten miscellany *Phoenix*, edited by Yu. Galanskov, Moscow, 1966, 379 (three hundred and seventy-nine) pages with cardboard covers. The contents of the magazine are as follows: 'You May Begin' (editorial article)[20]; A. Sinyavsky: 'What Is Socialist Realism?'[21]; V. Velsky: 'The Confession of Victor Velsky'[22]; Yu. Galanskov: 'Open Letter'[23]; 'Verbatim Record of the Discussion of the Pasternak Affair at a Meeting of Moscow Writers'[24]; A. Sinyavsky: 'In Defence of the Pyramid'[25]; 'Protest of the Creative Intelligentsia'[26]; 'Discussion of the Draft of the Third Volume of *The History of the Party* in the Institute of Marxism-Leninism by Old Bolsheviks'[27]; E. S. Varga: 'The Russian Road to Socialism'[28]; Letter by N. Bukharin[29]; Karaguzhin: 'Two Stories'[30]; O. Mandelshtam: 'Two Letters'[31]; E. Genri: 'Open Letter to the Writer Ehrenburg'[32]; 'Questions Put to the Writer E. Genri at a Lecture on Neo-fascism in Moscow University'[33]; G. Pomerants: 'Paper Delivered at the Institute of Philosophy'[34]; Yu. Galanskov: 'Organizational Problems of the Movement for Complete and General Disarmament and Peace throughout the World'[35]; Pomerants: 'Quadrillion'[36]; 'The Interrelation of Knowledge and Faith: an Exercise in Apologetics' by A. Dobrovolsky[37]; 'Description of Events in the Pochayev Monastery Today'[38]; 'Verses of Young People'[39]; Obituary.[40]

8. Twenty-nine (29) sheets of white unruled paper with a typewritten text. On the first sheet is written: 'Was not able to recall the quotations...'. On the second sheet the text starts with the words: 'Only Volodka Margulis was at my place all this time . . .' and ends: 'Too much . . .'. On the third page is written: 'The next day in Moscow . . .', and it ends: 'And so on in the usual spirit'. The fourth page begins: 'The writer Arkady Vasilev . . .' and ends: 'That is what the comparison showed'.

25

The fifth begins: 'In Odessa thieves . . .' and ends: 'A certain Soviet writer'. The sixth page begins: 'See quotation in footnote on page'. The seventh page begins: 'I was knocked off my feet . . .' and ends: 'I lay down against these marble walls'. The eighth page begins: 'Well, Svetlana . . .' and ends: 'The world, you understand?' The ninth page begins: 'Unable to recall quotation'. The tenth begins: 'We were ordered' and ends: 'The same again'. The eleventh page begins: 'I go, and dreaming myself . . .' and ends: 'will destroy the Soviet Republic'. The twelfth begins: 'Was impossible to reconstruct the quotations'. The thirteenth begins: 'See quotation in footnote on page'. The fourteenth begins likewise. The fifteenth begins: 'Quotations from the manuscript "The Place of the Fatherland Cannot be Reconstructed" '. The sixteenth page begins: 'See quotation in footnote on page'. The seventeenth page begins: 'The human foetus is known . . .' and ends: 'Paris 1961'. The eighteenth page begins: 'What are you laughing at' and ends: 'With which the court operated . . .'. The nineteenth page begins: 'This is not classicism either' and ends: 'The sense of our life . . .'. The twentieth page begins: 'Lenin is too like . . .' and ends: 'To become a god of immortality . . .'. The twenty-first page begins: 'He leant over the railings . . .' and ends: 'Of a sick imagination . . .'. The twenty-second page begins: 'Drunkenness is our native . . .' and ends: 'Washington 1965'. The twenty-fourth page begins: 'Detective Vitaly Kochetov . . .' and ends: 'Of our dumbfounded public . . .'. The twenty-fifth page begins: 'Let us with our combined effort . . .' and ends: 'With the blood-curdling hyperbole . . .'. The twenty-sixth page begins: 'So they should disappear for ever . . .' and ends: 'With all the sewage of the world'. The twenty-seventh page begins: 'If they summon me . . .' and ends: 'But I am not guilty . . .'. The twenty-eighth page begins: 'I now entrust . . .' and ends: 'Of the absurd and fantasy . . .'. The twenty-ninth page begins: 'If we have one little year . . .' and ends: 'Battles and achievements'. [List of quotations from books by Sinyavsky and Daniel referred to at the trial.]

9. Note-book in grey cardboard cover, on the first page of which is the entry: 'B 8-77-34, Ginzburg Alik', and on the last: 'Ekaterina Nik. D 1-17-72'.

10. Typescript on sheets of white unruled paper entitled: 'Anna Akhamatova: Pages from a Diary' on eight (8) sheets. The text begins with the words: 'And Lozinsky's death . . .' and ends: 'Fontanny dvor, 1937'.

11. Literary Almanac No. 1, July 1961, Moscow; typewritten text on forty-nine (49) pages.

12. Literary Almanac No. 2, June 1962, Moscow; typewritten text on sixty (60) pages.[41]

13. Typewritten miscellany 'The Russian Word, new series, No 2-3 (91-92), August-September 1966, Ryleyev Club, Moscow' on forty-six (46) pages, on the last of which is: 'editor Khokhlov'.[42]

14. Novel by V. Nabokov, *Invitation to a Beheading*, Paris Russian-language edition, 218 pages.

15. Typewritten text on sheet of white paper, 'Song of the Factionist Molotov', beginning with the words: 'I was an anti-party man . . .' and ending: '. . . come on, let's take a hair of the dog'.

16. Typewritten text on sheet of white paper 'The Lesbians' Wedding Song', beginning with the words: 'Though on watch . . .' and ending: ' . . . I love Belova'.

17. Typewritten text on sheet of white paper, beginning with the words: 'I look at the sky . . .' and ending: '. . . In truth, rose from the dead'.

18. Typewritten text on sheet of white paper 'Song of Freedom', beginning with the words: 'Birds did not fly . . .' and ending: 'Of my cold lips'.

19. Typewritten text on four (4) sheets, entitled 'Manifesto of Man', beginning with the words: 'Oftener and oftener . . .' and ending: '. . . On my body's marble, a cross'. [Poem by Yu. Galanskov, 'Manifesto of Man', 1961.[43]]

20. Typewritten text on eight (8) sheets. On the first is the text: 'Alexander Ginzburg. Tragi-comedy. Hot Pies'. The text ends: 'The pedlar woman's shouts as the curtain descends. 22-23.5.64'. [Comedy by Victor Kalugin, 'Hot Pies', evidently with an inscription to A. Ginzburg.]

21. Typewritten text on six (6) pages: 'G. Sapgir: Psalms of David. 1st psalm, 55th and 101st'.

22. Sheet of paper with entry: 'V 7-40-67, Yury Alekseyevich'.

23. Four sheets of checked paper with handwritten texts. On the first, text begins with the words: 'And Tito turned out to be . . .' and ends: 'You twist your love'. On the second correspondingly: 'Soviet Easter' and: 'You strike me across the mouth with a glove'. On the third is: 'Song of Freedom' and: 'Under the cloak of the bright yellow birch'. On the fourth is: 'Now rain, now snow' and: 'Intensification of the class war'.

24. Note-book in brown cardboard cover, forty-seven pages, checked paper with handwritten entries. On the first page the text begins with the words: 'My soul floated', on the last page is a pencilled entry: 'Lazaretny, 4, kv. 19, Golshtein G'.

25. One hundred and two (102) sheets of black carbon-paper with typewritten texts. The carbon-paper was in a small cardboard box together with standard sheets of white unruled paper. The carbon-paper was placed in an envelope and sealed with a wax seal (stamped).

26. Thirty (30) sheets of white unruled paper of standard size, in the same small box as the carbon-paper. Sealed in the same envelope as the carbon-paper (see item 25).

27. Typewritten text: 'Victor Mamonov, *Ordinary Holidays*. Alkhimiya Publishing House, Leningrad-Moscow, 1962', on twenty-seven pages.

28. FED-type films and twenty-five (25) processed items, seven unprocessed FED films and one cassette with a Kiev-Vega film. All the above-mentioned films were placed in three envelopes and sealed with a wax seal (stamped).

29. Tapes in cassettes, twenty-seven (27) in all, nineteen (19) of them

in 250 m cassettes, six (6) in 180 m cassettes and two (2) in 100 m cassettes. All the tapes were packed in a bag and sealed with a wax sealing stamp. [Items 15-18, 23 and 29: contemporary camp and city folklore recorded on paper and tape, collected by A. Ginzburg.]

At 15.20 hours A. I. Ginzburg's friends came to his flat: Pavel Mikhailovich Litvinov, born 1940, resident of Moscow, Frunzenskaya nab., dom 50, kv. 106, and Tatyana Mikhailovna Nekrasova, born 1938, resident of Moscow, Podsosensky per., d. 18, kv. 6. who were detained in the flat until the end of the search. The contents of the briefcase Nekrasova had with her was checked, nothing was confiscated.

At the end of the search, at 20.30 hours, Irina Sergeyevna Zholkovskaya, born 1937, resident of Moscow, 4-ya Tverskaya-Yamskaya, dom 10, kv. 2, arrived at Ginzburg's flat.

Besides the rooms occupied at present by Ginzburg, a search was conducted of two rooms belonging to him where repairs were being carried out, the wood-shed and also the corridor of the flat where some of Ginzburg's possessions are.

A statement was made by L. I. Ginzburg to the effect that the above-mentioned note-book and telephone entry on a sheet of paper, items 9 and 22, belonged to her.

There were no other statements or comments. The record was read by the investigator. Everything was correctly entered.

Search witnesses: Denisov, Kiryagina. Present: A. Ginzburg, L. Ginzburg. Investigator: Smelov. His assistants: Zabaluyev, Baryshev, Guganov, Semashkin, Khorinov. Copy of search record received by A. Ginzburg.*

Document II: 3

To the First Secretary of the Central Committee of the Soviet Communist Party, Comrade L. I. Brezhnev; to the Chairman of the Council of Ministers of the USSR, Comrade A. N. Kosygin; to the Chairman of the Presidium of the Supreme Soviet of the USSR, Comrade N. V. Podgorny; to the Procurator-General of the USSR, Comrade Rudenko; to the Chairman of the Committee of State Security under the Council of Ministers of the USSR, Comrade Semichastny; to the First Secretary of the Moscow City Committee of the Soviet Communist Party, Comrade Egorychev; to the editorial boards of the newspapers *Izvestia* and *Pravda*; to the editorial board of *The Literary Gazette*.

On 23 January 1967 the organs of the KGB arrested my son Alexander Ilich Ginzburg. I have not up till now been informed of the nature of the accusation brought against him. But in the warrant for his arrest it is stated that proceedings against him have been instituted under article 70 of the Russian Criminal Code.

At the end of 1966 my son was summoned to the KGB to discuss his

---

* The record is on twelve pages, each one of which is signed.

statement and the materials collected by him on the trial of the writers
A. Sinyavsky and Yu. Daniel.

During the 'discussion' it was demanded of him to declare who had
helped him collect these materials, and to whom and with what object
he had shown them. The threat was made that he would be tried for this
action if he did not 'correct' it. (He was urged: 'have pity on your mother'.)
And now the KGB's threats have been realized—my son has been arrested.

So, clearly Alexander Ginzburg is being charged under article 70 of
the Criminal Code (which concerns responsibility for anti-Soviet agitation
and propaganda) for compiling a collection of materials on an open
judicial trial, although he presented this collection to the USSR Supreme
Court and the KGB in the hope of a review of the case, which he regarded
as unjust. [L. I. Ginzburg is mistaken here. A. Ginzburg gave his collection
not to the Supreme Court, but to several deputies of the Supreme Soviet
and to the KGB.] There is nothing criminal in these actions. He acted
as any honest and principled man with a social conscience should act.
He openly declared his disagreement with the sentencing of two writers,
basing his statements on supporting documentary evidence. Disagreement
with one or another judicial decision of the judicial organs does not
signify anti-Soviet sentiments; any declaration of personal disagreement
is not illegal; this information collected by my son about an open judicial
trial cannot in itself be anti-Soviet.

It is impossible to believe that disagreement with one or another action
of the judicial organs, openly expressed, can be regarded as criminal in
our country. I am convinced that the accusation against my son is unlawful, that it is a mistake. But even more unlawful is his confinement in
prison during the investigation. Pre-trial arrest is an extremely severe
measure, an exceptional measure, taken in respect of criminals who
represent a danger to the public: gangsters, murderers, rapists or those
who try to escape justice. Alexander Ginzburg is not a gangster, not a
murderer, he has not tried to hide; on the contrary, when he had collected
the materials on the trial, he sent them to the Supreme Court and the
KGB, accompanied by a statement to which he affixed his name and
address. He worked and studied up to the very day of the arrest; when he
was summoned to the KGB for the 'discussion', he turned up at the
required time. There is not the least justification for his arrest. It is
unlawful and inhuman. It is a penalty inflicted before the trial, before
any legal guilt has been proved. It is a cruel measure of psychological
and physical coercion against a man. The accused's confinement to prison
(in the absence of any exceptional circumstances) does not help but
hinders true justice, just as do any other measures of physical coercion.

I regard it also as necessary to ask about the confinement of those under
investigation in prison. They have, after all, not yet been found guilty—
and they are being subjected beforehand not only to isolation, but to a
number of restrictions. Parcels are very limited: no more than five kilogrammes of provisions once every two months. Whatever the prison

rations for people under investigation, there are no grounds for depriving them of the provisions that relatives might give them or they themselves might like to purchase with the money conveyed to them. (In an investigation prison only ten-roubles worth of provisions may be purchased per month.) Not only the quantity, but even the kind of provisions is limited: butter, for instance, is not accepted; not more than 0·5 kg of sugar may be given—and this is for two months. Such a regime in an investigation prison is severe enough for a healthy man, but if the person concerned is not in good health, then the regime itself constitutes a method of physical coercion against him.

During the entire course of the investigation the prisoners are deprived not only of meetings with relatives, but even of correspondence. Even if the letters were inspected by the investigator it would be preferable; for total isolation from relatives is a very severe measure of moral coercion that may even destroy a man's mental equilibrium. And all this is carried out as regards persons who are perhaps guilty of nothing and who may be released before the trial or by order of the court!

The conditions of confinement of accused people in the KGB's investigation prison [i.e. the Lefortovo prison] cannot be regarded as humane, do not conform to the spirit of our justice and therefore must be eliminated.

I ask that my son Alexander Ginzburg be released immediately from prison. I also ask to be informed who sanctioned his arrest and upon what grounds. I also ask to be informed what is the nature of the accusation brought against my son, and precisely what actions of his the organs of the KGB regard as criminal.

Moscow Zh-180, Bolshaya Polyanka, d. 11/14, kv. 25   L. I. Ginzburg.
25 February 1967

Document II: 4

Reception Room

Presidium of the Supreme Soviet of the USSR   *To L. I. Ginzburg*
Your statement was, on 3 March 1967, sent for examination to the USSR Procuracy (City of Moscow) with the request that you be notified of the decision taken.

4 March 1967   Reception: V. Semerov

Document II: 5

Procuracy of the USSR

Moscow-Centre, Pushkinskaya, 15-a   *To L. I. Ginzburg*

Your statement has been received by the USSR Procuracy and sent on 3 March 1967, with the ref. no. 13/3-2403-60, to the City of Moscow Procuracy with the request that you be informed of the outcome.

Procurator of the department for the supervision of investigation in the organs of state security,

4 March 1967   Counsellor of Justice: [signature illegible]

Document II: 6

USSR Procuracy
Procuracy of Moscow City
No 07-10   *To Citizen L. I. Ginzburg*
6 March 1967   Moscow Zh-180, B. Polyanka,
Novokuznetskaya ul., 27   d. 11/14, kv. 25

I must inform you that your statement has been considered by the City of Moscow Procuracy. There are at present no grounds for altering the type of restraint—detention under arrest—exercised on A. I. Ginzburg. I must at the same time explain that he was arrested with the approval of the Procurator.

Deputy Procurator for the City of Moscow,
Senior Counsellor of Justice Pavlov

Document II: 7

Comrade Ginzburg!

Your letter, copies of which you sent to many organizations, has been received. The subject specifically broached in the letter can be decided in substance by these organizations.

Letters department of *Pravda*

No 38616/0   Kochmarov
13 March 1967

Document II: 8

USSR Procuracy
Moscow-Centre, Pushkinskaya, 15-a   *To Citizen L. I. Ginzburg*
20 March 1967   Moscow Zh-180, B. Polyanka,
No 13/3-60-67   d. 11/14, kv. 25

Your statement has been received from the Central Committee of the Soviet Communist Party and has been considered.

I must inform you that as regards your son, A. I. Ginzburg, there are valid grounds for instituting proceedings and an investigation is being carried out.

Procurator of the Department for the Supervision of
Investigation in the Organs of State Security,
Senior Counsellor of Justice Pokhlyobin

Document II: 9

CONVERSATION BETWEEN GUY LE CLERC
AND [*the Soviet writer Yury*] KAZAKOV[44]

'You have underground literature in your country, why is that?'

'For the most part it's verse that has not yet been accepted for publication,' answers Kazakov. 'It's illegal, but it generally gets published in the end. For example, Evtushenko wrote "Stalin's Heirs"; no one dared print it, but it was reproduced clandestinely. Evtushenko was disturbed by the distortions that occurred as a result. He wrote to Khrushchev sending him the original text of the poem and Khrushchev published it in *Pravda*.[45] But there exist, besides, some very young people—not older than twenty —who think that Paustovsky and Akhmatova are worthless (Kazakov uses a harsher expression), that the publication of a work is a sign of its mediocrity, that a work of genius cannot and should not appear in print. This is the view of Ginzburg, the chief editor of the review *Syntax*. He is spiritually as repulsive as he is physically. (Kazakov starts stammering in disgust.) It has been going on for ten years already. I meet them in Leningrad, in the writers' club where they drink hard, the women paying, and go into ecstasies over what they have not written. A writer's work is tough and serious. If you have something to say, it should not bother you if it is refused publication. In the final analysis, there's always a way open for the new. The "underground writers" are extremely few in number. They are as far removed from literature as the daubers of the rue Tertre are from painting.'

'Daniel and Sinyavsky operated underground, but they are true writers, aren't they?'

'I don't know anything new about them. I find it unpleasant to talk about them. I was not present at the trial. I signed a letter[46] in which I asked that their freedom and place in society be given back to them in so far as they acknowledge their mistakes. Together with my colleagues I undertook to guarantee their future conduct. But one must remember that they wrote different sorts of books—some for the Russian people, others which were intended to be sent abroad. This is the most infamous thing a writer can do. When Pasternak and Akhmatova were meeting with difficulties "from above", they kept silent, but they did nothing against their convictions. Daniel and Sinyavsky are two-faced. However, public censure would have been sufficient in their case, a tribunal of sorts where we would have frankly admonished them.'

Figaro Littéraire, 16 March 1967[47]

Document II: 10

RECORD OF SEARCH (Confiscation)
City of Moscow, 21 July 1967
Search begun at 1.40 hours; completed at 10.50 hours.
Agent-in-charge Sumerov of the Investigation Department of the

Public Order Directorate [POD] of the City of Moscow Executive Committee for the Leningrad District, on the basis of the decision of the Investigation Section of the POD of the City of Moscow Executive Committee for the Leningrad District, dated 5 July 1967, with regard to carrying out a search (confiscation) on the premises of citizen Yury Timofeyevich Galanskov, residing at 3-i Golutvinsky per., dom 7/9, kv. 4, in the presence of the following persons who were requested to act as search witnesses:

1. Mikhail Konstantinovich Korotkov, Moscow V-485, selo Konkovo, d. 65.

2. Vyacheslav Mikhailovich Vazhenov, Varsonofevsky per., 4, kv. 20 [a KGB official's house], presented an order for the surrender of valuables.

The following items were confiscated in the search:

1. Small note-book in brown binding with addresses and telephone numbers.

2. Eight pages torn from a note-book, 8 × 12 cm, with notes of a 'Conversation with Guy le Clerc' and other matters.

3. Two typewritten sheets containing 'Conversation with Guy le Clerc' and a speech by 'Soloukhin'. [The reference is to an interview with (*the Soviet writer Vladimir*) Soloukhin in the same issue of *Figaro Littéraire*.]

4. A sheet of white paper, 9 × 12 cm, with the entry: 'Korolyov Yury Pavlovich, Moscow 1-328, Beskudnikovsky bulvar, d. 5, korpus 1, kv. 53.'

The items listed above, numbering four as designated, were confiscated and removed to the Leningrad District police-station.

Complaints and statements during search: none.

Signatures: of person subjected to search, Antonova, sister*; of witnesses: 1. Korotkov, 2. Vazhenov. Official who conducted search: Sumerov. A copy of the record of the search was received by Antonova.

Document II: 11

RECORD (Inventory of property seized)

City of Moscow, 21 July 1967

Investigator and agent-in-charge Sumerov of the Investigation Department of the POD of the City of Moscow Executive Committee for the Leningrad District, on the basis of the decision of 5 July 1967 regarding criminal case No. 29394 [case of a group of Moscow and Leningrad currency operators], for the purpose of bringing a civil action or of a possible confiscation, in accordance with the requirements of articles 175 and 176 of the Russian Code of Criminal Procedure, in the presence of witnesses: 1. Mikhail Konstantinovich Korotkov, Moscow V-489, selo Konkovo, 2. Vyacheslav Mikhailovich Vazhenov, Varsonofevsky per., 4,

---

* As Yu. Galanskov's father, T. S. Galanskov, is illiterate, his sister signed for him.

kv. 20, made an inventory of property belonging to Yury Timofeyevich Galanskov and located in kv. 4, dom 7/9, 3-i Golutvinsky pereulok:

Item	Quantity	Quality and Value
1. 'Rekord' Television set No. A-1575262 B	One	150 roubles

Statements of persons present during the drawing-up of inventory: citizen T. S. Galanskov stated that the 'Rekord' television set belonged to him. Owner of the property: Antonova, sister. Witnesses: Korotkov, Vazhenov. Investigator: Representative of the Leningrad District POD Sumerov.

I have received a copy of the inventory and all the above-mentioned property and I commit myself to keep it intact.

I have been warned of my responsibility concerning the embezzlement, alienation or concealment of the above property in accordance with article 185 of the Russian Criminal Code.

Antonova

Document II: 12

City of Moscow, 5 September 1967

Major Eliseyev, senior investigator in the Investigation Section of the Directorate of the KGB under the Council of Ministers of the USSR for the City and Region of Moscow, together with the following witnesses: Evgeny Alekseyevich Naumov, resident at Bibliotechnaya ul., dom 23, kv. 28, Stanislav Feliksovich Kimlovich, resident at Leninsky pr-kt, dom 99, korp. 122, kv. 89, in the presence of Lyudmila Ilinichna Ginzburg, in accordance with the requirements of articles 169-171 and 176-177 of the Russian Code of Criminal Procedure, on the basis of the decision of the Moscow and Moscow Region KGB of 4 September 1967, carried out a search in flat 25, house 11/14, B. Polyanka Street.

It was explained to the above-named persons that they were entitled to be present during the entire course of the investigator's activities and to make statements regarding any of these activities. In addition, it was explained to the witnesses that it was their duty under article 135 of the Russian Code of Criminal Procedure to attest to the act, procedures and result of the search.

The search was begun at 13.00 hours and completed at 17.00 hours.

Before the search was begun it was suggested to L. I. Ginzburg that she voluntarily surrender the items mentioned in the search warrant. L. I. Ginzburg took an army ticket No. 0730158 in the name of Alexander Ilich Ginzburg from the sideboard and handed it to the investigator, stating that she had no other personal documents of her son.

Subsequently a search was carried out of the places of general use of flat No. 25, of the wood-shed belonging to Ginzburg, of two rooms occupied by L. I. Ginzburg.

During the search the following items were discovered and confiscated: Nothing was discovered and confiscated. The army card in the name of Alexander Ilich Ginzburg handed over by L. I. Ginzburg before the search was taken to the KGB offices.

During the course of the search Anatoly Tikhonovich Marchenko, born 1938, resident of Aleksandrov, ul. Novinskaya, dom 25, and Larissa Iosifovna Bogoraz-Brukhman, resident of Leninsky pr-kt, dom 85, kv. 3, visited the flat of L. I. Ginzburg. They were in the flat until the conclusion of the search.

KGB officials Ryazantsev, Steblev and Kulikov took part in the search. There were no statements or comments made by those taking part in the search. The record was read by the investigator. It was correctly made.

Witnesses: Naumov, Kimlovich. Owner of apartment: Ginzburg. Search conducted by: Eliseyev, Ryazantsev, Steblev, Kulikov.

Document II: 13

To the Chairman of the Council of Ministers of the USSR, Comrade A. N. Kosygin; the Chairman of the Presidium of the Supreme Soviet of the USSR, Comrade Podgorny; the Procurator-General of the USSR, Comrade Rudenko.

In 1966 my son Alexander Ilich Ginzburg produced a collection of materials on the Sinyavsky and Daniel case and transmitted it to government departments, as he considered that this case ought to be reviewed. As I have learnt, this collection contains published materials and letters to official institutions, expressing at great length the most diverse views on this matter.

On 23 January 1967 my son was arrested by organs of the KGB. He was charged under article 70 of the Russian Criminal Code—the same article under which Sinyavsky and Daniel were convicted.

He has been held under arrest for ten months already, although according to the law not more than nine months of pre-trial confinement in prison is permissible.

The period between the Procuracy handing a case over to the court and the actual trial should not exceed twenty-eight days. Ginzburg's case was handed over from the Procuracy on 26 October, since when a month has elapsed and the case has not only not been heard, but, according to my information, has not yet reached a court. Thus, my son's detention in prison without a trial is being inadmissibly prolonged.

These very serious violations of the laws—and the other violations about which I have already written in my first letter of February 1967—disturb me a great deal. I am afraid that the laws may also be violated later, during the court examination, and that this will affect my son's fate.

I received no answer at all to my first letter, which was sent to nine bodies. I ask you to consider the present letter and to give it a detailed answer.

Moscow Zh-180 Bolshaya Polyanka, d. 11/14, kv. 25   L. I. Ginzburg
25 November 1967

Document II: 14

The Procuracy of the USSR
Moscow-tsentr, Pushkinskaya, 15-a   *To L. I. Ginzburg*

Your statement of 26 November 1967 regarding the case of A. I. Ginzburg was re-directed on 30 November 1967, with the ref. no. 13/3-1425-63, to the City of Moscow court, to which the case has been handed for detailed scrutiny, and it is there that you should apply.*

Procurator of the Department for the Supervision
of Investigation in the State Security Organs

2 December 1967   Counsellor of Justice [signature illegible]

Document II: 15

The Procuracy of the USSR
Moscow-tsentr, Pushkinskaya, 15-a   *To L. I. Ginzburg*

Your statement of 26 November 1967, which arrived at the USSR Procuracy from the Presidium of the USSR Supreme Soviet, was re-directed on 15 December 1967, with the ref. no. 13/1425-63, to the Procurator of the City of Moscow with the suggestion that you be informed of the outcome.†

Procurator of the Department for the Supervision
of Investigation in the State Security Organs

16 December 1967   Counsellor of Justice [signature illegible]

Document II: 16

To the Procurator-General of the USSR; the Chairmen of the Supreme Court of the RSFSR, and the Moscow City Court; the Chief Editor of the newspaper *Izvestia*. Copies to: Lawyers S. L. Ariya, D. I. Kaminskaya

---

* On 11 December 1967 when, as the defence was informed, the hearing of the case was supposed to commence, L. I. Ginzburg applied to the City of Moscow court, but received a verbal answer from the office that the case had not even reached the court. The deputy Chairman of the Moscow City court, L. Mironov, confirmed this. After this L. I. Ginzburg received a new answer from the USSR Procuracy (see Document II: 15).

† No answer came from the Procurator of the City of Moscow, evidently because the trial opened on 8 January 1968.

and B. A. Zolotukhin. [At this time Dobrovolsky had not yet taken lawyer V. Ya. Shveisky.]

It is known to us that in the immediate future the trial will take place of citizens Ginzburg, Galanskov, Dobrovolsky and Lashkova, arrested in January 1967.

We wish to attend this trial, as information in the press of previous trials that have interested us has either been inadequate, as the Sinyavsky and Daniel case, or has been altogether lacking.

People have been admitted to such trials according to special lists and passes. Others wanting to enter, including friends and sometimes even relatives of the defendants, have not been admitted on the grounds of insufficient places in the court. In this way formally open trials have been turned into closed ones, and the principle of the publicity of legal proceedings, guaranteed by the Constitution, has in fact been violated.

We insist on our right to be present at the impending trial and ask that free entry into the court be assured and adequate seating be provided.*

Moscow, 30 November 1967

Document II: 17

To the Procurator-General of the USSR; the Chairmen of the Supreme Court of the RSFSR, and the Moscow City Court; the Chief Editor of the newspaper *Izvestia*. Copies to: Lawyers S. L. Ariya, D. I. Kaminskaya and B. A. Zolotukhin.

DECLARATION

Many of us addressed a letter to you in which the signatories insisted on their right to be present at the imminent judicial examination of the case of Galanskov, Ginzburg, Dobrovolsky and Lashkova. It was then assumed that the trial would be declared an open one.

After this letter had been sent to you, rumours arose that the trial would be a closed one. Only a few days remained till the commencement of the trial and there was no longer sufficient time to check the validity of these rumours. If they were false, so much the better. But our civic duty—to demand observation of the laws regarding the publicity of legal proceedings (article 111 of the Constitution of the USSR and article 18 of the Russian Code of Criminal Procedure)—impels us now to make this declaration.

As far as we know, the defendants are being charged under article 70 of the Russian Criminal Code (anti-Soviet agitation and propaganda), and Yu. Galanskov, in addition, under article 88 of the Russian Criminal Code (violation of the laws on currency operations). Neither of these articles concerns matters connected with state secrets or those squalid

---

* For list of signatories see p. 399. Ed.

not state secrets shd not be closed under pd of lawlssn

practices which give legal grounds for holding judicial sessions in camera. Cases under these articles were regularly tried behind closed doors in the past, but this system was one of lawlessness. Fortunately such cases have of late begun to be tried in open court, and any rumours of the possibility of a return to the sombre practices of the past is naturally a cause of concern to citizens. The crucial significance of the publicity of judicial proceedings lies in the fact that publicity is at the basis of all other judicial guarantees, and for that reason we cannot tolerate even isolated violations of the principle of publicity. If exceptional circumstances justifying a closed examination of certain matters should crop up in the impending trial, respect for the principle of publicity requires that all the other matters be examined in open sessions and that the entire trial be organized in such a way that the public should be able to attend it.

Furthermore, we are aware of certain circumstances in the conduct of the case of Galanskov, Ginzburg and the others that are cause for alarm. The accused were arrested in January, the investigation was prolonged for the maximum permitted period of custody (nine months). And after the case was handed to the Moscow City Court on 26 October, the period allowed by law to pass before the beginning of the trial was exceeded (articles 221 and 239 of the Russian Code of Criminal Procedure), and even then the accused were not released from custody, although there were no reasonable grounds for fearing an attempt to escape the course of justice on their part.

Kozlov's suppt argm on discrs of obsrvy laws to ensr justice

In view of our natural concern with regard to these circumstances we insist particularly on the rigorous observation of the laws regarding publicity during the course of the impending trial, we demand that in accordance with the law this trial take place in public and we ask that free access be assured to the public at all the open sessions.*

Moscow, 8 December 1967

Document II: 18

To the Moscow City Court. Copies to: A. N. Kosygin, L. I. Brezhnev, N. V. Podgorny and Lawyer B. A. Zolotukhin.

According to rumours circulating in Moscow, the Moscow City Court will, within the next few days, begin hearing the case of A. Ginzburg.

Many of the circumstances connected with the case of A. Ginzburg, who was arrested about a year ago, cannot fail to arouse the alarm of the public: the unprecedented length of the year's pre-trial imprisonment, the absence in our press of any news whatsoever about the reasons for the arrest of Ginzburg, and the prolonged investigation.

Those of us who know A. Ginzburg personally do not doubt his integrity and decency. His basic interests lay in the field of culture, he was not

* For list of signatories see p. 399. Ed.

engaged in political activity as such, and the collection of documents compiled by him (including articles from our press and other official documents) concerning the case of the writers Sinyavsky and Daniel, which deeply disturbed public opinion, cannot constitute sufficient grounds for his arrest and trial. All this cannot help to clear the atmosphere of a society which not long ago witnessed mass rehabilitations of persons sentenced on false charges. The abnormal circumstances created oblige us to ask the Moscow City Court to give the case of A. Ginzburg special consideration and to ensure the absolute publicity of the proceedings, the unprejudiced selection of witnesses and wide coverage of the trial in the press.*

[Moscow, January 1968]

* For list of the thirty-one signatories see p. 399. Ed.

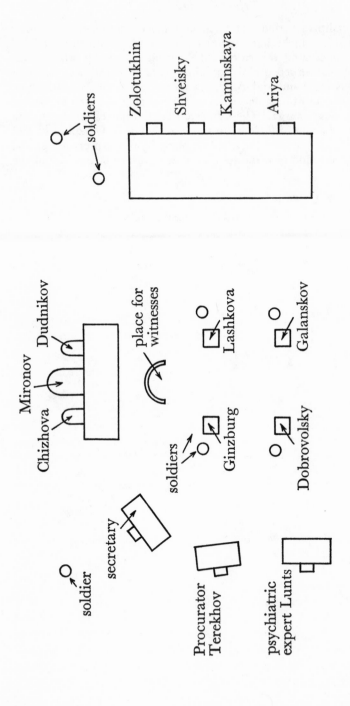

Zolotukhin
Shveisky
Kaminskaya
Ariya

soldiers

Mironov
Chizhova
Dudnikov

place for
witnesses

Lashkova

Galanskov

soldiers

Ginzburg

Dobrovolsky

secretary

soldier

Procurator
Terekhov

psychiatric
expert Lunts

Courtroom seating 150-200 people

═ III ═

THE TRIAL

Session of the Judicial Collegium on Criminal Cases of the Moscow City Court 8–12 January 1968

Members of the court: Chairman L. K. Mironov, People's Assessors S. G. Dudnikov and G. V. Chizhova, Secretary A. I. Fomicheva; with the participation of Procurator G. A. Terekhov and defence counsels B. A. Zolotukhin, D. I. Kaminskaya, S. L. Ariya and V. Ya. Shveisky.

It is, unfortunately, impossible to present a full verbatim report of the trial. During the sittings neither an official tape-recording nor an official stenographic report was made. The only official document is the record of the trial made by the secretary of the court, which contains only the sequence of events and a summary of all the speeches. It is the usual procedure that all participants in the trial afterwards examine this record, to enter their comments and amendments. In this particular instance, however, the court refused to accept every one of the lawyers' comments regarding errors in the record. But even in its incomplete form the record was not published anywhere, nor was it possible to examine it in the office of the court.

The present record is based: (a) on verbatim records made during the trial by several persons present in the room; (b) on the oral accounts of several of those present in the room, tape-recorded immediately after a given sitting had ended; (c) on a thorough interrogation of most of the witnesses soon after they had given their evidence in the trial, or on records made by themselves in writing of their own testimony. All this information has been correlated, carefully checked and made completely accurate. Wherever the direct speech of the participants in the trial is given, this is based on a stenographic record (in some cases made simultaneously by a number of different people). Where it was impossible to make such a record, or if the records were confiscated at the exit to the court, speeches and remarks are given in summary form. The sentence handed down is based on the text of the officially attested copy. Several matters of legal procedure have been almost everywhere omitted, as is specially mentioned in footnotes.

8 January

The sitting of the court was due to begin at 10.00 hours. At 9.30 hours Ginzburg, then Lashkova, Galanskov and finally Dobrovolsky were led into the empty room and given four separate chairs. A soldier was standing by each of them. The defendants were not permitted to look round or talk to each other. After fifteen minutes the public was let in. Then came the counsel for the defence, each of whom approached his or her client: Kaminskaya, Galanskov; Zolotukhin, Ginzburg; Shveisky, Dobrovolsky; Ariya, Lashkova. About 10.00 hours the Procurator, Terekhov, and the forensic medical expert, Lunts, came in together, followed by a secretary. Secretary, Procurator and expert took their seats to the right of the judge, the defence counsel to the left. At precisely 10.00 hours the clerk said: 'Rise, the court is in session!' Everyone stood up. The first to enter was People's Assessor Dudnikov, after him the Chairman, Judge Mironov, then People's Assessor Chizhova.

CHAIRMAN OF COURT (henceforth JUDGE). Please be seated. I declare this session of the Moscow City Court Judicial Collegium for Criminal Cases open. Criminal case No. 266 will be heard, in which Galanskov, Ginzburg, Dobrovolsky and Lashkova are being charged under article 70 paragraph 1 of the Russian Criminal Code and Galanskov, in addition, under article 88 paragraph 1 of the Russian Criminal Code.

THE SECRETARY reports on the arrival in court of the Procurator, the accused, defence counsel and the expert.

JUDGE. Galanskov, stand up. (Galanskov stands up.) Galanskov Yury Timofeyevich, born 19 June 1939. Is that your correct surname, first name and patronymic?

GALANSKOV. Yes, it is.

JUDGE. Russian, USSR citizen, born in the city of Moscow, non-party member, with secondary education, married, no previous conviction, prior to his arrest employed in the State Museum of Literature, resident of Moscow, 3-i Golutvinsky pereulok, dom 7/9, kv. 4. Is all that correct?

GALANSKOV. Yes.

JUDGE. Have you received the indictment? Do you recall when?

GALANSKOV. Yes, I have received it. On 29 October.

JUDGE. You may sit down. (To Ginzburg) Ginzburg, stand up. (Ginzburg stands up.) Ginzburg Alexander Ilich, born 21 November 1936. Is that your correct surname, first name and patronymic?

GINZBURG. It is.

JUDGE. Jewish, USSR citizen, born in the city of Moscow, non-party member, with secondary education, bachelor, no previous conviction,* prior to arrest an auxiliary worker in the State Museum of Literature, resident of Moscow, Bolshaya Polyanka, dom 11/14, kv. 25. Is all that correct?

GINZBURG. Yes.

JUDGE. Have you received the indictment? Do you recall when?

GINZBURG. Yes, I have received it. On 29 October.

JUDGE. You may sit down. (To Dobrovolsky) Dobrovolsky, stand up. (Dobrovolsky stands up.) Dobrovolsky Aleksei Alexandrovich, born 13 October 1939. Is that your correct surname, first name and patronymic?

DOBROVOLSKY. Yes, it is.

JUDGE. Russian, USSR citizen, born in the city of Moscow, non-party member, with secondary education, married, with children, no previous conviction,* prior to arrest bookbinder in the State Museum of Literature, resident of Moscow, Kalanchevskaya ul., dom 4, kv. 16. Is all that correct?

DOBROVOLSKY. Yes.

JUDGE. Have you received the indictment? Do you recall when?

DOBROVOLSKY. Yes, I have received it. On 29 October.

JUDGE. Sit down. (To Lashkova) Lashkova, stand up. (Lashkova stands up.) Lashkova Vera Iosifovna, born 18 June 1944. Is that your correct surname, first name and patronymic?

LASHKOVA. Yes, it is.

JUDGE. Russian, USSR citizen, non-party member, no previous

---

* Since, according to Soviet law, convictions are struck off after a certain period, Ginzburg and Dobrovolsky, because of the period that had elapsed since they had served their sentences, were regarded as unconvicted. In actual fact previous convictions are always taken into account by the court without regard to the length of time that has elapsed.

conviction, with secondary education, not married, prior to arrest a laboratory assistant in the preparatory faculty of Moscow University, resident of Moscow, Kropotkinskaya ul., dom 13, kv. 9. Is all that correct?

LASHKOVA. Yes.

JUDGE. Have you received the indictment? Do you recall when?

LASHKOVA. On 29 October.

JUDGE allows Lashkova to sit down and announces the composition of the court; he introduces the persons acting as state prosecutor, defence counsel, expert, secretary. He further explains to the accused and other participants in the judicial examination their right to challenge the composition of the court or any of the judges, the Procurator, the secretary or the expert,* and also the right of the accused to make complaints about actions of the Procurator and the court. Then he points out that the accused and their defence counsel have the right to make certain requests if they so desire.

GINZBURG requests that his fiancée Irina Zholkovskaya be admitted to the courtroom—'the only person close to me who is able to attend the court at this time'.†

ZOLOTUKHIN supports his client's application.

KAMINSKAYA requests that Galanskov's relatives, his mother, father, wife and sister, be admitted to the courtroom.

JUDGE (to clerk). Let them in and find places for them.‡

GALANSKOV. I have a request to make. I should like to know more about the People's Assessors, where they work, whether they have taken part in court sessions before. I should like them to describe themselves.

JUDGE (having consulted with the Assessors). The People's Assessors are workers and office workers of Moscow; they have taken part in court sessions before.

GALANSKOV. That is not much, I should like them to give further details.

JUDGE. Galanskov, I have already told you that they are workers and office workers of Moscow. That is sufficient. You may sit down. (Galanskov sits down.) The court will proceed to the reading of the indictment. (He reads out the indictment.)

---

* According to article 59 of the Russian Criminal Code a challenge may be made where 'circumstances give grounds for believing that the Judge (Procurator, expert, etc. —compiler's note) has some personal, direct or indirect, interest in the case'.

† Ginzburg means that his mother cannot be admitted for the time being, having been summoned to appear later as a witness.

‡ They were admitted roughly at the beginning of the reading of the indictment. Dobrovolsky's relatives (including his mother) were in the room from the very beginning.

The Trial

THE INDICTMENT

in the case of A. I. Ginzburg, Yu. T. Galanskov,
A. A. Dobrovolsky and V. I. Lashkova

On 10 and 16 January 1967 materials—'A Letter to Brezhnev' and 'An Open Letter to Sholokhov'*—containing fabrications defaming the Soviet political and social order, were handed in to the KGB reception by Citizens Golovanov and Tsvetkov. The preliminary investigation established that the letter signed by Yu. Galanskov was written by him and typed out in several copies with the help of Lashkova in December 1966. In addition, Citizens Golovanov and Tsvetkov, in their statement to the KGB, wrote that they had received this material for duplication, but when they realized the nature of its contents, had decided to hand it over to the KGB.

In October 1966 several Western radio stations and newspapers announced the appearance in the West of a collection of materials on the Sinyavsky and Daniel trial. It was reported that the compiler of the collection was Alexander Ginzburg. The journal *Grani*, No. 62, published part of the material from this collection, which in Western radio reports was called *The White Book. The White Book* created a stir when it appeared in the West. A 'Radio Liberty'[48] broadcast of 10 December 1966 was devoted to it. Initially *The White Book* was circulated illegally in the USSR, then one copy of it reached the West. The collection included two anti-Soviet documents which defame the Soviet political and social order, namely: a leaflet signed 'Resistance', and 'A Letter to an Old Friend'.[49]

Investigations carried out in 1961 and 1964 established that A. Ginzburg held anti-Soviet views and harboured in his flat literature hostile to our country and system. The materials of the investigation carried out in 1964 include depositions by Ginzburg which confirm this.†

In 1960 A. Ginzburg produced a magazine entitled *Syntax* containing literary materials in which a number of internal and external events in the life of our country were dealt with on the basis of incorrect premises.

At that time A. Ginzburg used to meet foreigners frequently and maintained friendly relations with them. At an American exhibition in the Sokolniki park he met two American citizens, Sjeklocha and

---

* The reference is to the letter of twenty-five representatives of the Soviet intelligentsia to the Central Committee of the Soviet Communist Party protesting against the revival of Stalinism, and the 'Open letter' from Galanskov to Sholokhov about the Sinyavsky and Daniel trial, both of which were published in *Phoenix*. (See notes 23 and 26. Ed.)

† There follows an unreconstructed quotation.

45

Mead, from one of whom he subsequently received Djilas's book *The New Class* and other literature hostile to the Soviet system.

A. Ginzburg condemned his own behaviour, whereupon the investigation considered it possible to drop the case, thus giving him the chance to start afresh. But he continued to pursue his anti-Soviet activity. In 1966 he compiled a tendentiously selected collection of materials on the Sinyavsky and Daniel trial. With the help of the typist Lashkova, Ginzburg produced no fewer than ten copies of this collection, one of which was sent abroad through Galanskov and published in No. 62 of the journal *Grani*, issued by the foreign émigré organization, the NTS. As Dobrovolsky has testified in the investigation, Ginzburg had foreign connections since 1962 and subsequently handed them on to Galanskov.

In 1966 Ginzburg participated in the production of the miscellany *Phoenix*, which contained these anti-Soviet items: 'The Confession of Victor Velsky', 'An Open Letter to Sholokov', the article 'The Russian Road to Socialism', an article of Sinyavsky's, 'What Is Socialist Realism?' and 'An Account of Events in the Pochayev Monastery Today'.

From a Swede visiting Moscow in June 1966 Ginzburg obtained anti-Soviet clippings from foreign papers and circulated them by giving them to [*the poet*] Gubanov.

In addition, Ginzburg harboured tape-recordings of two anti-Soviet songs in his flat.

It was established, by means of a textual and stylistic analysis, that the author of 'A Letter to an Old Friend' and the leaflet signed 'Resistance' was probably Ginzburg.

Ginzburg also wrote a letter to Kosygin which remained undelivered and was included in the collection of materials on the trial of Sinyavsky and Daniel.

Yu. GALANSKOV held anti-Soviet views and carried out anti-Soviet agitation and propaganda. In April 1966 he wrote 'An Open Letter to Sholokhov', which is anti-Soviet in content, containing fabrications defamatory of the Soviet political and social order. With Lashkova's help fifteen copies of this letter were made; it was included in the miscellany *Phoenix* and it subsequently got abroad.

In December 1966 Galanskov, with Ginzburg's help, assembled materials and produced a miscellany under the title *Phoenix, edited by Yu. Galanskov*, which contained these anti-Soviet items: 'The Confession of Victor Velsky', the article 'The Russian Road to Socialism', an article of Sinyavsky's 'What Is Socialist Realism?', 'An Open Letter to Sholokhov' and 'An Account of Events in the

Pochayev Monastery Today'. He received the slanderous article 'An Account of Events in the Pochayev Monastery Today' from Lashkova and included it in the miscellany; with the help of Ustinova and Kamyshanova he produced a number of copies of the anti-Soviet material 'The Confession of Victor Velsky' and included both these anti-Soviet items in the miscellany. From Ginzburg he received a film of the anti-Soviet article 'The Russian Road to Socialism', attributed to Academician Varga, and with Lashkova's help made several copies and included it in *Phoenix*.

In January 1967 Galanskov sent *Phoenix* abroad via a foreigner called Nadya, who worked on the journal *Grani*. Galanskov agreed to see this foreigner at a meeting with a foreigner called Philip in June 1966. In November 1966 Galanskov met a foreigner called Genrikh at the Kropotkinskaya metro station, received from him money in Soviet roubles and foreign currency, books of an anti-Soviet nature, a hectograph and paper for cryptography. It was then that *The White Book* was sent out by Galanskov via Genrikh for publication in the West.

In December 1966, in violation of the currency regulations, Galanskov sold 200 dollars at the rate of three roubles to the dollar through Entin and Borisova, but for the remaining 200 dollars he received a pack of mustard-plasters.

The money received from Genrikh in Soviet roubles (more than 2000), the anti-Soviet literature, the hectograph and the paper for cryptography, were handed over by Galanskov to Dobrovolsky for safe keeping; the intention was to use this Soviet money to purchase a co-operative flat for conspiratorial meetings.

In autumn 1966 Galanskov, with Lashkova's help, wrote a coded letter in which were to be found the numbers 101, 102, 103, etc., also A-66. Of this letter a single copy was made. At the same time Galanskov asked Dobrovolsky to write a letter on the cryptography paper, he himself composing the text. The return address was fictitious.

It was established by means of a textual and stylistic analysis that the author of 'An Open Letter to Sholokhov' was Galanskov, and he can probably be regarded as the author of 'The Confession of Victor Velsky'.

A. DOBROVOLSKY held anti-Soviet views, conducted anti-Soviet agitation and propaganda and harboured and circulated literature of an anti-Soviet nature. Entering into criminal relations with Galanskov and Lashkova, he helped duplicate the slanderous document 'An Account of Events in the Pochayev Monastery Today', which subsequently went into the miscellany *Phoenix*.

From Galanskov he received anti-Soviet literature published by the NTS, a hectograph and paper for cryptography, all of which he kept in his flat.

He circulated this literature, passing it on to Kats and Lashkova for reading.

V. LASHKOVA, having fallen under Galanskov's and Ginzburg's influence, conducted anti-Soviet agitation and progaganda from the summer of 1966; she entered into criminal relations with Galanskov and Dobrovolsky. For Galanskov she typed out fifteen copies of his 'Open Letter to Sholokhov' and five copies of the article 'The Russian Road to Socialism'.

In September–November 1966, having received from Galanskov and Ginzburg materials for the collection on the Sinyavsky and Daniel trial, she made five copies of them, one of which subsequently reached the West and was published in *Grani*, No. 62.

In summer 1966 Lashkova made twelve copies of the slanderous document 'An Account of Events in the Pochayev Monastery Today' for Dobrovolsky, and subsequently this material was included in *Phoenix*.

Having received from Dobrovolsky anti-Soviet literature to read —the pamphlet 'Solidarism Is the Idea of the Future' and the magazine *Nashi Dni* [*Our Times*], No. 35[50]—she circulated these items, giving Kushev the pamphlet to read and Levitin the magazine.

Criminal proceedings having been instituted against him, A. GINZBURG denied the accusation and in the preliminary investigation testified:

that he was, indeed, the compiler of the collection of materials on the Sinyavsky and Daniel trial, but did not regard either the collection itself, or the individual pieces in it as anti-Soviet; that the materials included in the collection were typed by himself with the help of Vera Lashkova in about ten copies. Ginzburg testified also that he had handed over the clippings from foreign newspapers to Gubanov. As regards the two anti-Soviet songs, Ginzburg testified that he had tape-recorded these songs not for circulation but for his collection.

The fact of Ginzburg's compilation of a collection of materials on the Sinyavsky and Daniel trial is confirmed by his and Lashkova's testimony to the effect that they knew each other and that Lashkova had typed out these materials. Further confirmation is provided by the carbon-paper confiscated in the search of Ginzburg's home and used, as has been established, to type out the items in this collection. In addition there is: the copy in the case materials of *The White Book* published in France, on the title page of which appears: 'Compiler Alexander Ginzburg'; Ginzburg's own testimony to the effect that he had shown a few copies of the book to several persons; the testimony of the witness Stolyarova to the effect that in November 1966 Ginzburg showed *The White Book* to [*the writer*] Ehrenburg.

In the part of the indictment regarding Ginzburg's complicity in producing the miscellany *Phoenix*, his guilt is confirmed:

by the miscellany *Phoenix*'s editorial which, as appears from the text, was written not by one but several persons (the pronoun 'we' being used in it) and the authorship of which, on the basis of a textual and stylistic analysis allowing of certain approximate conclusions, may be attributed to Galanskov and Ginzburg;

by Ginzburg's testimony that he read Galanskov's 'An Open Letter to Sholokhov' when it was still in manuscript;

by Dobrovolsky's testimony that Ginzburg gave Galanskov the film of the article 'The Russian Road to Socialism', attributed to Academician Varga and subsequently placed in the miscellany *Phoenix*; by the copy of the miscellany *Phoenix* confiscated from Ginzburg's flat during the search.

The conveyance of *Phoenix* abroad is confirmed by Dobrovolsky's testimony that he heard from Galanskov of the conveyance of this miscellany to the West through the foreigner called Nadya.

Ginzburg's and Galanskov's joint work on *Phoenix* and *The White Book* is further confirmed by the fact that, according to their testimony, they had been on friendly terms since 1959. Dobrovolsky testified to this too.

The fact that Ginzburg harboured the two anti-Soviet songs in his flat is confirmed by the tape-recordings confiscated from him during the search.

The fact that Gubanov was handed clippings from foreign newspapers of an anti-Soviet nature is confirmed by the testimony of Gubanov himself at the preliminary investigation.

The investigation has shown that Ginzburg held anti-Soviet beliefs as far back as 1960. In spite of the preventive measures of an educative nature frequently applied in his case by the relevant bodies, he nevertheless continued to engage in anti-Soviet activity.

In view of the above, Alexander Ginzburg is, therefore, charged with violation of the law as specified under article 70 of the Russian Criminal Code.

Criminal proceedings having been instituted against him, Yu. GALANSKOV did not admit that he was guilty as charged and declared that his actions were not criminal.

49

From the evidence given by Galanskov himself at the time of the preliminary investigation, the following has been established:

that from one of the foreigners visiting him Galanskov received a hectograph, anti-Soviet literature, paper for cryptography and anti-Soviet leaflets issued by the Possev publishing house. In June 1966 he learned from the foreigner called Philip, who had come to Moscow, of the intended visit of an NTS emissary. In November this emissary, a foreigner called Genrikh, visited Moscow, met Galanskov and gave him microfilms of the works of Sinyavsky and Daniel, and also money amounting to 560 (?) dollars and 300 roubles;

that Galanskov compiled the miscellany *Phoenix* and included in it five criminal pieces. With Lashkova's help Galanskov produced five copies of *Phoenix*, one of which he gave to a foreigner called Nadya visiting Moscow, for her to convey to the West. He promised this same Nadya to collect information on matters that interested her and received from her paper for cryptography and two addresses he was to use when writing abroad. In accordance with Nadya's request, Galanskov wrote two letters in December 1966, one of which dealt with Galanskov's attitude to the NTS, the other with the mutual relations between members of [*the literary group*] SMOG;

that Galanskov sold 400 dollars through Entin and Borisova.

Although Galanskov renounced this testimony in the course of the preliminary investigation, the investigation considers his renunciation superficial and considers that the previous evidence given by him corresponds to the facts.

This is also confirmed by the evidence given by Dobrovolsky during the preliminary investigation which the investigators consider fully reliable. Galanskov's criminal activity is confirmed by the following testimony of Dobrovolsky to the effect that:

Galanskov told him, Dobrovolsky, about the NTS and collected and conveyed various materials to it; that Galanskov took from Lashkova one copy of the article 'An Account of Events in the Pochayev Monastery Today' for dispatch to the West; that Galanskov supported Ginzburg's intention to send *The White Book* abroad and achieved this through the foreigner called Genrikh, who had come to Moscow; that Galanskov, with Ginzburg's help, compiled the miscellany *Phoenix* and gave one copy to the foreigner called Nadya to take to the West, she being an associate of the journal *Grani*; that Galanskov gave Radziyevsky, in order to get it printed, a copy of 'An Open Letter to Sholokhov' of which he himself was the author; that in 1966 Galanskov received anti-Soviet literature published by the NTS, in which certain facts of Soviet life were interpreted slanderously; that Galanskov also received money in Soviet and foreign currency; that he, Dobrovolsky, saw fifty-dollar notes at Galanskov's; that Galanskov gave him, Dobrovolsky, dollars to sell; and that during the course of 1966, Galanskov gave him about 2000 roubles to build a co-operative flat in his, Dobrovolsky's, name, which was to be used for conspiratorial purposes.

Galanskov's guilt, as charged, is also confirmed by the established fact that at the end of November 1966 Dobrovolsky, on Galanskov's request, gave Radziyevsky 'An Open Letter to Sholokhov', the record of the discussion of the draft of the third volume of the *History of the Party* by Old Bolsheviks, and other material, to have it printed.

Furthermore, Galanskov's guilt is also confirmed by the testimony of the following witnesses:

by Lashkova's testimony that approximately in October– November 1966 she typed for Galanskov one coded letter about the interrelationship of certain numbers, and a second one dealing with some disagreement between the author of the letter and another person, neither of the letters being addressed to anyone; that she, Lashkova, was present at a meeting between Galanskov and Dobrovolsky at the Lenin Library metro station and saw Galanskov hand some literature to Dobrovolsky; that Galanskov bought a type- writer for her and at about the same time showed her some dollars;

by Khaustov's testimony that Galanskov had anti-Soviet views, that Galanskov showed him the verbatim record of the trial of Sinyavsky and Daniel, their photographs, and also some leaflets; that in summer 1966 he, Khaustov, learnt from Galanskov that he was collecting materials for a new miscellany; and that in the spring of 1966 he read 'An Open Letter to Sholokhov' at Galanskov's flat;

by Epifanov's testimony that in June 1966 he arranged a meeting between Galanskov and the foreigner called Philip;

by Batshev's testimony that Galanskov brought Lashkova material for *The White Book*; that Galanskov made Lashkova type out a great deal for him, Galanskov;

by Golub's testimony that Galanskov was in an anti-Soviet state of mind in 1962-63 and in her presence spoke of an allegedly inade- quate degree of freedom in our country; that Galanskov wished to set up some kind of apparatus for the duplication of literature;

by Entin's testimony that with Borisova he sold 400 dollars for Galanskov, 200 dollars initially for 600 roubles and subsequently when, trying to sell a further 200 dollars, he was tricked and instead of money received a pack of mustard plasters;

by Borisova's testimony that together with Entin she sold 400 dollars;

and by Danilov's testimony that Borisova sold the dollars through him.

Galanskov's guilt is also confirmed by the material evidence filed.

In view of the above, Yu. Galanskov is, therefore, charged with violation of the law as specified under articles 70 and 88 paragraph 1 of the Russian Criminal Code.

Criminal proceedings having been instituted against him, A. DOBROVOLSKY admitted that he was fully guilty as charged and testified that in summer 1966, with Lashkova's help, he made twelve copies of the article 'An Account of Events in the Pochayev Monastery Today'; that he, Dobrovolsky, received for circulation from Galanskov pamphlets published by the NTS and circulated them, giving them to Lashkova and Kats; that he received from Galanskov the newspaper *Possev* in the form of eight leaflets, a hectograph, paper for cryptography and also over 2000 Soviet roubles; that on Galanskov's request he gave Radziyevsky 'An Open Letter to Sholokhov' and other material to be printed; that he harboured anti-Soviet literature he had received from Galanskov in his flat, and also the newspaper *Possev*, a hectograph and money in excess of 2000 roubles.

In view of the above, Aleksei Dobrovolsky is, therefore, charged with violation of the law as specified under article 70 of the Russian Criminal Code.

Criminal proceedings having been instituted against her, V. LASHKOVA admitted that she was guilty as charged, and testified that in autumn 1966 she received from Ginzburg material relating to the Sinyavsky and Daniel trial, of which she made five copies; in December 1966, on Galanskov's request, she made twelve copies of 'An Open Letter to Sholokhov' and five copies of 'The Russian Road to Socialism'; that in summer 1966 she made twelve copies for Dobrovolsky of the defamatory document 'An Account of Events in the Pochayev Monastery Today', containing fabrications that slandered the Soviet social and political system; that from Dobrovolsky she received anti-Soviet literature to read—the pamphlet 'Solidarism Is the Idea of the Future' and the magazine *Our Times*, No. 35—and circulated them by handing them on to Kushev and Levitin.

In view of the above, Vera Lashkova is charged with violation of the law as specified under article 70 of the Russian Criminal Code.

On the basis of the above:

The Trial

ALEXANDER GINZBURG is charged with establishing links with the NTS; with transmitting material to the West for publication; with circulating slanderous anti-Soviet literature in the USSR; with compiling a collection of materials on the Sinyavsky and Daniel trial in association with Galanskov in 1966; with writing a provocative letter addressed to Kosygin which was not sent; with helping Galanskov produce the miscellany *Phoenix* which was subsequently sent to the NTS; with receiving from Sweden in June 1966 clippings from foreign newspapers of an anti-Soviet nature in Norwegian, Danish, Italian and French and passing them on to Gubanov; with harbouring two songs of an anti-Soviet nature recorded by tape-recorder with a view to circulating them.

YURY GALANSKOV is charged with establishing links—in order to weaken and undermine the Soviet government—with the anti-Soviet émigré organisation, the NTS, to which he sent various materials; with receiving anti-Soviet literature and leaflets from the NTS and circulating them in the USSR, also with receiving cryptography and duplicating equipment (a hectograph), currency in dollars and Soviet roubles; with collecting, together with Ginzburg, material for *The White Book*; with arranging for its duplication and with dispatching it to the West through a foreigner called Genrikh; with producing in co-operation with Ginzburg the miscellany *Phoenix*, making five copies of it, one of which he sent to the NTS through the foreigner Nadya; with compiling and printing the slanderous anti-Soviet document 'An Open Letter to Sholokhov' and giving one of the copies of this letter to Dobrovolsky to be duplicated; with giving Dobrovolsky other anti-Soviet articles for duplication; with receiving during the course of 1966 for circulation anti-Soviet literature from abroad published by the NTS, namely: the pamphlet 'Solidarism Is the Idea of the Future', the magazine *Our Times*, No. 35, the books *The Power of Ideas*[51] and *At the Price of a Spiritual Feat*[52], the newspaper *Possev*[53] in the form of eight pamphlets of an anti-Soviet nature; with receiving at the same time 560 dollars and over 2000 roubles, a hectograph, and cryptography equipment; besides this, Galanskov is charged with violating the currency regulations.

ALEKSEI DOBROVOLSKY is charged with entering into criminal relations with Galanskov and Lashkova, conducting anti-Soviet agitation and propaganda, habouring in his flat money, anti-Soviet literature published by the NTS, a hectograph and, paper for cryptography, all handed to him by Galanskov; with duplicating, with Lashkova's help, the slanderous anti-Soviet document 'An

Account of Events in the Pochayev Monastery Today'; with receiving
for circulation NTS literature from Galanskov, namely: the pamphlet
'Solidarism Is the Idea of the Future', the books *The Power of Ideas*
and *At the Price of a Spiritual Feat* and the magazine *Our Times*, No. 35,
with spreading this literature by giving the pamphlet and the magazine to Lashkova to read, and giving Kats, for the same purpose, the
pamphlet; with receiving from Galanskov the newspaper *Possev* in
the form of eight leaflets of an anti-Soviet nature to be duplicated;
with receiving from Galanskov and giving to Radziyevsky 'An Open
Letter to Sholokhov' and 'The Russian Road to Socialism' to be
printed.

VERA LASHKOVA is charged with having, under Galanskov's
and Ginzburg's influence, conducted anti-Soviet agitation and
propaganda from the summer of 1966; with typing copies of material
for a tendentious anti-Soviet collection on the Sinyavsky and Daniel
trial, the so-called *White Book*, which includes the anti-Soviet leaflet
signed 'Resistance' and the anti-Soviet letter 'Letter to an Old
Friend'; with typing for Galanskov copies of anti-Soviet materials
for *Phoenix*; with typing twelve copies of the slanderous article 'An
Account of Events in the Pochayev Monastery Today' for Dobrovolsky and passing one of these copies on to Galanskov; with receiving
the pamphlet 'Solidarism Is the Idea of the Future' and the magazine
Our Times, No. 35, from Dobrovolsky in November 1966 to read;
with giving Kushev the pamphlet and Levitin the magazine so that
they should be circulated and read.

A fifteen-minute recess is announced. Afterwards the
sitting is resumed.

JUDGE. Galanskov, you will rise. Is the meaning of the indictment
clear to you?

GALANSKOV. No, it is not clear.

JUDGE. What do you mean, it is not clear? You understand with
what you are being charged?

GALANSKOV. I do not understand the meaning of the indictment.

JUDGE. What do you mean, you do not understand? You understand that you are being charged with anti-Soviet activity?

GALANSKOV. I understand that, but I do not understand the
meaning of this indictment.

JUDGE. Good, if at least you understand *that*, do you plead guilty?

GALANSKOV. No.

JUDGE. Be seated. Ginzburg, you will rise. Is the meaning of the
indictment clear to you?

GINZBURG. It is clear.

JUDGE. Do you plead guilty?

GINZBURG. No.

JUDGE. You may be seated. Dobrovolsky, you will rise. Is the meaning of the indictment clear to you?

DOBROVOLSKY. Yes, it is clear.

JUDGE. Do you plead guilty?

DOBROVOLSKY. I plead guilty in full.

JUDGE. You may be seated. Lashkova, you will rise. Is the meaning of the indictment clear to you?

LASHKOVA. Yes.

JUDGE. Do you plead guilty?

LASHKOVA. Yes.

JUDGE proposes the order of the judicial investigation: interrogation of the accused, the witnesses and the expert. He asks whether there are any objections.

> No one raises any objections. The court decides on the order in which the evidence is to be examined.* Then a one-and-a-half hour recess is announced, after which the interrogation of the accused commences.

INTERROGATION OF ALEKSEI DOBROVOLSKY

JUDGE. Dobrovolsky, stand up, approach the bench and tell us everything you know about this matter.

DOBROVOLSKY. I should like to begin my testimony by explaining how I, a man raised in a Soviet family and in a Soviet school, was able to commit a crime directed against the Soviet government. During the course of my year in prison I have frequently asked myself this question. In 1956 I finished my tenth year of school. At the time I, like all Soviet young people, was under the influence of the 20th Party Congress, which had exposed the cult of Stalin's personality and liberated people's minds. On finishing school, I started work in the *Moscow Pravda* printing works. I did not try to get into a higher educational establishment. . . . I was brought up to revere the person of Stalin. . . .

JUDGE. Keep to the facts, Dobrovolsky!

STATE PROSECUTOR (from now on PROCURATOR). Tell us when and under what circumstances you became acquainted with the other accused.

---

* This order was not observed, as some of the witnesses did not arrive in time, and others did not turn up at all.

DOBROVOLSKY. I became acquainted with Lashkova in a youth circle interested in questions of literary creation. One day an article entitled 'An Account of Events in the Pochayev Monastery Today', describing certain arbitrary acts on the part of the police, came into my possession. I believed what was said in this article, and considered it my duty to acquaint the public with it. I asked Lashkova to re-type this document for me. She re-typed it but failed to return one of the copies to me, saying that she had given it to Galanskov, who could bring it to the notice of the foreign public. In this way I began meeting Galanskov. Then he got me a job in the Museum of Literature and there I became acquainted with Ginzburg. I was only on nodding terms with him, we scarcely ever talked, and we never once discussed political questions. But Galanskov and I discussed political questions a great deal and agreed that in the USSR there was no freedom of speech, freedom of the press and so on—that is, everything that's laid down in the Constitution. A struggle for democracy was essential, but as such a struggle was subject to KGB persecution, it had to be illegal.

PROCURATOR. Who got you the job in the Museum of Literature?

DOBROVOLSKY. Galanskov.

PROCURATOR. What do you know about Galanskov's connections abroad?

DOBROVOLSKY. When Galanskov gave me the hectograph I naturally asked where he had got it from. He answered that from 1962 he had had connections abroad and had got them from Ginzburg. He said that he met foreigners visiting Moscow and received literature, cryptography equipment, hectographs and money in dollar and Soviet notes from them, that he himself collected and passed on to them manuscripts and documents of a tendentious nature that circulated from hand to hand.

PROCURATOR. Is the literature that Galanskov obtained from abroad literature published by the NTS?

DOBROVOLSKY. Yes.

PROCURATOR. So one can say that Galanskov has connections with the NTS?

DOBROVOLSKY. No, that is only my assumption. He spoke not of connections with the NTS but of foreign connections.

PROCURATOR. Did Ginzburg speak to you of the existence of foreign connections?

DOBROVOLSKY. No.

PROCURATOR. But Galanskov referred to Ginzburg and how he established links abroad?

DOBROVOLSKY. Yes.

PROCURATOR. Which particular foreigners visiting Moscow came to your place?

DOBROVOLSKY. No one came to my place, they came to Galanskov and Ginzburg.

PROCURATOR. On whose behalf did these foreigners come to Moscow?

DOBROVOLSKY. I don't know, I did not discuss political matters with them.

PROCURATOR. Did they mention the journal *Grani* in conversation?

DOBROVOLSKY. Yes, Nadya said that she was associated with this magazine.

PROCURATOR. Is *Grani* a magazine published by the NTS?

DOBROVOLSKY. Yes.

PROCURATOR. Tell us about the visits of foreigners to Ginzburg and Galanskov. Where did they meet and what did they exchange?

DOBROVOLSKY. I learnt from Galanskov that Ginzburg was collecting material for *The White Book* and that Galanskov was helping him. Lashkova was typing it. According to Galanskov, the purpose of producing this book was to acquaint our public and the public abroad with material on the Sinyavsky and Daniel trial. It was planned to convey this book to the West, which was accomplished through the foreigner called Genrikh. Galanskov gave him *The White Book* and received from him a microfilm and money in both dollars and Soviet roubles.

PROCURATOR. How did you hear about Genrikh?

DOBROVOLSKY. Galanskov introduced me to him.

PROCURATOR. What did Genrikh say to you?

DOBROVOLSKY. He said nothing.

PROCURATOR. Tell us where this meeting took place?

DOBROVOLSKY. At the Kropotkinskaya metro station.

PROCURATOR. Who told you to go there?

DOBROVOLSKY. I was at Vera Lashkova's. Galanskov phoned and asked me to come to the Kropotkinskaya metro station. It was approximately in late October, early November 1966. Galanskov did not tell me why I should go to the metro station. When I arrived at the Kropotkinskaya metro station, Galanskov appeared with this foreigner. Then there was a conversation between the two of them. I did not hear what was said. That evening, at Potasheva's, Galanskov told me that *The White Book* had been conveyed to the West that very day. That Genrikh was an NTS emissary I learnt only during the investigation. When Galanskov had finished work on the magazine *Phoenix*, he waited for the arrival of a messenger from abroad. Then came Nadya, an associate of the magazine *Grani*. I learnt this—that she was an NTS emissary—only during the investigation. She arrived in Moscow for the [*Orthodox*] Christmas of 1967 [*7 January*]. Galanskov sought me out at her request, she being a believer. I took her to the Troitse-Sergiyeva monastery [*in Zagorsk near Moscow*]. Galanskov later told me that he gave Nadya a copy of *Phoenix*.

PROCURATOR. Did Galanskov tell you that *Grani* was a magazine published by the NTS?

DOBROVOLSKY. No.

PROCURATOR. What is 'Possev'?

DOBROVOLSKY. It is the NTS publishing house.

PROCURATOR. Did you know this before the investigation?

DOBROVOLSKY. Yes.

PROCURATOR. Then you might have taken note of the fact that the magazine *Grani* bears the imprint of the Possev publishing house.

DOBROVOLSKY is silent.

PROCURATOR. Did you, Galanskov and Ginzburg, receive anything from abroad?

DOBROVOLSKY. Galanskov received dollars from Genrikh. The NTS literature he probably received earlier from some foreigner I don't know. Galanskov gave me the following books out of that bunch: *The Power of Ideas*, *At the Price of a Spiritual Feat*, the pamphlet 'Solidarism Is the Idea of the Future', the magazine *Our Times*.

PROCURATOR. Are these all books published by Possev?

DOBROVOLSKY. Yes.

PROCURATOR. When and in what circumstances did Galanskov give you these books?

DOBROVOLSKY. In Lashkova's presence, in October 1966.

PROCURATOR. Why did he give you this literature? Did you ask for it?

DOBROVOLSKY. Yes.

PROCURATOR. Did you want to familiarize yourself with NTS literature?

DOBROVOLSKY. Not only that. Previously Galanskov had given me books of a religious nature.

PROCURATOR. Did Galanskov tell you that he had been receiving this kind of literature from abroad since 1962?

DOBROVOLSKY. No, he said that he had had foreign connections since 1962.

PROCURATOR. Did Galanskov give you a bundle of leaflets?

DOBROVOLSKY. Yes, he gave me a hectograph and eight leaflets, which were to be duplicated. At first I agreed, but when I had read these leaflets through carefully, I changed my mind.

PROCURATOR. Did you tell Galanskov of this?

DOBROVOLSKY. Yes.

PROCURATOR. What did Galanskov say to that?

DOBROVOLSKY. He said that I should keep the hectograph and the leaflets at home.

PROCURATOR. Were the leaflets anti-Soviet?

DOBROVOLSKY. Yes.

PROCURATOR. And were there other occasions when you were given Possev pamphlets by Galanskov?

DOBROVOLSKY. No.

PROCURATOR. When Galanskov asked you to come to the Kropotkinskaya metro station, did he say why?

DOBROVOLSKY. No, he didn't.

PROCURATOR. Didn't he ask you to keep a look-out?

DOBROVOLSKY. Yes, that was exactly my function. While they talked I kept a look-out to see if anyone was following them.

PROCURATOR. You touted,[54] so to speak.

DOBROVOLSKY. Yes.

PROCURATOR. Was there an occasion when you were handed books at the Lenin Library metro station?

DOBROVOLSKY. Yes. Galanskov and Lashkova came to the metro and, in Lashkova's·presence, Galanskov gave me some books published by Possev, five or six in all. That was in October 1966.

PROCURATOR. During the investigation you said it was in November–December.

DOBROVOLSKY. I can't remember exactly when it was.

PROCURATOR. Precisely what books did Galanskov give you at the time?

DOBROVOLSKY. *The Power of Ideas, At the Price of a Spiritual Feat,* the pamphlet 'Solidarism Is the Idea of the Future'. . . .

PROCURATOR. What ideas are contained in the Solidarism pamphlet?

DOBROVOLSKY. The idea of solidarism.

PROCURATOR. What is the pamphlet about?

DOBROVOLSKY. About the NTS programme.

PROCURATOR. Is the NTS programme anti-Soviet?

DOBROVOLSKY. Yes.

PROCURATOR. And did you hand this pamphlet over to the State Security organs?

DOBROVOLSKY. No, I got interested in it. I kept several of the books, and some I gave to Lashkova and Kats. When they returned what I'd given them, I gave some of the books back to Galanskov, and some I kept.

PROCURATOR. Was Lashkova present when you were given the books by Galanskov at the metro?

DOBROVOLSKY. Yes.

PROCURATOR. What books did you give Kats?

DOBROVOLSKY. I can't remember exactly. I think it was 'Solidarism Is the Idea of the Future' and *Our Times*.

PROCURATOR. And what books did you give Lashkova?

DOBROVOLSKY. 'Solidarism Is the Idea of the Future'. It's hard to say exactly which books I gave to whom.

PROCURATOR. So, all the literature you received from Galanskov was literature published by the NTS?

DOBROVOLSKY. Yes.

PROCURATOR. Tell us how you admitted Lashkova to the NTS.

DOBROVOLSKY. I did not admit her to the NTS, there was just talk of her enrolment. I could not admit her to the NTS, as I am not a member of the NTS myself and have not got the authority.

PROCURATOR. Tell us about this conversation.

DOBROVOLSKY. Galanskov asked me to explain to Lashkova several passages in the Solidarism pamphlet that she did not understand. At the end of this pamphlet there is a kind of section of rules, where it is stated that admittance to the NTS can take place in the presence of two other NTS members. I said that one could do without the two or three members, that I could admit her on my own. But I did not have sufficient reason for saying this.

PROCURATOR. So you told Lashkova that you yourself could admit her into the NTS?

DOBROVOLSKY. Yes, that is what I said. I said it to bolster my and Galanskov's authority.

PROCURATOR. Galanskov's authority as a representative of the NTS?

DOBROVOLSKY. Yes.

PROCURATOR. And did you explain to Lashkova that the NTS was an anti-Soviet organization? Did you explain the basic idea of the NTS, that it called for terror, engaged in spying, called for the creation of armed detachments?

DOBROVOLSKY. I did not know that myself, it is not in the pamphlet.

PROCURATOR. But you yourself have read other literature where this is spoken of.

DOBROVOLSKY. Yes, I have, but I did not give it to Lashkova to read.

PROCURATOR. But you yourself have read it?

DOBROVOLSKY. Yes.

PROCURATOR. So, you knew all this?

DOBROVOLSKY. Yes.

PROCURATOR. Then why did you support the NTS?

DOBROVOLSKY (is silent for a while). I did not altogether support it. . . . What I want to say is that if I myself read their literature and gave it to others to read, it still does not mean that I agreed with their programme.

PROCURATOR. Even so you did agree with their views to some extent?

DOBROVOLSKY. Yes, to some extent I did.

> The Judge announces a 10-minute recess. Then the
> interrogation is resumed.

PROCURATOR. What do you know about the delivery to the NTS by Ginzburg and Galanskov of 'A Letter to an Old Friend' and the leaflet signed 'Resistance'?

DOBROVOLSKY. I can only speak about the delivery of *The White Book* as a whole. I know that those documents were in *The White Book*.

PROCURATOR. We are only concerned with those two documents.

DOBROVOLSKY. I did not see them individually, I only saw them in *The White Book*.

PROCURATOR. Tell us how they were conveyed abroad for publication.

DOBROVOLSKY is silent.

PROCURATOR. Tell us how they came to be in *The White Book*, how they were typed, how they were handed over. The whole story.

DOBROVOLSKY. I knew that Lashkova was typing *The White Book* for Ginzburg at his request. Galanskov urged Lashkova to finish the typing quickly, as they were expecting a messenger from abroad to whom they were to give *The White Book*. When I glanced through it at Lashkova's place, I noticed the two documents in it.

PROCURATOR. In what way was it intended to convey *The White Book* abroad?

DOBROVOLSKY. Through the foreigner called Genrikh.

PROCURATOR. Through an NTS representative?

DOBROVOLSKY. Yes.

PROCURATOR. Who passed on the book?

DOBROVOLSKY. I've already said that I do not know exactly. All I know is that, according to Galanskov, the book was passed on.

PROCURATOR. And who compiled *The White Book*?

DOBROVOLSKY. Ginzburg in the main.

PROCURATOR. And who wrote 'A Letter to an Old Friend' and the 'Resistance' leaflet?

DOBROVOLSKY. I don't know.

PROCURATOR. Who had put them into the book?

DOBROVOLSKY. I don't know.

PROCURATOR. Anyway, the collection had been compiled?

DOBROVOLSKY. Yes.

PROCURATOR. And Genrikh's arrival was awaited?

DOBROVOLSKY. Yes.

PROCURATOR. The book was to be conveyed through him?

DOBROVOLSKY. Yes.

PROCURATOR. It was handed over to him secretly?

DOBROVOLSKY. Yes.

PROCURATOR. And why do you think that was?

DOBROVOLSKY. I think that if they had wanted to hand over the magazine *Ogonyok* [*a Soviet weekly*] they would not have tried to hide the fact.

PROCURATOR. So it was done secretly because there were anti-Soviet documents in the book?

DOBROVOLSKY. Yes, there were anti-Soviet documents in it.

PROCURATOR. And they were frightened of the responsibility?

DOBROVOLSKY. Yes.

PROCURATOR. And is that how their NTS ties came to light?

DOBROVOLSKY. Yes.

PROCURATOR. Tell us about your conversation with Kats about the NTS. How did you introduce her to NTS literature?

DOBROVOLSKY. I gave Kats two books: *The Power of Ideas* and the magazine *Our Times*.

PROCURATOR. Who initiated you into the activity of the NTS? Who introduced you to the tasks and methods of this organization?

DOBROVOLSKY. No one introduced me to it.

PROCURATOR. But where did you learn about this organization?

DOBROVOLSKY. From Galanskov.

PROCURATOR. What did he tell you about the NTS?

DOBROVOLSKY. That such an organization existed. He sketched out its programme for me and asked me to talk to Kats about it.

PROCURATOR. So you talked to Kats on Galanskov's behalf?

DOBROVOLSKY. Yes.

PROCURATOR. You spoke about the aims and tasks of this organization?

DOBROVOLSKY. No. All I said was that such an anti-Soviet organization existed. I did not talk to her about the aims and tasks. Kats will confirm that.

PROCURATOR. No, Kats says something different; she says that you introduced her to the aims and tasks of the NTS and to its rules.

DOBROVOLSKY. That's not what she says.

PROCURATOR. She does. (He reads Kats's testimony to the effect that Dobrovolsky had introduced her to the aims of the NTS and to its rules.)

DOBROVOLSKY. Yes, that is so. I gave her the rules.

PROCURATOR. Did you do this on the instructions of Galanskov?

DOBROVOLSKY. Yes.

PROCURATOR. And did you talk to Lashkova on this subject?

DOBROVOLSKY. No, I did not.

PROCURATOR. So you gave Kats 'Solidarism Is the Idea of the Future' and *The Power of Ideas*?

DOBROVOLSKY. Yes, also *The Power of Ideas*, I think.

PROCURATOR. What else do you know about Galanskov's foreign connections?

DOBROVOLSKY is silent.

PROCURATOR. Did Galanskov speak to you about the nature of the connection with the NTS?

DOBROVOLSKY. Yes, the NTS link was maintained through messengers and through correspondence in cryptography.

PROCURATOR. What kind of cryptography precisely?

DOBROVOLSKY. By means of a special paper.

PROCURATOR. Did you ever use it?

DOBROVOLSKY. Yes.

PROCURATOR. Tell us about it.

DOBROVOLSKY. I didn't do the writing. Lashkova wrote at my request. I do not know what she wrote, as something was already written on the sheet when Galanskov gave it to me. Galanskov asked me to use this paper for a letter to Oslo. The address was on a separate sheet. Some kind of text had to be composed. I said that I would write it but Galanskov warned me that my handwriting was known to the KGB. Then I went to Lashkova and asked her to write the following text on the sheet: 'Dear Jan, your parcel has been received. Please send some new records.'

PROCURATOR. This was an open text?

DOBROVOLSKY. Yes.

PROCURATOR. Written on paper?

DOBROVOLSKY. Yes.

PROCURATOR. And there was another text written by using the special paper?

DOBROVOLSKY. I have forgotten the technique now.

PROCURATOR. What did this text actually signify?

DOBROVOLSKY. I didn't know. Galanskov told me that the records could have any titles.

PROCURATOR. But as he did not write it himself, but instructed you to do so, did you realize that the text contained something criminal?

DOBROVOLSKY. Yes.

PROCURATOR. Did Galanskov receive parcels from abroad?

DOBROVOLSKY. Yes.

PROCURATOR. When, where, how?

DOBROVOLSKY. I don't know. I know about this from what he said.

PROCURATOR. What was in these parcels?

DOBROVOLSKY. Literature published by the NTS and other literature.

PROCURATOR. What was the conversation you had about automatic lockers?

DOBROVOLSKY. There are automatic lockers in railway stations, one person puts something in a locker and then another one who knows the number of the combination can come along and take it out.

PROCURATOR. Who told you about these lockers?

DOBROVOLSKY. Galanskov.

PROCURATOR. Why did he tell you about it?

DOBROVOLSKY. He said one could get parcels that way.

PROCURATOR. Did he tell you that he himself had received anything that way?

DOBROVOLSKY. No.

PROCURATOR. Did Galanskov show you letters received from abroad?

DOBROVOLSKY. Yes. He showed me one letter, but he did not inform me of its contents. He told me they were some kind of instructions, but he didn't say what exactly. It looked like a text with certain sentences underlined in different coloured Indian inks.

PROCURATOR. When did Galanskov show you this letter?

DOBROVOLSKY. I don't remember.

PROCURATOR. From whom did you obtain the hectograph and the money?

DOBROVOLSKY. From Galanskov.

PROCURATOR. When?

DOBROVOLSKY. The hectograph in October–November 1966, the money in December 1966.

PROCURATOR. How much money did you receive?

DOBROVOLSKY. 2000 roubles.

PROCURATOR. What for?

DOBROVOLSKY. It was a question of purchasing an [*as yet unbuilt*] co-operative flat in my name. As I understood it, this flat was needed to receive foreigners. Although the flat was to be in my name, the real owner was to be Galanskov.

PROCURATOR. Why didn't Galanskov want to build the flat in his own name?

DOBROVOLSKY. He didn't want to attract attention.

PROCURATOR. And where is this money now?

DOBROVOLSKY. It was confiscated from me during the search.

PROCURATOR. Did Galanskov show you foreign currency?

DOBROVOLSKY. Yes, fifty-dollar notes.

PROCURATOR. Does this prove that he had foreign connections ?

DOBROVOLSKY. Yes.

PROCURATOR. What did Galanskov do with the dollars?

DOBROVOLSKY. He wanted to exchange them for Soviet currency.

PROCURATOR. So, he violated the currency regulations, but got taken for a sucker himself*: he got mustard plasters instead of money. I imagine they would come in handy for him right now.

GALANSKOV says something in a low voice to the Procurator.

PROCURATOR. How many dollars did Galanskov exchange?

DOBROVOLSKY. I did not know before being arrested.

PROCURATOR. Where did he obtain these dollars?

DOBROVOLSKY. Galanskov himself said he received this sum from Genrikh.

PROCURATOR. That's the Genrikh to whom he sold *The White Book*! How much did he get for it?

GALANSKOV. I protest. That is a provocative question.

JUDGE. Galanskov, you are interrupting the hearing!

DOBROVOLSKY (answering Procurator's question). I don't know.

* The Russian expression used—'Prokrutit dinamu'—is thieves' slang.

PROCURATOR. So, you know from whom he received the dollars, but you do not know how much.

DOBROVOLSKY. Yes.

PROCURATOR. Why did Galanskov give you a hectograph?

DOBROVOLSKY. To duplicate leaflets with.

PROCURATOR. What was the nature of these leaflets?

DOBROVOLSKY. Anti-Soviet.

PROCURATOR. What were they about? What were the titles of these leaflets?

DOBROVOLSKY. One of the leaflets was about the Sinyavsky and Daniel trial and the other gave a short account of the NTS programme. I cannot remember the contents of the other leaflets.

PROCURATOR. Were there no more attempts to set up a conspiratorial flat? Did you make such attempts?

DOBROVOLSKY. I did. On Galanskov's instructions, I spoke to friends of Lashkova—Maslova and Ustinova—but we weren't able to find a flat.

PROCURATOR. Did Ginzburg help in getting *The White Book* to Genrikh?

DOBROVOLSKY is silent.

PROCURATOR. I am asking you, did Ginzburg help in getting *The White Book* to Genrikh?

DOBROVOLSKY. All Galanskov told me was that it had been handed over; by whom precisely, I do not know. I never discussed the matter with Ginzburg.

PROCURATOR. Tell us what foreign currency transactions you engaged in.

DOBROVOLSKY. None. Galanskov gave me 50-dollar notes to change. I looked for someone who could change the money but didn't find anyone. Galanskov found someone himself.

PROCURATOR. Did Galanskov give you Soviet money?

DOBROVOLSKY. Yes. Galanskov paid the typists Ustinova and Kamyshanova through me, but these were all insignificant sums.

PROCURATOR. And did he give you money to buy a typewriter?

DOBROVOLSKY. Yes, in September 1966 Galanskov gave me 100 roubles to buy a typewriter for him. I bought one. A 'Civic Appeal' was typed on that machine.

PROCURATOR. So Galanskov gave you money for a typewriter to be used for typing anti-Soviet leaflets?

DOBROVOLSKY. Actually, the leaflets weren't regarded as criminal by the investigating bodies.

PROCURATOR. Where was the typewriter kept?

DOBROVOLSKY. At my place.

PROCURATOR. And did Lashkova use it?

DOBROVOLSKY. I do not remember.

PROCURATOR. Did Galanskov speak to you about the money received from Genrikh?

DOBROVOLSKY. Yes, a few days after the meeting with him took place, but he did not say what sums were involved.

PROCURATOR. For what purpose did Genrikh give Galanskov this money?

DOBROVOLSKY. To help Galanskov carry out the work he was engaged in.

PROCURATOR. An NTS representative gave Galanskov dollars and roubles for Galanskov's use in pursuing his criminal activity, is that so?

DOBROVOLSKY is silent.

PROCURATOR. Did the leaflets contain a call to strike blows at the organs of Soviet authority?

DOBROVOLSKY. I do not remember.

PROCURATOR. From whom did you receive the book *At the Price of a Spiritual Feat*?

DOBROVOLSKY. From Galanskov.

PROCURATOR. Under what circumstances?

DOBROVOLSKY. At the Lenin Library station, in the presence of Lashkova. I read it alone, and gave it no one to read.

PROCURATOR. Why did Galanskov give you this book?

DOBROVOLSKY. To read.

PROCURATOR. He was trying to educate you in the spirit of the principles set forth there.

DOBROVOLSKY. Yes.

PROCURATOR (quoting). 'Salvation from the communist yoke can be achieved only through war . . .' and so on. You should have informed the authorities about this. Did you feel solidarity with him?

DOBROVOLSKY. Yes.

PROCURATOR. Were the other books also of an anti-Soviet nature?

DOBROVOLSKY. Yes.

PROCURATOR. And did you receive them from Galanskov?

DOBROVOLSKY. Yes.

PROCURATOR. Did you write other letters on Galanskov's instructions?

DOBROVOLSKY. Yes, one more letter.

PROCURATOR. How was it written?

DOBROVOLSKY. It was written by hand on three sheets. Galanskov gave it to me. I went to Lashkova and in my presence she typed the

67

letter out from the manuscript. Afterwards I returned both the letter and the original manuscript to Galanskov. One copy of the letter was made, on thin paper. I can't remember the contents now. I think Galanskov was disagreeing with someone.

PROCURATOR. Was it typed in the usual way?

DOBROVOLSKY. Yes.

PROCURATOR. So the first letter was typed out in an unusual way and the second in the usual way?

DOBROVOLSKY. Yes, with the first letter the text was not visible on the page, but with the second it was typed out in the usual way.

PROCURATOR. When was it you wrote the first and when the second?

DOBROVOLSKY. It's hard to answer that question. Around autumn 1966, I can't say more exactly.

PROCURATOR. What conspiratorial steps did you take at meetings with foreigners and when you received parcels?

DOBROVOLSKY. At the meeting with Genrikh I watched Galanskov and Genrikh for some time as they walked.

PROCURATOR. What else?

DOBROVOLSKY is silent.

PROCURATOR. Did Galanskov tell you that books and parcels should not be sent to your address?

DOBROVOLSKY. Yes, he did. I was on the KGB's books.

PROCURATOR. How do you know? What makes you think so?

DOBROVOLSKY. It seemed like that to me.

PROCURATOR. To whose address did the parcels come?

DOBROVOLSKY. I don't know. Galanskov had the addresses, as he told me in November 1966.

PROCURATOR. And what can you tell us about your talks with Ivanova about a flat?

DOBROVOLSKY. I wanted to find out whether NTS literature could be kept in her flat. She is a friend of Lashkova's.

PROCURATOR. Did she agree to this?

DOBROVOLSKY. No.

PROCURATOR. Why didn't you keep it at your place?

DOBROVOLSKY. I did keep it there. Everything was found at my flat.

PROCURATOR. Why was it necessary to keep some at Ivanova's too?

DOBROVOLSKY. I didn't want to keep it at my place any longer.

PROCURATOR. What did Lashkova type for you? I am asking you only about anti-Soviet documents.

DOBROVOLSKY. She typed twelve copies of the article 'Events in the Pochayev Monastery Today'.

PROCURATOR. When was that?

DOBROVOLSKY. In September 1966.

PROCURATOR. Why did you give her this article to type?

DOBROVOLSKY. I believed the facts stated in it to be true and considered it my duty to acquaint the public with these facts.

PROCURATOR. How do you assess the article now?

DOBROVOLSKY. I can't assess it at all. I don't know whether these things actually happened or not.*

PROCURATOR. Obviously the proper thing to do would have been not to have had it typed?

DOBROVOLSKY. Yes, obviously.

PROCURATOR. And why did you want the whole world to learn the facts set out in this article?

DOBROVOLSKY. I considered it my duty. I believed the article to be true.

PROCURATOR. Where was it placed afterwards?

DOBROVOLSKY. In *Phoenix*.

PROCURATOR. Who was the compiler?

DOBROVOLSKY. Galanskov.

PROCURATOR. Where was *Phoenix* sent?

DOBROVOLSKY. Abroad.

PROCURATOR. Through whom?

DOBROVOLSKY. Through Nadya.

PROCURATOR. How did Nadya introduce herself?

DOBROVOLSKY. As an associate of *Grani*.

PROCURATOR. But that's an NTS magazine! Do you regard this article as anti-Soviet?

DOBROVOLSKY. If it contains slander, then it's anti-Soviet.

PROCURATOR. What else did you ask Lashkova to type?

DOBROVOLSKY. Nothing else.

PROCURATOR. What do you know about the circulation of 'The Confession of Victor Velsky', 'The Russian Road to Socialism' and the letter to Sholokhov?

DOBROVOLSKY. Galanskov put 'The Confession of Victor Velsky' into his miscellany *Phoenix*. I read the story. It's in two parts: the first concerns the hero's life; the second deals with philosophical and religious questions. The first part of this work is anti-Soviet.

PROCURATOR. And what can you tell us about the two other

---

* The article deals with police persecution of the Pochayev monks and their expulsion from their monastery in the Western Ukraine.

works: 'An Open Letter to Sholokhov' and 'The Russian Road to Socialism'?

DOBROVOLSKY. 'An Open Letter to Sholokhov' is anti-Soviet. I passed it on to Radziyevsky who was in a position to have it printed. Galanskov wanted to send this letter to scientists and cultural workers in the Soviet Union. Varga's article . . .

PROCURATOR (interrupting him). The article is only attributed to Academician Varga, in actual fact it is not his article!

DOBROVOLSKY. I learnt this only during the investigation. At Galanskov's request, I had this article typed by Ustinova. Then Galanskov paid her off through me. Ustinova herself merely typed the article, she did not study its contents.

PROCURATOR. That's why she isn't in the dock too! So, these three works were subsequently included in *Phoenix*?

DOBROVOLSKY. Yes.

PROCURATOR. How many copies of each article were typed?

DOBROVOLSKY. Five copies of 'The Confession of Victor Velsky' and five of 'The Russian Road'. 'The Letter to Sholokhov' was not typed.

PROCURATOR. What was Ginzburg's connection with the article 'Russian Road to Socialism'?

DOBROVOLSKY. According to Galanskov, this article was given to him by Ginzburg, who had it at home on film.

PROCURATOR. When was this?

DOBROVOLSKY. In the autumn. I do not know the circumstances. I learnt of this from Galanskov.

PROCURATOR. Did Galanskov warn you to be careful when he asked you to type this article?

DOBROVOLSKY. Yes.

PROCURATOR. What expressions did he use?

DOBROVOLSKY. I don't remember.

PROCURATOR. Did he warn you to be conspiratorial?

DOBROVOLSKY. Yes.

PROCURATOR. So he realized that this article was anti-Soviet and that circulating it could lead to charges being brought?

DOBROVOLSKY. Yes.

PROCURATOR. You have seen the article confiscated from Galanskov? Is it the same article that Ustinova typed?

DOBROVOLSKY. Yes, it is the same one.

PROCURATOR. And is the 'Open Letter to Sholokhov' referred to in this case the same one?

DOBROVOLSKY. Yes.

PROCURATOR. How were *The White Book* and *Phoenix* signed when they were sent to the NTS abroad?

DOBROVOLSKY. *The White Book* was signed: 'Compiler A. Ginzburg', *Phoenix*: 'Edited by Yu. Galanskov'.

PROCURATOR. So Galanskov gave you the letter to Sholokhov?

DOBROVOLSKY. Yes.

PROCURATOR. And who wrote it? Did Galanskov not tell you?

DOBROVOLSKY. No.

PROCURATOR. And where did it end up?

DOBROVOLSKY. In *Phoenix*.

PROCURATOR. So all the activity you have been telling the court about—yours, Galanskov's, Ginzburg's and Lashkova's—was of an anti-Soviet nature?

DOBROVOLSKY. Yes.

PROCURATOR. Galanskov's and Ginzburg's articles, the money, the NTS connections, etc., it was all of a criminal, anti-Soviet nature?

DOBROVOLSKY. Yes.

PROCURATOR. And can one reckon that all this was done with anti-Soviet intent?

DOBROVOLSKY. Yes.

PROCURATOR. I have finished.

JUDGE. Has the defence any questions to put to the accused?

DOBROVOLSKY'S DEFENCE COUNSEL SHVEISKY (henceforth SHVEISKY). What led you to this?

DOBROVOLSKY. I began my evidence with that. When I was seventeen, I was expelled from the Komsomol for opposing the unmasking of the cult of [*Stalin's*] personality at a district committee meeting. After that I started digging into questions that interested me. I began to take an interest in politics. I began finding faults with things. I felt this to be an assertion of myself as a thinking person. But I was incapable of understanding these complex matters and I got caught up in contradictions. I had neither father nor older brother to set me on the right path. . . . And the Komsomol workers I turned to brushed me aside. Freedom of speech does not mean freedom to fabricate slander against our Soviet regime. I was sentenced for anti-Soviet statements. I was nineteen at the time. And I did not admit my guilt as I felt I had been unjustly treated. Nor did I draw the correct conclusions during my term of imprisonment, as I was surrounded by nothing but followers of Bandera* and

* Stepan Bandera (1909-59): Ukrainian nationalist leader murdered in Munich in 1959 by a KGB agent. Ed.

Vlasov* in the camp. When I came out, I still held the same views. At that time the errors being committed by Khrushchev gave support to my views, and I identified the errors with the party line. I chose to emphasize only the hardships and defects in our life. In my biased way, all I saw was the dark side of things and I didn't want to look at what was bright and most important in our life. I even fell mentally ill. I interpreted the Sinyavsky and Daniel case as a violation of democratic norms, and began to believe that we had turned away from Lenin's path after his death. And I took part in the circulation of the 'Civic Appeal' about the trial.[55] I regarded this to be my duty as a citizen. At this time I met Galanskov. You know the rest.

SHVEISKY. Did Galanskov ask you about your connection with the NTS?

DOBROVOLSKY. No.

SHVEISKY (quotes). 'Galanskov asked me about my connection with the NTS. I told him that, after reading NTS pamphlets I had come to the conclusion that the NTS was a group of embittered people cut off from the homeland.' Isn't this what you said during the investigation?

DOBROVOLSKY. Yes, I did.

SHVEISKY. If you already realized this at the time, how could you pass on NTS literature to others?

DOBROVOLSKY. I based myself on the principle that 'the forbidden fruit always tastes sweeter'. I should like to point out that I didn't give anyone the most anti-Soviet literature, for instance *At the Price of a Spiritual Feat*.

SHVEISKY. Did you engage in literary activity? What did you yourself write?

DOBROVOLSKY. 'The Interrelation of Knowledge and Faith.' This article was included in *Phoenix*.

SHVEISKY. Is there anything criminal in it?

DOBROVOLSKY. No, I have not been charged with it.

SHVEISKY. Are there any other articles of yours?

DOBROVOLSKY. Yes, philosophical-religious ones.

SHVEISKY. And did you write on political subjects?

DOBROVOLSKY. Yes.

SHVEISKY. Is the letter from the monks of the Pochayev monastery the only document in *Phoenix* that came through you?

---

* Andrei Vlasov (1900-46): Red Army general captured by the Germans in 1942, active in 1944-45 as leader of the Russian anti-communist movement on German-held soil. Executed in Moscow. Ed.

DOBROVOLSKY. Yes.

SHVEISKY. Was it your desire that this document get into *Phoenix*?

DOBROVOLSKY. I was neither for nor against it. When I heard from Lashkova that the document might be published abroad, I demanded its return.

SHVEISKY. Did you know that this document would be published abroad, and did this accord with your wishes?

DOBROVOLSKY. Yes, it did.*

SHVEISKY. Is 'Events in the Pochayev Monastery' among the materials published by *Grani*?

DOBROVOLSKY. No.

SHVEISKY. Were 'The Confession of Victor Velsky' and 'The Russian Road to Socialism' published in *Grani*?

DOBROVOLSKY. No.[56]

SHVEISKY. How do you explain this?

DOBROVOLSKY. Obviously because of the contents.

SHVEISKY. How did 'The Pochayev Monastery' come into your possession?

DOBROVOLSKY. Through my friend, the late Mark Dobrokhotov.

SHVEISKY. Did you try to verify the facts described in this piece?

DOBROVOLSKY. No, I accepted it on trust.

SHVEISKY. From whom—Dobrokhotov?

DOBROVOLSKY. No, the monks. They had written it, after all.

SHVEISKY. Which books did you pass on for reading and to whom? As I understand it, you gave Lashkova 'Solidarism' and *Our Times*, Kats *Our Times* and *The Power of Ideas*, and Kushev the pamphlet 'Solidarism'. Is that correct?

DOBROVOLSKY. It seems to me there is a misunderstanding here. I was on distant terms with Kushev. I gave him nothing.

SHVEISKY. Did you notice that the Possev leaflets were dated August 1966?

DOBROVOLSKY. Yes.

SHVEISKY. What did this mean?

DOBROVOLSKY. That they were to be duplicated in August. That is how Galanskov explained it to me.

SHVEISKY. Why then were they not duplicated?

DOBROVOLSKY. I read through them and refused to duplicate them.

SHVEISKY. And why precisely did you refuse?

DOBROVOLSKY. The Procurator has read out some quotations

* There is no obvious explanation for Dobrovolsky's apparent inconsistency here. Ed.

from these leaflets here. They contain calls to undermine the Soviet government.

SHVEISKY. So this was a voluntary rejection of criminal activity?

DOBROVOLSKY. Yes.

SHVEISKY. But why did you keep a hectograph in your home?

DOBROVOLSKY. It was confiscated from me during the search and nothing was printed on it.

SHVEISKY. On the one hand you did not wish to print the leaflets because they were anti-Soviet, and on the other you admit that your actions were anti-Soviet. What exactly do you regard as anti-Soviet in your activity?

DOBROVOLSKY. I gave people anti-Soviet literature to read.

SHVEISKY. When were you in a psychiatric hospital for the first time—in 1954?

DOBROVOLSKY. Yes.

SHVEISKY. And criminal charges were brought against you in 1958?

DOBROVOLSKY. Yes.

SHVEISKY. What were the reasons for your being in a psychiatric hospital?

DOBROVOLSKY. I wanted to quit civilization and live in the bosom of nature.

SHVEISKY. Where did you want to go—to a little garden, or a public garden?

DOBROVOLSKY. I didn't want to live in the town. . . . It's hard to explain.

SHVEISKY. How do you feel now about the activities you are being tried for?

DOBROVOLSKY. I admit that by my actions, which previously seemed correct to me, I have been playing into the hands of the enemies of the Soviet government, the NTS.

SHVEISKY. Is the anti-Soviet orientation of the NTS clear to you?

DOBROVOLSKY. Yes.

GALANSKOV'S DEFENCE COUNSEL KAMINSKAYA (henceforth KAMINSKAYA). Dobrovolsky, you have said that you are confirming the evidence given by you at the preliminary investigation. Have I understood you correctly?

DOBROVOLSKY. Yes.

KAMINSKAYA. When were you arrested?

DOBROVOLSKY. 19 January 1967.

KAMINSKAYA. When were you first interrogated?

DOBROVOLSKY. The same day.

KAMINSKAYA. Did you give the same evidence then as now?

DOBROVOLSKY. No, at that time I tried to deceive the investigation.

KAMINSKAYA. You admitted giving Radziyevsky literature to duplicate?

DOBROVOLSKY. As everything I said at the time was a lie, it's hard for me to remember now exactly what lie I dreamed up then.

KAMINSKAYA. Did you know that Radziyevsky had handed on these documents for duplication?

DOBROVOLSKY. Yes.

KAMINSKAYA. You evidently knew how they got to Radziyevsky?

DOBROVOLSKY. I gave them to him.

KAMINSKAYA. But you denied that at the first interrogation?

DOBROVOLSKY. I don't remember.

KAMINSKAYA. When were you interrogated after that?

DOBROVOLSKY. Almost every day. I don't remember exactly.

KAMINSKAYA. I'll remind you. You were questioned on the 20th, the 21st. . . . Don't you remember the evidence you gave then about your personally having passed the material on to Radziyevsky?

DOBROVOLSKY. I think. . . . It's hard for me to answer that question. I don't remember.

KAMINSKAYA. Don't you remember the interrogation of 21 January, at which not only the investigator was present? The Assistant Procurator was there as well.

DOBROVOLSKY. I don't remember. There was often someone else besides the investigator present at my interrogations.

KAMINSKAYA. Was the evidence you gave at this interrogation true?

DOBROVOLSKY. The evidence I gave on 25 March 1967, five days after my return from the Serbsky Institute, was true.

KAMINSKAYA. Am I to take it that up to this point you did not give true evidence?

DOBROVOLSKY. Yes.

KAMINSKAYA. And subsequently your evidence was true in all respects?

DOBROVOLSKY. Yes.

KAMINSKAYA. Did you admit that you gave Radziyevsky the material yourself?

DOBROVOLSKY. Yes.

KAMINSKAYA. Didn't you testify that Galanskov had instructed you to do this?

DOBROVOLSKY is silent.

KAMINSKAYA. When was your article 'The Interrelation of Knowledge and Faith' written?

DOBROVOLSKY. In 1966, in the second half of the year.

KAMINSKAYA. Before you got to know Galanskov?

DOBROVOLSKY. It's hard for me to answer that question.

KAMINSKAYA. What was your object in giving this article to Galanskov?

DOBROVOLSKY. So that it would be put in *Phoenix*.

KAMINSKAYA. Did you know how *Phoenix* was to be circulated?

DOBROVOLSKY. Yes.

KAMINSKAYA. Were you seeking personal gain in placing this article in *Phoenix*?

DOBROVOLSKY. I wanted to receive a fee.

KAMINSKAYA. Who was the first foreigner you met?

DOBROVOLSKY. A French journalist called Gabriel.

KAMINSKAYA. When and where did you meet him?

DOBROVOLSKY. On 6 August 1966, in Delone's flat.

> The Judge announces a ten-minute recess. Then the interrogation is resumed.

KAMINSKAYA. What did you discuss with him?

DOBROVOLSKY. Literary matters.

KAMINSKAYA. Did you, perhaps, talk about some literary group?

DOBROVOLSKY. Yes, we talked about the Smogists.

KAMINSKAYA. Did you ask this foreigner any questions yourself?

DOBROVOLSKY. Yes, I did, but I can't remember exactly now. . . . I gave him my article. I wanted it to be printed.

KAMINSKAYA. Did you discuss this article with any other foreigner?

DOBROVOLSKY. Yes, with Genrikh. He told me my article had been published in some Catholic weekly.

KAMINSKAYA. What else did he tell you?

DOBROVOLSKY. He gave me moral encouragement and said that the fee would be transferred to me.

JUDGE. Stick to the point, Comrade lawyer!

KAMINSKAYA. I am questioning the defendant on the materials of the case.

JUDGE. I would ask you to confine your questions to the facts of the indictment.

KAMINSKAYA. Did Genrikh tell you this at his first meeting with you?

DOBROVOLSKY. No, at the second.

KAMINSKAYA. Who else was present at this meeting with Genrikh?

DOBROVOLSKY. The two of us.

GINZBURG'S DEFENCE COUNSEL ZOLOTUKHIN (henceforth ZOLOTUKHIN). Did you discuss the NTS with Genrikh?

DOBROVOLSKY. No.

ZOLOTUKHIN. Did you discuss the NTS with Nadya?

DOBROVOLSKY. No.

ZOLOTUKHIN. Where did you learn about their NTS affiliations?

DOBROVOLSKY. I became convinced of this after my arrest. Before the arrest I merely assumed as much.

ZOLOTUKHIN. What were you working on before the arrest?

DOBROVOLSKY. I was working on a piece about the immortality of the soul.

ZOLOTUKHIN. Tell us briefly about the basic idea of this work.

JUDGE. The question is out of order—it has no bearing on the case. I have just asked defence counsel Kaminskaya to keep to the indictment.

ZOLOTUKHIN. I am interested in the defendant's personality.

JUDGE. The court is not concerned with the defendant's creative work. The court is concerned with a criminal case.

ZOLOTUKHIN. What significance did this work have for you?

JUDGE. The question is out of order.

ZOLOTUKHIN. How would you describe your relations with Galanskov?

DOBROVOLSKY. We were not on bad terms.

ZOLOTUKHIN. Do you consider that there was mutual trust between you?

DOBROVOLSKY. Yes,

ZOLOTUKHIN. How often in the autumn of 1966 did you visit Galanskov at his home?

DOBROVOLSKY. Every day. I had lunch with him there.

ZOLOTUKHIN. And did you visit him apart from that?

DOBROVOLSKY. I did.

ZOLOTUKHIN. Did you ever see him working on the miscellany *Phoenix*?

DOBROVOLSKY. I did not see manuscripts at his home, but I saw printed works.

ZOLOTUKHIN. Were you interested in the identity of the contributors using pseudonyms?

DOBROVOLSKY. No.

ZOLOTUKHIN. But what did you say on this question at the investigation?

DOBROVOLSKY. I don't remember.

ZOLOTUKHIN. Don't you remember that you asked him about this, but he did not answer? That is what your testimony in the investigation record states.

DOBROVOLSKY. Perhaps.

ZOLOTUKHIN. If the relationship between you and Galanskov was one of trust, why didn't Galanskov tell you who the pseudonyms stood for?

DOBROVOLSKY. I did not insist on it.

ZOLOTUKHIN. How often did you visit Lashkova in autumn 1966?

DOBROVOLSKY. Frequently.

ZOLOTUKHIN. Did you find her at work?

DOBROVOLSKY. Yes.

ZOLOTUKHIN. What was she typing?

DOBROVOLSKY. She was typing *The White Book.*

ZOLOTUKHIN. Can you say anything about how hard she was working?

DOBROVOLSKY. Towards the end she began to work terribly hard, as a messenger was expected from abroad.

ZOLOTUKHIN. Do you know when the messenger arrived and whether Lashkova managed to finish off the work in time?

DOBROVOLSKY. He arrived a little while after the work had been finished, about two to three weeks after.

ZOLOTUKHIN. Did you send Galanskov a note from the Serbsky Institute?

DOBROVOLSKY. I did.

ZOLOTUKHIN. What did it say?

DOBROVOLSKY. I don't remember.

ZOLOTUKHIN (quotes). 'Yura, I beg you, for the love of god, you know I gave Radziyevsky nothing. Why don't you tell? I'll be put in prison.' Dobrovolsky, why did you write: 'Believe me, I can't go to gaol now. I must finish my research.' How do you explain your request?

DOBROVOLSKY. I cannot answer that question.

ZOLOTUKHIN. What kind of search for *Phoenix* did you propose to the KGB on 15 February 1967?*

DOBROVOLSKY. I don't remember. I refuse to answer that question.

---

* In February Dobrovolsky offered the KGB his help in the urgent searches being made for the remaining unconfiscated copy of *Phoenix*, as otherwise, in his own words, it 'would go abroad'. Later on he testified that *Phoenix* had already supposedly been conveyed abroad in December 1966.

LASHKOVA'S DEFENCE COUNSEL ARIYA (henceforth ARIYA). Who introduced you to Lashkova?

DOBROVOLSKY. Batshev.

ARIYA. In what professional capacity did you know Lashkova?

DOBROVOLSKY. As a typist.

ARIYA. You employed her as a typist?

DOBROVOLSKY. Yes.

ARIYA. Obviously she read the material as she was typing it?

DOBROVOLSKY. Yes.

ARIYA. Did you tell Lashkova of your indignation on reading 'Events in the Pochayev Monastery'?

DOBROVOLSKY. Yes.

ARIYA. So she believed everything discussed in this work to be true?

DOBROVOLSKY. Yes.

ARIYA. You said that, on Galanskov's request, you told Lashkova about the NTS. And you told her you could enrol her in the NTS.

DOBROVOLSKY. That is not the correct way of putting it. I did not suggest that she join the NTS.

ARIYA. How should it be understood?

DOBROVOLSKY. Lashkova herself asked me to tell her about joining the NTS.

ARIYA. And what was your answer? That you could enrol her on your own?

DOBROVOLSKY. It was an irresponsible statement.

ARIYA. Did Lashkova agree to join the NTS after this statement of yours.

DOBROVOLSKY. No, she was just asking me in general terms.

ARIYA. You saw material for *The White Book* at Lashkova's. Was it the complete book or individual items?

DOBROVOLSKY. It was separate items.

ARIYA. Can you say whether all the items that subsequently went into *The White Book* were there?

DOBROVOLSKY. No, I don't know.

ARIYA. You testified that towards the end of the work Lashkova put on the pressure as a messenger was expected from abroad. Who told you about the supposed arrival of the messenger?

DOBROVOLSKY. Galanskov.

ARIYA. Lashkova said nothing to you about him?

DOBROVOLSKY. No, Lashkova said nothing to me.

ARIYA. You are charged with giving Lashkova NTS literature to read?

DOBROVOLSKY. Yes.

ARIYA. Do you accept this formulation of the indictment?

DOBROVOLSKY. Yes.

ARIYA. Did Lashkova give anyone this literature?

DOBROVOLSKY. I warned her not to give it to anyone.

ARIYA. When did she return this literature to you?

DOBROVOLSKY. After about a month.

ARIYA. Did she tell you that she had given it to anyone to read?

DOBROVOLSKY. No.

JUDGE. Who got to know Lashkova first—you, Ginzburg or Galanskov?

DOBROVOLSKY. I don't remember.

JUDGE. Did you introduce Lashkova to Ginzburg and Galanskov, or did she get to know them herself?

DOBROVOLSKY. She herself.

JUDGE. Do you have a family?

DOBROVOLSKY. Yes.

JUDGE. A wife and child?

DOBROVOLSKY. Yes.

JUDGE. A daughter, a son?

DOBROVOLSKY. A son.

JUDGE. Did your wife know of your activity?

DOBROVOLSKY. No.

JUDGE. Do the defendants have any questions to put to Dobrovolsky?

GALANSKOV. From your testimony it follows that you never asked for 'Events in the Pochayev Monastery' to be sent to the West?

DOBROVOLSKY. No, I did not ask for that.

GALANSKOV. Did I receive one or two copies of this article from you?

DOBROVOLSKY. You received nothing from me. You received it from Lashkova.

GALANSKOV. Did you give this article to anyone else apart from Lashkova for typing?

DOBROVOLSKY. Yes.

GALANSKOV. For what purpose?

DOBROVOLSKY. So as to circulate it.

GALANSKOV. You have testified that I used to visit Titov once a month. Do you confirm this testimony?

DOBROVOLSKY. Yes.

GALANSKOV. On what do you base this testimony?

DOBROVOLSKY. On what my friends have told me.

GALANSKOV. Who specifically?

DOBROVOLSKY. Bukovsky.

GALANSKOV. You state that you saw instructions on film at my home and then you contradict yourself when you speak of instructions printed on paper, several lines of which were underlined with different coloured Indian inks.

DOBROVOLSKY. I saw instructions printed on paper.

GALANSKOV. Where was that?

DOBROVOLSKY. I don't remember.

GALANSKOV. Did you and I discuss this at all?

DOBROVOLSKY. I don't remember.

GALANSKOV. Was anyone else there at the time?

DOBROVOLSKY. No.

GALANSKOV. Do I understand you correctly to say that no one besides yourself saw this letter?

DOBROVOLSKY. Yes.

GALANSKOV. I want you to recall your testimony about the microfilm. . . .

DOBROVOLSKY. I testified about a film of works by Sinyavsky and Daniel.

GALANSKOV. Delone testifies that he saw dollars in your possession. What were the circumstances?

DOBROVOLSKY. It was in a café.

GALANSKOV. Why did you have these dollars with you?

DOBROVOLSKY. I was carrying them on me in the hope of finding someone who could sell them.

GALANSKOV. Did you ask anyone?

DOBROVOLSKY. Everyone.

GALANSKOV. Whom precisely?

DOBROVOLSKY. Bukovsky, Titov.

GALANSKOV. What sum was discussed?

DOBROVOLSKY. No sum was discussed.

GALANSKOV. Whom else did you ask?

DOBROVOLSKY. I don't remember. . . . Khaustov.

GALANSKOV. How could Khaustov help you?

DOBROVOLSKY. I thought he knew some currency operators.

GALANSKOV. And Bukovsky?

DOBROVOLSKY. The same with him.

GALANSKOV. Did you speak about your own dollars or someone else's?

DOBROVOLSKY. I spoke about dollars in general.

GALANSKOV. In view of the fact that the Procurator has asked a question about the sale of *The White Book* I should like to know precisely how you understood him?

DOBROVOLSKY. Metaphorically.

GALANSKOV. Did you give any evidence about the sale of *The White Book*?

DOBROVOLSKY. No, absolutely not.

GALANSKOV. Did you say you received books from me once?

DOBROVOLSKY. Yes.

GALANSKOV. Did you give evidence about a briefcase and some money?

DOBROVOLSKY. Only about a briefcase. There was no money.

GALANSKOV. Do you remember the colour of this briefcase?

JUDGE. The question is out of order—it has no bearing on the case.

GALANSKOV. Did you take the books from me with or without a briefcase?

DOBROVOLSKY. With a briefcase.

GALANSKOV. Which books did you receive at the time?

DOBROVOLSKY. 'Solidarism', *The Power of Ideas, At the Price of a Spiritual Feat.*

GALANSKOV. In other words, all the books you listed during the investigation?

DOBROVOLSKY. Yes.

GALANSKOV. May one assume that this was in late November?

DOBROVOLSKY. Yes.

GALANSKOV. Was there snow at the time?

JUDGE. The question is out of order.

GALANSKOV. What was I dressed in?

DOBROVOLSKY. I don't remember.

GALANSKOV. Tell us how I introduced you to Genrikh.

DOBROVOLSKY. It was at the Kropotkinskaya metro.

GALANSKOV. You testified that you saw a bundle of dollars at my place. What were the circumstances?

DOBROVOLSKY. We called and you showed me the bundle.

GALANSKOV. Was someone else present?

DOBROVOLSKY. No.

GALANSKOV. Did you speak to anyone about this?

DOBROVOLSKY. No.

GALANSKOV. How many days did you spend with Nadya?

DOBROVOLSKY. The first time, about ten to fifteen minutes, and the second time—the whole day; I took her to the Troitse-Sergiyeva monastery.

GALANSKOV. Tell us about your first meeting with her.

DOBROVOLSKY. It was at Lermontovskaya metro, when you introduced me to her.

GALANSKOV. Where did Nadya go then?

DOBROVOLSKY. I don't know.

GALANSKOV. How did you meet afterwards?

DOBROVOLSKY. We had agreed how to meet beforehand.

GALANSKOV. How long did you spend at the monastery with her?

DOBROVOLSKY. The whole day.

GALANSKOV. Did you see her afterwards?

DOBROVOLSKY. No.

GALANSKOV. You testified that you saw her before her departure.

DOBROVOLSKY. Yes, I saw her again the next day.

GALANSKOV. Did you call on anyone with her?

DOBROVOLSKY. No.

GALANSKOV. Didn't you call on Sitnikov with her?

DOBROVOLSKY. No.

GALANSKOV. Titov?

DOBROVOLSKY. I did.

GALANSKOV. For what reason?

DOBROVOLSKY. Titov is a religious artist.

GALANSKOV. Did you testify that when I came to Potasheva's I told you that *The White Book* had been sent to the West?

DOBROVOLSKY. Yes.

GALANSKOV. How was that?

DOBROVOLSKY. There were a large number of people at her place. Then you arrived and told me. No one heard more.

GALANSKOV. Was there nobody near by when I was speaking to you about this?

DOBROVOLSKY. No.

GALANSKOV. Are there any other persons who know about these words?

DOBROVOLSKY. No.

GALANSKOV. Can you state the exact position in the room where I spoke these words to you?

DOBROVOLSKY. I was in the entrance hall. I rang. You and some girl opened the door to me.

GALANSKOV. What else happened?

DOBROVOLSKY. You told me that *The White Book* had been handed over.

GALANSKOV. Did the girl hear this?

DOBROVOLSKY. She may have done.

GALANSKOV. You had one copy of the pamphlet 'Solidarism Is the Idea of the Future'?

DOBROVOLSKY. Yes.

GALANSKOV. Where is this pamphlet now?

DOBROVOLSKY. I don't remember.

GALANSKOV. To whom did you pass it?

DOBROVOLSKY. Kats.

JUDGE. Was it typed out?

DOBROVOLSKY. One was printed, and the other was typed.

JUDGE. Where has it got to now?

DOBROVOLSKY. I don't remember.

GALANSKOV. I testified that I handed on through you the story....

JUDGE (interrupts). The question is out of order.

GALANSKOV. In your testimony you refer not only to conversations with me, but also to conversations with Ginzburg?

DOBROVOLSKY. Would you be more precise?

GALANSKOV. You testified that a foreigner was supposed to come to [*the mathematician*] Esenin-Volpin. You testified that you learnt this from conversation with Ginzburg. When and where did you talk to Ginzburg?

DOBROVOLSKY. In the Museum of Literature.

GALANSKOV. Do I know Esenin-Volpin?

JUDGE. The question is out of order.

GALANSKOV. Describe our conversation about check-rooms.

DOBROVOLSKY. I can't remember.

GALANSKOV. You spoke about a film of the article 'The Russian Road to Socialism'. Did you see this film yourself?

DOBROVOLSKY. Yes.

GALANSKOV. How did you find out that this film belonged to Ginzburg?

DOBROVOLSKY. I have already said how.

GALANSKOV. When you mentioned this film, why did you also mention the quarrel I had with Ginzburg in Lashkova's flat?

DOBROVOLSKY. I heard about it from Lashkova.

JUDGE. Who was in Potasheva's flat the day of the meeting with Genrikh, when *The White Book* was handed over to him?

DOBROVOLSKY. Potasheva, Ustinova, Lashkova, Timofeyeva.

GALANSKOV. What was my interest in Ustinova at the time?

DOBROVOLSKY. I don't remember.

GALANSKOV. Was Ustinova at Potasheva's?

DOBROVOLSKY. Yes, she was.

JUDGE. Are there any more questions? Sit down, Dobrovolsky, that's enough.

The court then proceeds to the interrogation of Vera Lashkova.

INTERROGATION OF VERA LASHKOVA

JUDGE. Lashkova, stand up, approach the bench and tell us all you know about the present case.

LASHKOVA. Before giving my evidence, I should like to say that I plead guilty as regards the facts, but I do not regard my activity as anti-Soviet.

JUDGE. Tell us how you became acquainted with the other defendants.

LASHKOVA. I first became acquainted with Dobrovolsky; Batshev introduced us in January 1966. It was a chance friendship.

PROCURATOR. This friendship was not linked with any activity?

LASHKOVA. No, it was a chance friendship. Then I became acquainted with Galanskov, and in September 1966 he introduced me to Ginzburg. I met Galanskov through Kaplan, as Galanskov needed a typist. My acquaintanceship with Ginzburg was due to the fact that he gave me typing work. I met him on returning from Siberia.

PROCURATOR. Why did you go there?

LASHKOVA. I went to see Batshev.*

PROCURATOR. What was your concern with Batshev?

LASHKOVA. I felt I had to go to him.

PROCURATOR. How did you find the money to go? After all, you were not working at the time.

LASHKOVA. I was working before my trip to see Batshev. I visited him because we are friends and I felt I had to give him some support.

JUDGE. Before you got a job at Moscow University you were not working?

LASHKOVA. No.

JUDGE. Who supported you?

LASHKOVA. Nobody.

JUDGE. Tell us how you typed for Ginzburg.

LASHKOVA. Once I had received the materials for the book from Ginzburg and agreed on a fee with him, I started work. I finished by

* The young poet Batshev, a member of SMOG, was exiled to Siberia for five years in 1966 as 'a person leading a parasitical life'.[57]

mid-November 1966. I typed 'A Letter to an Old Friend' in part. Unlike the other items, where I made five copies, I typed six or seven copies of this letter. As regards the 'Resistance' pamphlet, it wasn't I who typed it. I saw it—it was going round Moscow—I saw it in the book, but I didn't type it myself.

PROCURATOR. What did you type for Dobrovolsky?

LASHKOVA. Verses on religious subjects, 'Events in the Pochayev Monastery Today'. I typed 'Events' first for Dobrokhotov and then for Dobrovolsky. In June 1966 Dobrovolsky asked me to do some typing work, he took me to Mark Dobrokhotov, and the latter asked me whether I could type a certain work for him. It wasn't a big job, the document was already typed, but it had been revised subsequently and had to be re-typed. It was very truthfully and sincerely written. It was addressed to certain official bodies. I typed six copies of this document. I did not consider this document anti-Soviet. Then I typed another six copies for Dobrovolsky. In all twelve copies. I was paid ten roubles by Dobrokhotov. At first I didn't want to take this money from him—it was too large a payment. But he told me that the money had been put aside especially for the re-typing of this work and I took it.

PROCURATOR. What do you know about the NTS?

ARIYA. According to the law, the accused may first relate everything having a bearing on the case and afterwards questions should be put. I ask you to allow Lashkova to tell the whole story herself first.

JUDGE. I see no irregularity in the Comrade Procurator asking a question.

PROCURATOR. What do you know about the NTS?

LASHKOVA. I first heard about the NTS. . . . I can't really call the reference in the newspaper reports on the Brooke trial[58] the first time. . . . I first heard about it from Dobrovolsky. I don't remember how the conversation arose. I heard that it was a White émigré organization that published certain works.

PROCURATOR. Have you seen the magazine *Grani?*

LASHKOVA. No, I have only seen the magazine *Our Times* and the Solidarism pamphlet.

PROCURATOR. Who gave you these?

LASHKOVA. Dobrovolsky, to read.

PROCURATOR. Did you realize that this was anti-Soviet literature?

LASHKOVA. The magazine *Our Times* contains a lot of complicated material, which I didn't start reading. I read the article about what happened in Novocherkassk.[59]

PROCURATOR. And the Solidarism pamphlet?

LASHKOVA. The first section of this pamphlet dealt with some rather complicated philosophical system—I hardly understood a thing. The second section, containing the NTS programme, is anti-Soviet.

PROCURATOR. Why did you take anti-Soviet literature?

LASHKOVA. At the time I did not know it was. I realized that only after I had read through it.

PROCURATOR. Did Dobrovolsky tell you not to give these books to anyone?

LASHKOVA. Yes.

PROCURATOR. Where were these books published?

LASHKOVA. I don't remember.

PROCURATOR. Did Dobrovolsky also give you sheets of paper with a typed text?

LASHKOVA. I don't think so.

PROCURATOR. Your testimony states that you received *Sphinxes*[60] too.

LASHKOVA. That has nothing to do with *Grani*.

PROCURATOR. How many times did you receive literature?

LASHKOVA. Once. I received the Solidarism pamphlet and *Our Times*.

PROCURATOR. To whom else did Dobrovolsky give literature?

LASHKOVA. He certainly gave literature to Kats and apparently to Kushev.

PROCURATOR. Did he give them these particular books?

LASHKOVA. I don't know, he and I never talked about it specifically.

PROCURATOR. How do you explain why he did this?

LASHKOVA. I don't know.

PROCURATOR. So, you came to the conclusion that 'Solidarism' was anti-Soviet literature. Is that so?

LASHKOVA. It is.

PROCURATOR. To whom did you pass on the literature received from Dobrovolsky?

LASHKOVA. *Our Times* I showed to Krasnov and the Solidarism pamphlet to Kushev.

PROCURATOR. Why did you do this?

LASHKOVA. As regards Levitin (Krasnov), some of the material —not criminal—interested me.

PROCURATOR. And the pamphlet? Why did you give it to Kushev?

LASHKOVA. I was curious to find out how he'd feel about this question.

PROCURATOR. What other anti-Soviet publications did you pass on, and to whom?

LASHKOVA. None.

PROCURATOR. You gave nothing to Gubanov?

LASHKOVA. No.

PROCURATOR. Did the episode at the Lenin Library metro actually take place?

LASHKOVA. Yes.

PROCURATOR. Tell us what happened. When was it?

LASHKOVA. I think it was in October 1966.

PROCURATOR. Why were you there?

LASHKOVA. It took place late in the evening. Galanskov and I had to go to a certain place and first went to the metro. Then Dobrovolsky came and Galanskov gave him five books—I don't know exactly which ones.

PROCURATOR. What kind of books were they?

LASHKOVA. I didn't see. In the metro I asked Galanskov what kind of books they were and he told me he'd explain later.

PROCURATOR. From Galanskov's extreme caution in handing over the books to Dobrovolsky, did you conclude that they were books published by the NTS?

LASHKOVA. Yes.

PROCURATOR. So what books were they exactly, didn't you see?

LASHKOVA. I did not see.

PROCURATOR. Did you give Levitin *Our Times*?

LASHKOVA. Only for a few minutes. He just glanced through it.

PROCURATOR. And did Kats give you anything?

LASHKOVA. She showed me the Solidarism pamphlet, but in a typewritten copy. I did not start reading it.

PROCURATOR. Did Galanskov ask you to type some coded letter? When was this, what were the circumstances?

LASHKOVA. It was in autumn 1966. I typed one copy of a letter on tissue-paper in his flat. I think there was no name and no address. It wasn't all in code, only a few sentences.

PROCURATOR. What were these sentences in code like roughly?

LASHKOVA. There were some figures. I think 101, 102, 103. . . . Apparently it was about some mutual relations.

PROCURATOR. Didn't you ask Galanskov what it all meant?

LASHKOVA. No.

PROCURATOR. Did he himself ask you to type this letter?

LASHKOVA. Yes. I typed it in his presence.

PROCURATOR. And where is the original of this letter?

LASHKOVA. I don't know. Probably destroyed.

PROCURATOR. So there was no address?

LASHKOVA. No.

PROCURATOR. Did Galanskov explain to you why this letter was needed?

LASHKOVA. No.

PROCURATOR. Why didn't you ask him about it?

LASHKOVA. I wasn't interested.

PROCURATOR. And did Dobrovolsky ask you to write a letter for him?

LASHKOVA. Yes, once. It was at the beginning of autumn. I was at home, Dobrovolsky came to see me and asked me if I could write a few lines for him. I said I could. I'm now bound to say that I may make a mistake as regards describing the technique of writing this letter. I may not have been completely correct in what I said at the investigation, because I can't remember what was placed under what. The letter was written in such a way that I could not see the written text afterwards. There was some thick sort of carbon-paper. The text written by me was about records, about a Jan.

PROCURATOR. And did you also write the visible text?

LASHKOVA. Yes.

PROCURATOR. What was it?

LASHKOVA. I don't remember. All I can say is that both the first and second texts were on commonplace subjects.

PROCURATOR. What was written in the first text?

LASHKOVA. 'Dear Jan, greetings. Your parcel has been received. The records have arrived.'

PROCURATOR. This was already on top of the text that had been written earlier?

LASHKOVA. I can't remember.

PROCURATOR. Anyway, it was cryptography?

LASHKOVA. Yes. But I don't recall the technique.

PROCURATOR. What did Dobrovolsky do with the letter?

LASHKOVA. He put the thick sheet in his pocket and the text into an envelope. I wrote the address, I think it was Oslo, on the envelope.

PROCURATOR. What was the return address?

LASHKOVA. I don't remember.

PROCURATOR. You said in the investigation that the return address was fictitious.

LASHKOVA. Yes, that is what Dobrovolsky told me.

PROCURATOR. What was Dobrovolsky's purpose in sending this letter?

LASHKOVA. I don't know.

PROCURATOR. Weren't you interested in finding out?

LASHKOVA. No.

PROCURATOR. How is that—you write a letter abroad and don't even wonder what it's for?

LASHKOVA. At the time I wasn't interested.

PROCURATOR. So you don't know whether they sent these letters to the person they were addressed to?

LASHKOVA. No.

PROCURATOR. When did you write the letter for Galanskov?

LASHKOVA. I can't remember exactly, it was in the autumn.

PROCURATOR. And for Dobrovolsky?

LASHKOVA. In October 1966.

PROCURATOR. Where did all this take place?

LASHKOVA. In Galanskov's flat and in mine.

PROCURATOR. Was there anyone else present?

LASHKOVA. No.

PROCURATOR. Tell the court about your conversation with Dobrovolsky about the procedure for admission to the NTS.

LASHKOVA. I became curious about this after I had read the NTS books. I asked him what the NTS was, what it did, who were its members. He told me. Then I asked how one enrolled as a member of the NTS. He told me. That's all.

PROCURATOR. Why did you ask Dobrovolsky this? Initially you turned to Galanskov, didn't you?

LASHKOVA. Yes.

PROCURATOR. Why did you have this conversation with Dobrovolsky?

LASHKOVA. It was in my flat. Galanskov and I went into the kitchen and there I said that I would like to learn more about the activity of the NTS. But then Dobrovolsky came up to me and told me all about it.

PROCURATOR. Why did you go into the kitchen with Galanskov to talk?

LASHKOVA. The NTS isn't the Soviet communist party. (Laughter in court.)

PROCURATOR. Did you ever come across the expression 'fighting units'? Tell us about it.

LASHKOVA. I first heard about it from Batshev. I can't remember how the conversation occurred.

PROCURATOR. Did you never encounter the expression in the letter you wrote?

LASHKOVA. Yes, I've already spoken about that. There was some sort of reference to 'fighting units' in a letter of Galanskov's, but I cannot remember exactly.

PROCURATOR. Tell us why you gave Galanskov one copy of the article 'Events in the Pochayev Monastery'? You received it from Dobrovolsky. Did he say you could give it to Galanskov?

LASHKOVA. I didn't ask. I typed out six copies of this article and kept one for myself. I was disturbed by the facts described in it.

PROCURATOR. Why did you hand it on to Galanskov?

LASHKOVA. I'll come to that in a moment. I described this letter from the monks to my friends. One day I came to Galanskov's place, not especially for that reason, and after I had told him about it, he asked me to bring him a copy. Later, after I had already given Galanskov the article, Dobrovolsky asked where my copy was. I said I had given it to Galanskov. Then Dobrovolsky started swearing and demanded it back. I did not know that Galanskov might circulate this document. I just gave it to him to read.

PROCURATOR. You knew that Galanskov was assembling material for a collection?

LASHKOVA. No, I didn't know that.

PROCURATOR. But is this document slanderous?

LASHKOVA. I don't know.

PROCURATOR. So, you believed it and decided to circulate this document?

LASHKOVA. No, I didn't decide to do that.

PROCURATOR. Did you see any foreign currency at the homes of any of the defendants, dollars for instance?

LASHKOVA. Yes, I saw a non-Russian note at Galanskov's.

PROCURATOR. Did you ask him what these notes were?

LASHKOVA. Not notes, a note. One.

PROCURATOR. A note?

LASHKOVA. Yes. And he said it was in dollars; I asked if it was a lot, he said it was.

PROCURATOR. Did he say where he got it?

LASHKOVA. No.

PROCURATOR. He didn't tell you, but you are stating that Galanskov had dollars and that he showed you a single note. Is that right?

LASHKOVA. Yes. One I saw. . . .

PROCURATOR. What do you know about a duplicating machine?

LASHKOVA. Which?

PROCURATOR. If there was more than one, then all of them?

LASHKOVA. I don't know anything.

PROCURATOR. Did you have any conversations about a duplicating machine?

LASHKOVA. There was one, but I didn't take part, though I was present. And it wasn't about a duplicating machine, it was about some sort of hectograph. Dobrovolsky arrived at my place with two strangers. He didn't talk to them in my room but in the little closet attached to my room.

PROCURATOR. So, Dobrovolsky invited two men to your flat and discussed a machine with them?

LASHKOVA. I didn't hear their conversation, it was later that I found out what they had been talking about. I can't remember how I found out, whether Dobrovolsky told me. . . .

PROCURATOR. Did Dobrovolsky talk to you about a duplicating machine?

LASHKOVA. He asked whether I had ever worked such a machine.

PROCURATOR. Did Dobrovolsky mention these men by name?

LASHKOVA. No.

PROCURATOR. You haven't heard the surname Tarasov?

LASHKOVA. I seem to have.

PROCURATOR. Did Ginzburg and Galanskov hurry you when you were typing *The White Book* and *Phoenix*?

LASHKOVA. You mean Ginzburg as regards *The White Book* and Galanskov with *Phoenix*? Ginzburg did not hurry me, he kept on giving me material, but there was no hurry.

PROCURATOR. That is not what you said during the investigation: 'I typed *The White Book* under considerable pressure, working eight to ten hours a day; Ginzburg hurried me, I did not know why. There was no special rush with *Phoenix*.'

LASHKOVA. Let me explain. *The White Book* is a bulky work while *Phoenix* is smaller and I did not type it all. Also, I typed it when I was already working at Moscow University, and it wasn't hard for me to type it then.

PROCURATOR. Do you realize why he hurried you? Have you heard of Genrikh?

LASHKOVA. I can say that I was not pushed to any definite completion day.

PROCURATOR. Did you type 'A Letter to an Old Friend' and the 'Resistance' leaflet?

LASHKOVA. I typed 'A Letter to an Old Friend', but not the leaflet.

PROCURATOR. Who wrote these two works?

LASHKOVA. I don't know.

PROCURATOR. From whom did you receive the materials for *The White Book*?

LASHKOVA. I received the whole lot from Ginzburg alone. Galanskov had no connection with *The White Book*.

PROCURATOR. Did any conversation about a flat take place in your presence?

LASHKOVA. Yes, there was a conversation between Ustinova and Dobrovolsky. It was Dobrovolsky who started this conversation. He said he had an aged relative who had to be looked after. He could apply for wardship of this relative. He said it was necessary to have a flat to which it would be possible to come freely. Nothing came of this conversation.

PROCURATOR. Did you take part in any conversation about addresses for parcels?

LASHKOVA. Yes, but whether it was with Dobrovolsky or Galanskov I can't remember exactly. It was to do with people to whose addresses books could be sent. I suggested my own.

PROCURATOR. Why didn't they take advantage of it? Were they frightened of uncovering the conspiracy?

LASHKOVA. I was not part of a conspiracy. I don't know why.

PROCURATOR. Which anti-Soviet document did you type?

LASHKOVA. The letter to Sholokhov, which I typed, I took as a personal protest on the part of its author; whether it is anti-Soviet or not, I can't tell.

PROCURATOR. Didn't this sentence occur in it: 'Here in the USSR there were camps which surpassed Hitler's in their scale'?

LASHKOVA. I don't remember. It should be looked at as a whole.

PROCURATOR (quoting). 'A sea of human blood was spilt on Soviet soil.' If this had been about the occupants, all right. We regard this letter as anti-Soviet. What other anti-Soviet articles did you type?

LASHKOVA. I don't know.

PROCURATOR. This is not what you said during the investigation. Here is your testimony of 12 September 1967: 'When I read "An Open Letter to Sholokhov", I asked Galanskov if he was not frightened'. Galanskov told you he was not frightened, didn't he?

LASHKOVA. Yes.

PROCURATOR. And after this conversation you typed seven copies of the letter?

LASHKOVA. Yes. All this letter contains is strongly worded attacks on Sholokhov.

PROCURATOR. Is the 'Resistance' leaflet anti-Soviet?

LASHKOVA. I did not type it.

PROCURATOR. But according to your testimony during the investigation, this leaflet was of an anti-Soviet nature. Do you confirm this opinion?

LASHKOVA. I cannot remember the contents of this leaflet.

PROCURATOR (quotes). 'Political cavemen. . . . We challenge you to resist.' How do you regard that?

LASHKOVA. I don't know. (Laughter in court.)

PROCURATOR. In your testimony at the investigation you gave a definite opinion.

LASHKOVA is silent, then makes some response, but very quietly.

PROCURATOR. Does the pamphlet 'Solidarism Is the Idea of the Future' contain ideas of an anti-Soviet nature?

LASHKOVA. Yes.

PROCURATOR. Do you admit that you are guilty of anti-Soviet activity?

LASHKOVA. Yes.

PROCURATOR. How do you regard your activity?

LASHKOVA. Disapprovingly.

PROCURATOR. How will you live in the future?

LASHKOVA. Differently.

PROCURATOR. Do you intend to renounce this activity?

LASHKOVA. Yes, I do intend.

PROCURATOR. And you will live as an honourable citizen of the Soviet Union?

LASHKOVA (is silent for a short while). I have already said I intend to renounce this activity.

JUDGE asks whether the defence has any questions.

ARIYA. Why did Ginzburg collect materials on the Sinyavsky and Daniel trial?

LASHKOVA. He and I did not discuss this.

ARIYA. To whom were these materials addressed?

LASHKOVA. To the Chairman of the Council of Ministers, Kosygin, and to the Presidium of the Supreme Soviet. Ginzburg intended sending these materials somewhere.

ARIYA. Was there any talk of conveying these materials abroad?

LASHKOVA. No.

ARIYA. When you had finished the work did he tell you that he wanted to send these materials abroad and not to those addresses?

LASHKOVA. No.

ARIYA. You did not type all the material that subsequently went into *The White Book*?

LASHKOVA. During the investigation I saw only the documents published in *Grani*. I did not see the complete *White Book*. I do not know it in full.

ARIYA. Did you type certain of the articles?

LASHKOVA. Yes, I typed the protests of the intelligentsia, some newspaper articles, the verbatim report of the trial. I do not know what proportion of the whole book I typed. Ginzburg brought me the material in parts.

ARIYA. Was there any reference in your conversations with Ginzburg to the title *White Book*, or did you speak of materials on the Sinyavsky and Daniel trial?

LASHKOVA. I do not remember; I don't think *White Book* was mentioned as a title.

ARIYA. Were you concerned how Ginzburg was going to pay you for your work?

LASHKOVA. Yes, we agreed that Ginzburg would provide for me: give me money and bring provisions.

ARIYA. For Galanskov you typed 'An Open Letter to Sholokhov' and 'The Russian Road to Socialism'. The following statement of yours has been filed: 'To Galanskov from his forced-labour typist Lashkova. I request leave for an indefinite period.' This statement is evidently facetious?

LASHKOVA. Yes.

ARIYA. Dobrovolsky has testified that you did not want to type for Galanskov, but you had his typewriter and typed your work for Moscow University on it.

LASHKOVA. Yes, I did my university work on his typewriter. He wanted to collect it, and finally he did.

ARIYA. When you took on typing work, did you read it first or did you start typing immediately?

LASHKOVA. I typed automatically without reading. Especially 'The Russian Road', which I typed from a photocopy.

ARIYA. Do you use a ruler when typing?

LASHKOVA. Yes, always. I never read 'The Russian Road' at all, and I didn't read 'A Letter ' before typing it.

ARIYA. As regards the events described in the work 'Events in the Pochayev Monastery Today', are you now convinced they are a lie?

LASHKOVA. I do not know.

ARIYA. Now as regards the NTS literature. Why did you get this literature from Dobrovolsky?

LASHKOVA. To read.

ARIYA. You are charged with receiving it for the purpose of circulating it; do you acknowledge this?

LASHKOVA. No.

ARIYA. Do you consider that the wordings 'to read' and 'to circulate' are comparable?

LASHKOVA. No, I do not.

ARIYA. Is 'Solidarism' anti-Soviet literature?

LASHKOVA. Yes.

ARIYA. To whom did you give this pamphlet?

LASHKOVA. To Kushev.

ARIYA. Were you trying to arouse anti-Soviet feelings in Kushev?

LASHKOVA. No.

ARIYA. Then what was your reason in giving him it?

LASHKOVA. I gave it to him to have a look through at home.

ARIYA. And he told you nothing about having seen it before? The circulation of this pamphlet is charged against both you and Dobrovolsky.

LASHKOVA. No, I do not remember.

ARIYA. How do you explain giving Kushev this pamphlet?

LASHKOVA. I was curious to find out what he thought of it.

ARIYA. Did you understand the philosophical part of this pamphlet?

LASHKOVA. Poorly.

ARIYA. When you read it yourself, did it awaken some echo in you?

LASHKOVA. No.

ARIYA. This material was in your possession for about a month?

LASHKOVA. I think it was less. I cannot remember exactly, but I don't think it was longer than ten days.

ARIYA. During those ten days did you have the opportunity of giving the pamphlet to a large number of people to read?

LASHKOVA. No.

ARIYA. What sort of family do you come from?

LASHKOVA. A worker's.

ARIYA. When you were helping, did you realize that the documents you were typing were strongly worded? Did you realize that your assistance constituted a crime against the state?

LASHKOVA. No.

ARIYA. How long have you been in prison?

LASHKOVA. A year.

ARIYA. Do you regret that you engaged in activity of this kind?

LASHKOVA (thinks for a long time). No, I do not regret it.

ARIYA. Perhaps you have not understood my question?

LASHKOVA. No, I have understood it.

ARIYA. But you said that you would not engage in it in the future any more?

LASHKOVA. Yes.

ARIYA. In the evidence you wrote that you did regret it?

LASHKOVA. Not quite that. . . .

ARIYA. Do you confirm this statement of yours?

LASHKOVA. Yes.

JUDGE. What are your parents?

LASHKOVA. My father is pensioned, my mother is a cook.

JUDGE. Where do they live?

LASHKOVA. In Smolensk.

JUDGE. How is it that you live apart from them?

LASHKOVA. I'd prefer not to answer that question.

JUDGE. Did you join an institute?

LASHKOVA. Yes, I tried to join an institute many times, but I did not pass the exam. Later I joined the Institute of Culture's faculty of stage management. At the time of my arrest I was in my second year.

ARIYA. When were you detained?

LASHKOVA. 17 January 1967.

ARIYA. Here is your testimony of 18 January, which forms the basis of the indictment against you. Did you give it before you were under arrest?*

LASHKOVA. Yes.

The Judge announces a recess till 9 January, 10.00 hours.

The court sitting of 8 January ends at about 20.30 hours.

9 January

The court sitting begins at 10 a.m. with

FURTHER INTERROGATION OF VERA LASHKOVA†

THE PEOPLE'S ASSESSOR CHIZHOVA (henceforth referred to as CHIZHOVA). Lashkova, yesterday I still did not understand whether

---

* Arrest is a separate operation from detention. Ed.

† Here and later, procedural details relating to the beginning of sittings, the entry of the court-members, etc., are omitted.

you regret your actions or not. First you said one thing, then another.

LASHKOVA. I don't regret having helped the other accused, but I am sorry that my actions have perhaps done harm to my people.

KAMINSKAYA. Did Dobrovolsky speak to you about his intention of producing a periodical on the lines of *Phoenix?*

LASHKOVA. No, he didn't.

KAMINSKAYA. But in the preliminary investigation you gave the following evidence in this connection: 'In a conversation with me, Dobrovolsky mentioned that he was planning to produce a periodical in the winter and that I would probably have to type it.'

LASHKOVA. That conversation was very general. I can't tell you anything about it in detail. I don't remember.

KAMINSKAYA. Was Dobrovolsky planning to produce this periodical alone?

LASHKOVA. I don't remember.

KAMINSKAYA. At the preliminary investigation you stated that he was planning to produce it alone.

SHVEISKY. Did Dobrovolsky talk to you about the aims he had in mind in planning to publish this periodical?

LASHKOVA. No, he didn't.

PROCURATOR. Tell us the details of your conversation with your acquaintance Iva Ivanova about her flat. Did you, during your discussion, ask her if you were free to use the flat for any purpose whatsoever?

LASHKOVA. Yes, I had such a conversation with her.

PROCURATOR. Did you type anything while wearing rubber gloves?

LASHKOVA. Yes. The 'Civic Appeal'.

PROCURATOR. Why did you put on rubber gloves while doing this?

LASHKOVA. To get a feeling of adventure. (Laughter in the courtroom.)

PROCURATOR. Tell us in detail how you typed wearing rubber gloves.

LASHKOVA. It's difficult anyway to type in rubber gloves. I only wore them while placing sheets of paper in the typewriter. After that I took them off.

PROCURATOR. But tell us, please, Lashkova—where did you get these rubber gloves?

LASHKOVA (after a pause). Galanskov gave them to me.

PROCURATOR. Are these the gloves that figure in this trial? The ones that were confiscated from Dobrovolsky?

LASHKOVA. No, they are not the same gloves. I typed wearing thin gloves. The gloves confiscated from Dobrovolsky were a thick pair.

JUDGE. Do the accused have any questions?

GALANSKOV. Vera, tell me, please, what kind of relations existed between us? Didn't we have a conversation in which I asked you how you felt about me? Did you then say that you felt very fond of me and even loved me?

LASHKOVA. Yes.

GALANSKOV. Can I assume that you typed for me from motives of pure friendship?

LASHKOVA. Yes.

GALANSKOV. Tell me, please, did I often bring you all kinds of food and cook meals for you?

LASHKOVA. Yes, often.

GALANSKOV. When it was necessary to wallpaper your room afresh, did I do it for you?

LASHKOVA. Yes.

GALANSKOV. Tell me, please, Vera, how many copies in all of my letter to Sholokhov did you type?

LASHKOVA. I don't remember.

GALANSKOV. In the summer of 1966, you typed four copies of the letter for me, working in my house. Is that so?

LASHKOVA. Yes.

GALANSKOV. But later you typed another five copies of the letter for me?

LASHKOVA. Yes.

GALANSKOV. How much in all did you type for me and how much time did you need for this work?

LASHKOVA. I don't remember.

GALANSKOV. Tell me, please, Vera, did I warn you to take precautionary measures when I gave you the letter to Sholokhov for typing?

LASHKOVA. No.

GALANSKOV. Tell me, please, did I warn you to take any kind of precaution when you were typing 'The Russian Road to Socialism'?

LASHKOVA. No.

GALANSKOV. Did a conversation take place between us, in which I told you that if you were ever summoned by the KGB, then, if the question should arise, you were not in any way to try and deny that I gave you material and that you typed it?

LASHKOVA. Yes, you told me that.

GALANSKOV. Vera, don't you remember the incident with the gloves in detail? I can remind you: I placed the paper in the typewriter wearing the gloves. You never wore the gloves, you only typed the text.

LASHKOVA says nothing.

GALANSKOV. Vera, why did you call my wife a bourgeois woman?

LASHKOVA says nothing.

GALANSKOV. Perhaps because her parents earn a lot of money?

LASHKOVA. I don't know exactly how much they earn. I know it's quite a lot.

GALANSKOV. Tell me, please, were you present at the metro station of the Lenin Library at the time of the incident discussed in court?

LASHKOVA. Yes, I was present.

GALANSKOV. Tell me, did I give any books to Dobrovolsky?

LASHKOVA. Yes, you did.

GALANSKOV. What evidence do you have for saying this?

JUDGE. Galanskov, you have already dealt with explanations of personal relationships! Ask more specific questions.

GALANSKOV. I have no more questions.

GINZBURG. Tell me, please, Vera, did you place the paper in the typewriter yourself or did somebody help you?

LASHKOVA. I did it myself.

> After this the court passes on to the interrogation of Yury Galanskov.

INTERROGATION OF YURI GALANSKOV

JUDGE. Galanskov, stand up and come here. What have you to say to the charges?

GALANSKOV. I wish to say that I don't understand the meaning of the accusations made against me. I have never, in my life, had anti-Soviet sympathies and I am not anti-Soviet now. I have always been a proletarian democrat and a supporter of the dictatorship of the proletariat.

JUDGE advises Galanskov to stick to the point.

GALANSKOV declares that, first of all, he will confine himself to the charges made under article 70 of the Russian Criminal Code, and will leave his evidence concerning article 88 of the Russian Criminal Code to the end of the interrogation. Then he renounces all the evidence given by him during the [preliminary] investigation and states that he can explain his motives for giving false evidence.

JUDGE. But you admit that you took part in the production of *Phoenix* and *The White Book?*

GALANSKOV. I admit it, and I have never denied the fact that I did indeed produce and edit the miscellany *Phoenix*. I want to relate how I came to compile it. At first, the miscellany was intended to be a collection of articles on pacifism. Later, under the influence of the trial of Sinyavsky and Daniel, the miscellany gradually changed, grew and was finally transformed into the miscellany that you see before you. I am charged in connection with five allegedly anti-Soviet articles which I put in the miscellany. These include 'The Confession of Victor Velsky', 'The Russian Road to Socialism', Sinyavsky's article 'What Is Socialist Realism?', the article on 'The Events at the Pochayev Monastery Today', and my 'Open Letter to Sholokhov'. I should like to begin by saying that I have never considered these works to be anti-Soviet and do not now consider them so. I can explain my reasons to the court.

GALANSKOV now attempts to prove that the articles allegedly incriminating him are not anti-Soviet. He tries to analyse each one of them separately.

JUDGE repeatedly interrupts him, saying that this is not a literary argument and that the court is not interested in literary criticism.

PROCURATOR. When did you become acquainted with the other accused?

GALANSKOV. I got to know Ginzburg in 1960. Gorbanevskaya introduced me to him. Ginzburg was arrested some time after we met. After his arrest I continued to visit his mother and I was on good terms with her. When Ginzburg returned from the labour camp we became closer friends. We never shared each other's political views. I was always a democrat and considered Ginzburg a liberal. We hardly talked about politics. We never took part in the same enterprises. Therefore, there can be no question whatever of my having worked on *The White Book* or of Ginzburg having taken part in the production of *Phoenix*.

PROCURATOR. Then how do you explain the confiscation of a copy of *Phoenix* from Ginzburg?

GALANSKOV. Simply that I forgot a copy at his house when I visited him just before the search.

PROCURATOR. Why did you obtain a photocopy from Ginzburg of the article 'The Russian Road to Socialism'?

GALANSKOV. I obtained that copy from Faingol, and not from Ginzburg.

PROCURATOR. How did you meet Lashkova?

GALANSKOV. I met Lashkova through Kaplan, as I needed a typist. Kaplan offered me two typists and I chose Lashkova.

PROCURATOR. How did you meet Dobrovolsky?

GALANSKOV. Bulovsky introduced me to him. That was in the summer of 1966.

PROCURATOR. And you lost no time in dragging him into your connections with the NTS?

GALANSKOV states that he has never had any personal connections with representatives of the NTS and has never obtained literature, money or anything else from them. The evidence of Dobrovolsky that he, Galanskov, had received money from Genrikh is an utter and complete fabrication. He also states that he has never sent *Phoenix* or *The White Book* to the NTS or abroad in general. Galanskov does not deny that he met two foreigners in the course of 1966.

PROCURATOR. Tell us about this in more detail.

GALANSKOV. My meeting with the foreigner called Genrikh took place in reality like this. One day Dobrovolsky and I agreed to meet outside the Udarnik cinema. In case I was delayed and could not get there in time, Dobrovolsky gave me two telephone numbers through which I could get in touch with him. I was to phone either him or Lashkova. When I got to the Udarnik Dobrovolsky was no longer there. Then I phoned Vera and when I found out that Lyosha [i.e. *Dobrovolsky*] was at her place, I went there. When I arrived, Dobrovolsky told me that we would have to go to the Kropotkin-skaya metro station in order to meet someone. A little later he and I left Lashkova's and went to the Kropotkinskaya metro station. After a while a man appeared, whom Dobrovolsky took aside to a news-paper kiosk and they talked about something. What exactly they were talking about, I don't know. After some time Dobrovolsky and the foreigner, referred to in court as Genrikh, left the metro station together and, walking along the street, continued their conversation. I was walking some distance behind them and so did not hear what they were talking about. Then I left them alone for a while, saying that I had to go into one of the houses for a while and would soon catch them up. Then I went to Lashkova's to see whether my friend Ustinova was there. After that I caught up with the two of them again and we all went together in the direction of Sveta Potasheva's house, where we had agreed to spend the evening. When we got to her house Dobrovolsky asked me to accompany Genrikh to the metro station while he himself went into Potasheva's house. I accompanied Genrikh as far as the metro. We hardly talked at all on the way. He asked if I had read some religious article. I replied that I had. I didn't talk to him about anything else; we didn't talk about politics, much less about NTS. When I had taken Genrikh to the metro station, I returned to Potasheva's house. I rang the bell; the door was opened to me not by Dobrovolsky, but by some girl. I went inside. There were a great many people there. I immediately went to the radio, sat down by it and tried to tune in to some music. Then Ivanova came up to me and asked me to dance. I went off to dance with her and didn't talk to anyone except my partner.

GALANSKOV also states that, at Dobrovolsky's request, he gave the foreigner called Genrikh a copy of the Leningrad periodical *The Bell*. This took place at the Udarnik cinema during Galanskov's second meeting with Genrikh. The name 'Genrikh' was invented by Galanskov himself. As evidence of this he cites a phrase from his personal confrontation with Dobrovolsky, in which Dobrovolsky asked him, 'Why do you call this foreigner Genrikh?' After this personal confrontation the foreigner was referred to even in Dobrovolsky's testimony as Genrikh.

PROCURATOR. And Nadya? Did you talk to her about NTS?

GALANSKOV. As to the foreigner called Nadya—I can say that I never knew she belonged to the NTS. I never talked to her on any occasion about political subjects or about NTS. I was at home when someone unexpectedly knocked at the door. When I opened the door, there was a girl standing on the threshold. She said she would like to talk to me about something and asked me to come out into the street. When I had gone outside, she told me that she was a visitor from abroad, that she had been given Dobrokhotov's address and had been to his house, but he had not been at home. So she had decided to turn to me and asked me to help her find someone. She could not tell me the exact address. She only remembered that it was somewhere in Shchelkovskaya, and that his surname was Chernitsyn. I asked her if perhaps Chernitsyn could be the name of the district Chernitsyno, and not a surname. I knew there was such a district near Shchelkovskaya.* She said no, it was a surname. As I knew that Dobrokhotov was a friend of Dobrovolsky's, I decided that the girl's visit had something to do with Dobrovolsky. I accompanied the girl, who was called Nadya, to the trolley-bus and rode with her as far as the Lenin Library metro station, and there we agreed to meet the next day at the Lermontovskaya metro station. I had decided to ask Dobrovolsky to come with me to meet Nadya. The next day I arrived at the agreed time at the metro. Dobrovolsky also came. After Nadya's arrival we all stood there together for about ten

* The district behind the Izmailovsky Park, near the metro station Shchelkovskaya.

minutes. Then Dobrovolsky went off somewhere with Nadya. From the fact that Dobrovolsky was not surprised at meeting Nadya and did not question her or myself, and from the fact that Nadya did not introduce herself to him in any way, I deduced that Dobrovolsky had known of Nadya's proposed visit to Moscow. And there was something else. When I was showing Dobrovolsky Chernitsyn's address, Nadya came up and he said: 'I know, it's for me'. I did not see Nadya again. I have absolutely no idea whether Nadya is a member of the NTS or whether the foreigner by the name of Genrikh is a member of the NTS.

PROCURATOR questions Galanskov about the parcels and the nature of his connections with the NTS.

GALANSKOV emphasizes several times during the interrogation that until his arrest he knew nothing of the NTS and had received no parcels from abroad.

PROCURATOR interrupts Galanskov several times, citing evidence given by the latter during the preliminary investigation.

GALANSKOV answers each time by saying that he has renounced his former evidence and will not answer any questions relating to it.

PROCURATOR. Tell us of your meeting with the foreigner called Philip.

GALANSKOV. In the summer of 1966 Epifanov phoned me at work and said that he would be arriving in a short while outside the Literary Museum, where I was working at the time. Epifanov did not come alone; he brought along with him a foreigner called Philip. Epifanov told me that Philip was a student from Paris, and that he was interested in meeting young poets, including members of SMOG. As Epifanov knew hardly anybody in SMOG and had heard quite a few times from me that I knew some of them well, he brought the foreigner to me. Having introduced us, Epifanov left.

PROCURATOR questions Galanskov about the letter in code typed at his request by Lashkova.

GALANSKOV answers that this letter was addressed to his acquaintance Batshev and had no connection with the NTS. He also says that during his studies at the Historical Archives Institute he had always been interested in classification—a subject devoted to the study of the coding systems used in classifying library books. That was why he had written a letter to Batshev in such a manner. The numbers used in the letter refer to the names of the individual members of SMOG.

PROCURATOR. Why did you do this?

GALANSKOV. I have always been interested in conspiracy.

PROCURATOR. In what connection?

GALANSKOV. I hope in the future to become chairman of the Committee of State Security and it will doubtless be useful to me then. (Laughter in the courtroom.)

PROCURATOR asks if it is true that some of his testimony at the preliminary hearing was true and some untrue. Why did the true parts not contradict the lies absolutely?

GALANSKOV replies that he is a good psychologist and that it cost him nothing to make use of a few established facts and then fabricate round them for the rest of his testimony. He did this to help the preliminary investigation tie up the loose ends, so that in this way the investigation would come to an end sooner.

JUDGE asks if the defence has any questions.

KAMINSKAYA. Do you consider the work 'The Confession of Victor Velsky' to be anti-Soviet?

GALANSKOV. I do not.

KAMINSKAYA. Do you consider the article 'The Russian Road to Socialism' to be anti-Soviet?

GALANSKOV. I do not.

KAMINSKAYA. Do you consider the article 'An Account of Events at the Pochayev Monastery Today' to be anti-Soviet?

GALANSKOV. I do not.

KAMINSKAYA. Why exactly do you not consider these works to be anti-Soviet?

GALANSKOV tries to explain.

JUDGE interrupts him, saying that this is a trial and not a literary argument.

KAMINSKAYA. When exactly and in what circumstances did you write the 'Open Letter to Sholokhov'?

GALANSKOV. The idea of writing the letter occurred to me in March 1966, when I was in a psychiatric hospital. In April of that year, when I left hospital, I wrote the letter.

KAMINSKAYA. What was your general state at this time?

GALANSKOV. I was very depressed at the time.

KAMINSKAYA. Have any of the articles that you are charged with in *Phoenix*, been published in *Grani* or in any other NTS publication?

GALANSKOV. No.

SHVEISKY. How do you explain why you changed your testimony so many times during the preliminary investigation?

GALANSKOV. At first I gave false evidence with the idea of taking the charges against Dobrovolsky on myself. I did this because this was not Dobrovolsky's first trial and because he had a family—a wife and a child. And I gave way to Dobrovolsky's pleas, as I realized I would have to answer for *Phoenix* anyway. Later, when the interrogator began to reveal to me Dobrovolsky's evidence about me—evidence of an absolutely crazy, unreal nature—I understood that I could not take such a line in relation to him any longer. And I renounced my testimony. After this the interrogator, in one of our conversations, told me that if I started to change my testimony, it might do harm not only to me personally but to all the other accused. And that if I persisted in this, all of us would be sent to the Siberian mines. I could not imagine Lashkova, who weighs forty kilogrammes, in the Siberian mines. So I decided to stick to my former testimony.

JUDGE. Do the accused have any questions?

DOBROVOLSKY. Have you ever heard from me that I share the views of NTS, that I agree with its programme?

GALANSKOV. No.

DOBROVOLSKY. Have I ever portrayed the NTS in a favourable light?

GALANSKOV. No.

KAMINSKAYA says that she would like to make a statement.

JUDGE. Please do.

KAMINSKAYA states that the work 'The Confession of Victor Velsky' is not an article, but a story consisting of two parts. The first part is a description of an individual's destiny—it tells of a young man's life, exposed to the heavy ordeals of existence. The second part is philosophical and consists of a debunking of the hero. The first part of the story had been found to be anti-Soviet, while the second part, much longer, had hardly figured at all in this trial, nor did it figure in the indictment, in spite of the fact that precisely this part of the story contained the explanation, causes and origin of the hero's anti-Soviet views, which had served as a reason for declaring the first part of the story anti-Soviet.

The Judge declares a recess of half an hour. After that the interrogation continues.

JUDGE invites Galanskov to tell the court of his illegal currency deals.

GALANSKOV says it is true that he took first 260 dollars and then 300 dollars from Dobrovolsky. Dobrovolsky gave him this money so that he could buy a typewriter for Dobrovolsky in a foreign currency shop. As there were no typewriters at that time in the foreign currency shop, Galanskov had kept the money at his place for a time. Then Entin came to see him from Leningrad. Seeing the dollars in Galanskov's home, he offered to exchange them for him through some friend, who lived in the hotel Ukraina and could manage to exchange the money officially. Galanskov consulted Dobrovolsky, to whom the money belonged, and having obtained his consent, gave Entin 200 dollars to be exchanged. Entin changed the dollars into 600 roubles. Then Galanskov decided to keep as many dollars as would be necessary for a typewriter. (He thought the typewriter would cost about 160 dollars.) The rest he gave to Entin so that he could exchange this as well. However this time Entin was deceived and given a packet of mustard plasters instead of money. After this Galanskov gave all the remaining money, both dollars and roubles, back to Dobrovolsky.

DOBROVOLSKY asks Galanskov why he maintains that he, Dobrovolsky, gave him the dollars when in reality it was he himself who had given Dobrovolsky the dollars and roubles.

GALANSKOV replies that this is not true.

KAMINSKAYA questions Dobrovolsky extensively as to when and in what circumstances he allegedly received money from Galanskov.

DOBROVOLSKY answers that he doesn't remember exactly.

LASHKOVA. I should like to ask Dobrovolsky a question.

JUDGE. Please do.

LASHKOVA. Dobrovolsky, don't you remember having a conversation with me, in the autumn or thereabouts, in which you said you wanted to buy a second-hand car for which you would pay immediately, and asked me if I had a friend who could sell you a car?

DOBROVOLSKY. No, there was no such conversation.

LASHKOVA. I assert that there was such a conversation and I ask the court to take it into account.

After this the court passes on to the interrogation of Alexander Ginzburg.

INTERROGATION OF ALEXANDER GINZBURG

JUDGE. Ginzburg, stand up and come here. What have you to say to the charges?

GINZBURG. First of all, I want to make it clear that I am not a poet, writer or journalist, but only an ordinary person. In addition, I have never been anti-Soviet. My declaration in the year 1960, about which so much was said in the charges, I made eight years ago after six months of solitary confinement and on the fifth day of a hunger strike. It did not express my true convictions and I have long since renounced it. As to my present-day views, I would like to treat them in more detail. Lenin in one of his last works, 'Better less but better' ...

PROCURATOR (interrupting). It is unnecessary to quote Lenin in court.

JUDGE upholds the Procurator's objection.

ZOLOTUKHIN expresses a protest.

JUDGE rejects his protest.

GINZBURG tells of his attitude to the trial of Sinyavsky and Daniel, of the public reaction to this trial throughout the world, and compares this reaction to the protests against the persecution of the Greek democrats. (Laughter in the courtroom.)

JUDGE forbids Ginzburg to talk about the trial of Sinyavsky and Daniel, as sentence has already been passed on them, and the whole question has nothing to do with this trial.

GINZBURG. I wanted to compile an objective collection relating to that trial, to include everything available to me, and send it to the leaders of our state.

JUDGE. Did you write about this to the Supreme Court of the USSR?

GINZBURG. No.

JUDGE. Why?

GINZBURG. I knew that many letters sent there had remained unanswered. I decided to choose a more effective way—to put together the most objective collection possible and show it to influential people, so that they could inform the leaders of our State. So in November 1966 I showed it to the writer Ehrenburg and some other deputies.

PROCURATOR. Name them.

GINZBURG. I refuse.

PROCURATOR. Why?

GINZBURG. It's enough that I am being tried on account of that collection of materials. I wouldn't like to see anyone else besides us in the dock.

PROCURATOR. Where did you obtain the material from foreign newspapers?

GINZBURG. In libraries; I also bought them at kiosks and asked people who subscribe to these papers to lend them to me.

PROCURATOR. Name these people.

GINZBURG. I refuse on the same grounds I refused to name the deputies.

PROCURATOR. Who helped you to put together this material?

GINZBURG. Nobody. I compiled it all myself.

PROCURATOR. Who translated the foreign newspapers?

GINZBURG. I did.

JUDGE. What languages do you know?

GINZBURG. With the help of a dictionary I can translate from English. I can also translate from French, but with difficulty. German I learnt at school. (Laughter in the courtroom.)

PROCURATOR. Who typed the collection?

GINZBURG. Partly myself, partly Lashkova. She did not type all the material. For example, she didn't type the leaflet 'Resistance'.

PROCURATOR. Did you take the whole collection to her at once or in parts?

GINZBURG. In parts.

PROCURATOR. On what terms did she type for you?

GINZBURG. I paid her money and sometimes bought her food.

PROCURATOR. When did she finish typing the material for the collection?

GINZBURG. About November 1966.

PROCURATOR. With what aim did you include in your collection anti-Soviet documents—the leaflet signed 'Resistance' and 'Letter to an Old Friend'?

GINZBURG. In the first place, I don't consider them anti-Soviet; they contain no slanders, no deliberately false fabrications and no calls for insurrection. Secondly, I was striving to make my collection as objective as possible and to present in it all points of view concerning that trial. So that even if I had considered those documents to be anti-Soviet, I nevertheless would have had to include them in my collection for the sake of objectivity. I repeat, I was not intending to circulate the collection among the public, but wanted to pass it on to the higher levels of the government and party.

PROCURATOR. What was your purpose in writing the letter to Kosygin which you included in your collection?

GINZBURG. I wrote the letter to express my opinion about the conduct of the trial and to declare that I did not consider the works of the writers concerned to be anti-Soviet. I thought then, and I still think so now, that if I don't agree with something, it is my duty to express my disagreement openly.

PROCURATOR. Then why didn't you send the letter to the person to whom it was addressed?

GINZBURG. I consider that an infamous accusation.

JUDGE reproves Ginzburg.

GINZBURG. I acted sincerely and with clean hands. I sent the letter to the addressee. If it didn't get there, I am not to blame. I sent six letters to my lawyer from prison, but he didn't receive any of them. That does not mean that I didn't send them.

PROCURATOR. When did you meet Galanskov and what kind of relations existed between you?

GINZBURG. I think it was in 1959, and he was introduced to me as a poet. From 1960 to 1962 I was in prison. He often came to our house. When I returned, we used to meet, but not very often. He used to come to our house and was on very good terms with my mother. From 1966 onwards we worked together as labourers at the Literary Museum.

PROCURATOR. Did he help you with *The White Book*?

GINZBURG. No. I, and I alone, compiled it.

PROCURATOR. Did you help Galanskov to compile the miscellany *Phoenix*?

GINZBURG. No, I haven't even seen the collection.

PROCURATOR. Why was a copy of *Phoenix* found at your home?

GINZBURG. Galanskov said that he forgot it in our home. He put it on a shelf near the door, where it was found during the search. I have already testified that I have neither seen nor read the collection. Galanskov's testimony on this subject tallies completely with mine.

PROCURATOR. Did you give Galanskov a photocopy of the article 'The Russian Road to Socialism'?

GINZBURG. No, I did not. Galanskov has stated this already. A friend gave it to him—he has already spoken about this.

PROCURATOR. When did you meet Lashkova?

GINZBURG. In autumn 1966, the end of September, beginning of October.

PROCURATOR. With what purpose?

GINZBURG. I needed a typist. She agreed to type for me and I brought her money and food in return.

PROCURATOR. When did you meet Dobrovolsky?

GINZBURG. In 1960 at a psychiatric examination in the Serbsky Institute. After that we did not meet again for many years. Then we met again in November 1966 when he came to work as a bookbinder at the Literary Museum. Galanskov and I were working as labourers at the same museum. Dobrovolsky himself correctly described our relationship as 'Good morning and Good-bye'. Galanskov and myself, as a rule, worked in different museums—branches of the Literary Museum—and very rarely met Dobrovolsky. We never discussed anything with him. As to his evidence regarding myself, it is without exception hypothetical and unreliable. It is supposed to be based on words spoken by Galanskov, in spite of the fact that Galanskov denies all these statements attributed to him. This also applies to his evidence that in 1962 I allegedly passed on my connections with foreign countries to Galanskov. I ask you to consider that until 1960 no such connections had been detected as regards me; there was not even any mention of them during the 1960 investigation in connection with *Syntax*, and from 1960 to 1962 I was in a labour camp, so I am unable to understand what connections Dobrovolsky is talking about. The same is true of his testimony that I allegedly gave my consent to Galanskov over sending my collection abroad, which Dobrovolsky knows about from Galanskov, although he stresses that he himself saw nothing and knows nothing for certain. The same also applies to his testimony that I allegedly gave Galanskov a film of the article 'The Russian Road to Socialism'. The following examples of his testimony are also typical. Dobrovolsky has never once been in my house in my company. Perhaps he has been there at some time in my absence with Galanskov, but I don't remember. Nevertheless he gave evidence that I had a secret depository in my house which he, Dobrovolsky, claimed to have seen. However, after two searches no such secret depository was found in my house. This is not surprising, as Dobrovolsky's evidence is a slander and a fabrication. And I want to say something else about Dobrovolsky's evidence. I have every reason for asserting that information was passed not only from Dobrovolsky to the investigator but also vice versa. For instance, Dobrovolsky stated at the beginning of the preliminary investigation that he had never seen the collection of material on the Sinyavsky–Daniel trial. Nevertheless at the end of the investigation he called the collection biased, criminal, etc., almost in the same phrases in which it is described in the indictment. Moreover, he was the only one amongst us to be allowed extra deliveries of parcels and the relevant documents on this are available in the case materials.

JUDGE. You said that you were convicted in 1960. On what charge?

GINZBURG. I took some exams on behalf of a friend, but the trial was really concerned with the periodical *Syntax*, which I had been compiling at that time. However, because there had been no specific breach of the law, the proceedings under article 70 of the Russian Criminal Code were abandoned, but I was convicted under article 196, paragraph I of the Criminal Code and sentenced to two years' imprisonment.

CHIZHOVA. Where did you work after you left school?

GINZBURG. I worked in various places—as a lathe-operator, librarian and actor and I studied journalism at Moscow State University. Just recently I have been working at the Literary Museum as a labourer and studying at the Institute of Historical Archives.

PROCURATOR. Tell us of your connections abroad with the émigré organization NTS.

GINZBURG. I have had no connections with the NTS, nor with any other such organizations.

PROCURATOR. But in your article 'Answer to Mr Hughes' published in the paper *Evening Moscow* in 1965, you yourself wrote that you knew two of the guides at the American Graphics Exhibit.

GINZBURG. Yes, that is true, but they are not connected with any organization. We met at the Exhibition and spoke only about art.

PROCURATOR. In the same article you yourself wrote that the periodical *Syntax* had been published in *Grani*, which is an NTS publication.

GINZBURG. In the first place—I didn't write that, it was added to the article by employees of the paper without my consent. It is not the only addition made to that letter, which I was forced to write. At the time I attached no great significance to this detail about *Grani*. Secondly, I don't even know in what year *Syntax* was published in *Grani*. When I was arrested in 1960 *Syntax* was not finished. I was in a labour camp until 1962 and when I returned I had other things to do. So I know nothing of how and when *Syntax* got abroad.

PROCURATOR. But surely it is no accident, Ginzburg, that your writings are used abroad by our enemies?

GINZBURG. Our enemies use anything. There is, for instance, an American edition of Kochetov's *Secretary of the Regional Party Committee** with a foreword by Kerensky. So what shall we do about it—put Kochetov in jail?

PROCURATOR. How did your *White Book* come to be published abroad?

GINZBURG. In the first place, I never called that collection *The White Book* and I don't know where the title came from. Secondly, I have already said that I have no knowledge of how my writings reached the West. It was not my aim to send it to any Western publishing house. I wanted it to reach the higher levels in our state. I wanted to ask for a review of the sentence on Sinyavsky and Daniel, as I considered that sentence to be unjust.

PROCURATOR. How did it get into *Grani*?

GINZBURG. During the preliminary investigation I was given the opportunity to look at some numbers of *Grani*. In *Grani*, No. 62, there are some documents which were also included in my collection, among them Ginzburg's 'Letter to Kosygin', the leaflet 'Resistance'

---

* This very Stalinist book by Vsevolod Kochetov first appeared in the USSR in 1961. Ed.

and 'Letter to on Old Friend'. Nowhere is it stated that this material was taken from my collection. My name is mentioned only once— ' "A Letter to Kosygin" by A. Ginzburg, editor of the periodical *Syntax*'—that is all. I would like to remark that if I had myself sent the letter to *Grani* I would have described myself differently. I am not so proud of *Syntax* as to refer to it eight years later. The publication of these few documents does not prove that I sent my collection to *Grani*.

PROCURATOR. But in *Grani*, No. 63, there is an editorial note that 'Ginzburg has done an enormous amount of work in compiling a collection of materials about the trial of Sinyavsky and Daniel'.

GINZBURG. Nothing is said in that note about my having sent my collection to *Grani*. The editorial note proves nothing.

ZOLOTUKHIN. What month is *Grani*, No. 63?

PROCURATOR. But it's a weekly magazine!

JUDGE (looking at the cover). No, it comes out three times a year. This number is March 1967.

ZOLOTUKHIN. But the French edition of Ginzburg's collection came out in February 1967 under the aegis of the publishing house 'La Table Ronde' (shows the book). So *Grani*, No. 63, in inserting this editorial comment, may have had in view the French edition of *The White Book* which is on exhibit in this trial.

GINZBURG. I did not, in any case, send my collection to any of these publishing houses.

PROCURATOR. Tell the court about the meeting with the Swede.

GINZBURG. I never had any meeting with a Swede. In June 1966 a woman friend of mine, whom I will not name, rang me and said that there was a Swedish student in Moscow who wanted to meet somebody from SMOG. Later I rang Gubanov[61] and his wife Basilova and asked whether they would like to meet a Swede who was interested in SMOG. They agreed. Then I gave my friend their address. That's all. I did not even plan to meet the Swede.

PROCURATOR. Where did you obtain the anti-Soviet newspaper cuttings which you gave to Gubanov?

GINZBURG. I have already said that I included in my collection some comments of the foreign press about the trial of Sinyavsky and Daniel. In the course of my work I got hold of papers in Norwegian, Danish and Italian. I don't know these languages but I noticed the word SMOG in large Roman letters. The same was true of a paper in French. I had no need of these papers. I didn't understand the contents of the articles but I realized they were about SMOG and sent them to Gubanov, one of SMOG's members. I don't know and could not know the contents of these articles, as I don't know Norwegian, Danish or Italian. I speak French badly and read it only with the help of a dictionary. I did not even begin to read that article, as it was not about the trial of Sinyavsky and Daniel.

PROCURATOR. Where did you obtain the two songs of an anti-Soviet character?

GINZBURG. I had a large collection of contemporary songs written by amateurs. During the search many recordings, among them these two songs, were confiscated. In my opinion, there is nothing anti-Soviet about them—they are merry musical jokes. Perhaps they could be considered to be evidence of bad taste but not of anti-Soviet feeling. One is about a whale and three herrings, the other is a parody of Tolstoy's *Anna Karenina*, which was written, as everybody knows, in the nineteenth century. It is true that the song speaks, in a humorous context, of Lenin's work *Lev Tolstoy as a mirror of the Russian Revolution*, but since this work was written ten years before the establishment of Soviet power, even a mockery of it cannot be described as an 'anti-Soviet action'. In my presence a procurator [name unintelligible] laughed merrily while listening to these songs.

JUDGE. Does the defence have any questions?

ZOLOTUKHIN. Tell me, Ginzburg, have you read the testimony of Schaffhauser, the NTS courier arrested in January 1967?

GINZBURG. Yes.

ZOLOTUKHIN. What was taken from him?

GINZBURG. A note-book containing notes on various Soviet writers and public figures, what they were working on and what their views were.

ZOLOTUKHIN. Besides Galanskov and yourself, whom else did the notes concern?

GINZBURG. I don't remember exactly; there were various writers, for example Aksyonov.

ZOLOTUKHIN. Did you know the NTS agent Mikulinskaya?

GINZBURG. I could not have known her—she visited the USSR in March 1967 when I had already been arrested.

JUDGE. Do the accused have any questions?

GALANSKOV. Do you say that I visited your home in company with Dobrovolsky?

GINZBURG. No. I said that in principle you could have, but I was not present if you did.

GALANSKOV. I have never visited your house together with Dobrovolsky.

DOBROVOLSKY. I protest! Ginzburg said that I . . .

JUDGE (interrupts him). Dobrovolsky, your protest is rejected. Ginzburg was expressing his personal point of view.

At this point the interrogation of the accused comes to an end. According to the usual practice of court proceedings, . the interrogation of witnesses now begins.

KAMINSKAYA requests the calling of citizen Grigorenko into court as a witness, as he can give important evidence concerning the money discovered in the search of Dobrovolsky's flat.

PROCURATOR asks that this request be denied because of Grigorenko's being of unsound mind.

JUDGE after consultation on the spot with the assessors, suspends judgment on the question until a report has been made on Grigorenko's present mental condition by the Psycho-Neurological Health Centre where he used to be registered; and asks the secretary of the court to send to the Centre a request for it. He then declares a break in the proceedings until 10 January at 10.00 hours.

The sitting ends at 17.30 hours.

10 January

The court sitting begins at 10.00 hours with the decision
on yesterday's request by defence counsel Kaminskaya
about calling citizen Grigorenko as a witness.

JUDGE states that the report on Grigorenko's mental condition has been received and he reads it. The report states that in 1964 Grigorenko was judged to be of unsound mind and diagnosed as a schizophrenic by a forensic-psychiatric diagnosis team. After this he was confined for a year's treatment in the special Leningrad mental hospital. Upon his discharge from the hospital he was registered as a schizophrenic with a Psycho-Neurological Health Centre.*

After the reading of this report the court consults on the
spot and then refuses Kaminskaya's request.

PROCURATOR requests the calling into court of the witness Nicolas Brox Sokolov, arrested in Moscow in December 1967. The Procurator explains his request by saying that Brox Sokolov's evidence includes facts directly relevant to the case.

JUDGE asks the opinion of the defence and the accused.

THE DEFENCE COUNSELS state that they would like first of all to acquaint themselves with the testimony of Brox Sokolov before he is called into court and with the records of the investigation. The accused are of the same opinion.

* See on this Documents IV: 13 and IV: 14, pp. 250 and 252.

PROCURATOR answers that Brox Sokolov's case has only just begun, that the investigation has yet to explain various circumstances connected with the case, and that it is a case of state importance so that the record of the investigation cannot be made public.

JUDGE refuses the request of the defence counsels on these grounds.

THE DEFENCE COUNSELS request that, in that case, they should be shown only the parts of the investigation relating to the case in hand, and not the whole transcript of the investigation.

The court, after consultation on the spot, decides to refuse the request of the defence counsels and to grant the request of the Procurator about calling into court the witness Nicholas Brox Sokolov. Then the interrogation of the witnesses begins.*

INTERROGATION OF THE WITNESS MASLOVA†

JUDGE. What can you tell us about the facts of the case?

MASLOVA. What are you interested in knowing?

PROCURATOR. Which of the accused do you know? When and in what circumstances did you meet?

MASLOVA. I got to know Lashkova about three years ago. I have been on very good terms with her all that time. I even lived with her at one time. About seven months before her arrest I met Dobrovolsky and a little later I met Galanskov, in both cases at Lashkova's flat. I met Galanskov in October or thereabouts. After that I met Galanskov three times in all. I hardly knew Ginzburg. I saw him at Lashkova's once but I really don't remember when and in what circumstances.

PROCURATOR. Tell us, what kind of people gathered at Lashkova's, what sort of conversation went on there and what were their general attitudes?

MASLOVA says that a lot of people usually gathered at Lashkova's that they talked about various subjects, including politics, art and literature.

---

* Various parts of the trial are left out from this point on: the establishment by the judge of each witness's personal particulars, the cautioning about penalties for refusing to give evidence (article 182 of the Russian Criminal Code, up to six months) and for giving deliberately false evidence (article 181 of the Russian Criminal Code, up to seven years), the taking from the witness of a signed statement that his rights and duties have been explained to him, the clarification of the witness's relation to the accused (is he a member of the family? etc.). Also omitted are a few of the judge's procedural questions during interrogations, for instance: 'has the defence any questions?' etc.

† Tatyana Maslova, twenty-two years old, an artist's model, called by the Prosecution.

PROCURATOR. What exactly did they say?

MASLOVA. I don't remember.

PROCURATOR reads the evidence of Maslova at the preliminary investigation where she stated exactly who used to gather at Lashkova's and what they talked about.

MASLOVA says that it was true that a certain critical attitude was characteristic of these conversations, but she found it difficult to say how exactly it was expressed.

PROCURATOR asks if Maslova had ever heard Lashkova say anything which seemed anti-Soviet to her. Was the NTS mentioned in her presence?

MASLOVA says that although she saw Lashkova every day, she had never heard anything anti-Soviet from her and had certainly never heard anything about the NTS from her. She had never had any conversations with Lashkova about politics. Neither had she ever heard any anti-Soviet remarks from Galanskov, Ginzburg or Dobrovolsky.

PROCURATOR. Tell me, please, did all the conversations take place in your presence? Were there no occasions when some of Lashkova's visitors went out into the kitchen and had some kind of discussion there?

MASLOVA. Yes, there were such occasions.

PROCURATOR. Did Dobrovolsky offer to rent a room for you, so as later to turn it into a conspiratorial meeting place or a store-room for NTS literature?

MASLOVA. It was completely different. I had nowhere to live, I wanted to rent a room for myself and I asked my friends to help me find a room. I made this request to Dobrovolsky as well. I never had any other conversations with Dobrovolsky about renting a room.

PROCURATOR. Did you ever interrupt Lashkova while she was working?

MASLOVA. Yes, I did. As far as I know Lashkova worked at Moscow University at that time and brought work home with her.

PROCURATOR. Did you know what exactly Lashkova was typing?

MASLOVA. It never interested me and Lashkova never talked to me about it.

PROCURATOR. Did you ever see any anti-Soviet literature in Lashkova's flat?

MASLOVA. No, I didn't.

PROCURATOR asks Maslova to repeat her testimony concerning the room. Did he [Dobrovolsky] offer to help her find a room or did she ask him about it?

MASLOVA answers that she asked Dobrovolsky to find her a room.

DOBROVOLSKY asks whether he had ever mentioned to her that he would like to use the room for any purpose whatsoever.

MASLOVA answers that he had not.

GALANSKOV. In connection with the evidence you gave at the preliminary enquiry, do you remember if I was ever at Lashkova's when there was a gathering, what I said exactly and to whom?

MASLOVA. I can't remember exactly but I often saw you at Lashkova's.

GALANSKOV. That's enough.

JUDGE. Maslova, you are free to go.

INTERROGATION OF THE WITNESS KAMYSHANOVA*

JUDGE. Tell us what you know of the facts of the case.

KAMYSHANOVA. I ask the court to put questions to me.

PROCURATOR. Which of the accused do you know?

KAMYSHANOVA. I know Galanskov, Lashkova and Dobrovolsky.

PROCURATOR. Do you know Ginzburg?

KAMYSHANOVA. I never knew Ginzburg.

PROCURATOR. When and in what circumstances did you meet the accused? When did you meet Lashkova?

KAMYSHANOVA. I have known Lashkova for quite some time, two or three years. Natasha Ustinova brought her to my house; she sometimes visited me and I used to visit her house. In the last months we saw each other very rarely.

PROCURATOR. When did you meet Dobrovolsky?

KAMYSHANOVA. In November 1966 at Ustinova's birthday party.

PROCURATOR. When did you meet Galanskov?

KAMYSHANOVA. In October 1966.

PROCURATOR. And you have known Lashkova for a long time?

KAMYSHANOVA. Two or three years.

PROCURATOR. What do you know about the criminal activities of the accused?

KAMYSHANOVA. I have noticed nothing criminal in their activities.

PROCURATOR. What did you type at the request of the accused —at whose request specifically? Did you receive any payment for it?

KAMYSHANOVA. I typed 'The Diary of Victor Velsky'. Galanskov asked me to, through Dobrovolsky. I was paid about twenty roubles for the work.

* Irina Kamyshanova, twenty-four years old, a typist, called by the Prosecution.

PROCURATOR. Who paid you this money?

KAMYSHANOVA. I think it was Galanskov. Yes, it must have been Galanskov.

PROCURATOR. Whom did you give the work to?

KAMYSHANOVA. Dobrovolsky, I think. They were both at my place on that day. They were both asking questions about the work while I was typing it, so I got the impression they both wanted the work.

PROCURATOR. Do you know who else was typing this work?

KAMYSHANOVA. I heard that one or two pages were typed by Vera Lashkova and a few by Natasha Ustinova.

LASHKOVA. I ask the witness to answer this—does she really know if I typed anything at all from this work?

KAMYSHANOVA. No, I can't swear to it, I only heard something about it.

PROCURATOR. What else did you type for Galanskov?

KAMYSHANOVA. I don't remember.

PROCURATOR. In your evidence at the preliminary investigation you stated that you typed Pomerants's 'Quadrillion'. Is that true?

KAMYSHANOVA. Yes, I think so.

PROCURATOR. What were you paid for this work?

KAMYSHANOVA. There weren't many pages. I think it was about twenty roubles again.

PROCURATOR. Do you know that 'Quadrillion' was printed in the periodical *Grani*?

KAMYSHANOVA. No, I didn't. I have never heard of such a periodical.

PROCURATOR. I have no more questions.

JUDGE. Witness, tell the court if you read what you were typing.

KAMYSHANOVA. I read the 'Diary' very superficially. I read the 'Gospel of Victor Velsky'.

CHIZHOVA. That was the second part—the religious one?

KAMYSHANOVA. Yes.

JUDGE. What impression did it make on you?

KAMYSHANOVA. The religious part was very interesting. The 'Diary' on the other hand, seemed to me like the ravings of a madman.

JUDGE. Did you read this phrase in the first part, which is incidentally referred to in this case as 'The Confession of Victor Velsky'? (quotes) 'I hate this regime . . .'*

KAMYSHANOVA. Perhaps.

* The end of the quotation was unintelligible.

JUDGE. And did you, a Soviet woman, while reading such a phrase, remain quite calm? Didn't you consider it anti-Soviet?

KAMYSHANOVA. In the first place, I have already said what impression the 'Diary' made on me, and secondly, there are words contradicting that phrase later on.

JUDGE. We did not see that.

KAMYSHANOVA. No, there were such words. You only have to read on.

JUDGE. Very well, thank you. Does anyone have any questions?

DOBROVOLSKY. I would like to ask the witness if she and I often met at gatherings?

KAMYSHANOVA. Yes, quite often at one time.

DOBROVOLSKY. And we had conversations there, yes?

KAMYSHANOVA. Yes, people usually talk in company.

DOBROVOLSKY. Did you ever hear any anti-Soviet remarks from me?

KAMYSHANOVA. Yes, I did.

DOBROVOLSKY and JUDGE (together). What remarks exactly?

KAMYSHANOVA. Once when he was drunk I heard Dobrovolsky say that he hated the existing regime which had deprived him, the son of a noble family, of the good things of life that his grandfather, for instance, had enjoyed, and that he too might have enjoyed. He also said that one day there would be a different sort of regime, under which he would not be the least important person. (Laughter in the courtroom.)

JUDGE. How did you react to these statements of Dobrovolsky's?

KAMYSHANOVA. At first, I paid no attention because Dobrovolsky, as I have said, was drunk. But later, having thought it over, I told Dobrovolsky we would have to break off our friendship.

SHVEISKY. Witness, you are a Soviet citizen. How could you not have paid any attention to these remarks? It's one thing when a drunk uses indecent language, but quite another when he makes anti-Soviet statements.

KAMYSHANOVA. I have already said that on reflection I decided to have nothing more to do with Dobrovolsky.

SHVEISKY. Why did you say nothing of this at the preliminary investigation?

KAMYSHANOVA. I was not asked.

SHVEISKY. You were asked about the matter generally and you should have mentioned this to us.

KAMYSHANOVA. I answered specific questions. No such question was asked.

JUDGE. Does anyone have any questions?

GALANSKOV. The witness remembers our conversation. . . . What was my reaction to this matter?

KAMYSHANOVA. Yes, I told Yury Galanskov about this conversation with Dobrovolsky. It was he who advised me not to have any further dealings with Dobrovolsky.

GALANSKOV. Didn't Dobrovolsky's behaviour at that time strike you, witness, as somewhat strange?

KAMYSHANOVA. Yes, it did a little.

JUDGE. The witness cannot answer that question. The question will be stricken from the record.

GALANSKOV. I only wanted to say—Oh, very well. (Sits down.)

JUDGE. The witness is free to go.

DOBROVOLSKY. I wish to make a statement.

JUDGE. Please do.

DOBROVOLSKY. I wish to give the court an explanation. The point is that the witness is a close friend of Galanskov's wife, Olga Timofeyeva, who has been present during this trial. This has influenced the evidence of the witness.

GALANSKOV. I wish to say that Olga Timofeyeva is indeed present at the trial, but . . .

JUDGE (interrupting). Galanskov, your statement has been erased. The witness is free to go.

KAMINSKAYA. I want to ask the witness a question. Did you tell the truth, and only the truth, in the court?

KAMYSHANOVA. Yes.

KAMINSKAYA. All right, thank you.

JUDGE (to an official). Escort the witness out.

KAMYSHANOVA. I would like to remain present in court.

JUDGE. There is no room in the courtroom. We can't allow you to stay.

KAMYSHANOVA. I can stand.

JUDGE. No, you must go.

INTERROGATION OF THE WITNESS KUSHEV*

JUDGE. What can you tell the court about the facts of this case?

KUSHEV. I request the court to ask me specific questions. I find it difficult to think of something to say.

* Evgeny Kushev, twenty-one years old, a poet sentenced to one year's suspended imprisonment in 1967 under article 190-3 of the Russian Criminal Code for his part in the demonstration of 22 January 1967 asking for the liberation of Galanskov, Dobrovolsky, Lashkova and Radziyevsky. Called by the Prosecution.

JUDGE. Tell us which of the accused you know.

KUSHEV. I know Vera Lashkova, Galanskov and Dobrovolsky.

JUDGE. How did you meet the accused, when and in what circumstances?

KUSHEV. I got to know Vera Lashkova through friends we had in common. The others I met through her at her flat. I think that is how, I don't remember exactly.

JUDGE. Procurator, please continue.

PROCURATOR. What kind of a relationship did you have with Lashkova and Galanskov in connection with the periodical *Kolokol* [*The Bell*]?

KUSHEV. I asked Vera Lashkova to type three copies of this periodical for me, which she did. I left the original with her.

PROCURATOR. During the preliminary investigation you stated that you talked to Galanskov about this. Is that so?

KUSHEV. No, I renounced that evidence.

PROCURATOR. But Galanskov was interested in this subject?

KUSHEV. I think he asked me about the Leningrad trial in Vladimir Bukovsky's flat, but we couldn't discuss it as there were too many people there.

PROCURATOR. Who produced *The Bell*?

KUSHEV. The Leningrad organization arrested in 1965.[62]

PROCURATOR. Could Galanskov have taken Lashkova's copy of *The Bell*?

KUSHEV. I don't know, perhaps he did, perhaps not. I suppose he could have.

PROCURATOR. What NTS literature did you get from Lashkova and Dobrovolsky?

KUSHEV. I read various NTS pamphlets.

PROCURATOR. What pamphlets exactly?

KUSHEV. I think they were 'Solidarism Is the Idea of the Future', *Our Times* and *The Power of Ideas*.

PROCURATOR. I have no more questions.

JUDGE. Tell me, do you consider these books to be anti-Soviet?

KUSHEV. It's all written there in black and white—that the NTS is carrying on an unremitting and spirited struggle against the Communist regime. Yes, I consider these works anti-Communist, if you like, and anti-Soviet.

JUDGE. They gave you these books themselves? I suppose they tried to convert you?

KUSHEV. No, I myself asked them to give me these books to read.

JUDGE. Tell us how this happened.

KUSHEV. Once Dobrovolsky and I were talking about the Russian Liberation Army [Vlasov's army][63] and he told me that he had an interesting pamphlet on the subject.

JUDGE. And you took this pamphlet from Dobrovolsky?

KUSHEV. Yes, I did.

JUDGE. Did you give it back to Dobrovolsky?

KUSHEV. Yes, I gave it back.

JUDGE. And what books did you borrow from Vera Lashkova?

KUSHEV. I find it difficult to remember exactly which pamphlets I borrowed from Lashkova and which from Dobrovolsky. I think I borrowed from Lashkova *The Power of Ideas* and *Our Times*.

LASHKOVA. I haven't even seen *The Power of Ideas* myself.

JUDGE. Lashkova says that you borrowed from her the pamphlet 'Solidarism Is the Idea of the Future'.

KUSHEV. Perhaps I did.

JUDGE. And you also borrowed the same pamphlet from Dobrovolsky?

KUSHEV. Yes.

JUDGE. So you borrowed it from Dobrovolsky and also from Lashkova?

KUSHEV. I must have borrowed it twice.

JUDGE. I call on the defence.

SHVEISKY. Tell me—you have, of course, read in these pamphlets the arguments against the Soviet system. What kind of system should it be changed to, according to the ideas of NTS?

KUSHEV. What do you mean?

SHVEISKY. You went to school, didn't you? What sort of education did you have? You understand what I'm talking about, surely?

KUSHEV. Their new system is based essentially on solidarism.

PROCURATOR. I consider that this is not the place to discuss the principal aims of the NTS. We all know quite well what the NTS is. It is a hostile, anti-Soviet organization.

JUDGE. Tell me, Kushev, didn't it seem strange to you that the accused kept such literature in their homes? They gave it to others to read, passed it round. . . . How do you explain your own unhealthy interest in this sort of literature?

KUSHEV. I read it out of academic interest, thirst for knowledge, if I can put it that way. I wasn't interested in where it came from. I didn't even think about that.

ARIYA. Tell us, how you would describe Vera Lashkova? What were her interests?

KUSHEV. Vera is a very interesting person. She loved literature, the theatre, poetry and art. She wasn't interested in politics, even international politics.

ARIYA. You mean Vera wasn't interested in political questions and problems?

KUSHEV. No, I never heard any political opinions from her at all.

KAMINSKAYA. Tell me, do you know of any subversive activities by Yury Galanskov, my client?

KUSHEV. I don't know of any subversive activity by Yury Galanskov. I only know that he was the editor of the miscellany *Phoenix-66* and I can't say if it is subversive or anti-Soviet.

KAMINSKAYA. Did Galanskov ever ask you to do anything for him? Did he ever give you any literature?

KUSHEV. No, Galanskov never asked me about anything or gave me anything.

JUDGE. Do the accused have any questions?

LASHKOVA. I ask Kushev to remember exactly what pamphlet I gave him.

KUSHEV. I've already said that I don't remember exactly.

JUDGE. Witness, come to the table and take a look—which of these pamphlets did you borrow from Lashkova?

KUSHEV (leafing through the pamphlets). I remember. I asked Lashkova to lend me 'Solidarism Is the Idea of the Future' and *Our Times*. I borrowed *The Power of Ideas* from Dobrovolsky. It contains the article on the Russian Liberation Army, 'The Tragedy of the Third Power', which interested me.

JUDGE. Which means you were interested in Poremsky's[64] article on Vlasov's army? And you took the other booklets from Lashkova?

KUSHEV. Yes, I took them from Lashkova after I had looked through her library at her home.

JUDGE. And you gave them back? You didn't give them to anybody? You didn't discuss them with anyone?

KUSHEV. No, I didn't give them to anyone or discuss them.

JUDGE. In your testimony at the preliminary investigation you said that, when visiting Vera Lashkova you saw her typing L. Chukovskaya's letter to Sholokhov which was to be included in *The White Book* and that this book was being compiled by her friend A. Ginzburg. Do you confirm this?

KUSHEV. Yes, this is known by everyone.

JUDGE. But you personally did not know Alexander Ginzburg?

KUSHEV. No, I didn't, to my regret. (Stir in the courtroom.)

JUDGE. What do you know about him?

KUSHEV. I know that he compiled *The White Book*. (Stir in the courtroom.)

JUDGE. I ask the accused if they have any more questions for Kushev.

GINZBURG. Tell me, please, did you—during your interrogation by the KGB—state that you had read the leaflet signed 'Resistance'?

KUSHEV. Yes, I've read it.

GINZBURG. Do you remember what it is about?

KUSHEV. Yes, I do. The pamphlet is about the unlawful expulsion of forty students from Moscow University who attended a protest meeting—more specifically a meeting demanding an open trial for Sinyavsky and Daniel.

GINZBURG. Are the facts described in the pamphlet true?

KUSHEV. As far as I know Moscow University expelled forty students. Consequently they are true.

GINZBURG. And how long before your arrest did you read the pamphlet?

KUSHEV. About a year and a half before my arrest.

JUDGE. This leaflet includes the following: 'Police thugs committed this blatant outrage, operating in cowardly fashion through the administrative bureaucratic structure to take reprisals against the dissenters. However the habits of the dogs only emphasize the characteristics of the trainers.' Is that 'true' as well?

KUSHEV. That's not fact but judgment.

JUDGE. No, that's also fact. What is your opinion of it?

GINZBURG. I protest. You don't have the right to ask Kushev such questions.

JUDGE. Yes, of course, he is unable to judge what constitutes anti-Soviet propaganda and what doesn't. He is also not bound to give his opinion of such literature. For the moment it's not him we're trying.

GINZBURG. Tell me, have you written to the investigator about a book which is held against you?

KUSHEV. Yes, I have. This is *The White Book* about the events in Hungary in October 1956.

JUDGE. This does not interest the court.

GINZBURG. No, it must interest the court. Is it a book published in the Soviet Union?

KUSHEV. Yes, it was published in Moscow, but in the court records . . .

JUDGE (interrupting). We don't need this evidence!

KUSHEV. . . . . it was said to be anti-Soviet and published by the

NTS publishing house Possev. That is why I wrote about it to the KGB investigator.*

JUDGE. Witness, you are free to go. Do you wish to tell the court anything else concerning the accused?

KUSHEV. No, I don't want to say anything else. I wish to remain in the courtroom.

JUDGE. There's not enough room; it's stifling and there's no room to move. There's nothing for you to do here. Go home.

KUSHEV. You are violating Article 283 of the Russian Code of Criminal Procedure.

JUDGE. Never mind that. Escort the witness out!

INTERROGATION OF THE WITNESS USTINOVA†

JUDGE. Do you know any of the accused present in the court?

USTINOVA. Yes, I know all the accused.

JUDGE. What can you say about their activities?

USTINOVA. I request that the court ask me specific questions.

PROCURATOR. Did you know about the involvement of the accused in anti-Soviet activities?

USTINOVA. No, I didn't.

PROCURATOR. Did you ever hear any statements from them which were directed against the Soviet system?

USTINOVA. No, I never did.

PROCURATOR. Did you ever receive any anti-Soviet literature from them?

USTINOVA. No, I didn't.

PROCURATOR. Did you type material for *Phoenix*?

USTINOVA. Yes, I did. The beginning of Velsky's article—I don't remember what it was called.

PROCURATOR. Who gave you the typewriter and material for typing?

USTINOVA. Dobrovolsky.

PROCURATOR. It seems that the typewriter was out of order and you took it to be repaired. At whose request?

USTINOVA. Yes, there was a letter missing on the typewriter and I took it to be repaired at Dobrovolsky's request.

PROCURATOR. Did he give you money for these repairs?

---

* This refers to *The White Book* published by the Information Bureau of the Council of Ministers of the Hungarian People's Republic about the events of 1956 and reprinted in Russian in Moscow 1957.

† Natalya Ustinova, twenty-five years old, a typist, called by the Prosecution.

USTINOVA. Yes, he did.

PROCURATOR. Why did you take the typewriter to another place? Why did you not leave it in your home?

USTINOVA. I thought it would be better not to keep it in my place, especially as, just before Vera's arrest, she came to visit me for some reason and catching sight of the typewriter said that it should have been at the bottom of the River Moskva long ago. I paid no attention to her words at the time but I realized what she had meant much later.

PROCURATOR. Why did you not continue with this type of work?

USTINOVA. I left for Leningrad and couldn't finish it. What I had completed was collected while I was away.

PROCURATOR. Did you receive any money for the work you had done?

USTINOVA. Yes, I did.

PROCURATOR. From whom?

USTINOVA. From Dobrovolsky.

PROCURATOR. When you were all together, were there any occasions when Lashkova and Dobrovolsky left the room together?

USTINOVA. Yes, there were such occasions.

PROCURATOR. They went out because they didn't trust you?

USTINOVA. No. Why? When people are at a party and somebody leaves the room, whether it was Dobrovolsky with Lashkova or anyone else, it doesn't mean that they don't trust the rest of the company.

PROCURATOR. Did Galanskov give you anything to type?

USTINOVA. No, he didn't. Unfortunately, we didn't know each other very well.

PROCURATOR. Did you ever see Lashkova typing when you came to visit her?

USTINOVA. Yes, I did.

PROCURATOR. And what exactly was she typing? Did she tell you?

USTINOVA. No, she didn't. I didn't ask her as I knew she worked at Moscow University and brought work home.

JUDGE. Very well, you are free to go.

INTERROGATION OF THE WITNESS SEREBRYAKOVA*

JUDGE. What does the witness know about the facts of the case?

SEREBRYAKOVA. I know about this matter through Vera Lashkova, with whom I shared a flat until my marriage. I was astonished

* Nina Serebryakova, twenty-two years old, a student, called by the Prosecution.

when she was arrested because I had never thought Vera could do anything that would get her into the dock. My mother informed me of her arrest by telephone the same evening. There was a typewriter at Vera's. I don't know where she got it from as I felt that if she didn't want to talk about it, it wasn't my business.

PROCURATOR. Which of Vera's friends do you know?

SEREBRYAKOVA. Galanskov, Dobrovolsky—he often came.

PROCURATOR. You named more people at the preliminary investigation.

SEREBRYAKOVA. At the preliminary investigation the names were read to me. At the moment it's difficult for me to think clearly. Kushev used to come.

PROCURATOR. Ginzburg? Kats? Batshev?

SEREBRYAKOVA (remembering). Yes, and him. I also know Lyuda Kats and Batshev.

PROCURATOR. Did you see what Vera was typing?

SEREBRYAKOVA. I didn't see exactly what she was typing. I don't have an inquisitive nature.

PROCURATOR. What did Vera give you to read?

SEREBRYAKOVA. She gave me the discussion on the draft of the third volume of the *History of the Soviet Communist Party*. I also saw some material about the trial of Sinyavsky and Daniel. I know she worked at Moscow University and she often had to do urgent work. That's all, I think.

PROCURATOR asks her if she had ever heard any anti-Soviet statements from Lashkova; was the NTS mentioned in her presence; had she seen any NTS literature?

SEREBRYAKOVA answers that she had never heard any anti-Soviet statements from Lashkova nor had she heard anything about the NTS from her. She had never seen literature published abroad in Lashkova's flat, much less literature published by the NTS.

PROCURATOR. That's all, as far as I'm concerned.

ARIYA. I have a question for the witness. How would you describe Vera as a person?

SEREBRYAKOVA. Perhaps my description will be a little subjective, but I have known her all my life and I can't find anything but good to say of her. I have known her constantly, apart from the short period when Vera lived with her parents in Smolensk. Vera is an exceptionally sincere and decent person, and has an outstanding personality. Vera has had a very hard life. She has lived in constant poverty. Her parents have not helped her at all.

ARIYA. When was Vera left on her own?

SEREBRYAKOVA. Vera came to live in Moscow in her mother's old room when she was sixteen. At first, she lived with a friend of her mother's. Then this friend moved to where she lives permanently, I think in Krasnystroitel street. I remember a time when Vera was living on forty-two roubles a month. Naturally one extreme led to another.

ARIYA. Was Vera a modest person?

SEREBRYAKOVA. Yes, very much so.

JUDGE. Very well, the witness is free to go.

INTERROGATION OF THE WITNESS L. KATS*

JUDGE. Tell us all you know of the facts of this case.

KATS. Please, ask me questions.

PROCURATOR asks which of the accused she knows. Had she heard anything from them about the NTS? Did she receive NTS literature from them?

KATS answers that she knows all the accused, but she had only heard of NTS from Dobrovolsky and it was he who had given her some books published by NTS.

PROCURATOR. And didn't Galanskov talk to you about NTS and give you books?

KATS. No, Galanskov didn't talk to me about it or give me anything.

PROCURATOR. What about Lashkova?

KATS. Perhaps she did.

PROCURATOR. What exactly did she give you?

KATS. I don't remember exactly.

JUDGE. Come to the table and have a look. Which books were given you by Dobrovolsky and which by Lashkova?

KATS (looking). Dobrovolsky gave me *The Power of Ideas*, and I think Lashkova gave me 'Solidarism Is the Idea of the Future', but really I'm not sure.

PROCURATOR. Did you take part in typing *Phoenix* and *The White Book*?

KATS. No.

PROCURATOR. And did you see Lashkova typing?

KATS. I saw her typing, but I never asked her what she was typing. I'm not the inquisitive sort.

PROCURATOR. What were your relations with Lashkova?

KATS. I consider her my close friend.

* Lyudmila Kats, twenty-one years old, a librarian, called by the Prosecution.

PROCURATOR. And what did you say to each other about the pamphlets you read?

KATS. We didn't discuss them.

PEOPLE'S ASSESSOR DUDNIKOV (henceforth referred to as DUDNIKOV). But, witness, you read the pamphlets, didn't you? Surely you understood they were anti-Soviet? Did you discuss your opinion of them with anyone else?

KATS. No, I didn't.

DUDNIKOV. How can that be? When I read something I always discuss it with my friends.

KATS. Well, I don't.

JUDGE. But Dobrovolsky was giving you blatantly anti-Soviet literature. How could you, a Soviet woman, have any dealings with him after that?

KATS. I didn't then know that he would turn out to be such scum.

DOBROVOLSKY. I ask the court to·protect me from the attacks of the witness.

JUDGE. Kats, you are free to go.

KATS. I wish to stay in the courtroom.

JUDGE. You may stay.*

INTERROGATION OF THE WITNESS VINOGRADOV†

JUDGE. Tell us what you know of the facts of this case.

VINOGRADOV. I request the court to ask me questions.

PROCURATOR. When did you meet the accused?

VINOGRADOV. I met Lashkova five years ago, Dobrovolsky three years ago and Galanskov two years ago, but I didn't know Ginzburg at all.

PROCURATOR. What can you tell us about the political opinions of the accused?

VINOGRADOV. Lashkova preferred not to talk about her opinions. Galanskov is a socialist and democrat. Dobrovolsky is an anti-Stalinist.

JUDGE. In your testimony at the preliminary investigation, on 16 October 1967, you stated that when you told Galanskov that you

---

* A few minutes later, after the interrogation of Vinogradov, a recess was declared. Afterwards L. Kats was not allowed back into the hall, and in addition, the Court Commandant Tsirkunenko, a KGB colonel, told her: 'If you had given different evidence, we would have allowed you to return to the courtroom.'

† Vladimir Vinogradov, twenty-two years old, a radio-technician, called by the Prosecution.

were an anarchist, he told you that he was a supporter of socialist syndicalism on the Yugoslav model.

VINOGRADOV. Yes, that's true.

JUDGE. Did Dobrovolsky and Galanskov say to you that in the Soviet Union the level of freedom did not correspond to the level of social development? And that the Constitution was allegedly being violated?

VINOGRADOV. It is indeed being violated, not only 'allegedly'. As for the rest of the question, that was my own phrasing of the opinions expressed to me by the accused.

PROCURATOR. Did Dobrovolsky give you a portrait of Nicholas II [*reigned 1894-1917*] to photograph?

VINOGRADOV. Yes, he did. But I don't remember whether I succeeded in photographing it or not. I think I did.

PROCURATOR. Didn't it surprise you that Dobrovolsky had a portrait of Nicholas II hanging on the wall?

VINOGRADOV. That's his business. You'd be surprised what people have hanging on their walls.

PROCURATOR. Did you take part in the pasting up of leaflets on 4 December 1966?

VINOGRADOV. Yes, I did.

PROCURATOR. Who helped you to put them up?

VINOGRADOV. Dobrovolsky and Ustinova.

PROCURATOR. Did you read the leaflets?

VINOGRADOV. Of course, I have to know what I'm sticking on walls.

PROCURATOR. Where did you stick the posters?

VINOGRADOV. In MIIT,* the Engineering Institute, MRAST† and on the streets.

JUDGE. You gave evidence that you asked Galanskov for the works of Daniel and Sinyavsky published abroad and that he gave you the article by Academician Varga 'The Russian Road to Socialism' so that you could photocopy it.

VINOGRADOV. Yes, he also told me that there was nothing criminal in the article.

JUDGE. You read this article attributed to Varga?

VINOGRADOV. Only four pages; the negatives and prints were bad.

JUDGE. You didn't read such excerpts as this for instance . . . [quotation unintelligible]

* MIIT—Moscow Institute of Transport Engineering. Ed.
† MRAST—Moscow Technical College of Radio Construction. Ed.

VINOGRADOV. Excerpts do not show the character of a work as a whole, especially not that excerpt.

JUDGE. Very well, here is another—'The dictatorship of the proletariat conceived by Marx and Lenin is being transformed into the dictatorship of the party bureaucracy and an oligarchy of top officials'.

VINOGRADOV. Unfortunately, I didn't read as far as that excerpt.

PROCURATOR. Do you know anything about the criminal activities of the accused?

VINOGRADOV. You can't call their activities criminal until the trial finishes.

PROCURATOR. I mean the criminal activities they have been accused of.

VINOGRADOV. No, I know nothing about them.

PROCURATOR. I have no more questions.

JUDGE. Does the defence have any questions?

ARIYA. Notes of conversations were confiscated from you. When you speak of 'Vera' in these notes, do you mean Lashkova?

VINOGRADOV. It depends on the context.

ARIYA. For instance, in that part of the conversation where you say that Lashkova and Kushev regarded their activities as something of a childish game?

VINOGRADOV. Yes, at that point I was undoubtedly talking about Lashkova.

GALANSKOV. Don't you regard socialist syndicalism as a form of social self-government?

JUDGE. We will not discuss that question.

DOBROVOLSKY. There has been an attempt here to make me look ridiculous. I should explain that I collect ikons, on one of which there was a picture of Nicholas II.*

JUDGE. The witness is free to go.

VINOGRADOV. I ask to be allowed to remain in the hall under the terms of Article 283 of the Russian Criminal Code of Procedure.

JUDGE. It is precisely under the terms of Article 283 that you will leave the courtroom.

VINOGRADOV. That doesn't surprise me—it's not the first time you have violated the law.

> After the interrogation of Vinogradov the court declares a recess of half an hour. After that the questioning of the witnesses is resumed.

* This statement by Dobrovolsky about an ikon with Nicholas II on it is meaningless.

INTERROGATION OF THE WITNESS EPIFANOV*

JUDGE. Where do you work?

EPIFANOV. I haven't worked since 1 November 1967 and I'm being supported by my mother.

JUDGE. What was your last place of work?

EPIFANOV. At the Moscow Regional Scientific Research Institute for Clinical Research.

JUDGE. In what capacity did you work there?

EPIFANOV. I worked as a technician.

JUDGE. Do you know the accused?

EPIFANOV. Yes, I know them all. Ginzburg and Galanskov since the spring of 1966, Dobrovolsky and Lashkova since the summer of 1966.

JUDGE. Tell us what you know of the facts of this case.

EPIFANOV. I don't know the substance of the charges and request the court to ask me more specific questions.

JUDGE. Tell the court what you know of the meetings the accused had with foreigners.

EPIFANOV. I know only of one meeting the accused Galanskov had with a foreigner. In the summer of 1966, I don't remember exactly when, a foreigner calling himself Philip phoned my house. He said that he was a student from Paris and asked me to put him in contact with young poets and members of SMOG. We agreed to meet at the University metro station. I knew hardly any young poets, but I had often heard from Galanskov that he knew them well. I rang him at work and we agreed that I should come and see him. I met Philip later and took him with me to the Literary Museum where Galanskov was working. I called Galanskov outside, introduced him to Philip and explained why I had brought him. Then I went away and left them together.

PROCURATOR. Did Philip give anything to Galanskov or Galanskov to Philip?

EPIFANOV. No, I didn't see them giving anything to each other.

PROCURATOR. What do you know of Galanskov's meetings with a Swede?

EPIFANOV. Nothing.

GALANSKOV. I protest against the question.

JUDGE. The accused Galanskov will speak only when the court permits it.

KAMINSKAYA. Comrade Chairman, I protest against the Procurator's question. There is nothing in the indictment about

* Alexander Epifanov, twenty-three years old, a student, called by the Prosecution.

133

Galanskov meeting a Swede. That question is outside the jurisdiction of the court.

ZOLOTUKHIN. Comrade Chairman, you have refused many of our questions, but never the Procurator's questions, which have gone beyond the bounds of this hearing.

PROCURATOR. Comrades Defence Counsels, what is the point of all this emotion? Especially when the witness has said that he knows nothing of these meetings.

JUDGE. Comrade Procurator, you may continue your questioning.

PROCURATOR. I have finished.

JUDGE. Witness, you stated that you know the accused. Did they ever show you any typed texts?

EPIFANOV. No, they showed me nothing.

JUDGE. Did Ginzburg say anything to you about *The White Book* or *Phoenix*?

EPIFANOV. No, he didn't. I only heard about *The White Book* after Ginzburg's arrest.

JUDGE. Here in front of me lies your evidence at the preliminary investigation: 'A few days after Philip's meeting with Galanskov, I asked Galanskov why he had come to visit him and Galanskov told me sharply that it was no business of mine.' What have you to say about that evidence?

EPIFANOV. I gave my most recent evidence about the meeting between Philip and Galanskov during a personal confrontation with Galanskov. I explained then that I had not been precise in my previous evidence because I did not remember the events very well. Therefore I ask the court to consider this evidence given during the personal confrontation to be my last and final word.

JUDGE. I call on the defence.

KAMINSKAYA. Witness, when were you personally confronted with Galanskov?

EPIFANOV. I don't remember exactly—on 27-28 June 1967, I think.

KAMINSKAYA. I have the 23rd written down.

EPIFANOV. Yes, that's right.

KAMINSKAYA. At that time you testified 'A man calling himself Philip phoned me and asked me to put him in contact with members of SMOG'. Do you confirm that?

EPIFANOV. I do.

KAMINSKAYA. You testified further 'I hardly knew the members of SMOG, but Galanskov had told me he knew them well. I rang Galanskov and agreed on a meeting with him'. You confirm this?

EPIFANOV. Yes.

CHIZHOVA. Witness, did you have Galanskov's permission to bring Philip to him?

EPIFANOV. No, I didn't say anything about Philip to Galanskov over the phone. I simply asked him to meet me.

KAMINSKAYA. That means you brought Philip to Galanskov on your own initiative?

EPIFANOV. Yes.

JUDGE. Did you tell Philip where you were taking him?

EPIFANOV. Yes, I did.

JUDGE. And what did Philip say? Did he know Galanskov?

EPIFANOV. No, Philip said that he didn't know Galanskov, but had heard of him in connection with Galanskov's demonstration in front of the American Embassy.

CHIZHOVA. And what was this demonstration about?

EPIFANOV. Galanskov went by himself to the Embassy and protested against the United States' aggression in the Dominican Republic. . . .

JUDGE. I erase that question—it is irrevelant. Does anyone else have any questions?

GALANSKOV. Tell us about the Court of Arbitration by which you were about to be tried.

JUDGE. I refuse that question.

KAMINSKAYA. Why do you refuse that question?

JUDGE. There is nothing about it in the indictment and Article 283 of the Procedural Code states that 'The chairman must refuse questions which are irrelevant'. Does anyone else have any questions?

CHIZHOVA. Witness, you said that you knew the accused. Describe their characters to us.

EPIFANOV. What do you mean by 'characters'?

CHIZHOVA. Well, what do you know of their opinions, their social and political convictions?

EPIFANOV. In the first place, I know the accused in different degrees. I have met Dobrovolsky and Lashkova only a few times, when I hardly spoke to them, so I can say nothing about them. And when I was introduced to Ginzburg and Galanskov, they were told I was unreliable—I talked too much. Ginzburg told me that it was impossible to discuss anything seriously with me, so I can't tell you anything about them.

CHIZHOVA. But you often went to visit Ginzburg. What did you talk about?

EPIFANOV. Ginzburg and Galanskov are educated people and very well read. It was always interesting to talk to them about literature and art. I borrowed books from Ginzburg. We sometimes went to the cinema together.

GINZBURG. Witness, who introduced us?

EPIFANOV. My uncle and his wife.

GINZBURG. Is your uncle much older than you?

EPIFANOV. Yes, he's forty-three years old.

JUDGE. Doesn't anybody have any more questions? Then escort the witness out.

INTERROGATION OF THE WITNESS POTASHEVA*

JUDGE. Tell us what you know of the facts of this case?

POTASHEVA. What exactly do you want to know?

JUDGE. Which of the accused do you know?

POTASHEVA. I know Lashkova, Dobrovolsky and Galanskov.

PROCURATOR. How did you come to meet them?

POTASHEVA. I got to know them through Galanskov's wife, Olga Timofeyeva. We studied together at the same institute.

PROCURATOR asks her if she had held any party in October at which Galanskov, Dobrovolsky and Lashkova were present.

POTASHEVA replies that she did.

PROCURATOR asks her questions about the party: who was present? What did they do? When did Dobrovolsky, Lashkova and Galanskov arrive?

POTASHEVA answers that a lot of people were there, mostly her fellow-students from VGIK.† As far as she can remember Lashkova arrived first, then Dobrovolsky and after that Galanskov.

PROCURATOR. Did you hear any of their conversations? Did any of their words or actions seem suspicious to you?

POTASHEVA. No, I heard nothing suspicious. There were a lot of people there, and I did not notice any suspicious actions—it was the usual sort of party.

PROCURATOR. And can you remember exactly when it took place—the date?

POTASHEVA. No, I can't. I only remember it was in October.

PROCURATOR. Tell me, didn't Dobrovolsky forget a book in your house?

POTASHEVA. Yes, in the morning Lashkova and Timofeyeva

* Svetlana Potasheva, twenty-two years old, a student, called by the Prosecution.

† VGIK—All-Union State Institute of Cinematography. Ed.

arrived and began to look for some kind of book. I found it for them and returned it.

PROCURATOR. Did you see any of the other accused?

POTASHEVA. No.

PROCURATOR. Dobrovolsky, what book was this?

DOBROVOLSKY. *The White Book.*

PROCURATOR. The book forgotten at Potasheva's by Dobrovolsky is an anti-Soviet document published in the West.

DOBROVOLSKY. No, that book had not been published in the West.

GINZBURG. This was *The White Book* about the events of 1956 published by the Hungarian Government.*

JUDGE. The court is not interested in that. The witness is free to go.

INTERROGATION OF THE WITNESS KHAUSTOV†

JUDGE. What can you tell us about the facts of the case?

KHAUSTOV renounces all the evidence he gave during the preliminary investigation. According to him, part of this evidence had been given while he had a high temperature and in reading the record of the interrogation he might have overlooked many inaccuracies made by the investigator in the record.

PROCURATOR. Which of the accused do you know and when did you meet them?

KHAUSTOV. I know all four of them. I met Galanskov on Mayakovsky Square in 1961.

PROCURATOR. What were you doing there?

KHAUSTOV. People were reciting poetry.

PROCURATOR. What, in the middle of the square? Didn't you have anywhere else to go?

KHAUSTOV. I don't know Ginzburg well—I've only met him

* This concerns *The White Book* about the events of October/November 1956 published by the Information Bureau of the Council of Ministers of the Hungarian People's Republic and republished in the USSR by the State Publishing House for Foreign Literature. In spite of the fact that this is an official publication sold freely in the USSR, *The White Book* led KGB investigators into error several times during the investigation, both because of its title (as Ginzburg's collection was published abroad under the title *The White Book*) and because of the events described in it—those of autumn 1956 in Hungary. See also the Interrogation of Kushev.

† Victor Khaustov, thirty years old, a worker, sentenced in 1967 to three years' imprisonment under article 190-3 of the Russian Criminal Code for taking part in the demonstration on 22 January 1967, demanding the release of Dobrovolsky, Lashkova, Galanskov and Radziyevsky, called by the Prosecution.

three times. I don't remember where I met him first. I met Dobrovolsky in 1965 and Dobrovolsky introduced me to Lashkova.

PROCURATOR. Did you often visit Galanskov at his home?

KHAUSTOV. Not very often.

PROCURATOR. Did you, in the summer of 1966, see some material on the trial of Sinyavsky and Daniel in Galanskov's flat?

KHAUSTOV. I saw some newspaper cuttings.

GALANSKOV. Witness Khaustov, tell me, what papers were these cuttings from?

KHAUSTOV. They were cuttings from Soviet papers.

PROCURATOR. And did you see the letter to Sholokhov?

KHAUSTOV states that in the spring or summer of 1966 he had read Galanskov's letter to Sholokhov in Galanskov's flat. He could not say whether the text was handwritten or typed, although in his evidence at the preliminary investigation he had stated it was handwritten, written by Galanskov himself. Khaustov also states that he knew Galanskov was planning to compile some sort of collection. He knew that this collection was called *Phoenix*—he had been told this by Ginzburg, whom he had met by chance on the street. Khaustov states that he had conversations with Galanskov about politics. Although Galanskov never expressed anti-Soviet sentiments, he, Khaustov, and Galanskov held the same opinions about certain questions, for instance, that it was impossible in the Soviet Union to make full use of the rights guaranteed in the Constitution: freedom of speech, of the press, of assembly, and so on.

GALANSKOV asks Khaustov to tell the court once more about the circumstances in which he saw the letter to Sholokhov in his flat. Galanskov maintains that Khaustov saw the handwritten text of the letter to Sholokhov in his flat, and that when Khaustov arrived at his flat he was in the process of rewriting this manuscript.

KHAUSTOV states that part of the letter was read to him by Galanskov and part of it he read himself. He did not know who the author of this letter was.

JUDGE asks if there are any more questions, and then allows Khaustov to be led away.*

INTERROGATION OF THE WITNESS LEVITIN†

JUDGE. Where do you work?

LEVITIN. As an accountant at the Church of Unexpected Joy.

* As Khaustov was serving a sentence he had been led into the courtroom under guard.

† Anatoly Emmanuilovich Levitin-Krasnov, fifty-two years old, an Orthodox writer, called by the Prosecution.

(Guffaws in the court.)

JUDGE. As a citizen of the USSR you must help the court and I ask you to tell only the truth. What can you say to cast light on this matter?

LEVITIN. In all fairness, I'm afraid I can tell you nothing, except that I know all the accused. If that can cast light on the matter, then I can tell you about it.

JUDGE. Begin with your friendship.

LEVITIN. As you see from my profession, I belong to church circles. Dobrovolsky is a believer and sometimes moves in church circles. We met in the home of our mutual friend, the late Mark Dobrokhotov. Vera Lashkova is my typist, since besides my official position I am also a writer on church affairs whose articles, as you probably know, are widely read among church people. At Vera Lashkova's house I saw Galanskov a few times and Ginzburg once. That is all I can tell you.

JUDGE. Did you know that Ginzburg was the author of *The White Book*?

LEVITIN. Yes.

JUDGE. How?

LEVITIN. From foreign radio broadcasts.

JUDGE. But in your evidence at the preliminary hearing, you stated that Ginzburg himself told you.

LEVITIN. No, I never said that. I said that Ginzburg told me, having come from the Procurator's, that the latter had accused him of producing *The White Book*. That's not quite the same thing.

JUDGE. What do you know about the miscellany *Phoenix*?

LEVITIN. I knew that it was planned to produce some kind of anti-Stalinist collection or journal. One of my articles was meant to figure in it. I was not against it because I saw nothing criminal in it. Once I met Dobrovolsky in the metro and he told me that they were planning to bring out a collection or journal. I tried to dissuade Alyosha from this enterprise. I remember the words I used: 'They will put you inside for this, even if you bring out Lenin's works in this way'. Alyosha said to me then: 'You've persuaded me—we won't print it'. But it turns out I didn't persuade him.

JUDGE. What did they say to you about the NTS?

LEVITIN. They didn't have to talk to me about the NTS. I knew what the NTS was before they were born.

JUDGE. No, what did they say to you about their ties with the NTS?

LEVITIN. Absolutely nothing.

JUDGE. But did you talk to them at all about the NTS?

LEVITIN. I really don't remember. There was very little I didn't discuss with them. I may have discussed NTS in the same way we discussed other organizations.

JUDGE. What do you know of their opinions?

LEVITIN. Like the majority of our intelligentsia . . .

JUDGE. Do you really have the authority to speak for the majority of our intelligentsia? Please speak only for yourself.

LEVITIN. Very well. Like many people I have met, they were dissatisfied with the very severe censorship, with the lack of enough religious liberty (here of course, I'm speaking from my pulpit)—in a word, they all wanted greater freedom of expression and nothing else.

PROCURATOR. What can you say about Galanskov?

LEVITIN. He's in poor health—a man with his nerves on edge.

PROCURATOR. It's obvious from the material before the court that you knew about the tourist who came from abroad to see Dobrovolsky. Didn't she come from NTS?

LEVITIN. Not in any way. She was a religious tourist and had come from foreign church circles.

JUDGE. Does the defence have any questions?

KAMINSKAYA. Have you heard that Galanskov took part in the production of the miscellany *Phoenix*?

LEVITIN. I heard that he took some part in it, but what he did exactly, I don't know.

SHVEISKY. Did you know that there was an article about Pochayev in the miscellany *Phoenix*?

LEVITIN. The investigator told me about it. He read me some of it, after which I was sure it was not my article.

SHVEISKY. Have you written about Pochayev?

LEVITIN. Yes, I have written three articles on that subject.

SHVEISKY. Were they written before your acquaintance with the defendants?

LEVITIN. Yes, I got to know them just after those events occurred.

JUDGE. Weren't you taken to court over these articles?

LEVITIN. No, and there was nothing in them for which I could be taken to court. . . .

JUDGE. Witnesses don't make speeches, but wait to be questioned. You have already answered the question.

ARIYA. From the material available to the court it can be seen that at the time of your meeting with representatives of public opinion[65], the deputy editor of the periodical *Science and Religion*, Grigoryan, said that he also knew of the events at Pochayev.

LEVITIN. Yes, I can repeat his exact words: 'You have written a great deal about Pochayev (this referred to me). I have done more for Pochayev, however, than you have. As soon as I heard of the events at Pochayev, I immediately phoned the Central Committee.'

ARIYA. Was Grigoryan telling the truth?

LEVITIN. I think so. He's a perfectly honest person and wouldn't lie.

ARIYA. Were those events a fabrication or not?

LEVITIN. Good heavens! No anti-religious activist and no member of the government has ever denied them.

SHVEISKY. Do you consider that Dobrovolsky's reaction, as a religious person, to the Pochayev events might have been especially sharp?

LEVITIN. Well, naturally. What religious person could approve of bestialities being committed against a monastery?

ZOLOTUKHIN. How did *Phoenix* come to be published abroad?

LEVITIN. I don't know.

ZOLOTUKHIN. How do your works come to be published abroad, then?

LEVITIN. I have no idea.

JUDGE. Have you ever given Dobrovolsky any books?

LEVITIN. I don't remember.

JUDGE. And did he ever give you any books published by the NTS?

LEVITIN. Never.

JUDGE. Did Lashkova ever give you any books published by the NTS?

LEVITIN. Once she showed me a book that had been published abroad. I don't remember its title.

JUDGE. Comrade Levitin, come here. Is this the book which Lashkova showed you?

LEVITIN. I don't remember.

JUDGE. Lashkova, is this the book you showed Levitin?

LEVITIN. Yes, that's it.

JUDGE. Did she urge you to read this book?

LEVITIN. No, she simply showed it to me as a literary curiosity.

JUDGE. Did she ever praise the NTS?

LEVITIN. Not at all. Knowing Vera, I regard it as inconceivable that she sympathized with the NTS.

JUDGE. You are free to go.

INTERROGATION OF THE WITNESS ENTIN*

JUDGE. What have you to say about this case?

ENTIN states that he should have been brought to trial, not on the charges at present made against him but together with Ginzburg, Galanskov, Dobrovolsky and Lashkova. He asks to be tried by the same court that is trying Galanskov and the rest because, firstly, he is directly concerned in the activities these people are accused of; secondly, he wholly shares their convictions, and is also a friend of Galanskov's. He says that he will give no evidence until charges are brought against him on this matter, and that otherwise he will give evidence only in answer to questions by the defence or by the accused themselves.

JUDGE warns Entin that he will bear full criminal responsibility for refusing to give evidence and that fresh criminal charges on that score will be brought against him.

ENTIN answers that it is all the same to him and that he wants only one thing—to be tried together with Galanskov and Ginzburg.

PROCURATOR. You consider that more honourable?

ENTIN. It's more logical.

PROCURATOR nevertheless tries to question Entin.

ENTIN refuses to answer, saying that he has already made a statement to the court and that he will give evidence only if he is asked by the defence or by the accused.

PROCURATOR. Are you really trying to have another charge brought against you?

ENTIN. Yes, that's what I'm trying to do.

JUDGE suggests reading Entin's evidence at the preliminary investigation.

ZOLOTUKHIN makes a statement that according to Article 286 of the Procedural Code the witness's previous evidence can only be read out if the witness is unavoidably absent from the court or if there is evidence of contradiction between the witness's testimony at the trial and his testimony at the preliminary investigation. In his opinion, the present situation meets neither of the requirements. Therefore he considers it impossible to read the record of Entin's interrogation at the preliminary investigation.

JUDGE answers that, in the present case, he finds there is precisely a contradiction in evidence, and therefore proceeds to read Entin's testimony:

* Leonid Entin, twenty-nine years old, without a regular job, at the time of the trial himself accused under article 88, paragraph 1, of the Russian Criminal Code for connections with Moscow and Leningrad currency speculators; called by the Prosecution.

'In the autumn of 1966, Entin together with Borisova came to Moscow. They stopped at Galanskov's flat and lived there for some days. Once Galanskov told Entin that he had some dollars and Entin himself offered to change them for him, through his friendship with Borisova. Entin knew that she had opportunities to change dollars. After this a conversation took place between Entin, Galanskov and Borisova, during which they decided to change the dollars into Soviet currency through some black-market currency dealers known to Borisova. Borisova knew a currency dealer—Danilov. She didn't have his telephone number, but found it in the directory. Borisova rang Danilov and asked if he could immediately buy some dollars from her. Danilov agreed. On the first occasion Galanskov gave Entin 100 dollars. Entin and Borisova took them to Danilov who paid them 300 roubles for the dollars—that is, at the very lowest rate of one to three. After this, Entin and Borisova offered to change all the remaining dollars in the same way for Galanskov. Galanskov agreed. When Borisova rang Danilov, he told her he would buy more and they agreed to a meeting. Danilov did not come to this meeting alone. There was a tall man with him called Sasha who was, judging from what he said, an important currency dealer. He told them about his huge currency operations and so on. Danilov said that he himself had no money and couldn't buy the dollars, and asked Entin and Borisova to accompany him to a nearby house where he said there was a man who could buy the dollars at once. Entin and Borisova went to this house, climbed up some floors and as the man who could buy the dollars didn't seem to be at home, they waited for some time on the landing. During this time Sasha, who had been brought along by Danilov, told them various stories about currency dealers. The man they were waiting for arrived after some time. Right there on the stairs Entin and Borisova gave Sasha 100 dollars to change, deducting the amount earmarked for Danilov, who had promised to buy some shoes for Borisova. After this Entin and Borisova went downstairs and waited outside. After some time Sasha came down and told Entin his friend would be down soon. The friend who had promised to buy the dollars soon came down. He was very drunk. When he approached Entin, Sasha disappeared somewhere. Entin suspected some kind of dirty trick in all this and began to ask the drunk for the money. The latter pushed some sort of package, wrapped in paper, into Entin's hand and said it was the money. When Entin, feeling that he had been tricked, began to ask the man for an explanation, the latter told him to clear off while the going was good and that he wasn't

143

going to get any money. Entin unwrapped the parcel he had been given and it turned out to be a packet of mustard-plasters. Entin and Borisova returned to Galanskov and told him about the incident. Galanskov had been disappointed and told Entin to provide compensation for the lost dollars. He asked Entin to get a useful job, establish himself at work, get into an institute and so on. Galanskov decided to try somehow to get back the money that had been stolen from Entin. A note was written. Entin did not remember who wrote the note—Galanskov or himself—as he was at that time under the influence of the drug 'phenomin', which he had been using for two years. What the note contained, Entin couldn't remember either. A meeting was arranged with Danilov, and Borisova gave him the note. The note was in a matchbox—there were also cartridges in it. Galanskov was present and after Borisova had given Danilov the note, he went off somewhere with Danilov. Entin didn't know what they talked about. He explained this episode in his life by the fact that Borisova was the first woman he had ever loved. She had always been adventurous; Entin tried in every way to be like her and therefore had decided to do this. He had changed the dollars not because he was usually involved in such matters—he hadn't even known how it was done.'

PROCURATOR, after this evidence has been read, tries to ask Entin a question concerning its truth.

ENTIN refuses to answer the question and repeats that until he is accused on the same charges as the defendants and is no longer a witness, he will not give any evidence.

GALANSKOV asks the court to allow him to question Entin himself.

JUDGE allows this.

GALANSKOV asks how Entin's own case is going and what charges are being brought against him.

ENTIN answers that at the moment he is being tried with sixteen other people, all of them completely unknown to him, and that this is another reason why he wants to be tried with Galanskov and not with those others. He faces a less severe sentence, it's true, than the one he would face in the Galanskov trial, but this does not deter him.

GALANSKOV asks him about the note.

ENTIN answers that the note contained some kind of threat addressed to the currency dealers, but that he can't remember its exact contents.

PROCURATOR. Did it say that if the money wasn't returned they would have to reckon with the NTS?

ENTIN. No, that I don't remember.

GALANSKOV questions Entin as to what time Entin changed the dollars on the first occasion, how much money he got, where he brought the money to Galanskov, whether Galanskov was at home when Entin brought the money, where Entin put the money on finding Galanskov not at home.

ENTIN confirms his testimony at the preliminary investigation, except for minor differences about the amount of dollars and Soviet currency and the time Entin brought the money to Galanskov. He says that he doesn't remember these things exactly, especially as he was then under the influence of drugs.

GALANSKOV questions Entin as to whether he remembers the episode when they both went with Borisova to Pushkin Square for a meeting with Danilov, during which the deception practised on Entin was meant to be explained. Did he, Galanskov, say to Entin that the money belonged to a religious fanatic? Did he point to a man in the square, a man with a moustache who was present at the meeting? Did he say that the money belonged to this man?

ENTIN answers that there was indeed a man with a moustache in the square, but he doesn't remember if Galanskov said the money belonged to him.

GALANSKOV asks if he had not repeatedly told Entin to prepare for the entrance exams to an institute, to come to Moscow and enter VGIK where he had been wanting to go for a long time, and that he had insisted on this because Entin was a talented film critic. (Laughter in the courtroom.)

ENTIN replies that all this is true.

JUDGE asks if there are any more questions, and then allows Entin to be led away.*

INTERROGATION OF THE WITNESS BORISOVA†

JUDGE asks Borisova to tell the court everything she knows about the facts of the case.

BORISOVA states that in autumn 1966 she came to Moscow together with Entin and stayed at Galanskov's flat. In Leningrad she had heard much that was good about Galanskov from very many people and this had interested her in Galanskov as an unusually good and kind person. She had seen this to be true because when she and Entin were living at Galanskov's flat, Galanskov had taken

---

* As Entin was under arrest awaiting trial he was led into the courtroom under guard.

† Irina Borisova, twenty-seven years old, a ballerina, called by the Prosecution.

great pains on their behalf, had given them meals and so on. Borisova's evidence agrees with Entin's about the exchange of currency, but she adds that in her opinion Galanskov himself did not need to change the dollars, he had no idea how they could be changed and didn't even know what to do with them.

PROCURATOR asks if Galanskov had asked her or Entin to change the dollars through the State Bank.

BORISOVA answers that she thinks ordinary Soviet citizens don't have the right to change dollars and that Galanskov had never asked her about this. She says that as she knows Galanskov to be an unusually honourable and honest man she was sure that the money Galanskov got for the dollars would have been spent on 'some honest, saintly deed and not in any way on himself'.

JUDGE asks if there are any more questions, and then allows Borisova to be led away.*

INTERROGATION OF THE WITNESS RADZIYEVSKY†

JUDGE. Which of the accused do you know?

RADZIYEVSKY. I only know Dobrovolsky.

JUDGE. Tell the court everything you know about this case.

RADZIYEVSKY. I met Dobrovolsky about a week before he gave me some material to duplicate for him. This material was in a parcel when I got it from Dobrovolsky. When I took the parcel from Dobrovolsky, I was a little drunk and so I could not deliver it to the destination that day and left it in my house, delivering it only the next day. This material should have been duplicated in the Gidrotsvetmetproyekt‡ establishment by two of my friends who worked there on some kind of duplicating machine. They took on all kinds of outside work, getting money for it. For duplicating the material I was to deliver to them, they were to get twenty-five roubles and I was to get five roubles.

PROCURATOR questions Radziyevsky about his personal confrontation with the worker Golovanov from Gidrotsvetmetproyekt when it was revealed on what conditions and in what way Radziyevsky had delivered the material to him.

---

* As Borisova was under arrest awaiting trial under article 88, paragraph 1, of the Russian Criminal Code she was led into the courtroom under guard.

† Paul Radziyevsky, twenty years old, a worker, arrested by the KGB in January 1967, but released soon afterwards, called by the Prosecution.

‡ The Hydraulic Engineering Non-ferrous Metals Research Institute? Exact name unknown. Ed.

RADZIYEVSKY confirms his evidence at the personal confrontation.

PROCURATOR. Tell me, Radziyevsky, did you read any of this material?

RADZIYEVSKY. No, I only opened the parcel and saw that it contained some typewritten sheets. I only saw the first page—there was something about Sholokhov on it. I don't remember exactly, but I think it was a letter by Sholokhov or to Sholokhov. I can't say anything more specific about the contents of this material. When I gave it to my two friends from Gidrotsvetmetproyekt they took the material to the KGB instead of duplicating it. After that I was arrested.

JUDGE asks if there are any more questions, and then allows Radziyevsky to go.

INTERROGATION OF THE WITNESS TSVETKOV*

JUDGE asks the witness to tell the court everything he knows about the case.

TSVETKOV states that he works at the Gidrotsvetmetproyekt and knows Radziyevsky. When Radziyevsky had given him the material to duplicate he had said that it was a discussion between old Bolsheviks about the draft of the third volume of the *History of the Soviet Communist Party*. Radziyevsky had told him that the material had to be duplicated because each old Bolshevik had to have a copy. When he had received the material and began to look it over he realized that it consisted of various strange writings which could be considered anti-Soviet. He didn't remember exactly what the material was about—he had read only part of some letter about Sholokhov and he didn't remember the title of the letter exactly. As it seemed to him that this letter contained anti-Soviet statements he had taken it to the KGB together with the rest of the material.

GALANSKOV. Please, tell me, does not the fact that you took this material to the Committee of State Security [KGB] probably indicate your civic vigilance?

JUDGE. The question is struck off.

GALANSKOV. Tell me, whom did you vote for in 1967 as your deputy to the District Soviet?

JUDGE. Question refused.

GALANSKOV. Then tell me, whom did you vote for in the Supreme Soviet?

* A. Tsvetkov, a worker, called by the Prosecution.

JUDGE. Question refused.

GALANSKOV. Have you attended a single election meeting this year or last year?

JUDGE. Question refused. The witness is free to go.

INTERROGATION OF THE WITNESS GOLOVANOV*

JUDGE asks the witness to tell the court all he knows about the facts of the case.

GOLOVANOV gives the same evidence as Tsvetkov, namely that he works at the Gidrotsvetmetproyekt, that he received a pile of papers from Radziyevsky, that he began to look through this material and was shocked to find that it did not correspond to his own convictions, and that he took it to the KGB.

GALANSKOV. Why did you consider the document concerning Sholokhov anti-Soviet?

GOLOVANOV. I read the document a long time ago. More than a year has passed since then and so I can't answer your question precisely. I can't tell you which parts exactly aroused my sincere indignation. In some parts the name of the great proletarian writer Gorky was mentioned without due respect and the Soviet writer Sholokhov was discussed in an offensive way.

GALANSKOV. Tell me, whom did you vote for in the District Soviet in 1967 as your deputy?

JUDGE. Question refused.

GALANSKOV. Tell me, whom did you vote for in the Supreme Soviet as your deputy?

JUDGE. Question refused. The witness is free to go.

INTERROGATION OF THE WITNESS MRS GINZBURG†

JUDGE asks the Procurator to begin questioning the witness.

PROCURATOR. Have foreigners visited your house?

MRS GINZBURG. No.

PROCURATOR. Tell me, have you had phone calls from Paris or Italy?

MRS GINZBURG. Yes, I have.

PROCURATOR. What did the people who phoned you from Paris talk about?

* V. Golovanov, a worker, called by the prosecution.

† Lyudmila Ilinichna Ginzburg, sixty years old, a pensioner, mother of Alexander Ginzburg, called by the Prosecution.

MRS GINZBURG. They phoned from a publishing house to tell us that my son's book had been published and was being widely read, discussed and approved of by French public opinion.

PROCURATOR. And what did the people who phoned you from Italy talk about?

MRS GINZBURG. About inviting some of the Soviet intelligentsia to go as a group to Italy. Among the people invited was my son— they wanted to invite him as well.

PROCURATOR. How did they know your telephone number?

MRS GINZBURG. I know it wasn't from me or from my son.

PROCURATOR. Well, in that case, how could they know your telephone number?

MRS GINZBURG. I've never spent any time thinking about that question.

PROCURATOR. Which of the accused has visited your house?

MRS GINZBURG. Galanskov. Also Lashkova came a few times.

PROCURATOR. Have you known Galanskov long?

MRS GINZBURG. Since 1959, I think.

PROCURATOR. What do you know of your son's anti-Soviet activities?

MRS GINZBURG. I know nothing about my son's anti-Soviet activities and I'm quite sure there never were any such activities.

PROCURATOR. When Galanskov came to your house, did he ever bring anything for your son?

MRS GINZBURG. Yes, he brought him some textbooks for the Institute.

PROCURATOR. And did he receive anything from your son?

MRS GINZBURG. I'm afraid I don't remember. Galanskov was always made to feel quite at home in our house and for all I know he might have borrowed some books from us.

PROCURATOR. Do you know Lashkova?

MRS GINZBURG. Yes, I've met her a few times.

PROCURATOR. Did Lashkova bring anything to your house?

MRS GINZBURG. No.

PROCURATOR. Did she take anything away from your house?

MRS GINZBURG. No.

PROCURATOR. I have no more questions.

JUDGE. Does anyone have any more questions?

GALANSKOV. I have. Please, tell me, witness, did I advise your son to enter the Institute?

MRS GINZBURG. You did, Yurochka [*affectionate form of Yury*].

F   149

GALANSKOV. Did I come to your house when he wasn't at home and when he wasn't spending the night there?

MRS GINZBURG. You did, Yurochka.

GALANSKOV. Did I advise your son to study English?

MRS GINZBURG. You did, Yurochka.

GALANSKOV. Witness, did I help you, did I buy you food?

MRS GINZBURG. Yes, Yurochka.

GALANSKOV. Did I go to the chemist's for you?

MRS GINZBURG. Yes, you did, Yurochka.

GALANSKOV. How long did I usually stay with you? One hour, two, three?

MRS GINZBURG. A long time—I don't really remember, Yurochka.

GALANSKOV. Did I visit you while your son was in the labour-camp?

MRS GINZBURG. Yes, you did, Yurochka.

JUDGE. The witness is free to go. You can stay in the courtroom— there is a free place over there.*

GINZBURG says that he would like to explain something.

JUDGE. Please do.

GINZBURG states that he would like to explain how exactly his telephone number could have got to the Paris publishing house and to Rome. According to him, ten days after his arrest, the agency France Presse had published an account of this in which his address and telephone number were mentioned.

INTERROGATION OF THE WITNESS BASILOVA†

JUDGE. What is the nature of your occupation?

BASILOVA looks surprised.

JUDGE. What is your profession?

BASILOVA. I'm a poet.

JUDGE. What organization do you belong to?

BASILOVA. I don't belong to any organization. I'm a poet.

JUDGE. What shall we write you down as? Are you a member of the Writers' Union or some other union?

BASILOVA. Write down what you like. You could say I was dependent on my husband and mother if you want to. I want to make a statement about the rest of my evidence.

---

* L. I. Ginzburg was allowed to stay in the hall, not as a witness but as the mother of one of the accused.

† Elena Basilova, twenty-three years old, a poetess, wife of the poet Gubanov, called by the Prosecution.

JUDGE (taking no notice). Which of the accused do you know?

BASILOVA. Alec Ginzburg.

JUDGE. Well, go on.

BASILOVA. Could the court be more specific as to what I'm to talk about?

JUDGE. Certainly. What questions does the State Prosecutor have?

PROCURATOR. Witness, tell me, did a Swede sent by Ginzburg come to your house?

BASILOVA. Not sent by Ginzburg—no. (Laughter in the courtroom.)

PROCURATOR. On the basis of your husband's evidence, a Swede came to your house in May 1965—bringing with him anti-Soviet literature.

BASILOVA. I ask the court to allow me to make a statement concerning my husband's evidence and my own also. (Laughter in the courtroom.)

JUDGE. Your testimony also bears evidence of this incident.

BASILOVA. That cannot be. I gave no such testimony.

JUDGE. Is this your signature, witness?

BASILOVA (looking at the record). It is. But I described the incident in a completely different way. (Laughter in the courtroom.)

JUDGE. Don't you recognize your own handwriting?

BASILOVA. No. This is evidently the investigator's handwriting.

JUDGE. Witness, don't play the fool. Your signature is below the evidence.

BASILOVA. Yes, but why don't you read out the evidence exactly as it is phrased?

JUDGE. It says here: 'This concerns the Swede whom Alec Ginzburg sent'.

BASILOVA. Yes, but that is not the end of the sentence, there are some brackets after that containing the following phrase: 'This is the Swede that Alec Ginzburg talked to me about on the telephone.' The whole sentence looks like this: 'This concerns the Swede whom Alec Ginzburg sent (i.e. the Swede whom Alec Ginzburg talked to me about on the telephone).' The main point of the sentence is this clarification which is put in brackets. The court for some reason emphasizes and even, as I notice, underlines, what comes before the brackets—that is, the incomplete and even subordinate part of the sentence which is a mere linking phrase between the general evidence and the specific point under discussion. (Laughter is going on all the time in the courtroom.)

JUDGE. The court will read your evidence in the way it considers necessary.

BASILOVA. In that case, I find it necessary to renounce that phrase because of its compromising nature. And I as a witness . . .

JUDGE (interrupting). What can you tell us about the matter before the court?

BASILOVA. Do I have the right to explain how the incident occurred and to clarify my evidence? (Laughter in the courtroom.)

JUDGE. Witness, do you realize that this is an unimpressive way to behave?

BASILOVA. No. If my evidence is unimpressive then the court shows its own unimpressiveness in calling such an unimpressive witness to give evidence.

JUDGE. Well, did a Swede visit you?

BASILOVA. Yes, but I don't understand what that has to do with the accused.

JUDGE. The accused sent him to your house.

BASILOVA. It happened like this. Ginzburg rang me up and asked if I wanted to meet a Swedish member of SMOG. Perhaps my husband and I would find him interesting. I asked him . . .

JUDGE (interrupting). Witness, stick to answering the questions asked by the court.

BASILOVA. I can repeat it. Alec Ginzburg told me over the phone that a Swedish member of SMOG had arrived. He asked me if my husband and I were interested. I asked who this Swede was, whether he was a member of SMOG. Was he a poet, an artist, a composer, since SMOG is an essentially creative movement, concerned only with art. In answer Alec Ginzburg told me he didn't know what his profession was, that he himself had not met him and had not talked to him. The Swede himself told me that he had not met Alec, when he arrived at my house. (Guffaws in the courtroom.)

JUDGE. That's enough, witness.

PROCURATOR. In your husband's evidence . . .

BASILOVA (interrupting). I want to make a statement.

JUDGE. Request refused.

BASILOVA. I shall make it all the same. I should like to know by what right the Committee of State Security has reduced my husband, already suffering from a psychological illness, to a state of mental breakdown by persecution, constant surveillance and other such methods; and then to question him in that state? Even worse, to use such evidence in court!

JUDGE (shouting). That is a slander on the organs of State Security. Witness, you will answer for that slander.

BASILOVA. It is not a slander. A doctor has to attend to my husband's condition. As his wife I want to know for what reason my husband was subjected to KGB interrogation, and if the court does not allow me to make a statement, I will take legal action. I want my husband to be left in peace. He is a poet, and the consequences could be very dangerous indeed.

JUDGE. Take the witness away.

ZOLOTUKHIN. I have a question for the witness. What can you tell me about Ginzburg?

BASILOVA. I love and respect Alec Ginzburg very much.

ZOLOTUKHIN. Is your husband registered with a psycho-neurological clinic?

BASILOVA. Yes.

ZOLOTUKHIN. Since when?

BASILOVA. Five or six years ago.

ZOLOTUKHIN. Was his illness diagnosed? What is it?

BASILOVA. Yes. Schizophrenia.

GINZBURG. I have a question. Tell me, witness, in your evidence did you mention the witness Gurevich-Sapgir? When did she visit you—before or after the Swede?

BASILOVA. I never even gave such evidence.

GINZBURG. Did the Swede know Russian or not?

BASILOVA. The Swede knew only 'Hello' and 'Goodbye' in Russian and he knew a little French. So we communicated mostly in silent gestures. It didn't last very long.

JUDGE. Take the witness away. Escort her out.

(In the courtroom noisy interruptions have been going on all the time.)

ZOLOTUKHIN (after Basilova has been led out) makes a statement in which he asks the court not to regard the evidence of the witness Gubanov at the preliminary investigation as wholly reliable even though this evidence figures in the indictment, since his wife, the witness Basilova, has given evidence that her husband is seriously ill mentally and was also in that condition at the preliminary investigation. This can be backed up by medical evidence. Zolotukhin emphasizes that Kaminskaya's request to call Grigorenko as a witness was denied precisely because Grigorenko, according to the report obtained from his psycho-neurological clinic, was mentally ill. Why then was Gubanov's evidence given such prominence, even included in the indictment and made the foundation of one of the episodes Ginzburg was accused in connection with—when Gubanov had been shown to be ill and had been in hospitals many times with the diagnosis of schizophrenia?

JUDGE, after conferring with his colleagues and consulting on the spot with the people's assessors, states that the court considers all this insufficient grounds for the exclusion of Gubanov's evidence from the indictment or from the materials of the case.

INTERROGATION OF THE WITNESS TOPESHKINA*

JUDGE. Tell us what you know of the facts of this case.

TOPESHKINA. I don't know anything about it. Perhaps you could ask me questions?

PROCURATOR. Have you bought an Olivetti typewriter?

TOPESHKINA. Yes.

PROCURATOR. From whom?

TOPESHKINA. From a friend of mine.

PROCURATOR. What is your friend's name?

TOPESHKINA. Stevens.

PROCURATOR. Did you give the typewriter to anyone?

TOPESHKINA. Yes, for a time.

PROCURATOR. To whom and when?

TOPESHKINA. Last autumn.

PROCURATOR. Autumn 1966?

TOPESHKINA. Yes.

PROCURATOR. To whom?

TOPESHKINA. To Timofeyeva.

PROCURATOR. Galanskov's wife?

TOPESHKINA. She wasn't his wife at the time.

PROCURATOR. For whom did you give her the typewriter?

TOPESHKINA. I gave her the typewriter for her friend Lashkova who was working at home . . .

PROCURATOR (interrupting). Why did you give her the typewriter?

TOPESHKINA. I was going to the country for a month, I didn't need it and Lashkova who was working at home . . .

PROCURATOR (interrupting). And what sort of material did Lashkova type on your typewriter?

TOPESHKINA. I don't know. She worked for the university. I don't know what kind of work she was doing.

PROCURATOR. Was the typewriter returned to you?

* Aida Topeshkina, thirty years old, a literary editor, called by the Prosecution.

TOPESHKINA. No.

PROCURATOR. Why?

TOPESHKINA. I was told it was confiscated during a search.

PROCURATOR. At whose house?

TOPESHKINA. I don't know.

PROCURATOR. Look at the accused. Is Lashkova among them? Which is she?

TOPESHKINA. That must be her. There are no other women here.

PROCURATOR. Answer this question. At Galanskov's house a visiting card was found belonging to an official of the Japanese Embassy—Minoru Tamba. Galanskov doesn't know how it got there.

TOPESHKINA. I might have dropped it and left it there.

PROCURATOR. Where did you get it?

TOPESHKINA. I know this man.

PROCURATOR. Why do you think it was you who left it at Galanskov's?

TOPESHKINA. I often visited his house and I sometimes spent the night there, so I could have dropped it.

PROCURATOR. You stated at the preliminary investigation that you met Tamba through an Englishwoman.

TOPESHKINA. Yes.

PROCURATOR. What was her name?

TOPESHKINA. Jill.

PROCURATOR. Did you visit her in Galanskov's company?

TOPESHKINA. Yes, once. There were a lot of people there—about forty.

KAMINSKAYA. You asked Galanskov to accompany you there? Why?

TOPESHKINA. I only asked him to a party—to drink and be happy.

KAMINSKAYA. And did he go there again?

TOPESHKINA. No.

KAMINSKAYA. Did he ask you to take him there again?

TOPESHKINA. No. He is a very shy man. He says that he doesn't like going to such gatherings, he doesn't know the language, feels shy of speaking and also feels bored.

GALANSKOV. Does the person named (Tamba) have any connection with me or with the charges?

TOPESHKINA. No, he's only connected with me.

GALANSKOV. Then why are you answering these unnecessary questions?

JUDGE. They are not unnecessary questions.

GALANSKOV. These irrelevant questions are dragging in another country, one of whose representatives here is the person named . . . (*Laughter in the courtroom.*)

JUDGE (*interrupting Galanskov*). What literature was confiscated from you during the search?

TOPESHKINA. No literature was confiscated from me.

JUDGE. What do you mean by that?

TOPESHKINA. What do you mean by the word 'literature'? Speeches by Sinyavsky and Daniel and a letter by Solzhenitsyn were confiscated from me.

JUDGE. And the 'Letter to an Old Friend'?

TOPESHKINA. I don't remember that one.

JUDGE. But here is your evidence, it's written down here—'Letter to an Old Friend'. You read it and signed it, didn't you?

TOPESHKINA. I don't remember that moment. It is possible to look at the record of the search; everything confiscated from me will be listed in it.

JUDGE. Why must we look at the record of the search? We have the record of your evidence.

TOPESHKINA. I don't remember, I could have confused Solzhenitsyn's letter with 'Letter to an Old Friend'. To clarify this you will have to look at the record of the search.

JUDGE. Where did you obtain the speeches of Sinyavsky and Daniel?

TOPESHKINA. I really don't remember, they were so widely read. I'm studying at the university—there almost everybody has a copy.

ZOLOTUKHIN. How long ago did you obtain them?

TOPESHKINA. I don't remember.

ZOLOTUKHIN. Right after their trial or some time later?

TOPESHKINA. I don't remember. I don't even remember when the trial was.

ZOLOTUKHIN. February 1965.

JUDGE (*to Zolotukhin*). Be accurate. Judging by your questions, dates are important here.

ZOLOTUKHIN. The trial was in February 1966.

KAMINSKAYA. Are you a friend of Galanskov's?

TOPESHKINA. Yes.

KAMINSKAYA. Do you have any children?

TOPESHKINA. Yes, two.

KAMINSKAYA. Did Galanskov help you with them?

TOPESHKINA. Yes, he used to stay with the children and he would collect them from their nursery school in the evening.

KAMINSKAYA. What were Galanskov's material circumstances?

TOPESHKINA. He was very poor—as poor as a church mouse.

KAMINSKAYA. And did his material circumstances change during this last year as far as you noticed? Did he begin to live more comfortably, throw money about?

TOPESHKINA. No. When I wanted to borrow some money from him to buy a coat for one of the children, he got it from his mother, to whom some relatives had sent it for some purchases.

KAMINSKAYA. Did you mention this before?

TOPESHKINA. Nobody asked me about it.

KAMINSKAYA. But in your evidence you say that he helped you.

TOPESHKINA. I've just mentioned a specific occasion when I borrowed thirty-five roubles to buy a coat for one of the children. Unfortunately I was only able to repay the money to his mother six months later.

KAMINSKAYA. Did Galanskov receive any literature from abroad?

TOPESHKINA. No, he didn't. He never gave me anything like that and if he had received anything I would certainly have known about it.

KAMINSKAYA. Are you close friends?

TOPESHKINA. Yes.

KAMINSKAYA. Was Galanskov interested in foreigners? Did foreigners visit him?

TOPESHKINA. No, he wasn't and they didn't. He never spoke to me about anything like that.

KAMINSKAYA. Did he have money in his flat—dollars?

TOPESHKINA. No, he didn't.

JUDGE. Are there any more questions?

GALANSKOV. I want to ask a favour. When you get home, kiss your daughter for me.

JUDGE. You are free to go.

TOPESHKINA. I want to make a statement concerning my evidence at the preliminary investigation.

JUDGE. Here we ask questions. We are not interested in your statements. You can go. (KGB Colonel Tsirkunenko, the Commandant of the court, pushes Topeshkina towards the exit.)

TOPESHKINA. I want to stay. I know that I not only have the right to stay, but it is my obligation.

JUDGE. Don't disrupt the court proceedings. There is no room left, it's stifling in here.

TOPESHKINA. All the same, I want to stay.

TSIRKUNENKO. Stop talking nonsense! Get out!

TOPESHKINA. I won't!

TSIRKUNENKO. Do you want the guards to be called?

TOPESHKINA. Call them! (Shouts from the courtroom—'Go and educate your children! What kind of education will they get? She's lost all honour and conscience! . . .' Tsirkunenko tries to push Topeshkina along.)

TOPESHKINA. Don't you dare touch me!

TSIRKUNENKO. I'm not touching you. You're being told to leave. You must obey the orders of the judge. There are many people here. (Shouts from the courtroom—'We're stifling. There's no room here!')

TOPESHKINA. If you're stifling, get up and give me your seat, but I'm staying. (Shouts from the courtroom—'Just listen to her! She should be looking after her children—but she isn't interested in that!' Topeshkina is led away.)

INTERROGATION OF THE WITNESS DOBROVOLSKAYA*

JUDGE asks which of the accused have visited her house and which of them she knows.

DOBROVOLSKAYA answers that Galanskov and Lashkova visited her, that they did not come often and came separately.

PROCURATOR asks if she knows anything about her husband's criminal activities.

DOBROVOLSKAYA answers that she knows nothing about this, that in any case she saw her husband rarely, since they worked on different shifts and were also both studying at institutes. She only knew that quite often Dobrovolsky was called away from his household chores and studies by various telephone calls and visitors unknown to her.

PROCURATOR asks about the money discovered at Dobrovolsky's flat after a second search.

DOBROVOLSKAYA answers that after the first search she found this money under the mattress of her bed, where her husband had obviously hidden it. This money was intended, as far as she could gather from her husband, for the building of a co-operative flat. Dobrovolsky had told her that he could possibly borrow quite a large sum of money from some friends and add it to the money he

---

* Galina Dobrovolskaya, twenty-seven years old, assistant in a bookshop, wife of Aleksei Dobrovolsky, called by the Prosecution.

had in the flat. It would be possible to build a co-operative flat with this money.

PROCURATOR asks if Dobrovolsky ever talked to her about the NTS or any such organization.

DOBROVOLSKAYA answers that she never had any conversations with her husband on such subjects.

JUDGE asks the witness to describe her husband's character.

DOBROVOLSKAYA says that Dobrovolsky is a very religious person, that he began to believe in God after he was released from the labour-camp, that Dobrovolsky has a wonderful relationship with his son.

JUDGE. Does the defence have any questions?

KAMINSKAYA. Please, tell me, Dobrovolskaya, did you write two letters to the KGB asking them to return the money confiscated in the search?

DOBROVOLSKAYA. Yes, I did.

KAMINSKAYA. Did you write one letter or many?

DOBROVOLSKAYA. I wrote two letters.

KAMINSKAYA. Tell me exactly what you wrote in these letters.

DOBROVOLSKAYA. I wrote in these letters that the money confiscated during the search at our flat belonged to Lyosha [*i.e. Dobrovolsky*] and that he must have borrowed it from someone. Besides that, in explaining where we could have got that kind of money, I wrote that Lyosha had recently inherited some.

SHVEISKY. Tell me, please, could Dobrovolsky have saved such a sum of money by himself on fifty roubles a month?

DOBROVOLSKAYA. No, he couldn't have.

ARIYA. Tell me, witness, do you have many ikons in your flat?

DOBROVOLSKAYA. Two ikons.

JUDGE. How can that be? Dobrovolsky collects ikons and you only have two in the flat?

DOBROVOLSKAYA. Two large ones and also some small ikons.

JUDGE. When did Dobrovolsky begin collecting ikons?

DOBROVOLSKAYA. I don't know exactly. I can't say.

JUDGE asks if she had noticed anything strange in her husband's behaviour.

DOBROVOLSKAYA. Yes, I did. He crossed himself, fasted and prayed.

JUDGE. Do the accused have any questions?

DOBROVOLSKY. Galya, what did the money you found under the mattress look like?

DOBROVOLSKAYA. It was in an envelope.

PROCURATOR. Was it a foreign envelope?

DOBROVOLSKAYA answers that it was a Soviet envelope. It had some numbers written on it. She explains that Dobrovolsky must have been calculating the amount of money inside and writing the total sum on the envelope.

DOBROVOLSKY asks if the money in the envelope was wrapped in paper.

DOBROVOLSKAYA. It was.

DOBROVOLSKY states that a criminological analysis of that paper had given the same result as an analysis of the paper the hectograph was wrapped in and also of the paper on which the newspaper *Possev* [found in his flat] was printed.

PROCURATOR. Tell me, witness, does this mean that the paper the money was wrapped in was NTS paper?

DOBROVOLSKAYA (confused). No, not NTS paper. . . .

PROCURATOR. I have finished.

DOBROVOLSKAYA. May I stay?

DOBROVOLSKY. I request that my wife be allowed to stay.

JUDGE. You may remain in the courtroom.*

INTERROGATION OF THE WITNESS TIMOFEYEVA†

JUDGE asks the witness to tell everything she knows of the matter in question.

TIMOFEYEVA says she met Galanskov about three months before his arrest. She only got to know of her daughter's intention of marrying him on about 20 December, a week before the marriage was registered. On 30 December she was invited to her daughter's wedding at the Galanskovs' house, where she talked for the first time to Galanskov, as before that she had only seen him two or three times. He had given her the impression of being a very shy person. They didn't have much of a conversation. She didn't know anything else about the business. (While giving her evidence she keeps looking at Galanskov.)

GALANSKOV. Witness, you should look at the judges while giving evidence.

KAMINSKAYA. Tell me, please, where did your daughter live after her marriage with Galanskov?

---

* G. Dobrovolskaya was allowed to stay, not as a witness but as the wife of one of the accused.

† Olga Timofeyeva, forty-five years old, Master of biological sciences, mother of Olga Timofeyeva (wife of Yury Galanskov), called by the Prosecution.

TIMOFEYEVA. With Galanskov, at his flat.

KAMINSKAYA. You have been in his flat. Can you describe the living conditions which your daugher shared with her husband?

TIMOFEYEVA. The conditions were awful. They left a terrible impression on me.

KAMINSKAYA. Did you have any conversation with your daughter in which you offered to help them to better their conditions?

TIMOFEYEVA. Yes indeed, we did have such a conversation. My husband and I were prepared to give them the money to build a co-operative flat, but only after they had lived happily together for about a year.

GALANSKOV. And if we had lived unhappily for that year, would you still have given us the money?

TIMOFEYEVA. In that case, of course not.

JUDGE asks if there are any more questions, and allows the witness to leave.

INTERROGATION OF THE WITNESS BROX-SOKOLOV*

JUDGE. Do you understand Russian?

BROX. Yes, I do.

JUDGE. What is your name?

BROX. Nicolas Borisovich Brox-Sokolov.

JUDGE. Your nationality?

BROX. Venezuelan.

JUDGE. Your place of residence?

BROX. In recent years—France.

JUDGE. You have been summoned to this court as a witness. Do you understand me?

BROX. Yes.

JUDGE. What is your native language?

BROX. Spanish.

JUDGE. Is an interpreter present?

SECRETARY. Yes.

JUDGE. The interpreter's name?

INTERPRETER. Yury Vasilievich Kirsanov.

JUDGE. Your level of education?

INTERPRETER. Higher education.

JUDGE. You have been summoned to this court as an interpreter.

---

* Nicolas Brox-Sokolov, twenty-one years old, a student, citizen of Venezuela, called by the Prosecution.

You will be held personally responsible if you are proved to have given a false translation. Do you understand?

INTERPRETER. Yes.

JUDGE (to Brox). You must tell the court anything that interests it. By the laws of our country you will be held criminally responsible if you give false evidence. (To the interpreter) Translate everything I have said into Spanish. He must tell the court that he understands this warning.

INTERPRETER begins to translate.

BROX interrupts him, saying that he has understood everything and will henceforth do without an interpreter.

PROCURATOR. The witness will tell us when and for what reason he came to the Soviet Union.

BROX. I flew here in an aeroplane on 23 December, arriving at about 8 o'clock in the evening. I came as a tourist.

PROCURATOR. Tell us what the NTS gave you to deliver here before your flight from Paris to Moscow.

BROX. I received five letters, five envelopes and two parcels.

PROCURATOR. Who gave you these?

BROX. A member of the organization called Zhenya.

PROCURATOR. You were to deliver these things to someone in the Soviet Union?

BROX. Yes, but I should like to add that I was to post the five envelopes and deliver the two parcels to someone.

PROCURATOR. Who gave you the name of the person you were to deliver the parcels to?

BROX. Another member of the organization who was in Paris at the time—called Victor.

PROCURATOR. When you say 'the organization', do you mean the NTS?

BROX. Yes.

PROCURATOR. What circumstances made you realize that Zhenya who gave you the two parcels and the envelopes came from the Federal German Republic?

BROX. In Paris on 11 December when Zhenya was talking to Victor, I heard that Zhenya had come from the Federal German Republic and was due to leave again the next day. The following day in the morning I met Victor again and he told me that he had just been to see Zhenya off at the station.

PROCURATOR. Did Zhenya say this in your presence?

BROX. Yes.

PROCURATOR. You overheard him?

162

BROX. I did.

PROCURATOR. Which town did Zhenya come from?

BROX. I don't know.

PROCURATOR. From what part of Germany?

BROX. From West Germany.

PROCURATOR. Tell me, were you given money?

BROX. I saw the money when I was arrested.

PROCURATOR. Were you given a special belt?

BROX. Yes.

PROCURATOR. You carried the parcels and the envelopes in the belt?

BROX. Yes. On 21 December, when I arrived in Paris, I was introduced to Zhenya. Victor met me at the station. There was also another member present, who had brought the special belt with him in which he had placed the two parcels. Zhenya came to see me in the hotel. He was wearing the belt with the two parcels and five envelopes in it.

PROCURATOR. And you put all this into your belt beneath your clothes?

BROX. Yes. When I met him on 21 December Zhenya told me he had brought this special belt for wearing beneath my clothes, so that the parcels wouldn't be seen.

PROCURATOR. Did you know what the parcels contained?

BROX. No. I was merely asked to deliver them out of friendship. Only in Moscow, when they were opened, did I realize they contained 3000 roubles, a hectograph and materials for cryptography.

JUDGE. Come here and look at these—are these the parcels?

BROX (looking). Yes.

PROCURATOR. Where were you arrested in Moscow?

BROX. In the Sokolniki Park.

PROCURATOR. Tell us what you know about Michael Slavinsky[66] whose lecture you attended in Grenoble.

BROX. When I was in Grenoble, I got a letter from an acquaintance inviting me to a lecture—this was at the beginning of June 1967. The person who wrote the letter said he got my address from Slavinsky. I didn't understand how Slavinsky could have known it, as I didn't know him at all. I was introduced to Slavinsky in the following way. The lecture was called 'Underground Literature in the Soviet Union'. After the lecture there was an exhibition of the works mentioned in the lecture. The next day I met Slavinsky again in a café. In November I met a certain girl. After we had been talking for some time, she asked me who this Mr Slavinsky was. I had seen

163

this woman before in the student hostel at Grenoble. She came to the university in November and said she would like to have a talk with me. We went to a café and there we talked. She said she was a representative of, or had been sent by, the NTS. It was then that I understood many other things which I hadn't understood till then. I realized that there was some connection between this meeting and the previous events. Then I asked the following question—'Who is Mr Slavinsky?' And she told me that he was an important figure in the Paris organization of the NTS.

PROCURATOR. What was this girl's name?

BROX. Tamara Volkova.

PROCURATOR. And what did you hear from Slavinsky and other representatives of NTS about Ginzburg, Galanskov and Dobrovolsky?

BROX. When I was listening to Slavinsky's lecture he mentioned the names of Ginzburg, Galanskov and Dobrovolsky.

PROCURATOR. And did Slavinsky say anything about *The White Book* in his lecture?

BROX. He said the NTS had received this book.

PROCURATOR. What other periodicals did Slavinsky mention in his lecture and which of them were shown in the exhibition?

BROX. During the lecture he mentioned *Phoenix-'61, Phoenix-'66, Sphinxes, The Bell, Syntax* and others that I don't recall at the moment. I remember only *Phoenix* from the ones at the exhibition.

PROCURATOR. What periodicals did you get from the NTS and what was published in them?

BROX. When I met Tamara Volkova in November 1967 she left me a small pamphlet which I think was the programme and statutes of the NTS and also the periodical *Grani*. I think *The White Book* was published in *Grani*.

PROCURATOR. Tell us, how many envelopes did you receive from the representatives of NTS and what was in them?

BROX. I received five envelopes. In each envelope there were five photographs—of Ginzburg, Galanskov, Dobrovolsky, Sinyavsky and Daniel and a leaflet from the publication *Possev*.

GINZBURG asks the court for the leaflet to be read out.

JUDGE refuses, saying it will be attached to the case materials and that the accused will soon be able to acquaint themselves with it.

The defence and the accused ask the court to allow them to acquaint themselves with all the material evidence. The court grants their request and they all peruse the photographs and leaflets.

PROCURATOR. Were addresses written on the envelopes?

BROX. Yes, they had on them the addresses of the senders and the addressees.

PROCURATOR. Were the addresses those of people living abroad or here in Moscow?

BROX. Here in Moscow.

PROCURATOR (showing him the photographs). Are these the photographs?

BROX. Yes. I've looked at them and read the writing on the backs —it says the same thing in four different languages.

PROCURATOR. You were supposed to post the envelopes in post-boxes?

BROX. At first I was told it would be necessary to post them in different post-boxes. I refused and said I would post them all in one post-box.

PROCURATOR. And they agreed that you should post them all in one post-box in Moscow?

BROX. Yes, in Moscow.

JUDGE. Does the defence have any questions?

KAMINSKAYA. No.

PROCURATOR. I ask that Dobrovolsky be shown the hectograph and cryptography paper. Look at them and tell me if they resemble the hectograph and cryptography paper Galanskov gave you?

DOBROVOLSKY. Yes. Exactly the same kinds of hectograph and paper were confiscated from me.

PROCURATOR. Of course, as all NTS hectographs are identical. Who gave them to you?

DOBROVOLSKY. Galanskov.

PROCURATOR. Lashkova, look at this paper for invisible writing confiscated from Brox. Tell me, is this the same sort of paper on which you wrote the letter abroad?

LASHKOVA. Yes, the same paper.

KAMINSKAYA. I have a question for Lashkova. Who brought you that paper?

JUDGE. That question has already been asked.

KAMINSKAYA. Comrade State Prosecutor has just asked Dobrovolsky a similar question, as to who gave him the hectograph. Dobrovolsky has just answered it. I am asking Lashkova a similar question.

JUDGE. Very well, then.

LASHKOVA. Dobrovolsky brought me the paper.

KAMINSKAYA. I have no further questions.

JUDGE. The witness is free to go.

GALANSKOV. I have a question for the witness. Can you tell us, witness, the addresses you were supposed to send the envelopes to?

BROX. I know the addresses were written on the envelopes. . . .

JUDGE. That will do.

GALANSKOV. Can you tell me, witness, how much money you brought with you?

JUDGE. You already know it was 3000 roubles.

GALANSKOV. Was there 3000 roubles in each parcel or in all the parcels taken together?

JUDGE. That question is irrelevant.

BROX. I should like to make a statement.

JUDGE. Please do.

BROX. I shall try not to take up too much of your time. I considered Ginzburg, Galanskov and Dobrovolsky as writers. In the French papers they were described as writers. Therefore I thought Ginzburg, Galanskov and Dobrovolsky were young writers who had been put in jail and that they had been treated unjustly. That was all I gathered from the press. My opinion was that they worked as writers. I only realized in November that Tamara Volkova belonged to the NTS. In the meanwhile the papers had written something about this trial. She asked me if I would like to help in some way —she knew that I intended to go to Moscow in December. At the beginning of December I met Tamara Volkova in Paris. She met me on my arrival at the station. She was accompanied by a man whom she introduced to me. I asked how I could help these young writers. They told me I would have to send five letters and perhaps a small parcel or two. One day before my departure I was told what I had to do. At that time I was in a position where I really couldn't refuse to take the parcels. It would have been embarrassing. The man I was told to meet here in Moscow, they told me, was someone who could perhaps help the young writers who were here under arrest. But now I realize I was deceived and deceived twice. The first time, when they told me that these people were writers. During this trial I have noticed that they are being tried not for what they wrote but for their ties with the NTS. And secondly, they told me the parcels contained only instructions and some material that could perhaps help them. When I was arrested, it turned out that the contents were not what they said. The parcels contained money, a hectograph, cryptography paper; all kinds of things—not at all what they had told me. I would like to say that I am sorry I involuntarily broke the laws of this country. My motive for wanting to visit this country was the wish to get to know the land where my parents were born. That was my only motive.

GINZBURG asks the court if the photographs found in the envelopes and the leaflet from the publication *Possev* are to be attached to the case materials.

JUDGE answers that until all the accused have finished looking at these documents, they will be at their disposal. Asks if there are any more questions for the witness and then orders him to be led away.*

INTERROGATION OF THE WITNESS SIMONOVA†

JUDGE asks the witness if she would like to make a statement.

SIMONOVA requests the court to ask her questions.

KAMINSKAYA asks questions concerning Galanskov's mental state.

SIMONOVA answers that during the time they lived together she noticed some eccentricities in Galanskov's behaviour: he was often irritable, he once brought home some sort of a stone, he was capable of breaking a lamp or anything else for no reason.

THE EXPERT LUNTS (henceforth referred to as LUNTS) asks if there were any witnesses besides herself who had noticed such strange incidents.

SIMONOVA answers that there were no other witnesses, she was alone. (Guffaws in the courtroom, shouts of 'Some were smuggled in'.)

LUNTS. And what did you do when this happened?

SIMONOVA. I cried. (Guffaws in the courtroom.)

JUDGE. Do you wish to tell the court anything else?

SIMONOVA. No.

JUDGE. You are free to go.

INTERROGATION OF THE WITNESS PINSKY‡

JUDGE asks the witness to tell everything he knows about the case.

PINSKY says that he can only describe Ginzburg's character. He met Ginzburg in 1962. They were drawn to each other through a common interest in literature. He considered Ginzburg a very

---

* As Brox-Sokolov was under arrest awaiting trial he was led into the courtroom under guard.

† Galina Simonova, twenty-seven years old, office worker, first wife of Yu. Galanskov, called at the request of Galanskov's lawyer.

‡ Leonid Efimovich Pinsky, sixty years old, literary critic, member of the USSR Writers' Union, called at the request of Ginzburg's lawyer.

interesting person, well-read and discerning about literature. He also knew Ginzburg to be an extremely honest person, sincere and upright. In his opinion Ginzburg could not have done anything dishonourable or dishonest.

JUDGE asks if anyone wants to question the witness, and then offers him a seat in the courtroom.*

> After this the Judge, having consulted the assessors, reads out the order of the next day's proceedings: the interrogation of the remaining witnesses, the interrogation of the expert, the speech for the Prosecution and speeches of the defence counsels. He asks the lawyers if they have questions for the expert and requests them to submit the questions in written form the following day. He then declares the court adjourned until 11 January at 10.00 hours. The court session of 10 January ends at 21.30 hours.

11 January

> The court sitting begins at 10.00 hours with further interrogation of witnesses.

INTERROGATION OF THE WITNESS STOLYAROVA†

JUDGE. What can you tell us about this matter?

STOLYAROVA. Please ask me questions.

JUDGE. When did you meet Ginzburg?

STOLYAROVA. Soon after Ginzburg's release from his first term of imprisonment. He came to see Ehrenburg,[67] whose secretary I was at that time, to thank him as a deputy for obtaining a Moscow residence permit for him.

PROCURATOR. Did he visit Ehrenburg after that?

STOLYAROVA. Yes. He visited Ehrenburg in November 1966 to consult him about the collection of documents he was working on about Sinyavsky and Daniel. He brought the manuscript, or separate documents, which he wanted to show him.

PROCURATOR. In your conversation with Comrade Eliseyev.‡ you said he brought a manuscript.

* The next day L. E. Pinsky was not allowed into the courtroom.

† Natalya Ivanovna Stolyarova, fifty-five years old, an interpreter, called by the Prosecution.

‡ This refers to Stolyarova's evidence at the preliminary investigation. Eliseyev is a KGB investigator.

STOLYAROVA. Yes, but I said at the time that I was not present during their conversation and that Ginzburg came with a parcel which I assumed contained a manuscript.

ZOLOTUKHIN. What was Ehrenburg's attitude to this work?

STOLYAROVA. He told me afterwards there was something he didn't like.

ZOLOTUKHIN. Do you know what it was exactly he didn't like?

STOLYAROVA. He didn't like the fact that Ginzburg had included excerpts from the bourgeois right-wing press instead of the well-known letter by Aragon and the statements of the left-wing intelligentsia, which in Ehrenburg's opinion would have more influence on our society. According to Ehrenburg, Ginzburg replied to this reproach by saying he would have been pleased to use these statements, but the left-wing papers in which they were published had not been on sale in our country.

JUDGE. You remember your conversation with Eliseyev? Here is the record of your evidence, signed by you, in which you say that no corrections or clarifications will be necessary.

STOLYAROVA. Yes, of course I remember.

JUDGE. You said then that you didn't know why Ehrenburg disapproved of Ginzburg's manuscript.

STOLYAROVA. That's quite true. But when I went back to work after that conversation I immediately asked Ehrenburg what he didn't like about Ginzburg's work and I received a reply.

ZOLOTUKHIN. Did Ginzburg tell you what he was going to do with this work when it was finished?

STOLYAROVA. Yes, he said he wanted to send it to the Supreme Court and also, I think, to the Supreme Soviet and other top-level institutions. He hoped he would be able in this way to better the lot of Sinyavsky and Daniel.

ZOLOTUKHIN. What was your relationship with Ginzburg?

STOLYAROVA. We were close friends.

ZOLOTUKHIN. What is your opinion of him?

STOLYAROVA. I consider him to be a very honest man, brave, talented and, most of all, a patriot—a real patriot, not a false one.

JUDGE. You are free to go.

STOLYAROVA. Permit me to stay in the hall.

JUDGE. You cannot, there are no seats left.

STOLYAROVA. There are some empty seats in the back rows.

JUDGE. Some more people will be coming soon. There's no room for you.

GINZBURG. I support Stolyarova's request.

JUDGE (shouting). Ginzburg! (To Stolyarova) You have been told there are no free places. You can leave. Comrade Commandant, escort Comrade Stolyarova out.

At this point the interrogation of the witnesses comes to an end. The Judge asks the Procurator, the defence lawyers and the accused to submit any questions they have in written form to the court's medical expert. Kaminskaya and Shveisky read out questions concerning the mental stability of their clients. The court refuses some questions. Then the expert Lunts is called on to speak.

STATEMENT OF THE EXPERT LUNTS*

In the opinion of the expert Lunts, all the accused are of sound mind. He spends quite a long time on the sanity of Galanskov and Dobrovolsky, saying that although they have both at various times been compelled to have treatment and have been registered at psycho-neurological clinics, the latest diagnoses on them by the Serbsky Institute of Forensic Psychiatry show that Galanskov is undoubtedly of sound mind and Dobrovolsky is likewise of sound mind, though the latter had also been noted as a psychopathic personality.

The defence argues with Lunts, citing previous medical diagnoses on Galanskov and Dobrovolsky, and the definition of schizophrenia given by Lunts himself in his textbook on forensic psychiatry. Lunts answers that the previous diagnoses were not correct and that in any case the condition of the accused could have changed since then. As for his definition of schizophrenia, it had become out of date. After this he asks the court if it has any further need of him and asks permission to leave. The Judge, after consulting with his colleagues, allows him to leave.

JUDGE asks if the State Procurator, the defence counsels or the accused have any requests or anything further to add.

PROCURATOR states that he has no requests to make.

THE DEFENCE COUNSELS ask for the right to base their speeches for the defence on the material evidence and to quote from some of the documents. They name the documents required.

JUDGE grants their request.

KAMINSKAYA asks permission to question Lashkova.

* Daniil Romanovich Lunts, professor of the Serbsky Institute of Forensic Psychiatry. To avoid errors only a short summary of Lunts's statement and questioning by the defence is given here because they were not recorded verbatim.

JUDGE. Please do.

KAMINSKAYA. Vera, don't you really remember the date of the party at Svetlana Potasheva's?

LASHKOVA. I can't remember the date exactly. (Thinks it over.) I remember that Galanskov and Olga had a conversation in which they mentioned it was her mother's birthday the following day.

KAMINSKAYA. Yura, do you remember the date of your mother-in-law's birthday?

GALANSKOV. Of course. 23 October.

LASHKOVA. May I make a statement?

JUDGE. Please do.

LASHKOVA. I insist that the conversation with Dobrovolsky about buying a car took place and ask for this to be included in the record.

JUDGE. Very well. Any more requests? I declare the judicial investigation over. I call on the State Prosecutor.

SPEECH OF THE STATE PROSECUTOR*

The Procurator devotes the first half of his speech mainly to a description of the NTS: its history, aims and methods, biographies of its leaders, sometimes quoting word for word phrases from the article 'The Depths' (*Izvestia*, 9 January 1968). He declares that the NTS is backed by the American Government and is a sub-department of the CIA, to whose authority it was transferred by the British Intelligence after the war. He states that the court has available a KGB report on the NTS being one of the sub-departments of the CIA. Later he talks of the connections existing between all the accused and the NTS, repeating the arguments in the indictment and also referring to the evidence of Mikulinskaya and Schaffhauser, which did not figure in the case. At this point he calls Ginzburg 'the leader of a secret NTS group in Moscow'. He speaks of Ginzburg and Galanskov compiling slanderous and biased collections including anti-Soviet documents, and of the accused receiving and circulating anti-Soviet literature. He refers a lot to the evidence of Dobrovolsky, emphasizing that Galanskov's statements about giving false evidence at the preliminary investigation in order to shield Dobrovolsky are false. In reality, according to the Procurator, Dobrovolsky in a previous secret conversation with Galanskov was to have shielded

---

* G. A. Terekhov, forty-five years old, senior assistant to the Procurator-General of the USSR. As the Procurator's speech was confiscated from the people who wrote it down before they left the courtroom, it is given here (to avoid the possibility of error) in the most abbreviated form. The speech lasted for about an hour and a half.

Galanskov, for which Galanskov promised to pay him 600 roubles. Later he dwells on the characters of the accused, saying that they had taken part in anti-social activities previously and had not wanted to follow the path of correction, even though they had had many opportunities of doing so. He speaks of the anti-Soviet opinions expressed by Galanskov and Ginzburg. Near the end he dwells on the sale of dollars by Galanskov through Entin and Borisova.

The Procurator considers the guilt of the accused to be proved and asks for the following sentences to be passed:

(a) On Galanskov, who was instrumental in establishing direct ties with the NTS, who took part in anti-Soviet incitement and propaganda, and who neither admitted his guilt nor repented his crimes—a sentence of seven years in a strict-regime labour camp under article 70, paragraph 1, and three years in a labour camp under article 88, paragraph 1, of the Russian Criminal Code; the latter sentence to run concurrently with the first.

(b) On Ginzburg, who maintained ties with the NTS and took part in anti-Soviet incitement and propaganda, who neither admitted his guilt nor repented his crimes—a sentence of five years in a strict-regime labour camp under article 70, paragraph 1, of the Russian Criminal Code.

(c) On Dobrovolsky, who was enticed into connections with the NTS by Galanskov, who did not play an active part, who admitted his guilt and repented of his crimes—a sentence of two years in a strict-regime labour camp under article 70, paragraph 1, of the Russian Criminal Code.

(d) On Lashkova, who acted under the influence of Ginzburg and Galanskov, did not play an active part, admitted her guilt and repented of her crimes—a sentence of one year in a strict-regime labour camp under article 70, paragraph 1, of the Russian Criminal Code.

(Stormy applause in the courtroom, shouts of 'Too little!')

Half an hour's recess is declared. Then the sitting is resumed.

JUDGE. The speech in defence of the accused Dobrovolsky will be made by defence counsel Shveisky.

SPEECH OF DEFENCE COUNSEL SHVEISKY*

Dobrovolsky has admitted his guilt in full, so I shall dwell only on the facts which could help his actions to be rightly judged.

* Vladimir Yakovlevich Shveisky, forty-five years old, member of the Moscow Collegium of Defence Lawyers.

Dobrovolsky says that he emerged as a thinking personality at a period of a general rethinking of values caused by the exposure of Stalin's cult of personality. As he was still a very young man at that time, and also politically immature, he regarded the events that had taken place very subjectively. When he emerged from this re-evaluation he tried to find the answers to the questions worrying him. In the end this led him to the dock. In 1958 Dobrovolsky was sentenced for making anti-Soviet statements. On his return from the camps, where he had been in the company of others like himself, he brought his mind to bear even more on the darker side of our way of life. He concentrated on questions which, in his opinion, were being decided unjustly in our life.

So much for Dobrovolsky's own explanations.

In this connection I wish to emphasize that no mistakes, errors or opinions can in themselves form the basis for bringing someone to trial. Article 125 of the Soviet Constitution gives a perfectly clear guide in that respect. It clearly states that the citizens of the Soviet Union are guaranteed the following by law: freedom of speech and the press, freedom of assembly and public meetings, freedom to hold street processions and demonstrations.

The actions of Dobrovolsky—the storing and circulation of NTS literature—are a different matter. The anti-Soviet character of this organization and the 'works' it publishes is quite obvious. It would be enough to read out the book confiscated from Dobrovolsky —Trushnovich's *At the Price of a Spiritual Feat.* It contains a direct call for a crusade against the Soviet Union, for the overthrow of its established system, and for the restoration of Russia. It is quite obvious that the circulation of such literature is contrary to our understanding of freedom of speech as this is directly harmful to our state.

The yearning of the Soviet people for increased democracy and a more important part for the citizen to play in the political and social life of our country is natural and legitimate yearning. This is now one of our most pressing tasks. It is, so to speak, Task No. 1. Without resolving it we shall not be able to resolve our other tasks. It was this that L. I. Brezhnev spoke of in his recent speech on the fiftieth anniversary of the Soviet state, when he emphasized that 'the perfecting of social relations, the development of socialist democracy and government, ideological and educational work—all this is one of our first and most important tasks'.

The creation of conditions for the many-sided development of the personality now assumes a particular significance. It is quite obvious that the Soviet people will not permit any return to violations of socialist legality and is determined to fight for the further development of democracy. But the storing and circulation of NTS literature by Dobrovolsky has nothing in common with this fight. Dobrovolsky, too, realizes this now. That is why he called his actions criminal in relation to his Fatherland and people. However, when sentence is pronounced I beg you to think also about the events of the past which had a great effect on the formation of the accused Dobrovolsky's opinions and on his actions.

There are two more circumstances which had a great influence on the behaviour of my client.

When he was still a pupil at school, serious deficiencies in his mental development were noticed. In connection with this, he was placed at the age of seventeen in a psychiatric hospital, where it was established that he was a psychopathic personality.

In the last few years Dobrovolsky has been placed more than once in a psychiatric hospital, where he has been diagnosed as a schizophrenic. In 1964, in connection with his new arrest, he was examined at the Serbsky Psychiatric Institute and was judged to be of unsound mind. Acting on this conclusion, the court committed him for compulsory treatment. He returned from the period of treatment only in the middle of 1965 and already in the first quarter of the following year [1966] he was again placed in a psychiatric hospital. He was there for two months and was diagnosed as having 'schizophrenia in a psychotic form'. The last diagnosis, carried out at the beginning of 1967 during the preliminary investigation, although pronouncing Dobrovolsky to be of sound mind, also declared him to be a psychopathic personality.

Naturally a person in such a state could not correctly interpret or evaluate the complex events of social and state life which were going on around him, nor his own place in these events. Dobrovolsky's psychopathic character showed itself above all in his typical moods of depression and despair. Thus a one-sided prejudice in his evaluation of events and facts was a natural consequence of the peculiarities of this psychopathic personality.

A strong influence in what happened to Dobrovolsky was his religious convictions. I would not touch on this question if it were not directly relevant to what happened. When Dobrovolsky got hold of 'An Account of the Events at the Pochayev Monastery Today'—an article written by monks telling of the crudest violations of the law allowed by certain local government officials—it made Dobrovolsky very angry. Before this, Dobrovolsky had written an article 'The Relationship between Knowledge and Faith', and was himself planning to enter a monastery. On receiving the monks' letter, Dobrovolsky believed completely in its trustworthiness and ran to Vera Lashkova's in order to duplicate it, circulate it and bring it to the attention of society.

In the indictment this letter from the monks, addressed to the leaders of our government, is described as a slanderous, anti-Soviet document. I strongly protest against that description.

Firstly, we do not possess any document telling us that the facts described in the letter have been investigated by anyone and proved to be false. Secondly, the monks' letter expresses a protest against specific violations of Soviet laws and there is nothing in it attacking Soviet power as the political foundation of our state. Thirdly, to regard this document as anti-Soviet merely because it contains criticisms of officials who allowed illegalities to take place would mean the suppression of criticism by the threat of a criminal trial for anti-Soviet propaganda.

As I have already said, Dobrovolsky took the letter to Vera Lashkova. Galanskov then received a copy through her. This led to Dobrovolsky's friendship with Galanskov. Knowing that the latter was working on producing the miscellany *Phoenix*, in which it was possible also to include the monks' letter and his own article, Dobrovolsky began to help Galanskov actively. Thus the partnership between these two began, to end in the arrest of both of them.

Dobrovolsky has stated here in court that his arrest was an escape from the double loyalties he was suffering in his life. In a letter written by Dobrovolsky to his family from prison he mentions a Greek poet who wrote about the sort of existence suffered by the shades of the dead who were barred both from heaven and from hell. Cursing their fate they wander on the banks of Charon.* No ray of light reaches them. Dobrovolsky writes that he finds himself in a similar position.

Dobrovolsky is now looking at the court with hope. Allow me to end my speech in defence of the accused Dobrovolsky also with hope.

JUDGE. The speech in defence of the accused Lashkova will be made by defence counsel Ariya.

* Here Dobrovolsky and also his defence lawyer make a mistake. Charon, in ancient Greek mythology, was not the name of an underworld river, but the name of the ferryman who carried the souls of the dead over the river of hell.

SPEECH OF DEFENCE COUNSEL ARIYA*

The Procurator in his speech made some new accusations against Lashkova which were not made against her earlier: indeterminate references to some kind of anti-social activity before 1966, references to some kind of connections with the NTS, the handing over of anti-Soviet literature to Lyudmila Kats.

There is no basis for such accusations in the case materials. There are no such charges in the indictment.

The Procurator in his speech went beyond the limits of the charges made against Lashkova. That is a violation of the law. Therefore the defence will not dwell on these accusations and will confine itself to discussing the charges made in the indictment.

The law considers anti-Soviet incitement and propaganda as one of the gravest crimes against the state. I consider that Lashkova is not a particularly grave offender against the state and cannot be judged according to article 70 of the Russian Criminal Code. Neither anti-Soviet intent nor anti-Soviet actions have been established in her case. And as regards her character as a whole, Lashkova cannot be considered a dangerous criminal.

This statement by the defence is based on a careful analysis both of the law and of the case materials. For this analysis to be truly correct, it is necessary above all to achieve a precise juridical definition of criminal anti-Soviet agitation and propaganda. If this is not strictly and correctly defined, then despite the requirements of legality, which is necessary to society, any critical statement, any expression of dissent, any criticism of government institutions, of people in authority or particular measures, could be made a reason for individual repression. We cannot help but notice this important fact—that the correct understanding of anti-Soviet agitation and propaganda in our law and judicial practice has undergone a historical change, and only in the sense of becoming more restricted in its application, not broader.

Article 58, paragraph 10, of the 1926 Criminal Code did not consider counter-revolutionary intent to be a necessary condition of criminal responsibility under this article. In other words, article 58, paragraph 10, of the 1926 Criminal Code made liable for conviction not only those who had wanted to harm the social and political system but also those who, having no counter-revolutionary intentions, knowingly admitted the possibility of such harm. This was a very broad understanding of a crime and was reaffirmed in the

* Semyon Lvovich Ariya, fifty years old, member of the Moscow Collegium of Defence Lawyers.

1928 Resolution of the USSR Supreme Soviet plenary session, 'On Direct and Indirect Intent in Counter-revolutionary Crimes'. And though ten years later, in 1938, the Supreme Soviet revoked this resolution, in judicial practice arraignment under article 58, paragraph 10, of the Criminal Code continued to be used in cases not only of direct but also of indirect intent.

In 1960 the new Criminal Code, in the text of article 70, stipulated direct anti-Soviet intent as a necessary condition of guilt under this article. That is the present position of the law with regard to intent.

The field of activities carrying a charge of anti-Soviet agitation and propaganda has narrowed even more obviously.

I will cite only one example. In the commentary to the 1926 Criminal Code there is a directive by the Presidium of the Russian Supreme Soviet (1934) that an appeal to others by lazy kolkhoz workers not to go to work on the collective farm must be considered as counter-revolutionary agitation. In our time such a directive would seem extreme and inappropriate.

In a certain scientific textbook published two years ago (there is no need to quote from it) we can read that the authors consider it impossible to arraign someone for an anti-Soviet crime for such acts as (a) offensive criticism of leading figures, (b) relating political jokes, (c) recounting hostile radio broadcasts, etc.

Thus, during the fifty years of Soviet power the concept of criminal anti-Soviet agitation and propaganda has narrowed sharply as regards both intent and nature of the activity.

And this is natural, for with the growth and strengthening of the Soviet state's power and might, attacks on it in speech or print have grown less dangerous for it.

The text of the law is the only correct criterion by which it can be judged what constitutes a crime. No arbitrary nor, much more, any broadening or elastic interpretation of the law is permissible.

Article 70 of the Russian Criminal Code sets out precisely the necessary elements constituting a crime: (a) direct anti-Soviet intent, i.e. the aim of subverting or weakening Soviet power; (b) proven slander, i.e. the obviously slanderous character of the information being spread; (c) directing of the slander against the Soviet social or political system (specifically against the system, not against particular institutions, people or measures). It is quite obvious that the notion 'system' may only include in its meaning what is clearly defined in chapters 1 and 2 of the Soviet Constitution, i.e. (1) the vesting of state power in the Soviets; (2) a socialist economic system and socialist ownership of the means of production; (3) labour as an honour and a duty for every citizen physically capable of work; (4) the leading role of the Communist Party; (5) the federal character of the state and the sovereignty of the Union republics; (6) a single citizenship for all Soviet citizens.

This is how the foundation of our law—the Soviet Constitution— defines our system of society and government. It follows that any attempts to include in the definition of 'system' anything not mentioned in the Constitution, and in this way to widen the interpretation of article 70 of the Criminal Code, must be regarded as an arbitrary and elastic interpretation not based on the law.

Starting from a precise, clear-cut formulation of the actual definition of the crime we must also evaluate the actions with which Lashkova is charged.

Above all it is impossible not to pay attention to the following circumstances. While all the other accused have to defend themselves against the accusation that they acted 'out of anti-Soviet sentiments', no one has accused Lashkova of anti-Soviet sentiments. Thus the charge against her can be formulated thus: although not anti-Soviet in attitude, Lashkova typed criminal texts and in two cases handed on criminal pamphlets.

From this, even without analysing the separate points of the indictment, it follows clearly that Lashkova had no anti-Soviet aims, that she had no directly anti-Soviet intentions such as are stipulated as a condition of conviction under article 70 of the Criminal Code. And this is not merely a chance omission in the charges against Lashkova. No evidence exists in the records of this trial showing Lashkova to have any anti-Soviet feelings. Lashkova did not type this material with the aim of undermining or weakening Soviet power. She had different reasons and aims.

We know from the trial record that Lashkova, due to unfavourable family circumstances, has lived alone and without help from the age of sixteen years. Even now Vera looks almost a child. We can understand how hard she must have found it to survive in the battle of life when she was a mere sixteen-year-old. From an early age she had to earn her own living. To earn money for her hard work as a typist—this was Lashkova's aim.

Ginzburg came to Lashkova for help because she was a typist, not because she was a fellow-thinker. She typed his collection for a fee. Dobrokhotov paid her for typing the material for Dobrovolsky. Vera used Galanskov's typewriter. She could not buy her own typewriter—while a typewriter was her living. Because of this she typed articles for Galanskov. And so it is established that Lashkova's aim was to earn money. Even if it were admitted that Lashkova knew that by typing the literary works of Ginzburg, Galanskov and Dobrovolsky she was allowing herself to harm society, even then one can talk only of indirect intent, and therefore her actions cannot be brought within the scope of article 70 of the Criminal Code.

The defence considers that these arguments concerning the facts of the typing incidents exclude the possibility of charging Lashkova under article 70 of the Criminal Code.

However, it is also necessary to examine other arguments concerning each work with which she is charged separately.

At Ginzburg's request Lashkova typed material about the trial of Sinyavsky and Daniel which later became known under the name of *The White Book*. *The White Book* as a whole is not stated as being anti-Soviet in the indictment. The Prosecutor, after groundlessly calling the collection about the trial of Sinyavsky and Daniel 'biased', cites only two documents in it as criminal in character: the leaflet 'Resistance' and 'Letter to an Old Friend'.

Lashkova's defence is not bound to go into an evaluation of the character of the leaflet since Lashkova has stated that she did not type it. Ginzburg has said he typed this leaflet himself. There has been no contrary evidence about this during the trial and therefore the charge of typing the leaflet 'Resistance' should be dropped from the statement of charges against Lashkova. The 'Letter to an Old Friend' perhaps contains some criminal statements. However, to evaluate correctly Lashkova's actions in typing for Ginzburg, among other things, the 'Letter to an Old Friend', it is necessary to cite the following circumstances.

The significance of this charge lies mainly in the fact that later the collection *The White Book* was sent abroad and was published in several countries. However, this fact has nothing to do with Lashkova since she didn't know and could not know that *The White Book* would be sent abroad, and she has not been accused of knowing it. In addition, Lashkova has stated that she knew from Ginzburg that the collection *The White Book* was being prepared only with the aim of being passed to the highest levels of power and to certain deputies of the USSR Supreme Soviet. This statement of Lashkova's is confirmed by Ginzburg, who stated that this was his aim in compiling the collection, that he spoke of this aim to Lashkova and that the aim was effected by him later. There is no evidence in the case materials contradicting Lashkova's statements as to for whom and for what aim she typed the text of the collection for Ginzburg. In addition, the witness Stolyarova has confirmed that a copy of the collection was given to I. Ehrenburg, deputy of the USSR Supreme Soviet. It has been established that another copy of the collection was given by Ginzburg to the Committee of State Security (KGB).

All this gives the defence the right to say that subjectively speaking Lashkova typed the collection including the 'Letter to an Old Friend', not with anti-Soviet intent but with the aim of passing this material to organs of the state and a small group of state officials. The collecting and typing of such materials for this stated high aim cannot be held to be criminal in any way. Therefore the typing of *The White Book* by Lashkova should be completely dropped from the charges against her.

Lashkova is likewise accused of typing two articles for the miscellany *Phoenix* compiled by Galanskov—'An Open Letter to Sholokhov' and 'The Russian Road to Socialism'.

The defence does not deny that the 'Open Letter to Sholokhov' is a criminal document. Besides this the letter contains some rude, almost vicious, expressions. We must admit that Lashkova, in typing this letter for money, should have understood and realized that she was being used to harm the prestige of our state. This is the only point in all the charges—that concerning the typing of texts—where the defence concedes a measure of guilt in Lashkova's actions. However, the clearly established and complete absence in Lashkova of any intent to undermine or weaken the Soviet system gives the defence grounds for stating that in connection with this action Lashkova should not be charged under article 70 of the Criminal Code, involving direct anti-Soviet intent, but only under article 190, paragraph 1, which does not involve such intent.

The question of Lashkova's typing the article 'Russian Road to Socialism', attributed to Academician Varga, must be resolved in a completely different way. This is a long article and very difficult to read. It is possible, by taking out of context certain phrases and paragraphs from this article, as the Procurator has done, to call the whole work 'criminal'. It's possible to quote various parts of this article which, taken out of context, will give a completely contradictory impression. To understand the real ideas of this work, it is necessary to follow the author's train of thought carefully and comprehend his main arguments. Lashkova typed this article without reading it carefully. We know this from her own evidence and from the statements of Galanskov. In the actual process of typing, the typist cannot concentrate on the ideas or style of particular passages and can fail to understand the meaning of the whole work.

We know that a typist can type correctly a scientific work whose contents she does not understand at all. Absorbed in the technical work of typing, how could the typist Lashkova understand the meaning of certain arguments in the article? She may have understood that the author was writing about Lenin's views on the aims of the Russian Revolution. Mechanically typing away on the typewriter, Lashkova may have noticed that the author gave a great deal of attention to Lenin's work *Notes on Our Revolution*. She may have gathered that in the author's opinion Stalin perverted Lenin's ideas and adopted impermissible methods of leadership. When she was glancing over the text certain phrases may have caught her eye giving her some impression of the author's sympathy for shining figures among the party leadership: 'side by side with the proletarian style of leadership, marked by its simplicity, humility and self-sacrifice, whose best representatives were Lenin, Sverdlov, Dzerzhinsky, Kirov—a different style of leadership gradually arose within the party'. Lashkova may have read phrases giving clear indications that the author excludes any return to capitalism: 'The Russian bourgeois world had not run its full course, and so it gradually began to manifest itself in the socialist world. . . . A return to that world is of course impossible, but it still . . . shows signs of existence and constitutes a great obstacle to the strong development of a new society.' In this way, typing the article out, but not studying or analyzing it, Lashkova may have considered the author to be on the side of Soviet power, a socialist economy and the party of Lenin. At the same time, if Lashkova noticed the strong criticism by the article's author of what he considers to be the negative side of our life, of the difficult heritage of Stalin in the life of the party and the country, she undoubtedly may have taken this as anti-Stalinist criticism, which is by no means necessarily anti-Soviet or criminal. There were certain foundations in the text of the article for such an interpretation. It is significant that although the article was sent abroad with the rest of the material from the collection *Phoenix*, it turned out to be unacceptable as anti-Soviet propaganda to the gentlemen of NTS and was not published in *Grani*. This is why the defence considers that Lashkova did not personally understand the criminal nature of this article and in typing it had no direct or indirect criminal intention. The defence asks that this part of the charges against Lashkova be dropped.

Lashkova is charged with typing at the request of Dobrovolsky several copies of a document called 'Letter of the Monks of Pochayev Monastery' and with passing one copy of this letter to Galanskov for inclusion in the miscellany *Phoenix*. The defence considers this charge to be groundless.

As we know, the letter contains a description of the lawlessness and physical force unleashed against the monks of Pochayev monastery by certain named officials. Even if the letter is admitted to be a fabrication and slander, then it is a slander not against Soviet power, not against our system of society and government, but against certain local officials. They are mentioned by name in the letter. But Lashkova did not consider the letter a fabrication or a slander. She believed this information and was indignant about the outrages described in the letter. Dobrovolsky confirmed this in court. The definition of the crime 'slander' always concerns intentionally false information. Lashkova believed the letter to be true. For her this document was not deliberately false. And not only Lashkova believed the document to be truthful. Levitin also believed it. He wrote and circulated his own articles in which he protested against the events at the Pochayev monastery. Grigoryan, the deputy editor of a leading party periodical, also believed it, even to the extent of taking measures to stop these violations of the law. We know he rang the Central Committee of the party about the matter and wrote a report about it. And finally, a most important point: can we today assert that the information in the letter is not true?

The document tells of the abuse of power by officials: arbitrariness, abuse of authority, the use of force. Has the Procuracy investigated these facts? There is no memorandum about it in the trial materials. Consequently there is no reason for considering the Pochayev letter to be untruthful. But I repeat that even if it is considered untruthful, it still contains no attacks on our system. Obviously then, this document should be excluded from the charges.

Lashkova is also accused of receiving two works published by the NTS from Dobrovolsky for the purpose of circulation: the pamphlet 'Solidarism Is the Idea of the Future' and the periodical *Our Times*. Dobrovolsky has already stated that he gave Lashkova the pamphlet and periodical to read. Lashkova is further accused of deliberately circulating the pamphlet to Kushev and the periodical to Levitin. Earlier I showed there was no foundation for alleging that Lashkova had any intention of weakening or undermining Soviet power. Let us see, then, how this so-called 'circulation' took place.

Kushev stated that he himself saw the pamphlet in her flat and asked to borrow it to read. Levitin says he looked through the periodical for only ten minutes and then put it down. In neither case did Lashkova take any initiative. On the contrary, she showed a disinterest and passivity hardly characteristic of a propagandist. Thus it is perfectly clear that neither the character of her action nor her intention can warrant a conviction under article 70 of the Criminal Code. The fact that she was in possession of criminal literature published by NTS proves her guilty only under article 190, paragraph 1, of the Criminal Code.

Of course, it cannot be said that Lashkova was motivated by money interest alone. She is a wiser and more complex person than that. She has a curiosity about everything new, even the dangerous and hostile, a wish to know and judge everything for herself. And this is not surprising. Let us consider in what circumstances the world-view of this generation to whom Lashkova belongs was formed.*

Ariya goes on to say that the greatest influence on the forming of a world-view by this generation was the ending of the Stalin cult of personality, the destruction of a hitherto unshakable authority. He refers to the political testament of Togliatti.[68]

It had turned out that 'something was rotten in the state of Denmark'—the actual process of de-Stalinization was proceeding in an unhealthy way for our society. A kind of 'ideological vacuum' arose and deficiencies in educational work prevented it from immediately being filled. The actions of Lashkova were the result of objective social phenomena—they were not her fault but her misfortune.

Ariya emphasizes that Lashkova is not a dangerous offender, and that her actions come under article 190, paragraph 1, of the Russian Criminal Code. Before determining the degree of her punishment the court must take into account her truthfulness during the trial, the absence of any harmful intention on her part (at this point Ariya refers to the stenographic record of a conversation between Vinogradov and Khokhlov calling the actions of Vera and Kushev 'childish pranks'), and her difficult life. He concludes by saying that her typing of the 'Open Letter to Sholokhov' and the fact that she gave people two NTS booklets to look at should be redefined as charges under article 190, paragraph 1, of the Russian Criminal Code, and should involve no imprisonment, while on the remaining charges Lashkova should be acquitted.

JUDGE. The speech for the defence of the accused Galanskov will be made by defence counsel Kaminskaya.

* From this point the closing speech of S. L. Ariya is abbreviated, as an exact record has not been preserved.

KAMINSKAYA asks that the court be adjourned until the following day as the defence of her client is very complicated and a voluminous amount of evidence is involved. She asks to be allowed the opportunity to prepare her defence more fully. In addition, it is already after eight o'clock and everyone is tired.

JUDGE nevertheless asks her to proceed with her defence.

ARIYA, ZOLOTUKHIN and SHVEISKY uphold Kaminskaya's request.

JUDGE (to Zolotukhin). Perhaps you would like to make your speech now?

ZOLOTUKHIN refuses.

JUDGE. Very well then. The court is adjourned until tomorrow, 12 January at 8.30 hours.

The court sitting of 11 January ends at 20.30 hours.

12 January

The court sitting begins at 8.30 hours with the continuation of the defence pleas.

JUDGE. The speech for the defence of the accused Galanskov will be made by the defence counsel Kaminskaya.

SPEECH OF DEFENCE COUNSEL KAMINSKAYA*

Galanskov is charged with offences under two articles of the Russian Criminal Code—articles 70 and 88, paragraph 1. Firstly, I should like to concentrate on those parts of the charges concerned with article 70.

You know that the charges under article 70 can be divided into two main parts: (1) Galanskov's part in compiling the collection of material about the trial of Sinyavsky and Daniel and Galanskov's compilation of the miscellany *Phoenix*; (2) the facts which give the Prosecution the opportunity of claiming that Galanskov maintained connections with the anti-Soviet émigré organization NTS. First of all, I should like to analyse the circumstances and facts concerning the first part of these charges.

The Prosecution states that Galanskov together with Ginzburg collected biased material about the trial of Sinyavsky and Daniel, that he organized its circulation and sent it abroad. First of all, I feel

* Dina Isakovna Kaminskaya, forty years old, member of the Moscow Collegium of Lawyers.

it my duty to remark that the Prosecution has produced no proof of Galanskov having assisted in the compilation of the collection of material about the trial of Sinyavsky and Daniel. Both at the preliminary investigation and during the trial Ginzburg has stated that he alone compiled this collection. From his first interrogation on 19 January, Galanskov has also maintained this, at no time changing his testimony. Not one of the witnesses interrogated has contradicted this. The accused Lashkova and Dobrovolsky have likewise consistently maintained that the collection was compiled by Ginzburg alone without anyone's help. Therefore I ask the court to drop this item in the charges against Galanskov.

The charges state that Galanskov compiled *Phoenix* with Ginzburg's help and produced four copies of it with Lashkova's help. In the opinion of the Prosecution, this miscellany contained five criminal articles. In other words, the Prosecution considers that the compilation of this miscellany by Galanskov is not criminal in itself; the basis of the charge is the fact that among other writings the miscellany contains five criminal articles:

—the 'Open Letter to Sholokhov' by Galanskov himself;

—the article 'The Russian Road to Socialism', attributed to Academician Varga;

—the article by Sinyavsky, 'What Is Socialist Realism?';

—the article 'An Account of the Events at the Pochayev Monastery Today';

—and the story of an unknown writer, 'The Confession of Victor Velsky'.

Whether Ginzburg helped Galanskov or not is a question for Ginzburg's own counsel.

I, as Galanskov's lawyer, will confine myself to a precise analysis of the incriminating articles.

Much has already been said during this trial about the article 'Account of the Events at the Pochayev Monastery Today' both by the defence for Lashkova and Dobrovolsky and by the witnesses. As a result it has been established that the events described in the article did in fact take place. Therefore the article cannot be in any way a slander on Soviet reality, but is merely a description of actual events.

As regards the article by Sinyavsky, 'What Is Socialist Realism?' the legally binding sentence passed by the Supreme Court of the RSFSR on Sinyavsky and Daniel deprive me of the right to analyse this article and argue about the definition of it as 'criminal'.

Among the works charged against Galanskov is 'The Confession of Victor Velsky'.[69] I should like to concentrate in detail on an analysis of this work. In the indictment 'The Confession of Victor Velsky' is called an article. This is a serious mistake which leads also to a mistake in the evaluation of this work. It is a work of fiction which like all works of fiction describes imaginary characters placed in imaginary situations. When analysing any work of fiction it is always important to understand whether or not the words of the hero express the underlying theme or inspiration of the work. Some things said by the hero in this story could be interpreted as anti-Soviet, but they are placed next to other phrases directly contradicting them.

The story consists of two parts. In the first part the story establishes a certain attitude towards the hero—directly connected with his action in falsely informing on his friends out of a false feeling of fear. The second part of the story, which is basically, from a philosophical viewpoint, allegorical, is constructed in a completely different way. This is what Velsky says about himself in the second part: 'I find it both sad and funny to read what I have written—it's like a storm in a tea-cup, how weak and pitiful this man is . . .'. And later on: 'There were only spiteful rejections, there were no ideals one could live for. . . . I cannot bear to read these pages over; all that is left for me is to commit suicide, but I can't even do that—I'm a coward'. From these quotations it is obvious that the second part concerns the dethronement of Velsky as hero.

In addition, I should like to bring the attention of the court to the second theme of the story—an absolute disenchantment with the emigration. To tell the truth, this is exactly why the story couldn't be and wasn't published in any émigré periodicals.[70] When Velsky, putting his dream into practice, breaks out into the 'free world' to the West he finds it corrupt and mercenary and realizes the illusory nature of the freedom he had so longed for. 'I've become a small cog in the mechanism of the big political game. I have to become a paid traitor.' And this is the sum total of Velsky's life: 'I am finished, finished, finished. I am not a portrait or a type—it's simply that my life turned out this way. . . .'

'The Confession of Victor Velsky' is a serious and unusual work. We could argue over its artistic qualities, but this is not a literary dispute. The meaning and contents of this work are as follows: there was a small, spiteful man who became a traitor, but even this man could not live as an émigré. He preferred madness to the mercenary prosperity of the Western émigrés. It was not by chance that this work found no editor or publisher in the West. I ask the court to exclude it from the 'criminal' documents.

Much has already been said at this trial about the 'Open Letter to Sholokhov' by Galanskov himself. Without doubt this letter can be considered sharply critical, rude and incorrect. But we must not forget that the idea of writing this letter came to Galanskov when he was in a psychiatric hospital. This has already been established during the trial. It explains the excessive emotionalism of the letter. The letter is intended as an answer to Sholokhov's speech at the 23rd Party Congress. This speech, according to Galanskov, by its contents and style provoked him into planning to write an answer to Sholokhov. I should like to mention that Galanskov's letter on the subject was not the only reaction to Sholokhov's speech. In the materials of the case there is another letter addressed to Sholokhov, and although it is written in a more reserved and tactful way, it contains basically the same criticism of the speech.* This trial is not concerned with deciding whether Sholokhov's speech was right or wrong. We know that Galanskov considered the speech inhuman and unjust, and also offensive in its form. We must also remember that this letter is addressed to one person and is a criticism of that person; it is not at all a criticism of the Soviet system as a whole. If this 'Open Letter' had confined its sharpest criticisms to Sholokhov himself and had not included a few general phrases, which have already been quoted here and whose criminal nature I cannot deny, I would have asked the court to exclude this document from the charges. As it is, I can only say that when Galanskov wrote this letter it was not his intention to subvert or undermine Soviet power.

Consequently, out of all the material published in *Phoenix*, I admit only two articles to be criminal in nature: Sinyavsky's article 'What Is Socialist Realism?'† (in view of the now binding sentence of the Russian Supreme Court) and the 'Open Letter to Sholokhov' —because of the considerations I have just outlined. However, that the actual works are admittedly anti-Soviet is quite insufficient reason for charging Galanskov under article 70 of the Russian Criminal Code. It is necessary also to prove anti-Soviet intent. What did Galanskov himself say in his editorial introduction to the miscellany *Phoenix* about his reasons for including Sinyavsky's article? 'I include it because of its qualities as literary criticism'. The absence of a direct intent or aim of weakening or subverting Soviet power excludes the possibility of charging Galanskov under

* This refers to L. K. Chukovskaya's letter included in Ginzburg's collection.
† The record of that part of D. I. Kaminskaya's speech where she analyses 'The Russian Road to Socialism' has been lost.

article 70, but the use of partly slanderous articles for his journal gives grounds for declaring his guilt under article 190, paragraph 1.

In the course of the investigation it was established that only four copies of *Phoenix* ever existed. Except for Dobrovolsky, who received an unbound copy from Galanskov, no one else read the miscellany. There has been absolutely no evidence that anyone else at all read it. Out of all the citizens of the Soviet Union, the circle of people who had got to know this miscellany was restricted to the editor and the contributor Dobrovolsky. Galanskov made no attempt to circulate *Phoenix* or give it to anyone to read. He himself said in court on this subject: 'I wanted to compile a collection of articles on pacifism and show it only to the authors of the works it contained'. I consider that Galanskov's guilt as editor and compiler of the miscellany *Phoenix* should be redefined according to article 190, paragraph 1.

Galanskov is likewise accused of giving Dobrovolsky his 'Open Letter to Sholokhov' with the alleged purpose of getting it typographically duplicated. I wish to draw the court's attention to Galanskov's absolutely uniform testimony on this point during the investigation. Throughout the trial he has admitted to being the author of the 'Open Letter' and the editor/compiler of the miscellany *Phoenix*, while he has always denied giving Dobrovolsky the 'Open Letter' for the purpose of duplication. Galanskov asserts that Dobrovolsky's evidence about this is slander. Let us try and examine this evidence of Dobrovolsky's.

However willingly Dobrovolsky has talked about his own crimes —and more particularly those of others—at the preliminary investigation and the trial, we must not forget that his evidence, like everyone else's, must be verified, especially as his evidence is that of a man under threat of conviction, directly concerned in the outcome of the case. And therefore, despite the unqualified confidence the court has shown in Dobrovolsky's evidence, it is necessary to examine it particularly carefully. I personally do not have any confidence in Dobrovolsky's evidence. During the investigation he changed it more than once. This man has lied to his close friends in his most secret and intimate letters—confiscated at the Serbsky Institute and now available to the court; he lied when he was, as he says, 'alone with his faith and God', he lied during interrogations and personal confrontations. The case records contain Dobrovolsky's first testimony given by him on the day of his arrest, 19 January 1967, and we also have the first testimony of Galanskov arrested on the same day. Galanskov said: 'I compiled *Phoenix* and I am ready to take full responsibility for it'. And what did Dobrovolsky say? 'I gave

Radziyevsky nothing, let him answer for himself.' Later forced against the wall in a personal confrontation with Radziyevsky he changed his evidence. He said: 'It was not I who gave Radziyevsky the "Open Letter to Sholokhov" but its author Galanskov.' And Dobrovolsky went on to describe with many lifelike details an alleged meeting between Radziyevsky and Galanskov at the Lermontov memorial.

Both in his first testimony and later Dobrovolsky lied. His only motive was to rid himself of responsibility, to transfer blame to somebody else. Perhaps this episode is not central to the charges against Galanskov, but it is very important because it testifies to Dobrovolsky's character.

To proceed. In his letters to the investigator, Dobrovolsky wrote that he had nothing to do with anything and asked to be shown the evidence against him. This is what he wrote on 13 March 1967 to the investigator, Major Eliseyev: 'I have tried to convince you of my innocence. I offered to be tested for my fingerprints on the copy of the "Open Letter" which was given to Radziyevsky—you refused. You are holding me here only on the evidence of Radziyevsky. The letter was given to him by Galanskov. Radziyevsky is testifying against me because he knows I am schizophrenic, thinking nothing will happen to me.' However, Radziyevsky had not given false evidence against him—he had told only the truth, as was later confirmed, and in the end Dobrovolsky himself had to admit it to be the truth.

In a letter to his family, confiscated at the time of the forensic-psychiatric diagnosis, he writes of his despair, horror and confusion at being imprisoned without cause since he had not committed any crime. As it turned out, Radziyevsky knew nothing of anyone called Galanskov. None of the witnesses has confirmed Dobrovolsky's story that it was not he, but Galanskov, who gave the 'Open Letter to Sholokhov' to Radziyevsky for the purpose of duplication. Why then did Dobrovolsky give the document to Radziyevsky for duplication? I don't exclude the possibility that he later intended to sell it. We know of an incident when Dobrovolsky sold a story by Solzhenitsyn to a friend (Galanskov) for five roubles. There may have been another reason. We know from the testimony of witnesses that Dobrovolsky wanted to compile his own anti-Stalinist collection. It's possible that the document was intended for inclusion in this collection of his.

Thus Dobrovolsky's evidence—coming from a man deeply concerned about the case's outcome—has found no confirmation, either during the investigation or in court. And therefore the charge accusing Galanskov of giving Radziyevsky the 'Open Letter to Sholokhov' for duplication should be excluded from the statement of charges against him. The same applies to the charge that Galanskov gave the article 'The Russian Road to Socialism' to Radziyevsky for duplication. This part of the charges was not even mentioned by the State Prosecutor in his speech.

I shall now turn my attention to the main part of the charges against Galanskov, his connections with the anti-Soviet émigré organization NTS. As regards this part of the charges Galanskov and his defence do indeed have a very complicated task. It is more complex because at the preliminary investigation Galanskov gave contradictory evidence on this subject. However, disregarding that, I consider that the Prosecution has not amassed sufficient facts to justify the basic charges about Galanskov having criminal connections with the anti-Soviet émigré organization NTS.

What is the Prosecution's basis for this?

Firstly, there is the existence of material evidence: the hectograph, the cryptography paper, the money, the literature published by NTS. This evidence was discovered at the time of the preliminary investigation. The Prosecution has other evidence too: the testimony of Dobrovolsky at the preliminary investigation and during the trial, and the testimony of Galanskov during a certain part of the preliminary investigation.

The Prosecution has no other evidence. I shall begin by examining the material evidence—the most important charges. The court knows that all this evidence—the hectograph, money, cryptography paper, anti-Soviet literature published by NTS—was found in Dobrovolsky's flat. The court also knows that Dobrovolsky's testimony about his own and Galanskov's relations with the NTS was only given after this evidence had been discovered at Dobrovolsky's flat. Consequently, this evidence does not in itself incriminate Galanskov. On the contrary, it could be used as evidence against Dobrovolsky. At the preliminary investigation Dobrovolsky gave evidence which was the only 'proof' of Galanskov's guilt. I am sure that if Galanskov had not partly confirmed this testimony by Dobrovolsky at the preliminary investigation the court could have no grounds for charging him with a connection with the NTS.

Now let us turn to Galanskov's testimony.

When judging the evidence of someone slandering another person, it is usually quite easy to understand the reason for his slander. It is more difficult to understand why a man should slander himself.

But in our legal experience we have quite often come up against this problem. I will not bore the court by trying to persuade it that to place full confidence in such evidence is very dangerous. This danger has repeatedly been pointed out in the instructions of high official bodies which state that the confession of the accused is not sufficient proof of his guilt. The continuing provision of such guidance by our leading institutions shows that this problem is still present.

What are my grounds for stating that the evidence which Galanskov at first gave during the preliminary investigation and which he then repudiated at the end of the preliminary investigation, at the time when article 201 of the Procedural Code was being signed is, as he now claims, false?

How does Galanskov himself explain his actions?

In the first place, he wanted to help Dobrovolsky. While he was at the Serbsky Institute undergoing a forensic-psychiatric diagnosis Galanskov received a note from Dobrovolsky which is available to the court: 'Yura, for the love of God, I beg you, take my guilt on yourself. I can't go to prison now, you know that.' As we know, he wrote quite a few notes like this to Galanskov. And Galanskov agreed to take the blame for Dobrovolsky's crimes.

Secondly, Galanskov has already spoken about his depressed state at that time, after living in prison conditions for so long. 'I agreed to Dobrovolsky's pleas and, realizing that I would have to answer for *Phoenix* anyway, took all the blame on myself,' said Galanskov.

I understand quite well that some people will find this convincing, others not. But I beg the court to remember that Galanskov is in a very bad state of health. He has stomach ulcers which give him great pain—we have the report of the medical commission about this. The illness has lowered his resistance and weakened his will. And without doubt the severe prison conditions have also played their part in this. The psychiatric diagnosis established Galanskov's sanity. But we know, and there are reports on this available to the court, that for many years serious divergences from the norm were observed, that in the Solovyov and Kashchenko hospitals he was diagnosed as schizophrenic, that even at the Serbsky Institute the doctors had to observe him for double the normal term, as they found it difficult to diagnose Galanskov's psychological state. And so, by giving this evidence, Galanskov may have wanted to bring the day of the trial nearer and so have a respite from his physical sufferings. But if the court is not convinced by all this and considers

Galanskov's evidence to be true, whereas I consider it to be self-slander, then I shall also dwell on the evidence brought by the Prosecution against Galanskov.

The court's evidence of Galanskov's guilt is based on Dobro-volsky's testimony. This testimony covers a great deal of ground. Galanskov is accused of meeting the foreigner Genrikh, whom the investigators consider to be an NTS agent, of giving him *The White Book* compiled by Ginzburg, and receiving in return some literature, the hectograph, the money, the material for invisible writing. You know that Genrikh has not been found and that therefore there is no proof that he belonged to the NTS. We know that Galanskov has not denied this meeting. He confirms that he did meet a foreigner called Genrikh at the Kropotinskaya metro station. The difference in the evidence, as between Galanskov's and Dobrovolsky's, lies in the fact that Dobrovolsky states that Genrikh visited only Galanskov and that he himself did not overhear any conversation with the foreigner; while Galanskov asserts the opposite to be true. Dobro-volsky supposes that *The White Book* was given to the foreigner during this meeting. I say he supposes this because apart from what Galanskov told him he has no way of knowing whether anything was given to the foreigner on that day or not—as he states that he himself saw nothing. This is what he says about it in his testimony: 'I emphasize again that I did not see the actual handing over of the book, that I only assume this took place from what Galanskov told me'. Dobrovolsky confirmed this in Galanskov's presence. During the same personal confrontation, he also said: 'I don't know who handed over *The White Book*. From what Galanskov told me I understood that it had already been handed over or would be in the near future.' He went on: 'I cannot say that *The White Book* was handed over at the Kropotinskaya metro station; there was a meeting with a foreigner but nothing changed hands.' As you see, his evidence is very vague and contradictory. Galanskov himself denies that he ever gave anybody the collection of materials about the Sinyavsky–Daniel trial which Ginzburg had compiled. The Prosecution has offered no other evidence that Galanskov sent *The White Book* abroad.

Dobrovolsky denies that the foreigner Genrikh came to visit him, but in the circumstances of the meeting there are indications which permit me to assert that the foreigner had come to visit not Galanskov but Dobrovolsky. Check this in any of Dobrovolsky's evidence: he has consistently stated that this meeting occurred in October 1966. He has also said it was on the same day as Potasheva's party. During the trial the date of that party was established as 22 October. In this respect, Dobrovolsky's evidence was confirmed. However it was later established from the testimony of Lashkova and Ginzburg that Lashkova finished typing the collection not earlier than 10 November 1966. Consequently, at the time of the foreigner Genrikh's visit to Moscow this collection was not even finished. So Ginzburg could not possibly have given the foreigner Genrikh the material compiled by Ginzburg about the Sinyavsky–Daniel trial in October 1966. There is another interesting detail about the circumstances of that meeting. Talking about his conversation with Genrikh while visiting some church, Dobrovolsky said: 'Genrikh told me that an article of mine had been published in some periodical. I don't remember through whom I sent the article abroad. Genrikh also told me that on his next visit he would bring me the royalties.' And when Genrikh asked Dobrovolsky in what currency he would like the royalties to be paid to him, Dobrovolsky replied: 'In roubles'. I call the court's attention to that most important moment. It seems strange to me that Dobrovolsky cannot remember specifically which article was referred to, if this was the only article Dobrovolsky had sent abroad. It is also strange that Dobrovolsky cannot remember which foreigner he gave the article to, if, as he says, Genrikh was the only foreigner he had met. It is strange that Genrikh whom he supposedly met by chance offered money specifically to Dobrovolsky and talked to him about his article. Are there not too many coincidences here?

Dobrovolsky states that there was also another meeting with a foreigner called Nadya, whom the investigators also consider to be an NTS agent. Galanskov admits meeting the foreigner Nadya. Dobrovolsky also states that Galanskov gave *Phoenix* to her during this meeting. Galanskov denies this. Dobrovolsky says Nadya came to visit Galanskov. Galanskov states that she came to visit Dobrovolsky.

I realize that the court has unqualified confidence in the evidence of Dobrovolsky. But I want to remind the court that a man's fate cannot be decided merely on the basis of a personal sympathy for Dobrovolsky, who has—I repeat—an interest in the outcome of this case. Consequently, in selecting from the evidence given by these two men, you must choose fairly certain items, while trying to find serious reasons for doing so. There is no evidence by witnesses about the meeting with Nadya and the handing over of *Phoenix*. Therefore I must turn to Dobrovolsky's own evidence.

In February 1967 Dobrovolsky wrote a note to the investigator, Major Eliseyev of the KGB. In it he wrote: 'I have been thinking over our conversation and I am ready to give the preliminary investigation the opportunity of finding the remaining copies of *Phoenix*. This must be done as soon as possible because a copy could be sent abroad. This must not be put off till later.' In March of that year, Dobrovolsky again wrote a note to Eliseyev: 'At the beginning of January Galanskov finished *Phoenix* and told me someone would come to take it abroad.' Thus Dobrovolsky has stated that up to the moment of Galanskov's arrest *Phoenix* had not been sent abroad. Dobrovolsky also said that, if released, he could not only find where *Phoenix* was, but also prevent it being sent to *Grani*. It is strange that the investigator did not react in any way to this and that Dobrovolsky was asked no questions on the subject. However, soon after this Dobrovolsky testified that he knew, from what Galanskov had told him, that *Phoenix* had been sent abroad. But one man's testimony is not sufficient if it is completely contradictory and unsupported by any witnesses. I contend that this evidence, being contradictory and finding no support in the records of the case, cannot be used for a charge against Galanskov that he handed *Phoenix* over to the NTS publishing house.

Dobrovolsky has stated that everything found during the search of his flat (hectograph, money, etc.) was given to him by Galanskov. Here we could repeat that Dobrovolsky is motivated by self-interest in this matter, especially as all this was found in his flat alone. The Prosecution upholds the truth of Dobrovolsky's evidence on this point by citing the interrogation of Schaffhauser, arrested as an NTS agent in Leningrad at the end of 1967.* This interrogation not only does not convince me, on the contrary it witnesses to the complete groundlessness of the charges against Galanskov. The NTS agent Schaffhauser came to the USSR only after, according to Dobrovolsky, Galanskov had given Dobrovolsky the hectograph, money, etc., and after the arrest of both Galanskov and Dobrovolsky. We know that a questionnaire was confiscated from Schaffhauser on his arrest, which was designed for finding out information about certain Soviet citizens, including the writer Aksyonov and others, and also about Galanskov. Schaffhauser's evidence makes the charges against Galanskov illogical and absurd, as it is obvious to everyone that one would first discover a man's opinions and only then give him a hectograph and money, not the other way round. I contend that these charges against Galanskov seem to me extremely contradictory and illogical.

I shall now turn to that part of the charges against Galanskov

* In fact Schaffhauser was arrested in January 1967 and sentenced in April. Ed.

which concerns the money allegedly given to Galanskov by the NTS. The money, like everything else, was found at Dobrovolsky's flat. Dobrobolsky's wife wrote many letters during the investigation asking for the money to be returned to her. Dobrovolsky claims that this money was given to him by Galanskov for the building of a co-operative flat in Dobrovolsky's name, the real owner of which would be Galanskov and which could then be used for conspiratorial purposes. I find this story of Dobrovolsky's completely unconvincing. At one time Dobrovolsky was sentenced under article 58, paragraph 10, of the Criminal Code; after his release he was under constant surveillance, including medical surveillance, as he had been diagnosed a schizophrenic. Was it logical that this co-operative flat should be bought in the name of a man whom the authorities were watching so closely? It would have been impossible to find a more unsuitable candidate. Besides, anyone familiar with the way in which obtaining these co-operative flats is organized will realize how difficult it would later be to transfer the flat to Galanskov; he would have had to try to do this as, if we are to believe Dobrovolsky, the real owner of the flat and the money. How can we put all this together? Dobrovolsky told us his wife did not know about his business affairs. But he had apparently talked to her about buying a flat, as she writes in one of her letters that they had been saving the money to buy a co-operative flat. If we believe Dobrovolsky when he says he wanted to build a flat for Galanskov, then how was he going to explain to his wife later that it was not their flat, that all their hopes and plans had been pure deception? Dobrovolsky explained that he had not told his wife directly that the money was Galanskov's but had hinted that he would be helped to build a flat, but for this to be done he would have to spend some time in a psychiatric hospital. Now, in court, his wife has repeated her evidence that the money was not earned, that she thought Dobrovolsky must have borrowed it from someone. She did not know on what conditions he had taken the money. This contradicts his own evidence. Entin's evidence indirectly supports Galanskov's, where the latter says the money did indeed belong to Dobrovolsky, not to himself, and that part of it was obtained as a result of an exchange of dollars. Entin said that Galanskov, giving him the dollars to change, told him they belonged to religious groups. All the witnesses at the preliminary investigation described Galanskov as a very poor man. He himself said: 'I am so poor I could not buy my wife a pair of stockings.' His mother works as a cleaner, his father as a lathe operator. Dobrovolsky, on the other hand, was described by Lashkova as a man who had the means to buy a car and asked her help in this, saying he could pay for it at once in cash. I contend that the money belonged to Dobrovolsky. I don't know whether he got it from the NTS or whether it was a legacy, as his wife wrote in her letter. Perhaps it was saved from his wages, perhaps it was given to him by his religious friends. I cannot select any one of these solutions in particular.

However, the Prosecution has no evidence, other than Dobrovolsky's bland assertions, that the money belonged to Galanskov and that he got it from the NTS. Galanskov himself categorically denies this, and Dobrovolsky's evidence is not supported by anyone or anything and is therefore invalid as proof.

To sum up, it is possible to say that none of the charges against Galanskov under article 70 of the Russian Criminal Code have been proved. Out of all Galanskov has been accused of, I regard as criminal only the two documents included in *Phoenix* by Galanskov: the 'Open Letter to Sholokhov' by Galanskov, and Sinyavsky's article 'What Is Socialist Realism?' As Galanskov lacks any anti-Soviet intent I ask the court to redefine his actions under article 190, paragraph 1, of the Criminal Code.

Finally, I shall turn to the charges against Galanskov connected with article 88, paragraph 1.

Firstly, I would like to call the court's attention to the fact that nobody, at any time, has said these dollars belonged to Galanskov. We only know he gave them to Entin to be changed. Nevertheless, a person is held responsible even if he is acting as a middle-man and receives no personal benefit. There was no personal benefit in this case, as the witnesses Entin and Borisova have confirmed. This episode in Galanskov's life was the only one of its kind; it happened by chance and is not characteristic of his personal attributes or his activities.

In addition, Galanskov has stated that he thought, from Entin's words, that the exchange was to take place officially, through someone having the proper authority. The court should judge that testimony in the same way as the other evidence, and in accordance with that evaluation judge the responsibility of Galanskov under article 88, paragraph 1, of the Criminal Code.

And finally, we must also think of the people concerned. I cannot understand why there was laughter in the courtroom when it was said that Galanskov carried out good and selfless deeds. I cannot understand why you laughed at the fact that he is a good man, that he visited an old woman, washed her floor for her, brought her medicine, that he helped a friend to bring up her children. Galanskov is a wonderful and good man; he wanted to fight everything he considered unjust. He demonstrated alone outside the American Embassy about the aggression in the Dominican Republic. He could not remain passive.

Galanskov has by nature strong feelings of personal responsibility and a high conception of citizenship. He has not sought riches for himself, a career, or fame—he only wanted righteousness to prevail.

I ask the court to remember that these young people are our children, not only in age but also because they have been brought up among us. They were not indifferent to what surrounded them, so we must not be indifferent in regard to them. We are largely responsible for their mistakes and errors and do not have the right merely to dismiss their fate with a wave of the hand.

JUDGE. The speech for the defence of the accused Ginzburg will be made by defence counsel Zolotukhin.

SPEECH OF DEFENCE COUNSEL ZOLOTUKHIN*

I wish to begin by saying that yesterday during the speech of the State Prosecutor a certain misunderstanding arose. When I talked to the Procurator after his speech, it became clear it was indeed a misunderstanding. However, I would like to make a statement on the subject.

The Procurator, in his speech, mentioned by chance that Ginzburg was the leader of a secret NTS group in Moscow.

JUDGE. The court realizes that this was a slip of the tongue.

ZOLOTUKHIN. In that case I can turn to a quiet, impartial analysis of the evidence.

The part of the indictment concerning Alexander Ginzburg contains seven specific charges:

(*1*) that Ginzburg compiled a biased collection of material about the trial of Sinyavsky and Daniel, with the intention of circulating it;

(*2*) that Ginzburg took part in producing the leaflet signed 'Resistance' and the 'Letter to an Old Friend';

(*3*) that Ginzburg wrote a provocative letter addressed to Kosygin and did not send it to the addressee;

(*4*) that he illegally sent to the NTS, through Galanskov, his collection of material about the trial of Sinyavsky and Daniel;

* Boris Andreyevich Zolotukhin, thirty-eight years old, member of the Moscow Collegium of Lawyers.

(*5*) that he helped Galanskov to produce the miscellany *Phoenix*, and give him a film of the article 'The Russian Road to Socialism', attributed to Academician Varga;

(*6*) that he gave Galanskov anti-Soviet extracts from papers in Norwegian, Danish, Italian and French;

(*7*) that he owned a tape-recording containing, among other things, two songs of an anti-Soviet character.

If I have understood the Procurator correctly, in his speech certain of these charges were dropped. If I am mistaken in this, I ask the Procurator to correct me.

Thus, the following charges have been dropped:

(*1*) that Ginzburg personally wrote or took part in the production of the leaflet signed 'Resistance' and 'Letter to an Old Friend'— the Procurator did not mention this in his speech;

(*2*) that he did not send the letter addressed to Kosygin—there was not a word about this in the Procurator's speech;

(*3*) that Ginzburg helped Galanskov to compile *Phoenix* by giving him a film of the anti-Soviet article 'The Russian Road to Socialism', as Galanskov stated during the trial that this film was given to him by Faingold, not Ginzburg; obviously taking Galanskov's testimony into account the Procurator did not mention in his prosecution speech any participation by Ginzburg in the compiling of the miscellany *Phoenix*;

(*4*) and finally, in the Procurator's speech nothing was said about the anti-Soviet songs confiscated from Ginzburg's flat, which figured in the indictment.

To sum up, we can say that the Prosecution has dropped four of the seven charges against Ginzburg; so there remain three charges, which I will examine in greater detail later.

Judging by the fact that the Comrade Prosecutor has not corrected me, I have obviously understood his speech correctly. (The Procurator says nothing.)

I would like to say more about one of the circumstances which has created the complex moral atmosphere prevailing in this trial. In his speech the State Prosecutor said more than once that Ginzburg held anti-Soviet opinions. As we know, a man's opinions in themselves are not liable to punishment. Apart from that, I consider there to be no proof that Ginzburg held anti-Soviet opinions not only at the time of the activities he's being tried for but even earlier. The Prosecution refers to Ginzburg's testimony of eight years ago, in 1960, when he was tried for his compilation of the periodical *Syntax*. At that time he was a young man. Finding himself in a very trying situation, he expressed certain views during his interrogation which he later repudiated and which he considered mistaken and wrong long before the present trial. The Procurator did not want to hear Ginzburg's explanation on this point, in which Ginzburg said he had given that testimony after eight months of solitary confinement, on the fifth day of a hunger strike, when he was in a serious condition physically and mentally. Testimony eight years old, given in severe conditions, is not legal proof. During the trial no evidence was produced that Ginzburg held anti-Soviet opinions at the time when he was compiling the collection about the trial of Sinyavsky and Daniel. Neither at the preliminary investigation nor during the trial itself did a single one of the many witnesses give evidence supporting this accusation.

What then were Ginzburg's motives in compiling the collection of material about the trial of Sinyavsky and Daniel?

The trial of Sinyavsky and Daniel was the first open trial in which two writers were charged in connection with the contents of their works. Before that instances were known of writers being criticized, being called anti-Soviet because of the contents of their works. This happened, for instance, with Bulgakov's *Days of the Turbins* and Pilnyak's *Mahogany*. We also remember the case of Boris Pasternak's novel *Doctor Zhivago*. But none of these writers were ever brought to trial for their works.

The Sinyavsky–Daniel trial was an unusual trial and thus it aroused great interest in the Soviet and world public. You remember how much attention was paid to it by our press, which devoted long articles to it. It is quite understandable that in these circumstances Ginzburg should have tried to read the works which served as evidence in the trial. He was interested in knowing exactly what kind of works a writer could be tried for. When he had read these works he felt they were not of a criminal character. And then he wrote his letter to Kosygin, expressing his point of view on the subject. This was written before the sentence was pronounced on Sinyavsky and Daniel which Ginzburg was waiting for. In February (1966) the verdict was pronounced. Even when an ordinary trial is being discussed, every person will have a different reaction to the verdict. Where a verdict like this is concerned, entailing serious problems, I think it may call forth even more varied responses. Ginzburg was among those who considered the verdict erroneous.

Here, during the trial, much has been said which has nothing to do with Ginzburg, namely about the anti-Soviet émigré organization NTS. The black shadow of the NTS has hovered over this whole trial. Precisely because of this I feel it my duty to say that disagreement with the result of the Sinyavsky–Daniel trial was expressed also by people whose ideological purity no one has questioned. I should like to mention the letter in defence of Sinyavsky and Daniel by sixty-two writers including Chukovsky,[71] Ehrenburg, Kaverin[72] and others. In this letter the authors state that they do not consider the activities of Sinyavsky and Daniel to have been anti-Soviet. I say this to emphasize that Ginzburg's reaction was not the only one of its kind.

Progressive Western society was likewise not indifferent to the trial. What was the reaction of those whom we rightly consider to be our country's friends? The collection of material about the trial of Sinyavsky and Daniel contains a letter by Aragon,[73] in which he disapproves strongly of the trial. [There follows a quotation from Aragon's letter.] The same collection contains a statement by the General Secretary of the British Communist Party, John Gollan, in which he expresses his disagreement with the trial.

Ginzburg considered the sentence unjust. Here I should like to ask a general question. What action should a citizen take if he feels this way? He could take a completely indifferent attitude to it or he could be roused to social action. The citizen could calmly watch an innocent man being led away under guard, or he could try to intercede for the man. I don't know which attitude the court would consider more worthy of respect. But I think the attitude that is not indifferent would be more that of a good citizen. This is a general question which can be applied both to small and to important trials, especially when a man is convinced of the rightness of his personal judgment. I hope that even the Prosecution does not doubt this.

Ginzburg did everything he could to help Sinyavsky and Daniel. Ginzburg was told, quite rightly, in this court, that in that case he should have applied to the Supreme Court of the USSR. Ginzburg did not do this. Why? Because many petitions to that court had remained unanswered. Ginzburg thought that if he collected all the material about the trial of Sinyavsky and Daniel and brought it to the notice of the higher institutions, this would be the most effective, indeed the only, way of helping Sinyavsky and Daniel. Ginzburg set about this task and finished it at the beginning of November 1966.

I now find it necessary to ask the question: 'Is this work criminal and anti-Soviet?' I find the answer in the phrasing of the charge, which does not consider the collection anti-Soviet, but biased. The prosecution sees bias in the fact that Ginzburg did not present the trial in an impartial light. Let us look at the collection and decide in what measure that accusation is justifiable.

The collection comprises 150 documents, which can be divided into three groups. The first consists of extracts from the Soviet and Western press about the beginning of the case. The second is a record of the trial itself. The third consists of extracts from the press and numerous letters from people about the verdict in the trial.

I state categorically, taking full responsibility, that the collection most painstakingly includes every account that Ginzburg could obtain from the whole Soviet press, both Moscow and provincial papers—a press expressing a point of view completely opposed to the views of Ginzburg and other opponents of the trial and the verdict. Thus both points of view are equally fully presented in the collection. Can this be called 'biased'? I should have called it objective. I maintain that Ginzburg included in his collection all the material—without exception—that he could obtain; and I ask the court to drop the charge against Alexander Ginzburg that the collection he compiled about the trial of Sinyavsky and Daniel is biased.

Ginzburg is also accused of including among the 150 documents in the collection two anti-Soviet documents: the leaflet signed 'Resistance' and the 'Letter to an Old Friend', which, it is alleged, give an anti-Soviet character to the collection. On this basis Ginzburg is charged with anti-Soviet incitement and propaganda. Ginzburg has himself explained in court that he does not consider these documents to be criminal. This is his own opinion, which may not appear convincing to the State Prosecutor. Ginzburg has also said in court: 'Even if I had considered them criminal, I would have had to include these two documents in the collection, as it was meant to show every kind of reaction from members of the intelligentsia, even reactions I would oppose, as I always strove for objectivity.'

And the collection does indeed contain widely differing points of view. It contains material on the necessity of increased democratization in this country, of more creative freedom, and of strengthening the international prestige of our country. And among this material Ginzburg included the leaflet 'Resistance' and the 'Letter to an Old Friend'. But in order to prove Ginzburg guilty under article 70 of the Criminal Code it is necessary to prove that he included these documents, which the Prosecution considers criminal, from anti-Soviet motives—with the aim of subverting or weakening Soviet power. However, even the Prosecution calls the collection only 'biased', not 'anti-Soviet'. Its aim was to obtain a revocation of the verdict, not to subvert the state. And as regards the texts themselves, criminal from the Prosecution's point of view, they must be proved to have as their aim the subversion or weakening of Soviet power. The inclusion of documents merely containing some slanderous phrases cannot be considered proof of guilt under article 70 of the Criminal Code.

This prompts the question: Perhaps this is an offence against article 190, paragraph 1? That depends on how Ginzburg was planning to circulate his collection. Ginzburg intended to distribute his collection inside the USSR, not to send it abroad as the Prosecution maintains. Ginzburg is charged with giving his consent to Galanskov, in October 1966, to send his collection to the periodical *Grani* through the NTS agent Genrikh. The question of the collection being handed over has already been outlined by the lawyer Kaminskaya when defending Galanskov, but as it is directly connected with the charges against Alexander Ginzburg, I shall also allow myself to touch upon this question.

There has been only one version of the handing over of the collection—based on the evidence of Dobrovolsky, who alleged that he knew, from what Galanskov had told him, that *The White Book* had been given to Genrikh; how, exactly, Dobrovolsky cannot tell us. Dobrovolsky states that Galanskov told him about this in the house of the witness Potasheva during the party there. Dobrovolsky also states that Lashkova, when typing this collection, was working very hard—allegedly to have it ready for the foreign courier. After the work was finished, it was not moved for two or three weeks. At the preliminary investigation Dobrovolsky insisted this was true and repeated it at the trial.

Lashkova has testified that she finished the work of typing the collection in November, but not before 10 November 1966. As I have already said, the handing over of the collection was said, in Dobrovolsky's evidence, to have taken place on the day of Potasheva's party. From the evidence of the accused Lashkova and Galanskov, who were at this party, and from the evidence of the witness Potasheva herself, it has been established that the party took place on 22 October. Therefore it took place no less than two weeks before Lashkova finished typing the collection. So all the evidence shows that in October 1966, when the foreigner Genrikh came to Moscow, the collection could not have been given to him, as it was not finished. The Prosecution has offered no other evidence as to how the collection was sent abroad, and there are no grounds for accusing Alexander Ginzburg of being concerned in this at all.

Why then did Dobrovolsky give such evidence? I think he had his reasons. We must not forget that Dobrovolsky's situation at the time of his arrest was little short of tragic. It was at his flat, and his alone, that all the material evidence—the hectograph, the money and the NTS literature—was discovered, evidence which was to give the prosecution grounds for charging the accused with connections with the anti-Soviet émigré organization NTS. We must also remember that Dobrovolsky had already been convicted once before of anti-Soviet activities. At the moment of arrest a man does not only fear the evidence which has already been discovered against him. He also fears additional circumstances which could be used as evidence against him. Dobrovolsky knew he had met four foreigners, had distributed literature published by the NTS, and had talked to Lashkova and Kats about the NTS. That is what Dobrovolsky was thinking about. He wanted to save himself, and in any way he could. The evidence for this is the note to Galanskov that Dobrovolsky wrote in the Serbsky Institute at the time of the psychiatric investigation, in which he begs Galanskov to take the blame for his crimes. He does not even recoil from giving false evidence. This man's moral principles allowed him to ask another prisoner to take the blame for his own crimes. If he slandered even Galanskov, his friend, then what did Ginzburg matter to him—a man whose acquaintance with him, according to his own testimony in court, was limited to 'good morning and goodbye'. And the investigation—as Dobrovolsky no doubt knew—was interested in Ginzburg and his collection.

And so, Comrade Judges, I consider that Dobrovolsky's testimony at that time, repeated during the trial, consists only of his own suppositions, is not only unsupported by any other evidence but even contradicted by the trial evidence.

Let us now look at Ginzburg's testimony. He states: 'I intended to, and I did, give this collection only to representatives of the state'. It is true that one copy of the collection was given to the KGB by Ginzburg. It is on the table in front of you. The investigation has established that Ginzburg showed a copy of the collection to Ehrenburg. The witness Stolyarova has confirmed she knows personally that Ginzburg showed the collection to Ehrenburg who, as we all know, is a deputy to the Supreme Soviet. Ginzburg declines to name the other deputies he showed it to, but this collection is now considered criminal and Ginzburg cannot name these people without obtaining their consent. And we can all understand that Ginzburg has no means of doing so.

And so we see that Ginzburg's evidence is at least partially substantiated. In addition, Ginzburg said at the preliminary investigation that he knew a copy of the collection had been given officially to the chairman of the Supreme Court. However, the investigators made no attempt to verify this statement.

I consider that Ginzburg had, personally, no part in the appearance of his collection in the West. We all know of the publication in the West of Galina Serebryakova's manuscript,[74] of the memoirs of Evgenia Ginzburg,[75] and so on. The witness Levitin, when asked in court how his articles had reached the West, said he had no idea. Thus a person may not know how his articles reach the West.

In conclusion, I should like to speak of Ginzburg passing to Gubanov the newspaper extracts which the prosecution considers anti-Soviet. It has already been established that this material was in the Norwegian, Danish and Italian languages, which Ginzburg does not know, and in French, which he knows very badly. As Ginzburg has said, he came upon the extracts by chance, when he was gathering material about Sinyavsky and Daniel from foreign papers. His attention was drawn to certain newspaper articles not connected with the Sinyavsky–Daniel trial, but which contained the word SMOG in large Latin characters: the court has had the chance to check this for itself. Not knowing, not being able to know, exactly what these articles contained, but realizing they were about SMOG, Ginzburg gave them to Gubanov, a member of SMOG. In order to prove a charge of distributing slanderous fabrications it is necessary to prove intent. That Ginzburg did not know, and could not know, the contents of these articles should prove the absence of any such intent. Consequently, he cannot be charged with circulating anti-Soviet material.

The witnesses Stolyarova and Pinsky have spoken of Ginzburg's integrity and honesty, of his undoubted intelligence, talent and courage.

I respectfully submit to the court that I need not dwell on Ginzburg's moral virtues, as, whether he is a good or an evil man, I can confidently state that he is not a guilty one.

To sum up, I should like to say that in my opinion the Prosecution has not provided enough evidence to charge Ginzburg with anti-Soviet activities.

I ask the court to pronounce a verdict of 'not guilty' on Alexander Ginzburg.

JUDGE. Does the State Prosecutor want to make any comment on the defence speeches?

PROCURATOR. No.

JUDGE. The accused Dobrovolsky may now make his final statement.

DOBROVOLSKY. Because of the fact that a lot of new accusations have been made against me here, I request the court to allow me ten or fifteen minutes to consult my lawyer so that I may repudiate these accusations in my final statement.

JUDGE. Dobrovolsky, no new accusations have been made against you. What Galanskov, Ginzburg or their counsel have said does not affect the charges against you: for you everything remains as it was in the indictment.

DOBROVOLSKY. All the same, I ask you to allow me an opportunity to prepare my statement.

JUDGE (after consulting the assessors). Very well, there will be a five-minute recess.

A five-minute recess. Then Dobrovolsky takes the stand.

FINAL STATEMENT OF DOBROVOLSKY

Some people here have tried to accuse me of having connections with the NTS and with illegal currency operations. I have no connections with either. I didn't even know anything about them before. I did not know exactly what the NTS was. I only understood what kind of an organization it is from the investigation and from the Procurator's speech, which opened my eyes to many things. I have tried to be as honest as possible during the investigation and trial. I have told the truth. If I had known this truth earlier, I would have told it earlier.

JUDGE. The accused Lashkova may now make her final statement.

FINAL STATEMENT OF LASHKOVA

I have been in prison for a year now and I've had a lot of time to think. I have never held anti-Soviet opinions and have never intended to weaken Soviet power.

I realize that my fault lies in the fact that I did not think seriously enough about these matters and others; if I had thought about them seriously enough, it's possible I would not have ended up here, in the dock.

In his speech for the Prosecution the Procurator called for a sentence on me of one year's deprivation of liberty. Consequently I can hardly ask the court for a lighter punishment.* But nevertheless, whatever the verdict may be, I wish to say that this final statement of mine is the first and last I shall make as an accused person.

JUDGE. The accused Galanskov may now make his final statement.

GALANSKOV. I am feeling very ill. I request the court to declare a recess.

JUDGE. Galanskov, this court cannot constantly be declaring recesses. You may make your final statement—proceed!

FINAL STATEMENT OF GALANSKOV

I wish to begin my final statement by saying that I do not admit myself to be guilty of the charges connected with article 88, paragraph 1, of the Criminal Code.

There is a tape-recording of my conversation with the investigator. During that conversation I corrected the investigator when he said I had sold dollars. I told him then, and I affirm now, that I did not want to sell the dollars but to change them officially. In addition, both Entin and Borisova testified that I personally had no need to change the dollars—Entin himself offered to do it for me. As I did not spend any of the money which I got as a result of the transaction, not even fifty kopecks on a meat-pie for myself, but gave it all back to Dobrovolsky, I do not admit myself guilty of any crime under article 88.

As for the charge under article 70 concerning connections with the anti-Soviet émigré organization NTS, I do not consider myself guilty of that either. Neither my testimony, nor Dobrovolsky's testimony, on which this charge is based, contains any proof of my guilt. I consider myself innocent and will always do so.

The Prosecution has told us many valuable facts about the NTS that were not known to anyone before. I understand that the organs of the KGB must have found the information very interesting. I also was interested to hear all this. But, in my opinion, the first part of the Procurator's speech, which was devoted to an examination of this subject, had no specific connection with this trial, nor, I hope, will it be able to influence unduly the verdict of this court.

The charges made against me are menacing in their social and political complexity. But it's not easy to frighten me.

My name has, indeed, been known in the West for some time. I am known as a poet and also because of my demonstration at the

---

* The period of imprisonment is considered to start from the date of arrest, i.e. for Lashkova from 17 January 1967.

American Embassy about the US aggression against the Dominican Republic. But, in the first place, I am not vainglorious and have never sought this kind of fame; secondly, this fact in itself is no evidence of any kind of connections with foreign, anti-Soviet organizations.

It is hard to frighten me because legal forms in our country are gradually but constantly taking on their rightful character. The Marxist potential of the Party is being restored all the time. The October Revolution, like all other revolutions having lived through a period of dictatorship, has turned out to be strong enough to survive that period undefeated and strong enough to preserve its revolutionary proletarian essence.

As concerns the purely legal parts of this case, life and the investigation have taught me to use my resources in the right way. I see no reason to try to prove myself innocent of the charges against me, as most of them are absolutely unfounded and have no connection with reality. I call upon the court to be impartial in its verdict on Dobrovolsky, Lashkova and myself. As for Ginzburg, his innocence is so obvious that the court can have no doubt of its verdict concerning him.

In conclusion I should like to speak about the field of social problems discussed in the miscellany *Phoenix*. I first intended *Phoenix* to be a pacifist journal, and the main reason influencing my change of mind was the trial of Sinyavsky and Daniel.

Among the material I asked to be attached to the case materials was my written opinion concerning the conduct of that trial. I asked to have it sent to the Central Committee of the Party and to the Ideological Commission. I think that the above-named organizations will be interested in this material and that it could have some effect on the fate of Sinyavsky and Daniel.

I feel that a reappraisal of that trial would play a great role in proving the enormous moral potential of socialism.

> The Judge declares a fifteen-minute recess. Then the session is resumed.

JUDGE. The accused Ginzburg may now make his final statement.

FINAL STATEMENT OF GINZBURG

I want to begin my final statement by expressing my thanks to the Prosecution for dropping the accusation of personal dishonesty against me—the accusation that I, having written a letter to Kosygin expressing my point of view about the trial of Sinyavsky and Daniel, did not send the letter to the person it was addressed to. I considered that accusation offensive.

Much has been said in this court about the NTS. I don't think that the State Prosecutor's opinion of this anti-Soviet émigré organization can be disputed in any way. I only wish to thank the State Prosecutor for not going so far as to number us with those who during the war killed, tortured and exterminated the Jews, for not directly accusing us of that kind of action. I shall now turn to the main point.

In this court, on 9 January, I have already tried to speak of my opinions and my motives for compiling the collection of material about the case of Sinyavsky and Daniel. I shall not repeat all that now. I only want to describe again briefly the reaction of public opinion to the trial of Sinyavsky and Daniel, and the circumstances in which I compiled this collection, which has now been made the basis of the charge against me.

When, on 9 January, I tried to speak about this, and compared the reaction of world opinion to the Sinyavsky–Daniel trial with the reaction to the trials of Greek democrats, there was laughter, which sounded more like snarling, in this courtroom. Nevertheless, I am going to speak about this again. The Procurator told us at some length that the NTS do not protest against the American aggression in Vietnam. What has that to do with the collection of material about the Sinyavsky–Daniel trial? I can refer to the first ninety pages of the collection lying before you. They contain, for example, a protest signed by, among others, Norman, who is at the moment in hospital with bayonet wounds received during a demonstration at the Pentagon against American aggression in Vietnam. This collection also contains protests signed by many other progressive people in the world. Perhaps the State Prosecutor is right about the attitude of the NTS to the war in Vietnam. But this is in no way connected with the collection which I compiled from all the material available to me about the case of Sinyavsky and Daniel, for the purpose of giving an objective picture of that trial and of world reaction to it, and of asking for a reappraisal of the case.

I am charged with including in my collection material which this court considers to be anti-Soviet. I refer to the leaflet signed 'Resistance' and the 'Letter to an Old Friend'. The defence counsels did not consider it their aim to dispute the Prosecution's arguments on this score. I find it necessary to discuss this, because if the court declares these documents to be criminal, then they cannot in future be defended by anyone, as was the case with Sinyavsky's article

'What Is Socialist Realism?' It is precisely because of this that I, as the compiler of the collection, consider it my duty to speak of these two documents.

First, the pamphlet 'Resistance'. The court knows what it is about. The facts set out in it are true, supported by witnesses, for instance Kushev. There has been no evidence by witnesses which proves these facts to be fabrications or slanders. During the court investigation this pamphlet was often quoted, particularly the words: 'The ferocity of the dogs only emphasizes the dispositions of their trainers.' The pamphlet does not refer by this to Soviet power as a whole. It refers only to the employees of the KGB organs who disrupted a public meeting and later expelled from the university forty students who had taken part in the meeting.

JUDGE interrupts Ginzburg, ordering him not to criticize the actions of representatives of the state security organs.

GINZBURG. I regard those actions as unlawful. If the court finds them lawful, the court takes that responsibility upon itself. I have already made statements on this subject in which I said that, in my opinion, the meeting in defence of Sinyavsky and Daniel was perfectly lawful and that nobody had the right to expel the participants from the university. Besides, the KGB employees acted in a rude and intolerable manner, and their actions are a dark blot on the reputation of that esteemed organization.

JUDGE again rebukes Ginzburg.

GINZBURG. So I consider this pamphlet is perhaps sharply critical in form but it is not directed against the Soviet state, only against the actions of certain KGB employees. Besides this, the pamphlet contains no slanders, no twisting of the facts; it contains only a rebuke to the authorities concerning a specific action. I ask the court to remove it from the list of anti-Soviet documents.

Now for the 'Letter to an Old Friend'. I have already said I don't know who wrote it. But I think it was someone who had known the horrors of Stalinist concentration camps. He writes: 'You and I have both known Stalin's times.' And the author talks of that period in a sharply critical tone. But that is not enough to class this document as anti-Soviet. In his speech on the fiftieth anniversary of the KGB, the chairman of the KGB, Andropov, said: 'We must not forget the time when political adventurers took over the leadership of our organization.' That is also what the author of the 'Letter to an Old Friend' calls for. Another excerpt from this letter has been quoted here: 'Gorky promoted a cannibalistic slogan—if the enemy doesn't surrender, he is exterminated.' First, this applies to the time I have just spoken of. Secondly, criticism of a single writer, even a great writer, is not criticism of the whole state. A man who lived through the horrors of that terrible period is bound to become agitated when he suddenly feels that, in his present life, he can see a return to the past; and then the expression of that concern is perfectly justified in being sharply critical. I maintain that the 'Letter to an Old Friend' contains no slander of the Soviet system, nor is it a call for the destruction of that system; and I ask the court not to classify this document as anti-Soviet.

As for the charge concerning my handing over to Gubanov of some newspaper extracts of anti-Soviet content, my counsel has offered a full and well-founded argument on that score, and I will not repeat it.

As concerns the charge that the collection of material I compiled about the trial of Sinyavsky and Daniel was given, with my consent, to the NTS by Galanskov—it has also been convincingly proved that this story is not only unsupported by evidence but even contradicts facts proved to be true during the court proceedings.

And so I am accused of compiling a biased account of the trial of Sinyavsky and Daniel. I do not consider myself to be guilty. I acted in this way because I was convinced I was right. My lawyer asked for a verdict of 'not guilty' on my behalf. I know that you will convict me, because so far no one accused under article 70 has been declared innocent. I shall depart peacefully to a labour camp to serve my term. You can send me to prison or to a labour camp, but I am sure no honest man will condemn me. I only ask the court for one favour: not to give me a shorter sentence than Galanskov. (Laughter in the courtroom, shouts of 'Longer, longer!')

JUDGE. The court will retire to consider its verdict.

> The judges retire for over four hours. At about 16.30 hours the usher calls out: 'The court will rise while the judges enter.' Everyone rises, the judges enter, in the same order as on the first day, and the presiding judge reads the sentence.

SENTENCE

in the name of the
Russian Soviet Federative Socialist Republic

12 January 1968, Moscow

The Judicial Collegium on Criminal Cases of the Moscow City Court, consisting of Presiding Judge L. K. Mironov—Deputy Chairman of the Moscow City Court—and People's Assessors S. G. Dudnikov and G. V. Chizhova, having—with the assistance of the Clerk of the Court A. I. Fomicheva and the participation of Procurator G. A. Terekhov, senior assistant to the Procurator-General of the USSR, and Defence Counsels B. A. Zolotukhin, D. I. Kaminskaya, S. L. Ariya and V. Ya. Shveisky—heard in open court the case of:

ALEXANDER ILICH GINZBURG: born on 21 November 1936; a Jew; citizen of the USSR; native of the city of Moscow; not a member of the Party; general secondary education; unmarried; no previous criminal record; until his arrest a general worker at the State Literary Museum; residing in Moscow, ul. B. Polyanka, No. 11/14, flat 25.

YURY TIMOFEYEVICH GALANSKOV: born on 19 June 1939; a Russian; citizen of the USSR; native of the city of Moscow; not a member of the Party; general secondary education; married; no previous criminal record; until his arrest a general worker at the State Literary Museum; residing in Moscow at 3-i Golutvinsky pereulok, No. 7/9, flat 4.

ALEKSEI ALEKSANDROVICH DOBROVOLSKY: born on 13 October 1938; a Russian; citizen of the USSR; native of the city of Moscow; not a member of the Party; general secondary education; married; has a child born in 1963; no previous criminal record; until his arrest a book-binder at the State Literary Museum; residing in Moscow, at Kalanchevskaya ul., No. 4, flat 16.

VERA IOSIFOVNA LASHKOVA: born on 18 June 1944; a Russian; citizen of the USSR; not a member of the Party; no previous criminal record; general secondary education; unmarried; until her arrest a laboratory assistant at the Preparatory Faculty of Moscow State Lomonosov University; residing in Moscow at Kropotkinskaya ul., No. 13, flat 9.

The accused Ginzburg, Dobrovolsky and Lashkova are charged with offences under article 70, paragraph 1, of the Russian Criminal Code, and the accused Galanskov under article 70, paragraph 1, and article 88, paragraph 1, of the Russian Criminal Code.

Having studied the evidence given during this judicial investigation, and having heard the arguments of the Procurator and the defence counsels, and the final statements of the accused, the Judicial Collegium *finds that*:

In 1965 the accused Ginzburg and Galanskov established criminal connections with the foreign, anti-Soviet organization calling itself

Narodno-trudovoy soyuz (NTS) [*People's Labour Alliance*] which is on the payroll of the United States Central Intelligence Agency.

The so-called People's Labour Alliance openly declares as its aim the overthrow of the existing system in the USSR and the restoration of the bourgeois way of life, through 'ideological and armed struggle with the Communist system'.

Ginzburg and Galanskov handed over to the NTS various slanderous anti-Soviet articles with the aim of getting them published abroad; Galanskov also received anti-Soviet material from the NTS, which he circulated within the Soviet Union.

In the summer of 1966 Galanskov and Ginzburg enticed Lashkova and Dobrovolsky into anti-Soviet activities. Lashkova and Dobrovolsky took an active part in duplicating and circulating anti-Soviet material, including that received from the NTS. Dobrovolsky also stored materials for invisible writing and for duplication of typed texts, which Galanskov had received from the NTS.

The anti-Soviet material sent abroad by Galanskov and Ginzburg was widely used in anti-Soviet, anti-Communist bourgeois propaganda against the USSR, including the publications of the NTS.

Each of the accused is guilty of perpetrating the following crimes:

(1) The accused GINZBURG carried on anti-Soviet incitement for a long time; established criminal connections with the foreign anti-Soviet organization calling itself the People's Labour Alliance; handed over for publication material containing anti-Soviet slanders which was widely used by the NTS in its written and oral propaganda against the Soviet Union, and also circulated in the Soviet Union material containing anti-Soviet slanders and published abroad.

In June 1966 Ginzburg received cuttings from foreign newspapers from a foreigner he met: they contained extracts from an article beginning with the words 'this ended in arrest and expulsion' and also the articles 'Appeal by Young Soviet Intellectuals to the Free World' and 'Call to the Free World'. (These two articles state clearly that the material had been provided for publication by the NTS periodical *Grani*.) They contained slanders against Soviet reality, and he circulated these articles by giving them to citizen Gubanov.

From February to October 1966 the accused Ginzburg, with the help of the accused Galanskov, compiled a collection which included the so-called 'Letter to an Old Friend' and a leaflet signed 'Resistance', which contained slanderous fabrications directed against the Soviet social and political system. This material included a direct call for opposition to authority and slanderous statements about the lack of personal and creative freedom in the Soviet Union. Thus, in the leaflet signed 'Resistance', it says: 'Obviously the authorities do not consider it necessary to safeguard in real life the freedoms proclaimed in the Constitution; on the contrary, they are inclined to uphold attacks on democracy and encourage direct or indirect violations of personal freedom' (vol. 9, p. 88, in the case materials).

In November 1966, with the help of Galanskov and Lashkova, Ginzburg produced about ten typewritten copies of the material he had compiled, including the 'Letter to an Old Friend' and the anti-Soviet leaflet signed 'Resistance'; he sent one of these copies through Galanskov to the NTS for publication. The texts named were published in the NTS periodical *Grani*, No. 62, and in other publications.

In the second half of 1966 Ginzburg helped Galanskov to compile a collection which included the following slanderous anti-Soviet material: 'Open Letter', 'The Russian Road to Socialism and its Results', 'The Confession of Victor Velsky' and 'Socialist Realism'.

In January 1967 Galanskov handed this collection to a representative of the NTS for publication. In the NTS periodical *Grani*, No. 63, there was an account of how this collection had been received and a short commentary on it. The so-called 'Open Letter' contains slanders on socialist society and on Soviet democracy and falsely claims that 'the revolutionary-humanist views of the Party have ceased to be humanist, the people have been reduced to the status of cattle, and the mythical Soviet man has failed to the same extent as the Soviet state itself has failed' (vol. 11, p. 131).

The article 'The Russian Road to Socialism and its Results' distorts the historical perspective of our country's development; it slanders Soviet reality and the economic measures carried out by the Soviet government.

'The Confession of Victor Velsky' is written in a spirit of hatred for humanity and of monstrous animosity towards the Soviet people's government. It contains infamous slanders on the Soviet people and the democratic foundations of socialist society. Thus, in the 'Confession' it says: 'I curse the Soviet State, which has defiled Russia. . . . It is built on lies and self-deception, it is essentially hostile to the best human impulses' (vol. 10, p. 53).

(2) The accused GALANSKOV carried on anti-Soviet incitement; established and maintained for a long time illegal connections with the foreign anti-Soviet organization NTS; more than once he met its representatives and sent to the NTS anti-Soviet material which was used in written and oral propaganda against the Soviet Union; received anti-Soviet material from the NTS and circulated it;

received foreign currency and Soviet money from the NTS, also materials for invisible writing and for duplication of typed texts for the purpose of carrying on anti-Soviet incitement.

During 1966 the accused Galanskov received from representatives of the NTS, who had come to visit him, the following anti-Soviet literature published by the NTS for the purpose of circulation: the pamphlet 'Solidarism Is the Idea of the Future', which describes the aims and organization of the NTS, urges ways and means, including armed warfare, of fighting against the existing socialist system in our country; the periodical *Our Times*, No. 35, which includes articles distorting certain measures and internal policies of the Soviet Communist Party and the Soviet government; the newspaper *Possev*, August 1966, containing attacks on the Soviet government and calling for a struggle against Soviet power; the books *The Power of Ideas* and *At the Price of a Spiritual Feat*, which contain calls for the overthrow of Soviet power and for purely terrorist action, and also practical advice on the setting up of illegal NTS organizations on the territory of the Soviet Union.

During the same period, Galanskov received, from the same members of the NTS, a hectograph, materials for invisible writing, and money to the amount of 560 dollars and more than 2000 roubles in Soviet currency, intended for use in anti-Soviet activities. Galanskov gave Dobrovolsky the hectograph and also the NTS literature he had been given for duplication and circulation.

From February to October 1966 Galanskov took part, together with Ginzburg, in compiling the collection which included the so-called 'Letter to an Old Friend' and the leaflet signed 'Resistance', containing slanderous fabrications about the Soviet social and political system.

In November 1966 Galanskov, with the help of Lashkova, typed copies of the above collection and, in the same month, during a meeting with an NTS representative called Genrikh who was visiting Moscow, gave him a copy of the collection for publication abroad.

The collection sent abroad was published in the NTS periodical *Grani*, No. 62, 1966, and in other foreign publications.

In the second half of 1966 Galanskov, with the help of Ginzburg, compiled a collection containing material of a slanderous, anti-Soviet character: 'Open Letter', 'The Russian Road to Socialism and its Results', 'The Confession of Victor Velsky' and 'Socialist Realism'. The articles named are distinguished by their anti-Soviet attitude and their slanders against the Soviet system and government. Galanskov, with Ginzburg's help, made five copies of this collection.

In January 1967 Galanskov, during a meeting with a representative of the NTS calling herself Nadya, who had come to visit him, agreed to send this collection abroad for publication, and during a later specially arranged meeting, handed the collection over to her.

A report about the receiving of this collection was published in No. 63 of the periodical *Grani*, and a short commentary on it was also given.

From October to November 1966 Galanskov prepared the anti-Soviet 'Open Letter' and, with Lashkova's help, had fifteen copies typed out. In January 1967, he gave one copy to Dobrovolsky and made arrangements with him about duplicating more copies for circulation.

During December 1966 and January 1967 Galanskov gave Dobrovolsky two anti-Soviet articles: 'The Russian Road to Socialism and its Results' and 'The Confession of Victor Velsky', for duplication and subsequent circulation.

In December 1966 the accused Galanskov, in contravention of the currency regulations, sold 400 dollars at the rate of three roubles to one dollar, through the agency of his friends Entin and Borisova.

(3) The accused DOBROVOLSKY, after entering into criminal connections with Galanskov and Lashkova, carried on anti-Soviet propaganda, duplicated, stored and circulated anti-Soviet material, and also stored materials for invisible writing and for duplication of texts, which Galanskov had received from the NTS.

From November to December 1966 Dobrovolsky received from Galanskov the following anti-Soviet literature sent by the NTS for circulation: the pamphlet 'Solidarism Is the Idea of the Future', the periodical *Our Times*, No. 35, the books *The Power of Ideas* and *At the Price of a Spiritual Feat*. In December 1966 Dobrovolsky circulated this literature, giving to Lashkova the periodical *Our Times* and the pamphlet 'Solidarism Is the Idea of the Future', to L. Kats the periodical *Our Times* and the book *The Power of Ideas*, and to Kushev the pamphlet 'Solidarism Is the Idea of the Future'.

At the end of 1966 Dobrovolsky received and stored in his flat the following material sent by the NTS for the purpose of anti-Soviet agitation: the anti-Soviet paper *Possev*, August 1966, in the form of eight sheets; a hectograph, and more than 2000 roubles in Soviet currency.

In December 1966 Dobrovolsky, with the help of Ustinova and Kamyshanova, produced for circulation five copies of the anti-Soviet text called 'The Confession of Victor Velsky'.

In January 1967, having agreed with Galanskov to duplicate for circulation the so-called 'Open Letter' containing anti-Soviet slanders, he received this letter and gave it to Radziyevsky for duplication in thirty copies.

In January 1967 Dobrovolsky, with the help of Ustinova, made five copies, for circulation, of the anti-Soviet text 'The Russian Road to Socialism and its Results', which Galanskov had given him.

(4) The accused LASHKOVA, in the summer of 1966, engaged in anti-Soviet propaganda, re-typed and circulated anti-Soviet literature. From October to November 1966 Lashkova received from Ginzburg and Galanskov texts containing anti-Soviet slanders: the 'Letter to an Old Friend' and the pamphlet signed 'Resistance'—and re-typed five copies of this material for circulation.

In the second half of 1966 Lashkova re-typed for circulation fifteen copies of the so-called 'Open Letter' and ten copies of the text called 'The Russian Road to Socialism and its Results', both of which contain matter of a slanderous anti-Soviet nature.

From November to December 1966, Lashkova received slanderous anti-Soviet material published by the NTS, namely: 'Solidarism Is the Idea of the Future', and the periodical *Our Times*, No. 35, which she circulated, giving the pamphlet to Kushev and the periodical to Levitin.

The accused Dobrovolsky and Lashkova have fully admitted their guilt in court.

The accused Ginzburg and Galanskov have not admitted themselves guilty of the charges brought against them.

The Judicial Collegium considers that the charges have been proved during the trial and that all the accused are guilty as charged.

The accused Dobrovolsky and Lashkova, having admitted their guilt, gave detailed evidence at the preliminary investigation and during the trial about their own actions and also about the crimes of the accused Ginzburg and Galanskov.

The guilt of the accused Dobrobolsky and Lashkova, apart from their confessions, is supported by the evidence of the witnesses Kats, Ustinova, Radziyevsky, Levitin, Tsvetkov and Golovanov about the duplication and circulation of anti-Soviet literature and other anti-Soviet slanders by Dobrovolsky and Lashkova.

From the report of the search (vol. 14, pp. 35-37) it can be seen that from Dobrovolsky were confiscated: the paper *Possev*, anti-Soviet literature, a hectograph, and money to the amount of more than 2000 roubles, which Galanskov had received from the NTS.

The charges against Ginzburg are supported by the testimony of the accused Ginzburg himself, in which he admitted compiling the collection and including in it the 'Letter to an Old Friend' and the leaflet 'Resistance'; by the evidence of the accused Lashkova that at Ginzburg's request she typed five copies of the material for this collection; by the evidence of the accused Dobrovolsky that Ginzburg compiled the above collection, and that Galanskov gave it, with Ginzburg's consent, to a representative of the NTS for publication abroad.

The fact that the NTS received and published this work of Ginzburg's is shown in the periodical *Grani* which is available as material evidence in the case materials (vol. 17, p. 87).

The fact that Ginzburg took part in compiling a collection which included the 'Open Letter' and other anti-Soviet material is supported by the evidence of Dobrovolsky, the confiscation of a copy of this collection from Ginzburg's flat, and also by the testimony of Ginzburg that he had read the manuscript of the 'Open Letter' while visiting Galanskov in his flat.

The existence of ties between Ginzburg and the NTS is supported by:

the evidence of Dobrovolsky that it was Ginzburg who put Galanskov in touch with the NTS and that Ginzburg and Galanskov knew of the arrival of the NTS agent Schaffhauser in the Soviet Union;

the evidence of the witness Brox Sokolov that, during a conversation with him, the NTS member Slavinsky named Ginzburg as a participant in underground activity in the Soviet Union;

the fact that the collection Ginzburg compiled was given by him to the NTS and was published in the periodical *Grani*.

That Ginzburg received from a foreigner newspaper cuttings from foreign papers containing slanderous anti-Soviet articles is supported by Ginzburg's own testimony in court and by the evidence of the witness Basilova. Ginzburg admitted giving the above newspaper cuttings to Gubanov. Basilova has confirmed that the cuttings were brought from abroad by a foreigner. The witness Basilova has also stated that Ginzburg fixed with Gubanov a meeting with the foreigner.

The charges against Galanskov have been proved by Galanskov's own evidence at the preliminary investigation that he had ties with the NTS, often met representatives of the NTS who came to visit him, compiled a collection which included the 'Open Letter' and other anti-Soviet material, and gave it to an NTS representative for publication abroad together with another collection which contained anti-Soviet material, i.e. the 'Letter to an Old Friend' and the leaflet signed 'Resistance'.

In addition to this Galanskov has admitted that on more than one occasion he received from the NTS anti-Soviet literature, a hectograph, materials for invisible writing, American and Soviet money, and that he also circulated the anti-Soviet literature he received from the NTS inside the Soviet Union.

The existence of ties between Galanskov and the NTS is supported by:

the evidence of Dobrovolsky that Galanskov met representatives of the NTS more than once, that he gave him anti-Soviet literature he had received from the NTS for circulation, that he also gave him the hectograph, the materials for invisible writing and more than 2000 roubles in Soviet currency; that Galanskov also asked him, with Lashkova's help, to type a letter for him on the cryptography paper —a letter later sent to the NTS—and also to find him a co-operative flat which could be used for receiving NTS correspondence and parcels;

the evidence of Lashkova that, at Galanskov's request, she typed a letter in code and, at Dobrovolsky's request, wrote a letter for him on invisible-writing paper, which were both sent to the NTS;

the fact that the anti-Soviet literature, hectograph and money, obtained from Galanskov, were discovered in Dobrovolsky's flat.

During the trial, the accused Galanskov repudiated in full his former evidence, denied taking part in anti-Soviet activities, and explained that he had slandered himself so as to shield Dobrovolsky.

The Judicial Collegium considers that Galanskov's evidence during the preliminary investigation was nevertheless true, as it corresponds with the evidence of Dobrovolsky and Lashkova, and with the facts of the case.

In addition, Galanskov did not show any convincing motivation for altering his evidence in court.

From the periodical *Grani*, No. 63 (vol. 17, p. 88)—available to the court—it is obvious that the collection compiled by Galanskov, with Ginzburg's help, was received by the foreign anti-Soviet organization NTS.

The evidence of the accused Lashkova, of the witnesses Kats, Khaustov and Vinogradov, support the charge accusing Galanskov of circulating libellous, anti-Soviet literature.

The contents of the texts named in the descriptive part of the sentence, of the literature received from NTS representatives by Galanskov, of the newspaper cuttings received from a foreigner by

Ginzburg—all bear witness to their libellous anti-Soviet character.

The evidence of the witnesses Entin and Borisova supports the charge accusing Galanskov of breaking the currency regulations. The accused Galanskov has not denied that the dollars were sold to unauthorized persons.

After evaluating the testimony of the accused, the contents of the literature they wrote, collected and circulated, the accumulation of proof gathered at the preliminary investigation and trial, the Judicial Collegium has come to the conclusion that, in carrying out their criminal activities, the accused Ginzburg, Galanskov, Dobrovolsky and Lashkova had as their aim the weakening of Soviet power. Consequently their actions are rightly defined as contravening article 70, paragraph 1, of the Russian Criminal Code.

Galanskov's breaking of the law is correctly defined as also contravening article 88, paragraph 1, of the Russian Criminal Code, as he, in selling dollars to unauthorized persons, was contravening the currency regulations.

Before deciding on the necessary punitive measures, the Judicial Collegium took into account the special danger of the crimes committed, and also the degree to which each of the accused was involved in the crime committed; the testimony given about the characters of the accused; and the sincere confession and repentance of their crimes by Dobrovolsky and Lashkova.

The Judicial Collegium cannot ignore the past behaviour of the accused Ginzburg. Since 1960 the Committee of State Security has more than once come across Ginzburg's anti-Soviet activities, and Ginzburg has promised to abandon his unseemly past and publicly criticized his own behaviour but then continued to carry on anti-Soviet propaganda.

The Judicial Collegium also takes into account that the accused Galanskov established close personal contacts with the NTS and received payment for carrying on anti-Soviet propaganda.

On the basis of the above conclusions, and in accordance with articles 301-303 and 312 of the Russian Code of Criminal Procedure, the Judicial Collegium on Criminal Cases of the Moscow City Court gives the following *verdict*:

YURY TIMOFEYEVICH GALANSKOV is found guilty of contravening article 70, paragraph 1, of the Russian Criminal Code, and article 88, paragraph 1, of the Russian Criminal Code, and is sentenced as follows: under article 70, paragraph 1, to seven years' deprivation of liberty without exile; under article 88, paragraph 1, to three years' deprivation of liberty without confiscation of property and without exile. On the basis of all the crimes committed, and according to article 10 of the Code, the final sentence on Yu. T. Galanskov is a term of *seven years'* deprivation of liberty in a strict-regime corrective labour colony, without exile and without confiscation of property.

Yu. T. Galanskov's term of imprisonment will run as from 19 January 1967.

ALEXANDER ILICH GINZBURG is found guilty of contravening article 70, paragraph 1, of the Russian Criminal Code and is sentenced to a term of *five years'* deprivation of liberty in a strict-regime corrective labour colony, without exile.

A. I. Ginzburg's term of imprisonment will run as from 23 January 1967.

ALEKSEI ALEKSANDROVICH DOBROVOLSKY is found guilty of contravening article 70, paragraph 1, of the Russian Criminal Code, and is sentenced to a term of *two years'* deprivation of liberty in a strict-regime corrective labour colony, without exile.

A. A. Dobrovolsky's term of imprisonment will run as from 19 January 1967.

VERA IOSIFOVNA LASHKOVA is found guilty of contravening article 70, paragraph 1, of the Russian Criminal Code, and is sentenced to a term of *one year*'s deprivation of liberty in a strict-regime corrective labour colony, without exile.

V. I. Lashkova's term of imprisonment will run as from 17 January 1967.

The degree of restriction of the prisoners Galanskov, Ginzburg, Dobrovolsky and Lashkova will remain that of detention under guard.

As regards the material evidence: the typewriters 'Moskva', 'Olympia' and 'Olivetti' will be confiscated; the anti-Soviet material —books, periodicals, newspaper cuttings, the paper *Possev*, leaflets, cryptography paper and hectograph—is to be preserved in the case materials.

The money confiscated from Dobrovolsky is to be turned over to the state as the fruits of crime.

The sentence may be appealed against to the Russian Supreme Court during the seven days following the sentencing, and for the prisoners Ginzburg, Galanskov, Dobrovolsky and Lashkova the appeal may take place during the seven days following the day on which they are handed a copy of the sentence.*

(Stormy, prolonged applause in the courtroom.)

The prisoners are led out of the courtroom. The court sitting ends at 17.00 hours on 12 January [*1968*].

[*Commentary*]

The trial took place in the Moscow City Court on Kalanchevskaya Street. According to reports from some of the accused and from their relations and many of the witnesses, conduct in the courtroom was extremely disorderly—the public kept up a constant din, shouting and drumming with their feet. The defence counsels protested on two occasions, but the judge did not accept either of these protests, saying: 'The public are only expressing their opinion'. The 'public', as might have been expected, consisted partly of KGB employees and partly of party activists sent by party district committees. The only relatives of the accused allowed into the courtroom were: Galanskov's father, mother, wife and sister, Ginzburg's fiancée and Dobrovolsky's mother. After giving their evidence Ginzburg's mother and Dobrovolsky's wife were allowed to stay in the courtroom. Galanskov's sister was not allowed into the courtroom after the third day. KGB officials obstructed the taking of notes by all the relatives except Dobrovolsky's wife; some of the notes that were taken were confiscated by KGB Colonel Tsirkunenko, who was acting as the 'Commandant of the Court'. (The real Commandant of the Court was removed for the duration of the trial.) The relatives were forbidden to talk to the witnesses, except for Dobrovolsky's mother, who had a long conversation with his wife before the latter gave evidence. All the witnesses were made to leave the courtroom after they had given their evidence.

As the trial began to attract more and more attention among the Soviet and world public, it became noticeable that the court tried

---

* Appeals against the sentence were made, and they were heard by the Court of Appeal on 16 April 1968 (see pp. 351-371). It should be noted that, under existing judicial practice, copies of the sentence are hardly ever handed to prisoners condemned under article 70 of the Criminal Code; they are only shown to the prisoners for a quick reading, although this is not stipulated either under law or in the published instructions on the subject. For example, Lashkova was allowed to read the sentence thoroughly only when on the point of entering the Court of Appeal. However, this practice has lately been changing, and prisoners have in a number of cases been given a copy of their sentence which they can keep for themselves.

both to shift its basic emphasis away from the compiling of the 'criminal' collections and over to the connections allegedly existing between the accused and the NTS, and also to play down the connection between this trial and that of Sinyavsky and Daniel. This is obvious merely from a comparison between the indictment with which the trial began and the statement preceding the passing of the sentences, with which the trial ended. It is indicative that, in the sentences, Sinyavsky, Daniel and Sholokhov are not even mentioned. From this angle it is interesting to note that the actions of the accused were not defined as falling under article 72 (organized activity aimed at committing especially dangerous crimes against the state, and also being a member of an anti-Soviet organization), but only under article 70.

After the sentence was pronounced, there was loud applause from the public in the courtroom, some of whom shouted 'Too little, too little!' The accused were immediately surrounded by soldiers, and were led out of the courtroom. Their relatives had no chance to say one word to them, except for Galanskov's wife who cried out 'Yurka!'

On the first day of the trial, on 8 January, relatives and friends of the accused began to gather outside the court at 9.00 hours, together with other people interested in the trial and foreign journalists. There was also a fairly large number of members of the operations squad of the Moscow City Komsomol Committee and employees of the KGB in civilian clothes. There were about 100 to 150 people standing outside the court. The main entrance was closed, guarded by a squad of police and by members of the operations squad wearing red armbands, who only allowed in those with special passes. All the others were sent to a courtyard entrance in the left wing of the building. Here was, open to the public, a corridor on the ground floor which led to the court offices. But the passage from this corridor to the right wing of the building, where the trial was due to take place, was also closed and guarded by a squad of policemen and by people in civilian clothes with armbands. The entrance to the staircase leading to the first floor, where the court chancellery is located, was also blocked by members of the operations squad with red armbands.

It soon became clear that no one was being allowed into the courtroom. From about 9.00 hours people were being allowed in through another entrance, but only if they had special passes issued by the KGB or by district party committees. Up to 11.00 hours even the relatives were not allowed into the courtroom and, after that time, only at the special request of the accused. Some of the citizens waiting outside the court building drafted a letter to the chairman of the Moscow City Court, Osetrov, and to the presiding judge, Mironov, asking to be allowed into the courtroom. The letter was signed by about thirty people, the majority of whom had signed an earlier petition for the trial to be held in open court ('Letter of the 116' and 'Letter of the 44'), and the letter was handed to the court chancellery. There was no reply. As there was only one copy of this letter, which was immediately handed to the chancellery, the compiler of this collection does not have its text.

The majority of those who had gathered in the corridor did not leave until the end of the first day's sitting. The KGB employees and members of the operations squad usually stood along the walls of the corridors and hardly talked to other members of the public, but they carefully listened to everything that was being said, quickly joining groups where they noticed a conversation beginning. At times disputes broke out between the friends of the accused and members of the operations squad about the aims of such trials and the way they were being conducted. There was no attempt to stop Soviet citizens from talking to the foreign journalists, the number of whom fluctuated between ten and twenty, but such conversations were listened to especially closely. The few incidents arose only because of attempts to take photographs: a man, either a member of the operations squad or a KGB employee, stood on the stairs, protected by other members of the operations squad, and frequently photographed everyone in the corridor. When one of the foreign journalists in turn tried to photograph him, he was immediately surrounded by KGB employees in civilian clothes who told the journalist not to do this. When some Soviet citizens protested against the fact that they were being photographed without their permission, they were told the man was a *druzhinnik* (i.e. a Komsomol volunteer assisting the police) and had that right; when they asked to be shown the *druzhinnik*'s credentials, they were told he was simply a private citizen. The same thing happened on every day of the trial; sometimes there were two photographers, and they not only took photographs from the staircase but in the corridor itself, from close up, under the protection of members of the operations squad.

During the mid-day recess some of the relatives of the accused came out from the courtroom into the corridor and talked to their friends—there was no attempt to interfere with this. On the following days, however, there was a change. For example, Yury Galanskov's sister, who was pregnant and who, feeling unwell in the courtroom, had gone out for a while, was not allowed back in.

On 9 January, at approximately 10.00 hours, about thirty to forty friends of the accused again gathered in the court corridor, together with an equal number of members of the operations squad and KGB employees in civilian clothes, and also a group of foreign journalists. As before, no one was allowed into the courtroom except for those specially invited, and there was again an attempt to write to the chairman of the court, requesting that friends of the accused be allowed into the courtroom. Twelve signatures were collected outside the court, backing this request, after which KGB employees intervened, stopped the collecting of signatures, and confiscated the letter. However, by some unknown means[76] this letter reached the West and was published in the periodical *Problems of Communism* (July–August 1968, vol. XVII, No. 4); a translation back into Russian of this text is given below [*i.e. in Litvinov's original Russian typescript*].

Document III: 1

To the Chairman of the Moscow City Court
Copy to Comrade Mironov, Presiding Judge

We the undersigned, among many others, addressed a previous letter to you requesting that you assure us, friends of the accused Ginzburg, Galanskov, Dobrovolsky and Lashkova, the right to be present at their trial.

In spite of the announcement that the trial would be open, not a single signatory of this letter has been admitted. Numerous guards, stationed at all the approaches to the courtroom where the hearing is being conducted, have let in only those who have passes. It is not known when, on what basis, and to whom these passes were issued.

The trial hearing on 8 January 1968 took place in a half-empty courtroom, while we stood outside in the cold all day, vainly hoping that, perhaps, you would answer our request.

Proceeding from the above, we hereby register an emphatic protest against the lawless manner in which a legally open judicial trial has in reality been turned into a closed one, and we again request that you permit all the undersigned to enter the courtroom.*

Three people were arrested outside the court, but were released after their papers had been examined. There was also an attempt to give false information to the world public about the events in the courtroom. On both the first and second days of the trial a woman would come out of the courtroom and, addressing herself mainly to the foreign journalists, gave out deliberately false information—for

* For list of the twelve signatories see p. 400. Ed.

instance, that she was a library employee and, having by chance heard of this trial, had freely attended it that morning, when there were still places left in the courtroom and people were being freely allowed in; she also said that all the accused had pleaded guilty, and so on.

On 10 January most of the witnesses were interrogated. As the witnesses had to leave the court immediately after giving evidence, they were able, on their way out, to give their impressions to the public gathered outside. From what they said, which tallied fully with the accounts given by the relatives present in court, the trial was being conducted in a way that involved serious violations of the law, and that an atmosphere of levity and indiscipline prevailed in the courtroom. This strengthened the impression many people had got at the beginning of the trial that the trial was prejudiced and unjust in character. Furthermore, all previous petitions to Soviet legal and administrative bodies and to the Soviet press had turned out to be useless. Faced with this, L. I. Bogoraz (Yuly Daniel's wife) and P. M. Litvinov, who had themselves been outside the court from the first day of the trial, decided to appeal to world public opinion, and in the first instance to Soviet public opinion, and to do this through the Western press. On the morning of 11 January their appeal was handed to foreign journalists around the court.

Document III: 2

To World Public Opinion

The judicial trial of Galanskov, Ginzburg, Dobrovolsky and Lashkova, which is taking place at present in the Moscow City Court, is being carried out in violation of the most important principles of Soviet law. The judge and the prosecutor, with the participation of a special kind of audience, have turned the trial into a wild mockery of three of the accused —Galanskov, Ginzburg and Lashkova—and of the witnesses, an unthinkable happening in the twentieth century.

The case took on the character of the well-known 'witch trials' on its second day, when Galanskov and Ginzburg—despite a year of preliminary incarceration and in spite of pressure from the court—refused to accept the groundless accusations made against them by Dobrovolsky and sought to prove their innocence. Evidence by witnesses in favour of Galanskov and Ginzburg infuriated the court even more.

The judge and the prosecutor throughout the trial have been helping Dobrovolsky to introduce false evidence against Galanskov and Ginzburg. The defence lawyers are constantly forbidden to ask questions, and the witnesses are not being allowed to give evidence that unmasks the provocative role of Dobrovolsky in this case.

225

Judge Mironov has not once stopped the prosecutor, but he is allowing those who represent the defence to say only what fits in with the programme prepared in advance by the KGB investigators. Whenever any participant in the trial departs from the rehearsed spectacle, the judge cries, 'Your question is out of order', 'That has no relation to the case', 'I will not allow you to speak'. These exclamations have been directed at the accused (apart from Dobrovolsky), at their lawyers and at the witnesses.

The witnesses leave the court after their examination, or rather they are pushed out in a depressed state, almost in hysterics.

Witness E. Basilova was not allowed to make a statement to the court —she wanted to relate how the KGB has persecuted her mentally sick husband, whose evidence, given during the investigation when he was in a certifiable state, plays an important role in the prosecution case. Basilova was expelled from the courtroom while the judge shouted and the audience howled, drowning her words.

P. Grigorenko submitted a request asking that he be examined as a witness because he could explain the origin of the money found on Dobrovolsky. (According to Dobrovolsky Galanskov gave him this money.) Grigorenko's request was turned down on the pretext that he is allegedly mentally ill. (This is not true.)

Witness A. Topeshkina was not allowed to make a statement to the court presenting facts to show the falsity of Dobrovolsky's evidence. Topeshkina, an expectant mother, was physically ejected from the courtroom while the audience howled at her.

The 'Commandant of the Court', KGB Colonel Tsirkunenko, did not allow witness L. Kats back into the court after a recess, telling her: 'If you had given other evidence, you could have stayed.'

None of the witnesses have been allowed to stay in the court after giving evidence, although they are even required to stay under Soviet law. Appeals by the witnesses on the basis of article 283 of the Russian Code of Criminal Procedure went unheeded, and the judge said sharply to witness V. Vinogradov, 'And now you're going to leave the court under article 283'.

The courtroom is filled with specially selected people—officials of the KGB and *druzhinniks*—to give the appearance of an open public trial. These people make a great noise, laugh, and insult the accused and the witnesses. Judge Mironov makes no attempt to prevent these violations of order. Not one of the blatant offenders has been ejected from the hall.

In this tense atmosphere there can be no pretence that the trial is objective, that there is any justice or legality about it. The sentence has been decided from the very start.

We appeal to world public opinion, and in the first place to Soviet public opinion. We appeal to everyone in whom conscience is alive and who has sufficient courage:

Demand public condemnation of this shameful trial, and the punishment of those guilty of perpetrating it!

Demand the release of the accused from arrest!

Demand a new trial in conformity with all the legal norms and in the presence of international observers!

Citizens of our country! This trial is a stain on the honour of our state and on the conscience of every one of us. You yourselves elected this court and these judges—demand that they be deprived of the posts which they have abused. Today it is not only the fate of the three accused which is at stake—their trial is no better than the celebrated trials of the 1930s, which involved us all in so much shame and so much bloodshed that we still have not recovered from them.

We are handing this appeal to the Western progressive press and ask that it be published and broadcast by radio as soon as possible. We are not sending this request to Soviet newspapers because that is hopeless.

Moscow V-261, Leninsky Prospekt, 85, flat 3   Larissa Bogoraz-Daniel
Moscow K-1, ul. Alekseya Tolstogo, 8, flat 78   Pavel Litvinov
11 January 1968

This appeal was broadcast, on the same day, in Russian and English by the BBC from London, and found a wide response among Soviet citizens, and also among people of progressive views in the West.

On 12 January, when the verdict was expected, a crowd began to gather outside the court in the morning which by noon had swollen to about two hundred people. On the initiative of A. S. Esenin-Volpin another attempt was made to ask the chairman of the court to let the friends of the accused into the court to hear the sentence. About fifty signatures were collected for this letter and it was handed in to the court, but there was no reply. As there was only one copy of this letter, which was handed in to the court chancellery, the compiler of this collection cannot provide its text.

When it became known that the court was about to pronounce sentence, all those waiting outside gathered in front of the main entrance. After the sentences had been read out the first to come out were the public who had been present inside the court. When they were asked what sentences the accused had received many answered 'They got too little!' or 'They didn't get long enough!', and, with angry faces, they ran to their cars through the crowd. Some were in KGB uniform. Then the relatives came out and, after them, the defence counsels, who were presented with bouquets of red carnations. By about six o'clock the crowd had dispersed.

═IV═

LETTERS AND
APPEALS BY
SOVIET CITIZENS

This section includes all the letters and appeals written by Soviet citizens in connection with the trial which are known to the compiler, or to which he has access: those addressed to Soviet and world public opinion, and also those sent to official Soviet state and party authorities. In the main they question whether the law was observed at the trial and demand that the case be retried at an open hearing. The compiler knows that not one of the letters to official authorities which he has included here received a reply.

The compiler regrets that he has not had placed at his disposal copies of any letters sent to official organs either approving the way in which the trial was conducted, and the sentences passed, or demanding a severer penalty. However, some letters addressed to him personally and sent also to the Union of Writers of the USSR and to Soviet newspapers, and published in them, indicate that Soviet public opinion was not so unanimous in its appraisal of the trial as might appear from a study of the material in this section.

Letters that Soviet citizens sent to Soviet papers in response to articles published about the trial are included in the section 'Press coverage of the case', since the compiler considered this more appropriate.

Document IV: 1

An Open Letter to a Professional Comrade

Colleague,
I hasten to write you this letter, an *open* letter to a workmate, because something irreparable may happen: we can remain silent this time, too,

but shall not be able to lay the blame on our ignorance or naiveté, because I already know about the letter-appeal by Larissa Daniel and Pavel Litvinov, I heard it in a BBC radio broadcast, the letter about the illegality which is rampant in your Motherland and mine, the illegality of the trial of our fellow publicists. It was a cry of despair and faith. Despair, because they gave their letter to foreign newspapers, having ceased to trust the integrity of our own; faith, because they know that someone will hear and respond, and I am grateful to them for believing in you and me *despite everything*. So, our fellow-citizens have been convicted because that poor boy Dobrovolsky slandered himself and them, just as used to happen to our near and dear ones during the Stalin repressions.

Now that you and I know these simple facts, we are left with one question to decide, and only one: do we believe them?

I do not believe that the convicted people were collaborating with the NTS; their writings are not subject to the jurisdiction of a criminal court.

You may have doubts, and that is natural. Well, speak them, let's put an end to them, let's demand a re-examination of the case, get it transmitted by radio and television for maximum publicity. That would put an end to my own doubts too: I must know—must know in order to live—whether my Motherland is aware of this illegality that has been perpetrated, or whether she is again condemning her children in ignorance, as in the not too distant past.

And if this is so, if our Motherland knows and is keeping silent, then I wish to ask that she place me too alongside those innocently convicted.

To me this action seems natural. That is why I feel embarrassed at being the first one to sign.

E. Shiffers, producer[77]

I am sending this letter to the paper *Soviet Culture* and to my personal friends.

Moscow, 15 January 1968

Document IV: 2

To: The USSR Supreme Court. Copies to: The Politburo of the Soviet Communist Party Central Committee and the Presidium of the USSR Supreme Soviet.

DECLARATION

During the last two years several political trials have taken place in Moscow and Leningrad, beginning with the well-known case of Sinyavsky and Daniel, and ending, for the present, with the trial of Ginzburg, Galanskov, Dobrovolsky and Lashkova. All these trials were held in an atmosphere of unnatural secrecy and of confused and untrue newspaper sensation. This alone is sufficient to make the careful observer realize that in the course of the preliminary investigation, and later during the actual trial, flagrant violations of Soviet law and constitutional norms were permitted—not to mention the unbearable moral atmosphere of these trials.

We lost our father during the mass repressions of the Stalin period. He was posthumously rehabilitated. We cannot accept the idea that the horror which our country and our people experienced during those terrible times of lawlessness and atrocities might be repeated, even on a small scale. Our fatherland, to which we have dedicated our lives, has endured countless sufferings in wars, in revolutions, and in the mutual extermination of our fellow-countrymen. And one of the most terrible of our sufferings was a lawlessness which sapped the spiritual and physical strength of our society. We cannot reconcile ourselves to new lawlessness, or our life and our work would lose their meaning and be reduced to a mere biological existence.

We demand a retrial of the cases of Sinyavsky and Daniel, Galanskov, Ginzburg, Dobrovolsky and Lashkova, and the cases of Bukovsky, Ogurtsov and others. And let them be open and public, so that light may be thrown upon the way the investigation was conducted, and on the essence of these cases. We demand light, openness, clarity! The right to make this demand is given to us by the very essence of the Constitution, by the concept of civil rights as we understand it, and by our human dignity, and our desire to see our fatherland splendid and pure—in big things as in small.

Leningrad D-194, ul. Petra Lavrova, 40,   Boris Borisovich Vakhtin[78]
kv. 15, tel. Zh 3 34 89
Leningrad D-41, Moika, 1/7, kv. 4,   Yury Borisovich Vakhtin[79]
tel. A 1 71 16
[January 1968]

Document IV: 3

To: The Editors of *Pravda, Izvestia, Morning Star*, Humanité and Unità.*

We, citizens of Leningrad, support the appeal by Pavel Litvinov and Larissa Daniel to Soviet and world public opinion and join with them in demanding a new, open hearing of the case of Galanskov, Ginzburg, Dobrovolsky and Lashkova on a legal basis.

We should like simultaneously to draw the attention of Soviet and world public opinion to the following fact: a group of Leningrad intellectuals has been held in prison here without trial for approximately one year. Taking into account the lessons we have learned from the Moscow trial,

* British Communist daily newspaper, formerly the *Daily Worker*. Ed.

we have every reason to assume that their trial too will be held without proper observance of socialist legality.*

[Leningrad, January 1968]

Document IV: 4

To: The Chairmen of the Moscow City Court, the RSFSR Supreme Court and the USSR Supreme Court, the Procurator of the RSFSR and the Procurator-General of the USSR. Copies to: the Chairman of the Presidium of the USSR Supreme Soviet, N. V. Podgorny; Chairman of the USSR Council of Ministers, A. N. Kosygin; Secretary-General of the Communist Party Central Committee, L. I. Brezhnev; Chairman of the Presidium of the Moscow City Collegium of Lawyers; defence counsels S. L. Ariya, B. A. Zolotukhin, D. I. Kaminskaya, V. Ya. Shveisky.

We, who appeared as witnesses at the trial of Galanskov, Ginzburg, Dobrovolsky and Lashkova, held at the Moscow City Court, 8-12 January 1968, protest at the violation of court procedure which was permitted with regard to ourselves.

Article 283 of the Russian Code of Criminal Procedure states: '. . . Witnesses who have been interrogated shall remain in the courtroom and *may not withdraw* before the completion of the judicial investigation without the permission of the court. The chairman *may allow* witnesses who have been interrogated to withdraw from the courtroom before the completion of the judicial investigation *only upon hearing the opinions of the prosecutor, the prisoner, and defence counsel*, or, in civil cases, of the plaintiff, the civil defendant and their representatives.'

Each one of us stated his wish to remain in the courtroom after giving testimony, referring to the above-mentioned article of the Russian Code of Criminal Procedure, and declaring that this was not only our right but in the first instance our obligation. Yet the Chairman of the Court, Deputy Chairman Mironov of the Moscow City Court, ordered all the witnesses out, punctuating his demand that they leave the room with rude shouts. The 'Commandant of the Court', KGB Colonel Tsirkunenko, was even more offensive and insulting. The demand that we leave the

* This is a reference to the members of the All-Russian Social-Christian Union for the Liberation of the People, whose trial was held on 14 March–5 April 1968 in Leningrad City Court. Seventeen people were convicted under articles 70 and 72 of the Russian Criminal Code to terms of imprisonment ranging from one year two months to seven years, for participating in the Union. Earlier, in November 1967, four leaders of the Union, Ogurtsov, Sado, Vagin and Averochkin, were convicted to terms of imprisonment ranging from fifteen to eight years under articles 64, 70 and 72 of the Criminal Code. The Union's aim was to remodel the Soviet state and social system on Christian principles. Its activities consisted essentially in recruiting new members and spreading religious and political literature.[80] [For list of the ten signatories see p. 400. Ed.]

room was either not supported by any kind of argument, or explained by a lack of seating-room and breathing-space, even though there were enough empty places.

We believe that a violation of established procedural practice of this kind calls in question the impartiality of the court.

We request that during the appeal hearing and also in the event of a retrial of this case, the appeal and supervisory bodies take into account the content of our statement as testimony to one of the flagrant violations of legality and of public access which were perpetrated at this trial.*

[Moscow, January 1968]

Document IV: 5

To: The Procurator-General of the USSR.

As you are obviously aware, in early January of this year the trial of Galanskov, Ginzburg, Dobrovolsky and Lashkova, charged under article 70 of the Russian Criminal Code, was held in the Moscow City Court.

As you are obviously unaware, this entire trial was conducted in conditions which involved a continuous violation of socialist legality. To be more specific, the violations were as follows:

(1) The period of detention of the accused during the preliminary investigation was considerably in excess of the maximum period stipulated by existing legislation.

This violation was evidently not necessitated by any special complications arising in connection with the elucidation of the facts of the case and could only have had the purpose of exerting psychological pressure on the accused before the trial—which is not permissible.

(2) The trial was officially declared an open one, but in fact it was nothing of the kind. Admission to the courtroom was by permit only, and even the closest relatives of the accused were admitted only after a deliberately humiliating delay and after the trial had already begun.

This violation of the right of public access to a legal hearing obviously cannot be justified by any ridiculous references to insufficient accommodation, and could only have had the purpose of avoiding that very publicity which would have precluded the subsequent violations of legality and procedural practice which took place during the trial and which were obviously planned in advance.

(3) The list—far from complete—of the violations committed during the trial, reads as follows: the court objected to defence witnesses for no reason and refused to hear them out; testimony favourable to the accused

* For list of the thirteen signatories see p. 400. Ed.

was rudely interrupted by the judge and not entered in the record; and, after testifying, the witnesses were ejected from the courtroom even though existing procedural law actually requires that witnesses remain in court until the end of the session.

The 'spectators' in court, consisting for the most part of disguised KGB agents, addressed mocking comments to the accused and to the witnesses who spoke favourably of them, and not once did the judge call them to order. The members of the court did not show the slightest intention of objectively examining the materials relating to the case, and obviously their sole aim was to convict the accused by fair means or foul. Consequently the blatantly false testimony of defendant Dobrovolsky, which contradicted every other testimony given, and which one can assume he gave after having been 'worked over' during the year-long investigation, was taken as absolute proof of the other defendants' guilt. Meanwhile the defence arguments, which absolutely proved the groundlessness of many of the accusations, were simply ignored by the court.

The experience of many trials in the past has shown, and those who organized this trial along *such* lines could not fail to be aware of this, that the result of all these violations is to discredit Soviet law in the eyes of the public both in this country and abroad, and that this does inestimable damage to the prestige of our state as a whole.

In accordance with the points I have listed, I request that you do the following:

(1) conduct a complete and detailed examination into all the violations and abuses which took place at the aforementioned trial, with the purpose of ascertaining their full extent and the identity of those who were personally responsible for their perpetration,

(2) hold an open trial of those guilty of these abuses under article 69 of the Russian Criminal Code, since there is direct evidence of a corpus delicti as specified in this article—to wit, activity directed towards the undermining of a state organ (the Soviet court as an organ of socialist legality) and with the aim of weakening the Soviet state (by damaging its moral prestige) and activity involving the exploitation of a state institution (the Moscow City Court),

(3) annul the sentences in the Galanskov case, since they were passed in conditions which involved criminal violations of socialist legality and were utterly unsuited to an objective examination of the case, and hold a new trial in conformity with all existing procedural norms, including the right of public access to a legal hearing. If not this, then at least annul the sentences,

(4) increase the procurator's powers of surveillance over the activities of our courts so that, in future, illegal actions which cast shame on our state will not be permitted.

Moscow G-351, Yartsevskaya ul., 18, kv. 27   G. S. Podyapolsky[81]
[January 1968]

Document IV: 6[82]

To: Members and Candidate Members of the Politburo of the Soviet Communist Party Central Committee.

International Human Rights Year has begun in the USSR with an unprecedented violation of human rights. At this very moment our Motherland has been nailed to a pillory of shame before the eyes of all mankind and the international communist movement. This has been done by official representatives of authority through a barbaric trial organized by organs of the KGB.

During the trial of Ginzburg, Galanskov, Dobrovolsky and Lashkova (held on 8-12 January this year), I, like many other citizens of Moscow, spent hours each day standing outside the court building and felt—with extraordinary bitterness—the injustice, and also the shame this trial was bringing on our country.

But all the same, despite this, I had not intended to write to you. I thought that the Politburo, for whom the interests of the party, the country and the international communist movement are surely paramount, would discover for itself what had transpired at the trial, and would react accordingly to world public opinion. However, the mendacious articles about the trial published in *Izvestia* (No. 15712) and *Komsomolskaya Pravda* (No. 13089) have compelled me to take up my pen.

For whom are these mountains of dirty lies intended? Certainly not for world public opinion! World opinion would not believe these lies, for it knows that this trial, though formally open, was in fact held in complete isolation from the outside world. F. Ovcharenko, writing in *Komsomolskaya Pravda*, is lying when he states that the courtroom was full and that workers and clerical staff from Moscow factories and offices were in attendance. Nothing of the kind—the trial was conducted in a half-empty room and was attended by precisely those persons who had no right to be there, employees of the investigatory organs (KGB), and a public carefully selected by those organs. Even the witnesses, who by law are required to remain in the courtroom after testifying, were dismissed despite their appeals and protests.

The KGB and the police took over not only the courtroom. They literally occupied the Moscow City Court building and its environs, flooding them with their agents. This was seen not only by us Soviet citizens but also by all the foreign correspondents who kept continual watch outside the court building. It goes without saying that none of them either was admitted to the courtroom.

Do these organs really believe that holding the trial in such complete isolation was in the interests of elucidating the truth to the fullest possible extent? No, they know as well as we do that truth does not fear the light, truth does not fear witnesses and observers. Only sordid affairs are carried on behind people's backs, in the darkness, in torture chambers.

If we examine the case from this point of view, we can see circumstances that in no way inspire confidence in what took place at the trial. The preliminary investigation, during which the accused were completely isolated from the outside world, lasted almost one year; this is in excess of the maximum permissible period of investigation, which itself is only allowed in exceptional cases. The members of the court and the Procurator were specially selected by the investigating organs; and even the accused were allowed to choose their defence counsels only ˜ om amongst those authorized by the KGB.* And as if that were not enough, it was even necessary to select a special audience! After all that, who could believe in the objectivity of the court?

In reality the court did not have any objective proof that the accused were connected with the NTS. Ovcharenko's statement that material evidence had been discovered in the apartments of the accused is a fabrication. The whole of the case for the prosecution rested on the utterly unsupported and clearly slanderous 'testimony' of Dobrovolsky.

This is a trial of a definite type, a provocation analogous to the trials which were staged in the days of Yagoda, Ezhov and Beria. The only difference is that in those days the authorities talked about 'enemies of the people', without concretely defining their crime, whereas nowadays they base their unjust sentences on the purest fabrications.

Indeed, these people were arrested for creating honest works of literature which even a specially chosen court could not deem anti-Soviet. For that reason they thought up the 'ties with the NTS'. The flimsiness of the charge can be judged, firstly by the fact that the Procurator for quite ridiculous reasons objected to defence witnesses who might have proved dangerous to the prosecution's case, and the court supported these groundless objections, and secondly by the introduction of Brox-Sokolov as a witness for the prosecution in a case with which he had no connection, direct or indirect. The tale of his notorious belt was supposed to create an appearance of the existence of some 'material evidence'.

This stupid venture has done grave damage to my Motherland. As a military specialist I would like to say that it is difficult even to estimate how many allies our country has lost, how many potential supporters our probable enemies have gained during this trial, not to speak of the moral, political and juridical aspects of the case. Not even our fiercest enemies could have done us greater harm.

The newspaper articles I mentioned earlier continue to damage us in exactly the same way. Only the few people who know nothing about the trial except what they have read in these articles are capable of believing such bare-faced lies. This latest action by the KGB can only arouse yet more indignation on the part of world public opinion.

Comrade members and candidate-members of the Politburo!

It is still not too late to make amends for the stupidity of bureaucrats

* The author is referring to established legal practice, according to which not all members of the Collegium of Lawyers have security clearance for cases in which the investigation has been conducted by the KGB.

concerned only with their own careers and not with the interests of the Motherland.

Look into the case and *you yourselves will be convinced* that the *charges* are absolutely *unfounded*. World public opinion has long since ceased to doubt it. And no one can change public opinion, especially not with such blatant lies.

In circumstances like these, the party and government leadership do not have the right to pose as impartial observers. In my opinion they are duty bound to demonstrate to the whole world that they took no part in this provocation, and with this in mind, to take measures to have the illegal sentences annulled, to put an end to the whole dirty business, and to impose severe punishment on those who plotted, prepared and carried out this provocation which is so shameful and harmful to our country.

Moscow G-21, Komsomolsky Prospekt 14/1,   P. Grigorenko
kv. 96, tel. 246 27 37
[January 1968]

Document IV: 7

To: Comrade Suslov, Soviet Communist Party Central Committee.

I cannot judge the degree of guilt of persons who in one way or another have been or are being subjected to repression, since I do not have sufficient information at my disposal. But one thing of which I am firmly convinced, and which I know, is that 'judicial' trials of the kind that took place in Moscow City Court from 8 to 12 January this year do enormous damage to our party and to the cause of communism in our country, and not only in our country.

We have celebrated the glorious [*fiftieth*] anniversary; we pride ourselves on our achievements in economics and technology; and yet when the United Nations has declared 1968 Human Rights Year, we are giving the enemies of communism the most powerful trump cards against ourselves. It is absurd!

We were naked, hungry and destitute, but we won, because we set greatest store by the liberation of man from subservience, outrage, lawlessness and so on. And we can lose everything if we forget 'whence hath come the Great October Socialist Revolution'.*

From the time of Radishchev† trials of writers have always been an abomination in the eyes of progressive thinking people. What were our home-grown bosses thinking of, shutting Solzhenitsyn's mouth,[83] playing

* This is a paraphrase of a quotation from the Russian Primary Chronicle: 'This is the tale of bygone years, from whence hath come the Russian land . . .'.

† Alexander Radishchev (1749-1802), a writer exiled to Siberia for his *Journey from St Petersburg to Moscow* (1790). Ed.

236

the fool with the poet Voznesensky,[84] 'punishing' Sinyavsky and Daniel with penal servitude, instigating KGB farces with 'enemies in our midst'?

One must not undermine the faith of the masses in the party; one must not speculate with the honour of the state, even if some political figure or other feels like putting a stop to *samizdat* within the space of six months. There is only one way to destroy *samizdat*—to promote, and not suppress, the development of democratic rights, to observe the Constitution, not violate it, to implement in practice the Declaration of Human Rights, as Vyshinsky signed it in the name of our state, and not ignore it.

Incidentally, I believe that article 20* of that Declaration reads: 'Everyone has the right to freedom of thought, conscience and religion. And every man has the right to freedom of opinion and expression; this right includes freedom to hold opinions without interference and to seek, receive and impart information and ideas through any media and regardless of frontiers'.

You know article 125 of our Constitution perfectly well, so it is not worth my quoting it.† I would merely remind you of V. I. Lenin's view that 'we need full and truthful information. And truth should not depend on the question of whom it is to serve.' (*Works*, fifth edition, vol. 54, p. 446.)

I am of the opinion that the persecution of young people (dissenters) in a country where more than fifty per cent of the population are under thirty is an extremely dangerous line, is adventurism.

It is *not* the toadies, *not* the public of yesmen (O lord, how they have multiplied!), *not* the mother's little darlings who will determine our future fate, but those very *rebels*, the most energetic, courageous and high-principled element in the young generation. It is stupid to see them as enemies of Soviet power, and it is ultra-stupid to let them rot away in gaol and make a mockery of them. For the party such a line is tantamount to self-strangulation. *Woe unto us*, if we are not able to come to an agreement with these young people. They will create, inevitably they will create, a new party. Take a look at history and you will be convinced of this: ideas cannot be killed with bullets, prisons or exile. He who does not understand this is no politician, no Marxist.

You remember, of course, the 'Testament of [*the Italian communist*] Palmiro Togliatti'. I have in mind this part of it: 'A general impression is created [*in the USSR*] of sluggishness and opposition in the matter of a return to Leninist norms, norms which used to guarantee both within the party and outside it great freedom of speech and discussion concerning problems of culture, art and also politics as well. We [*Italian communists*] find it difficult to explain to ourselves this sluggishness and this opposition, particularly in view of present-day conditions, in which the USSR is no longer encircled by capitalists and economic construction has made prodigious progress. We have always proceeded from the thought that

* These are in fact articles 18 and 19 of the Universal Declaration of Human Rights.
† The article guaranteeing freedom of speech, assembly and demonstration.

socialism is a system in which there exists the widest freedom for the workers, who participate in practice, in an organized fashion, in the management of all aspects of public life' (*Pravda*, 10 September 1964).

Who benefits from a policy of sluggishness and opposition? Only overt or covert Stalinists—political bankrupts. Remember: *Leninism—yes! Stalinism—no!* The 20th Party Congress has done its work [*by in 1956 denouncing Stalin*]. The genie is at large and cannot be driven back in! Not by any forces, not by anybody!

We are on the eve of the fiftieth anniversary of the Soviet army, we are on the eve of the consultative meeting of the fraternal communist parties—do not make the task more complicated for yourselves, do not darken the atmosphere in the country. On the contrary: Comrade Podgorny could amnesty Sinyavsky, Daniel and Bukovsky, and order a review of the case of A. Ginzburg and the others. (In this latter case the Moscow City Court permitted the grossest violations of legal procedure. Procurator Terekhov, Judge Mironov and the Commandant of the Court, Tsirkunenko, should be punished in appropriate fashion, basically for behaving like fools and abusing their power. One cannot achieve legality by violating the laws. We will not allow anyone to prostitute our Soviet courts, our laws and our rights. People like these 'judges' should be thrown out and never show their face again, for they are doing Soviet power more harm than all your NTSs, BBCs, 'Radio Libertys' and so on put together.)

Let *Novy Mir* once again print the works of Solzhenitsyn. Let G. Serebryakova publish her *Water-spout* in the USSR,[85] and E. Ginzburg her *Into the Whirlwind*—people know them and read them anyway, so why hide the fact?

I live in the provinces, where for every electrified home there are ten unelectrified ones, where even the buses can't get through in winter, and the post arrives weeks late. And if the news has got as far as us, and on such a large scale, then you can form some idea of what you have done, what sort of seeds you have sown throughout the country. Have the courage to correct the mistakes you have made before the workers and peasants take a hand in the matter.

I would not like this letter to be passed over in silence, since a party matter cannot be a private matter, a personal matter, nor, still less, a matter of minor importance.

I consider it the duty of a communist to warn the central committee of his party, and I insist that all members of the Soviet Communist Party Central Committee be acquainted with the contents of this letter.

The letter is addressed to Comrade Suslov for exactly this purpose.

With communist greetings!

Latviiskaya SSR, Kraslavsky raion   I. A. Yakhimovich,[86]
Chairman of the 'Gauna Gvarde'
Collective Farm

22 January 1968

Document IV: 8

To: The Russian Supreme Court. Copies to: *Izvestia* and *Komsomolskaya Pravda*, defence counsels B. A. Zolotukhin and D. I. Kaminskaya.

DECLARATION

I have acquainted myself with the speech made by Comrade B. A. Zolotukhin, defence counsel for A. Ginzburg, at the January 1968 trial, and also with the articles in the papers *Izvestia* and *Komsomolskaya Pravda* dealing with this trial. After comparing these documents I have concluded that the above-named organs of the press have misinformed the Soviet public by reporting on the trial in an extremely one-sided and tendentious fashion, and by giving false information which casts a slur on the honourable characters of at least some of the defendants. (I have in mind primarily A. Ginzburg, since I have not had an opportunity to acquaint myself with the documents relating to the other defendants.)

Moreover, I have acquainted myself with the appeal of L. Bogoraz and P. Litvinov to world public opinion. From it I learned that the trial of the accused Yu. Galanskov, A. Ginzburg, Dobrovolsky and Lashkova violated numerous laws laid down in the Russian Code of Criminal Procedure, and that the court strove not so much to ascertain the true facts of the matter and evaluate them from the viewpoint of Soviet law, as by hook or by crook to convict certain of the above-named persons.

All this put together alarms me as a citizen of my country. We must have guarantees against the possibility of a repetition of the bloody events that occurred at the time of the personality cult. An essential precondition for this is open public access to court proceedings—important both as a guarantee of public control over the courts' activities and as a means of developing the spirit of lawfulness and good citizenship in Soviet people—and also the strictest observance of Soviet laws.

I demand therefore that the court's verdict in the case of Yu. Galanskov, A. Ginzburg, A. Dobrovolsky and V. Lashkova be repealed, and that the case be reviewed with open public access and in accordance with Soviet laws.

Moscow 23 January 1968   B. V. Sazonov, philosopher[87]

Document IV: 9

To: Comrades L. I. Brezhnev, Communist Party Central Committee; Gorkin, USSR Supreme Court; Rudenko, USSR Procurator-General; Blokhin, President of the USSR Academy of Medical Sciences.

DECLARATION

During the trial of Ginzburg, Galanskov and the others, held in the Moscow City Court, my husband Pyotr Grigorevich Grigorenko was to have appeared as a witness at the request of defence counsel Kaminskaya.

The Chairman of the court, Mironov, refused to grant the request, giving as his reason a certificate from Psychiatric Clinic No. 1, Lenin District, which stated that Grigorenko was mentally unsound.

This certificate is a forgery, because in December 1965 my husband was judged by a medical fitness board to be mentally healthy and his case was removed from the register; since that time he has not even been summoned for a consultation. A certificate of health was presented to the court.

P. G. Grigorenko is in perfect health and working as a foreman at SU No. 20 [Construction office No. 20 of Moscow Building Trust], and he is also in charge of party classes as a propagandist. He has twenty people in his group, thirteen of whom are communists and seven non-party members.

So it turns out, then, that in one place my husband is a political instructor, while in another he is mentally abnormal. What is this— a mistake?

No, it is a complete disregard for the law, and it has been going on for more than four years.

On 1 February 1964, Grigorenko, a major-general by rank and a Master of Science, was arrested and charged with anti-Soviet activities, but instead of investigating the case they sent him to the Serbsky Institute, where he was adjudged mentally unsound. On the basis of that finding they sent him to the Leningrad prison hospital for compulsory treatment.

When I asked precisely when my husband had gone mad—since I had never noticed it—the investigators, Lieutenant-Colonel Kuznetsov and Captain Kantov, explained that his political views and his dissemination of them made him socially dangerous. I was told by some other investigators—lawyers—that my husband would be registered in the army reserve as a sick man, retaining his rank and pension as the law provides.

From party sources I learned that there is a regulation to the effect that mentally ill persons have temporarily to relinquish their party cards, and that when they have recovered their cards are returned to them.

Well, what happened next?

By Khrushchev's order of 29 August 1964 my husband was reduced to the ranks and expelled from the party as mentally unsound. All the patients in the hospital received sickness benefits except my husband. Murderers, rapists—the law was observed where they were concerned: another patient, Lieutenant-Colonel Shevchenko, who had stabbed his daughter to death, and Lieutenant-Colonel Burkovsky, who had shot three men, were retired into the reserve and kept their rank and pension.

On 29 April 1965 my husband was discharged from hospital as a second-category invalid. For ten months this second-category invalid and disabled war-veteran could not get a pension or a job. He was forced to work as a loader.

In December 1965 the medical fitness board at Psychiatric Clinic No 1, Lenin District, declared my husband mentally healthy and removed him from the register. But this was not followed by the restoration either of his party card or of his military rank, or of the pension he had earned by thirty-four years of honourable military service. Wounded on more than one occasion, they still refuse to give him a certificate of war disablement.

Everything I have related here is blatant arbitrariness. And the forged certificate presented in court was the culmination of all this arbitrariness. I see it as the prelude to new repressions against my husband.

I am filled with terror, the more so since during the years of the personality cult I lost my first husband, my sister and my brother-in-law, and was myself arrested.

As a communist and a citizen of the Soviet Union, I demand that my husband and family be protected from this lawlessness and this systematic persecution of myself and my children. I demand the complete restoration of my husband's rights as a party member and a citizen, and the reinstatement of his military rank.

Moscow G-21, Komsomolsky pr., 14/1,   Z. Grigorenko
kv. 96, tel. 246 27 37   member of the Communist Party,
25 January 1968   pensioner

Document IV: 10

To: Public Figures in Science, Culture and the Arts.

We, the signatories of this letter, appeal to you with words of deep alarm about the fate and honour of our country.

During recent years ominous symptoms of the restoration of Stalinism have appeared in our public life. The most striking of them is the repetition of the most terrible deeds of that time—the organizing of cruel trials of persons who dared to uphold their dignity and to defend their inner freedom, who made so bold as to think and to protest.

Of course, the repressions have not reached the scale of those years, but we have sufficient grounds for fearing that there are more than a few people among our state and party bureaucrats who would like to reverse the course of our social development. We have no guarantees that, if we allow this to happen in silence, the year 1937 [*the climax of the purges*] will not creep up on us again.

It will be a long time before we shall again see Andrei Sinyavsky and Yuli Daniel, condemned to long years of suffering solely because they dared to set down on paper what they believed to be the truth.

Victor Khaustov and Vladimir Bukovsky, young men, have been torn away from life for three years. Their entire 'crime' consisted in publicly expressing their disagreement with the draconic laws and penal measures which have once again nailed our country to the pillory. The

court = lawyers/men

coward Dobro

punishment meted out to them by the court was a model of cynical lawlessness and misrepresentation of the facts.

The latest trial, that of Galanskov, Ginzburg, Dobrovolsky and Lashkova, overstepped all limits in the way it trampled upon human rights. Even A. Vyshinsky [*prosecutor in the purge trials*] might have envied the organization of that trial: he at least tried to extort confessions of a sort and testimonies from witnesses. Procurator Terekhov and Judge Mironov did not consider it necessary even to go through the empty formalities of presenting proof.

Yury Galanskov, physically a very ill man, has been sentenced to seven years in a strict-regime camp. The sole and less than circumstantial proof of his guilt is the testimony of the mean-spirited coward Dobrovolsky.

Alexander Ginzburg has been sentenced to five years in a strict-regime camp regardless of all the testimonies of the witnesses and the material evidence of his innocence.

Maimed too is the life of Alexei Dobrovolsky, who at the trial played the sinister role of a Kostomarov.* If he has even a shred of conscience, thirty pieces of silver (a sentence of only two years' imprisonment) will be insufficient recompense for the contempt and ostracism which await this slanderer. Branded as a scoundrel who sent his comrades to their doom by slandering them out of base self-interest—the responsibility for this moral warping of Dobrovolsky lies to a large extent with our punitive organs.

The entire guilt of Vera Lashkova consists in her having typed a few texts and given books to her friends to read which from the court's point of view were of a criminal nature. She had paid for this with a year's imprisonment. But that is not all. In our country she will very likely be paying for it for a very long time, and she will pay dearly: her passport will be stamped and she will not be able to live, study or work in Moscow.† Such is the fate of the overwhelming majority of ex-political prisoners. (These are the unbearable conditions in which Leonid Rendel, for example, found himself when he returned in August 1967 from ten years in the camps of Mordovia. He is not only not allowed to live in Moscow, but has been forbidden to make even occasional visits to see his sick mother. Rendel has been placed under the supervision of the local authorities: every week he is obliged to report to the police, he is not allowed to leave his house after nine o'clock in the evening, he has even

---

* Evidently this is a reference to the role played by the historian N. I. Kostomarov (1817-85) during the investigation and trial in the case of the Brotherhood of Cyril and Methodius (1849), of which he was a member.

† According to a secret regulation, released prisoners who were sentenced under article 70 of the Russian Criminal Code are forbidden to reside in so-called 'régime' cities— Moscow, Leningrad, Kiev and others. However, since Vera Lashkova had served her entire term of imprisonment without leaving Moscow, the Moscow City police department gave her a Moscow residence permit for six months in July 1968, to be presented for either renewal or cancellation on expiry.

been forbidden to use the canteen in the village where he lives, and, lastly, the police can enter his house by force, search him, and examine his books, his papers and his belongings at any time of day or night. . . .)

The atmosphere surrounding the recent trial was yet another link in a chain of illegalities. The official organs shamelessly misinformed the Western communist press: on the day the trial began it was announced that a date had not yet been decided. When questioned a few days before the trial, Deputy Chairman of the Moscow City Court, Mironov, appointed judge in the case, said that no such case had been brought before the court.

People trying to get into the court were subjected to outright blackmail and contemptuous humiliation of their human dignity. The taking of photographs, constant shadowing, the checking of documents, eavesdropping on conversations—this is a far from complete list of what happpened while the court was settling accounts. One of the most frightening things was that among the spies there were some quite young people, teenage boys and girls. Instead of carefully reading and trying to think deeply about the complex problems of modern life, they had been asked to eavesdrop and inform. And this informing probably represents, from the point of view of the KGB, the very ideal of morality in young people which they contrast with the 'immorality' of Ginzburg who dared to stand up for people convicted without being guilty.

You are probably familiar with the letter of L. Bogoraz and P. Litvinov. With full responsibility we declare: every line of that letter is not merely the truth, but only a small part of the truth about the unprecedented outrages and humiliations inflicted upon the accused. The organization of the trial and the behaviour of the judge, who is under obligation to be completely impartial, in effect deprived the accused of their right to defend themselves and the jungle noises made by the so-called 'public' created an atmosphere of moral intolerance against the accused. There were people sitting in the courtroom leafing through newspapers, or dozing, and waking up only to clamour for a heavier sentence.

The authorities as usual organized the 'publicity' by exploiting the basest traits of specially chosen people: brute indifference to the fate of others, and a mindlessness which demanded neither information nor an analysis of the facts.

While in the courtroom the hysterical women and the Black Hundreds* dozed or jeered at the accused, outside in the ante-room, and later out in the frost, stood a throng of people who constituted the real public opinion: friends and relatives of the accused, and people who did not know the accused but who wished to know the truth—writers, artists, students and teachers.

For uninformed people, the central organs of the press prepared

* Originally the right-wing Russian chauvinist groups which carried out pogroms at the beginning of this century. Ed.

falsifications which contained either direct lies or tendentiously selected facts. The people who set themselves up as ideological mentors neglected one very important thing: 'It is essential to take not isolated facts, but the *whole complex* of facts bearing on the question under examination, without a *single* exception, since otherwise the suspicion will inevitably arise—and it is a wholly legitimate suspicion—that the facts have been selected or chosen arbitrarily, that instead of objective links and interdependence ... a subjective concoction is being presented, perhaps in order to justify some dirty business. This, after all, happens . . . more frequently than it would seem'. Those are the words of V. I. Lenin (*Works*, vol. 30, p. 351).

The inhuman treatment of intellectuals is the logical culmination of the atmosphere which has grown up in the last few years in public life. The naïve hopes for a complete purification of our public life with which the resolutions of the 20th and 22nd Party Congresses [*in 1956 and 1961*] inspired us, have not materialized. Slowly but surely the process of restoring Stalinism goes on. And here chief reliance is being placed upon our social inertia, our short memory and our bitter experience and acceptance of the absence of freedom.

Here are some of the landmarks in the revival of Stalinism in recent years:

(1) The name of J. V. Stalin has been cited from the highest platforms and in a wholly positive context. The papers have informed us of the applause which has greeted the mention of that name. But they have of course passed in silence over the fact that this was the applause of people with a servile hunger for a strong personality, people eager to justify their own conduct in the not too distant past.

How long must it have taken to pervert human nature to the point where people could applaud the murderer of hundreds of thousands of people, the organizer of tortures and torments!

(2) This might somehow be explained by a desire to interpret history objectively. Although having an objective attitude towards a hangman is also evidence of moral deformation, nevertheless one could still understand it.

But somehow there has not been enough objectivity to permit the truth to be told about several of V. I. Lenin's colleagues, the people who ran the Soviet state. One can, after all, without overstepping the bounds of party discussion, say honestly of these people that they did not organize acts of terrorism, did not indulge in espionage and did not sprinkle broken glass into foodstuffs. But even today official historians talk, for example, of the great services rendered during the Civil War by J. V. Stalin, who was then an ordinary member of the Revolutionary Military Council, while the activities of L. D. Trotsky, organizer of the Red Army and chairman of the Revolutionary Military Council, are not merely passed over in silence but are officially described as sabotage.

(3) As a result, the term 'cult of personality' has been all but banned

244

from our press. Artistic and scholarly works in which Stalin and the crimes of the Stalin period are criticized are prevented from going to press, or if they are already in the press the type is destroyed (the memoirs of B. Vannikov,* L. Slavin's book on Marshal Egorov, the frontline war diaries of [*the novelist*] K. Simonov, E. Ginzburg's memoirs and many, many others). Things have reached the point where Fedoseyev, a Central Committee member and director of the Institute of Marxism-Leninism, has recommended that the term 'cult of personality' be used only with reference to Latin-American dictators or to Mao Tse-tung.

(4) Not a single democratic beginning has ever been carried through to completion. Even now the literary or artistic tastes of time servers are law for the writer, the painter, the director, the reader and the artiste. In our film libraries films that would do great credit to our art are rotting; splendid paintings lie neglected in cramped studios or garrets. There is room in our literature for the paltry works of Kochetov and Smirnov, which among other things glorify Stalin. But only the fortunate few have been able to read Solzhenitsyn's *Cancer Ward.*

The attempt to fight against the so-called *samizdat*—uncensored literature—is doomed to failure. If there had been no *samizdat* in Russian literature, we would have lost Radishchev's novel [*1790*], Griboyedov's *Woe from Wit* [*1823*], and many of Pushkin's poems. And in our time, the careful appreciation of the unpublished word by a section of the reading public will ensure that the real creative work of our contemporaries is preserved for better times. The time-servers are powerless to do anything about it; the Zhdanovs† will fade into oblivion, but the art of an Akhmatova will enthral generation after generation.

Sensing this, the punitive organs resort to blatant forgeries, as they did in their absurd attempt to link Alexander Ginzburg, editor of the book on the case of Sinyavsky and Daniel, and Yury Galanskov, compiler of the literary and publicistic miscellany *Phoenix-66*, with the émigré organization NTS.

In the social sciences, the pernicious and irreversible dictates of political expediency are still imposed. Divergence from the truth means death for the scholar, but our modern historians, philosophers and political economists are forced to do it every day. If by chance a grain of truth does manage to find its way into print, the authors are persecuted. Examples of this are well known.

(5) Only recently the Crimean Tatar nation was rehabilitated. But the Soviet public hardly knows anything about it. Nor does it know that this people, which was the victim of a monstrous great-power crime, has been deprived to this day of the right to return to its homeland. And that those who try to do so are sent back or subjected to repressions.

* Ammunitions Minister during the Second World War. Ed.

† Andrei Zhdanov (1896-1948): leader of the post-war purge of literature and the arts. Ed.

(6) Many Soviet people regularly have the humiliating experience of being under surveillance.

All these are only a few examples from our public life.

Once again we remind you that silent pandering to the Stalinists and the bureaucrats who are deceiving the people and the leadership and stifling every signal, every complaint, every protest, leads logically to the most terrible thing of all: lawless reprisals against human beings.

It is in these conditions that we appeal to you, the people engaged in creative work, the people in whom our nation places infinite trust: raise your voices in protest at the imminent danger of new Stalins and new Ezhovs. On your conscience will lie the fate of the Vavilovs and Mandelshtams* of the future.

You are the heirs of the great humanist traditions of the Russian intelligentsia.

You have before you the example of the courageous behaviour of the contemporary progressive intelligentsia of the West.

We understand that you have been placed in such a situation, that each time you do your duty as citizens it is an act of courage. But after all, you have no choice: either courage or cowardly complicity in foul deeds; either risks or alliance with the Vasilevs and Kedrinas;† either giving up some privileges or joining the ranks of the yellow hack-writers from *Izvestia* and *Komsomolskaya Pravda* who consider themselves morally justified in publicly slandering people who have been subjected to outrageous injustices.

We want only a little: that our people should have the *moral right* to call for the release of Greek political prisoners.

And to have this, again only a little is needed: to obtain the release of our unjustly condemned fellow-citizens from their long years of imprisonment.

Remember: languishing in the cruel conditions of the strict-regime camps are people who have dared to think. Each time you are silent, the way is further paved for another trial. Little by little, because of your silent consent, there may come upon us a new *Nineteen Thirty-Seven*.

Moscow A-55, Novolesnaya ul., 18, korp. 2, kv. 83
Moscow, Ryazansky pr., 73, kv. 90
Moscow Zh-280, Avtozavodskaya ul., 5, kv. 75
January 1968‡

Ilya Gabai, teacher, editor[88]

Yuly Kim, school-teacher[89]
Pyotr Yakir, historian[90]

---

* Nikolai Vavilov (1887-1942) and Osip Mandelshtam (1891-1938), biologist and poet, both died in concentration camps. Ed.

† A. Vasilev and Z. Kedrina are members of the USSR Union of Writers and served as public prosecutors at the trial of Sinyavsky and Daniel.

‡ There exist two versions of this appeal. The second, definitive version is given here.

Document IV: 11

To: The USSR Procurator-General Rudenko and the Russian Supreme Court.*

In December 1967 letters were sent to various judicial and procuratorial authorities requesting that those who wished to attend the impending trial of Ginzburg, Galanskov, Dobrovolsky and Lashkova should be given the opportunity to do so. The signatories of those letters regarded it as their civic duty to insist that the trial really be an open one, since the public in our country had previously been faced more than once with flagrant violations of legality in a series of court proceedings which had to all intents and purposes been concealed from public opinion or been falsely presented to it. Such was the case, for instance, with the trial of Sinyavsky and Daniel, the trial of Khaustov, the trial of Bukovsky. All these trials had been declared open, but in practice this was not so. Only persons with permits were allowed into the courtroom, and who issued these permits and on what criteria, we do not know. And so a specially selected 'public' was present in the courtroom, while friends and even some close relatives of the accused were not able to attend.

It was only by violating the principle of open access that the KGB could—through the courts—settle accounts with people whom it found objectionable. For the accused, who acted within the framework of our Constitution and laws, and who in several instances voiced their support for the Constitution, demanded that legality be observed; but they were sentenced to long terms of imprisonment without reliable evidence of their guilt. At least, the public has no knowledge of any such evidence. Only in the absence of open access could material be printed in our press giving distorted accounts of the trial proceedings and grossly deceiving the reader as to the true content of those proceedings. (For example, the only published information about the trial of Bukovsky, in the paper *Evening Moscow*, reported that Bukovsky had pleaded guilty, although this was completely untrue.)

No answer was sent to the letters. None of the signatories received permission to attend the trial, which has just ended. Furthermore, the trial of Ginzburg, Galanskov, Dobrovolsky and Lashkova was marked by even more flagrant and senseless breaches of law and turned out to be a repetition of previous trials, but in even more sinister form.

All entrances to the Moscow City Court building were guarded by large numbers of KGB officers, *druzhinniks* and policemen denying entry to anyone who did not have special documents, the content of which they stubbornly refused to disclose. 'Court Commandant' for the duration of the trial was Tsirkunenko, a colonel of the KGB. Characteristically, even relatives of the defendants were not all, and not immediately, allowed

* This document became known as the 'Letter of the 79', and also as the 'Letter of the 52', since that was the initial number of signatures.

into the courtroom, although many of them carried legal summonses. The relatives of the defendants, witnesses and other citizens were treated rudely, threatened and insulted; photographs were taken of them, clearly in order to intimidate them, and eavesdroppers listened to their conversations. With the same aim of blackmail continuous surveillance was maintained over the relatives and close friends of the defendants for the period of the trial.

Everything was done to prevent any objective information from leaking out of the courtroom. For instance, Galanskov's wife and Ginzburg's fiancée were threatened with future reprisals, and were told that it would be the worse for the defendants if they took down an account of the proceedings. Unknown persons came out of the courtroom and tried to give completely false information to foreign correspondents, who themselves were not admitted to the court sessions.

Many of us were witnesses to these facts and are prepared to corroborate them.

The very fact that the organization which conducted the investigation was constantly involved in efforts to prevent the facts of the trial becoming known to the public is a mockery of justice intolerable in a civilized society. No judge who respects himself and his vocation had the right to conduct a hearing in such circumstances. And the fact that the trial proceedings were in every way kept from the public is sufficient ground for passing a vote of no confidence in the court and its verdict.

Therefore we cannot believe either in the fairness of the charges brought against Ginzburg, Galanskov and Lashkova, or in the truth or sincerity of Dobrovolsky's testimony on the basis of which they were accused of having had ties with the NTS. This testimony could not but remind us of the most sinister features of the trials of the thirties, when the accused were subjected to coercion during the investigation and slandered themselves and other people, as a result of which millions of people were shot, tortured and imprisoned in camps for decades at a time. In this connection it must without fail be noted that the accused in this case were held in a KGB investigation cell for a whole year, which is far in excess of all the terms stipulated in the Russian Code of Criminal Procedure.

Everyone knows that Ginzburg compiled a complete collection of material relating to the trial of Sinyavsky and Daniel; that Galanskov was the editor of the typescript literary miscellany *Phoenix*, the contents of which included a record of a discussion by old Bolsheviks on the draft of the third volume of the *History of the Party* and a record of the meeting of the Writers' Union at which B. Pasternak was expelled from its ranks; and, finally, that Lashkova had typed these materials. They had done this openly. They had put their signatures to all their works. They had tried to make public knowledge things that were being deliberately concealed. Soviet laws do not penalise such activities.

Are not these activities of the accused the true reason for their arrest, and is not the charge brought against them of having ties with a subversive organization (the NTS) a typical method of reprisal, a technique which has been with us since the days of Stalin?

These questions naturally arise in view of the deliberate violations of the principle of open access which were perpetrated at this trial. Is it not scandalous that people who spoke out openly and in support of openness were in fact tried and convicted secretly? A trial conducted and organized lawfully would not only have no fear of public scrutiny, but would welcome it in every way.

We demand a retrial of Galanskov, Ginzburg, Dobrovolsky and Lashkova by a new court acting in accordance with all the norms of legal procedure, and with a guarantee of full public access.

We demand further that those officials guilty of the flagrant breaches of legality during this trial be brought to account.*

Please send answers to the following address:
Moscow G-117, Pogodina ul., 2/3, kv. 91,
B. I. Shragin
27 January 1968

To: The USSR Procurator-General Rudenko and the USSR Supreme Court.

On 30 January 1968 a statement dated 28 January and signed by fifty-three citizens† was sent to you concerning the trial of Galanskov, Ginzburg, Dobrovolsky and Lashkova. The statement ended thus:

'We demand a retrial of Galanskov, Ginzburg, Dobrovolsky and Lashkova by a new court acting in accordance with all the norms of legal procedure, and with a guarantee of full public access.

'We demand further that those officials guilty of the flagrant breaches of legality during this trial be brought to account.'

Here find a list of a further twenty-eight citizens who signed the above appeal.‡

Moscow, 4 February 1968

Document IV: 12

To: The USSR Procurator-General, Comrade Rudenko.

Having acquainted myself with the appeal to world public opinion and to the citizens of the Soviet Union signed by P. Litvinov and L. Daniel, I feel compelled to appeal to you to lodge a protest against the verdict passed by the Moscow City Court in the case of Galanskov, Ginzburg, Dobrovolsky and Lashkova, heard on 8-12 January 1968, and to demand that the case be reviewed by a body of competent and honest lawyers,

* For list of signatories see p. 400. Ed.
† The statement was actually signed by fifty-two people and dated 27 January.
‡ For list of signatories see p. 400. Ed.

and that criminal proceedings be instituted against the persons guilty of violating Soviet laws by conducting the trial of 8-12 January 1968.

I ask you to ensure that when the case is reviewed, the courtroom will be freely accessible to any citizen who wishes to attend the hearing, and that the trial will be reported in detail in the Soviet press.

I ask you also to take steps against any attempts by KGB organs to persecute the writers of letters protesting at the trial of 8-12 January 1968.

You may obtain the text of the appeal of P. Litvinov and L. Daniel from the editorial offices of *Pravda* and *Izvestia*, or from the KGB, all of which obtained it from the Reuter agency; or you can ask the authors.

Respectfully yours,

Riga-tsentr, p/ya No. 298,   V. Potapenko[91]
ul. Revolyutsiyas, 41, kv. 10, tel. 7 17 87
[January 1968]

Document IV: 13

To: The Russian Supreme Court. Copy to: Defence counsel D. I. Kaminskaya.

This is an appeal to you by Pyotr Grigorevich Grigorenko.

The Moscow City Court, without giving any valid reasons, rejected defence counsel Kaminskaya's request that I be summoned to court as a witness, and so I am obliged to request that when the appeal lodged by Galanskov is heard, the following testimony of mine should be taken into consideration.

My own family has been friendly with the Dobrovolsky family for a considerable time, and hence it has often happened that some of the Dobrovolskys' domestic affairs have become known to myself and my wife, Zinaida Mikhailovna Grigorenko. We knew, among other things, that when Aleksei Dobrovolsky came out of a special psychiatric hospital in the summer of 1965, he and his wife G. Dobrovolskaya began saving money for a co-operative flat and often dreamed of the time when they would start living by themselves—just their family. Aleksei's mother, Natalya Vasilevna Dobrovolskaya, knew of their intentions too. Knew, and disapproved. What's more, she tried to win us over to her side. But we tried not to show our opinion, although we understood the young couple perfectly and sympathized with their intentions. .

In the autumn of 1966 Aleksei Dobrovolsky began to attend classes at an evening institute and consequently became a frequent visitor to my flat, where he would consult me on various problems. One evening in December he came to consult me about an essay he had been set on Lenin's work *The United States of Europe*. I noticed that he was upset about something, and asked him about it. He told me that his mother was making a great fuss over their intention to apply for a co-operative flat. He asked my wife to talk it over with her. She promised to do so and asked: 'But how are you off for money?' Aleksei replied that he and Galya had saved the money. And if it wasn't enough, they would need only a little bit more. But it was nothing to worry about, because he hoped that the priests would help him if necessary.

After the arrest of Dobrovolsky his wife frequently became distressed at the thought that it would now be a long time before her dream of getting a flat came true, since they had not even had time to send in their application and the money they had saved might gradually all be spent.

The day after the second search Galya Dobrovolskaya telephoned and told me with some trepidation that during the search they had taken some of *her* money. She begged me to advise her what to do. I went immediately to her flat and first of all ascertained how much money she had had. She answered:

'2300 roubles.'

'Why didn't you keep them in a savings-bank?'

'Alyosha had a passion for converting small notes into bigger and bigger ones, sorting them into piles, re-arranging them, counting and re-counting them. And anyway we were thinking of making our first payment soon.'

Then I asked her what I regarded as the key question:

'Are you sure that this was the money you and Alyosha were saving, and not some other money?'

'Yes, I'm sure,' she replied. 'It was from our earnings.'

At this point Dobrobolsky's mother came into the room.

'Natalya Vasilevna,' I said to her, 'Galya tells me that the money taken from her yesterday belongs to her and Alyosha, and that they had saved it from their wages. What do you think, could they have saved that much?'

With a certain amount of irritation, and in a reproachful tone obviously intended for Galya, she replied: 'Why not? After all, I feed them. They don't give a kopek towards the food.' (I and my wife had heard Natalya Vasilevna voicing similar reproaches on more than one occasion in the past.) 'And what's more,' she added, 'he got a legacy from his aunt.'

'Well, in that case,' I said to Galya, 'write a complaint to the head of the KGB's investigation department and to the Moscow City Procurator.'

At this Natalya Vasilevna remarked, 'I think she ought not to write. After all, we don't know yet what Alyosha is going to say about this money in his testimony.'

In reply to this, I asked them both once again if they were sure that the confiscated money belonged to them and had been earned by honest labour. Both confirmed this.

'Well then, you ought to write,' I said. 'Alyosha cannot testify something that does not correspond to the truth.'

To this, his mother commented, 'Oh, can't he just! You never would believe me, Pyotr Grigorevich; I've told you before and I'm telling you now, the man is mentally abnormal.'

'If that is so,' I said, 'all the more reason for you, as normal people, to testify only the truth and to stick to it.'

At Galya's request, I composed a draft complaint, and when I handed it to her I asked her to draw up a written account of when, from where and in what amounts she had received the money, since I wished to satsify myself once more that her statement about the money was true. She drew up an account, and I still have it in my possession.

There was no reply to G. Dobrovolskaya's complaint for over a month, and I advised her to write a second statement to the same authorities. At that time rumours had already begun spreading that Dobrovolsky was testifying that he had obtained this money from Galanskov. Hearing of my suggestion, Dobrovolsky's mother, evidently mindful of these rumours, protested vigorously, on the grounds that the complaint might 'do harm to Alyosha'. (Even then she did not doubt that the money belonged to Galya and Aleksei.) But Galya regarded the rumours about Alyosha's testimony as absurd and sent a second complaint.

On the eve of the trial, when the Dobrovolskys had already learnt from the defence lawyer that Aleksei was referring to the money as having been received from Galanskov, Dobrovolsky's mother demanded that Galya should retract in court her previous statements and testify 'the same as Alyosha'. Meanwhile, even at this juncture she did not manifest the slightest doubt within the family that the money had been saved by the young Dobrovolskys and not obtained from some other person. I was so incensed by this that I left, and have not set foot in that house again. I have not seen Galya again either, and I was pleasantly surprised to discover that she managed to resist the really formidable pressure exerted by Aleksei's mother, and kept to her original testimony. During the considerable time I have known the Dobrovolsky family I have formed a firm opinion of all its members, and I have no doubt that *it is Galya who is speaking the truth.*

Moscow, 31 January 1968   P. Grigorenko

Document IV: 14

To: The Russian Supreme Court. Copy to: Defence counsel D. I. Kaminskaya.*

During the trial of Galanskov, Ginzburg, Dobrovolsky and Lashkova, defence counsel Kaminskaya requested of the court that P. G. Grigorenko be summoned as a witness, so that his testimony might be heard on an important point: the origin of the money found during a search of defendant Dobrovolsky's flat. The court refused to have the witness summoned, stating that it was in possession of a certificate from Psychi-

* This document became known as the 'Letter of the Thirteen' and also as the 'Letter of P. G. Grigorenko's Friends'.

atric Clinic No. 1, Lenin District, attesting that P. G. Grigorenko was mentally unsound.

We do not understand how such a certificate could have been produced. In December 1965 P. G. Grigorenko was declared healthy by the medical fitness board of the same psychiatric clinic, and has not seen a psychiatrist since that time. (We enclose a copy of the certificate.)

We were all the more perplexed when the court refused to have Z. M. Grigorenko, wife of P. G. Grigorenko, summoned as a witness—in her case there were absolutely no grounds given.*

We know P. G. Grigorenko; he is healthy, perfectly normal and lucid in mind.

In view of this we ask the Russian Supreme Court to repeal the court's verdict in this case and to hold an enquiry to discover who issued the forged certificate of P. G. Grigorenko's mental abnormality†

Advice of receipt in possession of Khrabrovitsky.‡

Moscow, 31 January 1968

Document IV: 15

To: The Chairman of the Council of Ministers of the USSR, A. N. Kosygin. Copy to: The Russian Supreme Court.

Respected Aleksei Nikolayevich!
We are addressing ourselves to you concerning the trial of Yury Galanskov, Alexander Ginzburg, Aleksei Dobrovolsky and Vera Lashkova which ended in Moscow on 12 January.

Everything that is known about this trial testifies to its tendentious and preconceived character, and to gross violations of legal and procedural norms having been perpetrated during the court hearing. All this gives the impression that the harsh sentences meted out in the case (seven years for Yu. Galanskov, five for A. Ginzburg) were unjustified and arbitrary.

The articles about this trial published in *Izvestia* and *Komsomolskaya Pravda* shed no light on the essence of the case; on the contrary, one is struck by their failure to furnish substantial evidence or proof. All this brings our judicial organs into disrepute and quite naturally alarms the Soviet public, calling to mind the violations of legality which occurred during the period of the personality cult, with all their hideous and tragic consequences.

It is imperative that justice and legality be restored; it is imperative that this case be reviewed in an objective, responsible and humane fashion, at an *open* trial, in the presence of the general public, that accounts

---

* Actually neither D. I. Kaminskaya nor anyone else requested that Z. M. Grigorenko be summoned to court.

† For list of signatories see p. 401. Ed.

‡ Notification from Post Office confirming delivery of letter to addressee.

of the proceedings be published in the press, and that all the legal norms stipulated in the laws of our country and in the Soviet Constitution be observed.

We earnestly beg you to take measures to guarantee such a review.

B. Kozlovsky per., 7, kv. 16   A. Rappoport, philologist
                        I. Filshtinsky, Master of historical sciences

Moscow, 31 January 1968

Document IV: 16

To: The USSR Procurator-General. Copy to: P. M. Litvinov.*

We have heard Litvinov's appeal on the radio and read the newspaper articles about the trial of Galanskov, Ginzburg, Dobrovolsky and Lashkova.

We cannot understand from the papers what the real nature of the case was, what the facts about the trial and the way it was conducted are, of what exactly each [*of the defendants*] is accused, how legitimate the allegations are that all the defendants had ties with the NTS, and what Brox has to do with it all.

Litvinov's letter speaks of the violation of the most important legal norms. And if what is in that letter is the truth, then [*the whole thing*] really was a violation of legality.

And lastly, we know for a certainty not only that many people who wished to attend the trial were refused admittance, but that access was made difficult even for relatives and witnesses.

And so we wish for full publicity, and for the facts to be concrete, objective and sufficient in quantity, so that we should not be confused by the trial.

In view of the above-mentioned contradictions, we feel it imperative that an account of the trial proceedings should be published, particularly verbatim records of the speeches of the Procurator, the accused, the defence counsels and the witnesses.

                                M. A. Rozanov
                                K. Ya. Vinevich
                                B. S. Vinevich
                                A. M. Rozanova

[Moscow, February 1968]

Document IV: 17

To: The USSR Procurator-General, Comrade Rudenko; the Russian Supreme Court. Copies to: the Chairman of the Presidium of the USSR Supreme Soviet, N. V. Podgorny; the Chairman of the Council of

---

* This document became known as the 'Letter of the Four'.

Ministers of the USSR, A. N. Kosygin; the Secretary-General of the Communist Party Central Committee, L. I. Brezhnev; defence counsels Ariya, Zolotukhin, Kaminskaya, Shveisky.*

We have acquainted ourselves with the letter by Larissa Bogoraz and Pavel Litvinov concerning the trial of Yury Galanskov, Alexander Ginzburg, Aleksei Dobrovolsky and Vera Lashkova. We fully endorse the opinion of the authors of the letter and feel it incumbent upon us to issue the following statement.

From what we know about this trial it is clear to us that flagrant violations of legal norms were perpetrated during its conduct.

The trial, although declared open, was in fact held behind closed doors. A specially selected public was admitted to the courtroom by special passes in order to create an atmosphere of moral isolation around the accused. The noise and shouting of this public, the insults hurled at the accused and the witnesses, the mockery of the defendants' relatives— all this was supposed to create an impression of 'public indignation'. Meanwhile not one of the defendants' friends, and not one representative of those sectors of public opinion concerned about an impartial hearing was allowed to attend the trial. The people who gathered outside the court building every day in the hope of finding out something about the progress of the trial were subjected to rough treatment and provocation at the hands of the *druzhinniks*, the police and unknown persons in plain clothes. All of them were photographed many times and their conversations were constantly listened to by eavesdroppers. Witnesses were rudely ejected from the court as soon as they had testified, although the law obliges them to remain in court until the completion of the court investigation.

Numerous facts likewise indicate that the trial itself was of a blatantly tendentious character. From the very start the court sided with the prosecution. Questions put by the defence were frequently ruled out of order as having no relevance to the case. The accused and their defence counsels were required to keep strictly within the limits of the indictment and were not allowed to use material bearing on the case as a whole, whereas the Procurator was given full scope. Since none of the witnesses agreed with the basic points of the indictment, their interrogation was reduced to an empty formality: twenty-five witnesses were questioned in the space of one day; sometimes they were interrupted half-way through a sentence, and they were not allowed to make statements to the court. Quite unexpectedly Nicolas Brox-Sokolov was called in as a witness in the case although his testimony had no relevance to it. Evidently the authorities calculated that the mere fact of his presence at the trial would mislead the public.

The tendentious trial culminated in an equally tendentious verdict.

* This document became known as the 'Letter of the 224' and also 'Letter of the 170', because of the initial number of signatories.

The court fully satisfied the Procurator's demands, despite the fact that Galanskov, Ginzburg and their defence counsels convincingly refuted all the fundamental arguments of the prosecution. The part of the verdict which concerns Galanskov and Ginzburg either is completely unsubstantiated or rests on the testimony of Dobrovolsky, which neither the accused nor the witnesses corroborated. On the contrary, all the incriminating testimony and the material evidence (NTS literature, money, and the hectograph found at his flat) point only to Dobrovolsky himself, and he was given a far lighter sentence. One gets the impression that Dobrovolsky played a dark role in this trial and received a shorter term as his reward.

We are deeply disturbed at the conduct and outcome of this trial. During recent years there have been several cases of patent violations of legality and of the principle of public access at political trials (the case of Sinyavsky and Daniel, the Khaustov case, the Bukovsky case and others), and these violations have become increasingly more flagrant and obvious with each trial. And in this latest trial they have become completely arbitrary. As long as this arbitrariness is not stopped and denounced, no one can feel safe.

We insist that the case of Galanskov, Ginzburg, Dobrovolsky and Lashkova be reviewed, that the principle of public scrutiny be genuinely observed together with all legal norms, and that representatives of public opinion be present, chosen from among the signatories of this letter. We insist further that the persons guilty of organizing this trial and of bringing Soviet law into disrepute should receive the punishment they deserve.

(Enclosure: Appeal by L. Bogoraz and P. Litvinov, 'To World Public Opinion'.)

THE COLLECTION OF SIGNATURES TO THIS LETTER IS CONTINUING.*

5 February 1968

Please send answers to this letter to any of the following addresses: A. S. Volpin, Moscow A-445, Festivalnaya ul., 17, kv. 1; I. Ya. Gabai, Moscow A-55, Novolesnaya ul., 18, korp. 2, kv. 83; N. E. Gorbanevskaya, Moscow A-252, Novopeschanaya ul., 13/3, kv. 34; V. A. Krasin, Moscow A-445, Belomorskaya ul., 24, kv. 25; B. M. Ratnovsky, Moscow D-182, Pokrovskoye-Streshnevo, Tsentralnaya ul., 39.

The collection of signatures to this letter continued until the appeal hearing (16 April 1968), and on the eve of the hearing this addendum was sent to the addressees:

On February 5 this year the following letter was sent to you [text of

* For list of signatories see p. 401. Ed.

letter enclosed]. It was followed by a list of 170 people who signed it. Since then they have been joined by another 54 people.*

The appeal by P. Litvinov and L. Bogoraz, and also the five addresses to which we asked replies to be sent, are appended to the original appeal sent on 5 February.

[Moscow, April 1968]

Document IV: 18

To: The Chairman of the Council of Ministers, A. N. Kosygin. Copy to: P. Litvinov.

I have heard the declaration by P. Litvinov and L. Bogoraz protesting at the gross violation of legality and justice at the trial of Galanskov, Ginzburg and the others. The sincerity, the high principles and the great courage evident in the conduct of P. Litvinov and L. Bogoraz inspire trust in the facts reported by them.

Ovcharenko's article 'Lackeys' and Aleksandrov and Konstantinov's 'Bound by a Single Belt'† achieve the opposite effect: their unscrupulousness and their crude tone merely puts the reader on his guard. How is it possible to address oneself to public opinion and to Soviet citizens' sense of justice, all the while offering them this kind of verbal pig-swill instead of information! Lumped together here we have accounts of the activities and aims of the NTS, which are presented as the opinions of the accused themselves (an old method which has been totally discredited), and copious information about the contents of the belt belonging to the NTS agent Brox, a matter only remotely connected with the case of Galanskov, Ginzburg and the others. Meanwhile only a minimum of facts is given on the basis of which one could weigh the evidence against each of the accused suggesting that they were paid agents of the NTS.

Reporting details on the personalities of the defendants, the authors operate more often by way of insulting insinuations than by facts. 'In 1960 criminal proceedings were brought against him for swindling and forging documents. He spent two years in prison. In 1964 criminal proceedings were again instituted against him for similar unsavoury activities', writes Ovcharenko about Ginzburg. I have made special enquiries into the exact nature of the swindling and document-forging for which Ginzburg was convicted in 1960. He wanted to help a friend and took his examination for him, sticking his own photograph on the examination mark-book. And for this act, which is very common among students, the full force of the law was brought down upon Ginzburg, because he had already attracted the attention of the KGB by compiling the miscellany *Syntax*, that is, by activities of a completely different nature.

And why the attempt to cash in on Brox-Sokolov, who is to be judged at a completely separate trial along with the people to whom he was sent?

* For list of signatories see p. 401. Ed.   † See pp. 288 and 284. Ed.

Of course, his arrival on the eve of the trial with photographs of the accused seemed quite spectacular, but it cannot serve as evidence for the prosecution of Galanskov and the others. Brox knows nothing about the defendants. He believed the highly inaccurate information given to him by the NTS that they were writers. Convinced that Ginzburg and Galanskov were not known in our country as publicists, he churned out the old story which had been drilled into him: 'These are criminals being tried for their connections with the NTS'. But can the words of a rather too credulous Venezuelan drown the voice of Maxim Litvinov's* grandson?

I have heard extremely favourable opinions of P. Litvinov. And in August 1967 there was a programme on Moscow Radio which said how properly the communist M. M. Litvinov had brought up his children and grandchildren and what fine people they had turned out to be. The programme discussed a research officer at the Institute of Precision Chemical Technology, Pavel Litvinov (I hope that my reference does not bring any harm to the radio staff who prepared that programme).

Only the publication of a transcript of the trial will give the public a chance to decide if the court had enough evidence to prove whether the collections compiled by Ginzburg and Galanskov got into the hands of the Grani publishing-house at the authors' own request, whether any of the authors, and which, received fees and, most important, since even an affirmative answer to the first two questions does not prove that the defendants are paid agents of the NTS, whether there exists any other proof of the collaboration of each of the defendants with this organization.

In the article [*by Ovcharenko*] sweeping accusations are made indiscriminately against all the defendants, and no reasons are given for the difference in the sentences they received. Dobrovolsky's wholehearted repentance and the 'other circumstances'—whatever they are—which served as grounds for the court to exercise leniency with him alone, arouse the reader's suspicions. The experience of past years has shown that pleading guilty and giving evidence to confirm a friend's guilt do not always mean wholehearted repentance.

Galanskov and Ginzburg pleaded not guilty to having ties with the NTS, and the court brought the full weight of the sentence down upon them: seven years for Galanskov (the maximum under the relevant article) and five years for Ginzburg.

I agree completely with P. Litvinov and L. Bogoraz that political trials, which have recently become more frequent, should be held with full publicity as a matter of principle. After all, the first task of the courts and the press should as a matter of course be to convince those who are in doubt. Without this publicity, political trials of this kind will achieve exactly the reverse effect. Records of these trials should be printed in some kind of special publication accessible to every Soviet citizen.

Moscow, Telegrafnyi per., 7, kv. 13   I. Mezhova [*philologist*]
6 February 1968

* Soviet foreign minister 1930–39. Ed.

Document IV: 19

To: The Chairman of the Russian Supreme Court.

DECLARATION

I, Anatoly Levitin,[92] have in recent months attended two political trials in the capacity of a witness.* Now I feel it my duty to express my views on the case of Alexander Ginzburg and Yury Galanskov, who were sentenced in January 1968 by the Moscow City Court, and who have now lodged an appeal with you.

Consciousness of my responsibility before God and my conscience prevents me, the only Christian believer involved in this affair, from keeping a cowardly silence when the fate of two young men is being decided; my honour as a citizen and a former teacher who has spent most of his life among young people compels me to speak out firmly and straight-forwardly before the court on the subject of Ginzburg's and Galanskov's motives.

After the trial of Ginzburg and Galanskov had ended, articles were printed in *Izvestia* and *Komsomolskaya Pravda* flinging mud at the young people, and calling them lackeys and paid agents of the NTS. All these articles were written by journalists lacking the most elementary feeling of respect for the reader. After all, who would believe that two people who have been in and out of prisons and lunatic asylums since the age of twenty (although they were, as has now been established, perfectly sane), who have voluntarily condemned themselves to the life of hunted animals, who have lost the chance of a career and of leading a normal, peaceful life and raising a family—who would believe that their motives were base? Whatever our attitude to them, one thing is certain: we are dealing with men of principle.

What are their principles, and what were the motives behind their actions? Perhaps they wanted to restore the system of bourgeois land-ownership? Perhaps they wanted to be mill-owners and factory bosses?

I hardly know them, but even my superficial acquaintance is enough for me to be able to deny suppositions of this kind. It is difficult to imagine people more remote from any possessive feelings, more unpractical than these two men. They are people with a very highly developed sense of friendship; both of them would share their last crust of bread with a friend. Galanskov helped Ginzburg's mother, although he himself was poverty-stricken.

The authors of the newspaper articles have reproached Ginzburg and Galanskov for their frequent changes of profession. But what else could they do if they were everywhere dismissed and prevented from working normally?

What was it that Galanskov and Ginzburg wanted? The answer can

* In September 1967 I was a witness at the trial of Bukovsky, Delone and Kushev, held in Moscow City Court.

be given in one word: freedom. They wanted creative literature to be free from the cruel weight of censorship. They did not like the situation in which a great and truly Russian writer, Solzhenitsyn, is unable to publish his works, and another great and truly Russian writer, Pasternak, died a persecuted and vilified man, and many of his works have to this day not seen the light. They wanted the pen of the publicist to be freed from the censor's yoke, since only through free discussion of all the burning problems of the modern world can mistakes of the kind which occurred during the period of the personality cult be prevented. They wanted freedom of philosophical and religious belief, and could not accept the fact that Marxist philosophy is imposed by force, while any man who openly expresses his religious or idealistic outlook is deprived of the possiblity of doing the professional work for which he was trained. I do not have to look very far to find an example of this. I only have to take a few steps and pick up a mirror. It will show me the face of a middle-aged man with glasses, a typical teacher, who after exercising his profession for more than twenty years has now been forced to spend the last eight years living the life of a man of no fixed occupation, because he was dismissed from his school for his religious convictions.

Are Galanskov and Ginzburg alone in their convictions and their demands? No, they are not alone.

The year 1956—the year of the Twentieth Congress of the Communist Party—was a turning-point in the history of the USSR. At the present time it is still difficult to assess the significance of the events of that year. The idol that had held sway over the country for thirty years toppled; there began the agonizing process of re-examining the ideas in which a whole generation of people had grown up. People refused to accept the official authorities and decided they wanted to live in an independent way, to think for themselves, and to develop their own independent outlook. It was the hour of triumph for critical thought, and the Russian people (I am less interested in other peoples) made a great leap forward. The young generation changed completely, and to use the old methods of government became unthinkable. People of my generation remember well that in 1936, when the Constitution now in force was adopted, there was a great deal of talk to the effect that any constitution is merely a method of consolidating a situation which has arisen objectively in the country.

The time has now come to consolidate the changes that have taken place in people's consciousness during the last twelve years. In that time Russian thought has grown up and become surer. People's consciousness has altered: we all of us feel we are adults, and it only irritates us when we are watched over like babies and spoon-fed on pap.

V. I. Lenin always said that the most terrible things in politics were inconsistency and inertia. Conservative attempts to bring about a return to the thirties and forties only obstruct the progress of the Russian people

260

forward, compromise us in the eyes of the whole world (above all in the eyes of foreign communists) and hinder the fight against reaction. I will illustrate my thought with an example. About ten years ago the Metropolitan Nikolai invited me to write an article for the *Journal of the Moscow Patriarchate*, attacking the Jehovah's Witnesses. I was obliged to refuse his invitation point blank, for I cannot argue with people who are in prison. So it is now: I cannot argue in my articles with people whom I consider hide-bound reactionaries, for the sole reason that anything I say against them will be political denunciation.

Matters have reached the point where any honest writer who openly expresses his convictions runs the risk, if he is not imprisoned, of being thought a KGB agent. It is becoming embarrassing to express one's solidarity with the government, even on matters in which the government is absolutely right, for one is immediately suspected of being insincere.

All this is a consequence of the abnormal situation which has arisen through the government's refusal to face the objective facts. The question is, why do they have so little trust in the people and society? Do they really think that someone is intending to restore capitalism and overthrow Soviet power? And if not, then dictatorial methods are superfluous, and every restriction placed on freedom of conscience, scientific and philosophical thought, artistic creation and polemical writing is superfluous.

I do not know of what exactly Ginzburg and Galanskov are accused, and how much proof exists of their ties with the NTS, since witnesses were ejected from the courtroom after they had testified, and one can judge absolutely nothing from the newspaper reports, as they are so tendentious and prejudiced. But I am sure that Galanskov's and Ginzburg's motives were of the most honourable kind, and that if they did break the law in some way it was only through an excess of youthful zeal. This makes it possible to replace their imprisonment with a suspended sentence and release them from custody.

When I had finished giving my testimony, I heard the chairman of the court pronounce the three words: 'You are free!' Say those three words to Ginzburg and Galanskov, and you will immeasurably enhance the authority of the USSR all over the world. You will snatch the trump card from the hands of the anti-Soviet propagandists. You will give joy to millions of Russian people.

Let these three words ring out, and may they be the beginning of a new era of humanism in the land of Russia.

Moscow, Zh-377, 3-ya Novokuzminskaya, 23   An. Levitin (Krasnov)
9 February 1968

Document IV: 20

To: The Chairman of the Presidium of the USSR Supreme Soviet, Comrade N. V. Podgorny; The Procurator-General of the USSR, Comrade R. A. Rudenko.*

The trial of Ginzburg, Galanskov, Dobrovolsky and Lashkova, the manner in which the court proceedings were conducted, and the verdict, have raised the question of observance of legality. Everyone is familiar with the appeal by L. Bogoraz and P. Litvinov, which rang out around the whole world, and which contained evidence of the violation of legality in this affair. That appeal has so far elicited no official reply. The reports and articles which have appeared since the trial (in *Evening Moscow, Izvestia, Komsomolskaya Pravda*) prefer to avoid the problem of legality and strive to conceal the natural anxiety of public opinion. The ban on a press-conference by Ginzburg's mother and Galanskov's wife after the trial deepens this anxiety even more. Meanwhile sufficiently reliable documents are appearing (such as, for example, a statement by the citizens who were summoned as witnesses in the above-mentioned trial, which was sent, incidentally, to you too), which detail the violation of Soviet legislation on trials and of the principle of public access to the courts.

Legality has been violated, and this means that people have been put behind bars on insufficient legal grounds. Setting a precedent of this kind deprives the citizens of our country of their guarantee of security, and revives methods which have been condemned by the party and by the whole of our society.

We believe that all the material relating to this trial should be made available for detailed public scrutiny in accordance with existing law.†

Sender: I. V. Kvasha,
Moscow, Nemirovicha-Danchenko ul., 5/7, kv. 89
10 February 1968

Document IV: 21‡

To: The Secretary-General of the Communist Party Central Committee, L. I. Brezhnev; the Chairman of the USSR Council of Ministers, A. N. Kosygin; the Chairman of the Presidium of the USSR Supreme Soviet, N. V. Podgorny; the Chairman of the USSR Supreme Court, A. F. Gorkin; the USSR Procurator-General, R. A. Rudenko. Copies to: The editors of *Pravda, Izvestia, Komsomolskaya Pravda, The Literary Gazette, Evening Moscow*, defence counsel B. A. Zolotukhin.

We are appealing to you, shocked by the injustice of the trial of Alexander Ginzburg.

* This document became known as the 'Letter of the Eight'.
† For list of signatories see p. 403. Ed.
‡ This document became known as the 'Letter of the 121'.

It is clear to us from what we know of the court proceedings that A. Ginzburg was tried for compiling a collection of documents relating to the trial of Daniel and Sinyavsky; however, the verdict of guilty rested on the charge—which no one proved and for which there was no material evidence—of ties with the NTS. Our impression is strengthened by the articles which have appeared in our papers misleading the public, to say the least, and distorting the facts established in court. The unsubstantiated charge of ties with a certain anti-Soviet organization was brought as a means of dealing with the man who had compiled the collection of documents on the Sinyavsky–Daniel case.

We cannot consider this otherwise than as an attempt to resurrect the methods used at the 1937 trials.

The main point of the trial was obscured by facts irrelevant to the case, such as the sudden appearance, a year after the commencement of the investigation and a few days prior to the trial, of a Venezuelan subject armed with 'material evidence'.

We interpret the trial of A. Ginzburg as a direct sequel to the trial of Sinyavsky and Daniel.

We are in full agreement with defence counsel B. A. Zolotukhin's contention that the collection of materials compiled by A. Ginzburg is neither criminal nor tendentious.

Everything we know about the trial of A. Ginzburg gives us the right to request an immediate review of the case.*

Document IV: 22

To: The Secretary-General of the Communist Party Central Committee, L. I. Brezhnev; the Chairman of the USSR Council of Ministers, A. N. Kosygin; the Chairman of the Presidium of the USSR Supreme Soviet, N. V. Podgorny; the USSR Procurator-General, R. A. Rudenko. Copies to: Defence counsels S. L. Ariya, B. A. Zolotukhin, D. I. Kaminskaya, V. Ya. Shveisky and the editors of *Izvestia, Komsomolskaya Pravda, Literary Gazette, Moskovskii Komsomolets.*†

The signatories to this letter are extremely disturbed by the atmosphere created around the trial of Yu. Galanskov, A. Ginzburg, A. Dobrovolsky and V. Lashkova, by the way in which the trial was conducted and by its outcome.

It is no secret that this case has attracted public attention. Yet during the course of the hearing no information whatsoever concerning it was published. The trial was officially declared an open one, but in fact it was held behind closed doors. This very naturally gave rise to an atmosphere of suspicion, anxiety and mistrust.

---

* For list of signatories see p. 403. Ed.

† This document became known as the 'Letter of the 24' and also as the 'Writers' letter', since most of the signatories are members of the Writers' Union of the USSR.

The lengthy articles which appeared in *Izvestia* and *Komsomolskaya Pravda* after the trial only deepened this mistrust. The peremptory and yet strangely nervous tone of these newspaper articles, which were in the nature of a psychological attack on the trusting reader; the nebulous character of the argument and the obvious shortage of precise facts on the one hand, and the gravity of the accusations and their vagueness on the other; the formal openness of the trial, and its actual secrecy; all this taken together created an extremely dubious impression.

It seems very much as though the press was at a loss to find a sufficient number of concrete facts which were clear-cut and incontrovertibly proven. It seems very much as though the court which pronounced such severe sentences on two of the four defendants really did conduct itself in a manner which seriously violated the norms of Soviet jurisprudence.

All this arouses our anxiety.

All this arouses understandable concern among sincere friends of our country abroad, and at the same time it gives our ideological opponents yet another opportunity to present our society's morals and our democracy in an unfavourable light.

The fact that several 'open' criminal trials of political cases have been held within a comparatively short time, and in substantially similar conditions, evokes gloomy associations. The shameful trials of the thirties have not been and will never be erased from our memory; they also, as you know, were conducted 'openly' and reported in the press—as we now know—tendentiously and unscrupulously, and they even claimed justification according to the theory of 'the sharpening of the class struggle'.

Must we now, after celebrating the fiftieth anniversary of Soviet power, be witnesses to the resuscitation of the hypocritical methods of the past?

We insist on a new, unequivocally open and strictly objective court hearing, in full conformity with Soviet law.

We insist on demanding this in the interests of truth and legality, in the interests of the prestige of our socialist state and in the name of justice and humanity.*

[Moscow, February 1968]

Document IV: 23

To: USSR Procurator-General Rudenko and the Russian Supreme Court. Copies to: The Chairman of the Presidium of the USSR Supreme Soviet, N. V. Podgorny; the Chairman of the USSR Council of Ministers, A. N. Kosygin; the Secretary-General of the Communist Party Central Committee, L. I. Brezhnev; defence counsels B. Zolotukhin, D. Kaminskaya; the Editor of *Komsomolskaya Pravda*.†

* For list of signatories see p. 404. Ed.
† This document became known as the 'Letter of the 46' and also the 'Letter from Novosibirsk'.

The absence from our newspapers of any coherent and detailed information on the substance and progress of the trial of A. Ginzburg, Yu. Galanskov, A. Dobrovolsky and V. Lashkova, convicted under article 70 of the Russian Criminal Code, has aroused our suspicion and compelled us to seek information from other sources, namely from foreign communist newspapers.

What we have succeeded in finding out has made us doubt whether this political trial was conducted in conformity with all the legally stipulated norms, such as, for example, the principle of free access and publicity.

This causes us alarm.

Our sense of civic responsibility compels us to declare most emphatically that the holding of what are in fact secret political trials is, in our opinion, impermissible. We are alarmed at the thought that behind what are in effect the closed doors of the courtroom, illegal deeds may be perpetrated, unjustified sentences passed on the basis of unproven charges.

We cannot allow the judicial machinery of our state to be taken once more out of the control of the general public, and our country thus to be plunged once more into an atmosphere of judicial arbitrariness and lawlessness. We therefore insist that the verdict of the Moscow City Court in the case of Ginzburg, Galanskov, Dobrovolsky and Lashkova be annulled; we demand a retrial in an atmosphere of complete openness with scrupulous observance of all legal norms, and with publication of the findings in the press guaranteed.

We also demand that the persons guilty of violating the principle of openness and the judicial norms stipulated by law should be brought to account.*

Novosibirsk, 19 February 1968

Document IV: 24

To: The Secretary-General of the Communist Party Central Committee, L. I. Brezhnev; the Chairman of the USSR Council of Ministers, A. N. Kosygin. Copies to: The Presidium of the USSR Supreme Soviet; the USSR Procurator-General; the Chairman of the USSR Supreme Court; the Editors of *Pravda* and *Izvestia*; the Party State Control Committee; Aleksi, Patriarch of All Russia; the Moscow and Leningrad Collegia of Lawyers; V.Ts.S.P.S. [*All-Union Central Council of Trade Unions*].

CITIZENS!

I know, and you know even better, that a great number of declarations and protests have been sent to you concerning violations of the norms of Soviet criminal law—procedural and otherwise—which were perpetrated during the political trials of the writers A. Sinyavsky and Yu. Daniel, and of the representatives of the Russian intelligentsia Yu. Galanskov, A. Ginzburg and others. Several of these protests were addressed to the

* For list of signatories see p. 404. Ed.

Editors of *Pravda** and *Izvestia*. The signatories of these protests include (and indeed are for the most part) very fine and respected people.

If the violations of the norms stipulated by Soviet laws really did occur (and I do not doubt that they did, unless our country has a dual system of laws—one set out in official documents and another in unofficial ones), then these protests are wholly justifiable, and I would consider it my *civic duty* to put my signature to any one of them, and an *honour* to put it next to the signature of, let us say, Konstantin Paustovsky. But I wish to speak of something else.

I would think that the normal reaction of the relevant organs of the Procuracy, of the legal authorities and of the competent representatives of the public to the protests sent to them, would be to hold an investigation to ascertain if there did indeed occur violations of legality, and, if so, to punish those guilty of them and arrange retrials in accordance with legal norms. Apart from that, the protesters ought to be answered, at the very least in our progressive press, and informed either of the measures taken or that they themselves were incorrectly informed and legality was not violated.

Instead, these protests and statements are being sent for some reason to . . . the KBG offices in the signatories' district of residence. And it is not the points made in the protests that are being investigated. Oh no! *The writing of a protest* demanding the observance of Soviet legality is regarded as *an attack on the foundations of the existing order*, on the security of the state. Dossiers are being compiled on the signatories (or augmented, if they exist already). They are harassed with 'chats' (interrogations), these being punctuated by threats. The honest man, doing his civic duty, comes to be regarded as a disloyal citizen.

It is known that after the 20th Congress, the Soviet Communist Party did a great deal to strengthen legality. You are older than I am, and you know better than I that when legality begins to be violated by employees of the organs which exercise punitive power, the situation becomes not simply dangerous but mortally dangerous, and not merely for ordinary citizens but also for Secretaries of the Communist Party Central Committee and even for the Chairman of the Council of Ministers (although as a preliminary these people become 'former'). We have learned this from the historical experience of all the countries where socialism has triumphed, including our own. I feel it incumbent on me to remind you of this.

I would like to think that my letter will not be regarded by you as an attack on the Soviet social order. I would like to hope also that you for your part will do everything in your powers to restore the faith of your fellow-citizens in the purity of the Soviet Themis.

Furthermore I should like to say this to you—an amnesty of political prisoners has always—including in the light of history—been regarded as a

---

* Obviously the author has in mind *Komsomolskaya Pravda*.

progressive phenomenon, bringing great happiness to a great number of people and but few troubles (very rarely) to a few.

LeningradP-49   Orion Kvachevsky*
Mytninskaya naberezhnaya, dom 3, kv. 21
26 February 1968

Document IV: 25

To: The Secretariat of the Communist Party Central Committee. Copies to: The Presidium of the USSR Supreme Soviet; the USSR Procurator-General; the Presidium of the USSR Supreme Court; the Presidium of the Russian Supreme Court; defence counsels B. Zolotukhin, D. Kaminskaya.

Responsibility for everything that is done in the name of the Soviet State is borne by every citizen, and all the more so by every member of the Soviet Communist Party. Conscious of this responsibility, and despite the fact that all my previous declarations have gone unanswered, I consider it my duty as citizen and party member to write to you yet again, because I am unable *not* to write this letter.

(1) The trial of Galanskov, Ginzburg, Dobrovolsky and Lashkova has caused a new decline in the prestige of our country, and is a new defeat in the ideological struggle which is being waged throughout the world and here in our country.

(2) This trial is indicative of the fact that the persons who staged it have learned nothing from the political experience gained through the trials of Brodsky, Sinyavsky and Daniel, Khaustov, Bukovsky and others. Once again there have been investigators, Procurators and judges to give our opponents the arguments they desire and our friends cause for vacillation, disillusionment and indignation.

(3) This trial thus confirms what history has taught us: every time [*the authorities*] begin to 'reinforce' the ideological struggle and the programme of political education—and this inevitably means the introduction of administrative methods of repression as a substitute—every time the department of state security, the Procuracy and the courts begin to encroach upon cultural life with the aim of harassing 'ideological saboteurs', they do incalculable harm both to our culture and to our international prestige, and, in the final analysis, to the actual security of the state:

(*a*) during the years 1935-40, hundreds of thousands of Soviet citizens were arrested on charges of ideological crimes; they included a great number of scientists, writers and eminent artists, whose death or long imprisonment has noticeably impoverished our cultural life and set us back in scientific research:

(*b*) but during the same years, the fascist intelligence service was extremely effective, as we discovered when war broke out. The real spies thrived in that hysterical atmosphere of spy-mania, in that hunt for alleged 'enemies of the people', the whole of that universal, panic-stricken and therefore

---

* Geologist and brother of Lev Kvachevsky, who wrote Document V: 42 (pp. 338-40). Ed.

abortive and suicidal arbitrariness to which people have given the names of Ezhovshchina,* Berievshchina,* and, most accurately, Stalinshchina*;

(c) the staging of trials such as the ones mentioned above, and the persecution of talented young writers and stray miscreants on the literary fringes, of student malcontents, schoolchildren, 'Smogists', mentally unbalanced persons, and so on, turns of its own accord into an ideological 'tug-of-war', while at the same time it saps the strength needed to prevent the real damage being done by types such as Penkovsky, Runge and their like [*who successfully spied against the USSR while Soviet intelligence officers*].

(4) The concepts of *justice* and *humanity* are, unfortunately, regarded in this country as abstract and relative. The concept of *Leninist principles* is used so often that for many people it has actually become a rhetorical abstraction. Therefore I am appealing solely to political good sense, to a sober realization of what are the real interests of state and party.

Proceeding first and foremost from these interests:

(a) it is imperative that court verdicts which have done and are continuing to do us harm be reviewed;

(b) it is imperative that the Procurators, investigators and judges responsible for these trials be dismissed from their posts;

(c) it is imperative that the circumstances which have made these trials possible be revealed to the public, and that the point of view of both prosecution and defence should be presented in detail. It should be explained to that part of the public which has been genuinely misled by the information published in the newspapers and supplied by propagandists, why repression—when used as a means of ideological struggle and education—can only be harmful;

(d) it is imperative that the authorities concerned with public order and security, as well as the Procuracy and the courts, be debarred from interference in the ideological struggle and in cultural life. For there are a multitude of organizations, party, public, scientific and artistic, there are any number of qualified propagandists, scientists, writers, journalists and other people who can and must, in this fifty-first year of the existence of our state, carry on ideological polemics and political-education work without resorting to the 'arguments' of prisons and camps;

(e) it is imperative, lastly, to understand that all those who insist on trials and sentences of this nature, and on repressions in general in cases like these, are merely discrediting the state, and proclaiming its ideological and moral bankruptcy by maintaining that arbitrariness is necessary for its protection.

Moscow A-319, 1-ya Aeroportovskaya ul., 20, kv. 1, tel. 151 80 81

L. Z. Kopelev, Communist party member, member of the Union of Writers, critic, literary scholar, translator

27 February 1968

* Words signifying everything terrible connected with Ezhov (NKVD chief 1936-38), Beria and Stalin respectively.

Document IV: 26

To: The USSR Supreme Court; the Politburo of the Communist Party Central Committee; the Presidium of the USSR Supreme Soviet.

DECLARATION

'. . . and every State is such as its ruler's character and will make it. Hence, liberty has no dwelling-place in any State except that in which the people's power is the greatest; and surely nothing can be sweeter than liberty; but if it is not the same for all, it does not deserve the name of liberty.'

Marcus Tullius Cicero, *De re publica*, Book I, XXXI, 48

In January 1968 the entire world learned from foreign newspapers and radio broadcasts of the appeal made by Larissa Bogoraz-Daniel and Pavel Litvinov to world public opinion. The mere fact of an appeal by Soviet citizens who were unable to use the Soviet radio, television and press to publicize it, is an indication that constitutional norms are being violated in our country.

The fact that Soviet press reportage of the trial of Galanskov, Ginzburg, Dobrovolsky and Lashkova was minimal, belated and vague, owing to the atmosphere of secrecy in which the trial was held, indicates that all is not in order as regards the observance of the norms of legal procedure either.

These facts taken together have compelled me, a man who, every time he has heard about political trials in the USSR, has hoped in the depth of his heart that the BBC broadcasts were lies, or, at least, that this trial would be the last, to join my voice to those of Larissa Bogoraz-Daniel and Pavel Litvinov in protest.

These same facts cause me to fear that official persons of the Stalinist school have unlawfully assumed the right to deprive the citizens of the USSR of their right to speak out on radio, television and in the press; that the people who during the Stalin period found their vocation in the repression of Soviet writers and Soviet scientists (the followers of Gregor Mendel and Norbert Wiener*), and who quite recently became so petty and stooped so low as to chase after people who were fashionably dressed —that these wide-trousered squares who condemn jazz music and Western dances, having been defeated in those domains, have decided to begin all over again, and, arrogating to themselves the role of infallible literary critics with a monopoly over truth, have started to persecute writers. But one has only to remember how the fight against genetics led to the introduction of this science into our agriculture and medicine; the fight against cybernetics to the large-scale introduction of this science into our national economy and economic planning, into science and military matters; the campaign against Western fashions, jazz and dances,

* Austrian plant geneticist and American cybernetician, whose Soviet followers were mostly sent to camps. Ed.

to their becoming firmly established as part of our way of life; one has only to remember the story of the NPO,* to forecast the result of the present campaign against the progressive intelligentsia.

All these unnecessary, harmful activities on the part of the Stalinist caste have more than once caused a wastage of national potential and damaged the scientific, cultural, political and military prestige of the USSR.

I am certain that our party and government will show their determination, as they have done in the past, and put an end to the activities of Stalin's progeny, who are waging a struggle against those who point to shortcomings, rather than against the shortcomings themselves, thereby depriving our homeland of her finest sons and daughters, and that this time they will not allow the tragedy of 1937 to be repeated. For if measures are not taken, the Stalinists will extend their activity, which brings shame upon our state and the world communist movement, to other fields. I consider it shameful that there exists a censorship which deprives Soviet citizens of the opportunity to publish their writings in their own country, and which deprives them of the opportunity to obtain information about certain events in the USSR from Soviet radio broadcasts and the Soviet press, thereby leaving the door wide open for foreign radio stations.

Our country, as the first socialist state in the world, stems from the great socialist October Revolution, the declared aims of which were freedom of speech, freedom of the press and democracy. It ought to be the leader in these respects, for no achievements in any other respects can compensate for backwardness in democracy, just as the heart transplants carried out in the Republic of South Africa cannot compensate for the policy of apartheid pursued in that country, a country which for that very reason one cannot call a state.

Proceeding from the above points, I demand:

(1) that the cases of Sinyavsky and Daniel, Galanskov, Ginzburg, Dobrovolsky and Lashkova, the Bukovsky case, the Ogurtsov case and others be reviewed, that the findings of the court be published as widely as possible in the press, and also that these trials be broadcast on television and radio in order to make the issues of the cases absolutely clear and thereby deprive foreign radio stations of any scope for fabrication;

(2) freedom of speech and of the press, for all citizens equally.

Odessa 5, Industrialnaya ul., 44, kv. 4   L. N. Tymchuk, sailor
28 February 1968

Document IV: 27

To: The Chairman of the Moscow City Court, Comrade N. A. Osetrov.
Copies to: The editors of *Komsomolskaya Pravda* and *The Morning Star*.

* The meaning of these letters is unclear. Ed.

270

OPEN LETTER

On 8 January 1968, the first day of the hearing of the case of A. Ginzburg and the others, you were so kind as to grant me the opportunity of meeting you, and you answered a number of questions connected with the afore-mentioned trial.

One of them was the question of publishing the proceedings of the court.

You observed, quite reasonably, that 'to fill newspapers which come out in editions of millions with the proceedings of an ordinary case seems unnecessary'. And indeed, not one official document relating to this trial has appeared in the press. However, *Izvestia*, *Komsomolskaya Pravda* and various foreign papers have filled their pages with articles, reviews and even leaders (for instance, the British Communist Party paper, *The Morning Star*). The atmosphere of secrecy surrounding the trial, and the conflicting nature of the various reports of it, have combined to attract the attention of broad sections of Soviet and world public opinion. The absence of any official information has left the way open for fantasies on the part of some correspondents.

Typical in this respect is the article by Ovcharenko, assistant editor of *Komsomolskaya Pravda* (see that paper for 18 January 1968). It approxi-mates most closely to the genre of artistic writing, being a creative rearrangement and reinterpretation of almost all the materials of the preliminary and court investigations, evidently mixed with a certain amount of rumour. In a philippic devoted to the 'latter-day Hero-stratuses', Ovcharenko, as befits the author of an artistic work, interprets the facts in accordance with his own attitude to life, and heaps such accusations upon the heads of the defendants that the Procurator himself might well envy him. He turned out to be 'more catholic than the Pope'. I will not dwell in detail upon this artistic work; it is analysed in the attached letter.*

It appears that the relatives of the accused will have to take legal proceedings against Ovcharenko in accordance with article 7 of the Fundamentals of Soviet Civil Legislation.

Most curious too is a report by Mr Peter Tempest in *The Morning Star*, 13 January 1968, which states definitely that the most exotic witness for the prosecution, Brox-Sokolov, said in court: 'Slavinsky told me that Ginzburg was a member of an underground NTS group in Moscow.'

Do I have to prove that no such words were uttered at the trial? The defence counsel began his speech in defence of A. Ginzburg with these words:

DEFENCE. I would like to begin by saying that during the Procurator's speech there was a misunderstanding. I had a word with the Procurator after his speech, and I ascertained that it was indeed a misunderstanding. However, I wish to make a statement on the subject. In his speech, the

* The letters by Mrs L. Ginzburg and O. Timofeyeva to *Komsomolskaya Pravda* were attached. See pp. 324 and 328.

Procurator accidentally let fall the remark that Ginzburg was the leader of an underground NTS group in Moscow.

JUDGE. That was how the court understood it, as a slip.

DEFENCE. Then I can go on to a calm and unbiased analysis of the evidence.

Mr Tempest, naturally, could not attend the trial, and it is a known fact that when information is passed along a chain of correspondents, journalists, teleprinters and printing-presses, it can undergo various metamorphoses.

But all the same, the matter has gone too far! When the words of a Soviet Procurator are attributed to the anti-Sovietist Slavinsky, and the court assessors listening to him are confused with the NTS agent Brox-Sokolov, you have no other alternative than to admit your error and demand immediate publication of the official documents relating to what has now become a trial out of the ordinary.

Next, I should like to draw attention to the following part of our talk.

When I said that very close friends of the defendants (and I introduced myself to you as a friend of A. Ginzburg) were not being allowed into the courtroom, and that only specially selected persons had access, you replied: 'If we were to let all and sundry into the courtroom, there would just be no court big enough.' That is why a system of entry passes was introduced. I reminded you that two months before the trial began many friends of the accused sent you a letter requesting places in the courtroom. Your reply amazed me. You said: 'But Ginzburg has just stated in court that he has no friends.' As if that settled the question. Having known A. Ginzburg for ten years as an honest and decent man incapable of betraying his friends or denying them, I tried to elucidate the circumstances in which this statement was made. And it turned out that neither at the trial nor during the preliminary investigation had Ginzburg ever uttered such words. Evidently this was again some slip of the tongue.

And lastly, the third subject that came up during your talk with me was the discrepancy between the measures taken against the accused and the laws in force in our country.

I drew your attention to article 97 of the Russian Code of Criminal Procedure, which limits the maximum period during which the accused may be kept in custody to nine months. The commentary to this article has the following explanatory note: 'The period stipulated by law shall include the whole of that period of custody which qualifies as a measure of restraint. Therefore, included in the period of detention in custody shall be the time during which the case is being examined by the Procuracy and the court. If the case is referred back for further examination by a Procurator or court (including an appeal court) measurement of the length of time spent in custody is not started again from scratch; the period is calculated as from the [*original*] moment of detention, or the moment when the type of restraint is chosen.'

You heard me out and then answered: 'You have misread the Code of Criminal Procedure. Read it through once more'—and you busied yourself with your more pressing matters.

I wanted to tell you that I had read the Code of Criminal Procedure, that I had read the commentary to it, and the 'Fundamentals of Soviet Criminal Law', and the Decree of the Presidium of the Supreme Soviet passed on 3.9.1965—in other words, all the material which could possibly throw light on the question, and only then did I reach the conclusion that the accused were being kept in custody illegally.

But you rose slightly from your armchair and gave me to understand that the audience was over.

I took your words as the advice of a competent person experienced in jurisprudence, but it was only a few weeks later that I realized their profound significance. For indeed, when I re-read the Code of Criminal Procedure, I noticed that besides article 97, partial or complete violations had been perpetrated of at least another fourteen articles of the Code! They are as follows: articles 11, 25, 68, 70, 79, 221, 239, 276, 277, 283, 286, 292, 297 and 301. (I enclose with this letter a short account of these violations.) Really, this is a little excessive for just one trial. And a curious detail: persons guilty of violating article 97 must answer for this in accordance with the second paragraph of article 171 of the Russian Criminal Code, which recommends a penalty severer than that proposed in article 70 of the same Code—the article under which the defendants were charged. And finally, it must be regretfully noted that article 97 is still being violated now, while you read this letter.

Do I have to remind you that the year 1968 has been declared *Human Rights Year*, and that the mockery of human rights with which your establishment marked the start of this year is arousing the anxiety of all honest people in our country.

I think that you should, without fail, analyse carefully all the circumstances of the case, impose an administrative penalty upon the guilty persons, and make every effort to have the case of A. Ginzburg and the others reviewed.

Address to which reply should be sent:
Moscow Zh-28, Astakhovsky per., 1/2,   A. Shtelmakh [*engineer*]
kv. 123, tel. 297 49 32
16 March 1968

Enclosure to Document IV: 27

A short account of the violations of the Russian Code of Criminal Procedure which occurred during the judicial examination of the case of Galanskov, Ginzburg, Dobrovolsky and Lashkova, 8-12 January 1968.

Article 70. 'Any evidence may be offered by . . . any citizens . . .'.
The Procurator objected to Grigorenko, a witness who had offered to

give evidence on one of the basic points in the indictment. He stated that Grigorenko was 'at the present time of unsound mind'.

Citizen P. Grigorenko was once confined in a psychiatric hospital for his critical remarks about N. Khrushchev. At the present time he has been found to be mentally normal; he has been removed from the patients' register at the psychiatric clinic and is in charge of a political education group at his place of work.

Article 79. 'The conduct of a medical examination shall be obligatory: . . . (3) to determine the mental and physical state of the witnesses . . . when doubt arises as to their ability to grasp correctly circumstances which are of significance for the case, and to give correct testimony concerning them.'

There was no medical examination to determine the mental state of citizen P. Grigorenko.

Article 70. 'All the evidence collected in a case shall be subject to careful, thorough and objective verification on the part of a . . . Procurator and a court.'

All the evidence to support the charges brought against Galanskov and Ginzburg was given by defendant Dobrovolsky, an interested party. This evidence, however, was made the basis of the verdict of guilty. Evidence given by witnesses which contradicted Dobrovolsky's testimony and confirmed the innocence of Galanskov and Ginzburg on a number of points mentioned in the indictment was disregarded. For instance, the speech by the prosecution indicated that A. Ginzburg had given Galanskov a film of the article 'The Russian Road to Socialism', while Galanskov testified that he had obtained it from Faingolt.

Article 68: 2. 'In . . . the examination of a criminal case in court, the following shall be subject to proof: The guilt of the accused in committing the crime, and motives for the crime.'

The motives behind the actions which the accused were charged with committing were not examined; on the contrary, when the accused attempted to explain the motives underlying their actions, they were cut short.

Article 97. 'Detention in custody during the investigation of a case may not continue for more than two months. This period may be prolonged . . . up to three months, or, by the Procurator of the Russian Republic . . . to six months from the day of confinement in custody. Further prolongation of a period of detention in custody may be carried out only in exceptional instances by the Procurator-General of the USSR, for a period of not more than an additional three months.

Thus the total period of detention in custody as a measure of restraint during the investigation of a case is limited to nine months.'

(*Official Handbook for the Interpretation in Practice of the Russian Code of Criminal Procedure.*)

As we know, the defendants were arrested in January 1967, while their trial began in January 1968; in other words, the maximum period of detention in custody was exceeded by three months. Furthermore, in the commentary to article 97 (*Official Handbook*) we read: 'The period stipulated by law shall include the whole of that period of custody which qualifies as a measure of restraint. Therefore, included in the period of detention in custody shall be the time during which the case is being examined in the Procuracy and the court. If the case is referred back for further examination by a Procurator or court (including an appeal court), measurement of the length of time spent in custody is not started again from scratch; the period is calculated as from the [*original*] moment of detention. . . .' Thus, in accordance with article 97 of the Code of Criminal Procedure, the defendants should be released from custody at least before the appeal court makes its decision. The detention of these people in custody at the present time thus constitutes a violation of the law. References to the Decree of the Presidium of the USSR Supreme Soviet issued on 3 January 1965, in which it appears as though the limit placed upon the period of detention in custody does not apply to the period during which the case is in the hands of the appeal court, are not valid, since the Decree concerns only those cases which are referred *by courts* for further examination. 'These periods (that is, the periods of detention in custody mentioned in article 97 of the Code of Criminal Procedure. A.Sh.) do not include the period during which a case is in the hands of a court if, as a result of its examination by a court of first instance or an appeal court, the case is referred back by the court for further investigation.' ('In reply to an enquiry on the application of article 34 of the Fundamentals of Soviet Criminal Law . . .' see the section dealing with the calculation of periods of detention in custody as a measure of restraint against persons whose cases have been referred by courts for further investigation, *Gazette of the USSR Supreme Soviet*, 1965, No. 37, p. 533.) In the present instance, the court did not refer the case for further investigation.

Article 11. 'A Procurator shall be obliged to release immediately any person . . . kept in custody for more than the term provided for by law.'

The maximum term of detention in custody for the accused expired in October. The accused are still in custody at the present time.

Article 221. 'The question of sending a case for trial must be resolved by the judge or by the court in administrative session not more than fourteen days from the moment the case reaches the court.'

Article 239. 'Examination of a case in judicial session must be commenced not later than fourteen days from the moment a judge renders a decree, or an administrative session a ruling, to bring an accused to trial.'

The case of Galanskov, Ginzburg and the others was handed to the court in October 1967 and remained there for three months prior to the judicial hearing, which took place in January 1968, whilst articles 221 and 239 stipulate a maximum total period of only one month during which the case may be in the hands of the court.

Article 276. 'The court . . . must discuss each petition submitted (concerning the summoning of new witnesses. A. Sh.), must grant it if the circumstances which may be elucidated are of significance for the case or render a reasoned ruling refusing to grant the petition.'

The court refused to grant a petition to have the father of Galanskov's wife, V. N. Blyumkin, summoned, despite Galanskov's petition. The court gave no reasons for its refusal.

Article 277. 'In the event of the non-appearance of any of the participants in a judicial examination, or of a witness . . . the court shall hear the opinion of the prisoner and his defence counsel . . . concerning the possibility of examining the case, and shall render a ruling to continue the examination or to postpone it.'

Some witnesses did not appear at the judicial examination because they had not been notified. The procedure set forth in article 277 was not carried out.

Article 283. 'Witnesses who have been interrogated shall remain in the courtroom and may not withdraw before the completion of the judicial investigation without the permission of the court. The chairman may permit witnesses who have been interrogated to withdraw from the courtroom before the conclusion of the judicial investigation only after hearing the opinions of the prosecutor, the defendant and defence counsel. . . .'

About twenty witnesses were dismissed from the courtroom after giving testimony, despite their protests. Witness V. Vinogradov, who tried to assert his right to remain in the courtroom after giving evidence, in accordance with article 283, was told: 'And in accordance with article 283 you can get out of here'. The opinions of the accused and their defence counsels were not heard.

Article 25. 'The Procurator shall be obliged at all stages of a criminal proceedings to take the measures provided by law to eliminate any violations of law, regardless of who may be the source of such violations.'

No measures were taken to eliminate the violations which occurred during the judicial examination.

Article 286. 'The public disclosure in court of testimony which has been given by a witness during preliminary enquiries or the preliminary investigation proper may take place in the following instances: (1) if there exist substantial contradictions between such testimony and the testimony of the witness in court; (2) in the absence of the witness from the judicial session for reasons which exclude the possibility of his appearance in court.'

During the judicial examination, evidence given by witness Entin was publicly disclosed, although Entin was present in court, did not contradict the evidence given by him during the preliminary investigation, but, rather, refused to give any evidence without the permission of the defendants. Also the Procurator referred to evidence given by witnesses Batshev, Schaffhauser and Mikulinskaya, who were not present at the trial. Schaffhauser and Mikulinskaya are in prison, which considerably reduces the plausibility of the 'reasons which excluded the possibility of their appearance in court'. The protests of the defence counsels on this point went unheeded by the court.

Article 292. 'Documents attached to the file of a case or presented at a judicial session, shall be subject to public disclosure if they set forth or verify circumstances of significance for the case. Documents may be publicly disclosed at any moment of the judicial investigation . . . upon the petition of . . . the defendant or defence counsel. . . .'

The leaflets found on Brox-Sokolov and filed in the case were not publicly disclosed despite defendant Ginzburg's petition. Information on the NTS supplied by the KGB was also filed in the case, and this too was not disclosed at the trial.

Article 297. 'The court may not limit the duration of a defendant's final plea to a certain time, but the chairman may stop the defendant in instances when he touches on circumstances clearly having no relation to the case.'

During their final pleas the defendants were repeatedly interrupted, although their speeches were devoted to analysing the motives underlying their various actions.

Article 301. 'The verdict of a court must be reasoned.'

The defence counsels clearly demonstrated the groundless nature of a whole series of points contained in the indictment. The Procurator did not even attempt to refute their arguments during the pleadings. But when the verdict was pronounced, all that the Procurator had ever said was included in it, and even some things which he had refrained from mentioning in his final speech. In drafting its verdict the court disregarded the speeches for the defence.

Article 2. 'The Aims of Criminal Proceedings.'

'The aims of Soviet criminal proceedings are the speedy and complete uncovering of crimes, the conviction of the guilty and the securing of the correct application of the law, so that every person who commits a crime shall be subjected to a just punishment, and not a single innocent person shall be criminally prosecuted or convicted.

'Criminal proceedings must facilitate the strengthening of socialist legality, the prevention and eradication of crimes, and the education of citizens in the spirit of undeviating execution of Soviet laws and respect for the rules of socialist communal life.'

The examples noted above of gross violations of procedural norms indicate that, during the trial of Galanskov, Ginzburg and the others, the aims of judicial proceedings, as defined in article 2 of the Russian Code of Criminal Procedure, were not achieved.

Compiled by A. A. Shtelmakh

Document IV: 28

To: The Secretary-General of the Communist Party Central Committee, L. I. Brezhnev; the Chairman of the USSR Council of Ministers, A. N. Kosygin; the Chairman of the Presidium of the USSR Supreme Soviet, N. V. Podgorny.*

Dear Comrades!

We address ourselves to you on a matter which is deeply troubling various circles of Soviet society.

During the last few years there have been held in the Soviet Union political trials of young people belonging to the artistic and scientific intelligentsia. We are disturbed by these trials for a number of reasons.

First and foremost, we cannot but be alarmed at the fact that in the course of many of these trials the laws of our country have been violated. For example, all the trials in Kiev, Lvov and Ivano-Frankovsk in 1965-66, at which more than twenty people were sentenced, were held in camera, contrary to what is plainly and unequivocally guaranteed by the Constitution of the USSR, by the Constitutions of the Union Republics and by their criminal codes. Moreover, the closed nature of the trials facilitated further violations of legality in the course of the judicial examinations.

We are of the opinion that the violation of the principle of public legal proceedings is contrary to the resolutions of the 20th and 22nd Party Congresses on the restoration of socialist legality, is contrary to the interests of Soviet society, is a mockery of the supreme law of our country —the Constitution of the Union of Soviet Socialist Republics—and therefore cannot in any way be justified.

The principle of publicity includes not only an open judicial examination but also extensive and truthful press coverage of it. Lenin's demand is well known: that the broad masses should know everything, see everything and have the opportunity to judge everything, and that, particularly with regard to the punitive organs, 'the masses must have the right to know and check each step, however small, of their activity' (V. I. Lenin, *Works [4th edition]*, vol. XXVII, p. 186). Nevertheless, there was absolutely no reaction in our press to the political trials held in the Ukraine. And as for the Moscow political trials, the short notices about them which appeal not as the representative of anybody, but as an individual who have appeared in the press are more likely to perplex and offend the Soviet reader by their lack of respect for his common sense, than to give him real information about the cases heard and the course of the judicial examination.

It was this *de facto* lack of supervision and publicity that opened the way to violations of constitutional guarantees and procedural norms. It has become almost a rule that at political trials of this kind the court refuses to hear witnesses for the defence and restricts itself to prosecution witnesses. The facts quoted in the now widely-known open letter by

* This document became known as the 'Letter of the 139', and also as the 'Ukrainian letter'.

P. Litvinov and L. Bogoraz bear eloquent witness to the gross violations of procedural norms perpetrated in the course of the trial of Galanskov, Ginzburg, Dobrovolsky and Lashkova.

One is struck by the sinister fact that in many cases defendants are charged with uttering and advocating views which are in no way anti-Soviet, but only critical of individual phenomena in our public life, of obvious deviations from the socialist ideal and of obvious violations of officially proclaimed norms. For example, the journalist Vyacheslav Chornovil was tried by the Lvov regional court on 15 November 1967 for the sole reason that he had collected and submitted to official organs material revealing the illegal and juridically illiterate nature of the political trials held in the Ukraine in 1965–66.[93] And in spite of the fact that the prosecution was unable to bring any convincing charges against V. Chornovil and could not even present a single piece of evidence from any witness against him (of the two witnesses summoned by the prosecution, one failed to appear in court for unknown reasons and the other retracted his previous testimony and gave evidence in Chornovil's favour), in spite of the fact that the defence convincingly and clearly exposed the whole absurdity of the charge brought against Chornovil, the court nevertheless met all the demands made by the prosecution and sentenced the young journalist to three years' deprivation of freedom.

All these and many other facts indicate that the political trials held in the last few years are becoming a way of suppressing dissenters, a way of suppressing the civic activity and social criticism which is absolutely essential for the health of any society. They bear witness to the increasing restoration of Stalinism, against which I. Gabai, Yu. Kim and P. Yakir so vigorously and courageously warn in their appeal to leading figures in science, culture and art in the USSR [*see p.* 241]. In the Ukraine, where breaches of democracy are augmented and aggravated by abuses regarding the nationalities problem, the symptoms of Stalinism are manifesting themselves ever more overtly and blatantly.

We feel it our duty to express our deep alarm at what is happening. We call upon you to use your authority and your power to ensure that judicial and procuratorial organs adhere strictly to Soviet law and that difficulties and differences of opinion which arise in our socio-political life be settled in the realm of ideas and not handed over to the jurisdiction of the procuratorial and state security organs.*

[Kiev, April 1968]

Document IV: 29

To: His Holiness the Ecumenical Patriarch Athenagoras, Istanbul, Turkey.

CHRIST IS RISEN

Your Holiness: I am appealing to you and, in identical letters, to other distinguished representatives of the Christian world known to me; I

* For list of signatories see p. 405. Ed.

takes full responsibility for his words. I feel it my personal duty as a Christian to acquaint you with my impressions on reading the witness borne by Anatoly Tikhonovich Marchenko, who was recently released from the Potma concentration camp in the Mordovian Autonomous Republic, in his manuscript *My Testimony*[94] (Aleksandrov, 1967).*

It is not a matter of the accursed past, but of what is happening today.

(1) Political prisoners in gaols and camps today are being subjected to inhuman treatment. The conditions in which convicts are transported are nightmarish. Then, throughout the whole term of the sentence there is hunger, chronic malnutrition and sometimes downright torture by starvation. 2400 calories a day for each man, and for those who have committed offences—1300 calories. Forced labour, unendurably strenuous for men on such an inadequate diet. Living conditions which are a danger to health. Completely unsatisfactory medical treatment for the sick. The author came out of camp an invalid, deaf, through having been left untreated while suffering from suppurative meningitis. He bears witness and is willing to give evidence at an open trial—to the beating up of convicts, to the murder of would-be escapees, to the many and varied tortures and humiliations which reduced people to madness, self-mutilation and suicide. He describes the tyranny of the administration and the absolute futility of protest. The traditions of the Stalinist camps are with us today, and as strongly as ever: the suppression of the convict's human dignity and harsh reprisals against anyone who resists: deprivation of meetings, parcels and books, the punishment cell and the camp-prison, both with reduced food rations. All this together makes up what is called the 'strict-régime'. In reality it is a machine for accelerating death.

(2) Suffering alongside political prisoners in this machine today there are the so-called 'religiozniki' [*religious prisoners*]. The author writes: 'This is the word used to describe prisoners who are in gaol for believing in God. They aren't the only people who believe in God, there are other cons who believe as well. But the "religiozniki" are the ones who have been arrested and tried precisely because of their religion. And what variety there is! Muslims from the Caucasus and Central Asia, Orthodox Christians, Baptists, Jehovah's Witnesses, Evangelicals, Sabbatarians and many others. . . . The fanaticism of the 'religiozniki' is expressed only in the way they insist on retaining their own religious beliefs and rules. They are extremely quiet and humble people, men for the most part of about sixty or over, although there are young ones among them as well. Their attitude to imprisonment is somewhat different from that of the other cons: they take consolation from the fact that they are suffering for their God and their faith, and they are patient in bearing their sufferings and pain.'

---

* In July 1968 Marchenko was re-arrested and sentenced to one year in a strict-regime camp. Although formally tried under article 198 of the Russian Criminal Code (breach of passport regulations), one can assume that this was the KGB's revenge for Marchenko's book.

(3) The author became a close friend of the writer Yuly Daniel in the camp. Daniel and the writer Andrei Sinyavsky had been sentenced in 1966 to five and seven years of 'strict-régime' respectively, for their artistic writings, which displayed a critical attitude to present-day reality. Later, as we know, Alexander Ginzburg was sentenced to five years' strict-regime for compiling a collection of documents on the trial of those writers. Sentenced with him to seven years of the same murderous strict-regime, for compiling the manuscript literary miscellany *Phoenix*, was Yury Galanskov, a sick man.*

Unfortunately one cannot tell from Marchenko's witness how many other sufferers there are of this kind. Formally these people are considered criminal offenders, but they have neither committed nor contemplated any violence.

They only wanted to try and put into practice some of the human rights proclaimed as early as 1948 by the United Nations Organization; and these same human rights are also the religious duty of every man. A Christian is bound to be a complete man before God—a free man, to think freely, not to lie, not to dissemble with himself or with other people. . . . The persecution of a man for this freedom of personal convictions and for peaceful, truthful utterances is an encroachment by Caesar on what belongs to God. Such persecution is in essence a crime against humanity, against free, sacred humanity, which is given to us by God in Christ Our Lord. For this Christian principle, these representatives of the Russian intelligentsia, and others unknown to us, are suffering today under the strict-régime.

This, in short, is the evidence, and you can quite easily become convinced of its truthfulness if you so desire. I present it to the judgment of your Christian conscience. I am of the opinion that in our practical attitude to these facts today lies a test of the sincerity and spiritual strength of our Christianity.

Yours respectfully,

Sergey Zheludkov, priest

On the day of Saint Nicholas and Victory Day
9 May 1968
My address:
SSSR, Pskov 14, Pskovskaya ul., 6

I am sending identical letters to: The General Secretary of the World Council of Churches, Dr Eugene C. Blake, Geneva, Switzerland; His Eminence Cardinal Bea, Rome, Italy; His Eminence Cardinal Stefan Wyszinski, Warsaw, Poland; His Grace the Archbishop of Canterbury, Michael Ramsey, London, England; His Grace the Bishop of Woolwich,

* S. Zheludkov sent a special letter to the Communist Party Central Committee on the subject of the conviction of Galanskov and Ginzburg. Copies of this letter were confiscated from him by the police during his temporary detention, and the compiler of the present collection has been unable to obtain any of them.[95]

John Robinson, London, England; the President of the [*Prague*] Christian Peace Conference, Professor Josef Hromadka, Prague, Czechoslovakia; Archpriest Fr Alexander Shmeman, Professor at Columbia University and at the Orthodox Academy of Saint Vladimir, New York, USA; Archpriest Fr Vladimir Rodzianko, British Broadcasting Corporation, London, England.

Document IV: 30

To: The Chief Editor, *The Morning Star*.

Dear Comrade Chief Editor,
In January of this year your paper devoted a fair amount of space to information about the trial in Moscow of Galanskov, Ginzburg, Dobrovolsky and Lashkova. In view of the interest shown by your paper [*in the trial*], I am sending you this letter with the request that you print it. If for any reason it would be difficult or inconvenient for you to do so, please pass the letter on to any organs of the press which will agree to publish it.

At the end of April this year I obtained permission for a meeting with my husband Yury Galanskov, who is serving a term of imprisonment in one of the Mordovian strict-regime corrective labour camps. In a future letter I hope to describe in detail the conditions in which my husband is being kept and his state of health, but for the moment I only wish to carry out the following request made by him:

In the words of my husband, throughout the whole of his investigation, the KGB investigators repeatedly suggested that he give them information, or fabricate the same, discrediting Ginzburg and mentioning his alleged ties with the NTS. If he did this, they promised to show him the same clemency that was shown to Dobrovolsky at the trial. My husband asked me to make this as widely known as possible.

In other words, they wanted him to play the same provocational role in relation to Ginzburg as Dobrovolsky played in relation to himself. My husband refused to do so—and was given the maximum sentence.

As for Dobrovolsky, my husband believes that he is neither a KGB agent nor a villain, but a sick and broken man, deserving of pity and not censure. And this is the attitude he is trying to adopt in his camp as regards Dobrovolsky.

Respectfully,

O. Timofeyeva

Moscow, May 1968

═V═

PRESS COVERAGE
OF THE CASE*

This part contains all the articles and short items about the trial
(or connected with it) known to the compiler which have been
printed in the central Soviet press, and also all those readers'
responses which are known and available to the compiler.

As regards items in the official press the compiler would like to
point out that he has noticed the following sequence:

(1) the items of January 1968 are devoted mostly to the trial
itself:

(2) the items of late February–March are protests from Soviet
and foreign opinion against the trial and its coverage in the official
Soviet press;

(3) the items of April–May are part of the general newspaper
campaign begun after the 19th Conference of the Moscow Party
and the April plenum of the Party Central Committee;

(4) the items of June–August contain various mentions of the trial,
which, presumably, will continue to appear in the future.

All the items are arranged in chronological order. Items not
specifically about the trial or its coverage, and containing only brief
references to it, are presented in extract form.

[*The readers' responses, which start with Document V: 32, are also
arranged in chronological order.*]

Document V: 1

IN MOSCOW CITY COURT

The case of A. I. Ginzburg, Yu. T. Galanskov, A. A. Dobrovolsky and
V. I. Lashkova, charged under article 70 of the Russian Criminal Code,
was heard in Moscow City Court from 8 to 12 January.

On the basis of testimony by witnesses and by the defendants, as well as

* To avoid a lot of repetition this part of the book has been shortened by cuts. Ed.

material evidence, the court established that the above-named persons were guilty of having criminal ties with a foreign anti-Soviet organization.

The court sentenced Yu. T. Galanskov to seven years' deprivation of freedom, A. I. Ginzburg to five years, A. A. Dobrovolsky to two years and V. I. Lashkova to one year.

Evening Moscow, 13 January 1968

Document V: 2

BOUND BY A SINGLE BELT

We have written about him before (see *Izvestia*, No. 7, 1968). Brox-Sokolov came to the Soviet Union as an ordinary tourist, but his baggage, or more precisely his equipment, bore no relation to tourism. Brox turned out to be a guest with a false bottom. Around his waist was a belt holding a hectograph, cryptographic devices, packets of anti-Soviet literature and money—'donations' from that malicious foreign anti-Soviet organization the 'People's Labour Alliance'. Now he realizes that this belt is wound around his conscience like a gag.

Let us listen to what Brox himself has to say about it now. What happened, and how it happened. We shall run a little way ahead. The packets that Brox was to hand over to a 'certain person' in Moscow's Sokolniki Park contained photographs of people he did not know, and he probably did not suppose that he would make their acquaintance so soon and in such undesirable circumstances.

As is well known, the case of A. I. Ginzburg, Yu. T. Galanskov, A. A. Dobrovolsky and V. I. Lashkova, charged under article 70 of the Russian Criminal Code, was heard in the Moscow City Court from 8 to 12 January. Galanskov, Ginzburg, Dobrovolsky and Lashkova were in the dock and Brox was a witness at the trial.

Brox recently turned twenty-one. He celebrated his coming-of-age up to his ears in dirt. True, it seems as if he got into it through his *naïveté* and his great trustfulness of people who have made lies, slander and bribery their profession.

And so, the foreign guest who allowed himself to become the tool of an anti-Soviet organization living on hand-outs from the U.S. Central Intelligence Agency testified in court without having had time to carry out his assignments.

The witness Nicolas Brox-Sokolov is a citizen of Venezuela. He speaks Spanish, although he understands Russian and expresses himself quite well in it. But in order to preclude the possibility of there being a language barrier, the court offered him the services of a qualified interpreter. The witness was warned that he must speak only the truth and that he would be held criminally liable for false testimony.

Brox's life has not been a very eventful one. He was born in West Germany into a family of Russian émigrés. The parents after a short time went to Venezuela and became citizens of that country. The father thought that young Brox was sufficiently prepared to set out on an independent voyage over the stormy ocean of life. The son was sent to study in France, at the University of Grenoble. Subsequent events showed, however, that Nicolas Brox was not yet independent enough to fly solo.

The young student was perpetually surrounded with 'attention' on French soil. The impression was created that a certain Zhenya had come from West Germany for the express purpose of making the acquaintance of the 'nice Russian'. This pleasantly tickled Brox's vanity—for he attributed it all to his own personal charm. It never occurred to him then that his Russian parentage, his knowledge of the Russian language, and finally his desire to visit the Soviet Union were the 'honey' which was attracting the agents of the émigré NTS rabble of spies and saboteurs.

These 'friends' hovered around Brox for quite a while, without disclosing, until some time had passed, either their membership of the NTS or their true intentions with respect to himself. They slipped him 'literature' containing vicious attacks on Soviet reality and whispered in his ears cock-and-bull stories about the Soviet Union. At some point in June 1967 they got him to go to a 'lecture'. Where, what, who—they did not explain. They whispered 'It will be interesting'. In Grenoble a certain Mikhail Slavinsky rocks the walls with feigned indignation and wailing, perfected by years of practice, about the 'unhappy lot of the Russian people'. Brox was introduced to him, but did not learn his surname until much later, in November. Obviously Slavinsky has every reason to remain 'unknown'. His tirades, overflowing with slander and malice, are given the exalted title of lectures. Here Brox learned from Slavinsky's lips that there were 'zealots of freedom' in the Soviet Union. Their names: Galanskov, Ginzburg, Dobrovolsky.

Who are these people? They all finished secondary school, but the prospect of serving Soviet society, the Soviet people, did not suit them. They prefer to keep quiet about their own biographies. There is nothing attractive about them. Their past lives, right up to the moment of their final fall, can arouse nothing but a sense of wariness. Look at Ginzburg. Where has he not worked! In Kimry he tried to get into the theatre as a lighting technician. But even this sort of work requires effort. It proved too much for Ginzburg. He tried his strength in a co-operative. Here, too, his 'talent' never revealed itself. He got a job as an assistant in a museum but actually continued to live off his mother, a pensioner. Sometimes he would leave a job, sometimes he would be dismissed for absenteeism. Finally he came into his own at swindling. He was caught and tried for it in 1960. In 1964 criminal proceedings were again instituted against him, but he was not deprived of his freedom: he was offered the chance to take the road of honest labour. But Ginzburg is not that kind of person. Morally and politically depraved, he sinks into the mire and links himself with the foreign anti-Soviet organization, NTS.

Another of the defendants is Galanskov. He, like Ginzburg, had endeavoured throughout his life to settle on society's neck, while at the same time missing no opportunity to cast slurs on it. Many times Galanskov's attention was drawn to his anti-social behaviour. But he did not desist.

And what about Dobrovolsky? He was not very far removed from his pals. Criminal conviction struck twice against him. But nothing helped reform him. One would like to think that his repentance and admission of guilt at the recent trial will open his eyes and help him embark at last on an honest path.

Lashkova too, the typist, was entrusted with quite specific assignments. She made copies of documents with anti-Soviet content, and circulated literature received from the NTS.

These are the people who responded to the appeal from the émigré rabble and began to collaborate with the NTS.

Brox recalls that a certain Tamara Volkova appeared briefly in the university corridors at Grenoble and was at Slavinsky's lecture. She was later presented to him, began a most vigorous indoctrination of him and introduced him to other NTS members. Volkova invited Brox to Paris from Grenoble. There two more premature 'friends' appeared on the scene; the student knew them only by their first names—Victor and Zhenya. Nevertheless, he undertook to carry out their 'trifling', but 'noble', commission. This involved nothing more nor less than a trip to the Soviet Union. The generous 'friends' gave Brox a belt lined with materials that were to be dropped into letter-boxes or handed over to a 'certain person' in Moscow who was to meet him at a pre-arranged place. In short, a perfectly 'innocent' request, and you'll do anything for a friend!

Binding Brox in the belt of his downfall, the CIA hirelings were aware that they were pushing a man on to a path that could strip him of his honest name and chosen career. But have the leaders of an espionage organization got time for ethics when their own affairs are going so badly? The boastful promises to their American bosses that have resounded for so many years from the nest of the 'People's Labour Alliance' have remained so many soap bubbles. The active centre of the émigré lair of criminals and traitors is empty. The shop of rogues has obviously proved unprofitable within the system of CIA espionage, sabotage and propaganda activities.

On the evening of 23 December 1967 a young foreign tourist emerged from an aeroplane at Moscow airport. It was Brox. The cursed belt gripped him like an iron hoop. He wore it for several days without taking it off or getting rid of the contents. Now it is all on show in the court as material evidence. Letters with return addresses. They were intended for certain persons in the Soviet Union, and their 'sender', it seems, does not live in France, or in West Germany, but apparently in the Soviet Union also! Five envelopes with photographs. In the photographs and in the dock are people known to Brox by hearsay—Ginzburg, Galanskov and Dobrovolsky. Money. A great quantity of Soviet money. A hectograph and cryptographic devices. Brox is in despair. He declares that until his arrest he knew nothing about the contents of the packets. Yes, admits Brox, everything lying on the courtroom table was taken from his belt at the time of his arrest, when he was about to hand over the contents to the addressee. Some of this 'property' is already familiar to the men sitting in the dock. Here too the NTS remained true to type. 'This is exactly like the hectograph that Galanskov gave me earlier', said defendant Dobrovolsky.

The court has finished questioning the witness, but Brox asks to be allowed to make a statement. 'I shall try not to take up much of your time,' says Nicolas Brox. 'I would remind you that at the time of Slavinsky's "lecture" I thought that Ginzburg, Dobrovolsky and Galanskov were writers. The newspapers in France spoke of them as writers. So I thought that they were young writers and had been imprisoned, that they had been treated unjustly. Only in November did I learn who Tamara Volkova was. At that time the papers were writing something about a trial. She asked me how I could help. At first I didn't understand what she was getting at. She knew I was planning to go to Moscow in December. At the beginning of December I met Volkova in Paris. . . . I arrived in Paris and met her at the station. There was another person with her. I asked what I could do to help. They answered: "Post five letters and maybe a small parcel". On the eve of my departure I learned what I would have to do. At that time I was in such a state that I found it impossible to refuse the parcel. It was unpleasant. The man whom I was to meet in Moscow was, they told me, also someone who could help the people under arrest here. But now I see that I was deceived, and deceived twice over. Once, when they told me that these were writers and were being tried for that. I see no writers. It is criminals who are being tried here for their ties with the NTS. And then again, when they told me that these packets contained nothing but materials that would help them. When I was detained, it turned out that they did not contain what I had been told they did. There was money, a hectograph, copying-paper— all kinds of things, and not at all what I had been told. I should like to say that I regret having unwittingly broken the laws of this country.'

Even the eyes of Brox, the NTS 'courier', were opened to the nature of the men who stood before the organs of Soviet justice as paid NTS agents. The criminal activities of Ginzburg, Galanskov, Dobrovolsky and Lashkova have been exposed in court not only by incontrovertible documents and expert opinions but also by the testimonies of witnesses who knew them well.

Muscovites present at the trial greeted the sentence with approval. For anti-Soviet agitation and propaganda, and violation of the regulations on foreign currency transactions, the Moscow City Court sentenced Yu. Galanskov to seven years' deprivation of freedom. His accomplices were sentenced as follows: A. Ginzburg to five years' and A. Dobrovolsky to two years' deprivation of freedom: and V. Lashkova to one year's deprivation of freedom. It was noted in the sentence that in determining the penalties the court had taken into account the personalities of the accused, the degree of their sincerity and repentance, and other circumstances.

Izvestia, 16 January 1968   T. Aleksandrov
                                                          V. Konstantinov

Document V: 3

LACKEYS

There is excitement among the sensation-seeking 'specialists on Russian affairs', the anti-Soviet propagandists of the White émigré gutterpress, the commentators of [*the radio stations*] 'Deutsche Welle', 'Voice of America' and all the rest. All the stops have been pulled out for a chorus of subversive howls about freedom, of which we, dear reader, are evidently being deprived. Pathetic and tearful petitions are already being tapped out in the West, and committees are even being set up for the purpose of rescue and rendering material and moral assistance. . . .

These 'well-wishers' are firmly convinced that crude summary justice has been meted out in Moscow to a group of talented young writers, the authors of widely known works, works loved by the people, selfless fighters for . . . but on this point we have heard the most diverse stories. One feels that the highly experienced commentators are finding it difficult to formulate a programme for these 'young talents'. Yury Galanskov, Alexander Ginzburg and Aleksei Dobrovolsky, solemnly promoted to the status of writers by the bourgeois press and called nothing less than 'outstanding poets and publicists', have not as yet come to be regarded as such in their own country. Their names mean absolutely nothing to the Soviet reader, since to this day not one of them can be credited with a single published line.

The furore was raised because the three of them together with Vera Lashkova, a laboratory assistant in the preparatory faculty of Moscow University, recently found themselves in the dock. And here we shall have to talk of things extremely remote from literature.

Who were the people brought to trial?

A. Ginzburg is typical. A first-year correspondence student at an archives institute, he is over thirty and has not yet found a fixed occupation. He has been a librarian, a lathe operator, a lighting technician in a theatre and a museum assistant, but most of the time he was supported by his mother. He never stayed anywhere long. He either gave up his job or was dismissed for absenteeism. Workers at the Moscow Sewage Purification Works (Mosochistvod) demanded that he be dismissed from the collective for anti-social behaviour and breaches of labour discipline. He was hiding a criminal in his apartment. In 1960 proceedings were brought against him for swindling and forging documents. He spent two years in prison. In 1964 criminal proceedings were again instituted against him for similar unsavoury activities.

The others are much the same as Ginzburg. Proceedings were brought against A. Dobrovolsky for pasting up hooligan leaflets in public conveniences. Yu. Galanskov also has had dealings with the police on more than one occasion as a violator of public order.

In short, where violation of the law is concerned, each one of them is already quite experienced; the same cannot be said of their writing.

That is what they were like yesterday. And today, under article 70 of the Russian Criminal Code, A. Ginzburg, Yu. Galanskov, A. Dobrovolsky and V. Lashkova are being made to answer for their crimes against the Soviet people.

The parasites of yesterday stand accused today of having criminal ties with the White émigré organization NTS, whose task is the overthrow of the existing order in the USSR and the restoration of a bourgeois régime; of obtaining from the NTS anti-Soviet literature and disseminating it in our country; of sending materials to the West that contain slanders on our people and our homeland; and of engaging in manipulations involving the receipt of currency from abroad.

The courtroom was crowded. Those present included relatives of the accused, workers and employees in the capital, journalists, representatives of enterprises and organizations with which the defendants had been connected at various times. . . .

The court closely studied the facts, the testimony of witnesses, the material evidence and the experts' findings. Questions. Answers. The citation of documents. The story of the fall of these latter-day Herostratuses was traced step by step.

We wanted our names to be known throughout the world,' declared Yu. Galanskov in court; before his arrest he had been working with Ginzburg as an auxiliary in a museum.

They had oriented themselves quite 'professionally' to the world of the dollar and of provocations. Galanskov and Ginzburg were fully aware of what was expected of them in that world and what they had to do to hear words of approval not only from the provincial rags put out by the NTS but also from fat and respectable weeklies with multicoloured covers.

Ginzburg and Galanskov, and the bookbinder Dobrovolsky who was lured into their company, passed from abstract declarations to active operations. They became paid agents of the NTS, the so-called People's Labour Alliance, a White émigré organization that formerly served Hitler and is now supported by the US Central Intelligence Agency. They collected slanderous materials denigrating the Soviet state and social system, amassed and made copies of them, and then secretly sent them abroad to be used by the bourgeois press.

But they were not working only 'for export'. Through special messengers who visit our country in the guise of tourists, they received NTS literature from abroad—pamphlets, books and leaflets, in which every line is steeped in hatred and bile and almost every page contains a call for terror.

Interrogation of the defendants disclosed some not unimportant details. Here is the testimony of A. Dobrovolsky:

PROCURATOR. What do you know about Galanskov's and Ginzburg's connections abroad?

DOBROVOLSKY. When Galanskov gave me the NTS literature and the hectograph, I asked him were he had got it all. Galanskov replied that he had had contacts abroad since 1962 and had established these contacts through Ginzburg.

PROCURATOR. With what organization abroad was contact maintained?

DOBROVOLSKY. Galanskov told me he was in contact with NTS.

When the homes of Ginzburg, Galanskov and Dobrovolsky were searched, dozens of anti-Soviet publications received from abroad were seized. They included the NTS programme and regulations, the White Guard paper *Possev*, published in the form of eight leaflets, the inveterate anti-Soviet journals *Our Times* and *Grani*, and writings by NTS ringleaders and ideologists. The materials which Galanskov received from his bosses contained recommendations and instructions on forms and methods of struggle against the Soviet system, including armed struggle, appeals for terrorist acts and for the organization of NTS cells on Soviet territory. The pages of these pernicious works were crammed with such statements as 'The destruction of the communist dictatorship in Russia will be the beginning of a process of cleansing and renewal throughout the whole world'. They literally dazzled the eye with their anti-Soviet terminology —'the communist yoke', 'liberation from communism', etc. And I repeat, Ginzburg and Co. not only ecstatically absorbed these publications, but also made every effort to propagandize them. As witness E. Kushev testified in court, they would accidentally, as it were, slip this NTS produce to unfortunate young people, their former schoolmates and acquaintances.

One of them was Vera Lashkova, who has just landed in the dock. At one time she had been attracted by the sham originality of her new acquaintances. Unstable by nature, and never having seriously thought out her political views, she succumbed to the attitudes of this trio and became an accomplice in their criminal activities. It was she who typed copies, in great quantities, of the slanderous and malicious materials that her friends were pursuing and ferreting out from morning till evening. She read the NTS literature they slipped to her, and offered it round to others. At times Lashkova experienced doubts and anxiety, but when reassured by her employers that there was nothing wrong in what she was doing, and by the more than generous pay she received per page, she soon calmed down. Of course, by the age of twenty-two one can already evaluate one's activities independently. But this simple idea did not occur to her until too late.

'I gave impermissibly little thought to facts I should have weighed strictly. Had I done this in time, everything might have turned out differently,' said V. Lashkova contritely in court.

Without detracting from the gravity of V. Lashkova's guilt, it should nevertheless be admitted that the part she played in the criminal game contrived by the NTS accomplices was to a certain extent incidental. But Ginzburg, Galanskov and Dobrovolsky—they are another matter. They knew what they were doing. That is why they always maintained the strictest conspiratorial secrecy. Their NTS friends helped them to do this. They agreed on a pre-arranged code and provided their protégés with special cryptographic devices.

When the homes of Ginzburg, Galanskov and Dobrovolsky were searched, espionage equipment was discovered—cryptography paper, hectographs, instructions, anti-Soviet literature and leaflets. All of these were used when the occasion arose. The testimony of defendant Lashkova is of interest in this connection.

PROCURATOR. Did Galanskov ask you to type some kind of coded letter?

LASHKOVA. Yes, I did type a letter for him.

PROCURATOR. Tell the court when and in what circumstances.

LASHKOVA. It was at Galanskov's. I made one copy, on tissue paper. The letter was not written to anyone in particular, at any rate there was no address. The contents of the letter were somewhat vague, because there were figures. I mean some sort of code. It was not completely coded, but certain words and phrases were in code.

PROCURATOR. What was the text like, roughly speaking?

LASHKOVA. There was something about 101, 102, 103 and so on. About the relationships between them.

PROCURATOR. 101 does not want to travel to 103?

LASHKOVA. I was talking of the relationships between the numbers.

PROCURATOR. It's impossible to do something at 104's flat. . . .

LASHKOVA. Yes, that's the letter.*

It was established in court that the volunteer NTS lackeys received from abroad large sums of money in American dollars and Soviet roubles. This was the payment for their treason. Through middlemen Yu. Galanskov sold the dollars to foreign currency speculators for roubles. These deals were not without incident. After receiving some fifty-dollar bills from Galanskov on one occasion, the black-marketeers managed to palm off on him in exchange a packet of mustard-plasters. But what can you expect among your own kind!

---

* The discrepancies between the above dialogue and the same dialogue as recorded by Litvinov on p. 88 are probably to be explained by the unreliable official recording of the proceedings; see Litvinov's remarks on p. 41. Litvinov's record is, in view of his persistent concern for accuracy, almost certainly reliable. Ed.

As for the rest, matters seemed to be proceeding successfully and on a manifestly increasing scale. One after another, NTS emissaries arrived from abroad in the guise of tourists. Brooke, an Englishman; Philip, a Frenchman; Schaffhauser, citizen of the Federal Republic of Germany; and Mikulinskaya, daughter of a colonel in the tsar's army—all of them hurried to look up Ginzburg, Galanskov and Dobrovolsky, giving them fat parcels of anti-Soviet literature and the latest instructions on how to obtain in exchange information of interest to them. Special messengers were sent to them from Paris, Stockholm, Heidelberg. Their names figured prominently in questionnaires compiled for NTS couriers. These zealous collectors of fake works were represented as budding titans of the pen. Who would not make the most of it all, in the circumstances?

Ginzburg laboured ceaselessly at compiling an entire collection of slanderous materials. He had got hold of, among other things, a 'Letter to an Old Friend', a typical example of the primitive anti-Soviet concoctions disseminated by our enemies. Under the guise of a discussion of events of the recent past, it drags in ideas deeply hostile to socialism and contains crude and slanderous fabrications which cast slurs upon the Soviet people and our country.

Soon there arrived from France an NTS emissary by the name of Genrikh. With Ginzburg's consent and approval, Galanskov secretly handed over to Genrikh the slander he had collected. The NTS journal *Grani* published the material forthwith and exultantly told its readers of its growing contact with the 'Russian underground'. Reactionary newspapers and journals, too, pounced greedily upon this pile of slander that had come their way and confidently unwrapped issue after issue. In West Germany the NTS publishing house Possev published Ginzburg's anthology in Russian and German. With a haste that left no doubt as to the motives, it was promptly published in France and Italy. And every copy bore the words: 'Compiled by A. Ginzburg'.

But his partners had new concerns. From the store-house of faked documents they compiled a new miscellany with the pretentious title of *Phoenix*. And on the title page: 'Edited by Yu. Galanskov'. Through a resourceful NTS emissary this compilation was conveyed to Paris. And once again *Possev* and *Grani* went into ecstasies. They passed the newly received materials on to the editors of bourgeois newspapers and magazines, and to radio stations, and all these made extensive use of them in their ideological sabotage against the Soviet Union.

This was followed by promises to acquaint the public with the 'latest' as soon as it arrived. However, for reasons beyond the control of messieurs the publishers and commentators, a sudden alteration had to be made in their carefully laid plans. In lieu of the promised messages of greeting came the announcement that the enterprising seekers after glory had been arrested.

Nevertheless, their dejection was short-lived. After all, this development was a sensation too. Here was a real opportunity to stir up yet another commotion about 'writers fallen victim to arbitrary rule'. And the merry-go-round of slander and fantastic fabrications was sent spinning in the opposite direction with renewed force.

Unfortunately, massive misinformation often accomplishes its purpose. If such celebrities as Nobel prizewinner François Mauriac, famous actor Jean-Louis Barrault and Françoise Sagan could swallow the bait, what about ordinary people who are not too experienced in such matters? It was precisely such inexperience and dangerous lack of responsibility that played such a filthy trick on the young Venezuelan Nicolas Brox-Sokolov when he arrived in the Soviet Union from Grenoble in December of last year.

Before his trip to our country, this fair-haired lad, still a mere boy, had attended a lecture by a certain Mikhail Slavinsky, devoted entirely to the 'problems' of the development in the USSR of underground literature which is illegally sent abroad. Nicolas, who had come to France from Venezuela only recently, could not know that he was dealing with an experienced and cunning intriguer specializing in slander and sabotage against the Soviet land and its people. In his time Slavinsky has been leader of the anti-Soviet 'Young Russia' youth organization in France, worked at the NTS centre in Frankfurt-am-Main (West Germany), headed a group of agents organizing provocations against Soviet citizens at the Brussels World Fair and engaged in preparing hostile acts on the eve of the World Youth and Student Festival in Vienna. He is now a member of the NTS leadership. It is most significant that this specialist in provocations and sabotage has changed his line and is now involved in so-called underground literature. Slavinsky declaimed at length and with inspiration on the subject of Ginzburg, Galanskov and Dobrovolsky, who have now come to grief.

After such an indoctrination, Nicolas was easily persuaded to render a small service to the suffering 'littérateurs'. Brox-Sokolov eagerly undertook to carry out the assignment, and girded himself with the secret belt concealing packages which he was to give to a 'certain person' in Moscow. How this ill-fated mission to the Soviet Union ended, and how the unfortunate Venezuelan became convinced of the bitter truth that he had been used as a pawn in someone's political scheming, readers will know already from what has been reported in our press.

I was present in the courtroom when Brox-Sokolov was giving his testimony as a witness in the case of Ginzburg, Galanskov, Dobrovolsky and Lashkova. Greatly agitated, and in a mixture of Russian and Spanish, this is what he said:

'I would remind you that at the time of Slavinsky's "lecture" I thought that Ginzburg, Dobrovolsky and Galanskov were writers. The newspapers in France spoke of them as writers. So I thought that they were young writers and had been imprisoned, that they had been treated unjustly. . . . The man whom I was to meet in Moscow was, they told me, also someone who could help the people under arrest here. But now I see that I was deceived, and deceived twice over. Once, when they told me that these were writers and were being tried for that. I see no writers. It is criminals who are being tried here for their ties with the NTS. And then again, when they told me that these packets contained nothing but materials that would help them. When I was detained, it turned out that they did not contain what I had been told they did . . . .'

Yes, it turned out that the contents of the packets were not at all what Nicolas had imagined. They were exhibited at the trial. Money intended not at all for charitable purposes. A hectograph and a packet of cryptography paper, exactly like the ones previously given to Galanskov by other NTS emissaries. Leaflets with anti-Soviet appeals, not unlike those that Ginzburg and his friends had been circulating. A familiar type-face! And five envelopes which Brox-Sokolov was to have dropped into letter-boxes, containing enlarged photographs of the defendants with a short text on the other side that ended with threatening demands for their immediate release.

One would like to think that as a result of Brox-Sokolov's admission of guilt, his statement, and the material evidence found on his person, those people in the West who were taken in by the sensation stirred up by the propaganda media will be brought to their senses. It is time they saw reason and took a sober look at the findings of the trial, which are more instructive than might seem at first sight. Instructive above all, because they provide clear-cut, convincing answers to all the questions raised by the case.

The masters of truth distortion, together with those who have not taken the trouble to reflect on what has happened, are doing their utmost to represent Ginzburg, Galanskov and Dobrovolsky as perfectly gentle creatures who, at worst, did not know what they were doing. This is followed by lengthy dissertations on the need to make allowances for their youth and the inevitable errors made by the young. Enough of this, gentlemen! We are not dealing with childish pranks. Nor with a mischievous pen wielded by youngsters who have just left their mother's apron-strings. The people who were on trial here have already left their boyhood far behind them. One of them is beyond thirty, two others almost that. Galanskov has already been married twice. Dobrovolsky has a son who has long been playing football. It is time that those fond of attributing all sins and abominations to youth realized that their argument is fallacious in principle, and utterly untenable in this case. These innocent lambs kept count of their 'rewards' with the calculation of seasoned merchants and maintained strict conspiratorial secrecy with the artfulness of hardened criminals. Strange reasoning indeed.

Dobrovolsky and Lashkova pleaded guilty and told the court everything, which, incidentally, was taken into account in determining their punishment. Ginzburg and Galanskov, on the other hand, continued to wriggle, to evade the issue whenever they could, and played unexpected tricks, although by the end they were driven into a corner by the material evidence and the testimony of witnesses. For example, both of them suddenly declared that they did not consider what they had done in collaboration with the NTS, an organization hostile to our people, to be anti-Soviet activity.

Well then, what are we talking about? What else is one to call their underhand abuse of their country, their traffic in the dignity of the Soviet man? What else is one to call treachery and vileness?

There was something else one could not help reflecting on in the court-room. It was the brazen, unpardonable speculation on people's interest in, and natural respect for, literature, on people's trust in the writer's personality, a tradition of long standing in our country. It was not for nothing that Ginzburg and Galanskov tried to push their way to fame and ardently wished to acquire a reputation as writers. There was far-reaching calculation here. They knew full well that nothing but general approval could be expected for sentences, no matter how severe, handed down to, say, speculators in foreign goods, currency speculators or spies. But the spectacle of a writer persecuted for his convictions is an entirely different matter. If a big enough fuss is made beforehand ('Help! They are infringing on freedom of creativity!'), then just look, not only will the man in the street prick up his ears but even more important persons will swallow the bait and express their sympathy. . . .

They called them 'writers'. But when it was ascertained that this role was clearly inappropriate to the defendants, they reclassified them as 'Moscow intellectuals'. What an 'intellectual' shuffle! What brilliant card-sharpers!

The criminal activities of Ginzburg, Galanskov, Dobrovolsky and Lashkova have been completely exposed. Their guilt has been incontro-vertibly proved by the testimony of a great number of witnesses, by numerous documents, material evidence and the authoritative findings of experts. Taking into account the personalities of the accused, the degree of their sincerity and repentance and also a number of other important circumstances the Moscow City Court sentenced Yu. Galanskov to seven years' deprivation of freedom and his accomplices in crime A. Ginzburg, A. Dobrovolsky and V. Lashkova to five years', two years' and one year's deprivation of freedom respectively. The Muscovites present in the courtroom greeted the verdict with applause and shouts of approval.

A. M. Gorky once remarked contemptuously, referring to the intrigues of the enemies of our state and their obsequious hangers-on: 'What poverty of thought! What destitution of spirit! And—what hypocrisy!' Almost forty years have passed since then, but our foes, both covert and overt, still confront us at critical moments in our lives in the same old spiritual rags. There is the same depressing paucity of ideas. Only maybe their hypocrisy has increased. The hypocrisy of the slanderers themselves and of those who clumsily try to shield and defend them.

Komsomolskaya Pravda, 18 January 1968   F. Ovcharenko

[*The following Documents have been omitted:* **V: 4,** '*A Lie has Short Legs*', Soviet Culture, *6 February 1968*; **V: 5,** '*How to Become Famous*' and '*The Littérateurs*', The Voice of the Motherland, *14 February 1968*; **V: 6,** '*Open Letter by Brox-Sokolov*', Izvestia, *26 February 1968*.]

Document V: 7

NO INDULGENCE!

Readers of *Komsomolskaya Pravda* write in about the renegades convicted by a Soviet court.

Since the publication in *Komsomolskaya Pravda* on 18 January this year of the article 'Lackeys', the editors have received a great number of letters in response. Our readers express their anger and indignation at the, criminal activities of Galanskov, Ginzburg, Dobrovolsky and Lashkova, who have sullied themselves by collaborating with White émigré rabble, by actions incompatible with the lofty title of citizen of the USSR. Dozens of letters contain words of contempt for those who have sold their consciences for pittances in dollars and evil-smelling popularity.

P. Zanyuk and S. Vinnikov, soldiers in the Soviet Army; V. Biryukov, a Moscow worker; B. Ermolayev from Leningrad, who fought in the Great Patriotic War; pupils of the tenth class at school No. 12 in Volgograd; schoolchildren from Kharkov; comrades Brekin and Bagrov, research officers, and comrade Trunova, a schoolmistress from the Moscow area; S. Mozhayev from Lugansk and V. Kudryashov from Chuvashia; L. Khokhlova, a student at Moscow University; V. Kupnevich of Enakiyev; N. Kushin from Zlynka station in Bryansk Region; A. Vyshensky of Sverdlovsk, and many, many others approve of the court's verdict and write of the strength of the love which Soviet people feel for their homeland and of the need resolutely to repulse all the intrigues and ideological sabotage devised by our foes and their hangers-on.

In the general stream of comments unreservedly supporting the newspaper articles and the court's decision in the case of the voluntary lackeys of the NTS, there were a few letters of a different tenor. Either because of inadequate information or because of confusion arising from misinformation by bourgeois propaganda reports, several readers—amongst whom there are even some writers—express doubts as to the justice of the charge brought against the criminals and lament the harshness of the sentences.

If this is really a sincere desire to understand the essence of the issue, then we think these doubters would do well to acquaint themselves a little more closely with the open letter from Brox-Sokolov published in *Izvestia* on 26 February. The man who was dragged into this dirty business by deception addresses himself to the leadership of the so-called People's Labour Alliance—an organization for espionage and sabotage which collaborated with the Hitlerites during the war and is now supported by the CIA. He writes: 'Mr Slavinsky and other gentlemen of the NTS, your writers Ginzburg, Galanskov and Dobrovolsky—and they are writers only in your imagination—are alive and well. I even saw them—in the prisoners' dock. True, I didn't have a chance to talk with them more closely, but I expect they too would like to thank you for the "literature" you sent them, and for which they are now having to answer before a court in their own country.'

Revealing the criminal connection of the men on trial with an organization hostile to the Soviet people, Brox-Sokolov makes the following, not uninteresting statement: 'At the trial I saw the same cryptographic equipment and proclamations that you had sent with me too, and that I had seen for the first time when I was detained. It was very clever of you, Mr Slavinsky, not to give me an opportunity before my trip to see all the things you were sending to Russia with me. You realized that I would have refused to take the goods and carry out your assignment if I had known what it was you were sending via me. And as for the question of whom all this was intended for, I have not understood to this day, since I saw no writers Ginzburg, Galanskov or Dobrovolsky; I saw only the defendants Ginzburg, Galanskov and Dobrovolsky, who had committed crimes against their country with your assistance. You have done a bad service to them, gentlemen of the NTS.'

And our readers are of exactly the same opinion, when they hold up to shame these traitors and renegades. We print below some of the comments received by the editor in reply to the article 'Lackeys'.

I have never written to a newspaper before, but this time I cannot refrain from expressing my indignation at the anti-Soviet activities of the Ginzburg, Dobrovolsky, Galanskov and Lashkova group. I cannot find words to express my contempt for these wretched people. I don't envy their mothers, giving birth to them and bringing up such traitors.

The Ginzburgs and their like have branded with shame not only themselves but their children, their wives and their mothers, too, if they have any. And the gentlemen from West Germany, the USA and other capitalist countries are wasting their resources for nothing on espionage. Money down the drain!

Kolpino, Leningrad   M. Kalashnikova, doctor

Collaboration with the enemies of one's own country is shameful. No one has ever been forgiven for such treachery. How can one talk of showing mercy to Galanskov and his accomplices? And what right have they to call themselves writers? Literature is for people who are powerful, talented and pure as crystal.

I have never heard of these 'writers', although I am a regular reader of journals and keep an eye out for new books. Of course, any graphomaniac can declare himself a writer. And if Ginzburg and Galanskov are being hailed as writers in the West, well, it's understandable. After all, they compiled and supplied our ideological enemies with lampoons against the Soviet people. But happily, literature does not start with slander. We have other springs, clear and honourable.

Oryol   I. Alekseyev, journalist

I and my comrades at work, having read the article in *Komsomolskaya Pravda* on 18 January, approve of the verdict at the trial of those pen-pushers. Only the most weak-minded character could stoop to such vulgarity and vileness.

Yes, they got what they wanted. Their names have beome famous as the names of traitors to the Fatherland.

V. Kzygach, private in the Soviet Army

I fought in the Great Patriotic War and was gravely wounded. How can I fail to feel pain when these vile creatures slander me and all the Soviet people, slander the entire Communist Party, of which I am a member?

The Soviet court has punished the slanderers justly. They should be branded with shame as lackeys of the enemies of our people.

I. Korchagin, Kalinin State Farm, Penza Region

However indignant the gentlemen in the West become, Soviet justice is and will be harsh with respect to those who dare to slander our Fatherland, our people, our system and our way of life, which our fathers secured for us, and which we preserved from German fascism during the Great Patriotic War.

Yaroslavl   P. Viskov

All week the raucous and corrupt 'Voice of America' has been shouting hoarsely over the waves: 'A Soviet court has unjustly convicted four Soviet writers!', 'Demand the removal of the judges from their elective offices!', 'Demand the immediate release of the four writers!'

Why do the war criminals of the NTS, using the 'Voice of America' radio station, howl so persistently and maliciously? Because they are bemoaning their own bitter lot and earning the dollars they are paid for their treason.

It was just such people as Ginzburg, Galanskov, Dobrovolsky and Lashkova that the great writer of the Russian land Aleksei Maksimovich Gorky meant when he wrote: 'There is nothing and no one with whom the traitor may be compared. Even the typhus louse would, I think, resent the comparison.'

Soviet people know that lice are dangerous as spreaders of disease, and that is why they render them harmless.

In the name of the Soviet people, the court has passed its just sentence, and these scum, once in their corrective labour colony, should be made to serve their term to the end. By unremitting physical labour they might atone for a small part of their great guilt before their Fatherland.

Kharkov   A. Rasnovsky

In *Komsomolskaya Pravda* for 18 January 1968 there was an article called 'Lackeys'.

A Soviet court has examined the case of Yury Galanskov, Alexander Ginzburg, Aleksei Dobrovolsky and Vera Lashkova, who were charged with criminal activities aimed against the Soviet system, and that means against the entire Soviet people.

But can the degree of punishment allotted to them repair the moral damage done to our country?

Judging by the information in the article, the criminal activities of Yu. Galanskov, A. Ginzburg, A. Dobrovolsky and V. Lashkova were not the naïve errors of youth, but every whit premeditated treachery, which had been going on for quite a few years.

> Students of the S. M. Kirov Institute of Chemical Technology:
> Sizarev, Pavly, Morozov, Zakusilo, Mingulov

Respected Editors!
I read the article 'Lackeys' in the issue of *Komsomolskaya Pravda* for 18 January 1968. I cannot find words to express my indignation at the anti-Soviet activities of Yu. Galanskov, A. Ginzburg and A. Dobrovolsky. Here is direct evidence of their crime, *corpus delicti*, as they say. One wonders if the penalty for these traitors to the Fatherland is not too lenient?
                        With respect,

Leningrad   A. Fyodorov, apprentice steel founder

Dear Editors!
This is the first letter I have written to *Komsomolskaya Pravda*. I am extremely upset by the article 'Lackeys'. After reading it, I am seething with rage that people nursed by the Soviet system, instead of showing their gratitude, can spit on the soul of our people and betray their Fatherland.

Pskov   A. Petrov, age 28

In Kursk, recently, lovers of literature honoured the memory of a talented writer, V. V. Ovechkin, a man who suffered a hard fate and who had the honest and fearless heart of a communist. His books are one of the many examples in Soviet literature of selfless service to our party and people.

For some reason, the Western press does not write about Soviet writers whose works are the conscience, the painful depths of their own people's soul, whose works affirm the ideals in the name of which the banner of October was hoisted over the Smolny by the hands of our grandfathers and great-grandfathers.

And it's strange to hear about some 'Soviet writers' who publish in so-called 'journals on the other side' and have not gladdened the hearts of our readers with a single work.

No, it is not a question of literary talent, but of the most elementary concepts of honour and conscience for any citizen who is a patriot for his country.

And, let's face it, the foreign patrons of Ginzburg, Galanskov and Dobrovolsky are not stirring up an anti-Soviet sensation around them for purely literary reasons.

These people evoke a feeling of contempt; they are people without an anchor, people who have not realized that the most terrible thing in life is to lose the moral right to call themselves sons of a great people, the people of Pushkin and Lenin.

Kursk   Egor Polyansky, writer

Komsomolskaya Pravda, 28 February 1968

[*The following Documents have been omitted:* **V: 8,** '*Crocodile Tears*', Pravda, *3 March 1968*; **V: 9,** '*Why Are You Silent about Leroy Jones?*', Literary Gazette, *6 March 1968*; **V: 10,** '*Waves of Sympathy*', Literary Gazette, *13 March 1968.*]

Document V: 11

REPLY TO A READER

The editors have received a letter from Comrade G. Novikov, a Leningrad reader. We are publishing this letter in full with a reply by the editor-in-chief of the *Literary Gazette*.

To the Editors of *Literary Gazette*

Esteemed Comrade Editor Chakovsky
I have been reading *Literary Gazette* for more than ten years with great satisfaction.

Especially interesting are the polemics and discussions on major literary problems. Sholokhov's speech at the last Writers' Congress rightly expressed alarm at the fact that very few young writers were represented (13%) and their voice was not fully heard.

That is why I believe that *Literary Gazette* makes a mistake in ignoring the campaign launched by the world press over the trial of the group of young writers, and, most important, is evading the question of its readers' interest in knowing the true situation, even if only within the bounds of counter-propaganda.

I expected *Literary Gazette* to carry comprehensive articles on this disturbing situation in the literary world. For it is not only a matter of the principles of legality at a trial being flagrantly violated; the problem of attitudes to the Soviet intelligentsia, to its creative enterprise and to freedom of opinion is growing more acute, and this is connected with the consequences of the cult of [*Stalin's*] personality. It is incomprehensible what considerations (I am tempted to say—considerations of expediency) allow you to ignore questions that are now so well known to the Soviet reader from radio broadcasts and the world press.

This is why I ask *Literary Gazette* to uphold its reputation and comment on the latest events in the writers' world.

With greetings and respect,

Leningrad   reader G. Novikov

Esteemed Comrade Novikov!
It is possible that you are right in reproaching *Literary Gazette* for failing to carry 'comprehensive articles' in connection with the campaign launched by the bourgeois press and radio after the trial of the anti-Sovietists. I will be frank with you: the editors of our *writers'* paper simply did not deem it necessary to make a *special* reply to bourgeois propaganda, which has had the audacity to pass off as Soviet *writers* people who have *never* (at least in our country) published *a single line anywhere*.

But evidently the propaganda has left its mark. Even you, Comrade Novikov, call this group of underground anti-Sovietists 'a group of young writers'. Why? *Only because* that is what they are called by the Voice of America, the BBC and Deutsche Welle?

If Western radio had been your only source of information about this trial, I would understand your delusion, although I would have thought that some intrinsic doubt, based on many years' experience and natural for a Soviet man, as to the purity of bourgeois propaganda's intentions, would put you on your guard in this instance.

But there exist other sources of information. Soviet ones. *Izvestia* wrote about the trial on 16 January 1968. *Komsomolskaya Pravda* reported it in detail on 18 January 1968. Perhaps these reports failed to satisfy you? Perhaps something in them seemed inaccurate or inadequately argued to you, or aroused doubt?

Maybe that is the case. And if you had sent a letter to the above-mentioned newspapers, setting out the specific points that puzzled you and asking for exhaustive explanations, I have no doubt that you would have received them. However, there are no such specific questions in your letter as published here.

Nevertheless, we feel a reply is needed. And not for the sake of 'counter-propaganda', as you put it, but to deal in depth with the questions you raised. So here you are.

Press reports and eyewitness accounts by people who attended the court proceedings are the natural and usual sources of information for the public about any trial.

We shall return to the eyewitnesses later. First—the press.

From its reports we learned of four people who linked themselves with a foreign counter-revolutionary organization, the NTS, that sets as its goal the overthrow of the socialist order in our country, collaborated with the Hitlerites in the last war and sullied itself with the blood of Soviet citizens.

This foursome received anti-Soviet materials from the NTS for clandestine circulation in our country, was involved in machinations with foreign currency supplied from abroad and sent slanderous materials to the West.

From an article published in *Komsomolskaya Pravda* we know that when the homes of Ginzburg, Galanskov and Dobrovolsky were searched, dozens of anti-Soviet publications from abroad were seized. They included the NTS programme and regulations, the White Guard paper *Possev* published as an eight-page pamphlet, the inveterate anti-Soviet journals *Our Times* and *Grani*, and writings by NTS ringleaders and ideologists. The materials Galanskov received from this organization and passed on to Dobrovolsky and Ginzburg contained recommendations and instructions on forms and methods of struggle against the Soviet system, including armed struggle, and appeals for terrorist acts and for the establishment of NTS cells on Soviet territory. These materials contained such assertions as, 'The destruction of the communist dictatorship in Russia will be the beginning of a process of cleansing and renewal throughout the whole world'; their terminology included expressions like 'the communist yoke', 'liberation from communism', etc.

These are the basic facts we know. From the dialogue between the Procurator and the defendants, which has also been quoted in published material, it is known that certain of the accused admitted their criminal ties with the NTS.

The others were convicted on objective evidence.

Now I would like to say the following.

As a Soviet citizen, I feel repugnance for the kind of activity that the defendants were engaged in. I have no reason not to trust the court or the information in the Soviet press and, consequently, no reason to doubt that these people were convicted in accordance with the laws of the Soviet Union.

I also want to say that, as a writer and publicist, I envisage other ways of protecting the public from anti-Soviet propagandists. I favour, if you like, a more severe punishment in moral terms. I think that if these four people were made to face a large audience consisting of workers and representatives of the intelligentsia, a gathering that would tell them exactly what it thought of them, and if, as a result, the anti-Sovietists were subjected to public ostracism, that would be a severer and more effective punishment. I would also like to add that people who find the

Soviet system odious and are tempted by the fate of Tarsis, who vanished into the Lethe of the West,[96] ought to be given the opportunity to share his fate. And instead of giving such people food and drink at the nation's expense in prisons or corrective labour colonies, the responsibility for their keep should be shifted on to the American, English or West German taxpayers. That is my frank opinion.

But let us return to the trial. We are told by people abroad that it was illegal. Why? Because it was 'closed'. What does that mean? Is it really the rule in bourgeois judicial practice to stage the trials of people who threaten the security of the capitalist system in New York's Lincoln Centre or London's Trafalgar Square? Do American courts perhaps send out invitations to Soviet correspondents humbly requesting them to attend trials involving the latest 'Red spy'? Has it never happened in American, English and other bourgeois courts that a court official, standing before the closed doors of the chamber where the case is being heard, has gestured helplessly and said regretfully:

'I'm sorry, gentlemen, but there are no seats, the courtroom is over-crowded. . . .'

And yet—oh, what magnificent propaganda casuistry! If foreign correspondents were not invited to the Moscow trial, it meant the trial was 'closed' and 'secret'. If they had been invited, the testimony of 'impartial eyewitnesses' would have been circulated, to present the accused as innocent lambs whose guilt was absolutely unproved.

Certain Soviet writers, who were not present at the trial, have tried to discredit it in their letter broadcast by the Voice of America. But why should I believe them and not, say, Professor V. Menshikov, Doctor of medical sciences; Professor A. Gromov, Head of the department of forensic medicine; or senior lecturers K. Tarasov and V. Tumasyan, Masters of philosophical and historical sciences? Why am I obliged to believe Litvinov and his proclamations, and not the letter written by the above-named scholars? Their letter, addressed to the USSR Writers' Union, says, among other things, the following: 'We, a group of teachers at Moscow Medical Institute No. 1, who attended the trial, are deeply angered by the fabrications contained in the statement by a group of writers; we protest resolutely against such actions, which are aimed at misinforming public opinion and discrediting Soviet legal organs. We did not see in the courtroom the persons who signed the statement, and we are puzzled as to where they obtained their information.

'All the defendants and witnesses—about forty were called—enjoyed complete freedom of speech. Relatives and friends of the defendants sat in the courtroom, and not one of them throughout the entire trial expressed any doubt as to the objectivity or conclusiveness of the investigation's findings.

'The trial proceeded in an atmosphere of calm, thorough and serious examination of the case. The defendants' guilt was obvious even to the layman. It was openly and sincerely admitted by Dobrovolsky and

Lashkova and corroborated by the testimony of witnesses, in particular Brox-Sokolov and others. Moreover, we were amazed at the patience of the Soviet state organs; they issued repeated warnings to the accused, but the latter drew no conclusions for themselves.'

Bourgeois radio stations allege that the courtroom audience consisted of handpicked people—plain-clothes 'KGB men', 'policemen', etc.

In which category should the authors of the above letter be placed?

Do you want yet another letter? With pleasure. It too is addressed to the Writers' Union, and concerns itself with the 'popularization' by bourgeois radio stations of the declarations of certain Soviet writers:

'We were present in the courtroom together with many other citizens. We declare that the open trial of Ginzburg, Galanskov, Dobrovolsky and Lashkova was conducted in accordance with all the established procedural guarantees of justice. . . .

'The actions of certain individuals who continue to sell abroad false information about the trial arouse profound indignation,' the authors of the letter go on to say. 'Persons who sign "protests" and speculate in freedom of convictions, and intellectuals who secretly hope to gain fame in the West, must realize that theirs will be neither glory nor popularity—only a shameless flirtation with our ideological enemies.'

This letter was signed by a number of teachers at the Moscow Motor Highways Institute—Comrades V. T. Efimov, G. F. Yudin, N. S. Kuznetsov, N. M. Vasilev, V. A. Elizarov, E. V. Starostin and I. I. Kravtsov.

The Writers' Union and the USSR Artists' Union also received a letter from a group of scientists at the All-Union Raw Minerals Research Institute—Comrades G. S. Momdzhi, N. D. Sobolev, Ya. D. Gotman, L. M. Shamovsky, A. D. Ershov, V. M. Grigorev and V. I. Kuzmin, all Doctors of Sciences and senior research officers. In their letter they protest at the attempt to discredit a Soviet court, an attempt that was 'immediately exploited by the hostile propaganda apparatus of a number of capitalist countries in order to reinforce the myth that political opposition to the policies of the Soviet communist party and Soviet government exists among the Soviet intelligentsia'. A letter with similar contents was sent to the Writers' Union by a group of workers (thirty people) at State Bearing Plant No. 1.

We are assured from abroad that because the courtroom audience was relatively small, the trial was 'closed'. A strange argument. If the court held one hundred people, it meant the audience was 'handpicked'. If it had held five hundred the argument would have been the same: after all, even hundreds can be 'handpicked'. . . . Are not the Western champions of human rights urging us to hold trials in public squares? Are they not implying that these are the conditions which will ensure a painstaking examination of the case and a calm atmosphere, remote from hysterical passions?

How is one to know? At any rate, I heard with my own ears an American radio transmission in the Russian language in which the usual accusations of 'secrecy' with respect to the trial of the four anti-Sovietists were followed immediately by a report that China had staged a trial of Mao Tse-tung's opponents in a stadium holding 20,000 people, after which the chief prisoners had been executed. . . .

Let us take another example, one recently reported in our paper.

A case was fabricated against the American poet and playwright Leroy Jones in 'full conformity' with the laws of the state of New Jersey. He was accused of illegal possession of a weapon. Penalties in cases of the kind in this American state usually do not exceed six months' imprisonment. Jones, however, was sentenced to three years' imprisonment and fined $1000. The whole point was that Leroy Jones is a fighter for civil rights for the Negro population. A journal with his poems figured in court as 'material evidence'. Before the sentence was passed the judge quoted verses by Jones. How many such trials are now being held in the United States, where fighters for civil rights and fighters against the dirty war in Vietnam are being judged in the name of the law!

The Moscow trial had nothing in common with such inquisitions. So on what basis, by what right, are those who organize and encourage judicial reprisals in the capitalist countries trying to teach us legal procedure and democracy!

Now let us talk about 'creative enterprise' and 'freedom of opinion'. It is essential, Comrade Novikov, for us to agree on the main thing: do you feel that freedom of opinion in our country should include freedom to call for the overthrow of the socialist system, freedom of contact with counter-revolution abroad and freedom to circulate its propaganda materials?

If so, then I resolutely differ with you. But if you are for freedom of criticism that presupposes as an indispensable condition the preservation and perfection of socialism, then I am completely with you. If you feel that criticism and self-criticism in our country must be developed even more actively (although to estimate the level of their development it is enough to direct one's gaze to the relatively recent past), then I agree with you here also.

Bourgeois propaganda has also put out the following version: the accused, it alleges, were not anti-Sovietists but zealots for improving Soviet life.

In this connection, Comrade Novikov, let us try to recall whether history has known a single case of a man engaging in hostile actions against his fatherland under the banner of hatred for it. No, he has always shouted about his love for his people, trying thereby to provide moral justification for his betrayal.

Now something else. A number of foreign writers, including several quite respected ones, came to the defence of the convicted men. Why? I think this can be explained by several factors. Firstly, even they are not immune to lies, especially when these lies are reproduced daily by all the propaganda media. Obviously these writers believe they are defending a just cause.

There are also those Western writers who profess the principle of 'fifty-fifty' or 'half and half'. They fear being suspected of having unqualified sympathy for communism and believe that if yesterday they signed a protest against the war in Vietnam or against racial persecution in the USA, today they must 'counterbalance' this by associating themselves with some action against our country. Finally, there are other factors. Writers who have failed to gain any fame through their literary works crave easy popularity and are willing to link their names with any sensation.

Well, and what about those Soviet people, including a few professional writers, whose letters, addressed to Soviet organizations, arrive with amazing synchronism and sometimes even ahead of time in America, Brtiain and West Germany? Incidentally, it was in connection with the broadcasting by bourgeois radio stations of one such letter that a number of Soviet citizens sent their protest to the Writers' Union. Perhaps you would be interested to hear my opinion of the authors of the letter, these Soviet writers? Well, in this case too, I do not want to 'tar them all with the same brush'. Obviously there are those among them who are sure that they are fighting for the restoration of the truth, although the amazing readiness of anti-Soviet radio stations to broadcast their letters should have put these comrades on their guard. I think that there are also others among them who, unlike Maupassant's Boule de Suif, cannot resist the temptation to flirt with their enemies. Particularly if this flirtation brings them the fame that it would take them so many years to win by their literary labours.

And—one last thing.

This is not the first year that all kinds of lying 'voices' have been devoting their broadcasts to Soviet writers. These broadcasts long ago turned into a sort of radio comedy series, in which Soviet writers are portrayed as people who dream day and night of a capitalist paradise. If one is to believe this bourgeois 'radio-illusion', our writers think of only one thing: how to sell their socialist birthright—if not for a mess of pottage, then, of course, for English porridge or American apple pie.

I want to say that this is an abominable, provocative lie. For many years I have known hundreds of writers—Moscow and Leningrad writers, Russian writers, Ukrainians, Belorussians, Uzbeks and others who live and work in our fraternal republics. As a writer, and simply as a Soviet citizen, I know that the overwhelming majority of people engaged in the complex, strenuous writer's trade are genuine citizens of the Soviet Union, staunch builders of socialist culture and communist society. And I would like to say this, too, for everyone to hear, in connection with the 'radio broadcasts' and 'world press' reports mentioned by you, Comrade Novikov.

In the concluding lines of your letter you call upon *Literary Gazette* to comment on 'the latest events in the writers' world'. If, as the contents of the letter imply, you mean that same trial and what is happening around it, then I should like yet again to correct you. This is not an event in the 'writers' world'. It is an episode in the ideological struggle. In the struggle which never ceases for a minute, the struggle in which all means are good, for our opponents, and the end justifies the means.

Literary Gazette, 27 March 1968   A. Chakovsky

[**Document V: 12**, '*With Us*' *by Nikolai Gribachyov*, Izvestia, *27 March 1968, has been omitted.*]

Document V: 13

MATERIALS OF 19TH MOSCOW CITY
PARTY CONFERENCE*

Speech by Comrade L. I. Brezhnev
at the 19th Moscow City Party Conference, 29 March 1968

. . . Our ideological opponents realize that they cannot shake the moral and political unity of Soviet society. But the bourgeois ideologists still hope somehow to influence the outlook of individual groups of Soviet people and dull their class consciousness.

All kinds of anti-Soviet organizations and services set up by the imperialists are hunting our morally unstable, weak and politically immature people. Sometimes their nets catch people greedy for self-advertisement, people ready to make their presence felt as loudly as possible, not by toil for the good of their country but by any politically dubious means, even going as far as praising our ideological opponents. Soviet public opinion severely condemns the shameful actions of these two-faced people. (Prolonged applause.) The renegades cannot expect to go unpunished. This is clearly shown by the many letters from working people and the resolutions passed at meetings of workers and employees at numerous enterprises and institutions in Moscow and other cities.

Our enemies in the camp of imperialism seize with extraordinary tenacity upon any manifestations of immaturity and vacillation among individual representatives of the intelligentsia. The imperialists are seeking to exploit these phenomena for their own interests in the ideological struggle against the socialist world.

But let them all know that workers in Soviet culture and the arts, like the entire intelligentsia of our country, always have stood, are standing now, and always will stand together with their people, together with the party of Lenin. (Stormy, prolonged applause.)

* In order of publication by the Soviet press. [The speeches by S. V. Mikhalkov and M. V. Keldysh are omitted. Ed.]

Leninism Is Our Banner [*slightly shortened*]
V. P. Trushin, First Secretary of the Moscow City Komsomol Committee

. . . We say with firm conviction that young Muscovites, like all Soviet girls and boys, follow the party, learn from it and dedicatedly put into practice its ideals. And any propagandist attacks, any speculation by Western ideologists seeking to sow scepticism and doubt amongst our young people, however subtle their methods, however cunning their designs, are doomed to complete failure. (Applause.)

. . . The recent meeting of the Moscow City Komsomol organization activists unanimously condemned the shameful posture of those who, speculating in concepts like freedom and democracy, stirred up a provocative scandal around the renegades.

History has more than once dealt a blow to such people, people who interpret freedom as the opportunity to set up their petty passions against the interests of the people and mock at everything that is sacred and precious to every Soviet man.

For us members of the Komsomol, as for all generations of Soviet people, there is and will be only one freedom—the freedom to fight for communism, for the happiness and joy of human toil! And to affirm this freedom we shall spare neither strength nor energy, nor our own lives. (Applause.)

Faithful to Lenin's Behest [*shortened*]
E. A. Pirogov, First Secretary of the Leningrad District Party Committee

. . . As an essential condition for the solution of scientific problems on a high technical level, we need well-trained, ideologically convinced research staff. There are, working in our research collectives, outstanding engineers and scientists, utterly devoted to our party's ideals. However, amongst the creative and technical intelligentsia there occasionally appear individual persons who forget to whom they owe their education, their professional stature and their material welfare. Some of these people who 'do not remember their parentage' take the path of slander against our party, our country and our people.

The actions of these people are an insult to our intelligentsia and evoke the anger and censure of the Soviet people. Having learned of these facts, communists and non-party members, and many collectives from the industrial enterprises in our district call in their letters and resolutions for decisive measures to be taken against such people.

Moscow Pravda, 3 April 1968

[*The following Documents have been omitted:* **V: 14,** '*Thank You, Communists*' Literary Russia, *5 April 1968*, **V: 15,** '*Soviet Artists Always with the Party*', Pravda, *10 April 1968*; **V: 16,** '*Always with the Party, Always with the People*', Moscow Artist, *19 April 1968*.]

Document V: 17

MEETING OF THE SECRETARIAT OF THE BOARD OF
THE MOSCOW WRITERS' ORGANIZATION [*shortened*]

A recent session of the Secretariat of the Board of the Moscow writers'
organization discussed the question of the writers who had signed statements in defence of the anti-Sovietists Ginzburg, Galanskov and the
others. The meeting was attended by Secretaries of the Board S. Mikhalkov, M. Alekseyev, B. Galin, L. Kassil, E. Knipovich, S. Narovchatov,
V. Rozov, V. Roslyakov, V. Ilin, V. Telpugov (party organizer, Moscow
City Party Committee), and Yu. Korolkov (deputy Secretary, Party
Committee).

The course of the discussion disclosed the unsavoury role of a number of
Moscow writers who have displayed inadmissible political dereliction and
lack of principle. It was noted that letters and statements of this kind were
food for our ideological enemies. Their publication by bourgeois propaganda organs was aimed at misinforming public opinion abroad, representing the political blackguards Ginzburg and Galanskov as writers.

The irresponsible actions on the part of certain writers evoked the
unanimous and severe condemnation of the members of the Secretariat.
They noted in their speeches that these actions were arousing legitimate
protests and indignation in writers' circles.

. . . The writer Yu. Pilyar, in a statement to the Secretariat, described
the circumstances in which he signed one of these letters:

'I was able to acquaint myself with the full text of the letter for the first
time in the Secretariat of the Moscow branch. Until then I had simply not
read the whole letter and consequently I could not have grasped its true
meaning, in particular its appraisal of Soviet justice, with which I
categorically disagree. . . . I consider my action in signing the letter to have
been thoughtless at the very least, and I am ashamed of my gullibility. . . .

'I am outraged that some dishonest and despicable people, without
asking the writer's permission, sent abroad this document which was
addressed to the Soviet leadership. Now that I have become acquainted
with the full text of the document, I cannot refrain from expressing my
condemnation of the organizers of this whole letter business, who so
abused the confidence of numerous writers. In any case, I never gave
anyone the right to make use of my name in any dubious statements
to be published outside my own country.

'In view of the foregoing, I withdraw my signature from the letter.'

The resolution taken by the Secretariat states, among other things,
that the irresponsible actions of certain writers 'were evidence of violation
by their authors of the regulation of the Writers' Union which makes it
the duty of its members to wage an ideological struggle against bourgeois
and revisionist influences'.

The resolution states further: 'Anyone who does not understand the full extent of his responsibility to the people in a period of uncompromising conflict between the two ideologies of socialism and capitalism, cannot call himself a Soviet writer'.

Literary Gazette, 24 April 1968

Document V: 18

A PLAYWRIGHT TAKES TO THE HUSTINGS [*shortened*]

. . . The action in the play *A Round Table With Sharp Corners* [by S. Mikhalkov and A. Nechayev] is taken from newspapers and broadcasts of the latest news. Biting and topical publicism becomes a perfectly legitimate dramatic genre when it serves a lofty aim, ardently champions public interests and follows the precept of patriotism, which guides our art.

. . . It was not so long ago that justice was meted out to that criminal 'quartet' of scum and renegades (presented by bourgeois propaganda as the noble conscience of our intelligentsia) who went into the service of the anti-Sovietists from the NTS. And the theatre is already giving playgoers an opportunity to glimpse what goes on behind the screen of this hostile organization, and how the enemies of our country plot their criminal actions. . . .

Pravda, 27 April 1968   N. Abalkin

Document V: 19

THE SCIENTIST'S LOFTY DUTY

. . . At the Moscow House of Scholars there was a meeting of the party activists of the USSR Academy of Sciences, dedicated to discussion of the resolutions passed at the April Plenum of the Party Central Committee.

The party activists of the Academy of Sciences condemned those who were rising to the defence of persons justly punished by a Soviet court for their anti-Soviet activities. The meeting called upon all scholars to display a high level of political consciousness and integrity in the ideological struggle between socialism and capitalism: every man should be ready to repulse any attempts by our enemies to disunite the progressive forces of the present-day and undermine socialist society from within.

Pravda, 27 April 1968

[*The following Documents have been omitted:* **V: 20,** '*Spring is Coming*', Evening Moscow, *30 April 1968*; **V: 21,** '*Condemnation of Carelessness, Lack of Principle and Slander*', Literary Russia, *1 May 1968*; **V: 22,** '*Light and Shade*', Pravda, *11 May 1968*.]

Document V: 23

CARRY ALOFT THE GLORIOUS TITLE OF SOVIET ARTIST [*shortened*]

RESOLUTION OF THE BOARD PLENUM OF THE MOSCOW BRANCH OF THE ARTISTS' UNION OF THE RUSSIAN REPUBLIC

. . . Eight artists and fine arts specialists, members of the Moscow branch of the Artists' Union of the Russian Republic, put their signatures to collective letters disputing the rightness of the court's decision with respect to the anti-Soviet group of Galanskov–Ginzburg.

Bourgeois propaganda promptly seized upon this fact and, armed with these letters, praised their authors to the skies. . . . To our deep regret, not one of the artists or specialists mentioned in Western radio broadcasts has raised his voice in protest, or publicly expressed his indignation at the use of his name by hostile propaganda.

. . . Moreover, as was later discovered, some of the signatories did not even have any idea of the substance of the case of the people for whom they had interceded.

. . . The artists of the capital city condemn the political dereliction and thoughtlessness displayed by N. I. Andronov, B. G. Birger, V. G. Veisberg, Yu. Ya. Gerchuk, I. N. Golomshtok, M. V. Ivanov, E. B. Murina and V. I. Polyakov, and pronounce a strict reprimand for the action they have committed, which goes against the political, civil and ethical norms guiding the lives of members of the Moscow artists' collective.

The Board and party bureau of the Moscow branch of the Artists' Union call upon all the members of the union to carry aloft the glorious title of Soviet artist, devoting their talent and knowledge to the creation of marvellous works celebrating the grandeur of the ideas of communism, that they may welcome in a befitting manner the centenary of the birth of V. I. Lenin.

Moscow Artist, 24 May 1968

[*The following Documents have been omitted:* **V: 24**, '*Alongside Lenin, Always, Everywhere and in Everything!*', '*Against Bourgeois Indifference*', Literary Russia, *24 May 1968*; **V: 25**, '*The Logic of the Fall*', Soviet Russia, *28 May 1968—about the Novosibirsk protest, see* **Document IV: 23**; **V: 26**, '*Fidelity, Unity, Conviction*', Literary Gazette, *29 May 1968*; **V: 27**, '*The Eternal Anxiety of the Artist*', Literary Russia, *31 May 1968*; **V: 28**, '*Decoy Duck*', Komsomolskaya Pravda, *9 June 1968*; **V: 29**, '*For Communist Ideals*', Soviet Culture, *20 June 1968*; **V: 30**, '*The Ideological Struggle and the Writer's Responsibility*', Literary Gazette, *26 June 1968—mainly about Solzhenitsyn.*]

Document V: 31

IN THE FIRING-LINE

The half-empty bus jolted along the road from the village. . . . On the back seat three youths were talking loudly. Actually, most of the talking was being done by one of them, a bit older than the other two. Clearly proud of being so 'well-informed', he was holding forth on the subject of the trial of Galanskov, Ginzburg and the others. 'They weren't allowed to say a word in defence of themselves,' I heard him say in a cocksure voice. His pals shook their heads sympathetically and demanded more details.

An elderly man sitting in front was listening to their conversation. Finally he could restrain himself no longer and turned sharply to face the speaker:

'Where did you get all that from?'

The youth frowned, disliking this unexpected interference.

'It wasn't in the papers,' he said condescendingly.

'Yes it was, and in great detail!' the man retorted. 'Only it wasn't at all the way you were explaining to your friends.'

Paying no attention to hostile looks from the story-teller, he went and sat with the lads.

'If a thief gets punished for stealing, it's considered perfectly in order. But as soon as these anti-Sovietists, these underground plotters, these dirty slanderers come into the dock people start shouting about illegalities being committed, human rights being trampled underfoot, and so on. Where's the logic? Traitors deserve a worse punishment than any old swindler. And that's what our court based itself on—strict accordance with the law. Read *Komsomolskaya Pravda* and you'll get a clear idea yourselves of the whole thing. And as for your friend, he heard the bell ring but had no idea where he was.'*

Noticeably dispirited, the lads got off at a stop along the way. The man went on further. This passenger was M. A. Ponomaryov, a worker at the Kamkabel factory.

These irresponsible, despicable people, these whisperers, these demagogues, sometimes crawl out from some hole or other and buzz around us. They spread absurd fabrications, blackening what is dear to us. Not everyone can bring himself to deal them a blow. Tough ideological training is necessary to make you speak out openly against something with which you do not agree, something which goes against your convictions and principles.

A. Vyatkin (our correspondent)

Perm
Soviet Russia, 3 July 1968

* Russian proverb. Ed.

The publications in the official Soviet press concerning the trial of the four evoked a lively response from readers, both those who were familiar with the circumstances of the case and those who learned of it solely from the newspapers.

Komsomolskaya Pravda printed some of the letters it received (see p. 299); however, only those letters were selected which approved both the sentences and the Soviet press coverage of the case. One can surmise that readers' appraisal of the trial was not so unanimous as might appear from the reader's letter published by *Literary Gazette* (see p. 300).

Included here are all the letters known to the compiler which were sent to the editors of Soviet papers in reply to their published articles concerning the trial, and letters to the USSR Journalists' Union. Not one of the papers to which they were addressed printed a single one of the letters, and their authors received no reply.

[*READERS' RESPONSES*]

Document V: 32

To: The Chief Editor of *Izvestia*.

On 16 January 1968, your newspaper, in its No. 12 issue, published an article by T. Aleksandrov and V. Konstantinov entitled 'Bound by a Single Belt' [*Document V: 2*]. This article cannot fail to evoke indignation, just as the farce of the Ginzburg–Galanskov–Dobrovolsky–Lashkova trial, with which the article is concerned, cannot fail to evoke protest.

The article 'Bound by the Same Belt' is outrageous in every respect. In the first place, it is utterly immoral, since its purpose is publicly to slander persons who cannot speak out in their own defence; the authors of the article resort to a dishonourable and base device, seeking to present the defendants in the most repulsive light: 'swindlers', 'criminals', 'depraved persons' and so on. Who gave T. Aleksandrov and V. Konstantinov the right to act thus? 'They [the defendants] prefer to keep quiet about their own biographies', write the authors. But people are judged—or rather, they should be judged—not for their biographies but for their criminal acts. Such slanderous devices have no place in a Soviet paper; they are the devices of the gutter press and cannot fail to arouse indignation.

In the second place, the article staggers one with the absolute groundlessness of its allegations. There is not a single argument, fact or piece of evidence in the article to support even one of the assertions made by its authors. Let us leave on the conscience of T. Aleksandrov and V. Konstantinov the unsubstantiated allegations of Ginzburg's 'swindling', his 'moral and political depravity' (!), Galanskov's 'endeavours to settle

313

on society's neck' and simultaneously 'cast slurs on it', and other similar assertions. But the article offers not one proof of the ties which allegedly existed between the defendants and the NTS. What has Brox-Sokolov to do with it? Can the fact that 'agents' of that organization gave Brox the names of the accused and instructed him to convey to the USSR packages with their photographs really serve as proof of their 'ties' with the NTS? If it was on the basis of such 'evidence' that the court found the defendants guilty, how can one speak of legality? And how, then, are we to view the authors of the article, who are covering up illegalities? If there are incontrovertible proofs of the ties between the defendants and the NTS, then why do T. Aleksandrov and V. Konstantinov not say a word about them?

Thirdly, certain facts are deliberately distorted in the article, while others are ignored. Yes, as the authors write, 'it is known' that this trial was held in Moscow on 8-12 January, but it was not through the announcements in the Soviet press that it became known. T. Aleksandrov and V. Konstantinov do not say that the Moscow trial was not a public, open one, as Soviet law stipulates; nor do they inform us that the 'Muscovites present at the trial' were not the general public, and that only 'selected persons' were allowed into the courtroom—those who had special passes. The authors of the article do not write that those Muscovites who had wished to obtain seats in the courtroom were not given the opportunity to attend the trial, that foreign correspondents were not allowed into the courtroom because of the 'lack of empty seats' (!!), and that the representative of an international organization for aid to political prisoners [*Amnesty International*] was refused access to the courtroom. T. Aleksandrov and V. Konstantinov do not say a word about these and other flagrant violations of legality and justice which were perpetrated at the trial. There is no mention in the article of the length of time the defendants were held in preliminary detention before the trial, which exceeded all the stipulated limits; there is nothing about the cynical disregard for procedural norms, beginning with the denial to objectionable witnesses of the right to speak, and the dismissal of witnesses from the courtroom after their testimony, and ending with the confiscation of notes made at the trial by, for instance, Ginzburg's fiancée and so on.

T. Aleksandrov and V. Konstantinov write of the 'approval' with which the specially selected public greeted the pronouncement of the verdict; but they say nothing about the protests of both the Soviet public and the public abroad and they are silent about the declarations made by P. Litvinov and L. Daniel. The authors of the article, having set themselves the thankless task of slandering the defendants in the eyes of society and portraying them as 'criminals', say not one word about the real charges—such as Ginzburg's compilation of *The White Book* on the trial of Sinyavsky and Daniel, the editing by Galanskov of the journal *Phoenix-66* and so on.

One cannot but view all this as a deliberate attempt to delude public opinion as to the real nature of the Moscow trial.

Whatever the motives that prompted T. Aleksandrov and V. Konstantinov to write this article and your newspaper to publish it, the appearance of such a piece is a stain on the honour of our country, in the same way that the conduct of trials like the one which has just ended is a stain on the honour of the state and on the conscience of all its citizens. And as a citizen of the country that has proclaimed the slogans of freedom and justice to the whole world, *I protest against the publication by your newspaper of the article by T. Aleksandrov and V. Konstantinov.*

As a citizen of the Russian Republic, in the name of which the shameful verdict was passed, *I protest against that verdict and against the judicial farce that was staged in Moscow.*

I demand an immediate, open and impartial re-examination of the case in court, in the presence of the general public and foreign correspondents.

I demand public condemnation of the practice of secret judicial reprisals against dissenters and punishment for those guilty of violating the rule of law.

I demand the restoration of truth and justice.

[*Gorky Region,*] Arzamas, ul. K. Marksa,   V. M. Voronin [*engineer*]
d. 20, kv.3
21 January 1968

Document V: 33

To: The Chief Editor of *Komsomolskaya Pravda* and the Party Committee of *Komsomolskaya Pravda*. Copy to: Board of the Journalists' Union.

On 18 January 1968 an article by F. Ovcharenko entitled 'Lackeys' [*Document V: 3*] was published in the newspaper *Komsomolskaya Pravda*. Each of us is acquainted with one or other of the convicted persons and knows the circumstances of the case, and on this basis we maintain that the article contains distortions of the facts and misinforms the reader. For instance, Ginzburg and Galanskov are depicted in a false light—as parasites. These allegations can be easily refuted by the actual employment records of the convicted persons, their testimonials and Labour Books.

Much more important and dangerous is the false information given about the case itself. For example, the article states: 'When the homes of Ginzburg, Galanskov and Dobrovolsky were searched, espionage equipment was discovered—cryptography paper, hectographs, instructions, anti-Soviet literature, and leaflets'. Nothing of the kind was discovered in the possession of either Ginzburg or Galanskov, in contrast to Dobrovolsky; this is obvious from the records of the searches, copies of which are in the case file and also in the possession of the relatives [*of the accused*]. According to F. Ovcharenko, the guilt of the accused was proven by 'the testimony of a great number of witnesses and the authoritative findings of experts'. In the first place, the only experts who figured in the trial were a psychiatric diagnosis team and they, as is well known, are competent to establish responsibility, but not guilt. In the second place, however one interprets the testimony of the witnesses, not one of them, not even Brox-Sokolov, confirmed the existence of ties between Ginzburg and Galanskov and the NTS.

We will not continue our enumeration of all the distortions of truth perpetrated in the article. Enough has been said to cast doubts on the professional integrity of the author of the article 'Lackeys'.

We think that such a scandalous instance in the practice of journalism should be made the subject of discussion in the editorial offices or in the Journalists' Union. In our opinion, the following ought to be invited to the discussion: relatives and close friends of the convicted persons, the judge, the Procurator, the defence lawyers, the witnesses summoned by both the court and the preliminary investigation, and the court recorder. We are confident that if all the interested parties are allowed to have their say, the truth will be established, the article 'Lackeys' will receive the judgment it deserves and the newspaper will publish a refutation.*

Moscow, January 1968

Document V: 34

To: The Board of the Journalists' Union of the USSR.

OPEN LETTER

I address myself to your organization because it bears the moral responsibility for the content of the Soviet press and, above all, of the central newspapers.

I want to examine the question of the good faith of the information provided by the press regarding the case of Ginzburg, Galanskov, Dobrovolsky and Lashkova, which was heard in Moscow City Court from 8 to 12 January 1968. Having no first-hand knowledge of the circumstances of the trial, I am attempting to draw my conclusions about it, as are all citizens who did not attend the trial, purely from press reports.

The first press reaction to the January trial was a brief announcement in *Evening Moscow* on 13 January 1968, which said that 'on the basis of testimony by witnesses and by the defendants, as well as material evidence, the court established that the above-named persons were guilty of having criminal ties with a foreign anti-Soviet organization'.

It is these three points—testimony by witnesses, testimony by the defendants and material evidence—that I shall examine as they are presented in our press and, more precisely, in the articles 'Bound by a Single Belt' by T. Aleksandrov and V. Konstantinov in *Izvestia* of 16 January 1968, and 'Lackeys', by F. Ovcharenko, in *Komsomolskaya Pravda* of 18 January. Let us see whether the elucidation of these three

* For list of the twenty-nine signatories see p. 406. Ed.

points in the newspaper articles really does lead the reader to the logical conclusion that the defendants had criminal ties with a foreign anti-Soviet organization.

First and foremost, what concrete information is given about the testimony of the witnesses?

Apart from an obscure reference in *Komsomolskaya Pravda* to E. Kushev, the only witness named is Nicolas Brox-Sokolov, a citizen of Venezuela. In the pages of the press he grows into the central figure of the trial, the chief trump-card of the prosecution. He is the main character in the article in *Izvestia*, where he is given more space than the defendants. 'Bound by the Same Belt' is not only the title of the article; it is the theme running through the whole text and between the lines. The authors' purpose is precisely this: to convince the reader at all costs that Brox-Sokolov and the four defendants belong to one and the same spy organization and thus are bound together by a single 'belt of downfall' (*Izvestia*). A similarly prominent role is given to Brox-Sokolov by *Komsomolskaya Pravda* in its efforts to argue the prosecution's case.

What, in fact, do we learn about Brox-Sokolov? We learn that he was recruited by the white émigré organization NTS (People's Labour Alliance), that he arrived in the Soviet Union from France as a tourist and was arrested as a spy. He was found to be wearing a belt concealing a hectograph, cryptographic materials and anti-Soviet literature. He also had on him photographs of the defendants.

'*Now it is all on show in the court as material evidence*', we read in *Izvestia*.

One might ask: how can spying equipment belonging to Brox, who came to our country in December 1967, convict people who were in prison under investigation from January 1967 to January 1968? Why have the four defendants been tied up with Brox in the same ill-fated belt?

Let us try to find the answer to this question by a more detailed analysis of what exactly Brox's mission was. It appears that the NTS agents who recruited Brox gave him to understand that his role was to render assistance to the four prisoners. 'Brox-Sokolov eagerly undertook to carry out the assignment and girded himself with the secret belt concealing packages which he was to give to a "certain person" in Moscow', says *Komsomolskaya Pravda*. From *Izvestia* we learn that the meeting was to take place in Sokolniki Park. So it follows from the press reports that Brox-Sokolov personally played the role of middleman.

Might we ask what exactly would have been this foreign aid to Soviet prisoners? Or, at least, what connection was there between Brox's mission and the fate of the defendants? To this question the newspapers give no answer.

Perhaps the person for whom Brox's packages were intended might be able to clarify the matter? Who is he? What is his name? What was he supposed to do? Why is this important link hardly ever mentioned, why is it omitted from the chain of the prosecution's case? Or didn't Brox offer the name of his partner? A likely tale! They used to say that a talker is a godsend to a spy. A spy like Brox-Sokolov is a godsend to the KGB.

By the way, the gentleman from Sokolniki is not the only person with whom the organization behind Brox intended to communicate through Brox. Amongst the items of material evidence that were 'on show in court', *Izvestia* refers to other letters, complete with return addresses, taken from the same belt. 'They were intended for certain persons in the Soviet Union. . . .' Again 'certain persons'! Would it not have been in the prosecution's interests really to name these people? Or did the KGB not manage to track down the addressees from the addresses given?

But let us suppose that the identities of all these 'certain persons' have in fact not been ascertained; let us suppose that these persons were indeed intending to render some unknown assistance to the prisoners. This still leaves open the question of how and in what respect the clandestine equipment found on Brox, and also the money, the letters and the photographs, for whomever they were intended, could incriminate the defendants? Why is it all cited as material evidence of the guilt not of Brox himself but of those whom he only 'knew by hearsay' (*Izvestia*)?

Now let us turn to Brox's testimony at the trial. If you can call it testimony. . . .

At the University of Grenoble, where he studied, Brox attended lectures by a certain Slavinsky who, as *Komsomolskaya Pravda* explains, is 'a member of the NTS leadership'. From Slavinsky's lips Brox learned that there were 'zealots for freedom' in the Soviet Union. 'Their names: Galanskov, Ginzburg, Dobrovolsky' (*Izvestia*). And that was the whole 'testimony'. Now I ask the reader to follow the paper's logic: if Brox-Sokolov declares in a Moscow court that a certain professor in Grenoble praised Ginzburg and Galanskov, and Moscow reckons that this professor is one of the NTS leaders, then it follows that the persons he praised must also be considered 'paid agents of the NTS' (*Komsomolskaya Pravda*).

In my opinion, there were no grounds whatsoever for Brox to appear in the January trial as a witness—especially as chief witness for the prosecution, which is how the newspapers depict him. And incidentally, this character assumed the functions not only of witness, but also of Procurator and even judge. He declared in court: '. . . they told me that these were writers and were being tried for that. I see no writers. It is criminals who are being tried here for their ties with the NTS.' None other than Brox-Sokolov presumes to predict the court's verdict on a case involving Soviet citizens! Where are the facts, where are the proofs. . . ?

By the way, a witness does not have the legal right to be present in the courtroom until he has given his testimony. If an exception was made for Brox, on what grounds? If he had not been present in the court before giving his testimony, how could he have known that the defendants were 'criminals'—or anything else? All by 'hearsay'?

It makes one wonder what Brox-Sokolov's true role was in the January trial.

It is noteworthy that the authors' attitude to the spy Brox is one of great indulgence, indeed of touching pity. At times one detects a note of tender emotion, when they talk of 'this fair-haired lad, still only a mere boy, who speaks Russian quite well' (*Komsomolskaya Pravda*). Admitting that Brox got 'up to his ears in dirt', the authors of the *Izvestia* article hasten to add: 'True, it seems as if he got into it through his naïveté and his great trustfulness of people. . . .' Sympathetically, they quote the following words from Brox's statement in court: 'I should like to say that I regret having unwittingly broken the laws of this country'.

An altogether different tone is adopted with regard to the defendants. Their biographies are painted in solid black—though I should say that this is not true for all the defendants to the same degree, Dobrovolsky being somewhat of an exception. But for Galanskov and Ginzburg there is no mercy. *Izvestia*, for example, tells us that Ginzburg 'came into his own at swindling'. And in 1960, as *Komsomolskaya Pravda* explains, 'proceedings were brought against him for swindling and forging documents. He spent two years in prison. In 1964 criminal proceedings were again instituted against him for similar unsavoury activities.' It would have done no harm to tell the reader that in 1960 Ginzburg had been taking a school examination for external students on behalf of a friend of his, and for this purpose had substituted his own photograph on the relevant certificates. This is certainly a breach of the regulations, but does it do such terrible moral discredit to Ginzburg? And further: who, except Ginzburg, was ever sentenced to two years' imprisonment for such an offence? I suspect that the real, underlying motive for Ginzburg's prosecution in 1960 had nothing to do with the forging of documents. And does the same not apply in 1964 on the second occasion?

Komsomolskaya Pravda is not too worried about the consistency of its opinions with regard to the personalities of Ginzburg and Galanskov, or about whether these opinions follow logically from the facts cited in the article.

The defendants are said to have conducted their affairs 'with the calculation of seasoned merchants'. And at the same time, we learn that 'after receiving some 50-dollar bills from Galanskov on one occasion, the black-marketeers managed to palm off on him in exchange a packet of mustard-plasters'. A fine merchant!

We learn that the defendants 'maintained strict conspiratorial secrecy with the artfulness of hardened criminals'. But the same article tells us that on the title-page of *Phoenix*, the miscellany which figured in the charges against Galanskov, there are the words: 'Edited by Yu. Galanskov'. And in the various editions of the collection of documents which constituted Ginzburg's crime stand the words: 'Compiled by A. Ginzburg'. How's that for conspirators! I am tempted to repeat the words of Ovcharenko: 'Strange reasoning indeed'. It would be interesting to know for what sort of reader these passages were intended.

Incidentally, the reader might like to know that the collection Ginzburg compiled was *The White Book*, which contained materials relating to the case of Sinyavsky and Daniel. It includes a transcript of the trial itself, Soviet and foreign press reaction to it, and public statements by various people in connection with the affair. Opinions both for and against Sinyavsky and Daniel are represented. *Komsomolskaya Pravda* mentions a 'collection of slanderous materials' but does not feel the need to inform the reader what sort of collection it is. I repeat: it is *The White Book*.

Now let us see how the testimony of the defendants themselves appears in the pages of the press and what confessions are contained in this testimony.

Both articles cite Dobrovolsky's testimony verbatim. We read in *Izvestia*:

'This is exactly like the hectograph that Galanskov gave me earlier,' said defendant Dobrovolsky.

And here is *Komsomolskaya Pravda*:

PROCURATOR. What do you know about Galanskov's and Ginzburg's connections abroad?

DOBROVOLSKY. When Galanskov gave me the NTS literature and the hectograph, I asked him where he had got it all. Galanskov replied that he had had contacts abroad since 1962 and had established these contacts through Ginzburg.

PROCURATOR. With what organization abroad was contact maintained?

DOBROVOLSKY. Galanskov told me that he was in contact with NTS.

And so, the testimonies of Galanskov and Ginzburg remain unknown to the reader, and from the testimony of Dobrovolsky there follow two things. Firstly, in relation to the other defendants, Ginzburg and Galanskov, Dobrovolsky appears as a witness for the prosecution, confessing not his own sins but those of other people. Secondly, it is revealed that the objects which served in court as material evidence of the guilt of all the defendants (the hectograph and NTS literature) were found at the home of *Dobrovolsky*. One cannot but begin to wonder: was it not perhaps *only at Dobrovolsky's* that these objects were found?

And when you think about it—are there any grounds for trying a group of people together? Why did Galanskov and Ginzburg find themselves in the same dock? Yes, *Komsomolskaya Pravda* calls them 'partners' and alleges that they 'compiled a new anthology with the pretentious title of *Phoenix*'. But why *they*? Why *partners*? No evidence of any literary collaboration between Galanskov and Ginzburg is cited; if one goes by what they signed openly, then the compilation of *The White Book* was the work of Ginzburg alone, and the compilation of *Phoenix* that of Galanskov and no other. Might there not be testimony by the compilers themselves on this point? The author of the *Komsomolskaya Pravda* article, Ovcharenko, alludes only once to Ginzburg's and Galanskov's testimony, putting it, for some reason, into his own words: 'Both of them suddenly declared that they did not consider what they had done in collaboration with the NTS, an organization hostile to our people, as anti-Soviet activity.' What does this mean? Does it mean that the defendants confessed to collaboration and to their ties with the NTS, as Ovcharenko would have us believe? Or does it mean that the defendants merely did not admit any anti-Soviet activity on their part, and that Ovcharenko himself is defining their activity as collaboration and linking it with the NTS? There can be no doubt that it is the second and not the first. The defendants simply denied the charges, otherwise the author of the article would certainly have cited their testimony verbatim, as he did in the instance of Dobrovolsky.

And so it was Dobrovolsky's testimony that was trusted implicitly at the trial. He received a short sentence (two years) as compared with Galanskov's (seven years) and Ginzburg's (five years). The authors of the newspaper articles do their best to differentiate between Dobrovolsky and his fellow-defendants (I will not say friends) to his advantage. *Komsomolskaya Pravda* refers to 'Ginzburg, Galanskov, and *Dobrovolsky, who was lured into their company*'. And *Izvestia* consoles Dobrovolsky thus:

'One would like to think that his repentance and admission of guilt at the recent trial will open his eyes and help him to embark at last upon an honest path.'

When one compares all the facts of the defendants' behaviour, and the other circumstances, it occurs to one that Dobrovolsky's role is somewhat analogous to the role of Brox-Sokolov.

But that would be more obvious to those who were present at the trial.

'Muscovites present at the trial greeted the sentence with approval,' says *Izvestia*.

Komsomolskaya Pravda is more precise: 'The Muscovites present in the courtroom greeted the verdict with applause and shouts of approval'.

I am one of the Muscovites for whom there was no room in the court.

In complete accordance with Soviet law which provides for open and public trials, a group of people submitted an application to the appropriate authorities requesting that permission be granted to attend the trial. We submitted the application in good time, so that no excuses could be made later on the grounds that the building was filled, etc.

I do not know which Muscovites attended the trial, but I can guess. I am among those Muscovites, as well as those people from other cities, who can only form an opinion on the January trial from the press. One expression used by the press was 'massive misinformation'. I shouldn't be surprised if readers apply this expression to something the author did not mean!

A. Yakobson, translator[97]

PS. I shall point out one detail—a contradiction of fact between *Izvestia* and *Komsomolskaya Pravda*. *Komsomolskaya Pravda* quotes from Brox's testimony at the January trial: '. . . they told me that these packets contained nothing but materials that would help them. When I was detained, it turned out that they did not contain what I had been told they did. . . .'

'Yes,' continues the author of the article, Ovcharenko, 'it turned out that the contents of the packets were not at all what Nicolas had imagined. They were exhibited at the trial. Money intended not at all for charitable purposes. A hectograph and a packet of cryptography paper. . . . Leaflets with anti-Soviet appeals. . . . And five envelopes, *which Brox-Sokolov was to have dropped into letter-boxes, containing enlarged photographs of the defendants* with a short text on the other side that ended with threatening demands for their immediate release.'

From this it follows quite clearly that the envelopes containing the photographs, which Brox personally was to have dropped into a letter-box, could not have been in the packages intended for delivery by hand to a mysterious stranger, for otherwise the other—and criminal—contents of these packages would not have been a secret to Brox. . . .

But here is the discrepancy: *Izvestia*, while maintaining, like *Komsomol-*

skaya Pravda, that 'Brox knew nothing about the contents of the packets until his arrest', also says that '*the packets* that Brox was to hand over to a certain person in Moscow's Sokolniki Park *contained photographs* of people he did not know. . .'.

So, are these not the same photographs that *Komsomolskaya Pravda* is talking about, and are the people on them not the same? We read on in the *Izvestia* article: 'Five envelopes with photographs. In the photographs and in the dock are people known to Brox by hearsay—Ginzburg, Galanskov and Dobrovolsky'.

Whom would you have us believe, *Izvestia* or *Komsomolskaya Pravda*?

There is only one thing here that is not open to doubt: that Brox, the chief witness for the prosecution, 'did not know' the defendants, and knew of them only 'by hearsay'. All the rest evokes astonishment: how Brox-Sokolov made a mess of his simple task and, straight after him, the authors of both the articles!

[Moscow, January 1968]   A. Yakobson

Document V: 35

To: The Editors of *Komsomolskaya Pravda*.

In your newspaper of 18 January 1968 you published an article by F. Ovcharenko entitled 'Lackeys'. In this article my son, Alexander Ginzburg, was represented in a false light and the circumstances of the court case against him were misreported. There is no need to dwell on every single point in the article where the facts are distorted (for example, the allegation that he was financially dependent on me, that he was faced with criminal proceedings in 1964, and so on). I will note only what I consider to be the most salient points.

Throughout the four columns of the article my son was continually referred to as a 'paid agent of the NTS' who 'propagandized' materials and publications of that organization, and apparently told the court about his 'activities in collaboration with the NTS'.

There was not one word spoken at the trial to the effect that my son had received payment from anyone whatever for the collection of documents he compiled. The Procurator, who referred to him as an 'NTS agent', himself admitted in court that he had made a mistake; evidently this 'mistake' also found its way accidentally into the text of the verdict. However, none of the materials relating to the case, none of the testimonies by witnesses and not one of the questions put by the prosecution even touched on this point. People who were present at the trial must be well aware of this—I wonder whether the journalist who has reported the trial proceedings was in the courtroom?

I do not know from what sources the author of the article got his information that 'espionage equipment', NTS instructions and leaflets were discovered during a search of Ginzburg's home. The official record of the search (a copy of which is in my possession) does not mention any hecto-graphs, NTS literature or cryptographic materials.

Nor was my son accused of anything of the kind at the trial.

There was nothing 'unexpected' in my son's refusal to admit at the trial that his activities were anti-Soviet. He did not 'suddenly declare it': he had asserted it from the very beginning of the investigation right up to the end of the trial.

The few examples I have quoted are sufficient for me to be able to call the article by F. Ovcharenko libellous and to demand the publication of a refutation.

I ask you to check the facts I have cited, as well as the other points in the article which concern Alexander Ginzburg, against the documents—the official search records and the transcripts of the judicial sessions. I ask you to inform me of the results of the check and to publish a refutation in your newspaper.

If the check is carried out dishonestly, or if my letter goes unanswered, I shall be obliged to bring proceedings against the author of the article and against the newspaper for the libel of my son Alexander Ginzburg.*

Moscow, B. Polyanka, 11/14, kv. 25   L. I. Ginzburg
23 January 1968

Document V: 36

To: The Editors of *Komsomolskaya Pravda*.

OPEN LETTER

On 18 January 1968 an article by F. Ovcharenko entitled 'Lackeys' was printed in your newspaper. Amongst the many distortions of the facts relating to the judicial trial and the characters of the convicted persons, there is one point in the article which directly concerns myself. I quote:

'And I repeat, Ginzburg and Co. not only ecstatically absorbed these publications but also made every effort to propagandize them. As witness E. Kushev testified in court, they would accidentally, as it were, slip this NTS produce to unfortunate young people, their former schoolmates and acquaintances.'

This is a glaring, deliberate lie. The author of the article was presumably in court and could not have failed to hear my words to the effect that I did not know Ginzburg at all. He could not have failed to hear the only passage in my interrogation that concerned Galanskov. I quote here from memory:

Defence counsel Kaminskaya (defending Galanskov): Do you know anything about Galanskov's criminal activities?

---

* Under Soviet law, Mrs Ginzburg cannot bring proceedings for slander until she receives from her son a warrant authorizing her to conduct the case in court on his behalf, in so far as the libellous attacks in the newspaper do not relate to L. I. Ginzburg herself.

Myself: I am acquainted with Galanskov, but I know nothing which might compromise him. I know he is the editor of the journal *Phoenix*, but I cannot judge as to the hostile character of the journal, as I have not read it.*

In essence, then, I corroborated in court only Dobrovolsky's and Lashkova's testimony to the effect that on my own initiative I borrowed from them three brochures published by the NTS to read. It does not follow from any evidence in the case that they 'slipped' me or anyone else these brochures. And moreover, I did not speak of any other persons.

So, first, Ovcharenko is libelling the condemned persons; second, he is deliberately generalizing from a particular episode; and third, he is trying, utterly unscrupulously, to depict me as a dishonourable man.

I demand that you publish my letter with an appropriate editorial retraction, but since I hardly expect you to do so, I am at the same time sending copies of this letter to my friends and acquaintances.

Moscow, G-99, Smolenskaya ul., d. 10, kv. 17   E. Kushev
24 January 1968

Document V: 37

To: Chief Editors of *Pravda*, *Izvestia* and *Komsomolskaya Pravda*. Copies to: The General Secretary of the Communist Party Central Committee, L. I. Brezhnev; the Chairman of the Council of Ministers of the USSR, A. N. Kosygin; the Chairman of the Presidium of the Supreme Soviet of the USSR, N. V. Podgorny; defence counsel B. A. Zolotukhin.

[slightly abbreviated]

(*1*) We, friends and acquaintances of Alexander Ginzburg, are deeply shocked at the conduct of his trial, at the sentence and also at the press coverage of the case (the article in *Izvestia*, 16 January 1968, and the article in *Komsomolskaya Pravda*, 18 January 1968). If we are to believe *Izvestia* and *Komsomolskaya Pravda*, Alexander Ginzburg is a parasite, a swindler, a malicious anti-Sovietist and, finally, a 'paid agent of the NTS'. We knew a different Ginzburg, an honest, selfless man ready to come to the aid of his friends; an emotional person with a keen sense of justice. How could there arise such a complete discrepancy between two images of the same person? Which of them is the false one? We have no doubt that it is the first one, and we shall try to show this.

(*2*) The articles in *Izvestia* and *Komsomolskaya Pravda* are not reports on the trial proceedings; at best they can be seen as an exposition of the prosecution's case and the sentence. Perhaps the speech by Ginzburg's defence counsel and the testimonies of witnesses do not contribute anything substantial to an understanding of the case? A reading of the transcript of B. A. Zolotukhin's speech at the trial is sufficient to convince one that the

* See p. 406.

reverse is true. It is clear from his speech that the course of the trial is presented in the above-mentioned articles in a completely arbitrary fashion. First of all, Ginzburg was never confronted with any concrete charges of having ties with the NTS, with the exception of the accusation of having consented to his *White Book* being taken abroad—and that was convincingly refuted by the defence. All the concrete charges included in Procurator Terekhov's summing-up related only to the collection of documents on the Sinyavsky–Daniel case. In the part of his speech which referred to Ginzburg, there was no mention of illegal currency operations, hectographs, leaflets or NTS literature. . . .

. . . And so, Ginzburg's 'crime' was the compilation of a book in defence of Sinyavsky and Daniel, and the persons who had condemned Sinyavsky and Daniel doubtless wanted to punish him for it. To this end they made use of his chance and very distant acquaintance with Dobrovolsky, on whose testimony the main part of the prosecution's case against Ginzburg was drawn up. Although Dobrovolsky could not tell the court anything concrete about Ginzburg's 'criminal ties', Ginzburg was nevertheless included among the ranks of anti-Sovietists and NTS members, and, through an accidental (?!) slip of the Procurator's tongue, he almost became head of an NTS group in Moscow.

Such is the story of Ginzburg's 'transformation' from a man who spoke out openly against what he considered an injustice to a 'paid agent of the NTS'.

(*3*) The newspaper articles about the trial (we shall consider only those parts of them which concern Ginzburg) also aimed to accomplish this transformation of Ginzburg. It is instructive to analyse the methods the papers use to compromise Ginzburg's character and activities.

(*a*) Both articles give an identical version of Ginzburg's biography, and it certainly does not stem from a careful acquaintance with the facts of his life. It is a false version, both factually and in its spirit. . . .

It is no secret to anyone that in 1960 the KGB conducted an enquiry on the basis of Ginzburg's having compiled the poetry journal *Syntax*; the case was dropped for lack of a *corpus delicti*.

We know what difficulties Ginzburg experienced after his release; he had to take jobs utterly inappropriate for a man of his knowledge and capabilities; he and his mother lived in conditions of great material hardship. Recently he tried to get into an institution of higher education in order to obtain qualifications and occupy a stable position in society and not be employed in casual work. In the autumn of 1966 he entered the evening department of the Institute of Historical Archives. However, for Ginzburg a stable position in life meant not only material sufficiency and the approval of his superiors; it also meant the satisfaction of his inner sense of justice. The need to set right a legal error perpetrated, as he considered, with respect to Sinyavsky and Daniel, was more important to him than his own welfare.

(*b*) In both articles no discrimination of any kind is made between the aims and nature of the activities of the accused taken individually; they are treated as a single group, in which certain functions were merely shared out. . . . When you read phrases like 'When the homes of Ginzburg, Galanskov and Dobrovolsky were searched, dozens of anti-Soviet publications received from abroad were seized', or 'When the homes of Ginzburg, Galanskov and Dobrovolsky were searched, espionage equipment was discovered—cryptography paper, hectographs, instructions, anti-Soviet literature and leaflets', you are tempted to ask the author: but on precisely which of the three persons named were these publications and this equipment discovered? . . . All of it was found at the home of Dobrovolsky, but he only got two years. Obviously it was more important to the author of the article to smear the character of Ginzburg than to inform his readers of the facts disclosed at the trial.

(c) In *Izvestia* the trial is reported against the background of the Brox-Sokolov story, and in a very general and indistinct form. This is done so as to create an impression that all the accused were connected with the persons who equipped Brox-Sokolov. But an attentive reading of the newspapers convinces one that neither the testimony of this man nor the objects found on him are in any way indicative of any connections between the accused and the NTS. They merely heighten the sinister atmosphere of the trial and allow the article's authors to make frequent use of the word NTS in the same breath as the names of the accused, which was evidently precisely their aim.

(d) The article in *Komsomolskaya Pravda* is constructed differently. Some aspects of the trial are reported in detail, namely the prosecution's summing-up and the testimony of the accused. We have to give the author his due: he did not distort those aspects of the proceedings which he found unsuitable for his purposes—he simply ignored them. There are no references in the article to the defence, while in fact Ginzburg's defence counsel Zolotukhin asked for an *acquittal* for his client: he did not talk of degrees of guilt or of extenuating circumstances—he insisted on *Ginzburg's innocence on all the points in the indictment.* . . . It is quite unclear [*from the article*] what the collection was that Ginzburg compiled, what its purpose was and what documents it contained. On the other hand, the author states in his article—on what basis we do not know—that Ginzburg was circulating anti-Soviet leaflets. There is also the completely untrue allegation that Ginzburg admitted to collaboration with the NTS.

(4) Such are the methods used to compromise the character and activities of Ginzburg. It may be that the authors of the articles consider them purely journalistic devices, the employment of which they justify as serving some lofty purpose. We cannot agree that the concealment or distortion of truth can facilitate the accomplishment of any lofty purpose whatsoever.

We are convinced that only a new and open judicial examination of Ginzburg's case, and a full and objective coverage of it by the press, can be of real benefit to society.

(5) Analysis of the articles in *Izvestia* and *Komsomolskaya Pravda* shows that their authors deliberately distorted a great number of significant facts in the trial of Ginzburg and the others, and also that they concealed many important facts from their readers. We feel that the appearance of such articles in the press has done harm to our society. We are highly indignant at the publication of these articles and demand that the persons to blame for their appearance be punished. . . .*

Moscow, 1 February 1968

Document V: 38

To: The Editors of *Komsomolskaya Pravda*.

OPEN LETTER [*slightly abbreviated*]

On 18 January 1968 an article by F. Ovcharenko entitled 'Lackeys' was published in the paper *Komsomolskaya Pravda*, concerning the trial of Galanskov, Ginzburg, Dobrovolsky and Lashkova, which ended on 12 January this year in Moscow City Court.

I was present at that trial and I am personally acquainted with all four defendants. I know the circumstances of the case. Therefore I consider it my duty, both civic and personal (I am the wife of Yury Galanskov, one of the condemned men), to protest at the gross distortions of fact perpetrated by the author of this article. These distortions are all the more inadmissible, since the author was present at the trial and had the opportunity to familiarize himself with the true state of affairs and present an objective account of the proceedings.

As I know that Alexander Ginzburg's mother has already written a letter similar to this one, I shall dwell only on those parts of Ovcharenko's article which directly concern Yury Galanskov.

It is true that Yury Galanskov is the editor and compiler of the miscellany *Phoenix*. He himself never denied this, from the day of his arrest to the trial. And it was probably this which constituted the real reason for his receiving such a harsh sentence: seven years' confinement in a camp.

I should like to say, first of all, that Galanskov carried on his work as compiler of that miscellany on his own: Ginzburg had no part in it. . . . Moreover, Galanskov repeatedly stated throughout the investigation and at the trial that he compiled *Phoenix* on his own.

The author of the article probably knew all this; and still he wrote: 'But his partners had new concerns . . . they compiled a new anthology with the pretentious title of *Phoenix*'. On the subject of pretentiousness I find it difficult to argue with a man who, in his article, uses expressions like 'the story of the fall of these latter-day Herostratuses', 'the same old spiritual rags' and others. But I maintain that it was not 'they' who compiled the anthology; it was compiled by Galanskov alone.

* For list of the ten signatories, see p. 406. Ed.

And what is this anthology?

F. Ovcharenko states that it was compiled from 'the store-house of faked documents'.

Here are the contents of *Phoenix*, as described in the official record of the search conducted on 17 January 1967: [*she quotes from the search record: see p.* 22].

The author might have obliged by naming in his article even one of the works contained in *Phoenix* which he could confidently call a fake. Judging by the fact that he did not do so, either he was writing a deliberate falsehood or he has no conception either of the ethical sense of the works or of the actual content of the miscellany.

Next. Let us leave on the author's conscience the assertion that 'through a resourceful NTS emissary [Genrikh] this compilation was conveyed to Paris'. Leave it, because this point from the prosecution's case is based exclusively on the testimony of none other than Dobrovolsky, and is not supported by anything else, and also because the next few lines of the article clearly contradict the real facts. The real facts indicate that *Phoenix* never found its way abroad.* Ovcharenko writes: 'And once again *Possev* and *Grani* went into ecstasies. They passed the newly received materials on to the editors of bourgeois newspapers and magazines and to radio stations, and all these made extensive use of them in their ideological sabotage against the Soviet Union.'

Since the author was present at the trial, he must know that the prosecution did not have at its disposal a single copy of *Phoenix* published by Possev or any other foreign publishing house. Not only was *Phoenix* in its entirety not published but not even its five articles which the court found to be criminal [*here enumerated*] were published either by *Grani* or Possev or any other foreign publishing house. This was established in court. An exception is the article by Sinyavsky [*on socialist realism*], which was published abroad many years before Galanskov compiled *Phoenix*. But perhaps the author has at his disposal information about even just one transmission by the Voice of America, the BBC or Deutsche Welle, which was devoted to any one of these, in the court's opinion, criminal works? Hardly, since there were no such transmissions; at any rate no mention was made of any such transmission.

And if we are to believe what the author writes, viz. that *Phoenix* really was conveyed to Paris 'through a resourceful NTS emissary', then does it not seem odd that neither *Grani* nor Possev who, to use the author's expression, 'went into ecstasies', found time to publish it during the next year and more, if only for use in 'ideological sabotage against the Soviet Union'?

All the more odd, since Ovcharenko goes on to allege that *Grani* and Possev had promised to 'acquaint the public with "the latest items" as soon as they arrived'.

---

* Galanskov's wife means the collection as such. But she is in fact mistaken. *Grani* announced receipt of the collection on 25 January 1967. It was, however, published by *Grani* only in instalments, from 1967 to 1970. See note 5. Ed.

On more than one occasion in his article the author writes of '*underhand* abuse of their country' and 'secret' conveying of materials abroad; he even says that Galanskov and Ginzburg 'maintained strict conspiratorial secrecy with the artfulness of hardened criminals'. Are these emotional assertions not contradicted by the fact that Galanskov and Ginzburg openly put their names to the anthologies they compiled? . . . Isn't this too glaring a breach of their 'strict conspiratorial secrecy'? Somehow it doesn't go very well with the 'artfulness of hardened criminals'.

Judging by the article 'Lackeys', F. Ovcharenko sees as an indisputable fact the charge that Galanskov and Ginzburg had ties with the anti-Soviet émigré organization, NTS.

What proofs of these ties does he offer? He writes: 'Their guilt has been proven incontrovertibly by the testimony of a great number of witnesses, by numerous documents, material evidence and the authoritative findings of experts'. Let us attempt a separate analysis of each of these 'incontrovertible proofs'.

(i) *The testimony of a great number of witnesses*
As we know, twenty-five witnesses appeared at the trial. Not one of these witnesses testified anything which might, however indirectly, be indicative of Galanskov's or Ginzburg's having ties with the NTS. And as for the witness to whom Ovcharenko devotes so much space in his article . . . it is clear even from Ovcharenko's article that Brox-Sokolov had no idea of any alleged ties between any of the condemned men and the NTS. He testified in court (I quote Ovcharenko): 'I thought that they were young writers and had been imprisoned, that they had been treated unjustly'. Incidentally, it was Brox-Sokolov himself, who had never set eyes on Galanskov or Ginzburg before, who was the only witness to express condemnation of them. 'It is criminals who are being tried here for their ties with the NTS,' he said. But these words, too, cannot serve as any kind of proof, since Sokolov, as he himself said, heard about all this for the first time from the KGB investigators.

The second witness to whose testimony Ovcharenko refers in his article is Kushev. I shall not analyse the part of the article which concerns his testimony, since he himself has already done so in his Open Letter to the Editors of *Komsomolskaya Pravda* (a copy of which I attach).* From this letter it is evident that Ovcharenko's allegation that 'Ginzburg and Co. . . . would accidentally, as it were, slip NTS produce to unfortunate young people' (Kushev's name is mentioned in this connection) is slander not only on Ginzburg and Galanskov, but on Kushev himself.

(ii) *The 'documents and material evidence'*
'When the homes of Ginzburg, Galanskov and Dobrovolsky were searched, espionage equipment was discovered—cryptography paper, hectographs, instructions, anti-Soviet literature and leaflets,' writes Ovcharenko.

* See document V: 36, p. 324.

Nothing of the kind was discovered at either Galanskov's or Ginzburg's home. This is confirmed by the official search records, copies of which are in the possession of myself and Ginzburg's mother. The only item of material evidence discovered at the home of Galanskov which figured in the trial was the miscellany *Phoenix*. All the objects Ovcharenko lists when he talks of 'espionage equipment' were found *exclusively* at the home of Dobrovolsky.

(iii) *The 'authoritative findings of experts'*

The only expert to speak at the trial was a psychiatrist. As you know, a psychiatric diagnostic team is competent to establish only the mental responsibility of the defendants, but under no circumstances their guilt of anything whatsoever.

So there are your 'incontrovertible proofs'.

I do not think there is any need to explain in detail why they do not and cannot confirm the existence of ties between Galanskov, Ginzburg and the NTS: on the contrary, they indicate, rather, that no such ties existed.

Galanskov and Ginzburg themselves testified at the trial that they had no ties with the NTS. . . .

. . . F. Ovcharenko not only makes the repeated assertion in his article that Galanskov and Ginzburg were in contact with the NTS; he even calls them 'paid NTS agents'. Here he is not only giving a distorted version of the facts and the trial proceedings: he goes as far as to make new accusations against Galanskov and Ginzburg, accusations which not only were not contained in the verdict but were not even in the Procurator's indictment. There was nothing at all said at the trial about 'paid NTS agents'. And the author of the article 'Lackeys' knows that. I hope he also knows that Galanskov and Ginzburg were tried under article 70 of the Russian Criminal Code, that is, for anti-Soviet agitation and propaganda, and not in any way for participation in an anti-Soviet organization. . . . Can one believe that the author had any doubts that the NTS is an anti-Soviet organization when he called Galanskov and Ginzburg 'paid NTS agents', and that 'paid agents' must be considered participants in it? And that participants in an anti-Soviet organization should be tried under article 72, and not 70, of the Russian Criminal Code?

It is clear to any unprejudiced reader of Ovcharenko's article that the proofs of Galanskov's criminality adduced in the article are manifestly inadequate. And I personally have every reason to suppose that the last thing Ovcharenko was aiming to do was to give the reader a lucid account of the essence of the political trial which took place. It was far more important to him simply to compromise and vilify people whose fate has become the subject of declarations by many, many public figures both in the Soviet Union and abroad (Ovcharenko himself cites several names) who have expressed their alarm and their desire to help the prisoners. Unfortunately, Ovcharenko only counters the moral authority of these declarations with one thing: lies.

331

For a start, he calls Yury Galanskov a parasite, while Galanskov was tried *not* as a parasite but as a man from a workers' family, who completed his schooling while working and was a worker at the time of his arrest. Next, Ovcharenko accuses Galanskov of self-interest, depicting him as someone who acted for his own profit. Again this is a false accusation. Everyone who knew Galanskov and his way of life will confirm that he never had any such motives, and never had a rouble to spare. Finally, Ovcharenko accuses Galanskov of vanity, of greed for fame. Can an author working on a youth paper really not admit even the possibility that there are people who act—albeit rashly—from lofty and purely ethical motives? People prompted, for instance, by their alarm at the fact that the implementation of the 20th and 22nd Party Congress resolutions on the restoration of Leninist norms and the democratization of public life has been, if not officially suspended, then at any rate slowed down. Does one really have to be in contact with an anti-Soviet organization in order to experience feelings of alarm on that account, or the desire to do something, to say something out loud?

But I do not intend in my letter to enter into an argument with Ovcharenko on that score: his prejudice and dishonesty are too obvious.

This letter has an entirely different purpose. I am sending it to the editors of *Komsomolskaya Pravda*, but as I know that previous letters of similar content have not been published, I will do all I can to see that it circulates as widely as possible amongst *Komsomolskaya Pravda*'s readers.

I consider this my duty, all the more since Yury Galanskov is now in prison and has no opportunity to defend himself in any way against this slander, or refute it, let alone bring a libel action against his slanderers.

Moscow, Zh-180, 3-i Golutvinsky per.,   O. Timofeyeva
d. 7/9, kv. 4
24 February 1968

Document V: 39

To: The Editors of *Komsomolskaya Pravda*

In front of me I have your paper (issue of 28 February 1968) and the letter by Alexander Ginzburg's mother protesting against what she calls the slanderous article published in that paper on 18 January 1968.* For the *n*th time I am confronted with the censored press 'wagging its tail like a dog' (as Marx put it) and the uncensored *samizdat*. And the problem arises: whom shall I believe? It would be difficult to verify the facts directly, for who would give me access to the materials relating to the trial of Ginzburg and Galanskov? There remains only one way—indirect verification. I shall try to explain to you why I do not believe the official version of this trial.

* i.e. Documents V: 7, V: 35 and V: 3 respectively. Ed.

Argument 1

Our press has not inspired any trust for a very long time. . . . Noisy, overwhelming articles about 'enemies of the people'—and subsequent quiet little items about 'heroes of the revolution and the civil war who suffered although innocent'; fanfares about the flowering of the villages —and shamefaced mention of the millions of peasants who died in the *artificial famine* of the 'thirties in the Ukraine (this, at any rate, is how Hero of the Revolution and the Civil War Admiral Fyodor Raskolnikov viewed the situation[98]); portraits of 'Gestapo agent' Tito—and the scarcely visible apology to the Yugoslav communist party [*in 1955*]; the persecution of Pasternak, which hastened the poet's death; the frenzied hullabaloo in 1963 during one of the periodic campaigns against culture; the adulation of 'our dear' current time-server N. S. Khrushchev—and [*after his fall in 1964*] the small doses of poisonous hints and thrusts about the voluntarist, ignoramus and so on; the lies about the 'anti-Semite' Sinyavsky, who supposedly hated even Chekhov (I have read his 'Graphomaniacs' and *directly* convinced myself of the falsity of the smears against him); the evil-smelling concoction in the journal *Perets*, directed against one of the best Ukrainian critics, [*Ivan*] Dzyuba.[99] Even truthful thoughts are dressed up in such an unworthy way by our press that one begins to doubt them. . . .

What a torrent of falsehoods, both exposed and still unexposed, pours from it—tyrants and sycophants are eulogized, filth is poured over our finest people, history is falsified (for example, the 'miraculous' transformation of Bogdan Khmelnitsky from a traitor to the Ukrainian people—see the pre-war edition of the *Great Soviet Encyclopaedia*—into a hero of the same people) and so on. This flood of lies, which began at the end of the 'twenties, never disappeared entirely—even during the thaw, from the 20th until some time after the 22nd Party Congress, when Khrushchev was trying to walk the tightrope of half-truths. In contrast to this torrent there is *samizdat*.

Are there any grounds for trusting the letter by Ginzburg's mother, the 'Appeal to World Public Opinion' by L. Bogoraz and P. Litvinov, the 'Appeal to Public Figures in Science, Culture and the Arts' of Gabai, Kim and Yakir? (Yakir is the son of the famous army commander who was martyred in Stalin's torture-chambers and slandered by the same press discussed above).

In my view, there are.

Or are they, too, 'insufficiently well-informed' and 'misinformed by bourgeois propaganda'? Or in the pay of the NTS, the CIA, the BBC or the Voice of America? I hope you have not sunk to such absurdities.

If they were lying, then the KGB and its affiliated organizations would take pleasure in bringing libel actions against them—and they would not even have to pass special laws like the deplorable article 190 of the Russian Criminal Code. And anyway courage cannot be bought.

333

Argument 2

If the trial of Ginzburg and his friends had been lawful, there would have been no fear of making it an open one. True, Ovcharenko states that there were in court 'representatives of enterprises and organizations with which the defendants had been connected at various times'. But Litvinov and Yakir maintain that they were stooges. And I believe them, not Ovcharenko, since I saw with my own eyes a similar trial of so-called 'Ukrainian nationalists' in 1965[100] and listened to the fantastically stupid explanations by court officials regarding the 'open-closed' nature of the trial.

If the trial had been lawfully conducted, then *Komsomolskaya Pravda* would have published the letter of Ginzburg's mother and publicly, with facts—facts admitted by the same Yakir or Litvinov (even *Komsomolskaya Pravda* would not suspect them of denying facts in the form of search records and trial records as described by L. I. Ginzburg)—would have proved the untruthfulness of her letter.

But—alas!—the times have passed when Bolsheviks proudly proclaimed: 'We don't fear the truth, as the truth works for us!' Their indirect heirs (the direct ones were destroyed in Stalin's torture chambers by Beria), the Thermidoreans of October [*1917*], fear truth. The most they can rise to is stereotyped and distorted quotations, thrown together at random.

After all, only with the truth would it have been possible to convince both our public opinion and the world's that the trial was lawful and just. For the times have passed when the naïve [*German writer Leon*] Feuchtwanger could persuade himself—at the trial of Radek, Pyatakov, Sokolnikov and the others—to believe in the comedy (till the end of his life he could not forgive himself for this).

Argument 3

The mendacity of the article is apparent even to the unaccustomed eye, unguided by past experience. The paper alleges that Ginzburg and Galanskov were 'paid NTS agents', and that they maintained 'strict conspiratorial secrecy' as befits agents of an anti-Soviet organization. And the same paper, in the very same article, writes that their 'concoctions' appeared abroad *under their own names*. But what about the conspiracy? Is all this conceivable? They ought at least to have learned how to lie in forty years of Thermidor!

Ovcharenko could not bring himself to name—among those who had 'swallowed the bait' of bourgeois propaganda—the people who signed the 'telegram of the fifteen' to Litvinov and Bogoraz–Daniel: Bertrand Russell (the conscience of Europe since the death of Romain Rolland), Igor Stravinsky, [*J. B.*] Priestley and the others.* But he did not fear to

* This telegram was in reply to Litvinov's and Mrs Daniel's appeal (Document III: 2). Dated 14 January 1968, it read: 'We, a group of friends representing no organization, support your statement, admire your courage, think of you and will help in any way possible.' The other signatories were: Yehudi Menuhin, W. H. Auden, Henry Moore, Julian Huxley, Paul Scofield, Mary McCarthy, Cecil Day-Lewis, Stephen Spender A. J. Ayer, Jacquetta Hawkes, Maurice Bowra and Sonia Orwell. Ed.

distort Yu. Galanskov's final speech—his words about his lack of any desire for glory.

. . . I think there is only one point where Ovcharenko speaks the truth: 'Their names mean absolutely nothing to the Soviet reader'. Yes, just as the name [*of the writer Mikhail*] Bulgakov meant nothing to young readers a few years ago, and as the name of [*the populist R. V.*] Ivanov-Razumnik[101] and many other names mean nothing to them to this very day. I pity those readers who do not know that there is a great Russian writer living and working in the land of Russia, Solzhenitsyn, the author of the novels *Cancer Ward* and *The First Circle*, and the plays *Candle in the Wind* and *The Tenderfoot and the Tramp* [*Olen i Shalashovka*]. I pity all the people who signed the letters published in *Komsomolskaya Pravda* on 28 February this year. They just didn't understand anything. Perhaps they will be ashamed later, as those who marched in their thousands and 'angrily' demanded death for Lenin's comrades-in-arms are ashamed today. For they are not all in the ranks of the Black Hundreds; rather, they are descendants of the old woman who added her faggot to the bonfire of [*the mediaeval Czech martyr*] Jan Hus. May God grant that they be cured of this 'saintly simplicity'. Then there will be no bonfires. . . .

I pity those who do not know, and do not wish to know, what has happened and is happening in their own land. In his letter to Stalin,[102] [*Admiral*] Raskolnikov wrote that the people would judge him for all he had done with our revolution. I hope that that time will come, and that both Stalin and his lackeys will be judged in accordance with the laws of our country, and not in disregard of them. Thus, too, as distorters of truth, will you, the Editors of *Komsomolskaya Pravda*, be judged in accordance with the laws of honour. Under those laws you have already merited the contempt of all honest men, as lackeys and false-witnesses of our time.

Kiev, March 1968   L. I. Plyushch, mathematician and engineer[103]

Document V: 40

To: The Chief Editor of the *Literary Gazette*, A. Chakovsky.

Citizen A. Chakovsky,

I have read your article 'Reply to a Reader' in No. 13 of the *Literary Gazette*; it contains, amongst other things, the following lines: 'instead of giving such people food and drink at the nation's expense in prisons or corrective labour colonies'. [*See Document V: 11.*]

In your article you assume the pose of a man with a civic conscience, as though you were genuinely concerned about our country's fate and prestige. A man in such a public position cannot justify himself by saying that he was unaware of something or ill-informed. If, indeed, you did not know until now, then you could have, and that means you should have known exactly how convicts in corrective labour colonies are fed, and at whose expense. However, it looks as if you do not even make any attempt to imagine it; as if this problem does not interest you; and as if the above-quoted lines from your article were written for the sake of stylistic beauty and for a more shattering exposure of the 'criminals'.

Not so much for you as for your readers, I shall give a more accurate, amended version of your lines.

A convict in a strict-regime corrective labour camp—all political prisoners are confined under this regime[104]—receives 2400 calories per day, the normal quantity for a seven- to eleven-year-old child: in the morning, a helping (about two glasses) of thin, watery gruel; for lunch, about the same amount of cabbage soup, made from rotten cabbage, and two spoonfuls of watery porridge; in the evening, two spoonfuls of the same porridge plus a piece of boiled cod the size of a matchbox. All this soup and porridge is supposed to contain a daily total of 20 grammes of fat (not butter, of course). With it you get 700 grammes of black bread and fifteen grammes of sugar per day. And that is all.

That is the standard ration. For 'obstinate' prisoners there is the so-called strict food regime, or punishment rations: in the morning, a mug of hot water; in the afternoon, 400 grammes of cabbage soup plus two spoonfuls of watery porridge; in the evening, the same-sized piece of boiled cod (without the porridge). The cabbage soup and porridge for punishment rations are cooked separately: they must not contain a single gramme of fat. Sugar is forbidden too. Black bread—450 grammes for the whole day. Altogether it amounts to 1300 calories (the normal quantity for a child of one to three years).

And that's the food and drink 'such people' get. And at whose expense? That's an interesting question.

The convict in a corrective labour camp works eight hours a day, forty-eight hours a week. It was in the [*Mordovian*] corrective labour camp [*complex*] of Dubrovlag that the television set you and your family watch was made, and the radiogram which (by pure accident, naturally) brought you the Voice of America; and your soft couch, and your writing desk. But don't imagine that the people who make your furniture and are given 'food and drink at the nation's expense' get off lightly. Convicts employed in 'light' furniture production as loaders (and they include former artists, writers, scientists and party or Komsomol officials) strain themselves unloading timber and stone by hand; in unhealthy workshops your former colleagues, polishing your desk perhaps, are losing their health irretrievably.

And for this they get: gruel, black bread, under-nourishment day after day for many years.

Was this what you had in mind when you wrote that the nation 'gives such people food and drink'? What a highly developed humanism is yours, writer A. Chakovsky!

Is that how the people, including the convicts of Dubrovlag, Vorkuta, Siberia and Kazakhstan, feed you and other writers, the 'nation's conscience'?

336

Maybe the lofty civic pathos of your article can be explained precisely by the fact that you get a bit more for it than just a bowl of gruel and a ration of black bread?

If you receive orders to answer this letter of mine, you will probably cite examples of how prisoners are treated in the USA or China. You might even go further than these two models and mention Greece or Southern Rhodesia. And why not refer to Hitler's concentration camps too? But you will certainly say nothing about Stalin's concentration camps, despite the fact that you call upon [*your readers*] to 'direct their gaze to the relatively recent past'.

But what is the state of affairs *in our country today*? That's where such a high-ranking citizen as you should first and foremost direct his civic pathos!

I would like this open letter to you to reach my fellow-citizens not through the Voice of America or the BBC, but through publication in your paper. Only then could one speak of the 'perfection of socialism', and our ideological enemies abroad would not be able to use the shameful facts cited here for their own purposes.

g. Aleksandrov Vladimirskoi obl.,   A. Marchenko, porter,
ul. Novinskaya, 27   former political prisoner[105]
27 March 1968

Document V: 41

To: The Chief Editor of the *Literary Gazette*, A. Chakovsky. Copy to: Pavel Litvinov.

In your article 'Reply to a Reader' (*Literary Gazette*, No. 13) you ask: 'Why am I obliged to believe Litvinov?'

And I, an ordinary reader, ask: Why am I obliged to believe you, Alexander Chakovsky, and the 'witness' Brox-Sokolov?

And here is *my* reply:

Litvinov acted on principle: he considered the trial of Ginzburg and Galanskov a dangerous illegality, so he is fighting with utter selflessness—and, moreover, at great risk—for the obligatory observance of elementary legal standards.

It is obvious that you have a short memory, and so naturally, you have 'no reason not to trust the court'. You always were, and are, ready and willing to call black white, and white black; the only principle you profess is the preservation of your own position and all the privileges that go with it.

And the hireling Brox-Sokolov was simply saving his skin by lying.

That is why, deprived as I am of information about the trial, I believe Litvinov, and not you or Brox-Sokolov.

Moscow, A-55, Uglovoy per.,   L. Kogan, cinema-worker
d. 2, kv. 126
27 March 1968

337

Document V: 42

To: The Chief Editor of the *Literary Gazette*.

OPEN LETTER

Citizen Chakovsky,

In No. 13 of the *Literary Gazette* I read the 'Reply to a Reader', signed by you. It is without doubt one of your most significant works, if only for its laconic style.

Your article raises questions of general interest, and I should like to make use of my right, as a reader, to reply.

I do not intend to enter into a polemic with you, since our moral criteria differ. I find it impossible to argue with a man whose spiritual mentors, in questions of morals, are probably officials of the internal state security service (and perhaps there is voluntary contact from your side too).

Therefore I shall attempt to amplify slightly the 'main thing' which you passed over in silence, and express some purely personal views.

You took the 'basic facts that we know' almost word for word from *Komsomolskaya Pravda*, but I am convinced that you had access to other information too.

It would not have done any harm to throw some light on the position taken by the defence counsels and the prisoners, since you say your aim was to deal with the question in depth.

I should like to point out the following:

Ginzburg and Galanskov did not admit their guilt, as in fact there was no guilt whatsoever in the case of Ginzburg, and basically none in the case of Galanskov. This was convincingly maintained by both Kaminskaya, Galanskov's counsel, and Zolotukhin, counsel for Ginzburg. Zolotukhin, a party member, easily dismissed all the points made by the prosecution and, for the first time in the history of political trials in our country, demanded his client's acquittal in accordance with existing state laws. It is all the more remarkable when one recalls that the defence, at trials of this nature, have in practice always supported the prosecution.

I will not analyse the details of the trial yet again. That has been done by others. I shall examine the problem of the 'vacant seats' in the courtroom, since you devote a suspiciously large amount of space to it.

I was not in Moscow at the time of the trial, but I did recently try to get into the political trial which is now drawing to a close in Leningrad.[106]

Apparently it is easy for the prosecutor at that trial to prove his case on the basis of existing state laws, and rumour has it that the accused have confessed fully to their guilt.

But despite the fact that we sent an official application to Pozdnyakov, deputy chairman of the Leningrad City Court, neither I nor a number of my acquaintances succeeded in gaining access even to that trial. People were admitted when they produced bits of red cardboard (and God knows who issues these passes).

338

I can state with authority that there were vacant seats in the courtroom, but people who stubbornly insisted on being admitted were approached by plain-clothes men, all, it seemed, cast in the same mould, who advised them to 'clear off'.

I am certain you are well acquainted with all this 'chemistry'. But you brush aside facts that do not accord with the attitude you have adopted, and since most of the facts belong to this category, you have to resort to devices with which the experienced reader is all too familiar: the citing of letters by 'indignant' citizens and entire 'indignant' organizations. It is all done according to the well-known models of evil memory. But then I read the curious phrase: 'Why am I obliged to believe Litvinov and his proclamations?' In that form, those lines read like a denunciation.*

I do not know of any proclamations by Litvinov, but I have read and heard the 'Appeal to Soviet and World Public Opinion' signed by L. Bogoraz and P. Litvinov, and the appeal to the Consultative Meeting in Budapest, which was signed by a further ten persons as well as the two named above.[107]

Perhaps you really do know of some proclamations. You might gladden our hearts by publishing just one of them, and then you can tear it to pieces with all the talent of an 'engineer of human souls', expose its poverty, stupidity, inappositeness and imperialist essence.

No, citizen Chakovsky, you are not capable even of that. You are unable to express yourself 'in depth' on the questions you raise, although you promise at the beginning of your article to do so, because 'deep down' your article is directed against the several hundred representatives of Moscow's intelligentsia whom you mention; you do not cite their arguments, since then you would have to publish their letters.

Your poorly concealed indignation at the fact that letters from representatives of the intelligentsia 'addressed to Soviet organizations, arrive with amazing synchronism and sometimes even ahead of time in America, Britain and West Germany' is understandable. Yes, it really is a little embarrassing. But your embarrassment is only due to the fact that, like all children of darkness, you fear the pale gleam of light which, reflected back from 'the West', returns to its source.

Notice, citizen Chakovsky, you yourself write that the letters were sent to Soviet organizations, and the 'West' was merely informing Soviet citizens that this had happened. The contents of any of those letters is hardly secret. But why was it precisely the radio stations of Britain, America and West Germany which became transmission links between the Soviet people and a section of its intelligentsia? (I hope you do not doubt that millions of Soviet citizens listen to the broadcasts of these stations.) Did the *Literary Gazette*, which always gives such detailed

* Because the word proclamation has overtones in Russian of militant political opposition. Ed.

339

coverage of the trials even of fascist criminals, perhaps find room for just one of the letters protesting at the judicial reprisals against Ginzburg and Galanskov, even if only for the sake of a polemic?

My answer: the *Literary Gazette* did not do so, although it has in the past eagerly published letters like the following:

'Pasternak has become widely known as a Judas, but we Soviet citizens stick to our own Soviet literature. (Mamontov, worker.)'

But perhaps these concoctions were retracted? Perhaps there was an announcement that the editors had been heavily penalized for their shameful deeds? There was not.

Well then, don't blame the mirror. . . .*

I was amused by your explanation of why writers abroad came to the defence of the convicted men. You think they are not immune to lies, while I think they have no illusions as regards you. And neither do I and the people who share my views, as you see.

In your opinion, political prisoners in the prisons and camps are given food and drink at the nation's expense.

I would just like to express my personal contempt of you for those lines, but I shall not dwell in detail on the point—in this matter you become an epistolary target exclusively for the pen of the past and present political prisoners of the concentration camps, their inmates from the time of Stalin up to 1968, *Human Rights Year*.

You engage, in your article, together with your colleague F. Ovcharenko from *Komsomolskaya Pravda*, in the spiritual debasement of citizens who turn to you for explanations.

The time will come when people will remember by their names all those who committed, encouraged and attempted to justify arbitrary acts, and then they will remember you too.

Leningrad, 4 April 1968   Lev Kvachevsky, engineer-chemist[108]

Document V: 43

To: The Editor of the *Literary Gazette*, A. Chakovsky.

OPEN LETTER

'. . . and we shall become the masters of information rather than the slaves of misinformation.'   J. R. Pierce, *Symbols, Signals and Noise*.†

Comrade Chakovsky!

Allow me to congratulate you on your article 'Reply to a Reader'. Thanks to it, I learned some interesting facts about the conditions under which the trial of Galanskov, Ginzburg, Dobrovolsky and Lashkova was held. For instance, I would never have imagined that the 'Sharikopodshipnik' ball bearing plant had such a healthy, united and unanimous

---

* Russian proverb: Don't blame the mirror if your mug is crooked.
† Hutchinson, London, 1962. Ed.

collective. Just think, what determination and community of interests! The plant collective became interested in the trial and secured places in the courtroom for thirty of its most worthy representatives. And the teachers at Moscow Medical Institute No. 1 and the Moscow Motor Highways Institute did not lag far behind the ball bearing plant collective nor did the scientists at the Raw Minerals Research Institute.

One is struck by the shared fate of the foreign correspondents. To a man they awaited invitations, and to a man were unable to get into the trial, since they evidently did not display such organizational flair as the Soviet citizens who submitted applications well in advance for representatives of their best production collectives to attend the trial, without waiting for invitations.

True, we too have our unorganized and undisciplined people, but they, again because of their lack of organization, did not get into the trial, since, in view of the wide public interest in the trial, only those who had made collective applications on behalf of the best collectives were admitted, apart from relatives of the accused and witnesses. But with such an élite from such model collectives gathered together in the courtroom, who could have any doubts as to whether or not they were *druzhinniks*? Of course, all these members of the public take an active part in the work of the people's *druzhinas*, otherwise they would not be the best people. The *druzhinniks* are at all times and on all occasions called upon to keep order and assist the police organs and, it goes without saying, the organs of state security. It is no secret to anybody that *druzhinniks* always receive instructions to that effect. How could these people protest against the actions of the trial's organizers if they were called upon to support them? For protest means disorder. Now it is clear why none of the persons who had signed protests were to be seen in court. And how could L. I. Bogoraz-Daniel and P. Litvinov dare to assert that the courtroom was filled with a specially selected public, KGB officers and *druzhinniks*?

You are right, Comrade Chakovsky: we have no need to follow the Maoist example. Let them rather learn from us. After all, the Stalin personality cult served as their model. We have no need to stage trials in stadia. But it does not do to forget that the twentieth century is the century of cinema, radio and television, and not the century of the inquisition. And even if a stadium could not accommodate all those who wished to attend the trial, there is plenty of room for everyone in front of the cinema or television screen.

Thank you very much, Comrade Chakovsky, for your concern for the Soviet taxpayer. In my ignorance I was unaware that a proportion of taxes goes towards the upkeep of convicts. Well, it's never been written about in our country before. And there was I thinking that all Komsomol constructions and the constructions needed by communism were built by convicts; but they are evidently sitting idle, thanks to the connivance of the prison authorities. What a blatant lie! In the same breath you slander both the authorities and the convicts. I do not believe you. I have no reason to believe either you or a press which prints articles like yours, articles that provoke more doubts than they resolve, or a court which conceals its affairs from the eyes of men.

Honest and courageous people act openly and boldly, as did L. I. Bogoraz-Daniel and P. M. Litvinov. For publication of the case materials, or a review of the case, will convict them of slander if their appeal is false. Would a man call for his own unmasking?

Therefore I believe them, and not you or the authors of articles like yours, which are in no respect a substitute for publication of the materials of the case.

Articles like yours, the publication of which calls for neither talent nor courage, will not dispel doubts but only reinforce them, will undo all the efforts of counter-propaganda, possibly even provoke a reaction in the opposite direction.

Meanwhile the minds of scholars are preoccupied now with political trials to the detriment of science, and this has already done irreparable damage to our country.

Yes, Graham Greene was right in saying that no bell tolls in your ears.[109]

I send you greetings for the First of May.

g. Odessa-5, ul. Industrialnaya, d. 44, kv. 4   L. N. Tymchuk, sailor*
27 April 1968

Document V: 44

To: The Chief Editor of the *Literary Gazette*, A. Chakovsky.

REPLY BY A READER [*slightly abbreviated*]

One can agree or disagree with your article 'Reply to a Reader'. However, it is not a monotonous lecture, but a lively, conversational speech. . . . One feels that you are arguing with a man while you respect his opinion, and that, as an experienced writer, you understand that even amongst our citizens views on public, social and political aspects of our life may not coincide, may differ slightly from the official line and not be say, 99·97 per cent identical. But that is not so terrible if we all, even the 'dissenters', have one and the same aim: the socialist, Leninist, democratic path of development for our country. . . .

. . . Now some people are speaking against the convicted men. It is so simple and completely harmless. But I shall never understand how one can strike a fallen man who has no opportunity to defend himself. How could they ever have sentenced Sinyavsky and Daniel for writings which were not to the taste of someone? And to such long terms!

What do I know about the trials of Sinyavsky and Daniel, Ginzburg and Galanskov, or Bukovsky? A few articles in the papers citing only the prosecution arguments. And where are the speeches of the accused, the

* Also author of Document IV: 26. Ed.

defence? You must agree that this is the most elementary condition for objective coverage of judicial proceedings.

To these and similar questions we have not to this day been given solid or convincing replies.

'Anti-Sovietists.' That is a very grave charge, equivalent to the expression 'enemy of the people' used during the bloody period of Stalin's dictatorship.

Now the appeal and protest by P. M. Litvinov and L. I. Bogoraz-Daniel, which contain evidence of gross violations of socialist legality at the trial in January of the young writers. . . . I have no reason to doubt the sincerity of P. M. Litvinov's and L. I. Bogoraz-Daniel's intentions. I am certain that they are persons of great culture and civic courage. Doctor Litvinov's higher university degree is the best testimony to his personal qualities.*

Their 'proclamations', to use your expression, result from the impossibility of writing in the press. From the non-publication of the letter by A. Ginzburg's mother to the editors of *Komsomolskaya Pravda* in defence of her son. There's objectivity for you! How can one talk of self-advertisement? Does L. I. Bogoraz-Daniel care about it, she who has suffered so much personal sorrow? Does Doctor P. M. Litvinov need it? Maybe I, a worker, dream as I write this letter, of seeing my name in bourgeois newspapers? What nonsense!

I simply want us to be objectively informed about everything that is happening in the world and in our own country, without this excessive emphasis on the ideological struggle to the detriment of the facts. Throughout February and March there was complete silence on the subject of the momentous political events in Czechoslovakia and insufficient coverage of recent events in Poland. Losses in Vietnam are being sustained not only by the American and South Vietnamese troops. . . .

. . . Reporting the alarming facts of the Nazi revival in West Germany or racial discrimination in the United States or the United Arab Republic, our press has simultaneously stopped mentioning de-Stalinization. Or do you think we have forgotten about the catastrophe of the year 1941 or the bloody nightmare of the 'thirties? Never. Just as I will never believe that the writer Solzhenitsyn, a brave and courageous man who spent the whole of the war at the front and was awarded medals for his service in battle, was a traitor.

These false rumours doubtless owe their origin a hundred per cent to the 'case' cooked up by Stalin's and Beria's hangmen, as a result of which Captain A. Solzhenitsyn was interned in a concentration camp in February 1945. The 20th and 22nd Congresses of the Soviet Communist Party fully restored his good name and the names of those who survived. How can there be any talk of 'erroneous' rehabilitations? Rubbish.

* The author of the letter is evidently basing his words on erroneous information put out by foreign radio stations. In reality P. M. Litvinov is not the holder of a Doctor's degree.

Why are you writers and journalists silent on this subject? It concerns a colleague of yours. Perhaps Captain A. Solzhenitsyn is an 'anti-Sovietist too? Or was the writer Graham Greene right in saying that no bell tolls in your ears. . . ?

With all best wishes,

Odessa   V. N. Kryukov, born 1930, machinist
29 April 1968

An appraisal of the trial, of the protests of the Soviet public, and of the repressive measures taken by the authorities, different from that in the official Soviet press, is given in the uncensored typescript journal *Human Rights Year in the Soviet Union*, published and circulated anonymously.[110]

Document V: 45

[*The first two parts of this document give a summary of the trial and list the main press articles on the case and the most important letters of protest, as included in this collection. Being available elsewhere[110], they are omitted here.*]

(III) The unprecedented extent of the movement of protest provoked a series of repressive measures.

(1) At the beginning of February 1968 Mrs L. I. Ginzburg, Irina Zholkovskaya (A. Ginzburg's fiancée) and Olga Timofeyeva (Galanskov's wife) were summoned to the Moscow Procuracy (obedience being legally compulsory when a witness is summoned, but, the notices making no mention either of the purpose of the summons or of the consequences of failure to appear, O. Timofeyeva did not answer the summons). Mrs Ginzburg and Zholkovskaya were subjected to a 'prophylactic interview' for allegedly spreading false information about the trial. The interview ended with a threat that article 190-1 of the Russian Criminal Code might be invoked.

Following this, L. Bogoraz, P. G. Grigorenko, P. Litvinov and P. Yakir were summoned for similar 'prophylactic interviews', but this time to the KGB offices (Litvinov did not obey either the first or the second summons, but later, in March, was called to the Moscow Procuracy). The content of the interviews was identical: all the persons summoned were warned that they should cease their 'public activities'. Pyotr Yakir, the son of Iona Yakir, the army commander *who was shot in 1937*, was told: '*You* aren't your father's spiritual heir! *We* are his spiritual heirs.' When Larissa Bogoraz said that she would not talk until she was allowed to make a statement about the grossly illegal methods of persecution practised in the case of former political prisoner Anatoly Marchenko, she was told that this statement was yet further evidence of her 'anti-social activities'. In a letter to Yu. V. Andropov, chairman of the KGB,

344

P. G. Grigorenko described his own lengthy interview, which had been full of threats—he too received no reply to his letter.

(2) On 14-15 February two of the active participants in the protests, Alexander Volpin, Master of physico-mathematical sciences, and Natalya Gorbanevskaya, a translator, were forcibly interned in psychiatric hospitals.

Without any warning, and without her parents' knowledge, Gorbanevskaya was transferred on 15 February from maternity clinic No. 27, where she was being kept with a threatened miscarriage, to ward 27 of the Kashchenko hospital. The decision to transfer her was taken in consultation with the duty psychiatrist of the Timiryazev district, and the transfer was said to have been motivated by the patient's requests to be discharged. On 23 February Gorbanevskaya was discharged from Kashchenko hospital as the psychiatrists admitted she was not in need of treatment.

On 14 February A. S. Volpin was taken from his home by the police and the duty psychiatrist of the Leningrad district [*of Moscow*], Albert Matyukov. The reason given was that Volpin had not reported for a long time to the psychiatric out-patients' department where he was registered (and to which he had not once been summoned during the past four years). He was put in ward 3 of the Kashchenko hospital, where he was roughly handled by the ward supervisor, A. A. Kazarnovskaya, and the house doctor, Leon Khristoforovich (who did not give his surname). On 16 February, on an order signed by I. K. Yanushevsky, chief psychiatrist of Moscow, Volpin was transferred to the No. 5 hospital at Stolbovaya Station, fifty kilometres from Moscow (this is a hospital mainly for chronically ill patients and also for petty criminals sent for compulsory treatment). Appeals made by his relatives to I. K. Yanushevsky remained unanswered. Only after an appeal addressed to the USSR Minister of Health, Academician B. V. Petrovsky, initially by Academicians A. N. Kholmogorov and P. S. Aleksandrov and then by a further ninety-nine academics (including the most eminent Soviet mathematicians: academicians, professors and Lenin prizewinners), was some improvement made in Volpin's situation. At the present moment he is back again in Kashchenko hospital, but in ward 32 which is quieter than ward 3.

The only official basis for such actions could be the instruction 'On the immediate hospitalization of mentally ill persons who constitute a danger to society' (see the collection *Health Legislation*, vol. 6, Moscow, 1963). In the first place, however, this is only official and not legal, since the very fact of compulsory hospitalization conflicts with articles 58-60 of the Russian Criminal Code, according to which compulsory measures of a medical nature are prescribed by a court. Moreover, the hospitalization of 'socially dangerous' persons directly conflicts with a fundamental principle of legality—that of the presumption of innocence, since it is a person who has actually *committed* an offence who is recognized as socially dangerous and this can only be decided by a court verdict.

Secondly, even this rather cruel and illegal instruction was flagrantly disregarded. A person sent to hospital must, within twenty-four hours of his arrival, be examined by a commission of three people—this was not done in either Volpin's or Gorbanevskaya's case. Their relatives were not informed, which is also obligatory according to the instruction. Finally, a commission appointed after the letters from the mathematicians merely established that Volpin was in need of treatment, and to some extent improved the conditions of his internment. According to the instruction, the commission is in any case bound to examine a patient once a month and, furthermore, to issue a finding not as to whether he is ill or not but as to whether his illness is still of the 'socially dangerous' type—if it is not the patient should be discharged into the care of relatives. The regular commission which met on 17 April also declared that Volpin needed to undergo another one and a half months of treatment.

(3) The next, and so far the widest wave of repressions affected communist party members who had signed one or other of the letters. All the district party committees in Moscow were sent copies or photostats of the letters, including even those whose authors had addressed them to the court and the Procuracy, without even sending copies to the Party Central Committee. The district committees went through the lists of signatories and hunted down 'their' party members. In almost all cases identical action was taken—expulsion from the party, regardless of whether the particular case had ever been considered at a meeting of the party organization.*

... At the same time as participants in the protest campaign began to be expelled from the party, the lawyer B. A. Zolotukhin, defence counsel for Ginzburg, was also expelled 'for adopting a non-party, non-Soviet line in his defence'. In his defence speech the lawyer had convincingly refuted all the prosecution's evidence and—for the first time in many years' experience of political trials—called for the complete acquittal of his client. After his expulsion from the party, B. A. Zolotukhin was removed from his post as head of the legal consultation department [*of the Moscow Collegium of Lawyers*].

All the expulsions involved violations of the Party Statutes—to the extent that some members were expelled without being given a hearing.

In the case of many persons (non-party-members) who had signed various letters, 'talks' were held at their place of employment and suggestions were frequently made that they should resign 'at their own request'. Some persons were deprived of foreign assignments already scheduled for them. Fresh lists of 'undesirable' authors appeared in editorial and publishing offices. Some manuscripts already scheduled for publication were rejected.

Yury Aikhenvald and his wife Valeria Gerlin were dismissed from their

* There follows a list of seventeen people expelled from the party, omitted here since all the known details relating to repressions are given in the index of names (see p. 413 ff.).

teaching jobs for signing the letter of the 170 (both had been victims of repression in Stalin's time).

Yury Glazov, Master of philosophical sciences, who signed the letter of the 80, the letter of the 170 and the appeal to the Budapest meeting, was dismissed from the Institute of the Peoples of Asia.

For 'staff reduction' reasons the following were dismissed from their jobs: Pyotr Grigorenko, from his post as engineer in a construction and installation office; Irina Kristi, junior research officer, from the Institute of Theoretical and Experimental Physics (letters of the 170 and the 99); and the head of a laboratory in the same Institute, Alexander Kronrod, Doctor of physico-mathematical sciences (letter of the 99). Sergei Vorobyov, an editor on the staff of the publishing-house Sovetskaya Entsiklopediya, was expelled from the Komsomol for having at a meeting expressed dissatisfaction with the methods of discussion: signatories of letters were being discussed, yet none of the persons present had read the letters.

> *Human Rights Year in the Soviet Union:*
> *A Chronicle of Current Events*, No. 1, 30 April 1968

Document V: 46

EXTRA-JUDICIAL POLITICAL REPRESSIONS 1968

In the first issue of the *Chronicle* there appeared a list of people expelled from the party for putting their signatures to letters concerning the trial of Galanskov, Ginzburg and the others, and for certain other 'ideological' offences. Names were given of persons who had been dismissed from their jobs. Since then, the number of people subjected to various kinds of repression or penalties has increased. A list follows, indicating the nature of and reasons for the repressive measures.*

A few episodes from the campaign to condemn the signatories to the letters
In Novosibirsk the main idea of the persecution campaign has become the endeavour to purge the Akademgorodok—that is, the university and institutes in the Siberian branch of the Academy of Sciences—of those people who signed the Novosibirsk letter. This endeavour has taken many forms, from more or less insistent suggestions that they should resign 'at their own request' (and many teachers, for example, have been offered jobs and apartments in Novosibirsk itself—anywhere but in the Akademgorodok), to outright threats. A 36-year-old corresponding member of the Siberian branch of the Academy of Sciences, R. Sagdeyev, suggested that they 'should all be driven out of Akademgorodok, let them go and load pig-iron'. Rumour has it that academician Trofimuk,

---

* There follows an enumeration of the collective letters and a list of persons subjected to various kinds of repression. The list is omitted here since all the known details relating to repressions are given in the index of names (see p. 413 ff.).

corresponding members Dmitry Belyayev and Slinko, and the Pro-Rector of the University, Evgeny Bichenkov, are distinguishing themselves in the persecution campaign. On the initiative of corresponding member Valentin Avrorin, Dean of the Humanities Faculty at Novosibirsk University, the department of mathematical linguistics there has been closed down; certain lecturers in the department had signed the letter. The existence of the philological department of the Novosibirsk Humanities Faculty, and the departments of Northern languages and Siberian literature at the Institute of Philosophy, History and Literature (Siberian branch of the Academy of Sciences) is threatened.

Three members of the Moscow branch of the Artists' Union, Boris Birger, Yury Gerchuk and Igor Golomshtok, were the subject of discussion at a meeting which condemned them purely verbally without imposing any sanctions upon them. Then the Presidium of the Board of the Union was summoned to a meeting, and neither the three members under discussion, nor five members of the Presidium who, it may be supposed, would have objected to sanctions, were informed of this. It was purely by chance that these five and Boris Birger learned of the meeting and came to it. Thanks to this, the resolution to expel all three members was not carried.

It is said that after the appearance in the press, especially in the *Literary Gazette* and *Literary Russia*, of phrases on the incompatibility of signing letters about the trial and remaining in the ranks of the Writers' Union, several writers (the names of Vasily Aksyonov, Evgeny Evtushenko and Vladimir Tendryakov have been mentioned) presented themselves in the offices of the Union Secretariat and declared on behalf of 100 (other versions say 120 or 150) members of the Union that if so much as one signatory were expelled from the Writers' Union, then they too would all of them leave its ranks.

It is said that a similar declaration was made by Veniamin Kaverin in his own name and on behalf of Pavel Antokolsky, Konstantin Paustovsky and Kornei Chukovsky.

During a discussion on eleven research officers in the Institute of Russian Language who had signed letters concerning the trial, a 32-year-old Master of philological sciences, Lev Skvortsov, distinguished himself by showing the greatest condemnatory zeal. This is roughly what he said: 'I know there is an anti-Soviet organization in Moscow, and its centre is in our Institute'. Lev Skvortsov is known to have served on the panel of textological experts during the investigation of the case of Galanskov and the others, but the findings of the panel were not submitted for consideration in court because of their hypothetical nature. It is said, for example, that one of the panel's conclusions was that 'A Letter to an Old Friend' was the joint work of Galanskov and Ginzburg, although it is evident to the unpractised eye, without resorting to stylistic and textological examination, that the document was written by a person of a different generation. Since the 'Letter to an Old Friend' was pronounced an anti-Soviet document by the court in its verdict, and was presented as such in the indictment, the full gravity of the accusation of authorship is clear.

News in Brief
In May Yury Galanskov and Alexander Ginzburg arrived in camp 17 of the Mordovian camps. Their address is: Mordovskaya ASSR, st. Potma, p/o Ozerny, p/ya ZhKh 385/17a. From the very first day they were set to work sewing mittens for special work clothing. After a short time Yury Galanskov was sent to the hospital camp for investigation because of a stomach ulcer. Working in a construction brigade in the same hospital camp is Aleksei Dobrovolsky. His address: Mordovskaya ASSR, st. Potma, p/o Yavas, p/ya ZhKh 385/3.

On 12 May, after three months' confinement in psychiatric hospitals, Alexander Volpin was discharged.

Information and addenda relating to issue No. 1 [of the Chronicle of Current Events]
In the report on the Moscow trial a sentence about the material evidence which figured in the trial was incorrectly formulated.

The main items of evidence were:

a copy of the miscellany *Phoenix-'66*, confiscated during a search of Galanskov's home;

a copy of the same collection, confiscated during a search of Ginzburg's home;

money, a hectograph, cryptography paper and NTS pamphlets, confiscated during a search of Dobrobolsky's home;

typewriters, confiscated during searches at the homes of various persons;

The White Book, which came out in France in February, and an issue of the journal *Grani*, published in March—both these appeared after the arrest of the defendants and, naturally, could not have been confiscated in the homes of any of them.

> *Human Rights Year in the Soviet Union: A Chronicle of Current Events*, No. 2, 30 June 1968

A List of Publications Used

Evening Moscow, newspaper of Moscow City Communist Party Committee and Moscow Soviet, appears six times a week.
Human Rights Year in the Soviet Union, typescript journal published anonymously, appears bi-monthly.

Voice of the Fatherland, newspaper published by the Soviet Government for Russian émigrés, appears twice weekly.

Izvestia (Sovetov deputatov trudyashchikhsya SSSR) appears six times a week.

Komsomolskaya Pravda, newspaper of the Komsomol Central Committee, appears six times a week.

Literary Gazette, newspaper of the Board of the Writers' Union of the USSR, appears once a week.

Literary Russia, newspaper of the Boards of the Writers' Union of the Russian Republic and the Moscow Branch of the Writers' Union, appears once a week.

Moskovskaya Pravda, newspaper of Moscow City Communist Party Committee and Moscow Soviet, appears six times a week.

Moscow Artist, newspaper of the Board of the Moscow Branch of the Artists' Union of the USSR, appears once a week.

Pravda, daily newspaper of the Soviet Communist Party Central Committee.

Soviet Culture, newspaper of the Ministry of Culture of the USSR and the Central Committee of the Union of Cultural Workers, appears twice weekly.

Soviet Russia, newspaper of the Soviet Communist Party Central Committee, appears six times a week.

═══ VI ═══

THE APPEAL HEARING*

Session of the RSFSR Supreme Court
Collegium for Criminal Cases
16 April 1968

Members of the Court: Chairman Ostroukhova, members of the Supreme Court Timofeyev and Lukanov; also participating were Procurator Terekhov and defence counsels Shveisky, Ariya, Kaminskaya and Zolotukhin.

The session commenced at 10 a.m. in the building of the RSFSR Supreme Court (Kuibyshev Street, Moscow). Present in the court-room were the mother and wife of Yu. Galanskov, the mother and fiancée of A. Ginzburg, the mother of A. Dobrovolsky, defendant V. Lashkova and approximately fifty other persons who had obtained special passes from the KGB and district party committees. None of the defendants' friends, and no foreign correspondents were admitted; they awaited the court's decision in the corridor. Prosecution and defence were represented by the same persons as in the court of first instance.

The atmosphere in court during the proceedings was calm. No one ventured any shouts or cheers.

. . . At ten o'clock exactly an official announced: 'Rise, the court is in session!' All rose to their feet; Ostroukhova, Timofeyev and Lukanov entered. Then they were seated.

The Chairman of the court (henceforward Judge) declared the judicial session open and announced the appeal hearing of criminal case No. 286. She announced the composition of the court and the name of the Procurator, and asked if any of the persons summoned to appear in the case had any requests. Kaminskaya, Zolotukhin and

* Abridged. Ed.

Shveisky requested that their clients be summoned to the judicial session, referring to statements made by the defendants themselves and filed in the case. The judge asked the opinion of the Procurator. The Procurator stated that he was not obliged to summon the defendants, since their testimony and their written comments on the record of the judicial hearing in the court of first instance were filed in the case materials.

The court adjourned for consultation for twenty minutes. Then its ruling was announced: that the defendants should not be summoned to the judicial session.

[*The Judge then summarizes the findings of the court of first instance, and reminds her audience of the sentences passed; she goes on to refer to the appeals lodged by the defendants.*]

... Ginzburg asks in his appeal for the verdict to be repealed and the case dismissed.

... Galanskov asks ... for the verdict to be repealed and the case closed.

... Dobrovolsky pleaded guilty on all charges and asks in his appeal that his actions be reclassified under article 190-1 of the Russian Criminal Code.

... Lashkova pleaded guilty, and her defence counsel Ariya asks in his appeal that her actions be reclassified under article 190-1 of the Russian Criminal Code and a punishment handed down that does not entail deprivation of freedom.

After a fifteen-minute break the session recommenced.

JUDGE. Lashkova, do you have anything to say?

LASHKOVA. No.

JUDGE. I call upon defence counsel Shveisky, representing Dobrovolsky, to speak.

SPEECH BY DEFENCE COUNSEL SHVEISKY

First of all, I am obliged to say that a number of the actions committed by my client Dobrovolsky are without doubt criminal offences. It was at his house that the NTS literature, the hectograph, cryptographic equipment and 2000 roubles were found. These facts, according to existing laws, constitute a *corpus delicti*. In his appeal, Dobrovolsky describes the motives which drove him to the commission of crime, and asks that his conviction under article 70 of the Russian Criminal Code be altered to one under article 190-1.

The distinction between articles 70 and 190-1 lies first and foremost in the question of whether the defendant acted with intent.

However, intent is a largely subjective concept; actions which appear outwardly identical can be classified differently according to the question precisely of intent. Dobrovolsky describes in detail in his appeal the motives behind his behaviour, and it is precisely this that gives me, his defence counsel, grounds for asking that his actions be reclassified from article 70 to article 190-1.

I should like in my speech to single out three basic questions:

(1) how Dobrovolsky's outlook on life was formed;

(2) certain psychological peculiarities of his personality;

(3) to what extent the actions committed by him support his assertion that he had no intent to undermine the Soviet social and political system.

I shall dwell initially on the first question—the conditions in which Dobrovolsky's personality was formed. [*Shveisky here repeats the argument advanced by him at the trial. See p.* 174.] His behaviour was the result not of hostility to the Soviet system, but rather of his political immaturity and his inability to grasp the profound historical changes taking place in our country at that time. . . . It is clear from Dobrovolsky's entire testimony, and from the text of his appeal, that he had no direct intent to overthrow Soviet power. . . . I consider that everything that happened to Dobrovolsky was the result of profound and grave delusions.

Now I should like to discuss the question of Dobrovolsky's mental state. The psychiatrists who conducted a forensic-psychiatric examination of Dobrovolsky during the investigation judged him to be of sound mind. However, they did establish the presence in him of serious mental abnormalities. These abnormalities, naturally, could not fail to exert an influence on Dobrovolsky's development and his views. Particularly when we remember, as I have already said, the complex time during which Dobrovolsky's attitudes were being formed. After all, even healthy persons often make mistakes in critical social situations.

Dobrovolsky's mental abnormalities first became evident when he was still in the 9th Class. That was when he began to take an interest in problems of existence and was attracted to anarchist ideas. . . . Soon after this, in 1955, he was registered with the district psychiatrist and put into hospital—this was completely unconnected with any criminal prosecution. . . . In 1964 he was diagnosed by a team at the Serbsky Institute as 'a profoundly psychopathic personality'. (Here I must draw your attention to one small but fairly symptomatic detail. In the official record of the judicial proceedings, as confirmed by the Moscow City Court Collegium, this date was entered erroneously as 1954. Naturally I submitted this observation with the aim of securing a correction of a small inaccuracy. However, this observation, like all the other observations made by all the other defence counsels, was not accepted.)

... Now I should like to put the question: how might psychopathy have affected the behaviour of Dobrovolsky? [*Here Shveisky quotes from two Soviet psychiatric textbooks*: The Psychiatrist's Terminological Dictionary *and* Forensic psychiatry *by Prof. G. V. Morozov.*] Consequently psychopathy must have an effect upon the entire personality behaviour. And I submit that when we evaluate the actions of Dobrovolsky we must not ignore this serious fact, which is extremely important for the whole case.

Let us now go on to the third question—the existence of anti-Soviet intent in Dobrovolsky's actions. . . . Outwardly, his actions might appear to make the question a superfluous one. . . . It was in his home, and only his, that NTS literature was discovered during a search. But as for Dobrovolsky's attitude to the literature—well, that is a more complex question. It is known that he gave it to a few people to read: Lashkova, Kats and Kushev. But he did not give these books to anyone except the three persons I have named, and they shared his views closely. And that suggests that he was not trying to use this literature for anti-Soviet purposes.

It is also known that it was precisely at Dobrovolsky's home that the leaflets and cryptographic equipment were found. No one can have the slightest doubt that they had been sent into our country with anti-Soviet intent. However . . . Dobrovolsky himself said: 'When I saw what they contained, I refused to duplicate them'. And indeed, the leaflets were dated August 1966, but when they were seized during the search of Dobrovolsky's house in March 1967, not one attempt had been made to circulate them. Also, the hectograph had not even been unpacked.

Dobrovolsky has been charged also with duplicating two articles of anti-Soviet content: 'The Confession of Victor Velsky' and 'The Russian Road to Socialism'. However, this crime too should be classified under article 190-1, not article 70, of the Russian Criminal Code.

A man convicted under article 70 is a malicious enemy, acting deliberately against the Soviet state. Dobrovolsky is not an enemy; he is a deluded man, and therefore he should be punished for his crime under article 190-1, and not article 70. Such a decision would also be a wise act of political expediency from the point of view of the trial's outcome.

I ask that the crimes committed by Dobrovolsky be classified under article 190-1 of the Russian Criminal Code and that his term of imprisonment be reduced to correspond with the length of time he has actually spent in custody.*

JUDGE. I call upon defence counsel Ariya, representing Lashkova, to speak.

SPEECH BY DEFENCE COUNSEL ARIYA

I should like to begin by saying that, in my opinion, this case does not merit the sensation that has grown up around it. However, the public interest in this case has demanded the most scrupulous observance by the court of procedural and legal standards. Nevertheless, one has to admit that neither the conduct of the trial proceedings, nor the bringing in of the verdict was on a high legal level. A whole series of violations perpetrated in the course of the trial leads one to have doubts about the sentences passed by the court. These violations are ammunition not only for the defence, and that should not be forgotten. One of them was the dismissal of witnesses from the courtroom after they had testified. Significant, too, was the attitude taken to observations by the defence relating to the official record of the judicial proceedings. All of us submitted observations and, fully aware of our responsibility, strove to make corrections and additions to the record. This is entirely natural, since the record is neither a verbatim shorthand one nor a tape-recording, and the secretary simply cannot prepare a complete document. A typical detail is, for example, the date 1964, which was erroneously recorded as 1954 (referring to Dobrovolsky's illness). Or the testimony of Lashkova, where two entirely separate documents, 'A Civil Appeal' and 'Resistance', which cannot in any respect be said to be one and the same thing, were combined as one item. Absolutely every one of the observations made by the defence, including the observations on these points, was judged untrue. But when, for example, Ginzburg made the same observations, they were accepted. Far be it from me to suggest that the court wished to insult the defence. But it displayed a lack of consideration, an unwillingness to probe into the facts; it brushed aside observations made by the defence. These and other procedural violations perpetrated by the court lead one to suspect that the court paid insufficient attention to the very core of the case,

* Evidently Dobrovolsky himself had calculated on obtaining a reduction of his term of imprisonment at the appeal hearing, since he had, after the hearing by the court of first instance, requested permission to meet KGB officials and 'give them a lot of new information'. The decision 'Permission granted' had been written on his request.

and to doubt not only the procedural aspect. Among the violations there are some of a more serious nature. On certain of the points raised in the indictment, the court did not bring any verdict at all. The charge is brought, but no verdict on it! The case is without precedent! With regard to Ginzburg, for instance, no verdict was brought on the part of the indictment concerning the tape-recordings. With regard to Lashkova, the charge of typing and circulating 'Events in the Pochayev Monastery Today' was eliminated, by virtue of its omission in the verdict which contains not a word about it. This contravenes articles 303 and 314 of the Russian Code of Criminal Procedure.

The defence's first request is that the defendants be judged not guilty as regards that part of the indictment which was omitted from the verdict.

Furthermore, Lashkova was found guilty in particular of typing for Ginzburg a leaflet signed 'Resistance'. Lashkova denies having typed it, and Ginzburg maintains that it was he who did so. A verdict was brought in on this point, but the court did not indicate why the testimonies of Ginzburg and Lashkova were judged invalid. Neither the case material nor the text of the verdict provides adequate justification for this. This is some indication of the professional standards of the court. [*Ariya goes on to make further criticisms of the court's apparently unreasoned conclusions.*] Ginzburg tells us that his sole aim in compiling [*The White Book*] was to deliver it into the hands of competent persons who would pass it on to our highest authorities. ... Thus Lashkova was typing the collection for delivery not abroad but into the hands of competent persons in our state. This does not constitute any *corpus delicti* whatsoever. It seems to me that this document too should be excluded from the charges against Lashkova.

For Galanskov, Lashkova typed the article 'The Russian Road to Socialism and its Results'. From the testimony of Galanskov it is clear that he took the article to Lashkova and she began to type it straight away without reading it first. I should say that this article is difficult to comprehend. And a typist might, during her brief acquaintance with it in the course of typing, interpret it as a non-criminal document. ... [*Ariya gives a résumé of the attitudes expressed by the article's author, and doubts whether the word criminal can be applied to the work. His argument is for the most part a repetition of that advanced by him at the trial, see p.* 180.] ... Therefore, I consider that this document should be excluded from the charges against Lashkova.

Lashkova typed—also for Galanskov—the 'Open Letter to Sholokhov'. There can be no doubt as to the criminal nature of this letter. ... But [*here Ariya makes the point made by him at the trial—see p. 178—that Lashkova's motives were financial, and not anti-Soviet*] if a person types not in order to undermine Soviet authority but to retain possession of a typewriter, his actions cannot be classified under article 70 of the Russian Criminal Code. . . . Lashkova was accused also of circulating with anti-Soviet intent copies of the booklets 'Solidarism Is the Idea of the Future' and 'Our Times' which she had received from Dobrovolsky. . . . The evidence given by Kushev and Levitin testifies to Lashkova's indifference, and not to any attempt to circulate this literature. . . . The verdict stated, too, that Lashkova pleaded guilty on all points. This, however, does not correspond to the truth. She did not plead guilty on all points. She was accused of intent, but while admitting to the facts, she always denied having had anti-Soviet intent. She said during the investigation that she had never had an anti-Soviet aim.

Lashkova comes from a workers' family; she is herself a labourer and accustomed to earn every kopek by the sweat of her brow. This should not be forgotten.

Furthermore, the conduct and course of this trial have given an untrue picture of the mood of our young people. Confusion of ideas and a tendency to criticism cannot be called an especially dangerous state crime.

In my opinion, the court must reclassify Lashkova's offence concerning the typing of the 'Open Letter to Sholokhov' and the possession of NTS literature under article 190-1 of the Russian Criminal Code; as regards the other parts of the indictment, the case should be dismissed and a punishment assigned to Lashkova under article 190-1 that does not entail deprivation of freedom.

JUDGE. I call upon defence counsel Kaminskaya, representing Galanskov, to speak.

SPEECH BY DEFENCE COUNSEL KAMINSKAYA

I ask for the verdict to be not repealed, but altered. In the section which gives a legal assessment of the actions committed by Galanskov, I ask that he be judged guilty on part of the indictment under article 190-1 of the Russian Criminal Code. Other parts of the indictment I consider unproven. They are:

(1) ties with the NTS;
(2) participation in the compilation of *The White Book*;
(3) engagement in anti-Soviet agitation;
(4) the duplication, through Dobrovolsky, of the 'Open Letter',

357

the article 'The Russian Road to Socialism' and the story 'The Confession of Victor Velsky'.

The verdict makes the assertion that the case for the prosecution on these points was based on the following: the fact that Galanskov had several meetings with NTS representatives and handed material over to them; the fact that it was Galanskov who procured the hectograph and cryptographic equipment; the fact that he obtained and circulated anti-Soviet literature; and that it was he who received money from the NTS in dollars and Soviet roubles.

I consider that there was not enough material in the case to warrant this assertion. Upon what does the prosecution base itself?

Firstly, on the testimony of Galanskov himself. [*Here Kaminskaya repeats her argument—see p. 190—that Galanskov's evidence should not have been taken at face value; he himself is one of the defendants; he was then in a difficult mental condition, and he is also a sick man physically; and he retracted parts of his initial testimony.*] To continue. The prosecution bases itself, too, on the testimony of Dobrovolsky. This is also the testimony of a defendant. [*Kaminskaya advances essentially the same argument as in the trial: that Dobrovolsky's testimony was contradictory and biased; he was an interested party and mentally unbalanced; the discovery at his home of material evidence is no proof of Galanskov's guilt; rather, it points towards Dobrovolsky himself.*]

Galanskov's guilt is said to be confirmed also by the testimony of Lashkova concerning the coded letter. To use this letter as evidence, one must establish what it contained and to whom it was sent. Lashkova said that it concerned relationships between numbers. Galanskov testified that he had written the letter to witness Batshev, and it concerned their mutual acquaintances. What is there to disprove this? Nothing. Neither in the court's verdict, nor in the case material are there any data about this letter or where it was sent. Consequently, it is impossible to assert that the letter was anti-Soviet and was sent to the NTS.

What other facts were judged proof of Galanskov's guilt? The fact that he received money. [*Here Kaminskaya again casts doubt upon Dobrovolsky's testimony regarding his and Galanskov's intention to purchase a cooperative flat; see p. 195.*]

The charge of handing over *The White Book* through a foreigner named Genrikh is one of the most important points in the case against Galanskov. . . . The meeting of which Dobrovolsky speaks, and which was also established by the court, took place on 22 October, that is, three weeks before work on *The White Book* was completed. This was established by cross-examination of defendants and witnesses, and even Dobrovolsky does not deny it.

I shall end my analysis of the central points of the prosecution by saying that it is the duty of the court to provide a reasoned justification for its verdict and to adduce proofs that do not awaken any doubts. It is essential to be in possession of concrete, proven facts. But here we have only the testimony of Galanskov and Dobrovolsky, which should in no respect be considered incontrovertible proof, especially as Galanskov and Dobrovolsky are mentally unstable.

Now I should like to say a few words on the subject of the delivery of *Phoenix* for conveyance abroad. . . . I cannot understand why Dobrovolsky's statement, that he could make available to the investigating organs the missing copies of *Phoenix*, did not awaken the attention or the interest of the investigators. . . . No questions were put to him about it. At the trial he refused to answer a question on the subject. The following was established beyond all doubt: Galanskov was the editor of *Phoenix*. He himself has never denied it. It was established that there were five copies of *Phoenix*, one of which Galanskov destroyed because of its illegibility. Consequently, there remain four copies. One of them, according to Galanskov, is at his home; two were seized during searches; yet another was given by Galanskov to Dobrovolsky. Where this copy is no one knows. Nadya met both Dobrovolsky and Galanskov. The court ought to have established, by way of objective proof, exactly which of the two handed *Phoenix* over to her. One cannot lay the whole blame on Galanskov, especially as there were no witnesses, and Nadya has not been discovered or interrogated. I consider that on this point of the prosecution's case, too, there are no substantial proofs of Galanskov's guilt.

There are no proofs either of Galanskov having participated in the compilation of *The White Book*. [*Here Kaminskaya quotes the testimony of Ginzburg, Dobrovolsky, Lashkova and Khaustov.*] What basis the court had when it brought in its verdict on this point is not clear. The next point in the case against Galanskov, which I consider unproven, is his duplication—through Dobrovolsky—of 'The Confession of Victor Velsky', 'The Russian Road to Socialism' and the 'Open Letter to Sholokhov'. This charge is based solely on the testimony of Dobrovolsky. [*Kaminskaya goes on to summarize her argument from the trial, noting the contradictory testimonies of Radziyevsky, Dobrovolsky and Galanskov, and the testimony of Lashkova and Levitin concerning Dobrovolsky's intention to publish a journal of his own. See pp.* 188-190.] These episodes are not adequately proven. Therefore I ask that they be eliminated from the charges against Galanskov.

But there are facts of another kind in the verdict, that is, facts upon which the court has, in my opinion, placed an incorrect interpretation.

They are the duplication of the 'Confession of Victor Velsky' and 'The Russian Road to Socialism', and their inclusion in *Phoenix*. . . . Two of my colleagues [*Shveisky and Ariya*] have already spoken about the article 'The Russian Road to Socialism'. I can only add that at the end of this article its author writes that we need reforms, and that they must be implemented only from above, that is, the author thinks they must be implemented by Soviet power. The 'Confession of Victor Velsky' was also judged criminal by the court of first instance. But we must not forget that it is a work of art, and that the events and persons described in it are fictitious. [*She describes briefly the content of the story; see p.* 185.] It is a very complex work, but in no respect an anti-Soviet one. Therefore, it must be removed from the list of works judged criminal.

I do not quarrel with the judgment of two works—the article 'What Is Socialist Realism?' by Sinyavsky, and the 'Open Letter to Sholokhov'— as criminal; but I ask that Galanskov's activities in connection with their inclusion in *Phoenix* be reclassified under article 190-1 of the Russian Criminal Code. [*Kaminskaya's remarks on the subject of these two works are essentially a repetition of the argument she advances on p.* 187.]

My colleagues here have laid great stress on the need for evidence of direct intent in order to be able to classify the accused's actions under article 70. I consider that in the case of Galanskov there was no direct intent. He was trying, perhaps wrongly, to fight against what seemed to him untruth. He thought that he ought personally to participate in everything. Perhaps he did not always rightly see what form his struggle should take. [*Kaminskaya refers here to Galanskov's demonstration outside the American Embassy in 1965 in protest at the invasion of the Dominican Republic.*] In his testimony he says of himself: 'I am a proletarian democrat, a Marxist'. If he had not included two criminal articles in *Phoenix*, I would ask for an acquittal on the charges under article 70, but he did include them, and so I am asking only for a reclassification of his actions under article 190-1.

As regards article 88, paragraph 1, of the Criminal Code, Galanskov requests in his appeal that the case be dismissed. As a lawyer, I realize that absence of self-interest cannot serve as grounds for acquittal. Therefore I cannot challenge the verdict in the part of the indictment pertaining to article 88, paragraph 1.

JUDGE. I call upon defence counsel Zolotukhin, representing Ginzburg, to speak.

The Appeal Hearing

Comrade members of the Supreme Court, the verdict of the Moscow City Court Collegium regarding my client Alexander Ginzburg should, in my opinion, be repealed.

I consider that the verdict ought to be repealed and the criminal prosecution of Alexander Ginzburg discontinued, with all the consequences ensuing from it.

I intend to offer you my views on the evidence which was adduced by the court of first instance and upon which its verdict was founded.

Of what exactly was Alexander Ginzburg found guilty?

(1) Of handing over, through Galanskov, in November 1966, to the foreign émigré organization NTS, the collection of materials compiled by him on the trial of Sinyavsky and Daniel.

(2) Of participating in the compilation of the collection entitled *Phoenix*, the editor and compiler of which was Galanskov.

(3) Of giving to Gubanov four newspaper cuttings of anti-Soviet content in the French, Italian, Norwegian and Danish languages.

(4) Of establishing criminal ties with the foreign émigré organization NTS.

(5) And, finally, of drawing Lashkova and Dobrovolsky into anti-Soviet activities.

At the centre of the indictment is the charge that Ginzburg handed over to the West, to the NTS, a collection of materials on the Sinyavsky–Daniel affair, also known as *The White Book*. The verdict states that in November 1966 Ginzburg, assisted by Galanskov and Lashkova, arranged for the collection to be typed, and that it was typed in ten copies, one of which was handed to the NTS through Galanskov for publication. Let us examine the evidence cited by the court as justification for this grave—I would even say terrible—accusation.

According to the verdict, the fact of the book being handed over was proved by the testimony of Dobrovolsky that Ginzburg compiled *The White Book* and Galanskov handed it over to NTS representatives with Ginzburg's knowledge and consent. In other words, the sole evidence for making this grave accusation is, as we see, the testimony of defendant Dobrovolsky. The mere fact that there was only a single piece of evidence for such an important point ought to have put the court on its guard. And when, moreover, that sole evidence turned out to be the testimony of a *defendant*, vitally interested in the outcome of the case, that ought to have prompted the court to especial caution. And furthermore, the court should have taken into consideration the mental state of this person, so vividly and expressively described by his counsel.

361

[*Zolotukhin goes on to summarize Dobrovolsky's testimony relating to the date of Genrikh's arrival in Moscow and the meeting at which* The White Book *was allegedly handed over to him. He notes the discrepancy between Dobrovolsky's story and that of Ginzburg, Lashkova and several witnesses.*]

How did the court of first instance verify Dobrovolsky's testimony, which it used as a basis for confirming charges against the other defendants? It would be natural to suppose that the court collated Dobrovolsky's testimony with other testimony given by defendants and witnesses. But this did not happen. And when we attempted to do it just now, we saw that Dobrovolsky's testimony does not stand up to scrutiny—it falls apart as soon as it is placed side by side with precisely established facts.

And yet another alarming point: when Dobrovolsky was looking through albums containing photographs of foreign citizens who had visited the USSR in the autumn of 1966, he did not find Genrikh among them; he could not identify him.

That is all that the court of first instance had at its disposal when it sentenced Alexander Ginzburg to a severe punishment for having 'handed over to the NTS through Galanskov for publication' a collection of materials on the Sinyavsky–Daniel affair. In my opinion, this charge is completely unfounded.

The second, and no less terrible, accusation made in the verdict is that Ginzburg had established criminal ties with the NTS. [*Here Zolotukhin cites evidence given by Dobrovolsky and Brox-Sokolov. See p. 202.*] An impartial analysis of this evidence shows that to attach any weight to it in reaching a verdict is utterly impossible. . . .

The court cites Dobrovolsky's words to the effect that Ginzburg allegedly put Galanskov in touch with the NTS. This is a concrete assertion which needs to have some sort of evidence to back it up. But there is nothing of the kind in the case. In another part of his testimony Dobrovolsky says that Ginzburg passed on to Galanskov his contacts abroad, but there is no talk of any organization called NTS. The verdict says 'ties with NTS', but Dobrovolsky said nothing about that, even during the preliminary investigation. [*He quotes Dobrovolsky's words, emphasizing their conjectural nature and calling the court's attention to article 309 of the Code of Criminal Procedure, prohibiting the bringing of a verdict based on speculation and conjecture.*]

The verdict is founded, too, on Dobrovolsky's testimony that Ginzburg and Galanskov allegedly knew of the imminent arrival in Moscow of Schaffhauser, an NTS emissary, thus confirming the existence of ties between them and that organization. What exactly did Dobrovolsky testify? [*He quotes Dobrovolsky's reference to a conversa-*

tion between Ginzburg and Galanskov from which Dobrovolsky gathered that a foreigner would arrive to see Esenin-Volpin.] That is all. We are not being informed of a fact; it is an interpretation placed by Dobrovolsky upon a conversation, and a conversation between other people at that. 'I gathered,' he says. And nowhere does he say that they were definitely talking of Schaffhauser and the NTS.

. . . Let us turn to the testimony of Brox-Sokolov. The verdict states that in a conversation with Brox, Slavinsky referred to Ginzburg as a participant in underground activity in the Soviet Union. Brox testified at the trial that he had attended a lecture given in Grenoble by Slavinsky entitled 'Underground Literature in the USSR'. . . . That is all. There is no record in the case of any private talks between Brox and Slavinsky, and I do not understand what material the court had at its disposal in making reference to such 'conversations'. [*Zolotukhin goes on to describe the content of Slavinsky's lecture, stressing that Slavinsky spoke only of what was already public knowledge through radio and press publicity—the fact that Ginzburg had compiled* The White Book, *a fact which Ginzburg never denied.*] Brox did not glean any new information at this public lecture. Thus, Brox-Sokolov spoke about the content of a public lecture, delivered by Slavinsky at Grenoble, and not at all about Ginzburg's underground activity in the USSR.

The court did not have any other evidence of Ginzburg's ties with the NTS. But what is more, there is in the case materials evidence of the *absence of ties* between Ginzburg and this émigré organization. We know that in January 1967 Schaffhauser, a West German citizen, was detained in Leningrad. At the time of his arrest a questionnaire was confiscated from him, by means of which people in the West wanted to obtain information about certain Soviet citizens, among them Ginzburg. . . . In the official record of Schaffhauser's interrogation he is quoted as saying that the purpose of these questions was to study the possibility of recruiting these people for future collaboration with the NTS. *Future.* I consider that this clears Ginzburg completely of the charge of having ties with the foreign émigré organization NTS. Taking all this into account, the judicial collegium ought either to have brought in a verdict of not guilty, or, on the basis of article 314 of the Russian Code of Criminal Procedure, to have indicated the reasons for its rejection of this evidence. However, the court collegium simply ignored these facts and rejected the evidence of Ginzburg's innocence without giving any reasoned justification.

And now I shall talk of the contents of the collection of materials on the Sinyavsky–Daniel case. The verdict states that the collection contains two criminal documents: the leaflet signed 'Resistance' and the 'Letter to an Old Friend'. The collection itself is not considered to be criminal, but was judged merely tendentious. What prompted Ginzburg to include these two documents in his collection?

. . . Ginzburg does not himself consider them anti-Soviet, and this fact ought to have been recognized by the court as of paramount importance, since it is an indication of the absence in Ginzburg of anti-Soviet intent. Ginzburg said that these documents were circulating widely in Moscow and had a direct bearing on the Sinyavsky–Daniel case: there was no reason not to include them in a collection intended for presentation to the supreme organs of government and to competent persons of official standing. [*Zolotukhin reminds the court that Ginzburg actually took one copy of* The White Book *to the KGB and showed another to Ehrenburg, a deputy of the Supreme Soviet. Was this an attempt to undermine Soviet power?*]

As defence counsel Ariya has already stated here, the presentation to the government of one's own country of any document, with the request that it be examined, does not constitute a *corpus delicti*. And I fully support his opinion on this point.

The charge has also been brought against Alexander Ginzburg that in collusion with Galanskov he compiled the miscellany *Phoenix*, which contains a number of items judged criminal and anti-Soviet. The evidence for this accusation is: the removal from Ginzburg's flat of one copy of this collection; the testimony of Ginzburg himself that in the spring of 1966 he had read in Galanskov's flat the 'Open Letter to Sholokhov', of which Galanskov was the author; and the testimony of Dobrovolsky that Ginzburg and Galanskov had compiled *Phoenix* together.

I shall begin with the last point. The fact is that, as I see it, Dobrovolsky did not give any such testimony in court. But since the observations which I noted concerning the official record met with the same fate as all the other observations made by all the other defence counsels, that is, putting it bluntly, they were not accepted, I am forced to treat this testimony of Dobrovolsky's as objectively existing fact, and to analyse it. Even after accepting this unsubstantiated allegation, the court did not support it with a single concrete fact, or cite a single concrete action. The fact that one copy of *Phoenix* was removed from Ginzburg's flat does not in any respect constitute proof that he participated in its compilation. The most serious accusation that the court could bring against Ginzburg on the basis of this fact would be a charge of possessing the miscellany.

[*But here Zolotukhin cites Galanskov's explanation of how* Phoenix *came to be in Ginzburg's flat, thus clearing Ginzburg even of that charge.*] As regards the 'Open Letter to Sholokhov', Ginzburg testified that he had read it in the spring of 1966 at Galanskov's flat [*but in a considerably shorter form than the version he saw in* Phoenix *during the preliminary investigation.*] But even if Ginzburg had read the version of the letter which was included in *Phoenix*, or even all the documents which went into *Phoenix*, either separately or in a single collection, that is still proof only that he was a *reader* of *Phoenix*, and in no respect its author or editor. Thus I hold the charge against Ginzburg of compiling *Phoenix* to be groundless and the evidence adduced by the court of first instance to confirm this charge utterly inadequate.

Alexander Ginzburg is charged with circulating in the USSR material of a slanderous, anti-Soviet nature, printed by foreign publishing houses. By this is meant the fact that Ginzburg gave to Gubanov four newspaper cuttings in the French, Italian, Norwegian and Danish languages. [*Here Zolotukhin cites Ginzburg's testimony proving that his intentions in doing so were not anti-Soviet.*] From Ginzburg's testimony we can see that the contents of these cuttings were unknown to him. But even supposing that he was aware of their contents, he did not 'circulate them in the USSR', but gave them to one of the Smogists, in order that that person might acquaint himself with what was being written about SMOG abroad.

The court judged these newspaper cuttings anti-Soviet on the grounds that they slandered Soviet reality. In connection with this, I should like to express an opinion of a legal character: one cannot equate the concept of 'Soviet reality' with 'the Soviet political and social system'. The first may be given as broad an interpretation as one wishes—one may include in it the work of individual institutions and persons representing them; whereas by the second we mean the whole political structure of the Soviet Union. And in this light, even those documents which the court judged anti-Soviet do not appear so, in the exact sense of the word.

Alexander Ginzburg has been charged with drawing Lashkova and Dobrovolsky into criminal activities. (Dobrovolsky, incidentally, was the subject of criminal proceedings under article 58-10 as long ago as 1957, as we can see from the case materials.) It is not clear, either, how Ginzburg could have drawn Dobrovolsky into criminal activities if, as Dobrovolsky himself said, they were not on familiar terms and they never had a single conversation on any serious topic. And Lashkova—she typed material for Ginzburg for inclusion in the collection on the Sinyavsky–Daniel case. One of these documents,

'Letter to an Old Friend', the court judged criminal. But Lashkova testified, both at the preliminary investigation and at the trial, that when bringing his material Ginzburg had mentioned to her his intention of sending his collection to the supreme organs of government. Consequently, there was no attempt on the part of Ginzburg to draw her into criminal activities. This accusation, too, I hold unproven and unfounded.

The verdict notes that from 1960 onwards the state security organs had more than once instituted criminal proceedings against Ginzburg for his anti-Soviet activity. They had indeed—on two occasions [*he quotes the dates*]; in both instances the case was dismissed for lack of a *corpus delicti*. Thus any reference to these cases, which were dismissed, constitutes a violation of article 13 of the Russian Code of Criminal Procedure.

And finally, my last point. When one is talking of an especially dangerous state crime which is classified under article 70 of the Criminal Code, it is essential to demonstrate that the aim of the accused was to overthrow or weaken Soviet power. [*Zolotukhin cites the verdict on this charge and objects* en passant *to the fact that all four defendants were accused indiscriminately*.] But none of the witnesses, and none of the defendants, not even Dobrovolsky, testified that Ginzburg had committed his actions with the aim of undermining or overthrowing Soviet power, and even the investigating organs judged the collection compiled by Ginzburg on the Sinyavsky–Daniel case not anti-Soviet but merely 'tendentious'.

Apart from everything I have listed, the verdict states that Ginzburg's guilt was proven by 'the aggregation of the materials examined by the preliminary and judicial investigations'. I have always objected to this vague formula, since aggregation of materials is not any kind of new proof and does not add anything to the arguments already advanced.

And so, I hold that the guilt of Alexander Ginzburg is unproven, and that justice demands the repeal of the verdict brought in on him and the dismissal of the case.

The Judge calls in conclusion upon Procurator Terekhov to speak as state prosecutor.

SPEECH BY STATE PROSECUTOR

I do not intend to deliver an indictment and analyse all the arguments put forward by the defence. To do so, I would need six or seven hours at least. But if I leave out some things, it does not mean that I am in agreement with what the defence has said. Certain commentators have been writing that my silence in the court of first instance, after the speeches of the defence, signified my agreement with them. And so I should like to tell them beforehand that I do not agree with a single argument advanced by the defence.

The Procuracy of the Soviet Union has instructed me to make known that it considers the verdict brought in the case of Ginzburg, Galanskov, Dobrovolsky and Lashkova just and lawful with respect to all the convicted persons.

The defence have lodged appeals requesting that Ginzburg be acquitted, and the offences of the remaining defendants—Galanskov, Dobrovolsky and Lashkova—be reclassified under article 190-1 of the Russian Criminal Code. Let us go back and examine the evidence upon which the court of first instance based its decision.

The guilt of defendants Dobrovolsky and Lashkova is confirmed —leaving aside their frank confessions in court—by the testimony of witnesses, and also by the discovery in their possession of material evidence.

The charge brought against Ginzburg has been proven by the defendant's own admission that he compiled the collection relating to the Sinyavsky–Daniel affair, also known as *The White Book*, which includes two anti-Soviet documents, 'Letter to an Old Friend' and the leaflet signed 'Resistance'; by the testimony of Ginzburg and Lashkova to the effect that she typed this collection; and also by the testimony of Dobrovolsky that Ginzburg compiled the collection, and Galanskov handed it over for publication abroad with Ginzburg's knowledge and consent. Publication of this collection abroad is confirmed by the journal *Grani* No. 62, exhibited in this case. Participation of Ginzburg in work on the miscellany *Phoenix-'66*, compiled by Galanskov, is confirmed by the fact that one copy of it was removed from his flat during a search, by the testimony of Dobrovolsky that Ginzburg and Galanskov worked together on it, and by the testimony of Ginzburg himself that he read, in manuscript form, the 'Open Letter to Sholokhov' written by Galanskov and included by him in *Phoenix*.

The anti-Soviet nature of Ginzburg's activities is confirmed by the testimony of witness Brox-Sokolov that Slavinsky, an NTS activist, in a private conversation with him, referred to Ginzburg as one of those engaged in the anti-Soviet underground struggle in the Soviet Union, as well as by the testimony of witnesses Gubanov and Basilova that Ginzburg gave them several newspaper cuttings of anti-Soviet content taken from foreign papers which he had obtained in the summer of 1966 from a certain foreigner. The fact that Ginzburg did not know, or had only a slight knowledge of the languages in which these newspaper articles were written, does not prove anything, since he could have enlisted the help of persons who did know those languages. Ginzburg had ties with the espionage and intelligence organization NTS—for some reason or other the defence counsel modestly refer to it not as an espionage but as a foreign émigré organization; but espionage is the exact description, and it is supported by the CIA. Ginzburg's ties with the NTS are confirmed by the testimony of Dobrovolsky that Ginzburg put Galanskov in touch with this organization, and that they knew of the impending arrival in the USSR of Schaffhauser, an NTS emissary.

[*The Procurator goes on to repeat, without adducing further arguments, all the points in the verdict which relate to Galanskov, Dobrovolsky and Lashkova.*]

Now I should like to discuss two of the defence's arguments.

The defence says that all the main points in the indictment—ties with the NTS, and the handing over of *Phoenix* and *The White Book* for publication abroad—are based solely on the testimony of Dobrovolsky, and Dobrovolsky was repeatedly exposed as a liar during the preliminary investigation and the trial; consequently, we ought not to have taken his testimony as the basis for the indictment. Is this true? Was Dobrovolsky really exposed as a liar? Let us see.

Did the collection entitled *The White Book* find its way abroad? Yes. Is it the collection that Ginzburg compiled? Yes, it is. All the copies of the collection are exhibited in this case, and also issue No. 62 of the journal *Grani*, in which *The White Book*, including two anti-Soviet documents, 'Letter to an Old Friend' and the leaflet signed 'Resistance', was published. It is interesting to note that, as we know, this collection was typed in only five copies; Ginzburg tells us where four of them are, but he refuses to answer the question of the fifth. Perhaps it was this very copy that found its way abroad?

Now I should like to go on to what we might call the 'trump card' of the defence—the question of the date of the party at Potasheva's home, which, according to the defence, conflicts with Dobrovolsky's testimony, and with the findings of the investigation relating to the handing over of *The White Book* and the date upon which it occurred.

The court established that the party at Potasheva's home took place on 22 October 1966. According to Dobrovolsky, it was on that very day that Galanskov gave *The White Book* to Genrikh, an NTS emissary who had arrived in the USSR. Lashkova states that she completed the typing of the collection in November, immediately after the October Revolution celebrations of 1966 [*which take place on 7 November*]. The defence concludes that *The White Book* could not, therefore, have been handed over on 22 October, since it had not yet been typed. A curious argument. Here I have issue No. 61 of *Grani*. It says that a number of Western publishing houses have announced the impending publication of *The White Book*. Similar announcements appeared in many foreign newspapers too: on 23 November in Sweden and Italy; on 16 November in Switzerland; on 15 November in France, in the paper *Le Monde*; and on 3 November in Italy.

[*The Procurator goes on to list those foreign papers which published announcements about the imminent publication of* The White Book.]

These announcements are conflicting to the extreme: some say that Galanskov is the compiler of the collection, others—Ginzburg, and still others—a group of Moscow intellectuals. There are also many contradictions in their reports concerning the identity of the people to whom the compiler handed or sent it: Podgorny, Kosygin or others. Finally, the Procurator refers to a note in an Italian paper dating from 19 October, to the effect that a group of Moscow intellectuals had compiled a collection of materials on the Sinyavsky–Daniel case and sent it to Podgorny. From this, the Procurator draws the conclusion that the defence's arguments have no basis, and that the collection *The White Book* had been completed as early as 19 October, and could have been handed over for publication abroad on 22 October.

The Judge asks if the defence would like to explain any additional points.

ZOLOTUKHIN. Regarding the fact that in our speeches and appeals we call the NTS a foreign émigré organization, and not an espionage and intelligence organization, I should like to say that we are using the phrasing of the indictment and verdict. And concerning the handing over of the collection of materials on the Sinyavsky–Daniel case for publication abroad, I should like to draw your attention to two points.

Firstly, the prosecution in this appeal hearing makes wide use of material from the foreign press. I object to the use of evidence of this nature, because the reports given by foreign journalists are conflicting in the extreme and have no basis. Moreover, we cannot summon these journalists to the court and check where, when, and in what circumstances they obtained their information. Therefore, their reports cannot be used as evidence.

Secondly, about No. 62 of *Grani*. It is not *The White Book by Ginzburg* that is published there, but a few documents which were also included in Ginzburg's collection. Ginzburg himself testified during the investigation and at the trial that it was not he who wrote the text of the documents which went into the book—apart from his personal letter to Kosygin; they were circulating widely in Moscow. Moreover, a verbatim record of the trial of Sinyavsky and Daniel was published in *Grani* way back in No. 58. To return to *Grani* No. 62, I wish to state that in it are published only thirty-six of the 150 documents which went into *The White Book*.

PROCURATOR. But among those documents was the leaflet 'Resistance' and 'Letter to an Old Friend', and that is all that we are interested in.

ZOLOTUKHIN. And I am interested not only in that, but in the fate of Ginzburg, and in justice generally. And so, *Grani* published only thirty-six documents, and not *The White Book* compiled by Ginzburg, as the Procurator, begging his pardon, put it.

KAMINSKAYA. The court collegium established that the typing of *The White Book* was completed in November 1966, and we, of course, are using, and must use, precisely these facts and dates. They can only be challenged in instances when some new evidence has appeared. But in such cases procedural norms require that the verdict be declared incorrect and the case be remitted for further examination. I hope that the comrade Procurator is not pursuing such an aim.

Now a few words about the allegation that Galanskov was circulating anti-Soviet literature. According to the Procurator, this is confirmed by the testimony of Kats and Lashkova. I ask the court to verify, by examining the case materials, that during the entire course of the preliminary and judicial investigations all the witnesses testified that they had not received a single item of anti-Soviet material from Galanskov. I think that an error slipped into the Procurator's speech and I ask the court to take this into account.

SHVEISKY. Here, as in the court of first instance, a dispute has arisen once again about the correctness and the truthfulness of Dobrovolsky's testimony. As defence counsel for Dobrovolsky, I cannot voice an opinion on this point, because that would take me beyond the bounds of the charge brought against Dobrovolsky. Moreover, I would like to repeat that Dobrovolsky did indeed admit to having himself read, and given to others to read, literature of an anti-Soviet nature, but the court had no evidence of Dobrovolsky's intent in doing so, and therefore I am repeating my request that the conviction of my client under article 70 be altered to one under article 190-1 of the Russian Criminal Code.

JUDGE. The court will adjourn for consultation.

The court spends an hour and a half in consultation. Then it announces its ruling: the verdict of the court of first instance is upheld, and the appeals are unheeded.

APPENDICES

APPENDIX 1

Witness N. B. Brox-Sokolov

[*This appendix is omitted, the material on Brox-Sokolov being for the most part either irrelevant to the Ginzburg–Galanskov case, or already included in other parts of the present collection. The four documents reproduced by Litvinov are: 'In the KGB' (article in* Izvestia, *3 January 1968); 'The Depths' (*Izvestia, *9 January 1968); 'A Familiar Name' (*Izvestia, *10 July 1968); 'A Sabotage Enterprise and its Finale' (*Izvestia, *11 July 1968.*]

APPENDIX 2

Report to Amnesty International concerning my
journey to Moscow in connection with the trial of
Ginzburg, Galanskov, Dobrovolsky and Lashkova

*[By Ingjald Soerheim, lawyer and secretary to the
Norwegian Parliamentary Labour Party]**

PREPARATIONS

On Saturday, 6 January, I was asked by Amnesty, Norway, if I would
be willing to go to Moscow for the trial that was reported to start on
Monday 8th. I applied immediately for a visa at the Soviet Embassy
here and ordered tickets through Norsk Folkeferie/Intourist.

I applied for a *tourist visa* and stated as 'purpose of journey', 'cultural
and organizational/professional contacts'. I consulted in this with Professor Torkel Opsahl, who tried to make a journey in December when the
trial was first announced. He first applied for a visa as an observer, but
the reaction in the Soviet Embassy being that they could not give him a
status as such, he proceeded to apply for an ordinary tourist visa. It is
very important in our view that this was not refused—the journey did
not come about because Intourist did not confirm the ticket order. (It
was first confirmed, but the confirmation was withdrawn with the explanation that it was based on a 'mistake'.) From this we made the conclusion
that the question of whether or not it was possible to observe the trial as a
tourist was not answered by the Soviet authorities. In fact, they made a
remark to Professor Opsahl that the question about attending the trial
was a question to be discussed with the authorities concerned—in Moscow. So, our procedure was based on what happened to Professor Opsahl.
It is rather automatic to obtain a tourist visa, and it was granted in the
afternoon (3.00 p.m. Oslo time) of Tuesday, 9 January, my air ticket was
ordered for Wednesday 10th at 12.50 p.m.

Amnesty International made a press statement in the afternoon of the
9th (enclosed)—about twenty hours before my departure from Oslo. We
wanted to make it quite clear before I left that my purpose was to attend
the trial and to obtain information about it.

Wednesday morning at 10.30 I had a telephone call from Mr Lebedev

* The original English-language text is given here, which Litvinov translated into
Russian. Ed.

376

who handles visa matters in the Soviet Embassy here. He was angry and said I had misinformed them about the journey. I protested at this and said that the statements in my application covered my purpose. I told him that I planned to discuss the possibilities of attending the trial with the authorities in Moscow on my arrival there. He told me that I went to the Soviet Union 'as a tourist and on a tourist visa'. I asked if this meant that it was incompatible with the status of a tourist to make contact with the judicial authorities in order to attend the trial and obtain information about it. I asked five or six times if he would state concretely what this meant—could I or could I not make such contacts being a tourist? He just repeated the answer 'you go as a tourist and on a tourist visa'.

It became clear that he had no authority to discuss this with me, and so we finished the conversation. He also told me that 'the trial is going to end today' (Wednesday). I asked if the radio message to that effect (Wednesday morning by AP) was correct and he confirmed this.

I will stress that the telephone call from the Soviet Embassy here was the only occasion where Soviet authorities put forward the question of my visa application. I have mentioned this for [*the interest of*] people here and some of the correspondents in Moscow, who think the purpose of the call was to have the back free for the Embassy people in case criticism should come from Moscow afterwards. The other purpose was, of course, to give a motive for me not to go at all.

As you will remember, we consulted with you on the telephone and decided to go.

THE STAY IN MOSCOW

Wednesday. I arrived in Moscow at 8.05 p.m., Wednesday, 10 January. There were no problems with the passport control. The customs officer made a very thorough search of my luggage, which consisted of clothes and three dictionaries and no literature of a controversial nature. I had been so cautious as not even to bring my copy of the RSFSR Penal Code, as it was in English, with an introduction by an American professor. None of the other passengers were searched, as far as I could observe. The search took place in a relaxed atmosphere and was the only incident in my connection with the authorities that can be described as unpleasant. I went to the Hotel Russia, where I stayed the three nights I was in Moscow.

Thursday. I went to Moscow City Court (Kalanchevskaya Ulitsa 43) in the morning. I brought the letter of accreditation from Mr Haaland on behalf of Amnesty International and a letter of introduction from the Norwegian Lawyers Association. The main entrance of the building was closed, and the guards told me to enter from the rear. I then came into a corridor of a wing of the building; the trial took place in the other wing. There was no communication between the wings, the corridor being barred with guards. It was not possible to see the entrance of the courtroom from the corridor in the open wing.

Before luncheon (2.00 p.m.), I made several attempts to establish contact with the presidency of the court and the judge, but without success. The clerks told me that the presidents all were in a session in the 'Presidium' (assembly of presidents). Between my attempts, I stayed in the corridor where the foreign correspondents and the public waited as well. The correspondents (up to twenty in number) told me that the Russians waiting there were some friends and relatives of the defendants, but the majority were—in their opinion—from the security police (KGB, which stands for: Committee for State Security). Their tasks seemed to be three: to watch what was going on in the corridor, to inform about the trial and to engage the attendants [*i.e. the defendants' friends*] in discussions. I was soon approached by a group of them. They behaved rather provocatively in the attempt to start a discussion with me; they asked me about myself and my opinion about the case. My reply was, of course, that I was not able to have an opinion as long as I was not admitted into the courtroom. They pressed the point, that I must have an opinion from what I had heard, but I insisted on my answer. Their questions showed that they were very well briefed about my person and my task. There was a photographer in the corridor (on Friday there were two) who took pictures of me several times, whenever new people talked to me. I was photographed from two-three metres range—no attempts were made to conceal the photographing.

After the luncheon, the typist in the President's office told me that the Vice-President Almazov was the man to ask for a permission card. I waited fifteen minutes in his office and was received by him and another Vice-President, Ryazhsky. The conversation lasted for about twenty minutes and was conducted in a polite but formal atmosphere. They answered in the affirmative the question whether the trial was open, but they said the courtroom was so crowded that it was impossible to get an admission card. This was the *only argument* I met. They stressed how very much they would have liked to help me, and regretted that this was not possible. It was Almazov that talked; Ryazhsky was silent except for some side-comments: 'Oh yes, it has been so crowded that I haven't been able to attend the last days myself.' I pressed very hard that I was probably the only foreign lawyer present, so it would have no practical consequences to let me in. I also argued along this line: some Russians say that the trial is reported in a biased manner by foreign correspondents. It would, therefore, be in the interest of the Soviet authorities to let me give an objective report. But Almazov only repeated that the day of the trial had come too late to our knowledge. I underlined the ideas and work of Amnesty and that my only purpose was to obtain the maximum of objective information about the trial and the defendants. He had no reactions to this.

The conversation ended—rather surprisingly—with Almazov taking my letters of introduction and accreditation, saying: 'I will try to see the judge, he is the only one who can make an exception for you.' He returned forty-five minutes later and said that the judge was too busy to consider my case. Almazov seemed very upset, but remained correct. I said that I was willing to wait for any opportunity to see the judge. I made several attempts through the office of the court, but was not able to establish contacts with the Judge Mironov.

Friday. I was at the courthouse twenty minutes before the proceedings were to start (10.00 a.m.), but was told that the trial had started earlier that day. The judge was occupied. Throughout the day I had numerous contacts with the administration of the court, the police, the Vice-Presidents I had met on Thursday, but it was not possible to talk to the judge, although I was told that there were several recesses. I even stayed in the courthouse during lunch time, but all in vain. I did not try to engage other channels, as for instance the Supreme Court of the RSFSR. There was no judicial decision for me to appeal [*against*], the only reason given was of a practical nature which evidently is not subject to revision by the higher court. Furthermore did the correspondents as well as others believe that the decision to close the courtroom had been taken on a very high political level, and that it was not subject to discussion. Another reason was that I would not take the chance to leave the courthouse and be told afterwards that 'when we decided to let you in, you were gone'.

At the end of the day I witnessed the relatives coming out from the main entrance after the sentence had been passed; according to the prosecutor the sentences were—Galanskov seven years, Ginzburg five years, Dobrovolsky two years and Lashkova one year. The scenes that occurred were very moving. Galanskov's wife had a broken leg and was carried to a taxi by Pavel Litvinov (who published a very strong protest against the trial together with the wife of Yuly Daniel) and the son of the sentenced writer Yuly Daniel. She seemed to be in a trance—she did not react to greetings from gathered friends. After her departure, the silence in the ice-cold evening (minus 25 degrees centigrade) was broken by the sobbing cries of an old woman—Galanskov's mother. She was also taken into a taxi and disappeared. The crowd (about 200) slowly dissolved.

Saturday. I started the day with telephone calls to the other judicial organs I had planned to contact in order to obtain information about the case. I soon found out that the offices were all closed on Saturday, and decided to go home that day instead of Monday morning as planned.

I left Moscow at 5.30 p.m. and there were no problems at the departure.

It was the evening newspaper—*Vechernyaya Moskva* [Evening Moscow] that brought the first news about the trial to the Soviet public. In a very short notice the names and the sentences were mentioned; it also said that they were sentenced for anti-Soviet activities.

OTHER CONTACTS

I avoided contact with individual citizens. I was watched all the time and thought it would serve the purpose of the trip and that of Amnesty best if I behaved strictly correctly—turning to the official organs in charge.

The Trial of the Four

REACTIONS OF SOVIET AUTHORITIES

In addition to what has already been stated, I would like to stress that I met *no argument against Amnesty* and its activities. The argument was practical—no space in the courtroom.

PUBLICITY

My journey was given wide coverage by press, radio and TV here. I was interviewed three times on the radio, [*plus*] a direct TV broadcast at the beginning of the evening news the night I returned; the Swedish TV interviewed me at Stockholm airport. Several newspapers had editorials about the trial, regretting and condemning the fact that the Amnesty representative was not admitted into the courtroom. The papers all condemned the harsh sentences.

Amnesty, Norway, will send you a publicity report.

I stressed the aims and ideas of Amnesty on every occasion, and the purpose of my journey.

WHAT TO DO NOW?

It is not easy to give suggestions. One obvious thing would be in my opinion to demand a *full report* of the trial, the accusations, the proceedings (in stenograms), the character of the sentence to be served, appeal possibilities, etc.

It is interesting that the accusation of currency speculation seems to have been dropped during the trial. It is difficult to advise you on the question of protest. There is very little information about the trial, the evidence, etc., but even if it was established that there had been a link with an organization like the NTS, the sentences are very hard; it is difficult to see how small groups of that type can represent a substantial threat to the Soviet State. Whether protests could have any effect is difficult to say, as it is to judge what the effects of protests would be on future possibilities for Amnesty in the Soviet Union. I am sorry that I am not able to give you advice on this point. But as I have pointed out, Amnesty was not attacked during my stay in the USSR or by the embassy people here.

SOME COMMENTS ON THE BACKGROUND

The trial against four young Soviet citizens, Ginzburg, Galanskov, Dobrovolsky and Lashkova, was first expected to take place in Moscow towards the end of 1967, but was postponed to 8 January. Little is known in detail about the accusations, it goes under the general label 'anti-Soviet activities', RSFSR Penal Code art. 70. Ginzburg is known to be accused of participating in the publishing in West Germany of *The White Book* about the Sinyavsky–Daniel case. Galanskov is accused of preparing and publishing a mimeographed periodical *Phoenix, 66*. Dobrovolsky and Lashkova were charged with assisting them in their activities, which the prosecutor claimed also included contact with émigré organizations like the NTS, and spreading of material from these. Lashkova's contribution is said to include the typing work. Dobrovolsky acted as a witness for the prosecution during the trial.

In articles after the trial (in the *Literary Gazette* and the government newspaper *Izvestia*) there are attempts to ridicule the defendants as writers or intellectuals, saying that they have not published anything in the Soviet Union. (If they are sentenced for what they have written, said or done in connection with publications in other countries it is difficult to see the relevance of this.)

Article 70 has a maximum penalty of seven years, which was the sentence given to Galanskov as well as to Sinyavsky more than a year ago. This trial was the fourth of known trials against intellectuals in a period of a year and a half. The earlier were the Sinyavsky–Daniel case, the Bukovsky case and the case against a group in Leningrad that was interested in religious philosophy. Some of the correspondents I met in Moscow saw these cases (as well as other events) as indications of a colder climate in the internal life of the Soviet Union. In this connection, it ought to be mentioned that liberalization has not come so far as to permit other foreign newspapers to be sold in the USSR than the communist ones. It is interesting that trials like these come to be known to the Soviet public, and still more interesting that protests occur against them. (Like the demonstrations outside the court and the publication, not in the USSR, of a protest like that of Litvinov and Mrs Daniel.) It is very difficult, indeed, to think of events like that during the Stalin period, where people simply disappeared.*

* Attached to the report is the appeal by Larissa Bogoraz and Pavel Litvinov *To World Public Opinion.* [*See p.* 225.]

APPENDIX 3

A Press Conference which did not take place

Report by A. A. Amalrik

On 19 January 1968 at the home of Mrs L. I. Ginzburg, there was to have been a meeting of foreign correspondents in Moscow with Alexander Ginzburg's mother, Mrs L. I. Ginzburg, and Yury Galanskov's wife, Miss O. V. Timofeyeva, at which Mrs Ginzburg and Miss Timofeyeva were to have given an account of the recently ended trial to the correspondents. However, because of intervention by the press department of the Soviet Ministry of Foreign Affairs, the meeting did not take place. The compiler of this collection requested A. A. Amalrik, who was at Mrs Ginzburg's home on that day, to inform him of everything he knew about the circumstances of this meeting which did not take place.

To: P. M. Litvinov,
Moscow, ul. Alekseya Tolstogo 8, kv. 78

Dear Pavel Mikhailovich,
In reply to your request that I tell you what I know about the meeting (which was never held) between Ginzburg's mother, Galanskov's wife and foreign journalists, I can give you the following information:

I have known Alexander Ginzburg's mother, Lyudmila Ilinichna Ginzburg, for many years, and I paid frequent calls on her during her son's investigation and trial. On 19 January 1968 I called on her at about eleven o'clock in the morning and found there Yury Galanskov's wife, Olga Timofeyeva. Both women were extremely agitated and were putting on warm clothes to go somewhere. I asked what was happening. They replied that they were expecting some foreign correspondents to arrive towards eleven on that day, and they intended to tell them about the circumstances of the trial of their son and husband. But they said that at 9.30 an assistant Procurator of Moscow's October District, P. P. Smekalkin, had arrived unexpectedly, told them that he knew of the impending meeting, which he referred to as a press-conference, and said that under Soviet law private individuals were forbidden to hold press-conferences in their own homes. He suggested that L. I. Ginzburg and O. Timofeyeva should go outside on to the street and meet the journalists there. And so they were dressing up to go outside. I asked if they were not afraid that P. P. Smekalkin wished thus to provoke them into causing some sort of street disturbance, in view of the possible traffic obstruction which might ensue, all the more so since the journalists would be arriving in cars. If this happened, the KGB agents could easily create a crowd and the semblance of disorder, and that would give them the opportunity to bring charges against L. I. Ginzburg and O. Timofeyeva under article 190-3 of the Russian Criminal Code. I advised them not to go out of the house, especially as there is in reality no such law as the one to which Smekalkin had referred. Then Mrs Ginzburg and Miss Timofeyeva decided to stay in the house, but they asked me too not to leave, in case of possible new provocations.

I asked them what they intended to talk about. They answered: about the circumstances of the investigation and trial, the numerous procedural violations and the fact that they had not been allowed to take notes in court. They intended also to refute the slanderous fabrications about their husband and son which had appeared in *Izvestia* and *Komsomolskaya Pravda*. I noticed that lying on the table were copies of the official records of searches conducted at Ginzburg's and Galanskov's homes, and also theatre programmes of productions in which Ginzburg had acted and diplomas awarded to him for his victories in sporting competitions.

At eleven o'clock a man came into the room and said he was one of the foreign correspondents invited to the press-conference. Because no one knew him or had invited him, and his appearance was suspicious, I asked him to show his journalist's identity card. He turned out to be an official of the Ministry of Internal Affairs' diplomatic corps service department [*UPDK*], V. Gritsan, who was attached to Associated Press as a photographer. However, as he had come alone, I suspected that he was not only a photographer but a KGB agent too, and with the consent of Mrs Ginzburg I asked him to leave, saying that there would be no press-conference. He looked pleased and said that he had, in fact, come to 'drop a hint' that they should not hold a press-conference, and he suggested that we should 'work out a formula' together, which he would take at once and release to the press. I replied that no one needed his hints; he should not release anything to anyone, but simply leave. After that, he left.

However, none of the journalists came. A neighbour dropped in to say that from her window she could see some people standing outside the house and turning back foreign correspondents' cars as they arrived. From our window we could see a few men walking up and down the courtyard below, looking like KGB agents. More than half an hour passed thus. I advised O. Timofeyeva to telephone one of the foreign news agencies and enquire if anyone would be coming. She rang Reuter's and asked why no one had come. The Reuter correspondent apologized and explained that the press department of the Ministry of Foreign Affairs had warned them and also other foreign correspondents in Moscow that if they went to L. I. Ginzburg's flat there would be 'grave unpleasantnesses'.

A little later, Mrs Ginzburg went shopping to buy something to eat with coffee and some fish for her cat. According to her, there were by that time no more foreign cars outside the house, but a considerable number of KGB cars were parked there, and also she was trailed by several agents while she did her shopping. After some coffee I sat there for about an hour longer and then went home. By then there were no cars outside Mrs Ginzburg's house, nor did I notice anyone trailing me.

Moscow G-2, Vakhtangova ul. 5, kv. 5   Andrei Amalrik
1 February 1968

APPENDIX 4

The 'Church' leaflet and related material

In June 1968 two independent attempts were made by foreign citizens to distribute in Moscow material in defence of political prisoners, among them Galanskov and Ginzburg.

On 6 June a Belgian, Roger de Bie, attempted to distribute a petition by the Flemish Action Committee for Eastern Europe [*Vlaams Aktiekomitee Voor Oost-Europa*] in defence of political prisoners in the USSR and leaflets with pictures of Galanskov and Ginzburg. He was expelled from the Soviet Union and the episode went almost unnoticed. More attention was attracted by another attempt. On 17 June three English people, Marian Janette Hammond, John Vivian Broughton and Peter John Careswell, tried to hand out a leaflet from the organization 'Church' which demanded the release of political prisoners in the USSR. All three were expelled from the Soviet Union also.

There follows below the text of the 'Church' leaflet and also an article from *Izvestia* and an item from the typescript journal *Human Rights Year in the Soviet Union* [:*A Chronicle of Current Events*] concerning the event.[112]

Document 1*

FREEDOM for GALANSKOV!

FREEDOM for the BAPTISTS!

FREEDOM for ALL the POLITICAL PRISONERS in the USSR!

[photos of Galanskov and Bertrand Russell with captions]

In recent years many of us in the West, who share the desire of the Soviet people to find a more humane and just alternative to the capitalist system of exploitation, have been saddened by the repressive actions taken by your great country against a small group of young writers and poets, whose only crime has been to assert that the concept of socialist justice contains within it the right to free experimentation with political and creative ideas, even if they are wrong ones.

We believe that justice and freedom are the indispensable bases of a great society, and that they depend on each other. It is clear to you and us that the capitalist system is founded on freedom without justice, and consequently there is not enough of either the one or the other. Events

* Text abbreviated, especially in places where Document 3 (below) reproduces it in full. Ed.

in the Soviet Union after the revolutions show that a powerful élite tried to create socialist justice without freedom. The only possible result of such a course is the absence not only of freedom but of justice too.

This simple truth became obvious in all its horror at the trial . . . which began in Moscow on 8 January 1968. This trial was a mockery of justice, involving violation of basic Soviet legal norms. We want to draw your attention to the statement by Larissa Bogoraz . . . and Pavel Litvinov . . . issued during the trial: [*Extracts follow—see Document III: 2*]

POLITICAL PRISONERS

[*Biographical notes on Sinyavsky, Daniel, Galanskov, Ginzburg and Bukovsky omitted here*]

Apart from these writers, we also know about 90 Ukrainian intellectuals, sentenced mainly in 1965 to long terms for demanding that level of cultural and political autonomy for the Ukraine which is guaranteed by the Soviet constitution. We have no further information about them.

The PERSECUTION of CHRISTIANS

Writers and intellectuals are not the only minority in the Soviet Union to prefer penal servitude to compromise with their conscience. At present about 200 Baptists are in prison for their faith. Some sections of the criminal code . . . are not, in their opinion, compatible with a Christian way of life, moreover (and this must interest ordinary Soviet citizens more) they contradict (1) a fundamental principle of the Soviet constitution [*the separation of church and state*] and (2) the Universal Declaration of Human Rights. . . .

By definition Christians are in the first instance subject to a supreme authority standing beyond any man-made authority. Thus any Christian may face the dilemma—to obey the law, or the command of conscience? Such a dilemma has arisen for many people throughout history. As you read these lines thousands of young and brave Americans are disobeying the law, preferring imprisonment to participation in the amoral war in Vietnam. . . .

STATEMENT by BERTRAND RUSSELL
[*See Document 3 below*]
WHO ARE WE?

. . . In January of this year we, like most of our comrades, were shocked by the Moscow trial . . . and demanded the immediate release of those convicted. *That is our demand now too, as these brave people are still in prison. A shameful stain will lie for ever on the Russian people if justice and freedom do not triumph in the Soviet Union.*

Document 2 [*abbreviated*]

CATCALLS FOR A FARCE ON MAYAKOVSKY SQUARE

. . . The 'tourists' said they were members of the organization 'Church', which is an alliance of churchgoers and anarchists, and that they had come to the Soviet Union especially to stage an anti-Soviet demonstration on one of the central Moscow squares. For this purpose they had secretly conveyed across the frontier 300 leaflets printed in England.

From the 'tourists' ' testimony it is clear that the circulation of leaflets was only a part of their plan. Upon arrival in Moscow they immediately contacted accredited American and English journalists there and informed them of the time and place of the impending provocation. In the naïve hope that their venture would be successful, the young Britons supposed that the Western journalists would manage to photograph a 'manifestation' which they calculated would attract the support of Muscovites. Not for nothing were they decked out in T-shirts covered with slogans in Russian. In that form it was important to get in front of a camera lens, surrounded by a 'crowd of sympathizers'. But how can one tell from a picture if people are sympathizers or not? The publication of these shots was to be the signal for a new anti-Soviet campaign in the bourgeois Western press.

But the organizers of the 'demonstration' met with bitter disappointment. Passers-by speedily put them in their place. . . .

. . . Their escapade was meant to play into the hands of groups hostile to our country and our people. Whether they liked it or not, Broughton, Careswell and Hammond were tools in the hands of people like Peter Reddaway[113] and those behind him, people who do not scruple to use any means in their struggle against the Land of the Soviets. . . .

Izvestia, 21 June 1968   M. Melasov

Document 3

'CHURCH' LEAFLET ON MAYAKOVSKY SQUARE

At six o'clock on the evening of 17 June, in Moscow's Mayakovsky Square, three young Britons made an attempt to hand out a leaflet calling for freedom for Soviet political prisoners. The young people, Janette Hammond, aged 20, John Careswell, aged 21, and Vivian Broughton, aged 25, were detained by representatives of the security organs and on the following day deported from the Soviet Union. They are members of the youth organization 'Church'. Formed a year ago, the organization is an alliance of Christian radicals, Marxists and anarchists. It is known for its many street demonstrations against American aggression in Vietnam. In January,[114] after the Moscow trial, its members organized a six-hour demonstration outside the Soviet Embassy in London.

The 'Church' leaflet is in no way of an anti-Soviet nature. Both the declaration it includes by Bertrand Russell and the words of the leaflet's authors themselves express the regret and anxiety felt by many friends of our country in the face of the repressive measures being taken in the Soviet Union against freedom of speech and conscience. The leaflet opens with pictures of Yury Galanskov and Lord Bertrand Russell and the slogans:

'FREEDOM FOR GALANSKOV! FREEDOM FOR THE BAPTISTS! FREEDOM FOR ALL POLITICAL PRISONERS IN THE USSR!' The leaflet contains brief informatory notes on five political prisoners—Andrei Sinyavsky, Yuly Daniel, Yury Galanskov, Alexander Ginzburg and Vladimir Bukovsky, and on the persecution of Baptists in the USSR. There is also an extract from the appeal 'To World Public Opinion' by Larissa Bogoraz and Pavel Litvinov, and the declaration by Bertrand Russell. The declaration follows, in slightly abbreviated form:

'There is an influential body of people in the West which is always ready to condemn as wicked anything that happens in the Soviet Union, whilst at the same time boasting of the "liberty" and "democracy" enjoyed in the so-called Free World. Such people live in a black-and-white world and show no willingness to judge questions on their merits. Those of us in the West who have struggled over the years against these Cold Warriors have welcomed the enormous changes in the Soviet Union in recent years, changes which have undoubtedly led to greater human happiness and freedom. These admirable developments are endangered by the mock trial just held in Moscow. So intolerably unjust were the procedures of the court that even the official journal of the British Communist Party felt compelled to publish its criticisms. The Soviet writers should be retried before an open court.'

Earlier, on 6 June, Roger de Bie, a representative of the Flemish Action Committee for Eastern Europe, handed out at the Arbatskaya underground station a petition by the committee calling for the release of political prisoners, and postcards with pictures of them. He too was detained and deported.

On 23 June Larissa Bogoraz and Pavel Litvinov made the following statement: 'We are deeply touched by the bold action of the three young Britons who openly demonstrated in defence of human rights in the Soviet Union. A few months ago we became convinced that our protest had evoked a response among leading cultural figures in Europe and America. We found this a tremendous moral support. Now we are overjoyed to see from the example of the Flemish and English [*demonstrators*] that progressive Western young people too understand the meaning of our struggle.'

Human Rights Year in the Soviet Union: a Chronicle
of Current Events, No. 2, 30 June 1968

APPENDIX 5

Criminal Code and Code of Criminal Procedure of the Russian Republic. Articles referred to in the text*

CRIMINAL CODE OF THE RUSSIAN REPUBLIC

Article 64. Treason.

(*a*) Treason, that is, an act intentionally committed by a citizen of the USSR to the detriment of the state independence, the territorial inviolability, or the military might of the USSR; defection to the side of the enemy, espionage, transmission of a state or military secret to a foreign state, flight abroad or refusal to return from abroad to the USSR, rendering aid to a foreign state in carrying on hostile activity against the USSR, or a conspiracy with the aim of seizing power, shall be punished by deprivation of freedom for a term of ten to fifteen years with confiscation of property, with or without additional exile for a term of two to five years, or by death with confiscation of property.

(*b*) A citizen of the USSR recruited by a foreign intelligence service for carrying on hostile activity against the USSR, shall not be subject to criminal responsibility if he has committed no actions in execution of the criminal assignment received by him and has voluntarily reported to agencies of authority his connection with the foreign intelligence service.

Article 69. Wrecking.

An action or omission to act directed toward the subversion of industry, transport, agriculture, the monetary system, trade, or other branches of the national economy, or the activity of state agencies or social organizations for the purpose of weakening the Soviet state, if such act is committed by making use of state or social institutions, enterprises, or organizations, or by obstructing their normal work, shall be punished by deprivation of freedom for a term of eight to fifteen years with confiscation of property, with or without additional exile for a term of two to five years.

* The text of the articles is taken from *Criminal Code of the RSFSR. Official text, as amended to 16 September 1966,* published by Yuridicheskaya Literatura, Moscow, 1966, and *Code of Criminal Procedure of the RSFSR. Official text with amendments to 23 June 1967,* published by Yuridicheskaya Literatura, Moscow, 1967. References to date of introduction of certain articles in their present amended form have been omitted throughout. The articles of the Code of Criminal Procedure referred to in Document IV: 27 have not been included, only because that document contains extensive quotations from the articles in question. [The translations used here are taken from H. J. Berman and J. V. Spindler, *Soviet Criminal Law and Procedure—the RSFSR Codes,* Cambridge, Mass., 1966. Ed.].

Article 70. Anti-Soviet agitation and propaganda.*

Agitation or propaganda carried on for the purpose of subverting or weakening Soviet power or of committing particular especially dangerous crimes against the state, or circulating for the same purpose slanderous fabrications which defame the Soviet state and social system, or circulating or preparing or keeping, for the same purpose, literature of such content, shall be punished by deprivation of freedom for a term of six months to seven years, with or without additional exile for a term of two to five years, or by exile for a term of two to five years.

The same actions committed by a person previously convicted of especially dangerous crimes against the state, or committed in wartime shall be punished by deprivation of freedom for a term of three to ten years, with or without additional exile for a term of two to five years.

Article 72. Organizational activity directed to commission of especially dangerous crimes against the state and also participation in anti-Soviet organizations.

Organizational activity directed to the preparation or commission of especially dangerous crimes against the state, or to the creation of an organization which has as its purpose the commission of such crimes, or participation in an anti-Soviet organization, shall be punished in accordance with articles 64-71 of the present Code.†

Article 88. Violation of rules on currency transactions.

Violations of rules on currency transactions, or speculation in currency or securities, shall be punished by deprivation of freedom for a term of three to eight years, with or without confiscation of property, with obligatory confiscation of the currency and securities, with or without additional exile for a term of two to five years.

Speculation in currency or securities as a form of business or on a large scale, or violation of rules on currency transactions by a person previously convicted under paragraph one of the present article, shall be punished by deprivation of freedom for a term of five to fifteen years with confiscation of property, with or without additional exile for a term of two to five years, or by death with confiscation of property.

Article 171. Exceeding authority or official powers.

Exceeding authority or official powers, that is, the intentional commission by an official of actions clearly exceeding the limits of rights and powers granted to him by law, thereby causing substantial harm to state or social interests or to legally protected rights and interests of citizens, shall be punished by deprivation of freedom for a term not exceeding three years, or by corrective labour for a term not exceeding one year, or by dismissal from office.

Exceeding authority or official powers, if accompanied by force, by use of weapons, or by actions which torment the victim and insult his personal

* This article is equivalent to article 58-10 in the 1926 Criminal Code of the Russian Republic.

† The articles defining 'especially dangerous crimes against the state'.

dignity, shall be punished by deprivation of freedom for a term not exceeding ten years.

Article 181. Knowingly giving false testimony.

The giving of testimony, known to be false, by a witness or by the victim, or of an opinion known to be false, by an expert, or of a translation by an interpreter which he knows to be incorrect and which is made by the interpreter in court or in the conduct of a preliminary investigation or enquiry, shall be punished by deprivation of freedom for a term not exceeding one year, or by corrective labour for the same term.

The same actions combined with an accusation of an especially dangerous crime against the state, or any other grave crime, or with artificially created proof of the accusation, or committed for a mercenary purpose, shall be punished by deprivation of freedom for a term of two to seven years.

Article 182. Refusal or evasion by witness or victim to give testimony, or by expert to give opinion.

The refusal or evasion by a witness or victim to give testimony or by an expert to give an opinion in a judicial session or in the conduct of a preliminary investigation or enquiry, or obstructing the appearance of a witness or victim or the giving of testimony by him, shall be punished by corrective labour for a term not exceeding six months, or by a fine not exceeding fifty roubles, or by social censure.

Article 190-1*. Dissemination of knowingly false fabrications discrediting the Soviet political and social system.

The systematic dissemination by word of mouth of knowingly false fabrications discrediting the Soviet political and social system, or the manufacture or dissemination in written, printed or other form of works of the same content, shall be punished by deprivation of freedom for a term not exceeding three years, or by corrective labour for a term not exceeding one year, or by a fine not exceeding one hundred roubles.

Article 190-3*. Organization of or active participation in group activities violating the public order.

The organization of, or active participation in group activities which grossly violate the public order or involve clear disregard for the legal demands of representatives of authority, or lead to a disruption of transport, or in the work of state or public institutions or enterprises, shall be punished by deprivation of freedom for a term not exceeding three years, or by corrective labour for a term not exceeding one year, or by a fine not exceeding one hundred roubles.

Article 196. Forging, manufacturing, or supplying forged documents, stamps, seals, forms.

Forging a certificate or any other document issued by a state institution or enterprise or public organization, which grants a right or a release from duties, for the purpose of utilization of such document by the forger

* Not included in Berman and Spindler edition, as these articles were added only in 1966. Ed.

himself or by another person, or supplying such a document, or making forged stamps, seals, and forms of state institutions or enterprises or public organizations for the same purposes, or supplying them, shall be punished by deprivation of freedom for a term not exceeding two years, or by corrective labour for a term not exceeding one year.

The same actions committed systematically shall be punished by deprivation of freedom for a term not exceeding five years, or by exile for the same term.

Using a document known to be forged shall be punished by deprivation of freedom for a term not exceeding one year, or by corrective labour for the same term, or by a fine not exceeding thirty roubles.

Article 198. Violation of passport rules.

The malicious violation of passport rules in localities where special rules of residence or registration have been introduced, if such violation takes the form of residence without a passport or without registration, and if the person has already twice previously been subjected to an administrative penalty for such violation, shall be punished by deprivation of freedom for a term not exceeding one year, or by corrective labour for the same term, or by a fine not exceeding fifty roubles.

CODE OF CRIMINAL PROCEDURE OF THE RUSSIAN REPUBLIC

Article 13. Administration of justice only by courts.

Justice in criminal cases shall be administrated only by courts. No one may be deemed guilty of committing a crime and subjected to criminal punishment except by the verdict of a court.

Article 18. Publicity of judicial examination.

The examination of cases in all courts shall be open, except in instances when this contradicts the interests of protecting a state secret.

In addition, a closed judicial examination shall be permitted, upon a reasoned ruling of the court, in cases of crimes of persons who have not attained the age of sixteen years, cases of sexual crimes, or other cases for the purpose of preventing the divulgence of information about intimate aspects of the lives of persons participating in the case.

The verdicts of courts shall in all cases be announced publicly.

Article 59. Circumstances barring judge from participating in consideration of criminal case.

A judge may not participate in the consideration of a case:

(1) if he is a victim, civil plaintiff, civil defendant, or witness, or if he has participated in the given case as an expert, specialist, interpreter, person conducting the enquiry, investigator, accuser, defence counsel, legal representative of the accused, representative of the victim, civil plaintiff, or civil defendant;

(2) if he is a relative of the victim, of the civil plaintiff, of the civil defendant or of their representatives, a relative of the accused or of his

legal representative, a relative of the accuser, of defence counsel, of the investigator, or of the person conducting the enquiry;

(3) if there are any other circumstances giving grounds to believe that the judge is personally interested in the case, directly or indirectly.

Persons related to each other may not be members of a court that is considering a criminal case.

Article 135. Participation of witnesses of investigative actions.

In an inspection, search, seizure, examination, or other investigative action, in instances provided for by the present Code, witnesses of investigative actions shall be summoned. At least two witnesses of investigative actions shall be summoned.

Any citizens not interested in a case may be summoned as witnesses of investigative actions.

A witness of investigative actions shall be obliged to certify the fact, contents and results of an action at which he has been present. A witness of investigative actions shall have the right to make remarks in connection with an action. Remarks of a witness of investigative actions shall be subject to being entered in the record of a particular investigative action.

Before the commencement of an investigative action in which witnesses of investigative actions participate, the investigator shall explain to them their rights and duties.

Article 169. Persons present during seizure and search.

The presence of witnesses of investigative actions shall be obligatory during the conduct of a seizure or search.

The presence of the person at whose dwelling-place a search or seizure is conducted, or of adult members of his family, must be secured during the search or seizure. In the event that it is impossible for them to be present, representatives of the management of the apartment house or of the executive committee of the rural or settlement Soviet of workers' deputies shall be invited.

Seizures or searches on premises occupied by institutions, enterprises or organizations shall be conducted in the presence of a representative of the given institution, enterprise or organization.

Persons at whose dwelling-place a search or seizure is conducted, witnesses of investigative actions, and representatives must be informed of their right to be present at all the actions of the investigator and to make statements pertaining to such actions for entry in the record.

Article 170. Procedure for conducting seizure and search.

It shall not be permitted to conduct seizure or search at night, except in instances not permitting delay. In undertaking a seizure or search, an investigator shall be obliged to present a warrant to such effect.

Where necessary an investigator shall have the right to summon an appropriate specialist to participate in the conduct of the seizure or search.

When conducting a search after presentation of a warrant, the investigator shall propose that the instruments of the crime, articles and valuables criminally acquired, or other articles or documents which might be of

393

significance for the case, be given up. If they are given up voluntarily and there are no grounds to fear the concealment of the articles and documents being sought, the investigator shall have the right to limit himself to removing what has been given up without conducting further explorations.

When conducting search and seizure, the investigator shall have the right to open locked premises and store-rooms if the owner refuses to open them voluntarily, but the investigator must avoid unnecessary damage to locks, doors and other articles.

The investigator shall be obliged to take measures to prevent the public disclosure of circumstances of the intimate life of the person occupying the premises, or of other persons, which are revealed during a search or seizure.

The investigator shall have the right to prohibit persons in the premises or place where the search is being conducted, as well as persons arriving at the premises or place, from leaving it or from communicating with one another or with any other persons until the completion of the search.

Article 171. Removal of articles and documents during seizure and search.

When conducting seizure and search an investigator must strictly limit himself to removing articles and documents which may have a relation to the case. Articles and documents prohibited from circulation shall be subject to removal regardless of their relation to the case.

All the removed articles and documents shall be presented to the witnesses of investigative actions and to other persons present and when necessary shall be packed and sealed at the place of the seizure or search.

Article 176. Record of seizure, search, impounding of property.

A record of a seizure, search, or impounding of property shall be drawn up in conformity with the requirements of articles 141 and 142 of the present Code. If, in addition to the records, a special inventory is drawn up of articles and documents removed or transferred for special safekeeping, the inventory shall be appended to the record. The record of the seizure, search, or impounding of property must contain an indication that the rights provided by article 169 of the present Code were explained to the persons present, and the statements made by them.

With respect to articles and documents subject to removal, it must be indicated whether they have been given up voluntarily or removed compulsorily, and in exactly what place and under what circumstances they were discovered. All the articles and documents removed as well as all the property inventoried must be enumerated in the record or the inventory appended to it, with a precise indication of quantity, size, weight, or individual indicia and, as far as possible, their value.

If in the seizure, inventory or impounding of property there have been attempts to destroy or hide articles and documents, or instances of breach of order on the part of the persons being searched or other persons, the record must contain an indication thereof and of the measures taken by the investigator.

Article 177. Obligation to hand over copy of record.

A copy of the record shall be handed to, and a receipt obtained from, the person at whose dwelling-place the seizure, search, or impounding of property has been conducted, or adult members of the family, or, in their absence, a representative of the executive committee of the rural or settlement Soviet of workers' deputies or the management of the apartment house.

If the seizure, search, or impounding of property has been conducted on premises belonging to an institution, enterprise or organization, a copy of the record shall be handed to the appropriate official and a receipt obtained from him.

Article 201. Acquainting accused with all materials of case.

If an investigator deems the evidence gathered to be sufficient for drawing up an indictment, and has fulfilled the requirements of article 200 of the present Code,* he shall announce to the accused that the investigation in his case has been terminated and that he has the right to become acquainted with all the materials of the case both personally and with the help of defence counsel, as well as to file petitions to supplement the preliminary investigation.

If the accused has not declared a desire to have defence counsel, all the materials of the case shall be presented to him for examination. In instances when the accused petitions to summon defence counsel to participate in becoming acquainted with the proceedings in the case, and in instances when defence counsel participates in the case from the moment of presentation of the accusation, the investigator shall present all the materials of the case to the accused and his defence counsel. In such instances the presentation of the materials of the case must be postponed until the appearance of the defence counsel, but not for more than five days. If it is impossible for the defence counsel selected by the accused to appear within the said period, the investigator shall take measures to summon another defence counsel. All the materials of the case shall be presented to the accused and his defence counsel in filed and numbered form. If during the conduct of the preliminary investigation use was made of film or tape-recordings, these shall be shown or played to the accused and his defence counsel. Upon request of the accused or his defence counsel the investigator shall have the right to allow them individually to acquaint themselves with the materials of the case.

If several persons are being prosecuted in the case, all the materials of the case shall be presented to each of them.

When the accused and his defence counsel have finished acquainting themselves with the materials of the case, the investigator shall be obliged to ask them whether they petition to supplement the investigation and in exactly what respect.

* Article 200. Acquainting victim, civil plaintiff, and civil defendant with materials of case.

The accused shall have the right, in the process of acquainting himself with the materials of the case, to copy necessary information from it.

Article 221. Bringing to trial.

If there exist sufficient grounds to consider a case in judicial session, a judge, without predetermining the question of guilt, shall render a decree to bring the accused to trial.

In instances when the judge disagrees with the findings of the indictment, as well as when it is necessary to change the measure of restraint selected with respect to the accused, the case shall be subject to consideration in an administrative session of the court. In this connection, regardless of the grounds for submitting the case for consideration by an administrative session, the court shall decide all questions pertaining to the administrative session.

The question of bringing to trial must be decided by the judge or by the court in administrative session not more than fourteen days from the moment the case comes to court.

Article 239. Time limits for considering case in judicial session.

Consideration of a case in judicial session must be commenced not later than fourteen days from the moment a judge renders a decree, or an administrative session a ruling, to bring the accused to trial.

Article 283. Interrogation of witnesses.

Witnesses shall be interrogated separately and in the absence of witnesses not yet interrogated.

The chairman shall ascertain the relationships among a witness and the prisoner and victim and shall propose to the witness that he communicate everything that he knows about the case. Thereafter the judges and accusers, as well as the victim, the civil plaintiff, the civil defendant, and their representatives, defence counsel, and the prisoners shall interrogate the witness. If a witness has been summoned to the judicial session upon a petition of one of the participants in the judicial examination, such participant shall put questions to such witness first. The chairman shall eliminate questions having no relation to the case.

Judges shall have the right to put questions to a witness at any moment of the judicial investigation.

Witnesses who have been interrogated shall remain in the courtroom and may not withdraw before the completion of the judicial investigation without the permission of the court.

The chairman may allow witnesses who have been interrogated to withdraw from the courtroom before the completion of the judicial investigation only upon hearing the opinions of the accuser, prisoner and defence counsel as well as of the victim, civil plaintiff, civil defendant, and their representatives.

Article 286. Public disclosure of testimony of witness.

The public disclosure in court of testimony given by a witness during an enquiry or preliminary investigation may take place in the following instances:

(1) if there exist substantial contradictions between such testimony and the testimony of the witness in court;

(2) in the absence of the witness at the judicial session for reasons which exclude the possibility of his appearance in court.

This rule shall extend as well to instances of public disclosure of the testimony of the witness which has been given in court.

The playing of tape-recordings is not allowed without previous public disclosure of the testimony contained in the appropriate record of inter-rogation or record of judicial session. A note shall be entered into the record of the judicial session to the effect that the tape-recording has been played.

Article 303. Questions to be resolved by court when returning a verdict.

When returning a verdict a court shall resolve the following questions in the conference room:

(1) whether the act which the prisoner is accused of committing did take place;

(2) whether such act constitutes *corpus delicti* and exactly which criminal law provides for it;

(3) whether the prisoner committed such act;

(4) whether the prisoner is guilty of committing this crime;

(5) whether the prisoner is subject to punishment for the crime committed by him;

(6) exactly what punishment must be assigned to the prisoner and whether it is subject to being served by the prisoner;

(7) whether there are grounds for deeming the prisoner an especially dangerous recidivist; what type of corrective-labour colony must be decided on for the prisoner when assigning him punishment in the form of deprivation of freedom;

(8) whether the civil suit is subject to satisfaction, in whose favour, and to what extent, and also, if a civil suit has not been brought, whether the material loss is subject to compensation;

(9) how to regard the material evidence;

(10) on whom and in what amounts court costs must be imposed;

(11) the measure of restraint with respect to the prisoner.

If the prisoner is accused of committing several crimes, the court shall resolve for each crime separately the questions indicated in sections 1–6 of the present article.

If several prisoners are accused of committing a crime, the court shall resolve these questions with respect to each prisoner separately.

Article 314. Descriptive part of verdict.

The descriptive part of a verdict of guilty must contain a description of the criminal act deemed proved, with an indication of the place, time, and method of its commission, and the nature of the guilt, motives, and consequences of the crime; the evidence on which the court's conclusions are founded and the reasons for which the court has rejected other evidence; indications of circumstances tending to mitigate or aggravate responsibility;

in the event that part of the accusation is deemed unfounded, the grounds therefor. The court shall be obliged also to adduce reasons for changing the accusation, if such has been done in court, and, when necessary, reasons relating to the measure of punishment selected. The court shall further be obliged to adduce the reasons for deeming the prisoner an especially dangerous recidivist, for the relief of the prisoner from punishment, the application of suspended conviction, as well as for the assignment of a punishment below the lowest limit provided by the criminal law for the given crime, for resorting to another, milder punishment, or for the assignment of a type of corrective-labour colony with deviation from the general rules. If there is more than one prisoner in the case, the enumerated indications must be made with respect to each of the prisoners individually.

The descriptive part of a verdict of acquittal shall set forth the substance of the accusation upon which the accused has been brought to trial; the circumstances of the case established by the court; it shall adduce the evidence serving as the basis for acquitting the prisoner, with an indication of the reasons explaining why the court rejects the evidence on which the accusation was founded. Inclusion in a verdict of acquittal of formulations that cast doubt on the innocence of the acquitted person shall not be permitted.

The descriptive part of a verdict of guilty or of an acquittal must contain the reasons underlying the decision of the court with respect to the civil suit or compensation of the material loss caused by the crime.

APPENDIX 6

Signatories to Letters and Appeals

II: 16, p. 36

G. Avrutsky, A. Aleksandrova, L. M. Alekseyeva, Yu. Apresyan, N. Arkhiyev, K. Babitsky, T. Bayeva, I. Belogorodskaya, M. Berzina, L. Bogoraz, I. Buimistr, M. Buras, V. Butko, E. Vaisberg, V. Vinogradov, T. Vinogradova, Yu. Vishnevskaya, A. Volpin, A. Vsesvyatskaya, G. Gabai, Yu. Gastev, S. Genkin, Yu. Gerchuk, E. Gilerova, E. Ginzburg, G. Gladkova, I. Golomshtok, R. Goldin, T. Svirepova, Sviridova, V. A. Sergeyev, E. Solovyova, B. Sukhotin, L. Tanyuk, Yu. Telesin, V. Telnikov, V. Timachev, A. Topeshkina, M. Tulchinsky, N. Gorbanevskaya, M. Grabar, P. Grigorenko, S. Gurvich, A. Daniel, Z. Dzeboyeva, G. Diptseva, R. Dobrushin, M. Domshlak, N. Evgrafov, A. Epifanov, B. V. Efimov, L. Ziman, M. Zlobina, L. Zubakova, A. Ivanov, Z. Kaganov, I. Kaminapova, A. Kaplan, M. Kaplan, L. Kasatkin, L. Kats, Yu. Kim, V. Kornilov, I. Korkhova, A. Kosterin, G. Kravtsova, I. Kristi, M. Ulanovskaya, N. Ustinova, M. Kharitonov, A. Khrabrovitsky, T. Khromova, S. Chirkov, A. Shaikevich, V. Shevchuk, B. Shlifshtein, B. Shragin, A. Shtelmakh, V. Lebedev, Yu. Levin, A. Levitin, N. Lisovskaya, P. Litvinov, T. Litvinova, S. Mar-Akulin, A. T. Marchenko, T. Maslova, Melnikov, I. Melchuk, V. Meniker, V. A. Mikhailov, E. Mikhina, A. Monastyrsky, V. Nemukhin, A. Nikolskaya, V. Nikolsky, S. Pisarev, O. Potapova, M. Puzikov, A. Pek, O. Rabin, L. Rubinshtein, I. Rudakov, A. Rusanov, V. Savenkova, N. Sadomskaya, A. Shuster, V. Shcheglov, V. Eidelman, G. Eidelman, Yu. Yukhnovets, E. Yakir, I. Yakir, P. Yakir, S. L. Yakir, A. Yakobson.

II: 17, p. 37

L. Alekseyeva, T. Bayeva, L. Bogoraz, A. Boltrukevich, A. Volpin, A. Vsesvyatskaya, G. Gabai, I. Gabai, Yu. Gastev, S. Genkin, E. Gilerova, G. Gladkova, N. Gorbanevskaya, A. Daniel, T. Kozavchinskaya, M. Kaplan, L. Kats, Yu. Kim, S. Kadzasov, R. Dobrushin, A. Korkhov, V. Lebedev, N. Lisovskaya, P. Litvinov, A. Marchenko, V. Ponomaryov, I. Rapp, V. Savenkova, Yu. Sapronov, E. Solovyova, V. Telnikov, V. Timachev, A. Topeshkina, N. Ustinova, M. Kharitonov, A. Shtelmakh, V. Eidelman, G. Eidelman, I. Yakir, P. Yakir, M. Postnikov, V. Skvirsky.

II: 18, p. 38

V. Aksyonov, member of the Writers' Union of the USSR*; B. Akhmadulina, member of the WU; A. Babayev, member of the WU, Master of philological sciences; B. Birger, artist, member of the Artists' Union of the USSR†; K. Bogatyryov, member of the WU; V. Veisberg, artist, member of the AU; I. M. Gelfand, corresponding member of the Academy of Sciences of the USSR‡; Yu. Glazov, Master of philological sciences; E. Golysheva, member of the WU; E. Grin, editor; A. Dobrovich, doctor; M. Zand, fellow of the Institute of the Peoples of Asia (IPA) of the AS; V. Ivanov, sector head at the

---

* Henceforth abbreviated as WU. Ed.
† Henceforth abbreviated as AU. Ed.
‡ Henceforth abbreviated as AS. Ed.

Institute of Slavonic Studies of the AS; M. Ivanov, member of the AU; F. A. Iskander, member of the WU; L. Keldysh, professor, Doctor of physico-mathematical sciences; E. Lyakhovich, translator; P. Novikov, member of the AS; N. Otten, member of the WU; L. Pinsky, member of the WU; A. M. Pyatigorsky, Master of philological sciences; I. Revzin, Doctor of philological sciences; Rozenfeld, professor, Doctor of biological sciences; K. Rudnitsky, member of the WU; D. M. Segal, fellow of the Institute of Slavonic Studies of the AS; E. Semeka, Master of historical sciences; N. Stolyarova, member of the Literary Fund; T. Tsivyan, Master of philological sciences; I. R. Shafarevich, corresponding member of the AS; Yu. Edlis, member of the WU; A. Yaglom, professor, Doctor of physico-mathematical sciences.

III: 1, p. 224

N. Gorbanevskaya, P. Litvinov, S. Genkin, Yu. Yukhnovets, P. Yakir, V. Telnikov, Yu. Levin, A. Shtelmakh, K. Babitsky, V. Nikolsky, P. Grigorenko, V. Timachev.

IV: 3, p. 230

E. Shashenkov, engineer; V. Fridman, engineer; Yu. Gendler, legal consultant; G. Aizen, engineer; L. Kvachevsky, chemical engineer; M. Zadorina, artist; I. Krutkov, worker and chemist; V. Dreyer, student; V. Kushev, biologist; T. Soidma, biologist.

IV: 4, p. 231

E. Basilova, V. Vinogradov, A. Epifanov, I. Kamyshanova, L. Kats, E. Kushev, A. Levitin, S. Potasheva, N. Serebryakova, G. Simonova, N. Stolyarova, A. Topeshkina, N. Ustinova.

IV: 11, p. 247

Yu. Apresyan, Master of philological sciences; Afanaseva, member of the Journalists' Union; L. Alekseyeva, editor; K. Babitsky, linguist; S. Belokrinitskaya, linguist; K. Bogatyryov, member of the WU; L. Belova, Master of philological sciences, member of Cinematographers' Union; N. Vvedenskaya, Master of physico-mathematical sciences; N. Vilyams, lecturer at the Moscow Institute of Precision Chemical Technology; E. Vinogradova, Master of fine arts; A. Velikanov, physicist; T. Velikanova, mathematician; E. Volkonskaya, linguist; S. Gindikin, Master of physico-mathematical sciences; Yu. Gastev, lecturer at Moscow University; M. Grabar, Senior lecturer at Moscow Institute of Aviation Technology; Yu. Glazov, Master of philological sciences; S. Goffe, fine arts specialist; P. Gaidenko, Master of philosophical sciences; Yu. Gerchuk, critic, member of the AU; I. Golomshtok, fine arts specialist, member of the AU; R. Dobrushin, Doctor of physico-mathematical sciences; V. Dybo, Master of philological sciences; Yu. Davydov, Master of philological sciences; M. Domshlak, fine arts specialist; V. Ivanov, Master of philological sciences; E. Kopeleva, proofreader in the Publications department of the Radio Committee; G. Korpelevich, graduate student, Moscow University.

[L.] Kasatkin, Master of philological sciences; L. Kapanidze, Master of philological sciences; L. Krysin, Master of philological sciences; O. Kiselev, actor; R. Minlos, Master of physico-mathematical sciences, senior research officer at Moscow University; I. Melchuk, Master of philological sciences; V. Meniker, economist; A. Ogurtsov, Master of philosophical sciences; V. Polyak, Master of physico-mathematical sciences; S. Pozharitskaya, Master of philological sciences; A. Pyatigorsky, Master of philological sciences; N. Podolskaya, Master of philological sciences; L. Pazhitnov, Master of philosophical sciences; Sedov, Master of historical sciences; N. Sadomskaya, Master of historical sciences; V. Skvirsky, geographer; E. Semeka, Master of historical sciences; L. Tanyuk, producer; Yu. Telesin, mathematician; M. Ulanovskaya, bibliographer; M. Feigina, historian; I. Faleyeva, sociologist; B. Shragin, Master of philosophical sciences; A. Yakobson, translator.

Appendix 6

I. Belogorodskaya, engineer; G. Bulatov, actor; Yu. Blyumental, musician; A. Blyumental, student at the Moscow City Institute of Culture; N. Gorbanevskaya, engineer-translator; P. Grigorenko, foreman at SU-20, Moscow Building Trust, formerly Major-General, Master of military sciences, senior lecturer; A. Grigorenko, senior technician; Gubanov, electrician; A. Daniel, schoolboy, tenth grade; N. Emelkina, officer worker; D. Zhitomirsky, Doctor of fine arts; A. Kosterin, writer, member of WU; A. Kaplan, Master of physico-mathematical sciences; M. Kazartsev, worker; G. Kravtsova, drainage engineer; O. Leonteva, Master of fine arts; V. Nikolsky, senior engineer; A. Pavlova, construction engineer; S. Pisarev, research worker; M. Puzikov, engineer; I. Rudakov; V. Teterin, office worker; M. Shaposhnikov; Yu. Yukhnovets, worker; A. Khrabrovitsky, literary scholar; A. Tsvetopolskaya, senior engineer; Utkina, senior engineer.

IV: 14, p. 253

A. Kosterin, A. Khrabrovitsky, M. Puzikov, N. Arkhiyev, V. Savenkova, M. Luchkova, I. Gabai, S. Pisarev, V. Luchkov, P. Yakir, A. Grigorenko, Yu. Grimm, Yu. Teslya.

IV: 17, p. 254

[I.] Avramenko, mathematician; G. D. Avrutsky, engineer; N. I. Azarova, Master of philological sciences; Yu. Aikhenvald, poet-translator; I. M. Akselrod, lecturer; A. Aleksandrova, student at the Pedagogical Institute; S. D. Albanov, architect (Magadan); T. V. Bagrovnikova, technician; T. Bayeva, student at the Institute of Historical Archives; M. Ya. Berzina, junior research officer; A. A. Bryandinskaya, mathematician; P. L. Vasilevsky, mathematician; L. F. Vasilev, lawyer; Yu. Vishnevskaya, salesgirl in bookshop; O. Volkova, research officer; Z. Volotskaya, junior research officer; A. S. Volpin, Master of physico-mathematical sciences; G. Gabai, schoolmistress; I. Gabai, editor; Yu. Gendler. lawyer (Leningrad); S. Genkin, mathematician; V. Gerlin, schoolmistress; V. A. Gershovich, mathematician; E. Gilerova, schoolmistress; G. Gladkova, editor; Yu. Glazov, Master of historical sciences; M. Glazova, Master of philological sciences; V. Golomidov, student at the Institute of Culture; R. Ya. Goldin, engineer; N. E. Gorbanevskaya, engineer-translator; A. V. Grib, Master of chemical sciences; V. V. Grikevich, engineer; V. N. Grishin, mathematician; M. E. Deza, Master of physico-mathematical sciences.

[Z.] Dzeboyeva, biologist; V. Demnin, mathematician; N. Dorokhova, secretary-typist; G. G. Durman, research officer; B. V. Efimov, office worker; L. M. Efimova, lecturer; E. Zhigunov, editor; Zavelsky, economist; Yu. Zaks, chemical engineer; L. Ziman, teacher; K. Kh. Zimina, architect; B. Zubok, student at a Medical Institute; A. Ivanov, historian; V. V. Ivanov, engineer, Master of technical sciences; V. S. Imshennik, senior research officer; A. Kanayev, geologist; M. Kaplan [*poet*]; L. Kats, librarian; G. Kashina, geologist; L. Kvachevsky, chemical engineer (Leningrad); A. I. Kibalchich, architect; A. Kim, doctor; Yu. Kim, schoolteacher; D. A. Kirtnits, Doctor of physico-mathematical sciences; Yu. I. Kiseleva, artist; E. Kolesnikov, engineer; G. Kopylov, Master of physico-mathematical sciences (Dubna); V. R. Kormer, engineer; A. Korkhov, office worker; I. Korkhova, economist; S. Korytnaya, critic; G. Krapivyansky, deputy director of an art college; V. A. Krasin, economist; A. G. Krasina, technician; I. Kristi, mathematician; T. Kuznetsova, airport clerk; V. Lebedev, editor; E. Lebedeva, journalist; A. E. Levitin (Krasnov), religious writer; Yu. K. Lekomtsev, Master of philological sciences; T. Loginova, student at a Pedagogical Institute; V. Luchkov, physiologist; M. Luchkova, engineer; I. G. Makarevich, student at the Institute of Cinematography; I. R. Maksimova, editor; A. Marchuk, artist; M. Meyerson, student at Moscow University; Yu. Metlin, geophysicist (Leningrad); V. Miloshevich, hydraulic engineer; Z. Mirkina, translator; V. A. Mikhailov, engineer; A. Muchnik, mathematician; G. Natapov, mathematician;

V. Nikiforov, engineer; T. Nikolayeva, Master of philological sciences; T. Nikolskaya, student of Leningrad University; Novikova, lecturer at a technical college; B. Ogibenin, Master of philological sciences; V. A. Pavlinchuk, junior research officer; L. G. Pavlovskaya, engineer; A. Plomper, pensioner; A. Povolotskaya, editor; G. Podyapolsky, geologist; M. Pozdnyak, engineer; G. Pomerants, library officer; V. Ponomaryov, physicist (Kharkov); A. Popov, geologist; O. Potapova, student at a Pedagogical Institute; N. Pryadkina, student at a Textile Institute; I. Rapp, Doctor of physico-mathematical sciences; Yu. Rapp (Kharkov), [*junior research officer*]; A. Rappoport, teacher; B. M. Ratnovsky, engineer; B. A. Reznikov, physicist; V. Romanov, bibliographer; I. G. Romanova, schoolmistress; V. Rubin, Master of historical sciences; M. Rubina, Master of biological sciences; V. Sannikova, worker at the Likhachyov [*car*] factory; A. Sambor, radio journalist; V. L. Svechinsky, architect (Magadan); D. M. Segal, linguist; V. A. Sergeyev, engineer; M. Sergiyenko, student; V. A. Sipachyov, chemist; M. Slonim, student of Moscow University; T. I. Smirnov, musical director of a kindergarten; E. V. Smorodinova, engineer; B. B. Sokhransky, engineer; E. Starikov, engineer (Kaliningrad); A. Starostin, physicist; E. L. Stepanov, librarian; G. Superfin, student, Tartu University [*in Estonia*]; E. Surits, translator; B. Sushko, laboratory assistant; T. Sushko, chemist; V. I. Tatarsky, Doctor of physico-mathematical sciences; Yu. Telesin, mathematician; V. Telnikov, teacher; V. Timachev, geologist; A. Topeshkina, editor; V. Tupitsyn, mathematician; V. Turchin, Doctor of physico-mathematical sciences; K. F. Turchin, junior research officer; I. B. Uspensky, Master of biological sciences; I. Fadeyeva, geologist; L. Fyodorov, engineer; N. Feldman, senior research officer in an archive (Sverdlovsk); L. M. Finkelshtein, lecturer in history of music; G. Freidin, translator; V. Fridman, engineer (Leningrad); B. Khazanov, mathematician; M. Kharitonov, editor; A. Khrabrovitsky, literary scholar; V. Tsyplakov, student, Institute of Energetics; Chilikina, lecturer; V. Shakhsuvarov, engineer; Shevtsova, Master of economic sciences; N. Shiryayeva, bibliographer; B. I. Shlifshtein, engineer-economist; I. Kh. Shmain, mathematician; A. A. Shtelmakh, engineer; S. Shtutina, engineer; A. Shuster, physicist; E. Shchedrin, physicist; V. Shcheglov, mathematician; G. Shchedrovitsky, Master of philosophical sciences; V. Eidelman, physicist; G. Eidelman, mathematician; K. O. Erastov, translator; T. D. Erastova, mother of six children (and biologist); A. Yulikov, student; I. Yakir, student of the Institute of Historical Archives; P. Yakir, historian; R. Yakir, engineer; A. Yakobson, translator.

Additional signatories to the same letter

M. V. Bagrovnikova, schoolmistress; A. A. Bezzubikov, fitter; A. V. Blyumental, student at the Institute of Culture; Yu. A. Blyumental, musician; T. Ventslova, writer and lecturer at Vilnius University [*in Lithuania*]; E. Glezin, construction engineer; I. Z. Goldenberg, philologist (Novosibirsk); A. Gribanov, philologist; I. V. Grimblit, engineer; V. Denisov, doctor; E. Dushechkina, philologist (Tartu); Evgenov, biologist; Isayeva, technician; Ya. I. Kazakov, instructor in ferro-concrete; I. A. Kovalevskaya, biologist; A. Kogan, musical editor; I. R. Konenko, Master of chemical sciences; P. Kortan, engineer; N. M. Krayevskaya, engineer; M. L. Levin, Doctor of physico-mathematical sciences; E. G. Maksimova, geologist; Yu. V. Maltsev, translator; V. Mamonova, translator; B. R. Maramzin, writer (Leningrad); I. Markovskaya, doctor; V. Markovsky, Master of technical sciences; N. N. Meiman, Doctor of physico-mathematical sciences; A. Mirkina, pensioner; E. V. Mirkina, translator; G. Model, philologist; Monina, fine arts specialist; V. Mylnikov, lecturer; E. Nitsberg, philologist; T. I. Olegina, schoolmistress; V. Pashkovsky, doctor; E. Petrov, research officer; V. Rokityansky, physicist; D. Silvestrov, engineer; L. E. Sotnikova, engineer; E. Stroyeva, editor; N. Stroyeva, musician; E. V. Syroyechkovsky, zoologist; A. Timofeyevsky, film script-writer; Yu. Titov, architect; M. Torchilina, pensioner; N. Trauberg, Master of philological sciences; L. Ulitskaya, geneticist; R. P. Fedorenko, Master of physico-mathematical sciences; I. V. Fomenko, graduate student; L. Ya. Khalif, poet; Z. Ya. Shapiro, Master of physico-mathematical sciences; V. Shvartsman, lecturer; L. M. Shulgina, student; D. Epshtein, translator (Vilnius).

Appendix 6

IV: 20, p. 262

M. V. Yudina, Professor of the Moscow Conservatoire; Yu. G. Shtein, film director; I. V. Kvasha, actor at the 'Sovremmenik' Theatre; F. V. Zbarsky, member of the AU; A. A. Abramov, Master of physico-mathematical sciences; I. Yu. Perskaya, Master of historical sciences; S. A. Abramov, student at Moscow University; M. N. Polenov, student at Moscow University.

IV: 21, p. 262

N. Adamyan, member of the WU; N. Andronov, member of the AU; E. Andronova-Leontovich, Doctor of physico-mathematical sciences; Yu. D. Apresyan, Master of philological sciences; P. I. Afanaseva, librarian and People's Assessor; M. Arapov, linguist; K. Babitsky, linguist; S. Belokrinitskaya, linguist; M. Berkinblit, junior research officer at the Institute for the Problems of Information Transmission of the AS; V. M. Bovsheverov, laboratory head, Master of physico-mathematical sciences; Bozhovich, Master of fine arts; Bodiyeva, junior research officer at the Institute of Chemical Physics of the AS; M. Bongard, laboratory head, Institute for the Problems of Information Transmission of the AS; Yu. Bregel, Master of historical sciences; I. K. Bunina, senior research officer at the Institute of Slavic Studies of the AS; N. G. Vainberg, mathematician; Garlinskaya, member of the Union of Cinematographers; I. M. Gelfand, corresponding member of the AS; V. P. Golyshev, translator; E. M. Golysheva, member of the WU; M. I. Grabar, senior lecturer in the department of mathematics, Moscow Institute of Aviation Technology.

[S.] Gurvich, senior research officer at the Institute of Atmospheric Physics of the AS; A. E. Gurvich, Doctor of biological sciences and professor at the Gamalei Institute of Epidemiology and Microbiology; Davydovskaya, electrical engineer; L. A. Diky, senior research officer and Master of physico-mathematical sciences; Dinaburg, engineer and mathematician, Institute of Chemical Physics of the AS; Yu. Dombrovsky, member of the WU; T. Elizarenkova, philologist.

[V.] Dybo, Master of philological sciences; N. Erofeyeva, architect; A. K. Zholkovsky, junior research officer in Machine Translation Laboratory, 1st Moscow State Pedagogical Institute of Foreign Languages; V. V. Ivanov, head of the structural typology section at the Institute of Slavic Studies of the AS; M. Ivanov, member of the AU; O. V. Zanchenko, mathematician; N. Zorkaya, Master of fine arts; Zubkovsky, junior research officer at the Institute of Atmospheric Physics of the AS; I. S. Zykina, chemist; M. I. Kaganov, Professor and Doctor of physico-mathematical sciences; Z. Kaganov, junior research officer and mathematician; V. N. Kadantsev, engineer; Kazakov, electrical engineer; M. A. Kallistratova, Master of physico-mathematical sciences; Kamenomostskaya, Master of physico-mathematical sciences; Kanevsky, mechanical engineer; L. Kasatkin, Master of philological sciences; N. Koder-Stepanova, Master of biological sciences and senior research officer at the Institute for the Problems of Information Transmission of the AS; L. Keldysh, Professor and Doctor of physico-mathematical sciences; E. Kobasova, electrical engineer; S. A. Kovalyov, Master of biological sciences and senior research officer at Moscow University; A. Kon, junior research officer at the Institute of Atmospheric Physics of the AS; L. Kopelev, member of the WU; V. Kornilov, member of the WU; K. M. Cook, translator; L. Krysin, linguist; A. P. Lavut, senior engineer at Moscow University; Yu. Levitansky, member of the WU; M. A. Leontovich, member of the AS; I. S. Lipkina, engineer; M. Loriye, member of the WU; G. Lyudmirskaya, lecturer; A. S. Marchukov, mathematician; Medvedovskaya, mathematician; I. Melchuk, Master of philological sciences; A. G. Meshkovsky, Doctor of physico-mathematical sciences; A. F. Miller, Master of physico-mathematical sciences; S. Mikhailova, engineer; I. Mokarik, mathematician; S. Morozov, architect; Mostovaya, mathematician, junior research officer at the Institute of Chemical Physics of the AS; D. Muravyov, editor in the Iskusstvo publishing-house; E. Murina, fine arts specialist; N. Naumov, member of the WU; S. P. Novikov, corresponding member of the AS; L. Ostrovskaya, architect; N. D. Otten, member of the WU; M. P. Petrov, junior research officer; L. E. Pinsky, member of the WU; N. Podolskaya, Master of philological sciences; K. M. Pokrovskaya, physicist; V. Polyakov, member of the AU; Posvyansky, mathematician; M. A. Pravorotova, engineer; A. V. Rabinovich, mathematician; I. Revzin, Doctor of philological sciences; Reznik, engineer; S. Reznikov, architect; V. M. Rodionov, Doctor of biological sciences at the Institute of Bio-medical Chemistry of the Academy of Medical Sciences; N. N. Romanova, mathematician; I. Rubanova, Master of fine arts; Yu. G. Rudoi, physicist; I. Ryazantseva, film scriptwriter; D. Samoilov, member of the WU; V. Sannikov, Master of philological sciences; A. Simonov, writer; A. Simolon, junior research officer at the Institute of Organic Chemistry of the AS; V. V. Smolyaninov, junior research officer at the Institute for the Problems of Information Transmission of the AS; E. M. Smorgunova, linguist; Yu. N. Sokolov, geophysicist; I. Solovyova, member of the WU; B. V. Sukhotin, Master of philological sciences; V. I. Tatarsky, Doctor of physico-mathematical sciences and senior research officer at the Institute of Atmospheric Physics of the AS; A. Timofeyevsky, film scriptwriter; L. Ya. Timoshenko, member of the WU; T. I. Tovstukha, junior research officer at the Institute of Automation and Telemechanics of the AS; V. N. Toporov, Master of philological sciences; M. R. Tulchinsky, Master of historical sciences; V. Khinkis, member of the WU.

[T.] Khodorovich, junior research officer at the Institute of the Russian Language of the AS; T. Tsivyan, Master of philological sciences; L. M. Chailakhyan, Master of biological sciences; L. K. Chukovskaya, member of the WU; B. Churganova, linguist; M. L. Shik, Master of biological sciences; V. Shitova, member of the WU; I. E. Shifrin, physicist; V. V. Shmidt, Master of physico-mathematical sciences and senior research officer at the Institute of Metallurgy; A. A. Shteinberg, physicist; A. I. Shub, physicist; S. M. Epshtein, senior laboratory assistant at the Institute of the Russian Language of the AS; K. Yusina, mathematician; A. Yaglom, Professor and Doctor of physico-mathematical sciences.

IV: 22, p. 263

Vasily Aksyonov, writer and member of the WU; Pavel Antokolsky, poet and member of the WU; Boris Balter, writer and member of the WU; Boris Birger, artist and member of the AU; Vladimir Voinovich, writer and member of the WU; Kamil Ikramov, writer and member of the WU; Fazil Iskander, writer and member of the WU; Veniamin Kaverin, writer and member of the WU; Yury Kazakov, writer and member of the WU; Naum Korzhavin, poet and member of the WU; Vladimir Kornilov, poet and member of the WU; Sergei Larin, critic and member of the Journalists' Union; Lev Levitsky, critic and member of the WU; Novella Matveyeva, poet and member of the WU; Oleg Mikhailov, critic and member of the WU*; Valentin Nepomnyashchy, critic and member of the Journalists' Union; Konstantin Paustovsky, writer and member of the WU; Yury Pilyar, writer and member of the WU*; Grigory Pozhenyan, poet and member of the WU; Mikhail Roshchin, writer and member of the WU; Benedict Sarnov, critic and member of the WU; Felix Svetov, critic and member of the WU; Fedot Suchkov, critic and member of the WU; Maria Yudina, pianist and Professor.

IV: 23, p. 264

G. P. Akilov, Master of physico-mathematical sciences; S. L. Andreyev, engineer; R. L. Berg, Doctor of biological sciences; Yu. Borisov, Doctor of physico-mathematical sciences; I. S. Alekseyev, Master of philosophical sciences; L. G. Borisova, graduate student (and sociologist); I. Vasserman, graduate student; E. B. Vishnevsky, junior research officer;

---

* O. Mikhailov and Yu. Pilyar later announced that they were withdrawing their signatures from the letter. For Yu. Pilyar's statement, see p. 309.

Appendix 6

L. Vyacheslavov, graduate student; A. V. Gladky, Doctor of physico-mathematical sciences; M. M. Gromyko, Doctor of historical sciences; I. Z. Goldenberg, lecturer; F. A. Dreizin, Master of philological sciences; V. E. Zakharov, Master of physico-mathematical sciences; G. Zaslavsky, Master of physico-mathematical sciences; K. Ilichyov, temporary graduate student (and physicist); E. S. Kositsyna, teacher; Kulakov, Master of physico-mathematical sciences; A. V. Klorin, engineer; L. A. Lozovsky, engineer; D. V. Likhach-yova, junior research officer; V. F. Menshikov, graduate student; B. Naidorf, teacher; R. Nakhmanson, Master of physico-mathematical sciences; S. I. Plitko, officer at the Systems Research Institute; V. S. Pertsovsky, teacher; B. I. Prilous, senior laboratory assistant; S. Rozhnova, graduate student [and historian]; N. V. Revyakina, Master of historical sciences; Sokolov, Master of physico-mathematical sciences; B. E. Semyachkin, junior research officer; N. A. Topeshko, engineer; E. Titov; L. A. Trishina, assistant in the department of general linguistics of Novosibirsk University; A. I. Fet, Doctor of physico-mathematical sciences; A. M. Fridman, Master of physico-mathematical sciences; N. N. Filonenko, graduate student; I. V. Khriplovich, Master of physico-mathematical sciences; I. N. Khokhlushkin, junior research officer; F. A. Tselnik, engineer; M. I. Cheremisina, Master of philological sciences; A. V. Shabat, Master of physico-mathematical sciences; A. M. Shalagin, engineer; E. Shtengel, junior research officer; G. S. Yablonsky, junior research officer; V. A. Konev, Master of philosophical sciences.

IV: 28, p. 278

S. Paradzhanov, film director, prizewinner at international film festivals; A. M. Korolyov, Master of physico-mathematical sciences; Yu. V. Tsekhmistrenko, Master of physico-mathematical sciences; I. S. Marchuk, artist; V. G. Bondarchuk, Master of physico-mathematical sciences; I. G. Zaslavskaya, Master of physico-mathematical sciences; A. F. Lubchenko, Professor and Doctor of physico-mathematical sciences, Lenin Prize winner; I. P. Dzyub, Master of physico-mathematical sciences; I. A. Svetlichny, writer; V. A. Vyshensky, mathematician; I. M. Dzyuba, member of the Ukrainian Writers' Union*; Z. S. Gribnikov, Master of physico-mathematical sciences; I. P. Zhadko, Master of physico-mathematical sciences; N. N. Grigorev, physicist; B. D. Shanina, physicist; M. I. Beletsky, mathematician; V. Bondar,· Master of physico-mathematical sciences; V. A. Tyagai, Master of physico-mathematical sciences; Yu. Kulyupin, Master of physico-mathematical sciences; V. Zuyev, physicist; O. G. Sarbei, Master of physico-mathematical sciences; P. M. Tomchuk, Master of physico-mathematical sciences; D. Abakarov, Master of Sport of the USSR; V. I. Sheka, Master of physico-mathematical sciences; G. P. Kochur, member of the UWU; V. O. Shevchuk, member of the UWU; L. Kostenko, member of the UWU; E. A. Popovich, writer; M. Kotsyubinskaya, writer; B. Kharchuk, member of the UWU; Z. Franko, writer.

[A.] Gorskaya, member of the Ukrainian Artists' Union; B. Antonenko-Davidovich, member of the UWU; B. Gopnik, member of the USSR Journalists' Union; A. V. Skorokhod, Professor and Doctor of physico-mathematical sciences, corresponding member of the Ukrainian AS; V. B. Bogdanovich, senior engineer; V. N. Orayevsky, Master of physico-mathematical sciences; V. Pokrovsky, physicist; P. Dibrova, senior engineer; A. A. Beletsky, Doctor of philological sciences; T. N. Chernyshyova, Master of philological sciences; Zh. Sklyarenko, physicist; T. Kalustyan, artiste, prizewinner at the Ukrainian vocalists' competition; Yu. D. Sokolov, Professor and Doctor of physico-mathematical sciences, corresponding member of the Ukrainian AS; Yu. M. Berezansky, Professor and Doctor of physico-mathematical sciences, corresponding member of the Ukrainian AS; E. A. Sverstyuk, writer; Yu. N. Kovalenko, Master of technical sciences; A. M. Taran, journalist; A. A. Bratko, Master of philosophical sciences; G. T. Krivoruchko, worker; T. A. Kolomiyets, member of the UWU; A. F. Sergiyenko, student; B. E. Tyufanov, engineer; G. V. Bolotova, shop-assistant; V. V. Linchevsky, student; V. A. Fomenko,

* Henceforth abbreviated as UWU. Ed.

student; M. R. Selivachiv, student; L. G. Orel, teacher; I. A. Chernenko, editor; A. T. Bolekhivsky, doctor; M. I. Paly, student; Ya. V. Konopada, doctor; V. V. Zdorovilo, engineer; N. P. Bezpalko, accountant; L. I. Yashchenko, member of the Ukrainian Composers' Union; T. R. Girnyk, philologist; I. I. Rusin, engineer; A. V. Zaboi, artist; V. O. Bezpalko, worker; B. F. Matushevsky, engineer; M. Yu. Braichevsky, Master of historical sciences; V. P. Savchuk, worker; D. Porkhun, pensioner; A. N. Dotsenko, senior engineer; B. D. Shirotsky, lawyer; V. G. Orel, engineer; R. O. Melnichenko, philologist; L. G. Prosyatkivska, teacher; L. I. Litovchenko, student; E. Ashpis, lecturer at the Conservatoire; A. G. Sitenko, Professor and Doctor of physico-mathematical sciences, corresponding member of the Ukrainian AS; I. Ya. Boichak, Master of philological sciences, member of the UWU; V. Kolomiyets, member of the UWU; L. Semykina, member of the Ukrainian Artists' Union; G. F. Dvorko, Doctor of chemical sciences; A. L. Put, Master of biological sciences; G. A. Bachinsky, Master of biological sciences; P. F. Gozhik, Master of geological and mineralogical sciences; G. F. Matviyenko, biologist; I. B. Lyurin, biologist; A. Shevchenko, journalist; L. Kovalenko, Master of philological sciences and member of the UWU; I. Drach, member of the UWU; N. Vingranovsky, member of the UWU; Yu. Serdyuk, member of the UWU; G. Sevruk, artist; A. Osinskaya, artiste; L. P. Karmazina, engineer; K. B. Tolpygo, Professor and Doctor of physico-mathematical sciences, corresponding member of the Ukrainian AS; A. Semyonov, engineer; V. Zaretsky, member of the Ukrainian Artists' Union; Semyonova, biologist; I. Litovchenko, member of the Ukrainian Artists' Union; Plaksy, artist; V. Nekrasov, writer, member of the UWU and State prizewinner; Komashkov, metal-worker; Nazarenko, electrician; Erdan, worker; Berlinskaya, worker; Nedoshkovsky, scaffolding erecter; Mogil, water-insulation engineer; Dyriv, electrician; Bulai, electrician; Manakeyev, worker; Vinograd, worker; Kasimchuk, foundry worker; Gromadyuk, concreter; Sugonyako, carpenter; Ryabokon, sewage purifier; Stefanchuk, water-insulation engineer; Petrov, water-insulation engineer; Gorbach, electrician; Tsebenko, driver; Chizhevsky, concrete fitter; Godun, stone-mason; Kirev, electric welder; Ivanenko, engraver; Serosh, metal-worker; V. Stus, writer; R. Dovgan, journalist; R. Korogodsky, fine arts specialist; A. Zakharchuk, artist; V. Lutsak, sculptor; V. Dovgan, sculptor; V. Bogoslovsky, doctor; Ya. Stupak, writer; Ya. Kendzor, worker; V. Yaremenko, writer. [*Names here transliterated from the forms given by Litvinov, which are mostly the Russian ones.*]

V: 33, p. 315

N. Gorbanevskaya, O. Timofeyeva, A. S. Volpin, L. I. Ginzburg, S. Chudakov, E. Galanskova [*Galanskov's sister*], V. Pokhodayev, E. A. Galanskova [*Galanskov's mother*] T. S. Galanskov [*Galanskov's father*], A. Boltrukevich, A. Topeshkina, A. F. Kiryagina (witness to search at Ginzburg's home), L. Kats, S. Genkin, V. A. Nikolsky, S. Shtutina, A. Povolotskaya, N. Svetlova [*later Alexander Solzhenitsyn's wife*], Karelin, Shchadrina, Shternfeld, A. Viktorov [*Galanskov's first cousin*], K. Galanskova [*Galanskov's aunt*], N. Viktorova [*Galanskov's first cousin*], A. Shtelmakh, E. Basilova, F. Kamyshanova, G. Kaganovsky, G. V. Galanskova [*Galanskov's first wife*].

V: 37, p. 325

S. Kadzasov, linguist; T. Kozavchinskaya, linguist; I. Korkhova, economist; A. Levitin, physicist; A. Khanukov, chief factory engineer; A. Avramenko, doctor; A. Shtelmakh, engineer; A. Dobrovich, doctor; G. Avrutsky, engineer; G. Starostina, economist.

NOTES

INDEX OF NAMES

NOTES

to the English edition

INTRODUCTION

1. *Protsess chetyryokh*, Amsterdam, 1971.
2. Full Russian text in R. N. Grynberg, ed., *Vozdushnye puti-Almanakh IV*, Grynberg, New York, 1965, pp. 279-303, shortened English text in *Encounter*, London, September 1964.
3. *The Demonstration in Pushkin Square*, London and New York, 1969.
4. See the first eleven issues in P. Reddaway, *Uncensored Russia: The Human Rights Movement in the Soviet Union*, London and New York, 1972, and issue 16 onwards in individual booklets published by Amnesty International, Turnagain Lane, Farringdon St., London, E.C.4.
5. See D. Weissbort, ed., *Natalya Gorbanevskaya*, Carcanet Press, South Hinksey, Oxford, 1972, pp. 135-54.
6. See, e.g., M. Bourdeaux, *Faith on Trial in Russia*, London and New York, 1971.
7. See pp. 344-49 and Reddaway, *op. cit.*, chapter 3.
8. See appendix 4.
9. See Reddaway, pp. 123-25.
10. See, e.g., Weissbort, *op. cit.*, pp. 113-15, for a letter from her and T. Velikanova in defence of Gorbanevskaya.
11. See Reddaway, pp. 139-40.
12. See *ibid.*, chapter 10, *passim*.
13. Anon, ed., *Istoriya odnoi golodovki*, Possev-Verlag, Frankfurt, 1971.
14. See *Possev*, Frankfurt, No. 8, 1970, pp. 5-6.
15. See Reddaway, pp. 225-26.
16. See *ibid.*, pp. 223-25.
17. See *The Listener*, London, 9 September 1971.

THE TRIAL OF THE FOUR

1. All published in *Grani*, Frankfurt, No. 58, 1965. Some of the poems are translated in Keith Bosley, ed., *Russia's Other Poets*, London, 1968. Published in New York as *Russia's Underground Poets*, 1968.
2. The text here mistakenly reads 'August'.
3. *Belaya kniga po delu A. Sinyavskogo i Yu. Danielya*, Frankfurt, 1967.
4. Published in *Grani*, No. 52, 1962. Some of the poems are translated in Bosley, *op. cit.*
5. Items from this have appeared in *Grani*, Nos. 63, 64, 65, 67, 68, 69, 70, 75. For translations of Galanskov's own articles see A. Brumberg, ed., *In Quest of Justice: Protest and Dissent in the Soviet Union Today*, London and New York, 1970, documents 48 and 62, and P. Reddaway, ed., *Russia's Other Intellectuals*, due for publication, London, 1973.
6. See below and note 14.
7. This appears to be inaccurate. According to interesting official documents he was sentenced to three years in 1958. See *Russkaya Mysl* (Paris), 7 March 1968; *Possev*, (Frankfurt) 6 October 1967.
8. Apparently inaccurate. See note 7.
9. In fact in 1930.
10. As the war proceeded, however, the NTS, which was closely involved in the Vlasov movement, evolved the line 'Neither Stalin nor Hitler'. Almost all their leaders were consequently arrested and put in German concentration camps. See, among

other books, W. Strik-Strikfeldt, *Against Stalin and Hitler*, London and New York 1970. On the NTS in general see Gordon Young, *The House of Secrets*, New York, 1959, and the booklet *NTS—National Alliance of Russian Solidarists*, Possev Verlag, Frankfurt, 1967.

11. See English translation in *Problems of Communism* (Washington D.C.), XVII, No. 5, 1968, 79-82. Russian text in *Grani*, No. 64, 1967, pp. 194-201.

12. English text in M. Bourdeaux, *Patriarch and Prophets: The Persecution of the Russian Orthodox Church Today*, London, 1970, pp. 98-115. Russian text in *Vestnik Russkogo studencheskogo khristianskogo dvizheniya* (Paris), No. 84, 1967, pp. 39-69.

13. Text not available. Presumably they were produced for the Constitution Day demonstration-gathering, which has taken place each year since 1965.

14. Full title of English edition: *The Demonstration in Pushkin Square*, London, 1969. Russian edition: *Pravosudiye ili rasprava: Delo o demonstratsii na Pushkinskoi ploshchadi 22 yanvarya 1967 goda*, London, 1968.

15. See note 11.

16. See English translation in Brumberg, *op. cit.*, document 75, Russian text in *Grani*, No. 67, 1968, pp. 134-43.

17. See Russian text in *Grani*, No. 66, 1967, pp. 3-34; English extracts in Brumberg, *op. cit.*, pp. 401-10, 437-44.

18. A reference to Radio Free Europe.

19. Text in Litvinov, *op. cit.* (note 14).

20. Russian text in *Grani*, No. 63, 1967, pp. 7-8, English to appear in Reddaway, *op. cit.*

21. English text in Abram Tertz, '*The Trial Begins*' and '*On Socialist Realism*', Vintage, New York, n.d.; Russian in his *Fantasticheskii mir Abrama Tertsa*, New York, 1967.

22. Russian text in *Grani*, No. 75, 1970, English text partly in Michael Scammell, ed., *Russia's Other Writers*, London, 1970, and partly in Reddaway, *op. cit.*

23. Russian text in *Grani*, No. 67, 1968; English in Brumberg, *op. cit.*, document 62.

24. Russian text in *Novyi Zhurnal* (New York), 83, 1966.

25. Russian text in *Grani*, No. 63, 1967; English in Brumberg, *op. cit.*, pp. 411-25.

26. Protest against re-Stalinization by 25 leading cultural figures. Russian text in *Possev*, 16 September 1966; English in Reddaway, *op. cit.*

27. Russian text in *Grani*, No. 65, 1967; English in *Survey* (London), 63, 1967, pp. 159-69.

28. This anonymous work was found in Varga's archive after his death and Galanskov, in his introduction to it, says he does not know whether or not Varga was the author. Varga's relatives have stated that he was not, and Western scholarly opinion supports them. Russian text in *Grani*, Nos. 68 and 69, 1968; English in *New Left Review* (London), 62, 1970 (extract).

29. English text in Reddaway, *op. cit.*

30. Russian text in *Grani*, No. 63, 1967; English in Brumberg, *op. cit.*, pp. 429-33.

31. Russian text in *Grani*, No. 63, 1967.

32. Russian text *ibid.*; English in Reddaway, *op. cit.*

33. English text *ibid.*

34. See note 16.

35. Russian text in *Grani*, No. 64, 1967; English in Reddaway, *op. cit.*

36. As note 35.

37. See note 11.

38. See note 12.

39. Russian texts in *Grani*, Nos. 64, 67, 68, 70; English translations in Brumberg, *op. cit.*, and Bosley, *op. cit.* (note 1).

40. English text in Reddaway, *op. cit.*

41. Neither item 12 nor item 11 has appeared outside the USSR.

42. Not available. This journal carried the description 'new series', as it was a revival of the journal of the same name which was closed by the authorities a century earlier.

43. Russian text in *Grani*, No. 52, 1962; English in Bosley, *op. cit.*

44. A realist prose-writer in the tradition of Konstantin Paustovsky. See, in English, his *The Smell of Bread*, London, 1965.
45. *Pravda*, 21 October 1962. English translation in Priscilla Johnson, *Khrushchev and the Arts*, Cambridge, Mass., 1965, pp. 93-95.
46. Russian text in A. Ginzburg, *op. cit.* (note 3), pp. 385-7; English in L. Labedz and M. Hayward, eds., *On Trial*, London, 1967, pp. 290-91.
47. Translated from Litvinov's Russian translation of the French original.
48. Radio Liberty broadcasts from Munich in various languages of the USSR. Radio Free Europe broadcasts from Munich in five languages of Eastern Europe excluding the USSR.
49. See Russian texts in Ginzburg, *op. cit.* (note 3), pp. 62-3, 405-415; English in, respectively, Reddaway, *op. cit.* and Brumberg, *op. cit.*, pp. 93-100.
50. Both publications of the NTS: *Solidarizm—ideya budushchego* and *Nashi dni*.
51. i.e. Aleksei Poremsky, *Sila idei*, Possev Verlag, Frankfurt, 1961.
52. i.e. A. R. Trushnovich, *Tsenoyu podviga*, Possev Verlag, Frankfurt, 1955.
53. A publication closely connected with the NTS. Until the end of 1967 it was a weekly newspaper, then it became a monthly journal.
54. The expression used—*stoyat na stryome*—is thieves' slang—Lit.
55. See Russian text in Ginzburg, *op. cit.*, p. 61; English in Reddaway, *op. cit.*
56. After the trial, however, they were. See *Grani*, Nos. 68, 69, 75.
57. See the text of the court sentence, also other details about Vladimir Batshev, and his poems, in *Grani*, No. 59, 1965, pp. 15-18; No. 61, 1966, pp. 3-17; No. 63, 1967, pp. 9-15; No. 70, 1969, p. 114; No. 71, 1969, pp. 7-10; and translations of his poems in Bosley, *op. cit.*
58. i.e. the trial of the Englishman Gerald Brooke, sentenced in Moscow in July 1965 for acting as a courier for the NTS.
59. i.e. the riots of June 1962 over food price rises, in the suppression of which several hundred people were killed. See Albert Boiter, 'When the Kettle Boils Over', in *Problems of Communism*, XIII, 1, 1964.
60. A literary underground journal published in *Grani*, No. 59, 1965, pp. 7-77. Some of the poems are translated in Bosley, *op. cit.*
61. Leonid Gubanov, poet associated with SMOG. See his poems and details about him in *Grani*, No. 59, 1965, pp. 28-32; No. 61, 1966, pp. 15-19; No. 69, 1968, pp. 107-8.
62. On this group, 'The Union of Communards', see L. P. Nestor's article in *Possev: Pyatyi Spetsialnyi Vypusk*, 1970, pp. 23-34, *passim*; and Galanskov's article of 1969 in *Possev* 7, 1970, pp. 31-34. For the text of 'Kolokol' see *Possev* 24, 1967; 1, 1968, pp. 11-13; 4, 1968, pp. 57-58; and translations in Reddaway, *op. cit.*
63. On this army see George Fischer, *Soviet Opposition to Stalin*, Cambridge, Mass., 1952, and Strik-Strikfeldt, *op. cit.* (note 10).
64. Vladimir Dmitriyevich Poremsky, president of the NTS.
65. For a record of that meeting (1965) see English text in Brumberg, *op. cit.*, document 46; Russian in Arkhiepiskop Ioann San-Frantsisskii, ed., *Zashchita very v SSSR* Paris, Ikthus, 1966, pp. 88-101.
66. See Michel Slavinsky, *La Presse Clandestine en U.R.S.S. 1960-1970*, Paris, 1970.
67. The Soviet novelist and publicist Ilya Ehrenburg (1891-1968).
68. Palmiro Togliatti, the Italian communist leader who died in 1964 and left a political 'testament' which was both anti-Stalin and critical of the slowness of de-Stalinization in the USSR.
69. See note 22.
70. It later appeared in *Grani*, No. 75, 1970.
71. Kornei Chukovsky, grand old man of Soviet letters.
72. Veniamin Kaverin, liberal prose-writer of the older generation.
73. Louis Aragon, the French communist writer.
74. Serebryakova's novel *The Water-spout* (*Smerch* in Russian) was first published in 1967 in Polish by the publishing-house Kultura in Paris.
75. Published in English as *Into the Whirlwind* in 1967, and in other languages.

76. Most probably it was reconstructed from memory by one of the signatories and then taken abroad by a foreigner.
77. Author of a *samizdat* work, *The Monk (Inok)*, not yet published in the West.
78. B. B. Vakhtin: a specialist on China and senior research fellow of the Institute for the Peoples of Asia, also a member of the Writers' Union. See his article and photograph in *Zhurnalist*, No. 1, 1967, pp. 66-71.
79. Yu. B. Vakhtin: a senior fellow of the Institute of Cytology and author of many articles published in, especially, the journal *Tsitologiya*.
80. For documentation on the case see M. Bourdeaux, *Patriarch and Prophets*, pp. 341-44, and P. Reddaway, *Uncensored Russia. The Human Rights Movement in the Soviet Union. The Annotated Text of the Unofficial Moscow Journal A Chronicle of Current Events* (Nos. 1-11). London and New York, 1972, chap. 19.
81. A geologist and a founder member in May 1969 of the Action Group for the Defence of Civil Rights in the USSR. See Reddaway, *Uncensored Russia*, chap. 7.
82. Litvinov's note in Russian edition: 'One copy of this letter was sent to the Central Committee of the Party in January 1968 by P. G. Grigorenko, and the second was confiscated from him by employees of the KGB when they searched his flat in November. Consequently the compiler did not have a copy of this letter in Russian at his disposal, and has given here a translation back into Russian from the English version which appeared in the journal *Problems of Communism*, XVII, July-August 1968. P. G. Grigorenko has confirmed that the letter published there was indeed written by him and sent to the Politburo.'

    The English text printed in this book is a new translation of Grigorenko's original text, a copy of which reached the West not long after the trial and was published in *Novoye russkoye slovo* (New York), 7 June 1968, and then in English in *Problems of Communism*. On Grigorenko, see Reddaway, *Uncensored Russia*, chap. 6.

    The above note makes it clear that after Litvinov's arrest on 25 August 1968 some editing tasks must have remained to be completed by others, with the result that the book was not finally ready till the end of 1968.
83. Alexander Solzhenitsyn's letter attacking censorship was not allowed to be read at the Fourth Writers' Congress in 1967, and his novel *Cancer Ward* was refused publication later that year. See L. Labedz, ed., *Solzhenitsyn: A Documentary Record*, London, 1970, pp. 64 *et seq.*
84. Andrei Voznesensky was at the last moment refused permission to travel to New York for a poetry festival in 1967. See his letter denouncing his treatment by officials in *Grani*, No. 66, 1967, pp. 168-9; English text in *Problems of Communism*, XVII, 5, Sept.-Oct. 1968, p. 55.
85. See note 74.
86. On Yakhimovich see Reddaway, *Uncensored Russia*, chap. 6.
87. B. V. Sazonov, philosopher at Moscow University. See report of his speech in *Sovetskaya pedagogika*, 7, 1965, pp. 20-21.
88. On Gabai see Reddaway, *Uncensored Russia*, chap. 6.
89. Kim: also a folk-singer and husband of Pyotr Yakir's daughter Irina.
90. On Yakir see Reddaway, *Uncensored Russia*, chap. 7.
91. Potapenko: an engineer whose long protest against the Sinyavsky–Daniel trial is printed in *ibid.*, chap. 2.
92. For some of Levitin's writings and details of his life see Bourdeaux, *op. cit.*, esp. pp. 255-314, and Reddaway, *Uncensored Russia*, chap. 16.
93. See his *The Chornovil Papers*, London, 1968, also Michael Browne, ed., *Ferment in the Ukraine*, London, 1971.
94. This book has achieved world renown and appeared in various languages. The English language edition which gives the most extensive documentation on Marchenko's fate, additional to his book, is that published by Penguin Books in 1971. The best Russian edition is *Moi pokazaniya*, Possev Verlag, Frankfurt, 1969. On Marchenko see Reddaway, *Uncensored Russia*, chap. 9.
95. This letter, evidently written in March or April 1968, was published in *Novoye*

russkoye slovo (New York), 2 December 1968. Zheludkov's personal letter to Litvinov of 30 March 1968 is published in both Russian and English in K. van het Reve, ed., *Letters and Telegrams to Pavel M. Litvinov*, Dordrecht, Holland, 1969, pp. 154-63, and English extracts are in Bourdeaux, *op. cit.*, pp. 339-41. His letter to Academician Sakharov of 12 March 1969 is in *Vestnik Russkogo studencheskogo khristianskogo dvizheniya* (Paris), 1969, no. 94, pp. 46-57, and his book *Pochemu i ya khristyanin* (*Why I too am a Christian*) is due to be published by Possev Verlag.

96. Valery Tarsis (b. 1906) came to Britain in 1966 to give some lectures, was promptly deprived of his Soviet citizenship, and stayed in the West. His first well-known book, *The Bluebottle*, was published in 1962 in Russian (*Grani*, No. 52) and, under the pseudonym Ivan Valeriy, in English. His famous *Ward Seven* appeared in 1965 (in Russian in *Grani*, No. 57). Possev Verlag has in recent years been publishing his collected works in twelve volumes.

97. Anatoly Yakobson: translator, poet and critic. A friend of Yuly Daniel, he wrote a strong defence of him in 1966; see Labedz and Hayward, *op. cit.* (note 46), pp. 135-39. In 1969 he was a founder member of the Action Group for the Defence of Civil Rights in the USSR: see Reddaway, *Uncensored Russia*, chap. 7. See also his praise for the Red Square demonstrators of 25 August 1968 against the occupation of Czechoslovakia in N. Gorbanevskaya, *Polden*, Frankfurt, 1970, pp. 495-97. An English translation of this book has appeared under the title *Red Square at Noon*, (London and New York, 1972).

98. i.e. in his letter to Stalin of 1939. See John Erickson, *The Soviet High Command 1918-1941*, London, 1962, p. 466, and Robert Conquest, *The Great Terror*, London, 1968, pp. 456-7.

99. On this article see Dzyuba's book *Internationalism or Russification?*, London, 2nd ed., 1970, p. xvii. Dzyuba signed Document IV: 28.

100. Almost certainly one of the trials discussed in V. Chornovil, *The Chornovil Papers*, London and New York, 1968.

101. See especially *The Memoirs of Ivanov-Razumnik*, London, 1965, which contain much editorial material, including an excellent bibliography.

102. See note 98.

103. Leonid Plyushch: in May 1969 a founder-member of the Action Group for the Defence of Civil Rights in the USSR. See Reddaway, *Uncensored Russia*, chap. 7.

104. More precisely, all political prisoners sentenced under the more serious political articles of the Russian Criminal Code, i.e. those in the section 64-88. Less serious political articles, like 190-1, need not involve the strict-régime.

105. Anatoly Marchenko (b. 1938), author of *My Testimony*. See note 94. On the Mordovian camps see also Reddaway, *Uncensored Russia*, chap. 10.

106. On this trial see footnote to Document IV: 3 on p. 231, note 80 above, and *Possev* 1, 1971, pp. 38-43.

107. The text of this important appeal, dated 24 February 1968, is in Reddaway, *Uncensored Russia*, chap. 3.

108. Lev Kvachevsky, the brother of Orion (see Document IV: 24) and Dzhemma (wife of Vladimir Borisov), was sentenced to four years in December 1968. See *ibid.*, chapters 19 and (on Dzhemma and Borisov) 11.

109. Graham Greene said this at a public meeting in London on 28 March 1968, organized by International PEN and addressed by various well-known writers. PEN's general secretary, David Carver, recorded in a letter to *The Times* (13 April 1968) that Mr Greene, 'after he had read a letter from Mr Chakovsky refusing to cooperate in Mr Greene's desire to give his Russian royalties to the wives of Sinyavsky and Daniel' concluded his speech thus: 'No bell tolls in Mr Chakovsky's ears; no thought that when we defend others we are defending ourselves. . . .'

110. A translation of the first eleven numbers of this journal (from No. 6 onwards called simply *A Chronicle of Current Events*) forms the core of Reddaway, *Uncensored Russia*. The journal has appeared regularly every two months since 30 April 1968, maintaining a remarkable level of accuracy and reliability. Chapter 3 of *Uncensored*

Russia contains all the *Chronicle*'s material on the trial of the four, and the reader is referred to that chapter for extensive annotation which is not reproduced here.

111. For materials on this demonstration see *Possev* 7, 1968, pp. 11-13.
112. For further details see *ibid.*, pp. 7-10, and the British press of 18 and 19 June 1968.
113. Broughton, as a friend of Reddaway, had asked for his help with the translation of the 'Church' leaflet, and told the KGB this when interrogated. Hence the attack on Reddaway, who replied in a comment in *The Times* of 22 June 1968.
114. An error: in fact on 17 February. See the *Observer* of 18 February 1968.

INDEX OF NAMES

This index of page numbers includes all the persons referred to in this collection. Names of persons who wrote or signed any article, appeal, declaration or letter included in it are followed by the number of the document as it appears in the collection. The index also contains details of extra-judicial repressions implemented against persons who signed letters condemning the method of conduct and the press coverage of the 'trial of the four' or expressing doubt concerning their legality. The compiler wishes to make clear that he is not in possession of all the details relating to these repressions, and, further, that there are indications that they will continue in the future. Thus the repressive measures taken against signatories to the letters are not represented in their entirety in this index.

As well as the ones used throughout the compilation, the following abbreviations will be found in the index:

D. = Doctor	Philos. = Philosophical
M. = Master	Phys. mat. = Physico-mathematical
Biol. = Biological	Sc. = Sciences
Hist. = Historical	Jun. = Junior
Art. = Art studies	Sen. = Senior
Tech. = Technical	Off. = Officer
Philol. = Philological	

For example, D.Phys.-mat.Sc. is read as Doctor of Physico-mathematical Sciences. Jun.Sc.Off. is read as Junior Scientific Officer.

Index

Alekseyev, I. S., M.Philos.Sc., IV: 23, strict party reprimand, 404

Alekseyev, M., member of board secretariat, Moscow branch WU, 309

Alekseyeva, L. M., editor, II: 16, II: 17, IV: 11, expelled from party and dismissed from post (Nauka Publishing House), 399, 400

Aleksei, Patriarch of All Russia, 265

Almazov, L., vice-chairman of Moscow City Court, 378-379

Amalrik, A. A., playwright, 382-384

Andreyev, S. L., engineer, IV: 23, 404

Andronov, N., artist, member of USSR AU, IV: 21, strict party reprimand, 311, 403

Andronova-Leontovich, E., D.Phys.-mat. Sc., IV: 21, 403

Andropov, Yu. V., chairman of KGB, 209, 344

Antokolsky, P. G., poet, member of USSR WU, IV: 22, strict party reprimand, 348, 404

Antonenko-Davidovich, B., writer, member of USSR WU, IV: 28, 405

Antonova, E. T., see Galanskova, E. T.

Apresyan, Yu. D., M.Philol.Sc., II: 16, IV: 11, IV: 21, 399, 400, 403

Aragon, L., French writer, 169, 200, 409 (note)

Arapov, M., linguist, IV: 21, 403

Ariya, S. L., defence counsel for Vera Lashkova, 18, 36, 37, 40, 41, 42, 79, 80, 86, 94-97, 115, 116, 123, 128-129, 132, 140, 159, 175-183, 211, 231, 255, 263, 351, 352, 355-357, 360, 364

Arkhiyev, N., II: 16, IV: 14, 399, 401

Ashpis, E., musician, IV: 28, 406

Athenagoras, Patriarch, 279

Averochkin, B., lawyer, sentenced in 1967 to eight years' imprisonment as one of the leaders of the All-Russian Social Christian Union for the Liberation of the People, 231

Avramenko, A., medical doctor, V: 37, 406

Avramenko, I., mathematician, IV: 17, 401

Avrorin, V., corresponding member of USSR AS, 348

Avrutsky, G. D., engineer, II: 16, IV: 17, V: 37, 399, 401, 406

Azarova, N. I., philologist, IV: 17, 401

Babayev, A., M.Philol.Sc., member of USSR WU, II: 18, 399

Babitsky, K., linguist, II: 16, III: 1, IV: 11,

IV: 21, defence of Master's dissertation postponed indefinitely, 399, 400, 403

Bachinsky, G. A., M.Biol.Sc., IV: 28, dismissed from post (Institute of Zoology of USSR AN), 406

Bagrov, Jun.Sc.Off., sent letter approving the sentence to *Komsomolskaya Pravda*, 296

Bagrovnikova, M. V., teacher, IV: 17, 402

Bagrovnikova, T. V., technician, IV: 17, 401

Balakirev, senior lieutenant in KGB, 21, 24

Balter, B., writer, member of USSR WU, IV: 22, expelled from party by Moscow City Party Committee, reprimanded with entry in personal file by Board Secretariat of Moscow branch WU, 404

Barrault, J.-L., French actor, 293

Baryshev, lieutenant in KGB, 24, 28

Basilova, E., poetess, witness at trial, IV: 4, V: 33, 113, 150-153, 217, 226, 367, 400, 406

Batshev, V., poet, sentenced in 1965 to five years' exile, amnestied in 1967, summoned to the trial as a witness but failed to appear, 51, 79, 85, 90, 104, 128, 277, 358, 408(note)

Bayeva, T., student, II: 16, II: 17, IV: 17, 399, 401

Bea, Cardinal, 281

Beletsky, A. A., D.Phys.Sc., IV: 28, 405

Beletsky, M. I., mathematician, IV: 28, dismissed from post, 405

Belogorodskaya, I. M., engineer, II: 16, IV: 11, 399, 401

Belogorov, I., clerk, father of Vera Lashkova, 14

Belokrinitskaya, S., linguist, IV: 11, IV: 21, 400, 403

Belova, L., M.Philol.Sc., member of USSR Cinematographers' Union, IV: 11, expelled from party by district party committee, then Party Control Commission replaced expulsion by severe reprimand, 400

Belyayev, D., corresponding member of USSR AS, 348

Berezansky, Yu. M., Professor, D.Phys.-mat.Sc., corresponding member of Ukrainian AS, IV: 28, removed from teaching post at Kiev State University, 405

Berg, R. L., D.Biol.Sc., IV: 23, dismissed from post (Institute of Molecular Biology in Siberian branch of USSR AS), 404

Beria, L. P., chief of state security organs (1938-53), 235, 334

416

Index

Index

Buras, M., engineer, II: 16, 399
Burkovsky, lieutenant-colonel, 240
Butko, V., II: 16, 399

Carsewell, P. J., British citizen, student, member of 'Church' organization, 385, 386-388
Cicero, M. T., 269
Chailakhyan, L. M., M.Biol.Sc., IV: 21, 404
Chakovsky, A., editor-in-chief of *Literary Gazette*, 300-307, 335, 337, 342, 411(note)
Chamarya, S. P., police witness at first search of Galanskov home, 21, 24
Chekhov, A. P., writer, 333
Cheremisina, M. I., M.Philol.Sc., IV: 23, dismissed from post (Novosibirsk State University), 405
Chernenko, I. A., editor, IV: 28, 406
Chernitsyn, 103-104
Chernyshyova, T. N., philologist, IV: 28, 405
Chilikina, A., lecturer, IV: 17, 402
Chirkov, S., II: 16, 399
Chizhevsky, worker, IV: 28, 406
Chizhova, G. V., people's assessor at the trial, 41-42, 97, 111, 119, 135, 211
Chornovil, V., journalist, sentenced in 1967 to three years' imprisonment for compiling a collection [of documents] concerning political trials in the Ukraine during 1965-66, 279, 410(note), 411(note)
Chudakov, S., journalist, V: 33, 406
Chukovskaya, L. K., writer, member of USSR WU, IV : 21, reprimanded with entry in personal file by Board Secretariat of Moscow branch WU, 124, 187, 404
Chukovsky, K. I., writer, 200, 348, 409 (note)
Churganova, B., linguist, IV: 21, 404
Cook, K. M., translator, IV: 21, 403

Daniel, A. Yu., son of Yuly Daniel, II: 16, II: 17, IV: 11, 379, 399, 401
Daniel, L. I. *see* Bogoraz, L. I.
Daniel, Yu. M., writer, sentenced in 1966 to five years' imprisonment for his literary activities, 3, 4, 8, 10, 11, 13, 14, 15, 18, 19, 20, 26, 29, 32, 35, 37, 39, 45, 46-54, 57, 66, 72, 81, 94, 101, 108, 111-114, 125, 128, 131, 138, 156, 164, 168, 169, 184, 185, 192, 193, 197-201, 204, 207-210, 222, 225, 229-230, 237, 238, 241, 245, 247, 248, 256, 263, 265, 267, 270, 281, 314, 326, 342, 361, 362, 364, 365, 366, 367-369, 370, 379, 380-381, 386, 388, 407(note), 410(note)
Danilov, A., currency speculator, 52, 143-145
Davydov, Yu., M.Philos.Sc., IV: 11, severe party reprimand, 400
Davydovskaya, engineer, IV: 21, 403
Delone, V., poet, given one year's suspended sentence in 1967 for participating in demonstration on 22 January 1967 against the arrest of Galanskov, Dobrovolsky, Lashkova and Radziyevsky, 18, 76, 81, 259
Demnin, V., mathematician, IV: 17, 401
Denisov, K. S., police witness at first search of Ginzburg's home, 24, 28
Denisov, V., medical doctor, IV: 17, 402
Deza, M. E., mathematician, IV: 17, 401
Dibrova, P., engineer, IV: 28, 405
Diky, L. A., M.Phys.-mat.Sc., IV: 2, 403
Dinaburg, mathematician, IV: 21, 403
Diptseva, G., II: 16, 399
Djilas, M., Yugoslav political writer, 7, 11
Dobrokhotov, M., church writer, 10, 73, 86, 139, 178
Dobrovich, A., medical doctor, II: 18, V: 37, 399, 406
Dobrovolskaya, G., wife of Aleksei Dobrovolsky, witness at trial, 158-160, 195-196, 221, 250-252
Dobrovolskaya, N. V., mother of Aleksei Dobrovolsky, 11, 221, 250-252, 351
Dobrovolsky, A. A., 3, 11-14, 15, 16, 17, 18, 20, 22, 25, 37, 40, 42, 43-107, 110-111, 114-115, 116-118, 119-124, 126-133, 135-141, 146, 158-160, 164-167, 170-171, 172-175, 178-179, 181-182, 185, 188-196, 202-206, 211, 212, 214, 215-221, 224, 225, 220-235, 239, 242, 247-249, 250-256, 258, 262, 263, 265, 267-270, 273, 274, 279, 282, 283-295, 296-300, 302, 303, 304, 313, 315, 316, 319-323, 325, 326-327, 329, 330, 331, 340, 349, 351-359, 361-366, 367-368, 370, 376, 379
Dobrushin, R., D.Phys.-mat.Sc., II: 16, II: 17, IV: 11, 399, 400
Dombrovsky, Yu., writer, member of USSR WU, IV: 21, strictly warned by Board Secretariat of Moscow branch WU, 403
Domshlak, M., art historian, II: 16, IV: 11, 399, 400
Dorokhova, N., typist, IV: 17, 401
Dotsenko, A. N., engineer, IV: 28, 406
Dovgan, R., journalist, IV: 28, 406
Dovgan, V. S., sculptor, member of

Index

Index

Khokhlov, V., editor of typescript journal *Russian Word*, 22, 26, 182

Khokhlova, L., student, sent letter approving the sentence to *Komsomolskaya Pravda*, 296

Khokhlushkin, I. N., Jun.Sc.Off., IV: 23, 405

Khorinov, KGB expert, 24, 28

Khrabrovitsky, A., literary scholar, II: 16, IV: 11, IV: 14, IV: 17 399, 401, 402

Khriplovich, I. V., M.Phys.-mat.Sc., IV: 23 405

Khromova, T., historian, II: 16, 399

Khrushchev, N. S., 12, 32, 72, 240, 274, 333

Kibalchich, A. I., architect, IV: 17, 401

Kim, A., medical doctor, IV: 17, 401

Kim, Yu., teacher, author and performer of songs, co-author of appeal 'To Public Figures in Science, Culture and Art', II: 16, II: 17, IV: 10, IV: 17, dismissed from school post, all contracts for singing appearances cancelled, 241-246, 279, 333, 399, 401, 410(note)

Kirev, worker, IV: 28, 406

Kirov, S. M., member of Bolshevik Central Committee Politburo, killed in 1934, 181

Kirsanov, Yu. V., interpreter at trial, 161, 162

Kirtnits, D. A., D.Phys.-mat.Sc., IV: 17, 401

Kiryagina, A. F., police witness at first search of Ginzburg's home, V: 33, 24, 28, 406

Kiselev, O., actor, IV: 11, 400

Kiseleva, Yu. I., artist, IV: 17, 401

Klimovich, S. F., police witness at second search of Ginzburg's home, 34, 35

Klorin, A. V., engineer, IV: 23, 405

Knipovich, E., member of Board Secretariat of Moscow branch WU, 309

Kobasova, E., engineer, IV: 21, 403

Kochetov, V. A., writer, 112, 245

Kochmarov, employee on paper *Pravda*, 31

Kochur, G. P., writer, member of Ukrainian WU, IV: 28, 405

Koder-Stepanova, N., M.Biol.Sc., IV: 21, 403

Kogan, A., musician, IV: 17, 402

Kogan, L. S., cinematographer, V: 41, 337

Kolesnikov, E., engineer, IV: 17, 401

Kolmogorov, A. N., mathematician, academician, 345

Kolomiyets, T. A., writer, member of Ukrainian WU, IV: 28, 405

Kolomiyets, V., writer, member of Ukrainian WU, IV: 28, 406

Komashkov, worker, IV: 28, 406

Kon, A., physicist, IV: 21, expelled from Komsomol, 403

Konenko, I. R., chemist, IV: 17, 402

Konev, V. A., M.Philos.Sc., IV: 23, severe party reprimand, 405

Konopada, Ya. V., medical doctor, IV: 28, 406

Konstantinov, V., journalist, V: 2, 257, 284-288, 313-315, 316

Kopelev, L. Z., literary scholar and translator, member of USSR WU, IV: 21, IV: 25, expelled from party by district party committee, dismissed from post (Institute of the History of the Arts), contracts for publication of books and articles cancelled, severely reprimanded by Board Secretariat of Moscow branch WU with entry in personal file, 267-268, 403

Kopeleva, E. L., proof-reader, IV: 11, 400

Kopylov, G., physicist, IV: 17, 401

Korchagin, I., V: 7, 298

Korkhov, A., clerk, II: 17, IV: 17, 399, 401

Korkhova, I., economist, II: 16, IV: 17, V: 37, 399, 401, 406

Kormer, V. R., engineer, IV: 17, 401

Kornilov, V., poet, member of USSR WU, II: 16, IV: 21, IV: 22, strictly warned by Board Secretariat of Moscow branch WU, 399, 403, 404

Korogodsky, R., art historian, IV: 28, 406

Korolkov, Yu., deputy secretary of Moscow branch of Russian WU party committee, 309

Korolyov, A. M., M.Phys.-mat.Sc., IV: 28, 405

Korolyov, Yu. P., 33

Korotkov, M. K., police witness at second search of Galanskov's home, 33, 34

Korpelevich, G., graduate student, IV: 11 400

Kortan, P., engineer, IV: 17, 402

Korytnaya, S., critic, IV: 17, 401

Korzhavin, N. M., poet, member of USSR WU, IV: 22, reprimanded by Board Secretariat of Moscow branch WU, 404

Kositsyna, E. S., schoolteacher, IV: 23, expelled from party, dismissed from school post, 405

Kostenko, L., poetess, member of Ukrainian WU, IV: 28, 405

Kosterin, A. E., writer, member of USSR WU, II: 16, IV: 11, IV: 14, 399, 401

423

Index

424

Index

Date Due